STRATEGIC ENTREPRENEURSHIP

FOURTH EDITION

PHILIP A. WICKHAM

Prentice Hall
FINANCIAL TIMES

Harlow, England • London • New York • Boston • San Francisco • Toronto
Sydney • Tokyo • Singapore • Hong Kong • Seoul • Taipei • New Delhi
Cape Town • Madrid • Mexico City • Amsterdam • Munich • Paris • Milan

For John

Pearson Education Limited
Edinburgh Gate
Harlow
Essex CM20 2JE
England

and Associated Companies throughout the world

Visit us on the World Wide Web at:
www.pearsoned.co.uk

First published in Great Britain in 1998
Second edition published in 2001
Third edition published in 2004
Fourth edition published in 2006

© Philip Wickham 1998
© Pearson Education Limited 2001, 2004, 2006

ISBN 978-0-273-70642-7

British Library Cataloguing-in-Publication Data
A catalogue record for this book is available from the British Library

Library of Congress Cataloging-in-Publication Data
A catalog record for this book is available from the Library of Congress

10 9 8 7 6 5
10

Typeset in Sabon by 35
Printed and bound by Ashford Colour Press, Gosport

The publisher's policy is to use paper manufactured from sustainable forests.

WITHDRAWN

STRATEGIC
ENTREPRENEURSHIP

Brief Contents

Contents

Chapter 20 Gaining financial support: issues and approaches 398

Supporting resources

Visit **www.pearsoned.co.uk/wickham** to find valuable online resources

For instructors
- Complete, downloadable Instructor's Manual
- PowerPoint slides that can be downloaded and used for presentations

For more information please contact your local Pearson Education sales representative or visit **www.pearsoned.co.uk/wickham**

Preface to the fourth edition

When the first edition of *Strategic Entrepreneurship* was conceived, entrepreneurship was only just beginning to properly establish itself as a distinct and free-standing field within organisational and management studies. In its early days, while exciting, the field had a tendency to be a bit of a magpie: it would 'steal' the bright shiny bits of other management disciplines. So we had 'entrepreneurial' marketing, 'entrepreneurial' finance, 'entrepreneurial' strategy and so on. This is not to be critical. Entrepreneurs did all these things (though they might not always have compartmentalised their activities in the same way as business schools organise learning), and it was important that the burgeoning field of entrepreneurship looked at the way entrepreneurs undertook them – not least because they were often very successful at doing them.

Nonetheless, as it matures, the field of entrepreneurship is developing its own content, agenda and concerns. The fourth edition of *Strategic Entrepreneurship* aims to reflect these in a more focused way. A number of changes have been made. While the book still retains the 'strategic window' metaphor as its core organising principle, some new material has been added, some old material withdrawn and the resulting content reorganised.

New material first. This falls into three main areas. First, interest in social or public entrepreneurship is growing rapidly, not least as the boundaries between the private and the public, and the self-interested and the charitable break down. *Strategic Entrepreneurship* has always taken the stance that entrepreneurship is a style of management, and this seems an ideal platform from which to take the lessons of for-profit entrepreneurship into not-for-profit entrepreneurship. Second, as the pace of globalisation builds, it is increasingly necessary that the student of entrepreneurship should have at least some insight into the role of entrepreneurship in global economic development and the debate this engenders. Finally, while the notion of the 'entrepreneurial personality' seems to be waning as a conceptual approach and research platform, the notion of entrepreneurial cognition is waxing to fill the space. The application of insights from cognitive psychology to developing understanding of the entrepreneur and the entrepreneurial process offers great promise and, again, the student of entrepreneurship should at least be aware of the issues and the agenda. Introducing some ideas on entrepreneurial cognition also allows a particular lacuna in the book to be addressed. While dismissing the notion of the entrepreneur as a risk taker from an *economic* perspective is, I still feel, quite proper, this does not exhaust the notion of risk from a cognitive, psychological or social viewpoint, and the entrepreneur engages with the concept at these levels as much as, if not more than, simply at the economic. In this edition I take the chance to address this lacuna.

Each of these three additions is represented by its own chapter, but all inspire new ideas to be drawn in throughout the text. Space is limited. New additions mean some material has to be lost. I have concentrated on those areas where it is only right the magpie gives back some of its shiny toys; especially those areas that are receiving less emphasis in modern courses in entrepreneurship as many traditional subject areas take a greater interest in their entrepreneurial aspects. As a result, they can be dealt with far more effectively in dedicated textbooks. In the main, these are topics such as general strategy, organisational development, marketing and finance.

The reorganisation is aimed at making the book a better tool for course design and support. It is not, I hope, so radical that traditional users of *Strategic Entrepreneurship* will not be able to find their way around the text. Previous users of the book will still recognise chapter titles. Those chapters that have been removed from this edition are still available on the text's dedicated website. The book now has a five-part structure.

Part 1: The entrepreneur as an individual (Chapters 1 to 5) addresses fundamental ideas on the definition and classification of entrepreneurs and psychological approaches to their characterisation. It also considers the growth in cognitive approaches to understanding entrepreneurship and brings in introductory ideas on the economic psychology of risk behaviour.

Part 2: The entrepreneur in the macroeconomic environment (Chapters 6 to 9) develops a largely economic perspective on the entrepreneur, considering different perspectives on the entrepreneur's function within the broader economic system. A new chapter on the role of entrepreneurship on economic development is now included. This new edition also introduces ideas on *social entrepreneurship* – entrepreneurial management outside the for-profit sector. The social responsibility of the entrepreneur to immediate stakeholders and the wider community is also considered.

Part 3: The entrepreneurial process and new venture creation (Chapters 10 to 15) focuses on the entrepreneurial process, in particular the identification of new opportunities, planning resource requirements and the initiation of the venture. The potential and limitations of *intrapreneurship* – entrepreneurship within the established organisation – are reflected upon.

Part 4: Choosing a direction (Chapters 16 to 20) brings some material forward (now ahead of the strategic window), as many students (quite properly) enter entrepreneurship through the portal of inventive creativity. The roles of entrepreneurial vision and mission in providing direction for the venture are considered.

Part 5: Initiating and developing the new venture (Chapters 21 to 28) is now dedicated to the strategic window metaphor, which is structured as it has been in all editions. The strategic window metaphor now acts as a template to integrate, and add to, ideas developed in the previous chapters.

The chapter on **researching entrepreneurship** has been moved to the end of the book so as not to disturb the main flow of ideas. There is a deeper discussion of the methodologies adopted for researching entrepreneurship. This should support the research themes section at the end of each chapter.

Other changes are relatively minor. One aspect of the book that many have found useful is the fulsome list of **suggestions for further reading** (updated in this edition – it is hard to keep up in this fast-growing field). These are particularly useful for students undertaking projects in entrepreneurship. However, the number of citations can lead to a feeling of 'where do I start?' So I have highlighted two (occasionally three, if short) papers as **key readings** that I feel provide a strong introduction to the issues raised in the chapter. These would make excellent tutorial reading at both undergraduate and postgraduate level. To maintain focus, I have also removed some of the older and less immediately relevant references from the suggestions for further reading. The full list of references can be found on the text's dedicated website.

The **research themes** have proved to be a well-received pedagogical extra, not just as inspiration for active research projects but also as tutorial discussion points. They have been retained and enhanced. Also to support tutorial activity, new and up-to-date **selected readings** based on *Financial Times* articles, with suggested discussion points, are included. The tutor will find a guide to using these articles in teaching in an Instructor's Manual on the website.

These changes do, I feel, reflect the very positive maturing of entrepreneurship as an independent discipline. As noted above, historical chapter titles have been retained so that those using the book on an established course that they wish to retain will still be able to guide students to the appropriate material. I hope the changes will meet with approval. If you encounter any problems, let me know.

Once again, my sincerest thanks to Matthew Walker and his team at Pearson, who have made the project both enlightening and enjoyable. Thanks also to the reviewers of the fourth edition and their positive, focused and illuminating comments: Mary Deuchar, Hertfordshire (UK); Laura Wilson, Southampton (UK); Doug Engelbrecht, Durban (South Africa); Louis Edwards, Glamorgan (UK); Pegram Harrison, Regents (UK); Roberto Floren, Nyenrode (Netherlands); Per Blenker, Econ (Denmark); and Anders Bordum, CBS (Denmark).

My personal thanks to David Allison, Ted Fuller, John Mark, John Wilson and colleagues too numerous to mention.

Philip A. Wickham
January 2006

Acknowledgements

We are grateful to the Financial Times Limited for permission to reprint the following material:

Page 47: Jonathan Guthrie 'Why is it better to be bootstrapped than well heeled', © *Financial Times*, 7 December 2005; 49: Jon Boone 'Jaeger owner sets up fund to support fashion students', © *Financial Times*, 26 January 2006; 68: Jean Eaglesham 'Dyson seeks to brush up industry's image', © *Financial Times*, 19 November 2005; 69: Andrew Baxter, FT report 'Saïd MBA was "best year of my life"', © *Financial Times*, 30 January 2006; 115: Jonathan Guthrie 'Why buy-out terms mean you should watch your back', © *Financial Times*, 1 February 2006; 117: Andrew Ward: 'A venture born of ignorance', © *Financial Times*, 21 December 2005; 155: Kevin Allison 'An alternative energy supply swimming against the tide', © *Financial Times*, 21 December 2005; 175: Jonathan Moules 'How start-ups are helping countries to catch up', © *Financial Times*, 18 January 2006; 188: Nicholas Timmins 'Private providers offered fresh opportunities in health shake-up', © *Financial Times*, 31 January 2006; 189: Andrew Baxter 'Course choices that help MBAs make the world a better place', © *Financial Times*, 30 January 2006; 213: Fiona Harvey and Richard McGregor 'The polluter pays: how environmental disaster is straining China's social fabric', © *Financial Times*, 27 January 2006; 216: Stefan Wagstyl 'New Bosnia chief makes boosting economy priority', © *Financial Times*, 31 January 2006; 230: Andy Webb-Vidal 'A shot of rum turns crisis into opportunity', © *Financial Times*, 25 January 2006; 233: Jonathan Moules 'The driving workforce behind a successful food distribution group', © *Financial Times*, 21 January 2006; 253: Jonathan Guthrie 'The geeks have inherited the earth – and it is hell for efficiency', © *Financial Times*, 25 January 2006; 269: Andrew Jack 'When language gives an industry the edge', © *Financial Times*, 26 January 2006; 271: Peter Marsh 'Entrepreneur fires broad attack on manufacturers', © *Financial Times*, 17 January 2006; 289: Paul Tyrell 'The security of mutual support', © *Financial Times*, 25 January 2006; Andrew Bolger 'Biotechnology chief lauds Scottish skills', © *Financial Times*, 6 February 2006; 298: Paul Tyrell 'Smart companies take on "intrapreneurial" spirit", © *Financial Times*, 25 July 2005; 301: Julian Birkinshaw and Andrew Campbell 'Know the limits of corporate venturing', © *Financial Times*, 9 August 2004; 314: Peter Marsh 'An ambitious man of steel', © *Financial Times*, 4 February 2006; 316: Michiyo Nakamoto and David Pilling with additional reporting by Barney Johnson 'Rakuten head hits out over accounting rules', © *Financial Times*, 23 February 2005; 330: William Hall 'Expansion boosts area's prosperity', © *Financial Times*, 23 February 2005; 332: Adrian Michaels 'Breaking with tradition in Italian business', © *Financial Times*, 28 February 2005; 343: Jon Boone 'Traditionalist embraces change', © *Financial Times*, 23 February 2005; 346: Deborah Brewster 'The chief executive who saved the best for last, © *Financial Times*, 25 July 2005; 369: Peter Marsh 'Dumpy bottles for baby prove a world beater', © *Financial Times*, 28 July 2005; 370: Tim Burt 'A business groomed for success', © *Financial Times*, 19 July 2005; 393: Ben King 'The entrepreneur who wants to give it all away', © *Financial Times*, 20 January 2006; 396: Adrian Michaels 'Mediobanca to target perceptions', © *Financial Times*, 15 September 2005; 422: Jonathan Moules

'Inventor taps into funding support', © *Financial Times*, 17 December 2005; 423: Alexander Jolliffe 'I am sceptical about people who are too smooth', © *Financial Times*, 22 January 2005; 437: Virginia Marsh 'The merino makes a break from the flock for a life of luxury', © *Financial Times*, 17 August 2005; 439: Jim Pickard 'As new investors rush in, old hands look further afield', © *Financial Times*, 17 August 2005; 452: Alicia Clegg 'Tricks of the truckers' trade', © *Financial Times*, 14 December 2005; 454: Chris Nuttall 'Way of the web: start-ups map the route as big rivals get Microsoft in their sights', © *Financial Times*, 17 November 2005; 472: Miranda Green 'College Friends with designs on selling arts and craft', © *Financial Times*, 16 January 2006; 473: Neil Buckley and Sarah Laitner 'Heineken increases Russian Portfolio with sixth buy in 12 months', © *Financial Times*, 18 August 2005; 510: Bertrand Benoit 'How the Mittelstand found its champion', © *Financial Times*, 23 March 2005; 513: Tim Johnston 'Rank to buy control of CCH Wood Products', © *Financial Times*, 18 August 2005; 549: Martin Arnold and Andrew Jack 'Ban the bureaucracy and bring in the bulldozers', © *Financial Times*, 17 October 2005; 551: Geoff Dyer 'South Beauty's chic chow plans to win the West, © *Financial Times*, 1 February 2006; 564: Neil Buckley 'The calm reinventor: man in the news A.G. Lafley', © *Financial Times*, 29 January 2005.

We are grateful to the following for permission to use copyright material:

Page 28: Syl Tang 'Football set to score stylishly' from the *Financial Times*, 21 January 2006, © Syl Tang; 30: Amy Raphael 'Clothes maketh the man' from the *Financial Times*, 14 January 2006, © Amy Raphael; 87: Stephen Overell 'Management training for the young' from the *Financial Times*, 7 November 2005, © Stephen Overell; 89: Emma Crichton-Miller 'TBA' from the *Financial Times*, 28 January 2006, © Emma Crichton-Miller; 157: Laura Cohn 'Breaking the mould in Notting Hill and beyond' from the *Financial Times*, 4 February 2006, © Laura Cohn; 177: Yasheng Huang 'What China could learn from India's slow and quiet rise' first published in the *Financial Times*, 24 January 2006, © Yasheng Huang; 251: Michael Schrage 'How and Why giveaways are changing the rules of business' from the *Financial Times*, 7 February 2006, © Michael Schrage; 487: Edi Smockum 'The personal touch' from the *Financial Times*, 17 September 2005, © Edi Smockum; 490: Dalia Fahmy 'Candy-coloured "blobjects" for all' from the *Financial Times*, 17 September 2005, © Dalia Fahmy; 563: Frank Partnoy 'When Disney wishes upon a Pixar' from the *Financial Times*, 25 January 2006, © Frank Partnoy.

Guided tour

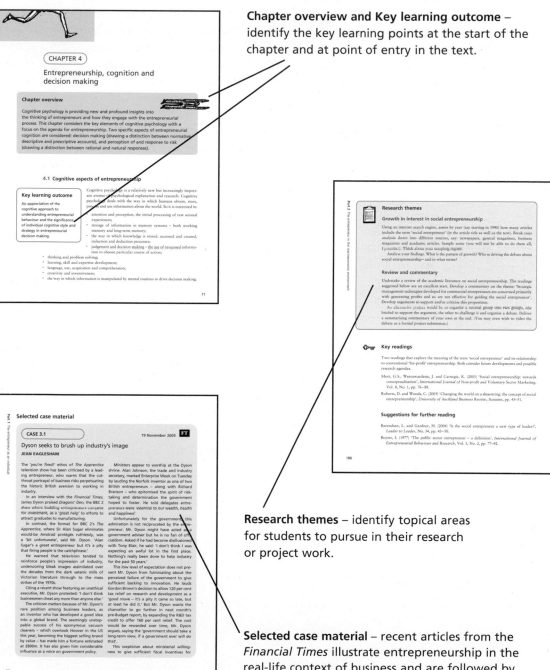

Chapter overview and Key learning outcome – identify the key learning points at the start of the chapter and at point of entry in the text.

Research themes – identify topical areas for students to pursue in their research or project work.

Selected case material – recent articles from the *Financial Times* illustrate entrepreneurship in the real-life context of business and are followed by discussion questions.

Prologue: entrepreneurship in the modern world

Of all those who feature in the management of the modern world economy, it is entrepreneurs who most attract our attention. We all take some view of them. We may see entrepreneurs as heroes: as self-starting individuals who take great personal risk in order to bring the benefits of new products to wider world markets. We may express concern at the pace of economic and social change entrepreneurs bring and of the uncertainty they create. We may admire their talents, or we may question the rewards they get for their efforts. Whatever our instinctive reaction to them, we cannot ignore the impact entrepreneurs have on our world and our personal experience of it.

The modern world is characterised by *change*. Every day we hear of shifts in political orders, developments in economic relationships and new technological advancements. These changes feed off each other and, increasingly, they are global. Developments in information technology allow capital to seek new business investment opportunities ever more efficiently. Success is sought out more quickly; failure punished more ruthlessly. Customers expect continuous improvement in the products and services they consume. Some have argued that the rate of change in the modern world is no different from, or even less than, what it has been in the past. This is probably true. But we do seem to be more acutely aware of change and consider it to be an *issue* more than past generations.

One of the key changes in the modern world is that businesses are having to become more responsive. In order to keep their place in their markets, they are having to innovate more quickly. In order to compete, they are having to become more agile. This is an issue not just for profit-making organisations but for all corporate bodies. The boundary between the world of the 'market' and the public domain is being pushed back and blurred.

Consequently, the world is demanding both more entrepreneurs and more *of* entrepreneurs. In the mature economies of the western world they provide economic dynamism. The fast-growing businesses they create are now the main source of new job opportunities. The post-war growth economies of the Pacific Rim (albeit with a recent stall) are driven by the successes of thousands of new ventures. It is individual entrepreneurs who must restructure the post-communist countries of eastern and central Europe and provide them with vibrant market economies (Benacek, 1995; Luthens *et al.*, 2000; Fogel, 2001; Peng, 2001; Puffer *et al.*, 2001; McMillan and Woodruff, 2002). Looking back over the fifteen or so years since the collapse of communism in the west, it seems this is proving to be a difficult challenge. In the developing world, entrepreneurs are increasingly meeting the challenge of creating new wealth and making its distribution more equitable (Ahwireng-Obeng and Piaray, 1999; Zapalska and Edwards, 2001; Trulsson, 2002).

Change presents both opportunities and problems. The opportunities come in the shape of new possibilities, and the chance of a better future. The problems lie in managing the uncertainty these possibilities create. By way of a response to this challenge, entrepreneurs must aim to take advantage of the opportunities while controlling and responding to the uncertainties. This response must be reflected in the way that organisations are managed. As we shall see, this is the fundamental responsibility of entrepreneurs. To make sense of this responsibility, and how it is managed, we must understand *entrepreneurship* in all its aspects.

This book aims to provide an insight into entrepreneurship that will be valuable to practising managers, to students of management (who will become the entrepreneurial managers of the future) and to those who research and investigate entrepreneurship. It is for those who want not only to be more informed about entrepreneuriship but also to be more entrepreneurial. It does this by taking a particular perspective on entrepreneurship. This perspective is readily summarised as follows:

- Entrepreneurship is a *style* of management.
- Entrepreneurial management aims at pursuing *opportunity* and driving *change*.
- Entrepreneurial management is *strategic* management, that is, management of the whole organisation, in a competitive environment.
- Entrepreneurism is an approach to management that can be *learnt*.

As we will discover, it is not easy to define, exactly, what an entrepreneur is, or is not.

This book takes a straightforward view. It contends that entrepreneurs are just *managers* who make *entrepreneurial decisions*. This book explores these decisions, what they are, what they involve, and the actions necessary to see them through.

Understanding is as much about recognising our misconceptions as it is about gaining knowledge. To a greater extent than other economic actors – managers, investors, bureaucrats – the entrepreneur is a somewhat mythical figure. If we are to get to grips with entrepreneurship and recognise the potential to be entrepreneurial, the myths that surround the entrepreneur must be dispelled. For example, this book rejects the notion that the entrepreneur is someone who is 'born' to achieve greatness. It also dismisses (with some important qualifications) the idea that entrepreneurs are behaviourally 'determined' by psychological forces beyond their control, or that the entrepreneur must have a particular type of personality to be successful. Rather, we will regard the entrepreneur simply as a manager who knows how to make entrepreneurial decisions and how to follow them through.

Discussion will not be limited to the issues of owning businesses or starting new ones. These issues may be an important part of entrepreneurship but they are not its entirety. Nor are they an essential component of entrepreneurship: what makes someone an entrepreneur is not their historical or legal relationship to an organisation but the *changes* they create both with it and within it. In addition to exploring entrepreneurial management, this book also intends to 'demystify' the entrepreneur. This is not an attempt to devalue them or the work they do. In fact, the opposite is intended. It recognises entrepreneurial success as the result of personal application, hard work and learning, not as some innate imperative. What this book does aim to do, above all else, is make entrepreneurship *accessible* by demonstrating that good entrepreneurship is based on management skill, and that the entrepreneurial path can be opened by managers who wish to follow it, and recognise that success follows from personal effort, knowledge and practice, rather than a pre-ordained destiny.

Key readings

Two papers that succinctly summarise the philosophy of a strategic approach entrepreneurship, a philosophy espoused by this book are:

Sandberg, W.R. (1992) 'Strategic management's potential contributions to a theory of entrepreneurship', *Entrepreneurship Theory and Practice*, Spring, pp. 73–90.

Thompson, J.L. (1999) 'A strategic perspective of entrepreneurship', *International Journal of Entrepreneurial Behaviour and Research*, Vol. 5, No. 6, pp. 279–96.

Both make good preparatory reading.

Suggestions for further reading

Ahwireng-Obeng, F. and Piaray, D. (1999) 'Institutional obstacles to South African entrepreneurship', *South African Journal of Business Management*, Vol. 30, No. 3, pp. 78–85.

Benacek, V. (1995) 'Small business and private entrepreneurship during transition: the case of the Czech Republic', *Eastern European Economics*, Vol. 33, No. 2, pp. 38–73.

Bettis, R.A. and Hitt, M.A. (1995) 'The new competitive landscape', *Strategic Management Journal*, Vol. 16, pp. 7–19.

Carroll, G.R. (1994) 'Organizations . . . the smaller they get', *California Management Review*, Vol. 37, No. 1, pp. 28–41.

Duane, I.R., Hitt, M.A. and Simon, D.G. (2003) 'A model of strategic entrepreneurship: The construct and its dimensions', *Journal of Management*, Vol. 29, No. 6, pp. 963–89.

Fogel, G. (2001) 'An analysis of entrepreneurial environment and enterprise devevelopment in Hungary', *Journal of Small Business Management*, Vol. 39, No. 1, pp. 102–9.

Luthens, F., Stajkovic, A.D. and Ibrayeva, E. (2000) 'Environmental and psychological challenges facing entrepreneurial development in transitional economies', *Journal of World Business*, Vol. 35, No. 1, pp. 95–110.

McMillan, J. and Woodruff, C. (2002) 'The central role of entrepreneurs in transition economies', *Journal of Economic Perspectives*, Vol. 16, No. 3, pp. 153–70.

Messeghem, K. (2003) 'Strategic entrepreneurship and managerial activity in SMEs', *International Small Business Journal*, Vol. 21, No. 2, pp. 197–200.

Moore, J.F. (1993) 'Predators and pray: a new ecology of competition', *Harvard Business Review*, May/June, pp. 75–86.

Peng, M.W. (2001) 'How entrepreneurs create wealth in transition economies', *Academy of Management Executive*, Vol. 15, No. 1, pp. 95–110.

Puffer, S.M., McCarthy, D.J. and Peterson, O.C. (2001) 'Navigating the hostile maze: a framework for Russian entrepreneurship', *Academy of Management Executive*, Vol. 15, No. 4, pp. 24–36.

Trulsson, P. (2002) 'Constraints on growth-orientated enterprises in the southern and eastern African region', *Journal of Developmental Entrepreneurship*, Vol. 7, No. 3, pp. 331–9.

Zapalska, A.M. and Edwards, W. (2001) 'Chinese entrepreneurship in a cultural and economic perspective', *Journal of Small Business Management*, Vol. 39, No. 3, pp. 286–92.

CHAPTER 1

The nature of entrepreneurship

Chapter overview

This chapter is concerned with developing an overarching and integrated perspective of the entrepreneur and entrepreneurship. It reviews the great variety of approaches that have been taken to characterise the entrepreneur, highlighting the lack of agreement on a fundamental definition. Three broad approaches are considered. The first defines the entrepreneur as a *manager* undertaking particular tasks. The second regards the entrepreneur in *economic* terms and concentrates on the function they have in facilitating economic processes. The third regards the entrepreneur in *psychological* terms as an individual with a particular personality.

The conclusions of the chapter are that the entrepreneur is best regarded as a *manager* and that entrepreneurship is a *style of management*.

1.1 What is entrepreneurship?

The word 'entrepreneur' is widely used, both in everyday conversation and as a technical term in management and economics. Its origin lies in seventeenth-century France, where an 'entrepreneur' was an individual commissioned to undertake a particular commercial project by someone with money to invest. In its earliest stages this usually meant an overseas trading project. Such projects were risky, both for the investor (who could lose money) and for the navigator-entrepreneur (who could lose a lot more!). The intertwining of the notions of entrepreneur, investor and risk is evident from the start. A number of concepts have been derived from the idea of the entrepreneur such as *entrepreneurial*, *entrepreneurship* and *entrepreneurial process*. The idea that the entrepreneur is someone who undertakes certain projects offers an opening to developing an understanding of the nature of entrepreneurship. Undertaking particular projects demands that particular tasks be engaged in with the objective of achieving

Key learning outcome

An understanding of the main approaches to understanding the nature of entrepreneurship. In particular, the distinction between the entrepreneur as a performer of *managerial tasks*, as an *agent of economic change* and as a *personality*.

specific outcomes and that an individual take charge of the project. *Entrepreneurship* is, then, what the entrepreneur *does*. *Entrepreneurial* is an adjective describing *how* the entrepreneur undertakes what they do. The fact that we use the adjective suggests that there is a particular *style* to what entrepreneurs do. The *entrepreneurial process* in which the entrepreneur engages is the means through which new value is created as a result of the project: the *entrepreneurial venture*.

But this is very general. Offering a specific and unambiguous definition of the entrepreneur presents a challenge. This is not because definitions are not available, but because there are so many: the management and economics literature is well served with suggested definitions for the term 'entrepreneur'. The problem arises because these definitions rarely agree with each other on the essential characteristics of the entrepreneur. Economists have long recognised the importance of the entrepreneur. But even in this discipline, known for its rigour, the entrepreneur remains an illusive beast. The difficulty lies not so much in giving entrepreneurs a role, but in giving them a role that is distinct from that of 'conventional' employed managers. Clearly, this is a distinction that is important but the difficulty is a long-standing one. Reviews of the issue by Arthur Cole, William Baumol, Harvey Leibenstein and James Soltow (all 1968) are still pertinent today and highlight issues still not fully resolved.

William Gartner (1990) undertook a detailed investigation of this matter. He surveyed academics, business leaders and politicians, asking what they felt was a good definition of entrepreneurship. From the responses he summarised ninety different attributes associated with the entrepreneur. These were not just variations on a theme. Many pairs of definitions shared no common attributes at all.

This suggested that the quest for a universal definition had not moved on since 1971 when Peter Kilby noted that the entrepreneur had a lot in common with the 'Heffalump', a character in A.A. Milne's *Winnie-the-Pooh*, described as:

> *a rather large and important animal. He has been hunted by many individuals using various trapping devices, but no one so far has succeeded in capturing him. All who claim to have caught sight of him report that that he is enormous, but disagree on his particulars.*

Gartner (1985) is led to conclude that 'Differences among entrepreneurs and among their ventures are as great as the variations between entrepreneurs and non-entrepreneurs and between new and established firms'.

While many definitions of the entrepreneur, or entrepreneurship, might be offered, any one definition is likely to result, in some cases at least, in a mismatch with our expectations. Intuitively, we know, or feel we know, who is, or is not, an entrepreneur. A particular definition will sometimes exclude those we feel from our experience are entrepreneurs or it will include those we do not think are entrepreneurs. This will be illustrated if we consider some of the attributes associated with the entrepreneur.

For example, the notion of *risk* is one that is often associated with the entrepreneur. But this fails to distinguish between entrepreneurs who progress ventures and the *investors* who accept *financial* risk in backing those ventures. Actually founding a new business has been suggested as a defining characteristic (by Gartner himself). However, many well-known entrepreneurs have revitalised an existing organisation rather than building a new one from scratch. Some definitions emphasise the importance of entrepreneurship in providing the economic efficiency that maximises investors' returns. Rewarding investors is important, but it is not the only objective that entrepreneurs pursue. Effective entrepreneurs work to reward all the stakeholders in their ventures, not just investors. Some actively seek profit-limiting social responsibilities. Innovation has also been suggested as a critical characteristic. However, innovation is an important factor in the success of all business ventures, not just the entrepreneurial. These points will be expanded upon in the discussion that follows.

We should not be disheartened by this apparent failure. Entrepreneurship is a rich and complex phenomenon. We should not expect, or even desire, that it be pinned down by a single, universal definition. Its variety presents endless possibilities and offers meaning to specific ventures. It is this that makes it so useful and inviting an idea. In any case, being able to define something is not the same as *understanding* it. This book will not offer a concrete definition of entrepreneurship as a starting point. A better approach is to develop a broad picture of the entrepreneur, to characterise entrepreneurs and explore the process they engage in and then move on to create an understanding of how entrepreneurship provides a route to new wealth creation.

As well as a managerial phenomenon, entrepreneurship has economic and social dimensions. The entrepreneur is an individual who lives and functions within a social setting. Entrepreneurs are not characterised by every action they take, but by a particular set of actions aimed at the creation of new wealth with their ventures. Wealth creation is a general managerial activity. Entrepreneurship is characterised by a particular approach to wealth creation. Recognising this gives us three directions from which we can develop an understanding. The entrepreneur can be considered as:

- a *manager* undertaking an activity – i.e. in terms of the particular *tasks* they perform and the way they undertake them;
- an *agent of economic change* – i.e. in terms of the *effects* they have on economic systems and the changes they drive; and as
- an *individual* – i.e. in terms of their *psychology*, personality and personal characteristics (including peculiarities in cognitive strategy and style) .

Each of these three aspects is reflected in the variety of definitions offered for entrepreneurship. The function of each perspective is not merely to characterise entrepreneurs but also to distinguish them from other types of people involved in the generation of wealth, such as investors and 'ordinary' managers. The next three sections explore each of these perspectives in more detail.

1.2 The entrepreneur's tasks

We recognise entrepreneurs, in the first instant, by what they actually *do* – by the *tasks* they undertake. This aspect provides one avenue for approaching entrepreneurs and the way in which they are different from other types of manager. A number of tasks have been associated with the entrepreneur. Some of the more important are discussed below.

Key learning outcome

An understanding of the tasks that are undertaken by, and which characterise the work of, the entrepreneur.

Owning organisations

Most people would be able to give an example of an entrepreneur and would probably claim to be able to recognise an entrepreneur 'if they saw one'. A key element in this common perception is *ownership* of the organisation.

While many entrepreneurs do indeed own their own organisations, using ownership as a defining feature of entrepreneurship can be very restricting. Modern market economies are characterised by a differentiation between the ownership and the running of organisations. Ownership lies with those who invest in the business and own its stock – the *principals* – whereas the actual running is delegated to professional managers or *agents*. These two roles are quite distinct. Therefore if an entrepreneur actually owns the business then he or she is in fact undertaking two roles at the same time: that of an investor and that of a manager. This is a distinction noticed as far back as 1803 by the classical French economist J.B. Say (Say, 1964 reprint).

So, we recognise many people as entrepreneurs even if they do not own the venture they are managing. In developed economies, sophisticated markets exist to give investors access to new ventures and most entrepreneurs are active in taking advantage of these to attract investors. For example, when Frederick Smith started the distribution company Federal Express he put in only around 10 per cent of the initial capital. Institutional investors provided the rest. Do we think less of him as an entrepreneur because he diluted his ownership in this way? In fact, most would regard the ability to present the venture and to attract the support of investors as an important entrepreneurial skill.

It should also be noted that 'ordinary' managers (whatever that means) are increasingly being given a means of owning part of their companies through share option schemes which are often linked to the company's performance. While this may encourage them to be more entrepreneurial it does not, in itself, make them into entrepreneurs.

Founding new organisations

The idea that the entrepreneur is someone who has established a new business organisation is one which would fit in with most people's notion of an entrepreneur. The entrepreneur is recognised as the person who undertakes the task of bringing together the different elements of the organisation (people, property, productive resources and so forth) and giving them a separate legal identity. Many thinkers regard this as an essential characteristic of the entrepreneur (for example, Bygrave and Hofer, 1991). The Indian academic R.A. Sharma (1980) sees it as particularly important for entrepreneurship in developing economies. However, such a basis for defining the entrepreneur is sensitive to what we mean by 'organisation' and what we would consider to constitute a 'new' organisation.

Many people we recognise as entrepreneurs 'buy into' organisations that have already been founded and then extend them (as Ray Kroc did with McDonald's), develop them (as George and Liz Davis did with Hepworth's, converting it into Next) or absorb them into existing organisations (as Alan Sugar did with Sinclair Scientific). Increasingly, management buyouts of parts of existing organisations are providing a vehicle for ordinary managers to exhibit their entrepreneurial talent.

A more meaningful, though less precise, idea is that entrepreneurs *make major changes in their organisational world*. Making a major change is a broad notion. It is too ill-defined and subjective to be the basis for a rigorous definition. But it does go beyond merely founding the organisation, and it differentiates the entrepreneur from the manager who manages within existing organisational structures or makes only minor or incremental changes to them.

Bringing innovations to market

Innovation is a crucial part of the entrepreneurial process. J.A. Schumpeter, the Austrian School economist (so called because he was one of a number of radical economists working in Vienna in the first half of the twentieth century), saw innovation as fundamental to the entrepreneurial process of wealth creation. A concise summary of his ideas can be found in a paper he wrote for the *Economic Journal* in 1928. Schumpeter saw entrepreneurs not so much as the lubricant that oiled the wheels of an economy, but as self-interested individuals who sought short-term monopolies based on some innovation. Once an entrepreneurial monopoly was established, a new generation of entrepreneurs came along with more innovations that aimed to supersede that monopoly in a process Schumpeter called 'creative destruction'. Peter Drucker proposed that innovation is the central task for the entrepreneur-manager in his seminal book *Innovation and Entrepreneurship* (1985). Entrepreneurs must do something new or there would be no point in their entering a market. However, we must be careful here with the idea of innovation. Innovation, in a business sense, can mean a lot more than merely developing a new product or technology. The idea of innovation encompasses any new way of doing something so that value is created. Innovation *can* mean a new product or service, but it can also include a new way of delivering an existing product or service (so that it is cheaper or more convenient for the user, for example), new methods of informing the consumer about a product and promoting it to them, new ways of organising the company, or even new approaches to managing relationships with other organisations. These are all sources of innovation which have been successfully exploited by entrepreneurs. In short, innovation is simply doing something in a way which is new, different and better.

The entrepreneur's task goes beyond simply *inventing* something new. It also includes bringing that innovation to the marketplace and using it to deliver value to consumers. The innovated product or service must be produced profitably, in addition to being distributed, marketed and defended from the attentions of competitors, by a well-run and well-led organisation.

No matter how important innovation might be to the entrepreneurial process, it is not *unique* to it. Most managers are encouraged to be innovative in some way or other. Being successful at developing and launching new products and services is not something that is witnessed only in entrepreneurial organisations. The difference between entrepreneurial innovation and 'ordinary innovation' is, at best, one of degree, not substance.

Identification of market opportunity

An opportunity is a gap in a market where the potential exists to do something better and thereby to create value. New opportunities exist all the time, but they do not necessarily present themselves. If they are to be exploited, they must be *actively* sought out. The identification of new opportunities is one of the key tasks of entrepreneurs. They must constantly scan the business landscape watching for the gaps left by existing players (including themselves) in the marketplace. Opportunity is the 'other side of the coin' as far as innovation is concerned. An innovation (a new way of doing something) is an innovation only if it meets with an opportunity (a demand for a new way of doing something).

As with innovation, no matter how important identifying opportunity is to the entrepreneurial process, it cannot be all that there is to it, nor can it characterise it uniquely.

The entrepreneur cannot stop at simply identifying opportunities. Having identified them, the entrepreneur must pursue them with a suitable innovation. An opportunity is simply the 'mould' against which the market tests new ideas. In fact, actually spotting the opportunity may be delegated to specialist market researchers. The real value is created when that opportunity is exploited by something new which fills the market gap.

All organisations are active, to some degree or other, in spotting opportunities. They may call upon specialist managers to do this, or they may encourage everyone in the organisation to be on the lookout for new possibilities. Like innovation, entrepreneurial opportunity scanning differs from that of ordinary managers in degree, not substance.

Application of expertise

It has been suggested that entrepreneurs are characterised by the way that they bring some sort of expertise to their jobs. As discussed above, this expertise may be thought to lie in their ability to innovate or to spot new opportunities. A slightly more technical notion is that they have a special ability in deciding how to *allocate scarce resources* in situations where *information is limited*. It is their expertise in doing this that makes entrepreneurs valuable to investors.

While investors will certainly look for evidence of an ability to make proper business decisions and will judge entrepreneurs on their record in doing so, the idea that the entrepreneur is an 'expert' in this respect raises a question, namely whether the entrepreneur has a skill *as an entrepreneur* rather than just as a particularly skilful and effective manager in their own particular area. Does, for example, Rupert Murdoch have a knowledge of how to make investment decisions which is *distinct* from his intimate and detailed knowledge of the media industry, backed up by good management and attributes such as confidence, decisiveness and leadership? Is it meaningful to imagine someone developing a skill in (rather than just knowing the principles of) 'resource allocation decision making' other than it being demonstrated in relation to some specific area of business activity?

It is not clear whether such a disembodied skill exists separately from conventional management skills. In any case, such a skill could not be unique to the entrepreneur. Many managers, most of whom would not be called entrepreneurial, make decisions about resource allocation every day.

Provision of leadership

One special skill that entrepreneurs would seem to contribute to their ventures is leadership. Leadership is increasingly recognised as a critical part of managerial success. Entrepreneurs can rarely drive their innovation to market on their own. They need the support of other people, both from within their organisations and from people outside such as investors, customers and suppliers.

If all these people are to pull in the same direction, to be focused on the task in hand and to be motivated, then they must be supported and directed. This is a task that falls squarely on the shoulders of the entrepreneur. And if the task is to be performed effectively, then the entrepreneur must show leadership. In an important sense, performing this task well *is* leadership.

Leadership is an important factor in entrepreneurial success and it is often a skill that is exhibited particularly well by the entrepreneur, but it is a *general* management skill rather than one which is specific to the entrepreneur. That said, an entrepreneurial path may give the manager a particularly rich opportunity to develop and express leadership skills.

The entrepreneur as manager

What can we make of all this? It would seem that the entrepreneur takes on no task that is fundamentally different (though it may be different in degree) from the tasks performed by ordinary managers at some time or other. We should not be surprised by this. After all, the entrepreneur is a *manager*. We may wish to draw a distinction between an entrepreneur and an 'ordinary' manager, but if we do so it must be in terms of *what* the entrepreneur manages, *how* they manage, their *effectiveness* and the *effect* they have as a manager, not the particular tasks they undertake.

1.3 The role of the entrepreneur

> ### Key learning outcome
>
> An understanding of the economic effects of entrepreneurial activity.

Entrepreneurs are significant because they have an important effect on world economies. They play a critical role in maintaining and developing the economic order we live under. We have already noted that entrepreneurs create new value. Understanding *how* they do this is of central importance if we are to draw general conclusions about entrepreneurship. This section is a preamble that outlines some key effects of entrepreneurial activity that are drawn into definitions of the entrepreneur. This is self-contained, but Chapter 6 will consider the role of the entrepreneur in more depth from the perspective of different schools of economic thinking.

Combination of economic factors

Economists generally recognise three primary *economic factors*: the *raw materials* that nature offers up, the physical and mental *labour* that people provide, and *capital* (money). All the products (and services) bought and sold in an economy are a mix of these three things. Value is created by combining these three things in a way which satisfies human needs.

Factors do not combine themselves, however. They have to be brought together by individuals working together and undertaking different tasks. The co-ordination of these tasks takes place within *organisations*. Some economists regard entrepreneurship as a kind of fourth factor which acts on the other three to combine them in productive ways. In this view, *innovation* is simply finding new combinations of economic factors.

Other economists object to this view, arguing that it does not distinguish entrepreneurship sufficiently from any other form of economic activity. While entrepreneurs do affect the combination of productive factors, so does everyone who is active in an economy. It is not clear in this view why entrepreneurship is a *special* form of economic activity.

Providing market efficiency

Economic theory suggests that the most efficient economic system is one in which unimpeded markets determine the price at which goods are bought and sold. Here, *efficient* means that resources are distributed in an *optimal* way, that is the satisfaction that people can (collectively) gain from them is *maximised*.

An economic system can only reach this state if there is *competition* among different suppliers. Entrepreneurs provide that efficiency. A supplier that is not facing competition will tend to demand profits in excess of what the market would allow and so reduce the overall efficiency of the system. Entrepreneurs, so the theory goes, are on the lookout for such excess profits. Being willing to accept a lower profit themselves (one nearer the true market rate), they will enter the market and offer the goods at a lower price. By so doing, entrepreneurs ensure that markets are efficient and that prices are kept at their lowest possible level.

Classical economics provides a good starting point for understanding the effects that entrepreneurs have on an economic system. However, business life is generally much more complex than this simple picture gives it credit for. Firms compete on more than price, for example. Chapter 6 will consider the way that different schools of economic thought view the role of the entrepreneur. And, as we shall discover in Chapter 18, when the strategies that entrepreneurs adopt are considered, the most successful entrepreneurs are often those who avoid competition (at least *direct* competition) with established suppliers.

Accepting risk

We do not know what the future will bring. This lack of knowledge we call *uncertainty*. No matter how well we plan, there is always the possibility that some chance event will result in outcomes we neither expected nor wanted. If we know the *likelihood* (probability) of various possibilities then uncertainty becomes *risk*. Some economists have suggested that the primary function of the entrepreneur is to accept risk on behalf of other people. There is, in this view, a *market* for risk. Risk is something that people, generally, want to avoid (individuals are risk averse), so they are willing to pay to have it taken away. Entrepreneurs provide a service by taking this risk off people's hands. They are willing to *buy* it.

An example should make this clear. We may all appreciate the benefits that a new technology, for example the digital recording of television images, can bring. However, there is a risk in developing this new technology. Financial investment in its development is very high. There is also a great deal of uncertainty. Competition between different suppliers' formats is intense. There is no guarantee that the investment will be returned. We now enjoy the benefits of digital technology and yet we, as consumers, have not, personally, had to face the risks inherent in creating it. In effect, we have delegated that risk to the entrepreneurs who *were* active in developing the technology. Of course, entrepreneurs expect that in return for taking the risk they will be rewarded. This reward, the profit stream from their ventures, is the *price* that customers have 'agreed' to pay (not explicitly, but by being willing to pay an addition cost for the goods provided) so that they can have the benefits of the product and yet not face the risk of developing it.

The idea that entrepreneurs are risk takers is one which reflects their popular image. The idea of accepting risk was important to the conception of entrepreneurship developed by the classical English economist John Stuart Mill in 1848. However, we must be very careful to distinguish between *personal* risk and *economic* risk. We may face personal risk by exposing ourselves to dangerous situations, climbing mountains for example, but this is not risk as an economist usually understands it. To an economist, risk results from making an *investment*. Risk is the possibility that the return from an investment may be *less* than expected. Or, to be exact, might be less (or more) than could have been obtained from an alternative investment that was available. As was pointed out in section 1.2, the role of the entrepreneur who manages the venture and that of the investor who puts their money into it are quite distinct.

So, acceptance of risk is actually something that *investors*, not *entrepreneurs*, do. However, the popular impression that the entrepreneur is a risk taker is not completely inappropriate. It recognises that entrepreneurs are good at managing in situations where risk is high; that is, when faced with a situation of high uncertainty they are able to keep their heads, to continue to communicate effectively and to carry on making effective decisions. In this sense, entrepreneurs do not accept risk as such, they convert uncertainty into risk (by quantifying it) on behalf of investors. The relationship between entrepreneurs and risk is quite subtle and will be explored further in section 11.7.

Maximising investors' returns

Some commentators have suggested that the primary role of an entrepreneur is one of maximising the returns that shareholders get from their investments. In effect, the suggestion is that they create and run organisations which generate long-term profits on behalf of the investors that are higher than would otherwise have been the case. This is another aspect of the entrepreneur's role in generating overall economic efficiency.

Investors will certainly look around for entrepreneurs who create successful and profitable ventures, although the view that entrepreneurs in the real world act simply to maximise shareholders' returns is questionable. Entrepreneurship, like all management activity, takes into account the interests of a wide variety of stakeholder groups, not just those of investors. Nor is it evident that investors demand that a firm maximise their returns whatever the social cost might be. Whereas Lord Hanson openly placed maximising shareholder returns at the top of his agenda, Anita Roddick would argue for a much broader range of concerns for The Body Shop.

Processing of market information

Classical economics makes the assumption that all the relevant information about a market is available to and is used by producers and consumers. However, human beings are not perfect information processors. In practice, markets work without all possible information being made available or being used (this is a theme that will be developed in section 6.3). One view of entrepreneurs is that they keep an eye out for information that is not being exploited. By taking advantage of this information, they make markets more efficient and are rewarded out of the revenues generated. This information is information about *opportunities*. The idea that entrepreneurs are information processors is in essence a sophisticated version of the idea that entrepreneurs pursue opportunities and provide competitive efficiency.

One of the ways in which smaller organisations may be more successful than larger competitors is that they may be more adept at spotting and taking advantage of unexploited information (an issue to be considered further in section 21.1).

In summary, entrepreneurs clearly play an important economic function. It is difficult, though, to reduce this to a single economic process in which the entrepreneur's role is different from that of other economic actors.

1.4 The entrepreneur as a person

Key learning outcome

An understanding of how different views of the nature of individual personality have been introduced into definitions of and understanding of the entrepreneur.

We are all different, not only in the way we look but also in the way we *act* and in the way we *react* to different situations. We talk of people having consistent *personalities*. Psychologists have long had an interest in personality and have developed a number of conceptual schemes and exploratory devices to investigate it. Some of these, and how they influence thinking about entrepreneurs, will be discussed in more depth in Chapter 3. This section sets the scene by considering six broad approaches to defining the entrepreneur as a person.

The 'great person'

An immediate reaction when faced with an entrepreneur, or indeed anyone with influence and social prominence such as a leading statesman, an important scientist or a successful artist, is to regard them simply as being special: as a 'great person' who is destined by virtue of his or her 'nature' to rise above the crowd. Such people are born to be great and will achieve greatness, one way or another. The 'great person' view can often be found in biographies (and not a few autobiographies) of entrepreneurs. It is a nice narrative and an inviting angle biographically or journalistically.

Entrepreneurs can certainly be inspiring, and may provide motivating role models. Generally though, the 'great person' view, however passionate, is not particularly useful. For a start it is self-justifying. If an entrepreneur achieves success, it is because they are great; if they fail then they are not. It is tautological. Further, it is not predictive. It can only tell us who will become an entrepreneur after they have done so (and achieved success). There is no test for greatness other than its expression. Furthermore, it assumes entrepreneurship is entirely innate. It sees no role for the wider world in influencing the initiation or progression of the entrepreneur's path. Most damaging, however, is the way it denies the possibility of entrepreneurial success to those who are not (or are not seen or do not feel themselves to be) born to be great persons.

Social misfit

Another view which forms a marked contrast to the great person view but which also has a great deal of currency is the idea that entrepreneurs are *social misfits* at heart. In this view someone is an entrepreneur for an essentially negative reason: they are unable to fit into existing social situations. As a result the entrepreneur is driven to create his or her own situation. It is this that provides the motivation to innovate and build new organisations.

Advocates of this view look towards both anecdotal and psychological evidence for support. Many entrepreneurs achieve success after comparatively unhappy and lacklustre careers working as professional managers. Often they relate their inability to fit into the established firm as a factor in driving them to start their own venture.

Some researchers who have studied the childhood and family backgrounds of entrepreneurs have noted that they are often characterised by privation and hardship which left the person with a lack of self-esteem, a feeling of insecurity and a repressed desire for control. This leads to rebellious and 'deviant' behaviour which limits the person's ability to fit into established organisations. Entrepreneurial activity, it is concluded, is a way of coming to terms with this. It provides not only a means of economic survival but also an activity which enables a reaction against anxiety left by psychological scars. If, as Schumpeter suggests, entrepreneurship is *creative destruction*, then the social misfit view certainly emphasises the entrepreneur as a creative destroyer.

While the idea of the social misfit may provide insights into the motivations of *some* entrepreneurs, any generalisation of this sort is dangerous. For every entrepreneur whose childhood was unhappy and involved privation, another can be found who was quite comfortable and happy. Many successful entrepreneurs recall being dissatisfied when working within established organisations. However, this is not necessarily because they are misfits in a negative sense. Rather, it may be because the organisation did not provide sufficient scope for their abilities and ambitions. This in itself may be demotivating and therefore managerial performance in an established firm is not necessarily a good indicator of how someone will perform later as an entrepreneur.

Personality type

The conceptual basis for the personality type view of entrepreneurship is that the way people act in a given situation can be categorised into one of a relatively limited number of responses. As a result, individuals can be grouped into a small number of categories based on this response. For example, we may classify people as *extrovert* or *introvert*, *aggressive* or *passive*, *spontaneous* or *reserved*, *internally* or *externally orientated*, etc. Each of these types represents a fixed category (there is more on such categorisation in section 4.1).

There is a common impression that entrepreneurs tend to be flamboyant extroverts who are spontaneous in their approach and rely on instinct rather than calculation. Certainly, they are often depicted this way in literature and on film. Detailed studies, however, have shown that all types of personality perform equally well as entrepreneurs. Personality type, as measured by personality tests (more on this in section 3.2) does not correlate strongly with entrepreneurial performance and success. For example, introverts are just as likely to be entrepreneurs as are extroverts.

Personality trait

The idea of personality *trait* is different from that of personality *type*. While a personality may be *of* a particular type, it *has* a trait. Whereas types are distinct categories, traits occur in continuously variable dimensions.

Psychologists distinguish three types of trait that are relevant to understanding personality.

- *Ability traits* relate to specific abilities such as problem solving, planning, innovativeness or negotiation skills. These may be learnt and are certainly developed by practice. The extent to which they reflect innate abilities is not clear and is a controversial issue.

- *Temperamental traits* are those concerned with public actions – 'how we do what we do'; for example, extroversion and introversion or internal versus external reference (whether we look inside ourselves or to the outside world for guidance and judgement on our actions) are temperamental traits.
- *Dynamic traits* are those concerned with internal motivation – 'why we do what we do'; they relate to internal drives.

In an influential study in the early 1960s, David McClelland identified a 'need for achievement' (along with various other characteristics) as the fundamental driving trait in the personality of successful entrepreneurs. Other factors which have also been viewed as important include the need for autonomy, the need to be in control of a situation, a desire to face risk, creativity, a need for independence and the desire to show leadership qualities.

While conceptually very powerful, the trait approach to the entrepreneurial personality raises a number of questions. To what extent are traits innate? Are they fixed features of personality or might they actually be learnt? To what extent are traits driven by external factors? How does a trait as measured in a personality test relate to behaviour in the real world? Is the same trait expressed in the same way in all situations? Does possession of certain traits lead to entrepreneurship or does pursuing an entrepreneurial career merely provide an opportunity to develop and express those traits? Do entrepreneurs simply act out the traits they feel are expected of them?

The idea of traits in the personality of entrepreneurs provides a very important paradigm for the study of entrepreneurial motivation. However, the available evidence suggests it is unwise to advocate, or to advise against, an entrepreneurial path for a particular manager based on the perception of traits they might, or might not, possess. This is a theme that will be returned to when the issue of personality testing and entrepreneurship is considered in section 3.2.

Social development approaches

Both personality type and trait are seen as innate. They are determined by a person's genetic complement (nature) or by early life experiences (nurture) or by some combination of both. (The relative importance of these two things and how they might interact is a highly controversial issue in social theory.) Personality type and trait are also seen as being 'locked into' a person's mental apparatus, and therefore relatively fixed. They can change only slowly or under special conditions.

The social development view regards personality as a more complex issue. In this view, entrepreneurship is an output which results from the interaction of internal psychological and external social factors. The view is that personality develops continuously as a result of social interaction and is *expressed* in a social setting rather than being innate to the individual. The way that people behave is not predetermined, but is contingent on their experiences and the possibilities open to them.

In this view, entrepreneurs are not born, they are *made*. While their predisposition may be important, it does not have any meaning in isolation from their experiences. A person is not, once and for all, entrepreneurial. He or she may, for example, decide to become an entrepreneur only at one particular stage in their life. Equally, he or she may decide to give up being an entrepreneur at another.

A number of factors are seen as significant to the social development of entrepreneurs. In general, they fall into one of three broad categories:

- *Innate* – factors such as intelligence, creativity, personality, motivation, personal ambition, etc.
- *Acquired* – learning, training, experience in 'incubator' organisations, mentoring, existence of motivating role models, etc.
- *Social* – birth order, experiences in family life, socio-economic group and parental occupation, society and culture, economic conditions, etc.

The social development model provides a more plausible picture of entrepreneurial behaviour than those that assume entrepreneurial inclination is somehow innate. Entrepreneurship is a social phenomenon. It is not inherent within a person, rather it exists in the interactions *between* people and with social situations. While entrepreneurs may actively grasp opportunities, they do so within a cultural framework. The social development approach is sophisticated in that it recognises that entrepreneurial behaviour is the result of a large number of factors, some internal to the entrepreneur, and others which are features of the environment within which entrepreneurs express themselves. However, this is also a weakness. While it identifies the factors which might influence entrepreneurship, it usually cannot say *why* they influence it. While social development models are good at indicating what factors might be involved in entrepreneurial behaviour, they often suggest so many factors that might be involved that their predictive power is limited. It can be very hard to test social development models empirically.

The role of personality in entrepreneurial inclination and success is a controversial area. In part this is because there is no general consensus of what the concept of personality actually means or refers to. As Chapter 3 reviews, there are several approaches to the notion of personality within different schools of psychology. Combine this with the lack of agreement on what (or who) constitutes an entrepreneur and the scope for debate will be evident.

Cognitive approaches

Cognitive science is the branch of psychology that attempts to develop an understanding of how we as humans obtain and process information and use it to make sense of the world. Its application to entrepreneurship is of growing importance. Cognitive insights into entrepreneurship are discussed fully in Chapter 4.

1.5 Entrepreneurship: a style of management

Key learning outcome

A recognition that entrepreneurship is a style of management aimed at pursuing opportunity and driving change.

The discussion so far has emphasised what the entrepreneur is *not*, as much as what they *are* because it is important to dispel certain myths about the entrepreneur. In particular, it is important to discount the theories that the entrepreneur is someone with a particular type of personality or that certain people are somehow born to be entrepreneurs. We must also recognise that the entrepreneur does not have a clear-cut economic role. However, we must now consider what the entrepreneur actually *is* by developing a perspective that will illuminate the way entrepreneurs go about their tasks *as* entrepreneurs rather than providing a potentially restrictive *definition* of the entrepreneur.

What we can say with confidence is that an entrepreneur is a *manager*. Specifically, he or she is someone who manages in an *entrepreneurial way*. More often than not they will be managing a specific *entrepreneurial venture*, either a new organisation or an attempt to rejuvenate an existing one. The entrepreneurial venture represents a particular management challenge. The nature of the entrepreneurial venture characterises and defines the management that is needed to drive it forward successfully. Drawing together the themes that have been explored in this chapter, it is evident that entrepreneurial management is characterised by three features: a focus on change, a focus on opportunity and organisation-wide management.

A focus on change

Entrepreneurs are managers of *change*. An entrepreneur does not leave the world in the same state as they found it. They bring people, money, ideas and resources together to build new organisations and to change existing ones. Entrepreneurs are not important as much for the *results* of their activities as for the *difference* they make.

Entrepreneurs are different from managers, whose main interest is in maintaining the status quo by sustaining the established organisation, protecting it and maintaining its market positions. This is not to deprecate a desire for equilibrium as an objective – it can be very important and is an essential ingredient in the effective running of a wide variety of organisations – but it is not about driving change.

A focus on opportunity

Entrepreneurs are attuned to opportunity. They constantly seek the possibility of doing something differently and better. They innovate in order to create new value. Entrepreneurs are more interested in pursuing opportunity than they are in *conserving resources*.

This is not to suggest that entrepreneurs are not interested in resources. They are often acutely aware that the resources available to them are limited. Nor does it mean that they are cavalier with them. They may be using their own money and, if not, they will have investors looking over their shoulders to check that they are not wasting funds. What it *does* mean is that entrepreneurs see resources as a means to an end, not as an end in themselves.

Entrepreneurs expose resources to risk but they also make them work by stretching them to their limit in order to offer a good return. This makes them distinct from managers in established businesses who all too often can find themselves more responsible for protecting 'scarce' resources than for using them to pursue the opportunities that are presented to their organisations.

Organisation-wide management

The entrepreneur manages with an eye to the *entire* organisation, not just some aspect of it. They benchmark themselves against organisational objectives, not just the objectives for some particular department. This is not to say that functional disciplines such as marketing, finance, operations management, etc. are unimportant. However, the entrepreneur sees these as functions which play a part in the overall business, rather than as isolated activities.

Entrepreneurial managers as venturers

In short, the entrepreneur is a manager who is willing to *venture*: to create change and to pursue opportunity rather than just to maintain the status quo and conserve resources. Of course, the effective entrepreneur does *all* these things when appropriate. There are times when the status quo is worth sustaining, and times when it is unwise to expose resources. Part of the skill of the effective entrepreneur is knowing when *not* to venture. However, when the time is right, the entrepreneurial manager *is* willing to step forward.

This is a 'soft' definition. There is no hard and fast distinction between the entrepreneur and other types of manager. This does not make the entrepreneur any less special, nor does it make what entrepreneurs do any less important. What it does do is open up the possibility of entrepreneurship. In being 'just' a style of management it is something that can be learnt. Managers can choose to be entrepreneurial.

An illuminating characterisation of entrepreneurship is offered by Czarniawska-Joerges and Wolff (1991), who use the language of theatrical performance rather than economics to distinguish among *management*, which is:

> *the activity of introducing order by coordinating flows of things and people towards collective action*

and *leadership*, which is:

> *symbolic performance, expressing the hope of control over destiny*

and *entrepreneurship*, which is, quite simply:

> *the making of entire new worlds.*

In conclusion, we can say that entrepreneurial management is characterised by its *whole organisation* scope, its objective of creating *change* and a focus on *exploiting opportunity*. These characteristics are shown in Figure 1.1.

1.6 The human dimension: leadership, power and motivation

Key learning outcome

An appreciation of the way in which the concepts of leadership, power and motivation are interrelated.

Entrepreneurs are managers, but they are not just any sort of manager. If we were to seek the one characteristic that distinguishes entrepreneurs from their more conventional colleagues it would most likely be found *not* in their strategic or analytical insights (though these are important) but in the *human dimension*: the way in which they use leadership and power and their ability to motivate those around them. Any discussion of entrepreneurship must, therefore, develop an insight into the ways in which leadership, power and motivation may be used as managerial tools.

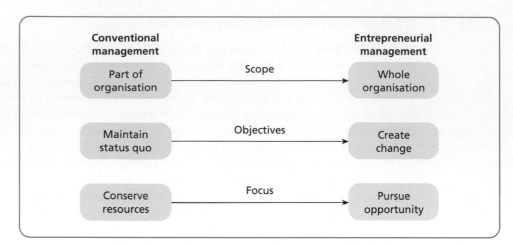

Figure 1.1 Conventional management and entrepreneurial management: a comparison

An economic perspective suggests that human organisations exist to process resources. The differentiation of labour within them allows that processing to be carried out more efficiently. However, once those resources are processed they must be distributed to the stakeholders who make up the organisation. That distribution is rarely on an 'equal' basis. Further, organisations are not just rational orderings of activities but are also the stages upon which their members act out the roles which define them. Hence any discussion of leadership, power and motivation must be willing to take its cues from a variety of perspectives: *functional* ones, which construe the organisation as a deterministic system, *interpretive* ones, which explore human experience within organisations, and *radical* ones, which question the way in which different individuals benefit from organisational life.

In light of this, no one definition can possibly hope to fulfil the complete potential of any of these concepts. However, it is important to give the ideas some kind of conceptual location, and basic definitions can be suggested as follows.

> *Leadership might be defined as the power to* focus *and* direct *the organisation.*
>
> *Power might be defined as the ability to* influence the course of actions *within the organisation.*
>
> *Motivation might be defined as the* process of encouraging *an individual to take particular courses of action.*

Leadership, power and motivation are distinct concepts but clearly any discussion of one will usually draw in the others since they are different aspects of the overall process of control over the venture. It is useful to regard them as different aspects of the approach the entrepreneur takes to controlling the direction of the venture (Figure 1.2).

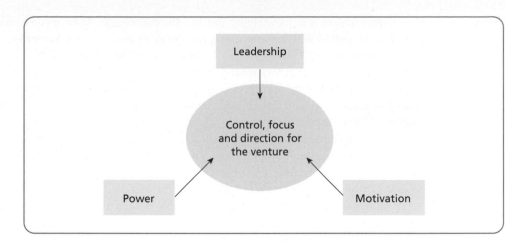

Figure 1.2 The dynamics of entrepreneurial control: leadership, power and motivation

Leadership, power and motivation come together in the means the entrepreneur chooses to shape and drive their venture in the *direction they wish to take it*. They are tools the entrepreneur adopts in order to turn their vision into reality, and as such, they lie at the heart of their project to create an entire new world.

> *It is important to recognise that entrepreneurial leadership, power and motivation cannot be confined within the formal organisation. They must extend beyond it to draw all the venture's stakeholders (its investors, customers and suppliers as well as its employees) together.*

Power

Power is a concept which appears to be central to successful management and which has resisted being reduced to a simple conceptual formula. To many people the term has a negative connotation. Power means power 'over' people. It suggests coercion and is something which must be curtailed. The biologist Edward O. Wilson (1975), for example, defined power as 'the assertion of one member of the group over another in acquiring access to a piece of food, a mate, a place to display, a sleeping site or any other requisite to the genetic fitness of the dominant individual'. However, an emerging idea is that power is not centred on an individual at all. Rather, it is a result of the structural factors that define how people work together and interact with each other. House (1988) offers a good review of the development of this idea.

However, if we define power as an ability to influence the course of actions within the organisation then power becomes a necessary feature of organisational life. Power is a feature of situations in which resources are limited and outcomes are uncertain. Under these conditions, actions *must* be influenced or the organisation would not be an organisation. In this respect, power is an inevitability and, like the organisation itself, it can be made to work for good as well as ill. Certainly, entrepreneurs must recognise the basis for power within their organisation and learn to use it both positively and effectively. This is an approach taken by Jeffrey Pfeffer (1981) in his important study, *Power in Organizations*.

Power must be distinguished from *authority*. Authority represents a *right* to influence the course of actions owing to the position that the holder of that authority has within the organisation. This right is not the same as *ability*. The way in which authority translates into power depends on how the people who make up the organisation regard the holder's standing and the position they occupy. Whereas one group may recognise the position, others may not do so. The entrepreneur may be given a high degree of ostensible authority by the social system in which they operate. The venture may 'belong' to them and be seen as the property of the individual entrepreneur. They will probably be seen as the chief executive, that is, the most senior decision maker. However, this in itself is no guarantee that they will actually have power over their venture. As with leadership, the entrepreneur's position *potentiates* power rather than provides it.

An important line of analysis sees power manifest itself as the control of different aspects of the venture. The relationship is reciprocal. Power gives access to control, and control provides a basis for power. Dimensions of control which are important for the development of the entrepreneur's power base are *resources*, *people*, *information*, *uncertainty*, *systems*, *symbols* and *vision*.

Motivation

Motivation, the condition that makes individuals undertake, or at least desire to undertake, certain courses of action, is a subject that has received a lot of attention from psychologists over the past hundred years. Because of its impact on organisational performance, it is of great interest to management theorists and practitioners. A number of approaches to its understanding have been developed. These approaches are varied, emphasise different factors and generally supplement, though at times they do contradict, each other. They all offer unique insights. They differ in the impact they have had on the understanding that has been gained of managerial motivation in general and on entrepreneurial motivation in particular. A major dichotomy exists between those theories that regard motivation as an outward expression of inner drives and those that regard motivation as something directed towards achieving externally defined and rewarded goals. Some approaches attempt reconciliation between these two factors. An understanding of entrepreneurship does however demand a distinction between an entrepreneur's ability to motivate themself and their ability to motivate those around them.

Self-motivation

Some important elements to address in terms of self-motivation are as follows.

Why am I doing this?
Good entrepreneurs know why they have chosen to be entrepreneurs. They constantly remind themselves why they have chosen the entrepreneurial path. The attractions of entrepreneurship can be understood in the way that the course fulfils economic, social and

self-developmental needs better than alternative routes open to the entrepreneur. Self-motivation must be built on an understanding that the option taken is one that is desirable.

Learning from mistakes

Like any other manager, entrepreneurs make mistakes from time to time. Sales may not be made or investment propositions may be rejected. Personal interactions may be mismanaged. Entrepreneurs are, however, very sensitive to the mistakes they make. This is not just because the consequences of the mistakes are greater than those made by other managers (although they may be) but because entrepreneurs present themselves as experts in managing their venture and its associated uncertainty. Errors of judgement cut to the heart of this role. They can be a great blow to the entrepreneur's confidence.

Of course, mistakes are an inevitable part of any managerial career, not just the entrepreneurial one. Effective entrepreneurs try to avoid mistakes by thought and preparation before entering situations, but when mistakes do occur they are met positively. The good entrepreneur does not try to deny the mistake or pass off responsibility to others. Rather, mistakes are regarded as an opportunity to learn. This means that ego must be detached from the incident and a cold analytical eye used to view the situation to identify a way of avoiding a similar mistake in the future.

Enjoying the rewards

All too often the entrepreneur can become so involved in running the venture that they forget to enjoy its rewards. At one level, this could mean spending the money that has been made. However, this consumption can only be a narrow part of the rewards of entrepreneurship. Money is rarely a complete motivating force for the entrepreneur and, in any case, significant financial rewards may only be accrued a long way down the line. The main rewards lie in the job itself: the challenges it presents, the opportunity to develop and use new skills, the power to make changes, the satisfaction of leadership, and so on.

Learning to recognise these rewards and to savour them is a major factor in developing and sustaining self-motivation.

Motivation of others

Once self-motivation has been achieved the entrepreneur is in a strong position to start motivating others. Motivation is a behavioural phenomenon. Individuals are motivated (or demotivated) by the way people act towards them. This behaviour is an integral part of leadership. It is sensitive to personality and situation. As such, motivating behaviour is a complex process although some common patterns of motivating behaviour can be identified. Figure 1.3 shows a framework for managing individual motivation. Its key elements are set out below.

Understanding personal drives

Before someone can be motivated it is important to recognise what they want to gain from their situation. Management occurs in a social setting and the needs which individuals bring to a situation are a complex mix of financial, social and developmental ones. The effective entrepreneur lays the groundwork for motivating the people in the venture to undertake specific tasks by involving them in the vision that has been created for the venture. This is achieved by communicating the role they will play in this vision and what they will get out of it.

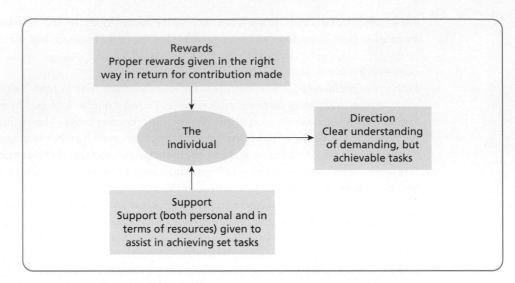

Figure 1.3 A framework for individual motivation

Setting goals

People are motivated not just in an abstract sense; rather, they are motivated to do something. In other words, motivation must lead somewhere. The entrepreneur is responsible for setting the goals that must be achieved. The degree to which these are specific objectives and the formality they take will be dependent on the situation, the entrepreneur's personal style and the cultural setting.

Whatever their form, individuals must recognise their goals and be able to locate them in relation to the goals of the organisation as a whole. Such goals should stretch the individual but also be realistic. They should demand effort but must be achievable given the personal and organisational resources the individual commands.

Offering support

Setting objectives is just the first step in motivating people. If people are to deliver, they require support. This can take the form of ongoing encouragement, advice, the provision of resources and influencing behind the scenes. The support offered should be commensurate with the level of the task and the demands on the person undertaking it. Effective motivation means giving people room to use their skills and insights but never letting them think that they are out on their own.

Using rewards

Rewards take a wide variety of forms. In character, rewards are the means that satisfy an individual's economic, social or developmental needs. In scope, the term 'reward' covers everything from a simple nod of approval from the entrepreneur to a complex deal offering a share in the financial performance of the venture. Whatever the nature of the reward, an entrepreneur who knows how to motivate understands how best to use it.

First, rewards must be *appropriate* for the task undertaken. They must match the individual's expectations of what the reward should be. Second, their magnitude must be right: too small and they can lead to cynicism; too large and they can engender suspicion. Third, rewards must be used on the proper *occasions*. Rewards which are given too freely (and this includes simple things like comments of approval) become devalued. Fourth, they must be seen to be *equitable*. If the reward structure for different individuals and groups is seen to be unfair then jealousy and conflicts can result.

A positive approach to sanctioning

The entrepreneur must occasionally resort to sanctioning individuals who fail to perform in an appropriate way. How this necessary task is handled is important not just for maintaining the motivation of the individual but also for the signals it sends to the organisation as a whole. In general, a positive approach to sanctioning is to be advocated. The objective of the sanctioning must be seen to be one of helping the individual to deliver at the proper level, not just as a punishment. It should not (primarily) be about what was done wrong in the past, but about how performance can be improved in the future. This should also encourage a forum which allows the issues to be discussed while personality and ego are put to one side. Indeed, it can provide an opportunity for the entrepreneur to show their goodwill. All in all, sanctioning, so far as possible, should be seen as a positive experience.

Summary of key ideas

- There is no universally agreed definition of entrepreneurship. The wide variety of definitions in the literature emphasise three aspects:
  - the entrepreneur as a *manager* undertaking particular *tasks*;
  - the entrepreneur as an *economic agent* generating particular *economic effects*; and
  - the entrepreneur as an *individual* of a particular *personality*.

- The idea that there is an 'entrepreneurial' personality which predisposes people to business success is far from clear and is controversial.

- Some important schools of thought on the entrepreneurial personality include: the great person, the social misfit, the personality type, the personality trait, social development and the cognitive.

- Entrepreneurial management may be distinguished from conventional management by:
  - a focus on change rather than continuity;
  - a focus on new opportunities rather than resource conservation; and
  - organisation-wide rather than specific-function management.

- *Leadership*, *power* and *motivation* are interrelated and interdependent tools which the entrepreneur can use to control the venture and give it direction.

- Leadership is the power to *focus* and *direct* the organisation. Entrepreneurial leadership is based on the communication of *vision*.

- Power is the ability to influence the *course of actions* within the organisation. Power is based on the control of *resources* and the *symbolic* dimensions of the organisation, particularly the vision which drives it.

- Motivation is the ability to *encourage* an individual to take a particular course of action. Motivation is based upon an understanding of drives and the ability to reward effort.

Research themes

This chapter has aimed at providing an introduction to the nature of the entrepreneur and the various attempts to define entrepreneurs as a distinct class of economic actors. As a starting point, it is right that this chapter highlights directions for the development of ideas later in the book. I wish to pick up on particular research ideas at these latter points, when understanding is fuller. So at this stage I will indicate some general research themes touching upon the definition of entrepreneurs.

Historical development of the concept of the 'entrepreneur'

Despite some very good reviews, a comprehensive account of the way in which the term 'entrepreneur' has changed over the past three hundred years or so would add a great deal of value. Much existing work deals with the concept in a formal sense within the economics and management discourses. Less has been done on its use within the psychology, anthropology or sociology fields. Also of interest might be its use in popular literature. How does the world in general see entrepreneurs? A good starting point for ideas and style would be the edited commentaries of Pollard (2000) on the representation of business in English literature.

Perceptions and associations with the concept of the 'entrepreneur'

Most people have some feelings about entrepreneurs (often quite strong ones) based on their knowledge and experience of them. I often run brainstorming sessions in which people are invited to suggest the ideas they associate with them. There is an opportunity to undertake this in a more systematic way, using an initial brainstorming to generate associations (for example, the entrepreneur is dedicated, is ruthless, works hard, and so on), classify those associations as positive or negative (good or bad) and then to quantify the findings in a second stage in which individuals are invited to rate their agreement with the idea (for example, strongly agree to strongly disagree). Originality would come from classifying respondents in a way that reflects their interaction with entrepreneurs (for example, only know about them from the news, have worked with one as an employee, have sold things to them, I am one!). Develop your own ideas on how respondents might be classified. Further originality would come from creating a pictorial representation (or mapping) of the results. Relationships between experience of the entrepreneur and attitudes towards them might then be revealed. Any good book on market research will guide details of an appropriate methodology. Gartner's classic 1988 study would be a good starting point.

Philosophical issues in defining the 'entrepreneur'

This is one for the more philosophically minded researcher. Definitions are things we find in dictionaries. But the nature of and the role of the knowledge contained within definitions are major issues in analytical philosophy (the branch of philosophy that deals with the relationship between knowledge, concepts, language and the world). For example, analytical philosophers distinguish between *ostensive* definitions – those that point to something – and *contextual* definitions – those that set out a list of criteria by which something is recognised. There are other issues, of course. Any good introductory book on analytical philosophy will discuss these issues. My recommendations would be the books by Grayling (1999) and by Hospers (1990). Both are excellent. The project should aim to take approaches to the definition of the entrepreneur and critically evaluate them using the relevant philosophical ideas. Think about answering the following questions. Why do we find it so hard to define entrepreneurs in an exact and universally agreed way? Is it something to do with our (lack of) knowledge of entrepreneurs (do we need more)? Are entrepreneurs inherently indefinable, or is our expectation of what a definition of the entrepreneur or entrepreneurship can (or should) do at fault?

Key readings

I normally only recommend two key readings but I think William Gartner's two papers should be read as a pair (neither are too long and are quite accessible). The Barton-Cunningham and Lischeron paper is slightly more conceptual in its approach but covers the difficulty in obtaining a definition very well.

Barton-Cunningham, J. and Lischeron, J. (1991) 'Defining entrepreneurship', *Journal of Small Business Management*, Jan., pp. 45–61.

Gartner, W.B. (1988) '"Who is an entrepreneur" is the wrong question', *American Journal of Small Business*, Spring, pp. 11–32.

Gartner, W.B. (1990) 'What are we talking about when we talk about entrepreneurship?', *Journal of Business Venturing*, Vol. 5, pp. 15–28.

Suggestions for further reading

Bacharach, S.B. and Lawler, E.J. (1980) *Power and Politics in Organizations*, San Francisco, CA: Jossey-Bass.

Baumol, W.J. (1968) 'The entrepreneur: introductory remarks', *American Economic Review*, Vol. 58, pp. 60–3.

Brockhaus, R.H. (1987) 'Entrepreneurial folklore', *Journal of Small Business Management*, July, pp. 1–6.

Bygrave, W.D. and Hofer, C.W. (1991) 'Theorising about entrepreneurship', *Entrepreneurship Theory and Practice*, Vol. 16, No. 2, pp. 13–22.

Cole, A.H. (1968) 'Entrepreneurship in economic theory', *American Economic Review*, Vol. 58, pp. 64–71.

Cromie, S. and O'Donaghue, J. (1992) 'Assessing entrepreneurial inclination', *International Small Business Journal*, Vol. 10, No. 2, pp. 66–73.

Cropanzano, R., James, K. and Citera, M. (1992) 'A goal hierarchy model of personality, motivation and leadership', *Research in Organisational Behavior*, Vol. 15, pp. 267–322.

Czarniawska-Joerges, B. and Wolff, R. (1991) 'Leaders, managers and entrepreneurs on and off the organisational stage', *Organisation Studies*, Vol. 12, No. 4, pp. 529–46.

Deakins, D. and Freel, M. (2003) *Entrepreneurship and Small Firms* (3rd edn). London: McGraw-Hill.

Drucker, P.F. (1985) *Innovation and Entrepreneurship*. London: Heinemann.

Emerson, R.M. (1962) 'Power-dependent relationships', *American Sociological Review*, Vol. 27, pp. 31–41.

Gartner, W. (1985) 'A conceptual framework for describing the phenomenon of new venture creation', *Academy of Management Review*, Vol. 10, No. 4, pp. 696–706.

Grayling, A.C. (ed.) (1999) *Philosophy 1*, Oxford: Oxford University Press.

Green, R., David, J., Dent, M. and Tyshkovsky, A. (1996) 'The Russian entrepreneur: a study of psychological characteristics', *International Journal of Entrepreneurial Behaviour and Research*, Vol. 2, No. 1, pp. 49–58.

Hamilton, R. (1987) 'Motivations and aspirations of business founders', *International Small Business Journal*, Vol. 6, No. 1, pp. 70–8.

Hargreaves Heap, S.P. (1998) 'A note on Buridan's ass: the consequences of failing to see a difference', *Kyklos*, Vol. 51, No. 2, pp. 277–84.

Hickson, D.J., Hinings, C.R., Lee, C.A., Schneck, R.J. and Pennings, J.M. (1971) 'A strategic contingencies' theory of intraorganizational power', *Administrative Science Quarterly*, Vol. 30, pp. 61–71.

Hisrich, R.D. and Peters, M.P. (2002) *Entrepreneurship* (5th edn). New York: McGraw Hill.

Hitt, M.A., Ireland, R.D., Camp, S.M. and Sexton, D.L. (eds) (2002) *Strategic Entrepreneurship: Creating a New Mindset*. Oxford: Blackwell.

Hofstede, G. (1980) 'Motivation, leadership and organisation: do American theories apply abroad?' *Organisational Dynamics*, Summer, pp. 42–63.

Hornaday, R.W. (1992) 'Thinking about entrepreneurship: a fuzzy set approach', *Journal of Small Business Management*, Oct., pp. 12–23.

Hospers, J. (1990) *An Introduction to Philosoplical Analysis* (3rd edn). London: Routledge.

House, R.J. (1988) 'Power and personality in complex organizations', *Research in Organizational Behaviour*, Vol. 10, pp. 305–57.

Kilby, P. (1971) 'Hunting the Heffalump', in Kilby, P. (ed.), *Entrepreneurship and Economic Development*. New York: Free Press.

Kirby, D.A. (2003) *Entrepreneurship*. London: McGraw-Hill.

Kuratko, D.F., Hornsby, J.S. and Naffziger, D.W. (1997) 'An examination of owner's goals in sustaining entrepreneurship', *Journal of Small Business Management*, Jan., pp. 24–33.

Kuratko, D.F. and Hodgetts, R.M. (2001) *Entrepreneurship: A Contemporary Approach* (5th edn). New York: Dryden.

Kuznetsov, A., McDonald, F. and Kuznetsov, O. (2000) 'Entrepreneurial qualities: a case from Russia', *Journal of Small Business Management*, Vol. 38, No. 1, pp. 101–7.

Lambing, P. and Kuehl, C. (1997) *Entrepreneurship*. Upper Saddle River, NJ: Prentice Hall.

Landau, R. (1982) 'The innovative milieu', in Lundstedt, S.B. and Colglazier, E.W., Jr (eds) *Managing Innovation: The Social Dimensions of Creativity, Invention and Technology*. New York: Pergamon Press.

Leibenstein, H. (1968) 'Entrepreneurship and development', *American Economic Review*, Vol. 58, pp. 72–83.

McClelland, D. (1961) *The Achieving Society*. Princeton, NJ: Van Nostrand.

Mill, J.S. (1848) *Principles of Political Economy with Some of their Applications to Social Philosophy*. London: J.W. Parker.

Morris, M.H. (2000) 'Revisiting "who" is the entrepreneur', *Journal of Developmental Entrepreneurship*, Vol. 7, No. 1, pp. v–vii.

Olson, P.D. (1986) 'Entrepreneurs: opportunistic decision makers', *Journal of Small Business Management*, July, pp. 29–35.

Olson, P.D. (1987) 'Entrepreneurship and management', *Journal of Small Business Management*, July, pp. 7–13.

Peterson, R.A., Albaum, G. and Kozmetsky, G. (1986) 'The public's definition of small business', *Journal of Small Business Management*, July, pp. 63–8.

Petrof, J.V. (1980) 'Entrepreneurial profile: a discriminant analysis', *Journal of Small Business Management*, Vol. 18, No. 4, pp. 13–17.

Pfeffer, J. (1981) *Power in Organizations*. Cambridge, MA: Ballinger.

Pollard, A. (ed.) (2000) *The Representation of Business in English Literature*. London: Institute of Economic Affairs.

Say, J.B. (1964) *A Treatise on Political Economy: Or, the Production, Distribution and Consumption of Wealth*. New York: A.M. Kelly (reprint of original 1803 edition).

Scherer, R.F., Adams, J.S. and Wiebe, F.A. (1989) 'Developing entrepreneurial behaviours: a social learning perspective', *Journal of Organisational Change Management*, Vol. 2, No. 3, pp. 16–27.

Schumpeter, J.A. (1928) 'The instability of capitalism', *Economic Journal*, pp. 361–86.

Schumpeter, J.A. (1934) *The Theory of Economic Development* (1961 translation by Redvers Opie). Cambridge, MA: Harvard University Press.

Seters, D.A. van (1990) 'The evolution of leadership theory', *Journal of Organisational Change Management*, Vol. 3, No. 3, pp. 29–45.

Sharma, R.A. (1980) *Entrepreneurial Change in Indian Industry*. New Delhi: Sterling Publishers.

Soltow, J.H. (1968) 'The entrepreneur in economic history', *American Economic Review*, Vol. 58, pp. 84–92.

Stanworth, J., Stanworth, C., Grainger, B. and Blythe, S. (1989) 'Who becomes an entrepreneur?' *International Small Business Journal*, Vol. 8, No. 1, pp. 11–22.

Tait, R. (1996) 'The attributes of leadership', *Leadership and Organisational Development Journal*, Vol. 17, No. 1, pp. 27–31.

Taylor, B., Gilinsky, A., Hilmi, A., Hahn, D. and Grab, U. (1990) 'Strategy and leadership in growth companies', *Long Range Planning*, Vol. 23, No. 3, pp. 66–75.

Thompson, J.D. (1967) *Organizations in Action*. New York: McGraw-Hill.

Vroom, V.H. (1963) *Leadership and Decision-making*. Pittsburgh, PA: University of Pittsburgh.

Watson, T.J. (1995) 'Entrepreneurship and professional management: a fatal distinction', *International Small Business Journal*, Vol. 13, No. 2, pp. 34–46.

Webster, F.A. (1977) 'Entrepreneurs and ventures: an attempt at classification and clarification', *Academy of Management Review*, Vol. 2, No. 1, pp. 54–61.

Wilson, E.O. (1975) *Sociobiology: The New Synthesis*. Cambridge, MA: Harvard University Press.

Zaleznik, A. (1977) 'Leaders and managers: are they different?' *Harvard Business Review*, May/June, pp. 67–78.

Selected case material

CASE 1.1

21 January 2006 **FT**

Football set to score stylishly

SYL TANG

It is one of those national clichés: Americans don't understand football (or soccer, as they call it). No matter how many times it has been suggested that the sport is about to penetrate finally the stars and stripes mindset, it somehow never takes off the way it has in the rest of the world.

But that may finally be about to change, if hip-hop mogul Jay-Z gets his way. His big idea? It's fashion – not an Olympic win or a gorgeous frontman – that will spearhead the revolution. You see, Jay-Z made a move earlier this year to buy into the football club Arsenal and he's not the only trendy US investor thinking football is about to go mainstream.

Recently Californian entrepreneur David Schulte bought Lotto, a 40-year-old clothing brand based in Treviso, and the number one soccer brand in Italy, dressing over

600 European players. No sooner had he made the purchase than – score – he launched Lotto Leggenda, a non-performance luxury line sold in boutiques such as Los Angeles's Fred Segal, Arrive in Miami, and Blue and Cream in New York. Schulte has a dream: design it and they will come.

'My goal is to get them to buy into the flavour of soccer,' he says. 'I don't know if I can get them to sit and watch every game. Soccer in the States is not defined by the local league; it's the globalisation, the lifestyle of the soccer player, a big-money sport.'

In fact it is the money that has prevented soccer from becoming a US phenomenon. Soccer's structure of two 45-minute halves does not lend itself to the way America broadcasts sports. The big networks have no interest in televising a game where there are no commercials for 45 minutes. But, says, Adidas's Abby Guyer, 'Broadband television could change all that. With the advent of new sports channels, on cable and now with in-demand, it's conceivable that big networks will offer in-demand in addition to regular programming.'

Indeed, the 2006 World Cup, being played in Germany, will receive national attention in America in a way the previous tournaments did not, if for no other reason than fans will not find themselves forced to watch games taking place in Asia at 3am.

'The traditional American view is that Americans don't care about soccer and because it's a pretty select group of people into soccer, Adidas has focused on the World Cup for soccer fans. But all of that will change in 2006,' says Guyer, pointing out that lately David Beckham has spent a lot of time in America. 'He has a lot to do with it. Americans may not know much about him as a player but he is the first well-known soccer name who wants to be a New York star.'

Schulte agrees that the globalisation of media and multinational excitement around Beckham has led Americans to consider football more seriously.

'Though it's an integral part of Europe, worldwide media has now made football players' lifestyle an integral part of culture. Beckham rents yachts, has a beautiful wife, drives a Bentley. It's a way of life that the hip-hop, high-end generations X and Y have bought into, that people want to emulate. That aesthetic is exported into our country. The tastemakers are looking for the next thing.

'There is an exoticism to the sport. Hispanic culture has crested: Colombian culture in Miami and Mexican culture in Los Angeles have become very important to America. Countries such as Italy, Brazil and Argentina have become travel destinations. Tastemakers are into them – and soccer happens to be the only sport that matters to those countries.'

Perhaps it began as long as four years ago, with a project Guyer herself conceived. Charged with marketing Adidas Lifestyle, the fashion-focused arm of the brand, she set out to prove that although soccer was not a 'mainstream American thing', in a city such as New York, with its huge expatriate community, it could, when targeted to fashion-specific acolytes, succeed.

'Maybe these are people who wouldn't watch a US National Football League game; who work in or are into fashion: that was the idea,' she says.

A photography exhibit by Kai Regan of soccer being played in Brooklyn and Queens was followed by a courier project by Adidas. Hand-chosen recipients were delivered a red plastic suitcase marked World Cup Survival Kit with the word 'Fanatic' on it in white. Inside were fashion-relevant items, such as fashionable jerseys, soccer socks and badges, and a magazine with people in fashion and music speaking about the best moments of the World Cup and musing on which team they themselves would play, alongside true soccer profiles, schedules organised in New York time, and interviews of top players. For fun, 'world cup aromatherapy', comic books and the matchbooks of the best bars at which to watch soccer were included.

With just 500 kits distributed by young women in soccer gear arriving in person at recipient's offices, Adidas created a phenomenon that spawned the first Adidas Fanatic soccer tournament. What started as one event instantly became an entire month of activities. Sixteen teams from hipster fashion companies and shops such as Alife signed up to play. The following year, posters that didn't even include date or time or any contact information drew 21 teams, from hip record labels, sneaker and skate shops, hotel groups, design magazines, marketing agencies such as Supreme, Fader, Tolkion, the TriBeCa

CASE 1.1 CONT.

Grand hotel, even The Diner in Brooklyn, a barbeque joint, to the 2003 Fanatic Redux.

The event was conceived for the media community – but one without pressure on fashion journalists: no media are asked to cover the Adidas element. Still, it led to the sport becoming front and centre with edgy fashion types. Two teams went on to recruit more teams and form a league that plays in Chinatown on Chrystie Street once a week, an area increasingly surrounded by hip boutiques.

But what's is all got to do with clothes? Guyer points out that 'soccer allows people to put national stuff on fashion.' She agrees with Schulte that luxury wear could lead to fandom. 'The fans always come first. For the whole of the rest of the world, soccer is their lifeblood and so it's authenticity first, then the clothing. However, people can arrive at fandom from a different path.'

Source: Syl Tang, 'Football set to score stylishly', *Financial Times*, 21 January 2006, p. 6. Copyright © 2006 Syl Tang.

CASE 1.2

14 January 2006 **FT**

Clothes maketh the man

AMY RAPHAEL

Johnnie Boden is skating around the sample room at his North Acton HQ on an office chair. It is a strange and slightly unnerving sight. He wears a light blue shirt, a blue jumper tied untidily around his waist, dark jeans, scuffed Camper shoes and plaster of Paris on his lower left arm. He thinks it's a bit excessive – he only broke his finger. When asked how, he pushes his right hand through his mop of dark red hair and launches himself a bit closer. 'Pub fight.' A pause followed by a broad smile. 'Actually,' he says slowly in his deep, high-class voice, 'I fell off my horse.'

With endless energy to burn, 44-year-old Boden seems unable to sit still. He politely announces he's thirsty, disappears to ask an assistant to fetch some water and then pounces on the jug when it arrives. He's warm so he jumps up and opens the windows, which are covered with a blown-up photo of boys and girls running free on an English beach, probably in Cornwall or Norfolk. The kids are in rude health and dressed, naturally, in the vibrant stripes and vivid floral patterns that have come to epitomise Mini Boden.

In the 12 years since he abandoned his career as a stockbroker and first thought of setting up a mail order clothing company for 'time-pressed people', Johnnie Boden has become so successful that his company's name has virtually become an adjective. A 'Boden woman' is around 40 (though she could be as young as 25 or as old as 55), she has a couple of children and works part-time from home. She is a Yummy Mummy, a modern lady who lunches. Her husband is a professional family man who happily accepts the clothes his wife presents to him. Their kids sleep in Mini Boden jersey pyjamas and, by day, throw on velour stripy hooded dresses or camouflage cargo pants.

With their combined income of £60,000, the Boden family is unashamedly middle-class and growing a little conservative, although apparently 20 per cent read *The Guardian*. Johnnie Boden, who was educated at Eton and Oxford, refers to his clients as being 'inner-directed'. All these facts, figures and terms point to substantial market research, which Johnnie claims is a fundamental part of the company's success in providing the Boden family with what it wants. Given that there is only one retail outlet (in Hangar Green, west London), the company has to research constantly its core customer base or it would have little idea of who makes up the half million active Boden regulars in Britain.

'People who buy Boden want to look fashionable but don't want to be enslaved by fashion. That to me really is a key thing.' In other words, they're not interested in making a statement with a label. 'Correct. That's a very good way of putting it. We started off with men's wear but now the vast majority of what we sell is women's wear and Mini Boden. And we know from the research that we're not appealing to the twenty-something woman who has to have Stella McCartney's latest outfit. We're for people who are slightly more self-confident, who don't need the labels. They like colour, and quirk is also an important factor.'

It is the quirkiness and whimsical nature of Boden's catalogues that define them. In Mini Boden, each bright colour photo of a child is accompanied by a caption with their name, age and future occupation (Milly, eight, surfer; Giorgia, seven, ballet teacher). In the women's catalogue, we discover that Natalie loves Chunky Monkey ice-cream. The personal touch is central too. Not only is the label Boden's signature but he appears to contribute some of the blurb too, sometimes even referring to his own three kids (aged 5, 8 and 11). 'My daughters wear these constantly at this time of year,' Johnnie himself writes of the stonewashed logo sweatshirt in the current Mini Boden catalogue.

The Boden empire, which last year saw a pre-tax profit of £10.4m on sales of £86m and this year hopes to achieve sales of £100m, combines the catalogue with an equally bright and 'fun' website. Although the catalogue has changed beyond recognition – in the early days it used line drawings before photography was an affordable option while friends were used as models until it all became too complicated – Boden says 'a lot of money' is being spent to improve the quality of the images on the website.

At times the privately owned company seems to bombard customers with catalogues and e-mails, each with constant special offers: '£10 off when you spend £30 or more plus FREE postage and FREE returns.' Boden insists it is not rashly sending out catalogues desperate to attract new customers but that it's done the research and the timing is scientific. 'We'd love to be able to send out one which would serve as our shop window for six months but unfortunately people just throw the catalogues in the bin or forget about them so we have to remind them by sending one every three weeks. In America you'd get one once a week.'

It was from America that Johnnie Boden took his inspiration and it is the US that is now proving to be something of a holy grail for him. 'I was a rather bad and unhappy stockbroker who was sent to the States. I saw how people could buy good-quality clothing from catalogues, which gave me the basic idea. We started selling to America in 2002 and it's doing fantastically well. It now accounts for about 20 per cent of our sales.' Though ambitious, Boden has no current plans to move into other territories, partly because America is a big country to conquer properly but also because he aims to double the UK mail order market by around 2010.

CASE 1.2 CONT.

His flourishing business must, I suggest, be the result of him being a perfectionist or workaholic but he shies away from labelling himself. In fact, he hates being labelled at all. He has found, of course, that with success comes public exposure – and the press have been quick to spotlight Johnnie Boden's Eton–Oxford background. On occasion he is seen more as a privileged Tory boy than a successful British entrepreneur. 'Oh yeah,' he grimaces, skating away to the other end of the sample room. 'All that bollocks.' He sighs. 'The problem, as David Cameron tells us, is that people are so obsessed with these things. They think because you have that kind of background, you must be a certain type of person.'

His rich voice drops to almost a whisper. 'I was privately educated and I don't really want to go into it but emotionally I probably was er . . . lots of things weren't great for me. But I don't deny my background gave me huge benefits which I'm using to my best – and, dare I say it, everyone's – advantage.' His voice rises again. 'I'm doing my best to sell fantastic clothes. The idea that we sell to a small clique is laughable. We do have a lot of customers in south-west London but that's simply where the money is. We only get about 12 per cent of our customers' clothing spend so the Yummy Mummy will be also be buying from M&S, Matalan, Jigsaw and Gap. Everybody shops around.'

While he's riled, I ask Boden about an article published in May 2003 where he is quoted as 'agreeing heartily' with a piece he had just read in *The Spectator* saying teenage delinquency is caused by working mothers. His face darkens. 'I don't want to comment because I was misquoted and it made me very cross. I didn't say what was attributed to me and I actually spoke to the journalist afterwards and it all got quite nasty . . . but it was her word against mine.'

So what does he really think of working mothers? 'My wife only doesn't work full-time now because she's got three children to look after. Most of the employees here are women and the ones who've had children tend to be very mature. Bringing up children brings an added dimension to your life. I'm completely relaxed about it.' He shrugs and points to the door. 'You can ask any of those women out there. Boden is extremely flexible.'

The point is Johnnie Boden has never pretended to be what he is not. In the very first press releases he mentioned his education and he has never pretended not to be a Tory. Similarly, he has never claimed that Boden has anything to do with high fashion. There are a handful of designers he admires – Matthew Williamson, Marc Jacobs, Clements Ribeiro – but his background is in the City and not in fashion. 'Absolutely. I'm not a designer but I've got quite a good feel for it. My job is working with designers and saying, "Left a bit, right a bit." In the early days, I had strong opinions about men's wear product and I still do . . . But I'm basically tweaking the design team's ideas.'

Boden, it seems, is quite happy with his world. 'I don't understand the whole catwalk industry and I'd look a bit of a prat if I tried to get involved. It's not really what we are about.' He roughs up his hair, fiddles with his plaster of Paris. 'As long as we can keep our finger on the pulse with things that really matter, I'm very happy not to be part of the fashion world. I don't really want to spend my life air kissing at catwalk shows . . .' He smiles triumphantly. 'Anyway, I've never been to a fashion show in my life.'

Source: Amy Raphael, 'Clothes maketh the man', *Financial Times*, 14 January 2006, p. 3. Copyright © 2006 Amy Raphael.

Discussion points

1. Compare and contrast David Shulte (Lotto) and Johnnie Boden (Boden) in terms of (a) their roles in making the economy work, (b) the tasks they undertake to develop their ventures and (c) (what you suppose) is special about them as personalities.

2. As entrepreneurs, in what way(s) are they different from 'ordinary' managers?

CHAPTER 2

Types of entrepreneur

Chapter overview

Classification often complements definition. It can sort items so that defining characteristics become evident. Definition then enables allocation of particular items to specific categories. However, classification can often be undertaken even if there is no clear definition available. This is so with the concept of the entrepreneur. As Chapter 1 makes clear, there is no single, unambiguous, universally agreed definition as to what an entrepreneur is. This chapter is concerned with outlining a variety of approaches taken to classify entrepreneurs. Consideration of social and public entrepreneurs is reserved until Chapter 7.

2.1 Classifying entrepreneurs

Key learning outcome

An understanding of how different types of entrepreneur might be distinguished.

Classification of entrepreneurs into different types provides a starting point for gaining an insight into how different types of entrepreneurial ventures work and the disparate factors underlying their success. This provides important insights to researchers of entrepreneurship, investors wishing to judge the opportunity to invest in new ventures, governments developing policy to support entrepreneurs, and to entrepreneurs themselves when creating strategies for their ventures. After all, we should not expect there to be a single formula for success. Some success factors may be more important to some entrepreneurs than others. What is important to sucess will depend on the type of venture the entrepreneur is undertaking, his or her motivations and the strategic approach taken. There are a number of potential classification schemes. This section aims to give a flavour of the approaches taken rather than a comprehensive review of all the schemes. There are two main approaches: either to classify the entrepreneurs *themselves* or to classify their *ventures*.

The most common types of entrepreneur encountered are either those planning to start up an initial venture, so-called *nascent* entrepreneurs, or those running a single business – *singular* entrepreneurs. Singular entrepreneurs at an early stage of venture development when they are still actively learning are referred to as *novice* entrepreneurs. An early move to classify singular entrepreneurs was to differentiate between *opportunist* entrepreneurs, who were interested in maximising their returns from short-term deals, and *craftsmen*, who attempted to make a living by privately selling their trade or the products they produced. Craftsmen were not so much interested in profits as in being able to earn a stable living from their specialist skills. The idea of the 'opportunist' entrepreneur is quite vague, and a later development was to replace the with two more definite types: the *growth-orientated* entrepreneur, who pursued opportunities to maximise the potential of their venture, and the *independence-orientated* entrepreneur, whose main ambition was to work for themselves. These latter entrepreneurs preferred stability to growth and so were willing to limit the scope of their ventures. Craft entrepreneurs can be subdivided into those whose main aim is to secure a steady income and are referred to as *income orientated*, and those who take the risk of expanding their business and face the challenge of changing their role from being craft operators to being managers of craft operators. Such entrepreneurs are called *expansion orientated*. The term 'craft' is historical. In modern usage it refers not just to artisans but to any entrepreneur who uses a particular knowledge or skill, in addition to general management skills, that can deliver market value. So it would include independent management consultants as much as producers of arts and crafts. In line with this, a further distinction might be made between craftsmen entrepreneurs whose expertise is based on *traditional skills*, those whose expertise is scientific or *technological* and those whose skills are of a *professional* nature.

The American entrepreneurship academic Frederick Webster (1977) considers classification schemes for both the individual entrepreneur and for their ventures. Four types of individual entrepreneur are recognised within his scheme. The *Cantillon* entrepreneur (named after the eighteenth-century French economist Richard Cantillon) brings people, money and materials together to create an entirely new organisation. This is the 'classic' type of entrepreneur, who identifies an unexploited opportunity and then innovates in order to pursue it. The *industry maker* goes beyond merely creating a new firm. Their innovation is of such importance that a whole industry is created on the back of it. They develop not only new products, but also a whole technology to produce them. Examples include Henry Ford and the mass production of motor vehicles, Thomas Edison and domestic electrical products, and Bill Gates with software operating systems. The *administrative entrepreneur* is a manager who operates within an established firm but does so in an entrepreneurial fashion. Usually occupying the chief executive or a senior managerial role, they are called upon to be innovative and to provide dynamism and leadership to the organisation, particularly when it is facing a period of change. An example here is Lee Iacocca's rejuvenation of the Chrysler Motor Company or Jan Carlzon's turnaround of the Scandinavian Airlines System (SAS). Nowadays, administrative entrepreneurs are often referred to as *intrapreneurs*. The *small business owner* is an entrepreneur who takes responsibility for owning and running their own venture. The business may be small because it is in an early stage of growth, or the owner may actually wish to limit the size of their business because they are satisfied that it gives them a reasonably secure income and control over their life.

Webster further classifies entrepreneurial ventures by the ratio of the amount that is expected to be received as a result of the venture's success (the *perceived payoff*) and the number of investors involved (the *principals*). Three types of venture are identified:

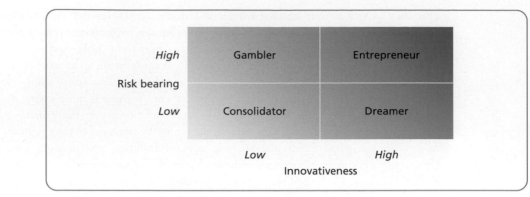

Figure 2.1 Landau's classification of entrepreneurial types

- *Large payoff: many participants* – i.e. a major venture with the risk spread widely over a large number of investors.
- *Small payoff: few participants* – i.e. a limited venture with the risk taken on by a few key investors only.
- *Large payoff: few participants* – i.e. a major venture with the risk taken on by a few key investors.

The remaining possibility – a small expected payoff with a large number of investors – is not considered to be a likely scenario.

Landau (1982) has proposed that the characteristics of innovation and risk taking discussed earlier might provide a basis for classifying entrepreneurs. He suggests that both factors are independent of each other and may be defined as high or low. This gives the matrix illustrated in Figure 2.1.

The *gambler* is the entrepreneur (or better, his or her venture) characterised by a low degree of innovation and a high level of risk. The gamble, of course, arises from the fact that without a significant innovation, the entrepreneur is taking a big chance in being better able to deliver value than existing players in the market. The *consolidator* is the entrepreneur who develops a venture based on low levels of both innovation and risk. This consolidates in that it is really, at best, a marginal improvement on what existing players are doing. Although risks are low, so too must be expected returns. The *dreamer* is the entrepreneur who attempts to combine a high level of innovativeness with low risk. All entrepreneurs would, of course, love to operate here. Many attempt to do so. However, Landau suggests the 'dream' cannot be realised. All innovation, by its nature, introduces risk. The more significant, and hence potentially valuable, the innovation, the greater the risk of the unknown. The final quadrant combines high innovativeness with high risk. This is where true entrepreneurs operate. They (or their investors) must accept risk, but by understanding their innovation and why it appeals to the market, they minimise and manage the risks.

Technology-based entrepreneurs are especially important in modern business as it is they who are taking advantage of new scientific developments, especially in the areas of information technology, biotechnology and engineering science, and offering their benefits to the wider world. Investors are attracted by the high growth potential of their ventures. Jones-Evans

(1995) offers a fourfold categorisation of such technology-based entrepreneurs based on their technical and commercial experience prior to making the move to entrepreneurship:

- The *'research' technical entrepreneur* – those whose incubation has been in a research environment. Two sub-types are suggested: *pure research* entrepreneurs, who have been based in academic research environments and who have not had significant commercial experience, and *research-producer* entrepreneurs, who while working in an academic or industrial research environment have had exposure to commercial decision making.
- The *'producer' technical entrepreneur* – those whose incubation has included an exposure to decision making in a commercial setting along with experience in technological development.
- The *'user' technical entrepreneur* – an individual whose main experience has been commercially based but has involved contact with, and the development of knowledge about, a technical development. This may be because they have been employed in its marketing or sales, or perhaps in procuring that technology for a business.
- The *'opportunist' technical entrepreneur* – one who has no previous exposure to a technology but has seen a commercial opportunity in relation to it and has pursued that with a new venture. Opportunist technical entrepreneurs may call upon a general technical knowledge base and are keen to develop an understanding of the new technology and what it offers. Eisenhardt and Forbes (1984) develop an international perspective of technical entrepreneurship.

This approach to classifying technical entrepreneurs is useful for two key reasons. First, it indicates the type of support the entrepreneur will need in order to drive the venture forward successfully. The research and producer technical entrepreneur, while in command of the technical aspects of what they are doing, may need support with the commercial management of their ventures. User and opportunist entrepreneurs may call upon dedicated technical experts to underpin their commercial moves. Second, it enables investors to judge the managerial balance of the ventures to which they are called upon to commit themselves. An investor seeks not only a good idea, but also one that has a clear market potential and is backed by a managerial team that can not only invent but also deliver that invention to the customer profitably.

Wai-Sum Siu (1996) has examined the types of new entrepreneur who operate in China and he gives a fascinating snapshot of the people behind this fast-growing economy. Basing his assessment on *employment*, *managerial*, *financial*, *technical* and *strategic* criteria, he identifies five types of entrepreneur. The *senior citizen* undertakes a venture to keep occupied during his or her retirement. The business is small and based on personal expertise. It is privately funded and has no long-term strategic ambitions. *Workaholics* are also retired but show more ambition for their ventures than do senior citizens. They often possess administrative experience and their businesses are bigger, drawing on a wider range of technical skills. Strategic goals may be explicit and employees may be invited to make a personal investment in the future of the venture. *Swingers* are younger entrepreneurs who aim to make a living from making deals. They may have only limited industrial and technical experience and rely on networks of personal contacts. Their ventures may be moderately large, but they tend not to have long-term strategic goals. The main aim is to maximise short-term profits. Funding is provided through retained earnings, family contributions and personal loans. *Idealists* are also younger entrepreneurs who run moderate-sized ventures. However, their motivation is based less on short-term profit and more on the sense of achievement and independence that running their own venture gives them. They serve a variety of end markets and their ventures may be based on high-technology products. Financing is through retained profits, family contributions and private investment. *High-flyers* are motivated in much the same way as idealists. However, their ventures are much larger, reflecting success in the marketplace. Again, a variety of products are offered. Corporate goals and strategy tend to be much more explicit than in the idealist's venture, and investment is drawn from a wider variety of sources, including institutional and international agencies.

2.2 Serial and portfolio entrepreneurship

> ### Key learning outcome
>
> An understanding of the types of serial and portfolio entrepreneurs, the motivation of the entrepreneur to lead a series of ventures and the strategy they adopt to do so.

The motivations of entrepreneurs are many and varied. As will be discussed in more detail later, entrepreneurs are driven by a desire for autonomy, prestige and a sense of achievement as much as, if not more than, by a desire to make money. This is most evident in that group of entrepreneurs who, having led one business success, move on to start another. Such entrepreneurs, called *serial entrepreneurs* (sometimes referred to as *habitual* entrepreneurs), gain their rewards from the establishment and building of businesses, not their long-term management. It is notable that some commentators, for example Gartner (1985), argue that once the building stage of the venture ends, then so does true entrepreneurship.

Serial entrepreneurs, as well as being particularly interested in the start-up and early growth phase of the venture, may also have particular decision-making expertise in these areas of business development, and therefore gain their personal competitive advantage in relation to managing this stage. Such skills might be reflected in an ability to spot new opportunities, to evaluate markets and in dealing with financial backers. An entrepreneur who can point to a record of success will also be a more attractive proposition to an investor than one who cannot. Further, the capital generated from an initial venture (retained profits or money made through its sale) may provide a source of funds to start up a further venture. The establishment of additional ventures may also reflect the strategic concerns of the entrepreneur. It may be that the competitive advantage gained in the initial business can be successfully transferred to a subsequent one. Further, several businesses may be a way of diluting risk. These strategic advantages must, of course, be measured against the risk inherent in the entrepreneur's spreading their attention over a broader area. Management buyouts and buy-ins are a fruitful area for serial entrepreneurs. According to Wright *et al.* (1997a) as many as a quarter of managers involved in buy-ins have previously held a significant equity holding as well as managerial responsibility in another venture. Westhead and Wright (1998) explore a range of factors that might encourage serial entrepreneurship, including geographical setting, managerial experience and financing, and find significant effects for a sample of US ventures. Rosa and Scott (1999) studied multiple start-up, cross-ownership and cross-managerial involvement in a sample of Scottish small businesses. They found these to be quite common and an important factor in high-growth businesses.

Serial entrepreneurs may be sub-divided into two types: those who start new businesses in sequence, only running one at any time, and those who run several businesses simultaneously.

The former are referred to as *sequential entrepreneurs*; the latter as *portfolio entrepreneurs*. James Dyson, who started the ball-wheelbarrow business before moving on to the cyclone vacuum cleaner business, is a good example of a sequential entrepreneur. Richard Branson, who has diversified his Virgin group into a number of different areas, is a portfolio entrepreneur. Wright *et al.* (1997b) have suggested that serial entrepreneurs might be classified in the following way:

- *Defensive serial entrepreneurs* are those who undertake subsequent ventures because of a forced exit from an earlier one. This need not be because it failed. It could be because the venture was sold, or floated on the stock market to pay off venture capital investment.
- *Opportunist serial entrepreneurs* are those who undertake subsequent ventures because they perceive the opportunity for financial gain, perhaps on a short-term entry–exit basis.
- *Group-creating serial entrepreneurs* are those who undertake serial entrepreneurship because creating a number of businesses is fundamental to the strategy they are pursuing. Two sub-types of group-creating serial entrepreneurs are suggested. *Deal-making serials* use acquisition as a major part of gaining the new businesses. *Organic serials* start new businesses from scratch and grow them.

This adds up to quite a comprehensive classification scheme, which is summarised in Figure 2.2.

We should not be overly determined to shoehorn individual entrepreneurs into one particular category. The classification of a particular entrepreneur may change over time. At some point all entrepreneurs are nascent and then novice. Most start with a single business. Serial entrepreneurs start off as singular entrepreneurs. A sequential entrepreneur may decide to retain a business before acquiring the next, and so then become a portfolio entrepreneur. At any one time, an individual entrepreneur may fall into more than one category. A portfolio entrepreneur may adopt a mixture of acquisition and organic growth to expand their portfolio. Strategic and financial objectives may be seen in parallel, or not be clearly delineated at all. The point of classification is to guide thinking, not regiment it.

Whatever the approach of the serial entrepreneurs, their desire to succeed with more than one business demonstrates the excitement that the entrepreneurial career offers.

2.3 Entrepreneurship and small business management: a distinction

> ### Key learning outcome
>
> An appreciation of why the entrepreneurial venture is distinct from the small business.

Both small business management and entrepreneurship are of critical importance to the performance of the economy. However, it is useful to draw a distinction between them since small businesses and entrepreneurial ventures serve different economic functions. They pursue and create new opportunities differently; they fulfil the ambitions of their founders and managers in different ways. Supporting them presents different challenges to economic policy makers. Drawing this distinction is an issue of classification. There are two possible approaches, namely to make a distinction between the characteristics of *entrepreneurs* and *small business managers* or between *entrepreneurial ventures* and *small businesses*.

The former is problematical. As discussed in section 1.4, the entrepreneur is not distinguished by a distinct personality type and there is no independent test that can be performed

Nascent
Planning to start a new venture. Venture not yet initiated.

Singular Running a single venture (**Novice** in early stages)	**Opportunist** Look for profitable deals	**Growth orientated** Grow business by increasing range of deals	
		Independence orientated Seek merely to retain independence	
	Craft Utilise personal skill or knowledge	**Expansion orientated** Grow business by expanding craft production capacity	
		Income orientated Seek merely to provide steady income for self and family	
Serial (or **habitual**) Involved in running more than one business	**Sequential** Running only one business at any one time. Leave one business before starting next	**Defensive** Start new business after (forced) exit from initial business	**Deal** New business obtained through acquisition of extant business
			Organic New business initiated and grown from scratch
		Opportunistic Leave initial business and start new business because of perceived better opportunity	**Deal** New business obtained through acquisition of extant business
			Organic New business initiated and grown from scratch
	Portfolio Run more than one business at one time	**Opportunistic** Add on new business because of perceived financial opportunity. No real strategic consideration	**Deal** New business obtained through acquisition of extant business
			Organic New business initiated and grown from scratch
		Group Add on new business because of perceived strategic opportunity. Long-term synergy between existing and new business	**Deal** New business obtained through acquisition of extant business
			Organic New business initiated and grown from scratch

Figure 2.2 A classification scheme for entrepreneurial ventures

to identify an entrepreneur. The question is consequently a matter of personal opinion. Some people may regard themselves as true entrepreneurs whereas others may judge themselves to be 'just' small business managers. This can be an emotive issue and it is not clear what benefits are to be gained by forcing people into different conceptual bags in this way. Rather than trying to draw a distinction between managers, it is more valuable to differentiate what they manage, that is, to differentiate between the *small business* and the *entrepreneurial venture*. There are three essential characteristics which distinguish the entrepreneurial venture from the small business.

Innovation

The successful entrepreneurial venture is usually based on a significant *innovation*. This might be a technological innovation, for example a new product or a new way of producing it; it might be an innovation in offering a new service; an innovation in the way something is marketed or distributed; or possibly an innovation in the way the organisation is structured and managed, or in the way relationships are maintained between organisations. The small business, on the other hand, is usually involved in delivering an established product or service. This does not mean that a small business is not doing something new. It may be delivering an innovation to people who would not otherwise have access to it, perhaps at a lower cost or with a higher level of service. However, the small firm's output is likely to be established and produced in an established way. So while a small business may be new to a locality, it is not doing anything essentially new in a *global* sense, whereas an entrepreneurial venture is usually based on a *significantly new* way of doing something.

Potential for growth

The size of a business is a poor guide to whether it is entrepreneurial or not. The actual definition of what constitutes a small business is a matter of judgement depending on the industry sector: for example, a firm with one hundred employees would be a very small ship-builder, but a very large firm of solicitors. However, an entrepreneurial venture usually has a great deal more *potential* for growth than does a small business. This results from the fact that the entrepreneurial venture is usually based on a significant innovation. The market potential for that innovation will be more than enough to support a small firm. It may even be more than enough to support a large firm and signal the start of an entire new industry. The small business, on the other hand, operates within an established industry and is unique only in terms of its locality. Therefore, it is limited in its growth potential by competitors in adjacent localities. A small business operates *within* a given market; the entrepreneurial venture is in a position to *create* its own market.

A word of caution is necessary here, since having the potential to grow is not the same as having a *right* to grow. If it is to enjoy growth, it is still necessary that the entrepreneurial venture be managed proficiently and that it compete effectively, even if it is creating an entirely new market rather than competing within an existing one.

Strategic objectives

Objectives are a common feature of managerial life. They take a variety of forms; for example, they may be formal or informal, and they may be directed towards individuals or apply to the venture as a whole. Most businesses have at least some objectives. Even the smallest firm should have sales targets if not more detailed financial objectives. Objectives may be set for the benefit of external investors as well as for consumption by the internal management.

The entrepreneurial venture will usually go beyond the small business in the objectives it sets itself in that it will have *strategic* objectives. Strategic objectives relate to such things as:

- *growth targets* – year-on-year increases in sales, profits and other financial targets;
- *market development* – activities actually to create and stimulate the growth and shaping of the firm's market (for example, through advertising and promotion);
- *market share* – the proportion of the market the business serves; and
- *market position* – maintaining the firm's position in its market relative to competitors.

These strategic objectives may be quantified in a variety of ways. They may also be supplemented by a formal mission statement for the venture. This is an idea that will be discussed more fully in Chapter 12.

The distinction between a small business and an entrepreneurial venture is not clearcut. Generally we can say that the entrepreneurial venture is distinguished from the small business by its *innovation*, *growth potential* and *strategic objectives*. However, not all entrepreneurial ventures will necessarily show an obvious innovation, clear growth potential or formally articulated strategic objectives, and some small businesses may demonstrate one or two of these characteristics. However, in combination they do add up to distinguish the key character of an entrepreneurial venture, that is, a business that makes significant changes to the world (Figure 2.3).

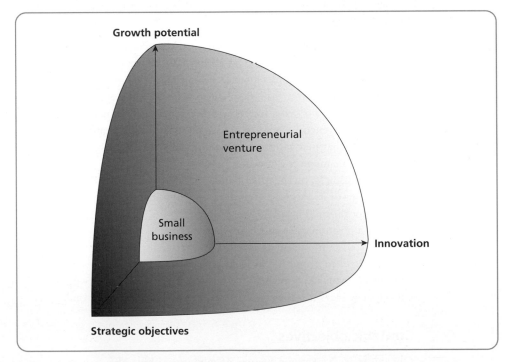

Figure 2.3 The difference between a small business and an entrepreneurial venture

Summary of key ideas

- Classification of entrepreneurs is important for a number of reasons, including research, government policy and investor analysis.

- An important approach classifies entrepreneurs on the basis of whether they are:
  - craft or opportunity based;
  - singular, sequential or portfolio;
  - income or growth motivated; and on
  - the strategy they use to expand the business.

- Entrepreneurial ventures may be distinguished from small businesses on the basis of:
  - the presence of a significant innovation on which the venture is founded;
  - the articulation of strategic objectives;
  - growth potential.

Research themes

Intuitive classification schemes

We human beings are inveterate categorisers. When presented with a new object, situation or problem, we tend to compare it to objects, situations or problems we have encountered before. We then group it with the most similar we have in our memory: we categorise. This influences the way we value new objects, react to situations and judge decisions, because we use values, responses and decision outcomes from our experience of stored categories to help us deal with the new. It would be an interesting project to see how naive individuals (those who have no prior knowledge of how entrepreneurs might be classified – this may include entrepreneurs themselves and those who work with them) approach the issue of classification. Prepare a series of short descriptions of entrepreneurial ventures (real or imagined – better that the subject has no prior knowledge of them). These should be of about 200–300 words. Make sure that they are matched in the types of information they contain but that there is variation in the details. Present these on separate sheets of paper to the subject. Have him or her sort them into two or more categories (you can leave the number to the subject or you may dictate the number of categories you want). Once the subject has done this, conduct an interview requesting that the subject explain why they have categorised as they have. Keep this flexible, and probe interesting details. How do such natural classification schemes match with the more formal schemes described in this chapter? Do different individuals agree on the final classification or is it highly variable? Do individuals use the same criteria or not? How does the way in which different subjects weight or prioritise particular features differ? Summarise by exploring what the findings say about the way in which individuals recognise and judge entrepreneurship.

▶

The effect of classification on judgement

For reasons related to those discussed above, we tend to judge things we know (or are told) are in the same category as more similar than things we know to be (or are told to be) in different categories. So if we provide descriptions of two categories and then present a description of an object, situation or decision problem, individuals' judgements will tend to vary if we suggest it falls into one category or the other *even if the descriptions remain the same*. For example, up to the year 2000, many businesses eagerly sought to classify themselves as dotcoms because they felt they would be favoured by investors. After the dotcom crash when internet stocks tumbled, most businesses were keen to shake off the label and emphasised the traditionality of their offerings. To a large extent, this reflects a change in investors' assessment of the dotcom category *as a whole*, not the prospects of *individual* businesses.

This raises an issue with the classification of entrepreneurs. Collecting entrepreneurs into one category will encourage decision makers to associate them and so bias their judgement. The study might progress as follows. Using the categorisation schemes discussed above, obtain or create short (500 word?) accounts of different types of entrepreneur, their ventures and their performance. Collect these into two categories: one high performing, the other low performing (call these the high- and low-context cases). Next obtain or create an account of a proposed new venture that might be classified with either the high- or low-performing groups (call this the probe case). Take two groups of subjects (at least 25 in each, ideally matched for age, sex and experience) and present each group with all the cases. For one group, associate (based on the classification scheme) the probe case with the high performers; for the other group, associate the probe with the low performers. So both groups have access to the same information; only the association of the probe case changes. Ask the two groups to judge the likely performance of the new venture. In principle, having access to the same information, they should, on average agree. But does the categorisation affect judgement of the venture's potential? Conclude by considering the implications of the findings for the way in which information about new ventures should be presented.

Cluster analysis of entrepreneurial ventures

Cluster analysis represents a variety of techniques for classifying items based on their descriptive characteristics. The methodology is somewhat mathematical but its principles only require basic algebra (a good introductory account of methods is provided by Aldenderer and Blashfield, 1984). The technique involves taking a collection (the more the better) of entrepreneurial ventures described in some detail (these may be from the same sector, or different ones). As a first stage, have a small group brainstorm on what the different characteristics of each venture are. Given this set of descriptive characteristics, then quantify them. Some characteristics (e.g. rate of growth, age of venture, number of businesses in portfolio) are directly numerical; others, such as degree of innovation, might require a judgement using a Likert scale (e.g. highly innovative, moderately innovative, and so on). Once each venture is quantified along each characteristic, apply an appropriate clustering technique and see what categories emerge (a number of software packages are available to do this). How does the categorisation change if the weighting of descriptive characteristics is modified? How do these 'empirical' categories match up with the 'prescriptive' ones described above? Is there a general case to be made for the classification scheme you have devised? How might the scheme be used to develop policy for the ventures in each category (e.g. governmental support, investment issues)?

 ## Key readings

The classic papers addressing the issue of entrepreneur classification. Accessible and still worth reading:

Carland, J.W., Hoy, F., Boulton, W.R. and Carland, J.C. (1984) 'Differentiating entrepreneurs from small business owners: a conceptualisation', *Academy of Management Review*, Vol. 9, No. 2, pp. 345–59.

Gartner, W. (1985) 'A conceptual framework for describing the phenomenon of new venture creation', *Academy of Management Review*, Vol. 10, No. 4, pp. 696–706.

Siu, Wai-Sum (1996) 'Entrepreneurial typology: the case of owner managers in China', *International Small Business Journal*, Vol. 14, No. 1, pp. 53–64.

Webster, F.A. (1977) 'Entrepreneurs and ventures: an attempt at classification and clarification', *Academy of Management Review*, Vol. 2, No. 1, pp. 54–61.

Carland *et al.*'s approach is a somewhat different from mine, but contrasts rather than contradicts. Useful to see how the same issue in entrepreneurship can be seen from different perspectives.

Suggestions for further reading

Aldenderer, M.S. and Blashfield, R.K. (1984) *Cluster Analysis*, Sage University Paper, Quantitative Applications in the Social Sciences series, No. 44. Newbury Park, CA: Sage.

Dunkelberg, W.C. and Cooper, A.C. (1982) 'Entrepreneurial typologies: an empirical study', in Vesper, K.H. (ed.) *Frontiers of Entrepreneurial Research*, Wellesley, MA: Babson College Centre for Entrepreneurial Studies, pp. 1–15.

Eisenhardt, K.M. and Forbes, N. (1984) 'Technical entrepreneurship: an international perspective', *Columbia Journal of World Business*, Winter, pp. 31–7.

Gartner, W. (1985) 'A conceptual framework for describing the phenomenon of new venture creation', *Academy of Management Review*, Vol. 10, No. 4, pp. 696–706.

Gartner, W.B., Bird, B.J. and Starr, J.A. (1992) 'Acting as if: differentiating entrepreneurial from organisational behaviour', *Entrepreneurship Theory and Practice*, Spring, pp. 13–31.

Jones-Evans, D. (1995) 'A typology of technology-based entrepreneurs', *International Journal of Entrepreneurial Research and Behaviour*, Vol. 1, No. 1, pp. 26–47.

Landau, R. (1982) 'The innovative milieu', in Lundstedt, S.B. and Colglazier, E.W., Jr (eds) *Managing Innovation: The Social Dimensions of Creativity, Invention, and Technology*. New York: Pergamon Press.

Miner, J.B., Smith, N.R. and Bracker, J.S. (1992) 'Defining the inventor-entrepreneur in the context of established typologies', *Journal of Business Venturing*, Vol. 7, No. 2, pp. 103–13.

Oviatt, B.M. and McDougall, P.P. (2005) 'Defining international entrepreneurship and modeling the speed of internationalization', *Entrepreneurship: Theory and Practice*, Vol. 29, No. 5, pp. 537–53.

Parker, S.C. (2002) 'On the dimensionality and composition of entrepreneurship', Durham Business School working paper.

Rosa, P. (1998) 'Entrepreneurial process of business cluster formation and growth by habitual entrepreneurs', *Entrepreneurship Theory and Practice*, Vol. 22, No. 4, pp. 43–61.

Rosa, P. and Scott, M. (1999) 'The prevalence of multiple owners and directors in the SME sector: implications for our understanding of start-up and growth', *Entrepreneurship and Regional Development*, Vol. 11, pp. 21–37.

Siu, Wai-Sum (1996) 'Entrepreneurial typology: the case of owner managers in China', *International Small Business Journal*, Vol. 14, No. 1, pp. 53–64.

Webster, F.A. (1977) 'Entrepreneurs and ventures: an attempt at classification and clarification', *Academy of Management Review*, Vol. 2, No. 1, pp. 54–61.

Westhead, P. and Wright, M. (1998) 'Novice, portfolio and serial founders in rural and urban areas (habitual entrepreneurs and angel investors)', *Entrepreneurship Theory and Practice*, Vol. 22, No. 4, pp. 63–100.

Westhead, P., Ucbasaran, D. and Wright, M. (2005) 'Decisions, actions and performance: Do novice, serial and portfolio entrepreneurs differ?' *Journal of Small Business Management*, Vol. 43, No. 4, pp. 393–17.

Westhead, P., Ucbasaran, D., Wright, M. and Binks, M. (2005) 'Novice, serial and portfolio entrepreneur behavior and contributions', *Small Business Economics*, Vol. 25, No. 2, pp. 109–32.

Wright, M., Robbie, K. and Ennew, C. (1997a) 'Venture capitalists and serial entrepreneurs', *Journal of Business Venturing*, Vol. 12, pp. 227–49.

Wright, M., Robbie, K. and Ennew, C. (1997b) 'Serial entrepreneurs', *British Journal of Management*, Vol. 8, pp. 251–68.

Wright, M., Westhead, P. and Sohl, J. (1998) 'Editors' introduction, 'Habitual entrepreneurs and angel investors', *Entrepreneurship Theory and Practice*, Vol. 22, No. 4, pp. 5–21.

Selected case material

7 December 2005

Why it is better to be bootstrapped than well heeled

JONATHAN GUTHRIE

I love American capitalism. It is so much shinier than the UK version. The numbers are bigger. The ups and downs are more melodramatic. Even the jargon is glossier, making the dreariest concepts seem exciting. The disreputable word 'debt', redolent in Britain of Mr Micawber, becomes the far snappier 'leverage'. Sacking Smith in Accounts because he seems a bit useless becomes 'delayering', which sounds clinical, not cruel.

'Bootstrapping' is another example. This means setting up a business with an embarrassing insufficiency of pecuniary wherewithal, as us Brits would describe it. Or, as *Bootstrapping*, a mass market US business book puts it, in very big Wild West-style letters on its front cover: 'Start and Grow a Successful Company with ALMOST NO MONEY'.

This struck a chord with me. The money mentioned by author Greg Gianforte, a Montana entrepreneur whose cover photo suggests he ropes steers for a hobby, is primarily equity capital. I have long thought that the government, the City and the financial media are unhealthily obsessed with this commodity. Few start-ups appear to need it. A recent UK survey showed only three per cent had sold shares to backers.

The TV series *Dragons' Den* fuels the urban myth that finding a wealthy shareholder is a natural part of setting up a business. If I was an aspiring entrepreneur, that would put me off. The private investors on the show have lots of cash. But you could fit their collective fund of charm and humility into a fruit fly's armpit. And leave room for the producer's heart.

Starting a business with ALMOST NO MONEY is a more appealing prospect than prostrating yourself before the show's chief Mr Nasty, mobile phones tycoon Peter Jones, while he laughs at your bald spot. Entrepreneurs have been starting businesses with zero capital for millennia. All you need is stock supplied on tick, or customers willing to pay for products you have yet to buy or create.

Would-be tech moguls have a peculiar fixation with early stage equity capital. Mr Gianforte, whose business RightNow Technologies sells customer service software, says: 'If you asked 100 recent MBA graduates how to start a [tech] business they would tell you to write a business plan, raise money, build a bonfire and start shovelling cash on to it.'

Mr Gianforte set up his company on more parsimonious lines in 1997, in offices at the back of an estate agency in picturesque Bozeman, Montana. There were no windows. 'We bought posters of the mountains in Wal-Mart and stuck them on the walls,' he recalls, because 'a bootstrapper only spends money when it is absolutely necessary.' The company now has sales of $85m (£49m) and a market capitalisation of $550m.

Max Bleyleben of Kennet, a venture capital firm with offices in London and Silicon Valley, says that bootstrapped tech businesses 'tend to be more efficient and better at adapting to changes in the market'. Start-ups can generate working capital, he suggests, by getting loans from software resellers and other partners. Alternatively, they can match cash-hungry product creation with cash-generative consulting.

Naturally, Mr Bleyleben still believes start-ups need VC money, otherwise he'd be out of a job. But a company should build up a few millions in turnover first, he says. That means the investor will typically get a smaller stake for a given outlay.

Chirag Shah co-founded Trading Partners, a UK supply chain technology company, without early equity backers. The investment bubble burst before any had signed up. Capital was thus limited to savings from the founders' former careers as 'vastly overpaid consultants'. Mr Shah says: 'We would go to customers, find out what they wanted, and start developing the product after we had sold it to them. Our programmers never slept and we took no salaries for two years.' Turnover is now into 'double-digit millions'.

StaffWare, a UK workflow software start-up, survived hand-to-mouth between 1988 and 1995, according to John O'Connell, one of its founders. It extracted development funding from big computing companies such as Unisys and ICL. And it charged software resellers a sign-up fee. StaffWare later floated on AIM [Alternate Investment Market] and was bought out for £130m last year, making Mr O'Connell a wealthy man.

He says: 'It is much better to be funded by your partners than the City, because it brings you closer to them.' But he adds that his seven years of bootstrapping were 'very tough, very unremitting'. Mr O'Connell says: 'I got good at walking tall while inwardly quaking with fear. You cannot make sales if you look and sound desperate.'

Starting a tech venture is now a lot cheaper than it was for Mr O'Connell because the cost of memory has plummeted. Superior programming languages have increased the productivity of each programmer. Widespread internet use has made promotion easier too.

Indeed, early stage tech investors who survived the shakeout of the early 1990s in the US are now getting the cold shoulder from some start-ups, says Mr Bleyleben. 'These no longer need to raise much money to get started,' he says, '$100,000 will do it, instead of $3m.'

Tech entrepreneurs on both sides of the Atlantic should therefore have increasing opportunities to scrutinise the bald spots of would-be 'dragons' beseeching them to sell a stake. After watching a characteristically haughty performance by the *Dragons' Den* panellists last week, I find that a pleasing prospect.

Source: Jonathan Guthrie, 'Why it is better to be bootstrapped than well heeled', *Financial Times*, 7 December 2005, p. 16. Copyright © 2005 The Financial Times Limited.

CASE 2.2

26 January 2006

Jaeger owner sets up fund to support fashion students

JON BOONE

Harold Tillman, the retail entrepreneur, has set up a scholarship fund to support fashion students in an attempt to address industry concerns that too many fail to fulfil their potential because of a lack of financial support.

Mr Tillman, the owner of the Jaeger brand, hoped his £1m gift to the London College of Fashion would help to give students the financial freedom that he had enjoyed. 'When I was a student in the 60s everything was basically paid for but we know that today there are several students a year who can't afford to go on and study at MA level. Because they have to repay their student loans, some of them end up taking professions they haven't even studied, and that is a huge loss to our industry.'

He called on other fashion and retail businesses to support emerging talent through scholarship and mentoring schemes.

'Fashion is worth around £10bn a year to Britain but it is only based around a very small network of businesses and I don't think those are aware of how much they rely on students coming through the system. We are not talking about the world class British designers . . . but about the general design pool that most businesses need.'

Philip Green, the retail entrepreneur, has spent £5m setting up a Fashion Retail Academy to give teenagers aged 16–18, the skills he said were lacking among recruits to his industry.

Frances Corner, head of the LCF, welcomed the donation and said: 'The creative industries are vital for our economic future and yet while China, India and Singapore are putting huge amounts into their creative businesses many people here don't seem to realise that in order to develop major fashion companies, designers need to be supported . . . when they are still at the one man band stage.'

In 2004, the clothing industry produced almost £4bn of goods and employed more than 90,000. If the textile industry is added, the combined sectors produce more than £9.5bn worth of goods at manufacturers' prices and employ 180,000 people. Overseas sales combined are worth more than £6bn at manufacturers' prices.

Mr Tillman's gift to the LCF will pay for 10 MA places at the college, which is celebrating its 100th anniversary this year. Graduates will also receive work placements at Jaeger or one of Mr Tillman's other businesses.

Ms Corner said with most government funding focused on undergraduates many fashion students who wanted to study further were unable to do so. 'This will be a huge help because students have to spend a lot of money on materials and producing a portfolio and many of them have considerable debt. Many . . . will want to start their own businesses, which obviously requires even more funding.'

Discussion Point

1. Using the scheme developed in the chapter, classify Greg Gianforte and Philip Green as entrepreneurs.

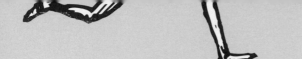

CHAPTER 3

The entrepreneurial personality

Chapter overview

This chapter builds on the initial discussion (section 1.4) of the role of personality factors in entrepreneurial inclination, motivation and performance. The difficulties in relating personality to entrepreneurship are explored, particularly in terms of instrumentalising these fundamental concepts. Different psychological theories of personality are introduced. An introductory account of the increasingly important role that cognitive psychology is playing in entrepreneurship studies is offered. The role of personality testing in predicting entrepreneurial behaviour is considered and some difficulties with it explored.

3.1 Personality and entrepreneurship: some theoretical issues

Key learning outcome

Recognition of some of the theoretical and methodological problems encountered in attempting to link the concepts of entrepreneurship and individual personality.

The idea that an entrepreneur is, in some way, a special sort of person is commonly held. Surveys that I conduct with undergraduates and postgraduates at the start of courses in entrepreneurship suggest that typically 85 per cent of students hold the belief that there is something unique about the personality of entrepreneurs. This belief is persistent. At the end of the course, in which the idea of the entrepreneurial personality is challenged, 65 per cent still retain this belief. The arguments put forward are accepted, but there is insistence that, intuitively, the idea still 'feels right'. Section 1.4 considered some general schools of thinking about the entrepreneurial personality and some issues with them. This chapter expands upon these preliminary ideas. The primary objective of this chapter is not to offer a resolution, but to explore the theoretical and methodological difficulties in settling the issue.

The claim that entrepreneurs have a special, or distinctive, personality is, ultimately empirical. It is something that can be examined and demonstrated to be right or wrong. The methodology for doing this has four aspects: the *instrumentalisation of entrepreneurship* and *personality*, the *ontology* of personality and theoretical *pragmatics*. It is useful to consider these in detail before moving on to consider different schools of thinking about personality.

Instrumentalisation of the concept of entrepreneurship

Instrumentalisation refers to the methodological approach taken to defining, characterising and measuring a variable that plays a part in some theoretical explanation. If the personality of entrepreneurs is to be compared with that of non-entrepreneurs then a strict specification of who is an entrepreneur is necessary. As was made evident in Chapter 1, this is not an easy question to answer. The specification must be in terms of economic function or managerial characteristics. It cannot be in psychological terms because this would make the theory self-fulfilling. The claim is that certain tasks, or economic causality, attract (or perhaps lead to the development of) particular personality types. We cannot use a method in which individuals judge who, from a sample of individuals, are entrepreneurial or not, unless we are sure that the judges are not using (explicitly or implicitly) presumptive personality criteria. A common criterion is simply that a person must have started their own business. An example here is the study by Blanchflower and Oswald (1998). This is useful, because it is quite specific and easy to observe and confirm. However, it is very broad as it includes small business managers as well as entrepreneurs who start and develop large ventures. It also excludes intrapreneurs. The context of, experience of and motivations for starting a business are highly variable. It would be surprising if all business starters were unified within a single personality type. More fruitful might be to use the way in which entrepreneurs are recognised by different schools of economic thinking (see section 6.1). However, here, we noted the difficulty in distinguishing entrepreneurs from other managers. It is a matter of degree. Issues such as identifying significant new opportunities (Austrian School), or being responsible for evaluating and responding to customer demand (heterogeneous demand school), or significantly moulding an organisation's resource base (resource-based view), or positioning a business in a particular sector (industrial organisational economic school) might be used as scales. A weighted average approach to assigning a numerical degree of entrepreneurship to individuals might then be adopted.

Instrumentalisation of personality

If entrepreneurial behaviour and effect are to be correlated with personality, then not only entrepreneurship but also *personality* must be a strictly defined concept. There is not, though, a universal agreement on what, exactly, personality is, what its theoretical underpinning should be or how it should be measured (even if it can be measured). The ways in which different schools of psychology see the personality concept is discussed in more detail below. Whichever conceptualisation is adopted, personality must be something that can be determined *independently* of the individual's specific domain of entrepreneurial activity. Otherwise there is the danger that the domain of activity predetermines personality allocations, once again making the theory self-fulfilling. For example, we may judge an 'eagerness to take risks' as a personality trait. However, entrepreneurs are in jobs where taking risks is (or is seen to be) a major part of their activity. Individuals in other jobs may not get the chance to take risks. This does not mean that, given the right circumstances, they would not be eager to take risks. If so, then risk taking *is* an aspect of that person's personality, he or she just has not had a chance to reveal it. If risk taking is regarded as (potentially) significant, then there must be a test for risk propensity independent of individuals' task contexts.

Ontology of personality

The way in which theories of personality are approached and constructed is sensitive to assumptions about the *ontology* of personality. Ontology is the branch of analytical philosophy that is concerned with the *existence* of concepts. Broadly, there are three positions. *Realism* is the view that a concept has an actual existence in the world independent of our understanding of it. It is there to be discovered through inquiry. *Positivism* proposes that only that which can be observed is real and that we should be suspicious of things we cannot observe. *Instrumentalism* is the view that concepts exist only in the sense that they provide accounts of the world that lead to useful and correct predictions. A realist view of personality would claim that personality is something that individuals actually have and it is the responsibility of research programmes to describe it. A positivist position might be more suspicious. Can we actually observe personality? If so, in what way? Do we need a concept of personality in addition to the notion of 'behaviour'? Personality might be regarded as a way of summarising consistencies and patterns in behaviour, but it is no more than a summary, not something directly observable. An instrumentalist position might claim that personality is a useful concept in that it allows us to account for and predict behaviour and we should accept its existence on this basis.

Theoretical pragmatics

The final aspect of a theory linking personality to entrepreneurship is its *pragmatics*. Broadly, what do we want the theory for and what do we want it to do? There are three positions with respect to this. A *descriptive* theory is based on independent observations of an individual's personality and their entrepreneurial inclination, behaviour and performance. It then describes correlations between the two. A descriptive theory is simply an account of the way in which the world works. A *normative* theory, on the other hand, goes further. It makes a claim that certain aspects of personality are *necessary* for effective entrepreneurial behaviour. A normative theory can be based on empirical observation within a descriptive theory but usually has an element of theoretical presumption that precedes empirical observation (for example, that entrepreneurs *must* be individuals who respond positively to change, whether or not this is actually observed). Normative theories direct descriptive theories in a particular direction, suggesting which factors are important and should be the basis of empirical study. Finally, *prescriptive* theories suggest that if one wants to be a successful entrepreneur then one should have (or adopt or develop) a particular personality type. Prescriptive theories are usually based on the edicts of normative theories or findings of descriptive theories.

Each of the above three types of theory has a different role. Descriptive theories are concerned with how the world is. They regard the personality–entrepreneurship link as a phenomenon that can be discovered and is meaningful in its own terms. Normative theories aspire to make predictions. Given a personality type, then the success or otherwise of that type in an entrepreneurial career can be predicted (to some degree). Personality testing of nascent entrepreneurs makes practical use of normative theories (see below). Prescriptive theories suggest pathways of development to entrepreneurs in that they suggest the personality characteristics entrepreneurs should aim to acquire if they are to be successful. They are important in programmes for education of entrepreneurs.

These different types of theory differ in the way they instrumentalise the personality concept and the ontology they ascribe to personality. Descriptive theories require that personality be something observable, measurable and independent of entrepreneurial activity. They may be comfortable with a positivistic or instrumental ontology. Normative theories are not so dependent on observable counterparts of personality. A normative theory may claim personality to be something that cannot be revealed in a positivistic or even instrumental sense, although this would reduce the validity of the theory to many researchers in the field. Prescriptive theories must limit themselves to aspects of personality that can be developed through conscious action, whether those aspects can be independently measured or not.

The ways in which the entrepreneur may be defined has been discussed in Chapter 1, and these will be expanded upon from an economic perspective in Chapter 6.

3.2 Schools of thinking on personality

Key learning outcome

An introductory understanding of the ways that different schools of psychology approach the concept of personality and the implications of those approaches for thinking about the personality of the entrepreneur.

Psychology, like economics, is a subject that is characterised by numerous schools that agree on some particulars and disagree on others. A fairly general definition of personality might be along the lines of:

A relatively stable pattern or profile of thoughts, feelings and actions that characterise a particular individual

or

What makes us unique.

Such definitions do not get us very far in making personality an observable and measurable concept. Although some advances have been made in this area by psychology, many psychologists are becoming suspicious of the notion of personality. It is interesting to note that the *Penguin Reference Dictionary of Psychology* (3rd edition, 2001) notes at the beginning to its entry on personality that the term is

> *One of the classic 'chapter heading' words in psychology. That is, a term so resistant to definition and so broad in usage that no coherent simple statement about it can be made – hence the wise author uses it as the title of a chapter and then writes about it without incurring any of the definitional responsibilities that go with introducing it into the text.*

As with entrepreneurship, it is not so much that no definition of personality can be found, but that we are embarrassed by riches. A number of different schools of psychology lay claim to the concept (and many other related ones) and offer often contradictory or non-comparable (the technical term is *incommensurate*) definitions.

Each school has its own theoretical underpinning and methodological approach. Critically, each sees the concept of personality in a different light. Before reviewing the leading schools it is worthwhile to consider what they agree upon. This will reveal the core of beliefs about what 'personality' is. Carver and Scheier (2000) develop a definition of personality that covers areas of general agreement across the different schools. They suggest personality is:

- *Organised* – it has a coherent unity and is not fragmented.
- *Active* – personality is maintained by and revealed through dynamic processes.
- *Physical* – personality is a psychological concept, but it is derived from physical (anatomical, neurophysiological) processes, particularly, but not exclusively, in the brain.
- *Causal* – personality determines how an individual will act and react in particular circumstances.
- *Regular* – the personality of an individual is consistent over periods of time, and leads to consistent patterns of behaviour.
- *Manifest* – it shows up in many different ways, including physical states, affective moods, personal feelings, decisions and actions.

Around this core, different psychological schools develop different interpretations of the personality concept. The more important are briefly reviewed below. Accounts of these different perspectives can be found in any good textbook on the psychology of personality. Phares (1987), Mischel (1999) and Carver and Scheier (2000) are recommended. A very accessible introductory account can be found in Jarvis (2000). For an excellent review of recent thinking on the nature of personality the more ambitious student might try David Funder's review in the 2001 *Annual Review of Psychology*.

Psychodynamic approaches

Psychodynamic approaches to personality see it as the result of a series of internal psychological processes that may work in harmony or in discord. The most famous exemplifier of the psychodynamic approach was the Viennese therapist Sigmund Freud (1856–1939). Freud suggested that such forces psychologically *determined* human behaviour. These were not always under conscious control. The unconscious mind played an important role and these forces were often manifest beyond awareness. Freud suggested three primary processes in the anatomy of the mind: the *Id*, which lies in the unconscious, relates to basic biological urges and impulses. It includes biologically determined instincts that demand immediate gratification. The Id is impulsive and irrational. The *Superego*, on the other hand, manages social behaviour and graces. The Superego, which lies in both the conscious and unconscious, maintains an individual's moral beliefs and is imparted by parents and socialisation processes. The *Ego*, which lies in the conscious mind, mediates between the Id and Superego. It helps the Superego keep the Id in check while making sure that the Superego is informed of the person's deeper wants and needs within the Id. The Ego is rational, calculating and plans ahead. Freud developed his theory based on the presumption that these three processes should work in harmony in a balanced, dynamic way and that if they were out of step then some form of mental strife or even illness would result. This strife took the form of three anxieties: *neurotic* anxiety, the belief that one's base instincts would take control (and so one would lose control of one's behaviour), and *moral* anxiety about actions one has taken (guilt, regret, embarrassment, etc.). These are derived from *reality* anxiety, justified (at least to self) beliefs that one is in some sort of danger. Motivation arises from the transformation of instincts within the Id. If these are not socially acceptable, then they must be transformed into actions that are. A number of psychologists have added to, and developed, Freud's thinking.

Freud divides psychologists. Some are intensely loyal to his ideas. Others dismiss his work as speculative, unscientific and not testable in any real sense. If the claim is made that entrepreneurs are so, because running one's own venture is a way of managing these anxieties (the 'misfit' school might have some sympathy with this idea) and that motivation arises from motive transformation, then these claims are not such that can be empirically validated through objective inquiry. It should be recognised that this is not of immediate concern to researchers who are adopting a subjective methodological approach (such methodologies are explored further in Chapter 28).

Dispositional approaches

A disposition is a tendency to act in a particular way in a particular situation. We may say of a person, she is outgoing, or alternatively, introspective. Some people are predictable; others less so. Some people look towards internalised values to judge their acts; others look outside themselves to others' reactions to judge their acts. And so on. Features like these are referred to as *traits*. Traits are dimensions. An individual may have more or less of a trait and be located somewhere along a spectrum. Eysenck (1975) suggested that two key traits were the introvert–extrovert dimension and the emotionally stable unstable dimension. Combining these two independently gave rise to four basic personality types: stable introverts were *phlegmatic*, unstable introverts were *melancholic*, stable extroverts were *sanguine* and unstable extroverts were *choleric*. A number of workers have developed a five-factor model of traits (see Carver and Scheier, 2000, p. 69). The five factors relate to the individual's characterisation in their approach to *power*, *love*, *work*, *affect* (emotionality) and *intellect*. The idea of traits is linked to some ideas in cognitive psychology (see below). Research has been conducted to see if entrepreneurs are drawn disproportionately from one particular trait group. The findings are generally negative; all trait groups are represented in entrepreneurs as they are in the wider population. However, there are issues of methodology and definition, and research continues.

Biological approaches

The term 'biological approaches' covers a range of approaches and might include the evolutionary approaches discussed below. Central, though, is the idea that personality is, fundamentally, a biological process. A specific idea is that personality is dictated by genes. If so, personality can be explained through genetics. At face value, this is quite convincing. After all, our genes dictate our bodies, so why not our minds as well? Environmental factors also play a part. We know that personality must, in part, be physically located, because personality can be changed by physical processes (alcohol, narcotics and brain lesions, for example). The central question is, to what extent is behaviour determined by genetics or environment?

Some evidence supporting the genetic claim has been obtained from twin studies. Identical twins share their genetic complement, while non-identical twins share just half (the same as any siblings). By assessing the personalities of twin-pairs separated at birth through adoption, any closer match between the personalities of identical twins over that of non-identical must be due to genetic factors. This area of research is highly controversial. Not least among the objections is the notion that the approach negates the role of society and personal experience in moulding personality. The study of individual genetic endowments has been transformed by modern DNA technology and the Human Genome Project. To my knowledge, no twin studies have been conducted on entrepreneurs, nor have the genetics of entrepreneurs been explored. Such studies will be an interesting, but frightening, prospect. Can we really imagine venture capitalists giving up reading business plans and talking to entrepreneurs and instead sending them off for DNA testing?

Evolutionary psychological approaches

Evolutionary psychology is based on the premise that modern human cognitive skills are the result of evolution through selective forces. Human beings were essentially 'completed' evolutionarily by about 100,000 years ago. Since then we have not changed significantly in terms of physical characteristics and mental architecture. So we cannot look to the modern world to explain our current repertoire of cognitive skills; rather we must look to that period in the late Palaeolithic when we became what we are. An important aspect of our situation then was the growing complexity of social interactions, motivated not least by the possibility of increasing welfare through the exchange of goods.

One of the more controversial claims made by evolutionary psychology is that our cognition is modularised. We do not have a single, integrated mental system. The human mind is composed of a series of systems that have evolved to deal with different decision situations. There is debate as to the extent to which these systems are integrated at a higher level. Accessible accounts of this idea, and the debate it has engendered, are given by Corballis and Lea (1999), Badcock (2000), Carruthers and Chamberlain (2000), Cartwright (2000), Oyama (2000), Wright (2000) and Barrett *et al.* (2002). Ofek (2001) gives an account of the economic basis of human evolution. By its nature, though, evolutionary psychology is talking about the psychology of human beings as a *species*, not at an individual level. Its concern is with our *common* psychological inheritance. So while it may offer an explanation of entrepreneurial behaviour in general, it is less well placed (at this time) to explain why one person decides to take on the role of entrepreneur and another does not.

Phenomenological approaches

The schools of thinking so far discussed share a belief in the commonality of personality. Individuals may fall into different categories, but within those categories, individuals 'share' a personality. The phenomenological approach takes issue with this. It emphasises the uniqueness of each individual and the irreproducibility of his or her historical and introspective experiences. It prioritises subjective experience over objective classification. Usually associated with the approach are two beliefs about human beings. The first is that humans are endowed with free will, the possibility of making choices for themselves. In practice, these choices may be restricted by both external and internal factors. In principle, though, these restrictions can be removed, freeing the individual to make free choices. Second, it regards humans as self-perfecting, drawn towards the 'good', in terms of health, welfare and personal maturity. The phenomenological approach is, to a greater or lesser degree, anti-positivistic (see Chapter 28). It does not concern itself with generalisations. It prefers to regard accounts of psychology as essentially personal narratives. There are some good phenomenological accounts of the psychological experiences of individual entrepreneurs, but, necessarily, they cannot be extended to the experience of others. Phenomenological approaches cannot explain why some people become entrepreneurs and others do not, simply because it does not set out to.

Behavioural approaches

Behavioural psychology was founded largely by the animal psychologist B.F. Skinner, who, in the late 1940s, studied behavioural conditioning in pigeons. He moved on to extend his ideas to humans. The basic postulates of behaviourism are that psychology must become a 'proper' science and so should concern itself only with what is observable (behaviour) and forget about the unobservable (introspection). In this respect, behaviourism is super-objective and at the opposite end of the scale to phenomenological approaches. Skinner's methodology was to connect human action directly to externally imposed stimuli without calling on the notion of mind as an intervening factor. As might be imagined, Skinner's ideas were, and still are, highly controversial. Skinner's rather brutal behaviourism quickly lost favour when its limitations in explaining some human actions were demonstrated (the most important area is in language development and performance). Some attempts were made to salvage the ideas, but behaviourism has largely been superseded by cognitive psychology (see below), which still connects actions to inputs, but calls upon personal cognitive processes as an intervening mechanism. Most studies into entrepreneurial psychology came at a time after behaviourism was in descent. Despite this, behaviourist ideas are still influential, often at the level of the metaphor. Do we not say entrepreneurs are stimulated by new opportunities? Or that making more capital available will encourage more people to become entrepreneurs? Or that certain social, cultural and economic conditions facilitate entrepreneurship? Unadorned with concern over what is actually happening in the individual mind to connect these stimuli to the response of becoming entrepreneurial, these are in essence behaviourist linkages.

Social-cognitive learning approaches

The social-cognitive learning school moves the debate from concern with personality as something, essentially at least, predetermined and 'in the head' of the individual to something that results from social experience and interaction. It places emphasis on personality as something that is, to a greater or lesser extent, imparted to the individual by others. Social-cognitive learning approaches are very diverse and this school is not unified by a single methodology or even theoretical outlook. However, there is agreement on the importance of learning in a social context. Leadership and the role of mentors are brought into play, as are personal learning styles and strategies. Life experiences such as exposure to incubating organisations are drawn in, along with antecedent (inherent, given) personality factors. This school is influential in the study of entrepreneurship particularly because of its flexibility in dealing with these issues, which are widely seen as relevant. A number of workers have developed social-cognitive learning models of entrepreneurship. An important example includes Cooper (1981), who suggested a model that included three sets of factors influencing entrepreneurial start-up: antecedent influences (those things inherent to the entrepreneur such as genetic endowment, education and life experiences), incubator organisation experience, and environmental experiences (including the availability of opportunities and resources).

The flexibility of the approach, while a strength, is also a weakness. In being able to call upon a wide range of factors, the approach loses specificity. It can fail to make clear predictions, and the move to entrepreneurship can always be accounted for given the range of explanatory factors available. This is not to say that the approach has not offered a number of important insights, especially when handled by researchers careful to control its methodology.

Attribution-based approaches

All of the ideas explored so far have assumed (implicitly at least) that personality is something we, as individuals, possess. Different schools disagree on how it is located and what its psychological underpinning is, but where it is located is not at issue. Attribution theories take a more radical approach and suggest that personality is not so much something an individual has, but is something awarded to individuals by others. Personality is in the eye of the beholder, not the beholden. Attribution theory was largely founded by H.H. Kelley (1973), who asked why individuals tended to assign objects to particular categories and specific events to certain causes. He concluded that individual decision makers were 'intuitive scientists' in that they used an intuitive analysis of variance to make assignments. In particular they looked at three factors: *consistency*, *distinctiveness* and *consensus*. The suggestion in attribution theory is that when allocating an individual of whom we have experience to a particular personality type (either a formal typing from psychological theory, or our personal intuitive categories), we decide across three factors, here applied to the label of 'entrepreneur':

- *Consistency* in the way in which an individual reacts – e.g. we always expect entrepreneurs to react positively and embrace new opportunities.
- *Distinctiveness* in that the individual reacts differently to those stimuli we regard as proper entrepreneurial stimuli, compared with how they react to stimuli we do not regard as such – e.g. we may expect an entrepreneur to be a tough negotiator in a business setting, but not so in his or her family life.
- *Consensus* in that the entrepreneur acts differently from those we do not regard as entrepreneurs. If *all* people react in a certain way, then there is no point in looking towards that action as a way of distinguishing entrepreneurs from others.

If we see that an individual is consistent in reacting positively to entrepreneurial stimuli, is distinctive in their response to specifically entrepreneurial stimuli and is of low consensus in that they react differently from most others, then we will label that person an entrepreneur. The important point to note is that it is *we* who are assigning that label, not the 'entrepreneur' her or himself. Kelley's attribution theory has been very influential in the social sciences (Figure 3.1). Within ten years of its publication, over one thousand papers in the social sciences were published citing it (see Kelley and Michela's review (1980) for an account of early application and developments of the theory). Important avenues of application are in investigating the way dispositions are attributed to an actor (e.g. Ajzen, 1971), the way in which individuals attribute success and failure to themselves or to external factors beyond their control (e.g. Bernstein and Stephan, 1979) and differences in attribution of causal effect between individuals involved in an event (actors) and those looking in on the event

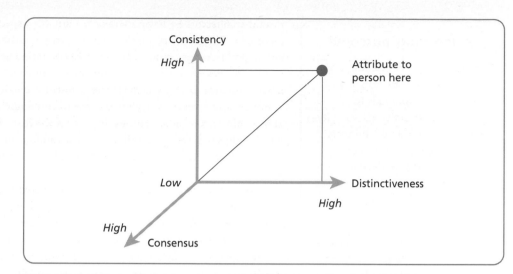

Figure 3.1 Kelley's attribution theory model and its application to the assignment of entrepreneurial personality

(observers) (e.g. Arkin and Duval, 1975). Despite the number of studies, however, I know of no research that utilises attribution theory specifically to explore how people assign the label 'entrepreneur' to other people. There is a clear research opportunity here.

The limitations of personality models

Personality is a concept of central importance in psychology. It plays a crucial role in aiding our understanding of the social interaction between people and it has both illuminated our understanding of, and enriched our appreciation of, the entrepreneur. However, it is important that we do not let an inappropriate idea of personality distort our view. There is no real evidence to suggest that there is a single 'entrepreneurial personality'. People of all personality types, attitudes and dispositions not only become entrepreneurs but become *successful* entrepreneurs. A consequence of this is that personality testing does not provide a good indicator of who will, or will not, be a successful entrepreneur. To be a successful entrepreneur takes many things: ambition, drive, hard work, effort in learning to understand a business and practice as a manager. But it does not demand a particular personality. Experience shows that a reserved introvert who carefully calculates their next move can look forward to as much entrepreneurial success as their more 'theatrical', and instinctive, counterpart. No one with entrepreneurial ambitions should ever dismiss the option of an entrepreneurial career because they do not feel they are the 'right type' of person. To do so reveals more about their misconceptions of entrepreneurship than it does about their potential.

3.3 Entrepreneurship and psychometric testing

Personality testing is part of a more general class of psychological tests generally known as *psychometric* tests. Psychometric tests aim to discover something about an individual's mental architecture by having him or her answer a specific series of questions. These may be on the basis of written answers ('pencil-and-paper' tests) or an interview, or a combination of the two. In addition to personality tests, psychometric testing includes general intelligence testing (such as the IQ test), tests for particular mental aptitudes and a series of techniques for examining psychological abnormalities. The most famous test here is the *Rorschach test*, in which subjects reveal what they see in a random pattern of ink blots (although few psychologists now take this particular test seriously).

Tests that aim to reveal an individual's personality (or personal outlook) face a number of challenges. First, the questions posed must be meaningful and relevant in revealing specific aspects of personality. As will be appreciated from the earlier discussion of schools of thought about personality, the relevance of particular questions will be sensitive to theoretical assumptions being made about what, exactly, personality is. Second, the responses must be correlated to particular personality factors with regard for proper statistical methods. Third, the subject must give honest answers to the questions. Their response should not be influenced by what they feel the investigator wants them to say, nor should they answer on behalf of the person they *want* to be, rather than actually *are*. Fourth, if the test is to have any value as a predictive tool, it must be demonstrated that the way in which the subject responds to the test matches up with the way they actually behave in the real world. Fifth, those aspects of personality revealed must be stable over time. All of these issues present significant methodological challenges and much of the research in the psychometrics field is aimed at resolving them (the interested student is referred to a standard work in the field such as Kaplan and Saccuzzo (1997) for details on methodology and research).

The challenges are particularly acute when it comes to testing the personality of entrepreneurs. Two groups have a particular interest in this area: researchers who are exploring the links between personality and entrepreneurial inclination, and investors who want to be able to predict the likely performance of an individual seeking financial support. Clearly, there is much sympathy between these two groups and they often work in collaboration. A number of tests have been developed for testing entrepreneurs. The most popular are the proactive personality disposition (PPD) and the entrepreneurial-orientation (EO) scale. Proactivity is defined as the extent to which individuals take action to control their environments. This proactivity is measured by asking subjects how they would react in a variety of situations. The assumption is that the more proactive a person is, the more likely they are to is to seek out and pursue an entrepreneurial career. Crant (1996) tested individuals' proactivity measures and then correlated them (along with variables such as sex, education and parental entrepreneurship) with intentions to start a business. The study found that proactivity correlated positively with intention. Becherer and Maurer (1999) tested the proactivity of 215 small business presidents and found that the president's proactivity correlated with the firm's overall entrepreneurial posture (as judged independently), but could not be correlated with the president's leadership style. The EO scale probes the entrepreneur's strategic outlook, rather than personality directly, and it can be applied to firms as well as to individuals. However, it is a psychometric test methodology. The test has eight items that ask, for example, whether the entrepreneur/entrepreneur's firm looks towards introducing new products, or prefers to rely on existing products, whether they tend to initiate actions that competitors react to, or vice versa, and whether the entrepreneur prefers bold, far-reaching acts to cautious incremental acts, and so on. Kreiser *et al.* report studies on the regularity of these orientations on an international basis (2002a) and explore how they are affected by environmental uncertainty (2002b). These authors give full details of the test. Weaver *et al.* (2002) also explore the effect of environmental uncertainty on entrepreneurial orientation.

The findings of studies using instruments such as the PPD and EO scale have produced mixed results. As noted above and in Chapter 1, it is fair to say that, at present, no real consensus has emerged as to the link between personality and entrepreneurial behaviour. No test has consistently and robustly demonstrated any clear, significant connection. (The research picture is a bit distorted because researchers, and journal editors, tend to prefer studies with positive results rather than negative. This is an issue in all walks of academic inquiry, not just entrepreneurship. The negative findings of the Blanchflower and Oswald study (1998) are a notable exception; see section 5.1.) However, research continues and new methodological advances in the future may make the picture clearer (my belief is that cognitive approaches have great potential and are likely to be the most valuable in the future).

Nevertheless, many venture capitalists do insist on prospective entrepreneurs undergoing personality tests before they are awarded investment funds. A number of agencies have started up offering this service to venture capitalists. If they are not going to reveal anything of value, why should they be willing to pay for them? The answer lies (and what follows is very much a personal view) not in personality tests as such, but in the wider nature of human decision making. We are impelled to make sense of the world. We like regularity and patterns (which is why we see faces and other objects in random ink blots). We like to connect events to clear, unambiguous causes, because then we can make decisions influencing them (or at least feel we can). Unfortunately many aspects of the real world are not connected through simple cause and effect chains; they are causally ambiguous. So we seek, and grasp at, simple explanations that give accounts of why contingencies happen. After all, no matter how often it is demonstrated that astrology, tarot card reading and handwriting analysis are sheer nonsense, with no predictive or explanatory power whatsoever, many people simply refuse to give up their belief in them, because in doing so they lose their ability to explain how the world works, something they value greatly. The decision by a venture capitalist to invest, or not, in a particular personality test is a major one. It is fundamentally a matter of judgement and that judgement is hard to explain (even good venture capitalists find it hard to explain *why* they are good). A lot of money and risk is involved. That risk is not just financial. The venture capitalist's reputation and career prospects are on the line as well. Anything that can externalise and objectify an investment decision will be valued. So some venture capitalists' belief in the value of personality testing is based not so much on the fact that it highlights the best investment opportunities, but if the final decision is the wrong one, the investor can point to something public and explicit that is outside his or her own judgement to explain why. In short, it is a self-defence mechanism. But such self-defence may be rational if the investor can safeguard his or her reputation using it.

Summary of key ideas

- The notion that entrepreneurs, as a group, share some aspects of personality that makes them different to non-entrepreneurs is intuitively appealing.

- However, establishing if this is so is problematical.

- Any theory linking entrepreneurship to personality must be clear on what the terms mean and how they can be (independently) measured (instrumentalised).

- This is a challenge with both concepts. It is particularly so with personality.

- Different schools of psychological thinking define, characterise and measure personality in different ways. Important schools include:
  - psychodynamic
  - dispositional
  - biological
  - evolutionary
  - phenomenological
  - behavioural
  - social-cognitive learning
  - attributional.

- Personality testing has been used as both a practical and research tool for evaluating and studying entrepreneurs. However, it is premature to suggest that such testing is unambiguously able to distinguish entrepreneurs from non-entrepreneurs.

- Cognitive approaches consider how humans acquire, store and process information in order to make decisions. Whether entrepreneurs (as a group) are distinct from non-entrepreneurs in their cognitive style and strategy is not yet clear, but it is the subject of extensive research.

- Entrepreneurs are decision makers. The experimental study of human decision making is a fast-growing area that promises to illuminate the way in which entrepreneurs think.

Research themes

Presumptions about entrepreneurial personality

As noted at the beginning of this chapter, many people feel, intuitively, that entrepreneurs have a particular sort of personality. This may be researched further using a Delphi technique. The first stage would be to identify a group of individuals (say 30–50) who might be expected to have developed such a belief – for example, practising entrepreneurs, people who work with entrepreneurs, management consultants, academics in the business field, supporting agencies, local and national politicians. Contact them, asking four open-ended questions. First, what do they think is and how would they define 'personality'? Second, how would they define the term 'entrepreneur'? Third, what personality characteristics would they associate with the entrepreneur and how are these different from the population as a whole? Fourth, what is the role of these personality characteristics in entrepreneurial success? Once the responses have been collected, go through them, coding the points raised. Different people say the same or similar things in different ways. Try to find the core issues in the responses to each question and summarise them as single words or propositions.

Next, set up a survey based on these propositions. Submit it to each of the original respondents, asking for the degree to which they agree or disagree with the propositions (a Likert scale may be used). Once the findings have been summarised (perhaps graphically), resubmit them to the respondents, getting their final view on the overall findings. You may ask if they would change their original opinion given the aggregated findings. As a final analysis, conclude the nature of people's presumption about the link between personality and entrepreneurial activity. Is this consistent or do people hold widely different views? Is there a core of assumptions? How might these presumptions affect the way in which entrepreneurs see themselves, the personality they aspire to and how those around them see them?

A literature review

There is an extensive literature on the relationship between personality and entrepreneurial inclination and behaviour. References to some of the key studies are given in the suggested reading. A search by an academic search engine will find many more. Consider these studies chronologically. Review each, asking how the concepts of entrepreneur and personality are instrumentalised, make evident the assumptions about the ontology of personality and expose the underlying pragmatics using the scheme discussed above. Are these aspects discussed explicitly in the study or are they implicit? How are the notions of 'entrepreneur' and 'personality' defined? What issues might there be with the instrumentalisations selected? How do they support the methodology used? Do the findings support the notion of an entrepreneurial personality or not? What is the current stage of knowledge and what issues remain to be investigated? Summarise by discussing the trends in these issues and map out directions for future studies.

Correlating entrepreneurial activity with personality

Identify a pool of individuals whom you (based on some explicit criteria that do not involve personality, for example managerial history or business type) consider to be entrepreneurs and a complementary set of individuals who are not. Ideally these should be matched for age, sex and sector they are working in. Construct a survey that asks those selected how they would react in certain (briefly described) situations. For example, how they would react if presented with a new business opportunity, or how they would deal

▶

with a leadership challenge, or would approach a particular negotiation (the EO scale may be adopted). The aim here is to have the subject reveal something about their personality. It is, of course, being assumed here that the subjects' approach to the situation is an indicator of personality (i.e. a rather behavioural definition of personality). Aim for around twenty or so situations. You may wish to limit subjects' responses to one of a few (four to six) options for each situation. These options may be found by coding responses from an open-ended preliminary study. Once the responses have been collected the next stage would be to have an independent group of judges (perhaps other students) assess the responses and categorise the individuals as entrepreneurial or not. How well does the categorisation judgement match up with the actuality of whether a subject is an entrepreneur or not (based on your initial definition)? Does personality (as revealed by the subjects' responses) provide a good lead indicator of who is, or is not, an entrepreneur? Might a better correlation be obtained if the entrepreneur is defined in a different way? In the summary, consider the limitations of this methodological approach and how it might be improved.

 ## Key readings

Many psychologically minded students of entrepreneurship have not given up on the notion of the entrepreneurial personality. Having been somewhat dismissive of the concept, it seems only fair that I recommend two recent studies that take a more positive view. Both also provide excellent reviews of the issues involved. From a more practical perspective is:

Chapman, M. (2000) '"When the entrepreneur sneezes, the organization catches a cold": a practitioner's perspective on the state of the art in research on the entrepreneurial personality and entrepreneurial process', *European Journal of Work and Organizational Psychology*, Vol. 9, No. 1, pp. 97–101.

Slightly more theoretical is:

Müller, G.F. and Gappisch, C. (2005) 'Personality types of entrepreneur', *Psychological Reports*, Vol. 96, No. 3, pp. 737–46.

You decide!

Suggestions for further reading

Ajzen, I. (1971) 'Attributions of dispositions to an actor: effects of perceived decision freedom and behavioural utilities', *Journal of Personality and Social Psychology*, Vol. 18, No. 2, pp. 144–56.

Amundson, N.E. (1995) 'An interactive model of career decision-making', *Journal of Employment Counselling*, Vol. 32, No. 1, pp. 11–21.

Arkin, R.M. and Duval, S. (1975) 'Focus of attention and causal attribution of actors and observers', *Journal of Experimental Social Psychology*, Vol. 11, pp. 427–38.

Badcock, C. (2000) *Evolutionary Psychology*. Cambridge: Polity Press.

Barrett, L., Dunbar, R. and Lycett, J. (2002) *Human Evolutionary Psychology*. London: Palgrave.

Becherer, R.C. and Maurer, J.G. (1999) 'The proactive personality disposition and entrepreneurial behavior among small company presidents', *Journal of Small Business Management*, Vol. 37, No. 1, pp. 28–36.

Bernstein, W.M. and Stephan, W.G. (1979) 'Explaining attributions for achievement: a path analytical approach', *Journal of Personality and Social Psychology*, Vol. 37, No. 10, pp. 1810–21.

Blanchflower, D.G. and Oswald, A.J. (1998) 'What makes an entrepreneur?', *Journal of Labour Economics*, Vol. 16, No. 1, pp. 26–60.

Brandstatter, H. (1997) 'Becoming an entrepreneur: a question of personality structure?', *Journal of Economic Psychology*, Vol. 18, No. 2/3, p. 157.

Carruthers, P. and Chamberlain, A. (eds) (2000) *Evolution and the Human Mind: Modularity, Language and Meta-cognition*. Cambridge: Cambridge University Press.

Cartwright, J. (2000) *Evolution and Human Behaviour*. London: Macmillan.

Carver, C.S. and Scheier, M. (2000) *Perspectives on Personality* (4th edn), Boston, MA: Allyn & Bacon.

Chell, E. (1985) 'The entrepreneurial personality: a few ghosts laid to rest', *International Small Business Journal*, Vol. 3, No. 3, pp. 43–54.

Chu, P. (2000) 'The characteristics of Chinese female entrepreneurs: motivation and personality', Journal of Enterprising Culture, Vol. 8, No. 1, pp. 67–84.

Cooper, A.C. (1981) 'Strategic management, new ventures and small business', *Long Range Planning*, Vol. 14, No. 5.

Corballis, M.C. and Lea, S.E.G. (eds) (1999) *The Descent of Mind: Psychological Perspectives on Hominid Evolution*. Oxford: Oxford University Press.

Crant, J.M. (1996) The Proactive Personality Scale as a predictor of entrepreneurial intentions, *Journal of Small Business Management*, Vol. 34, No. 3, pp. 42–9.

Eisen, S.V. (1979) 'Actor–observer differences in information inference and causal attribution', *Journal of Personality and Social Psychology*, Vol. 37, No. 2, pp. 261–72.

Eisenhauer, J.G. (1995) 'The entrepreneurial decision: economic theory and empirical evidence', *Entrepreneurship Theory and Practice*, Summer, pp. 67–79.

Escher, S., Grabarkiewicz, R., Frese, M., van Steekelenburg, G., Lauw, M. and Freidrich, C. (2002) 'The moderator effect of cognitive ability on the relationship between planning strategies and business success of small scale business owners in South Africa: a longitudinal study', *Journal of Developmental Entrepreneurship*, Vol. 7, No. 5, pp. 305–18.

Eysenck, H.J. (1975) *The Inequality of Man*, San Diego, CA: EdITS.

Funder, D.C. (2001) 'Personality', *Annual Review of Psychology*, Vol. 52, pp. 197–221.

Frese, M., Brantjes, A. and Hoorn, R. (2002) 'Psychological success factors of small scale businesses in Namibia: the role of strategy process, entrepreneurial orientation and the environment', *Journal of Developmental Entrepreneurship*, Vol. 7, No. 3, pp. 259–82.

Gilhooly, K.J. (1996) *Thinking: Directed, Undirected and Creative* (3rd edn). London: Academic Press.

Gimenez, F., Pelisson, C., Kruger, E.G.S. and Hayashi, P. (2000) 'Small firms' owner-managers construction of competition', *Journal of Enterprising Culture*, Vol. 8, No. 4, pp. 361–79.

Ginsberg, A. and Buchholtz, A. (1989) 'Are entrepreneurs a breed apart? A look at the evidence', *Journal of General Management*, Vol. 15, No. 2, pp. 32–40.

Hull, D.L., Bosley, J.J. and Udell, G.G. (1980) 'Renewing the hunt for the Heffalump: identifying potential entrepreneurs by personality characteristics', *Journal of Small Business Management*, Vol. 18, No. 1, pp. 11–18.

Jarvis, M. (2000) *Theoretical Approaches in Psychology*. London: Routledge.

Kaplan, R.M. and Saccuzzo, D.P. (1997) *Psychological Testing: Principles, Applications, and Issues* (4th edn). Pacific Grove, CA: Brooks/Cole.

Katz, J.K. (1992) 'A psychosocial cognitive model of employment status choice', *Entrepreneurship Theory and Practice*, Fall, pp. 29–37.

Katz, J.K. (1992) 'The dynamics of organizational emergence: a contemporary group formation perspective', *Entrepreneurship Theory and Practice*, Winter, pp. 97–101.

Kelley, H.H. (1973) 'The process of causal attribution', *American Psychologist*, Feb., pp. 107–28.

Kelley, H.H. and Michela, J.L. (1980) 'Attribution theory and research', *Annual Review of Psychology*, Vol. 31, pp. 457–1.

Kikul, J. and Gundry, L.K. (2002) 'Prospecting for strategic advantage: the proactive entrepreneurial personality and small firm innovation', *Journal of Small Business Management*, Vol. 40, No. 2, pp. 85–97.

Korunka, C., Frank, H., Lueger, M. and Mugler, J. (2003) 'The entrepreneurial personality in the context of resources, environment and the start-up process – a configural approach', *Entrepreneurship: Theory and Practice*, Vol. 28, No. 1, pp. 23–42.

Kreiser, P.M., Marino, L.D. and Weaver, K.M. (2002a) 'Reassessing the environment–EO link: the impact of environmental hostility on the dimensions of entrepreneurial orientation', *Academy of Management Best Papers Proceedings*.

Kreiser, P.M., Marino, L.D. and Weaver, K.M. (2002b) 'Assessing the psychometric properties of the entrepreneurial orientation scale: a multi-country analysis', *Entrepreneurship Theory and Practice*, Vol. 26, No. 4, pp. 71–94.

Kristiansen, S. (2002) 'Individual perception of business contexts: the case of small-scale entrepreneurs in Tanzania', *Journal of Developmental Entrepreneurship*, Vol. 7, No. 3, pp. 283–304.

Luthans, F., Stajkovic, A.D. and Ibrayeva, E. (2000) 'Environmental and psychological challenges facing entrepreneurial development in transition economies', *Journal of World Business*, Vol. 35, No. 1, pp. 95–110.

Markman, G.D., Balkin, D.B. and Baron, R.A. (2002) 'Inventors and new venture formation: the effects of general self-efficacy and regretful thinking', *Entrepreneurship Theory and Practice*, Winter, pp. 149–65.

McCarthy, B. (2003) 'The impact of the entrepreneurial personality on the strategy formation and planning process in SMEs', *Irish Journal of Management*, Vol. 24, No. 1, pp. 154–72.

McCline, R.L., Bhat, S. and Baj, P. (2000) 'Opportunity recognition: an exploratory investigation of a component in the entrepreneurial process in the context of the health care industry', *Entrepreneurship Theory and Practice*, Vol. 25, No. 2, pp. 81–94.

Minniti, M. and Bygrave, W. (1999) 'The microfoundations of entrepreneurship', *Entrepreneurship Theory and Practice*, Vol. 23, No. 4, pp. 41–53.

Minniti, M. and Bygrave, W. (2001) 'A dynamic model of entrepreneurial learning', *Entrepreneurship Theory and Practice*, Vol. 25, No. 3, pp. 5–16.

Mischel, W. (1999) *Introduction to Personality*. New York: Harcourt Brace.

Mitchell, R.K., Smith, B., Seawright, K.W. and Morse, E.A. (2000) 'Cross-cultural cognitions and the venture creation design', *Academy of Management Journal*, Vol. 43, No. 5, pp. 974–93.

Myers, D.G. (2002) *Intuition: Its Powers and Perils*. New Haven, CT: Yale University Press.

Neck, C.P., Neck, H.M., Manz, C.C. and Godwin, J. (1999) 'I think I can; I think I can: a self-leadership perspective towards enhancing the entrepreneur through thought patterns, self-efficacy and performance', *Journal of Managerial Psychology*, Vol. 14, No. 7/8, pp. 477–501.

Ofek, H. (2001) *Second Nature: Economic Origins of Human Evolution*. Cambridge: Cambridge University Press.

Oyama, S. (2000) *Evolution's Eye: A Systems View of the Biology–Culture Divide*. London: Duke University Press.

Phares, E.J. (1987) *Introduction to Personality* (2nd edn). New York: Scott, Foresman.

Robichaud, Y. and Egbert, R.A. (2001) 'Towards the development of a measuring instrument for entrepreneurial motivation', *Journal of Developmental Entrepreneurship*, Vol. 6, No. 2, pp. 189–201.

Shepherd, D.A. and Krueger, N.F. (2002) 'An intentions-based model of entrepreneurial teams' social cognition', *Entrepreneurship Theory and Practice*, Winter, pp. 167–85.

Stancill, J.M. (1981) 'Realistic criteria for judging new ventures', *Harvard Business Review*, Nov./Dec., pp. 60–71.

Uusitalo, R. (2001) '*Homo entreprenaurus*', *Applied Economics*, Vol. 33, pp. 1631–8.

Weaver, K.M., Dickson, P.H., Gibson, B. and Turner, A. (2002) 'Being uncertain: the relationship between entrepreneurial orientation and environmental uncertainty', *Journal of Enterprising Culture*, Vol. 10, No. 2, pp. 87–106.

Wright, R. (2000) *Nonzero: History, Evolution and Human Cooperation*. London: Abacus.

Yves, R., McGraw, E. and Roger, A. (2001) 'Towards the development of a measuring instrument for entrepreneurial motivation', *Journal of Developmental Entrepreneurship*, Vol. 6, No. 2, pp. 189–201.

Selected case material

CASE 3.1

19 November 2005

Dyson seeks to brush up industry's image

JEAN EAGLESHAM

The 'you're fired!' ethos of *The Apprentice* television show has been criticised by a leading entrepreneur, who warns that the cut-throat portrayal of business risks perpetuating the historic British aversion to working in industry.

In an interview with the *Financial Times*, James Dyson praised *Dragons' Den*, the BBC 2 show where budding entrepreneurs compete for investment, as a 'great help' to efforts to attract graduates to manufacturing.

In contrast, the format for BBC 2's *The Apprentice*, where Sir Alan Sugar eliminates would-be Amstrad protégés ruthlessly, was a 'bit unfortunate', said Mr. Dyson. 'Alan Sugar's a great entrepreneur but it's a pity that firing people is the catchphrase.'

He warned that television tended to reinforce people's impression of industry, underscoring bleak images assimilated over the decades from the dark satanic mills of Victorian literature through to the mass strikes of the 1970s.

Citing a recent show featuring an unethical executive, Mr. Dyson protested: 'I don't think businessmen cheat any more than anyone else.'

The criticism matters because of Mr. Dyson's rare position among business leaders, as an inventor who has developed a good idea into a global brand. The seemingly unstoppable success of his eponymous vacuum cleaners – which overtook Hoover in the US this year, becoming the biggest selling brand by value – has made him a fortune estimated at £800m. It has also given him considerable influence as a voice on government policy.

Ministers appear to worship at the Dyson shrine. Alan Johnson, the trade and industry secretary, marked Enterprise Week on Tuesday by lauding the Norfolk inventor as one of two British entrepreneurs – along with Richard Branson – who epitomised the spirit of risk-taking and determination the government hoped to foster. He told delegates entrepreneurs were 'essential to our wealth, health and happiness'.

Unfortunately for the government, this admiration is not reciprocated by the entrepreneur. Mr. Dyson might have acted as a government adviser but he is no fan of officialdom. Asked if he had become disillusioned with Tony Blair, he said: 'I don't think I was expecting an awful lot in the first place. Nothing's really been done to help industry for the past 50 years.'

This low level of expectation does not prevent Mr. Dyson from fulminating about the perceived failure of the government to give sufficient backing to innovation. He lauds Gordon Brown's decision to allow 120 per cent tax relief on research and development as a 'good move – it's a pity it came so late, but at least he did it.' But Mr. Dyson wants the chancellor to go further in next month's pre-Budget report, by expanding the R&D tax credit to offer 160 per cent relief. The cost would be rewarded over time, Mr. Dyson argues, saying the 'government should take a long-term view, if a government ever will do that'.

This scepticism about ministerial willingness to give sufficient fiscal incentives for innovation is matched by a concern about the impact of the government's broader policies, particularly on corporate tax. Some erosion of the manufacturing base through production moving offshore is inevitable, given both wage differentials and the increasing supply base in the Far East, says Mr. Dyson. But this need not be disastrous if Britain could retain and develop added-value manufacturing.

This corporate model is exemplified by the Dyson example, where a contentious decision to move the assembly line to Malaysia in 2002 has been followed by increased employment of designers and engineers in the UK. 'If that's the model for modern Britain, that's OK,' he says.

But he warns ministers not to take this vision of an added-value manufacturing sector for granted. Policies such as the increasing burden of corporate taxation might end up driving the entire sector offshore. 'It absolutely could happen. But we're a British company, I'm British, I like living here. I just hope the government makes life easier, not more difficult.'

CASE 3.2

30 January 2006

Saïd MBA was 'best year of my life'

FT REPORT ANDREW BAXTER

For Keely Stevenson, working as a hospice volunteer was the spark that first lit a long-term passion for social entrepreneurship, bringing her in a series of steps to Oxford University's Saïd Business School in 2004 – as one of the first Skoll Scholars to take the MBA.

In between have been so many different experiences that Ms Stevenson could almost be called a veteran social entrepreneur at the age of 28. Starting from the University of California Berkeley, where her research included projects on US public housing reform and microlending in Bangladesh, Ms Stevenson has had a rich variety of roles.

Among other things, she has been a Fellow at the United Nations, working on public outreach strategies; designer and manager of Social Edge, an online community for social entrepreneurs, a task she undertook while working at the Skoll Foundation; and interim executive director of ProWorld Service Corps, a social enterprise working in Peru, Mexico and Belize on community empowerment and social and economic development.

Even with this experience, however, she felt that doing an MBA would help her to make a bigger impact. 'I considered a masters in public policy,' she says, 'but decided I needed to build my finance and general management skills. I thought that using the academic framework of an MBA would be helpful, and I had not had any sort of management training.'

But which MBA? Although there are several MBA programmes in the US with social entries electives and other related activity,

CASE 3.2 CONT.

Ms Stevenson was attracted to the Oxford programme partly because the social entrepreneurship side was new and there was thus 'a chance to shape something,' but also because of its broad, entrepreneurial remit and its international character. 'It's really useful to get the perspective of someone from Kenya or Egypt,' she says.

The Oxford MBA was 'the best year of her life', says Ms Stevenson, and even by her standards was eventful. She spent the summer as an MBA intern/consultant at Triodos Bank, a social bank with offices in the UK Netherlands, Belgium and Spain. This, she says, was an important way to apply the skills learned in the MBA classroom, in a financial institution whose values and vision were aligned with her own.

A further opportunity to put classroom experience into practice came with Ms Stevenson's three-month strategic consulting project for an outside company or client, which for her and four classmates was South Africa's Royal Bafokeng tribe. Platinum was recently discovered on the 300,000-strong tribe's land, and it is now investing its wealth in designing world-class education, healthcare and economic and social development projects.

Following an invitation from Princess Tirelo Molotlegi, the MBA team stayed with the Royal family, which has begun a campaign called Vision 2020 to ensure the tribe is self-sustainable by 2020.

Ms Stevenson is now back in the US, looking for a job in microfinance and capital markets, a sector where the strong finance background she has developed as a result of the Oxford MBA should help her as she pursues her social entrepreneurial ambitions.

Source: Andrew Baxter, 'Saïd MBA was "best year of my life"', *Financial Times*, 30 January 2006, p. 6. Copyright © 2006 The Financial Times Limited.

Discussion point

1. 'All entrepreneurs share certain personality characteristics.' Discuss.

CHAPTER 4

Entrepreneurship, cognition and decision making

Chapter overview

Cognitive psychology is providing new and profound insights into the thinking of entrepreneurs and how they engage with the entrepreneurial process. This chapter considers the key elements of cognitive psychology with a focus on the agenda for entrepreneurship. Two specific aspects of entrepreneurial cognition are considered: decision making (drawing a distinction between normative, descriptive and prescriptive accounts), and perception of and response to risk (drawing a distinction between rational and natural responses).

4.1 Cognitive aspects of entrepreneurship

Key learning outcome

An appreciation of the cognitive approach to understanding entrepreneurial behaviour and the significance of individual cognitive style and strategy in entrepreneurial decision making.

Cognitive psychology is a relatively new but increasingly import-ant avenue of psychological explanation and research. Cognitive psychology deals with the way in which humans obtain, store, process and use information about the world. So it is interested in:

- attention and perception, the initial processing of raw sensual experiences;
- storage of information in memory systems – both working memory and long-term memory;
- the way in which knowledge is stored, accessed and created, induction and deduction processes;
- judgement and decision making – the use of processed informa-tion to choose particular course of action;
- thinking and problem solving;
- learning, skill and expertise development;
- language, use, acquisition and comprehension;
- creativity and inventiveness;
- the way in which information is manipulated by mental routines to drive decision making.

Cognitive psychology is very much an experimental science, with its findings based on repeatable experiments and the testing of hypotheses. Cognitive psychologists often develop systems models of information processing. There is no immediate claim that these systems have an anatomical or even neurological representation in the human brains; rather they are accounts of the way in which the brain works as a system.

Some cognitive psychologists talk of specific cognitive styles (which are relatively permanent features of an individual, though they may develop with learning) and strategies (which are specific to particular problems) that reflect the generalised ways in which humans process information. For example, when faced with a new problem some people call to mind methods they are already familiar with; others will seek out original and new solution methods; some people seek risky situations, others avoid them; some people are willing to make decisions with only a limited amount of information, others hold back until they are well informed. These are only examples. But these examples give a hint that entrepreneurs might be distinguished not so much by their personality, but by the cognitive strategies and styles they adopt (which may be related to personality but are not the same thing).

From this description of cognitive psychology it will be clear why interest has grown in the cognitive aspects of management in general and entrepreneurship in particular.

Cognitive psychology has made great strides in enhancing our understanding of human thinking. It is now recognised that we all have our own cognitive styles that we use to process information and that we adopt particular cognitive strategies when called upon to use that information in order to solve problems. Many of these strategies and styles resonate with our experiences of how other people approach challenges. We may, for example, note that some people are 'big-picture' – that is, they only like to take the essential, important facts into account when they first meet a new problem. Others are 'small-picture'. They like detailed and extensive information before attempting a solution. At other times we may recognise that some people prefer tried and trusted solutions; others are willing, eager even, to find new ways of doing things. At a deeper level, some people compartmentalise new information into a pre-existing set of categories and see new things in established terms. We may regard such people as relatively fixed in their thinking. Other people prefer to set up new categories and so see things in new ways. We may regard these as more open in their thinking. These general observations about how people work, however useful as rules of thumb, cannot be accepted at face value, though. Cognitive psychology is a science. It is concerned with establishing the well-defined and experimentally reproducible processes that are revealed through the actions taken in response to specific cognitive challenges. Cognitive processes are sometimes split into three types:

- *Perception processes* – these are concerned with how we see the world and gather information about it. Examples are *complexity–simplicity*, the number of dimensions that are used to categorise the world, *levelling–sharpening*, the use of existing or the creation of new categories to incorporate new information, and *verbalising–visualising*, the use of verbal or, alternatively, visual imagery to develop understanding.
- *Problem-solving processes* – these govern how information is used when an individual is called upon to make a decision. Examples include *scanning–focusing*, how much information is called in order to solve a problem, *serialism–holism*, referring to whether problems are approached in a linear, reducing way, or are dealt with as an integrated whole, and *adaptation–innovation*, the preference for established solutions or new solutions.

- *Task processes* – these are concerned with determining the way in which we approach particular jobs. Themes here include *constricted–flexible*, the preference for new types of task over established ones, *impulsive–reflective*, the tendency to act in a decisive or considered way, and *uncertainty accepting–cautious*, the willingness to take on tasks with an element of risk in them.

Stubbart (1989) and Hayes and Allinson (1994) provide full reviews of cognitive styles and their relevance to management. Cognitive styles and strategies may be linked to, and provide a basis for, what we consider to be personality. They are, however, distinct from it. Individuals may rely on well-honed cognitive approaches, but they are not necessarily invariant over time. Our cognitive approaches are subject to learning and may be modified, either intentionally or unintentionally, in the light of experience. Cognitive psychology is increasingly offering insights that can potentially account for and explain a number of aspects of the individual entrepreneur's inclination towards the entrepreneurial option and their engagement in the entrepreneurial process. Particularly important areas are:

- the influence of cognition on motivation and the entrepreneur's perceptions and valuation of the entrepreneurial option compared with conventional employment alternatives (e.g. Campbell, 1992; Katz, 1992a,b; Amundson, 1995; Eisenhauer, 1995; Robichaud and Egbert, 2001; Uusitalo, 2001);
- the impact of cognition on the individual's ability to spot new business opportunities (e.g. Minniti and Bygrave, 1999; McCline *et al.*, 2000; Keh *et al.*, 2002);
- the analytical skills of the individual and his or her ability to evaluate and make proper judgements about the value of that opportunity (see section 3.3);
- creativity in developing new innovations to capitalise on those opportunities;
- cognitive abilities in terms of considering competitive environments and dynamics (e.g. Giminez *et al.*, 2000; Luthans *et al.*, 2000; Frese *et al.*, 2002; Kreiser *et al.*, 2002a,b; Kristiansen, 2002; Weaver *et al.*, 2002);
- abilities in relation to 'strategic foresight', the potential to imagine future worlds and consider the outcomes of current decisions in relation to them (see section 16.4);
- judgement over what parts of the world are under personal control and which are not (do entrepreneurs overestimate their ability to control the world as compared with non-entrepreneurs?) (e.g. Neck *et al.*, 1999; Markman *et al.*, 2002; Shepherd and Krueger, 2002);
- the ability to judge risk (either realistically, or perhaps more positively than others, e.g. Stancill, 1981; Chaterjee *et al.*, 2003);
- skills in creating appropriate strategic approaches and plans (e.g. Escher *et al.*, 2002);
- abilities in relation to communicating with and persuading key stakeholders (e.g. Kamm and Nurick, 1992);
- social relationship skills in sustaining and maintaining the organisation (e.g. Katz, 1992);
- the ability to develop personal learning strategies in light of experience (e.g. Minniti and Bygrave, 2001).

The question of whether or not entrepreneurs (as a group) have a cognition (cognitive skills or strategy) that is different from non-entrepreneurs has been the subject of a number of recent studies. Buchanan and Di Pierro (1980) provide a historical and conceptual introduction to this issue. Mitchell *et al.* (2002) lay out the foundations for, and emphasise the potential of, a cognitive approach to understanding entrepreneurial behaviour and performance.

Forbes (1999) reviews studies of the role of management cognition (particularly decision heuristics and cognitive schemas) in entrepreneurship. Neck *et al.* (1999) develops the notion that 'thought self leadership', the process of self-influence through the cognitive strategies of self-dialogue and mental imagery, plays a role in entrepreneurial management, and Keh *et al.* (2002) examine the effect of cognitive processes on assessment of opportunities under risky conditions. The theme of cognition and its influence on entrepreneurship will be revisited in sections 7.3 and 5.6, where cognitive insights into entrepreneurship and culture and the start-up decision, respectively, will be considered.

It is probably premature to insist that entrepreneurs, as a group, share any particular set of cognitive approach. The 'best' cognitive approach in any situation is dependent on a particular situation. Entrepreneurial situations are as varied as any other type of situation. However, it is true that entrepreneurs do tend to be innovative, are receptive to new ideas and do set out to find new ways of doing things. How this general observation can be rationalised in terms of specific, well-defined cognitive strategies is a subject of much interest within industrial and organisational cognitive psychology.

4.2 Entrepreneurship and human decision making

Key learning outcome

An appreciation of the distinction between normative, descriptive and prescriptive accounts of human decision making, the *anchoring*, *availability* and *representativeness* biases that influence decision making and the dangers they present to the intuitive decision maker, and the use of prescriptive methods to improve decision making.

The making of decisions is a fundamental part of the human experience. We can imagine different outcomes and possibilities; we can judge that which we can act to influence and that which we must accept, and we have preferences for some outcomes over others. The study of human decision making is a rapidly growing field of inquiry, both in terms of fundamental decisional processes in cognition and in specific areas of professional decision making, particularly in management, medicine and law. Clearly, entrepreneurs are, if nothing else, *decision makers*.

There are three types of theory that aim to explain and predict decision making. The first are *normative* theories. Normative theories identify what is the best (optimal) decision in a particular situation and the process for making it. Such theories are based on sound logical and statistical methodologies. They are often based on an assumption that human beings are rational (they make best use of information) and are utility maximising (they want the best possible outcomes for themselves). Following groundbreaking work by mathematicians in the early post-war period, these theories are often expressed in highly mathematical terms. They underpin much work in management science and finance.

The second type of theory is *descriptive*. Descriptive theories provide accounts of the decisions people actually make. Their concern is with what people *really* do, rather than what they *should* do. Descriptive theories may also take on a mathematical form, but they are more likely than normative theories to be expressed in psychological terms.

The final type of theory is *prescriptive*. Prescriptive theories suggest ways individuals can improve their decision-making practice. They are usually expressed in pedagogical terms.

If humans were perfectly rational (in the formal economic sense) then there would be no difference between normative and descriptive theories and there would be no need for prescriptive theories. But we are not. For any specific decision problem there is usually a difference between what a normative theory predicts is optimal and what human decision makers actually do. Such a deviation between actual decision-making outcomes and theoretically optimal ones is referred to as a *bias*. A bias is not simply an error caused by not understanding the normative method, or laziness in applying it (after all, normative methods may be difficult to use). Errors would lead to decision outcomes being randomly dispersed around the normative mean. Biases are *consistent* (the bias is usually in one particular direction away from the normative), *prevalent* (they occur in a wide variety of decision contexts) and persistent (they are difficult to *eliminate*, even if the decision maker is informed of the normative method and is rewarded for using it). A few examples of biases are described below.

Anchoring bias

The anchoring bias involves using an irrelevant and spurious number to make a numerical judgement. For example, consider two (matched) groups of expert investors offered the same business plans with exactly the same information. Both groups are given a suggested investment price (with one group given a high price, the other a low price), then asked if that price is too high or too low and finally asked to give the price at which they would invest. It might be imagined that both groups would offer the same (average) investment price, but those initially given the high price tend to offer a higher (often much higher) fair price.

Availability bias

The availability bias involves using prominent instances that are in memory as the basis for making a judgement. Entrepreneurs (and investors) are often called upon to judge the frequency, probability or regularity of an event. For example, how likely is it that a business of a particular size, or operating in a particular sector, or led by a particular type of entrepreneur will succeed or fail? If information on actual numbers is limited (which it usually is) then we show a tendency to judge how frequently something occurs by how easily we can call an example to mind. But how prominent something is in our memory is consequential on many factors, regularity being only one. In fact, the less often something happens, the more likely it is to gain a lot of news coverage. (Plane crashes are rare, but dramatic; car crashes are frequent but not usually newsworthy – result: people will happily drive to an airport (taking, statistically speaking, quite a high risk) and then sit nervously on the plane where (again, statistically speaking) they are quite safe).

This can be significant in terms of entrepreneurial investment. During the dotcom boom, the news media were full of amazing internet success stories. They were cognitively available and so investors overestimated the chances of an investment's paying off. After the dotcom crash, the press was full of internet failures. These now became cognitively available and the precariousness of the sector was overestimated. Investors pulled their money out. Result: boom and bust overswings in investment.

Representativeness bias and base-rate neglect

The representativeness bias involves judging a sample or event as being more or less likely because it is felt to be more or less typical of a population or process. This can often result in *base-rate neglect bias* – ignoring background information in making judgements. In one study I conducted (Wickham, in press), decision makers were induced to think that highly unlikely statements about entrepreneurs were more likely to be true when they were combined with statements that were highly likely to be true, though statistically, the truth of an unlikely statement is not changed by combining it with a more likely one. However, the combined statement seemed more representative than the unlikely one on its own. Consider how this might influence judgement of business plans if unlikely events are linked to highly likely.

One manifestation of representativeness occurs when a pool of investors are given a description of an entrepreneur, which states, for example that 'he has a degree in computer science, is fascinated by technology, reads science fiction' and so on. It is then suggested that his business plan has been drawn at random from a pool of 100 that contains plans for high-tech ventures and retailing start-ups. The proportion of investors who suggest that the chance is the entrepreneur's plan is for a high-tech start-up does not change, whether they are told that the high-tech–retail mix of plans is 80:20, 50:50, 20:80 or even 1:99. Of course, the chance (of being selected randomly) of its being a high-tech falls across this range. And this should influence judgement – but it doesn't. This is referred to as *base-rate neglect*.

Other biases include *framing effects* – judgement changing on the basis of how information is contextualised (especially if positive or negative aspects of a problem are emphasised) – and a series of biases associated with judging correlation and causation.

Why do we exhibit such biases? Cognitive psychologists have suggested that these biases arise because individuals use deep-seated *heuristics* or practical 'rules of thumb' to make judgements rather than normative methods. It is important to recognise that using a heuristic, even if it leads to a bias, is not necessarily wrong. The human brain is a costly organ (in energy terms). The average man's brain will be about 2 per cent of his bodyweight, but it will use nearly one-quarter of all the energy he consumes. Heuristics are 'fast' and 'frugal'. Because they simplify problems, they offer up decisions quickly and do not use a lot of the brain's capacity. What matters is not so much that they get the answer 'wrong' occasionally, but that when they do, it does not matter too much. Normative methods give the 'right' answer, but take a lot of time (and brain power) to implement. The investment may not always be worth it.

The key point is that such biases can, at times, impact on the quality of decision making both for entrepreneurs and for those supporting them (especially investors). The issue is not so much one of the entrepreneur (and her supporters) eliminating heuristics – because they can be useful – but one of being aware that they may be present. The advantages and dangers of relying on intuitive (heuristic-based) decision making are explored by Myers (2002). Gigerenzer (2002) suggests practical methods for eliminating biases and improving decision making.

There is not space here to explore these issues further. An excellent, and quite accessible account of heuristics and biases in management decision making is Bazerman (2002). The student interested in exploring the theory in some depth is referred to the books by Plous (1993), Gilhooly (1996), Baron (2000) and Hastie and Dawes (2001), which offer good introductions to the issues. The contributions to Kahneman *et al.* (1982) and Kahneman and Tversky (2000) are also recommended but are more advanced.

4.3 Entrepreneurial confidence and overconfidence

Key learning outcome

An appreciation of the role of the *overconfidence bias* and how it can distort the decision making of entrepreneurs and their supporters.

As discussed in section 5.2, entrepreneurs need self-confidence. However, a number of studies have demonstrated that at time we all exhibit what are referred to as *positive biases*. A positive bias is said to occur when we make a judgement about ourselves that results in a view of ourselves that is more positive than statistical rules, or indeed basal experience, deems to be proper or hold to a view of the world that is overly optimistic. The term 'positive bias' refers to a range of judgements, but they probably have a common source. These include the following:

- An overconfidence in the veracity of declarative knowledge (knowledge of facts). This might lead an entrepreneur to overestimate their understanding of a market, product technology, customers or competitors.
- An overly positive self-rating of personal characteristics relative to base rates. Entrepreneurs often believe themselves to be better-than-average managers or negotiators.
- An overly positive belief in ability to make judgements under uncertain conditions. This can lead to decisions being made too quickly and before a proper evaluation has been made.
- An overly optimistic belief in the likelihood of desired outcomes. The positives loom larger than the possible negatives.
- Overconfidence in the prediction of own actions in a particular situation. That is, 'given a particular problem, I know what I will do and I know I will do it right!'
- Overconfidence in the prediction of actions of others in a particular situation. That is, 'I know how they (customers, investors, competitors, distributors, etc.) will react.'
- An excessive confidence in the security of position in negotiations.

Many of these facets support each other when judgements are made about the value of investments. A decision maker may both overestimate his or her ability to judge the information provided and be overly optimistic about the possibility of success. The over-confidence bias should not be interpreted to mean that every statement made by every entrepreneur should be downgraded because it is contaminated by overconfidence. The phenomenon says nothing about individuals or specific statements. It is a statistical effect. Ask 100 entrepreneurs how they rate their abilities, and more than 50 are likely to rate themselves above average. Not all are fooling themselves, but some must be! Busenitz and Barney (1997) found that overconfidence in personal ability and overoptimism for favoured outcomes play a role in entrepreneurial entry. Forbes (2005) found that entrepreneurs tend to demonstrate higher degrees of overconfidence than non-entrepreneur managers. Simon and Houghton (2003) examined how overconfidence affected the willingness of high-tech firms to introduce new products and found a positive correlation. A model linking over-confidence to entrepreneurial entry is developed by Bernardo and Welch (2001). It is not just entrepreneurs who are prone to overconfidence. Zacharakis and Shepherd (2001) found venture capitalists could also succumb.

4.4 Entrepreneurs and the human response to risk

Key learning outcome

An understanding of the distinction between syntactic (formal) and pragmatic (everyday) uses of the word 'risk' and how this influences discourse by and about entrepreneurs. An understanding of the concept of *risk aversion* and how it impacts on the relationship between entrepreneurs and investors. An appreciation of the *prospect theory* approach to understanding behavioural responses to risk and the role of entrepreneurs in managing investor ambiguity.

In section 1.3 it was suggested that while most people associate entrepreneurs with risk, it was in fact *investors* who are the risk takers. While accepting the logic of this argument, many feel uncomfortable with it. 'But don't entrepreneurs put their own money into their venture – mortgage their houses even!' Yes, often. But if so, the entrepreneur is acting as an investor as well. The roles are quite different. It just so happens that the same person is playing two roles (this is not to say that the fact that the same person is playing two roles at once is *trivial*. It may be a powerful signal that the entrepreneur has faith in the venture – see section 6.3). 'What about the entrepreneur's reputation!' Of course, but to an economist a person's reputation is only worth what it can add to their (properly discounted) future earnings. So putting one's reputation on the line is simply another form of investment.

By this stage, most people feel the argument has become a little slippery. It has not; it is just being strict. But they have a point. The strictness of the argument relies on a very formal definition of risk. And, as with many concepts that are used in everyday life, and are adopted as technical terms by specialists, the way the term is used (we say *pragmatically*) in everyday life may be different from the way in which it is used technically (we say *syntactically*).

Syntactically, risk is a distribution of outcomes (which have some financial value). Positive outcomes (getting more than we expect) add to risk as much as negative things (getting less than we expect). If two traders exchange risk (which happens every day in the insurance and financial markets), the one whose distribution of outcomes gets wider is gaining risk; the one whose distribution narrows is offsetting risk. But pragmatically, risk is the sense that 'something bad might happen'. The thing that happens need not have a direct financial value (though it might have an indirect cost) and it is the negative side – the bad – that concerns people, not the fact that things might turn out better than expected. In general, we do not like risk. If you were offered the chance to win £100 on the toss of a fair coin (you choose heads or tails – so 50 per cent chance of winning), would you pay £50 to enter? Most people would not. They expect a premium (a discount on the cost of entering the bet) to enter. This discount is a measure of the person's *risk aversion*. If you were willing to pay more than £50 (this is quite rare) then you would be referred to as *risk seeking*. If exactly £50, then *risk neutral*. Institutions demonstrate risk aversion as much as individuals. Venture capitalists are willing to invest in a new venture (in effect, buying risk from the entrepreneur) – but only if they get a premium (an excess return) for doing so.

Prospect theory

The syntactic (formal) interpretation of risk is highly mathematical. It is the one that informs economics, and from it management science and finance theory. It underpins insurance contracts. Work by mathematicians in the early post-war period developed a highly sophisticated normative model of risk and described the decisions a rational decision maker (one who wishes to maximise his or her possessions and uses information efficiently) should make. This is known as *expected utility theory*. These predictions were soon put to the test (and so behavioural economics was born) and it was quickly found that most decision makers did not follow them: again, they demonstrated biases. The most sophisticated descriptive model of how people really respond to risk was proposed by two psychological-economists – Daniel Kahneman and Amos Tversky – in 1979. This they titled *prospect theory*. Daniel Kahneman won the Nobel Memorial Prize in Economics in 2002 for this work. (Sadly, Amos Tversky died in 1996.) The Kahneman–Tversky paper is quite technical (though the mathematics is not too difficult and for those with some mathematical confidence and working through it is a fine investment). Fortunately, as with all profound ideas, the central themes can be described without recourse to equations. Prospect theory's proposals are best compared to those of expected utility theory. What follows applies to organisations as much as to individuals.

What are decision makers interested in?

According to expected utility theory, where they finish up – their final 'endowment'. According to prospect theory what they might gain or lose. This makes sense. If you find you have lost £10, you don't think, 'Well, I will adjust my endowment. There is the value of my house, my car, my savings. I will just deduct £10.' No, it is more natural just to think, 'Oh, no! I have lost £10.'

Is 'where are we now' important?

As far as expected utility theory is concerned, to a secondary degree. But this only arises because of the technical idea it locates the decision maker on his or her utility function. For prospect theory, the where are we now is of *fundamental* importance because it defines the reference point from which decision makers judge gains and losses. This makes sense. An entrepreneur may look towards some future state in which he or she has achieved certain things (towards a vision), but when it comes to taking actual and immediate decisions, it is the win or lose (relative to where he or she was before the decision) that seems to matter.

Do decision makers take risks?

According to expected utility theory – it depends. Generally speaking people are risk averse. They may be risk-seeking occasionally, but it is hard to predict when. Everything depends on a technical condition known as the shape of the individual's *utility function*. Prospect theory is much clearer. In the domain of gains (when people are winning), they are risk averse (they avoid or expect to be paid to take on risk). In the domain of losses (when people are losing), they actually become risk seeking (they are willing to take on risk – in principle, even willing to buy risk) This is counterintuitive, but it has been observed in a wide variety of situations.

Corporate risk behaviour has proved to be an interesting application because prospect theory makes a prediction that firms in a loss situation will take risks, whereas those in a winning situation will avoid risk – a prediction that is at odds with capital asset pricing theory (which suggests the reverse). Empirical evidence offers a good deal of support to the prospect theory position.

Do gains eliminate losses?

Expected utility theory would suggest yes. Finding £10 and then losing £10 should leave us feeling indifferent (provided there are no additional costs due to the gain and loss). However, prospect theory proposes 'loss aversion'. In other words, losing £10 hurts more than gaining £10 brings pleasure. So the gain–loss above would leave us feeling worse than when we started. This seems to fit with most people's intuitive experiences.

What about chance?

In expected utility theory (as in prospect theory), chance is brought in via the formal concept of probability. A probability is a measure between 0 (impossible) and 1 (certain to happen). Something that may happen has a probability between 0 and 1. Expected utility theory proposes that decision makers should take probabilities at face value. Prospect theory, on the other hand, suggests that decision makers distort probabilities. Specifically, they act as if low probabilities were higher than they really are (so they feel lucky when gains are made and unlucky when losses are suffered), and act as if moderate to high probabilities were lower than they really are (so people feel unlucky where gains are concerned and (relatively) lucky where losses are concerned). This distortion of probability has an interesting effect on risk taking. The feeling of being lucky at low probabilities may overcome the risk aversion in gains and so make people risk seeking. At the same time, the feeling of being unlucky at low probabilities in losses may overcome risk seeking and induce risk aversion. Have you ever wondered why the same person is often willing to pay for a lottery ticket with a very low chance of winning and, at the same time, pay for insurance for an unlikely loss – with both the lottery company and insurance company making a profit?

Does it matter how decisions are articulated?

According to expected utility theory, no. All that matters is the core information that the decision maker should be concerned with – outcomes and the chance of those outcomes. Superfluous information is stripped away. Logically equivalent presentations of the same decision problem elicit the same response. Prospect theory however suggests *framing* effects are important. A framing effect is the encouragement of risk aversion or risk-seeking behaviour by presenting the positive (gain, opportunity) aspects of a problem or negative (loss, threat) aspects, respectively. Strictly speaking, framing effects are not simply a matter of emphasis (though this is important) but one of restructuring a problem so that its logical content does not change.

The idea that losses induce risk-taking behaviour is at first sight counterintuitive. Surely, entrepreneurs take risks when faced with opportunities or gains? Sometimes they do, but human risk behaviour is quite subtle. A good example of risk seeking in losses is the *sunk cost* effect, the phenomenon where a manager, entrepreneur or investor continues to invest in a project long after it is clear that it will never offer a return (expected utility theory suggests a decision maker should care only about what happens in the future; what has happened in the past does not matter). McCarthey *et al.* (1993) examined decisions made by entrepreneurs to expand their business asset base and found that escalation of commitment under losses was frequent. Not just entrepreneurs are affected. One would expect an entrepreneur to put a positive spin on their venture's performance when communicating with investors. But close observation of entrepreneur–investor communications (see Guler, 2003, for example) has uncovered instances where the entrepreneur has played down performance in order (perhaps instinctively) to create a sense of loss in the investor, induce risk-seeking behaviour and encourage further sunk cost investment.

Prospect theory is enormously influential. It is based on psychological insights as much as economic theory and its explanatory power is considerable. It has been applied to a wide variety of managerial decision making and is being applied increasingly to entrepreneurial and venture capital decision making.

There is another decisional anomaly that is of interest. Consider the following two bets. In the first, a jar contains 100 marbles; 50 are red and 50 are white. You choose a colour. If your colour is drawn at random, then you will win £1,000. How much would you be willing to pay for a ticket to enter this bet? Now consider the following bet. A jar contains 100 marbles. Each is either red or white. But you do not know how many of each colour is in the jar. Again you choose red or white. If your colour is drawn, you win £1,000. How much are you willing to pay for a ticket to enter this bet? Most people are not willing to pay as much for the second bet as they are for the first. But statistical theory suggests both bets *must* be of the same value. This anomaly was demonstrated by Daniel Ellsberg in 1961.

The first case is formally referred to as one of risk, because probabilities are known. Strictly speaking, the second is known as one of *ambiguity* because probabilities are not known. It will be appreciated that most entrepreneurial decision situations are ones of ambiguity, not risk (though the word 'risk' is more commonly used). This test demonstrates that we tend to show an aversion to ambiguity (strictly speaking, an irrational aversion) that is different from, and additional to, aversion to risk. It is usually possible (at least in principle) to obtain insurance against risk. But it is not possible to insure against ambiguity. This revisits the point that the fundamental role of the entrepreneur is one not so much of eliminating risk as of their using their expertise and management skills to turn ambiguity into risk.

Summary of key ideas

- *Cognitive psychology* is a relatively new branch of psychology that is concerned with how humans acquire, process and act upon information about the world.

- It is of growing influence in the study of management in general and entrepreneurship in particular.

- Cognitive processes that are relevant to the study of entrepreneurship are:
  - *Perception processes* – how entrepreneurs see the world;
  - *Problem-solving processes* – how entrepreneurs address immediate challenges and bring creativity to bear;
  - *Task processes* – how entrepreneurs approach and undertake actions and related performance issues.

- *Decision making* may be studied from a *normative* or *descriptive* perspective. The normative is concerned with calculating from theoretical principles what the optimal course of action should be; the descriptive is concerned with observing and describing what human beings actually do.

- A systematic difference between a normative recommendation and an observed decision pattern is referred to as a bias.

- Three biases are influential in entrepreneurial decision making:
  - *anchoring bias* – using an irrelevant number or quantity to make a judgement;
  - *availability bias* – regarding how easy it is to call an instance to mind as a good guide to the the quantity, size or frequency of something;
  - *representativeness bias* – judging an item or situation on the basis of how typical it seems to be in relation to the population it might have been drawn from or the process that might have created it, and ignoring *base-rate* information that is also relevant.

- Entrepreneurs (and their supporters) may be subject to *positive or overconfidence biases* where they either rate their own abilities greater than statistical inference would suggest is proper or hold an overly positive view of the world.

- The normative approach to risk behaviour is referred to as *expected utility theory*. It is mathematically elegant but does a poor job of predicting and explaining real human risk behaviour.

- One of the best, and most successful, descriptive approaches to human risk behaviour is *prospect theory*. Prospect theory suggests that human decision makers:
  - are concerned about *gains* and *losses*;
  - make decisions from an initial *reference point*;
  - find that *losses hurt more* than gains bring pleasure;
  - *avoid risk* when winning, but *take risks* when losing;
  - *distort probabilities* – at low probabilities feel lucky when winning, feel unlucky when losing; the other way round at moderate to high probabilities;
  - are susceptible to *framing* – whether the positive or negative perspective on a problem is emphasised.

- Prospect theory is increasingly influential in the study of managerial risk taking generally and in the study of entrepreneurial risk taking in particular.

- In addition to an aversion to risk (where decisions are made knowing probabilities), decision makers show a separate aversion to *ambiguity* (where decisions are made without knowing probabilities) – even though this is statistically irrational.

- One perspective on the entrepreneur's fundamental task is that it is to use his or her knowledge, experience and skills to turn ambiguity into risk on behalf of investors.

Research themes

Heuristics and biases in entrepreneurial decision making: case study analysis

Develop a case study of an entrepreneurial start-up or period of significant business development. This may on the basis of already published secondary data or primary data obtained from interviews. Concentrate on getting information about key decisions by the entrepreneur and key stakeholders. Assess the decisions made and the outcomes that resulted. Is there any evidence that biases were present in the decision making? Focus on instances where anchoring, availability, representativeness and overconfidence might have come into play. How did these affect the quality of the decisions and the resulting performance of the business?

Concepts of risk: a content analysis

Content analysis is a research methodology in which communications (written, transcripts of speech or even visual images) are broken down into elements to see what constituent words, phrases or concepts are present.

The project involves developing an understanding of how the notion of risk and related terms such as uncertainty and ambiguity (and any other words you feel to be related) are used in real, practical discourse (contrasted with how the concepts are used in a formal economic sense).

Obtain a series of specialist dictionaries in the social and other sciences (e.g. economics, finance, sociology, psychology, anthropology, mathematics, plus any others you think relevant). Look up the key words and undertake a content analysis on the definitions offered. How do these compare and contrast? What terms, phrases and concepts are common to all? Which are unique to specific fields? You may attempt to produce a visual representation (a map) of how the key words relate to each other both within and across fields.

How does this conceptualisation of risk concepts relate to how the key words are used in a formal sense? How might it relate to how entrepreneurs (and key stakeholders) might use the terms? You may even conduct a survey of practitioners to find out.

Key readings

Three papers that provide an accessible account of common biases in managerial and strategic decision making are:

Roxburgh, C. (2003) 'Hidden flaws in strategy', *McKinsey Quarterly*, No. 2, pp. 26–39.

Wickham, P.A. (2006) 'How to be an effective – bias-free – decision-maker in an increasingly global economy', *Handbook of Business Strategy 2006*, Bradford: Emerald.

Wickham, P.A. (in press) 'Framing strategic messages for the growth-orientated organisations', *Handbook of Business Strategy 2007*, Bradford: Emerald.

The latter two include a preliminary set of test questions (useful preparation for a tutorial) that demonstrate how easy it is to fall for bias traps when making strategic decisions.

Suggestions for further reading

Amundsen, N.E. (1995) 'An interactive model of career decision-making', *Journal of Employment Counselling*, Vol. 32, No. 1, pp. 427–38.

Baron, J. (2000) *Thinking and Deciding* (3rd edn). Cambridge: Cambridge University Press.

Bazerman, M.H. (2002) *Judgement in Managerial Decision Making*. Hoboken, NJ: Willey.

Bernardo, A.E. and Welch, I. (2001) 'On the evolution and overconfidence of entrepreneurs', *Journal of Economics and Management Strategy*, Vol. 10, No. 3, pp. 301–30.

Buchanan, J.M. and Di Pierro, A. (1980) 'Cognition, choice, and entrepreneurship', *Southern Economic Journal*, Vol. 46, No. 3, pp. 693–701.

Busenitz, L.W. and Barney, J.B. (1997) 'Difference between entrepreneurs and managers in large organizations: biases and heuristics in strategic decision-making', *Journal of Business Venturing*, Vol. 12, No. 1, pp. 9–30.

Campbell, C.A. (1992) 'A decision theory model for entrepreneurial acts', *Entrepreneurship Theory and Practice*, Fall, pp. 21–7.

Chatterjee, S., Wiseman, R.M., Fiegenbaum, A. and Devers, C.E. (2003) 'Integrating behavioural and economic concepts of risk into strategic management: the twain shall meet', *Long Range Planning*, Vol. 36, pp. 61–79.

Eisenhauer, J.G. (1995) 'The entrepreneurial decision: economic theory and empirical evidence', *Entrepreneurship Theory and Practice*, Summer, pp. 67–79.

Ellsberg, D. (1961) 'Risk ambiguity and the Savage axioms', *Quarterly Journal of Economics*, Vol. 75, pp. 643–69.

Escher, S., Grabarkiewicz, R., Frese, M., van Steekelenburg, G., Lauw, M. and Freidrich, C. (2002) 'The moderator effect of cognitive ability on the relationship between planning strategies and business success of small scale business owners in South Africa: a longitudinal study', *Journal of Developmental Entrepreneurship*, Vol. 7, No. 5, pp. 305–18.

Forbes, D.P. (1999) 'Cognitive approaches to new venture creation', *International Journal of Management Reviews*, Vol. 1, No. 4, pp. 415–39.

Forbes, D.P. (2005) 'Are some entrepreneurs more overconfident than others?', *Journal of Business Venturing*, Vol. 20, No. 5, pp. 623–40.

Frese, M., Brantjes, A. and Hoorn, R. (2002) 'Psychological success factors of small scale businesses in Namibia: the role of strategy process, entrepreneurial orientation and the environment', *Journal of Developmental Entrepreneurship*, Vol. 7, No. 3, pp. 259–82.

Gigerenzer, G. (2002) *Reckoning with Risk: Learning to Live with Uncertainty*. London: Allen Lane.

Gilhooley, K.J. (1996) *Thinking: Directed, Undirected and Creative* (3rd edn). London: Academic Press.

Giminez, F., Pelisson, C., Kruger, E.G.S. and Hayashi, P. (2000) 'Small firms' owner-managers' construction of competition', *Journal of Enterprising Culture*, Vol. 8, No. 4, pp. 261–79.

Guler, I. (2003) 'Throwing good money after bad? Sequential decision-making in the venture capital industry', *Academy of Management Best Conference Paper 2003*.

Hastie, R. and Dawes, R.M. (2001) *Rational Choice in an Uncertain World: The Psychology of Judgement and Decision Making*. Thousand Oaks, CA: Sage.

Hayes, J. and Allinson, C.W. (1994) 'Cognitive style and its relevance for management practice', *British Journal of Management*, Vol. 5, pp. 53–71.

Kahneman, D. and Tversky, A. (1979) 'Prospect theory: an analysis of decision-making under risk', *Econometrica*, Vol. 47, pp. 263–91.

Kahneman, D. and Tversky, A. (2000) *Choices, Values and Frames*. Cambridge: Cambridge University Press.

Kahneman, D., Slovic, P. and Tversky, A. (1982) *Judgement under Uncertainty: Heuristics and Biases*. Cambridge: Cambridge University Press.

Kamm, J.B. and Nurick, A.J. (1992) 'The stages in team venture formation: a decision-making model', *Entrepreneurship Theory and Practice*, Winter, pp. 17–27.

Katz, J.K. (1992a) 'A psychosocial cognitive model of employment status choice', *Entrepreneurship Theory and Practice*, Fall, pp. 29–37.

Katz, J.K. (1992b) 'The dynamics of organizational emergence: a contemporary group formation perspective', *Entrepreneurship Theory and Practice*, Winter, pp. 97–101.

Keh, H.T., Foo, M.D. and Lim, B.C. (2002) 'Opportunity evaluation under risky conditions: the cognitive process of entrepreneurs', *Entrepreneurship Theory and Practice*, Vol. 27, No. 2, pp. 125–48.

Kreiser, P.M., Marino, L.D. and Weaver, K.M. (2002a) 'Reassessing the environment–EO link: the impact of environmental hostility on the dimensions of entrepreneurial orientation', *Academy of Management Best Papers Proceedings*.

Kreiser, P.M., Marino, L.D. and Weaver, K.M. (2002b) 'Assessing the psychometric properties of the entrepreneurial orientation scale: a multi-country analysis', *Entrepreneurship Theory and Practice*, Vol. 26, No. 4, pp. 71–94.

Kristiansen, S. (2002) 'Individual perception of business contexts: the case of small-scale entrepreneurs in Tanzania', *Journal of Developmental Entrepreneurship*, Vol. 7, No. 3, pp. 283–304.

Luthans, F., Stajkovic, A.D. and Ibrayeva, E. (2000) 'Environmental and psychological challenges facing entrepreneurial development in transition economies', *Journal of World Business*, Vol. 35, No. 1, pp. 95–110.

Markman, G.D., Balkin, D.B. and Baron, R.A. (2002) 'Inventors and new venture formation: the effects of general self-efficacy and regretful thinking', *Entrepreneurship Theory and Practice*, Winter, pp. 149–65.

McCarthey, A.M., Schoorman, F.D. and Cooper, A.C. (1993) 'Reinvestment decisions by entrepreneurs: rational decision makers or escalation of commitment?' *Journal of Business Venturing*, Vol. 8, No. 1, pp. 9–24.

McCline, R.L., Bhat, S. and Baj, P. (2000) 'Opportunity recognition: an exploratory investigation of a component in the entrepreneurial process in the context of the health care industry', *Entrepreneurship Theory and Practice*, Vol. 25, No. 2, pp. 81–94.

Minniti, M. and Bygrave, W. (1999) 'The microfoundations of entrepreneurship', *Entrepreneurship Theory and Practice*, Vol. 23, No. 4, pp. 41–53.

Mitchell, R.K., Busenitz, L., Lant, T., McDougall, P.P., Morse, E.A. and Brock-Smith, J. (2002) 'Towards a theory of entrepreneurial cognition: rethinking the people side of entrepreneurship research', *Entrepreneurship Theory and Practice*, Winter, pp. 93–104.

Myers, D.G. (2002) *Intuition: Its Powers and Perils*. New York: Harcourt Brace.

Neck, C.P., Neck, H.M., Manz, C.C. and Godwin, J. (1999) 'I think I can; I think I can: a self-leadership perspective towards enhancing the entrepreneur through thought patterns, self-efficacy and performance', *Journal of Managerial Psychology*, Vol. 14, No. 7/8, pp. 477–501.

Plous, S. (1993) *The Psychology of Judgement and Decision Making*. New York: McGraw-Hill.

Poltis, D. (2005) 'The process of entrepreneurial learning: a conceptual framework', *Entrepreneurship: Theory and Practice*, Vol. 29, No. 4, pp. 399–424.

Robichaud, Y. and Egbert, R.A. (2001) 'Towards the development of a measuring instrument for entrepreneurial motivation', *Journal of Developmental Entrepreneurship*, Vol. 6, No. 2, pp. 189–201.

Shepherd, D.A. and Kreuger, N.F. (2002) 'An intentions-based model of entrepreneurial teams' social cognition', *Entrepreneurship Theory and Practice*, Winter, pp. 167–85.

Simon, M. and Houghton, S.M. (2003) 'The relationship between overconfidence and the introduction of risky products: Evidence from a field study', *Academy of Management Journal*, Vol. 46, No. 2, pp. 139–49.

Stancill, J.M. (1981) 'Realistic criteria for judging new ventures', *Harvard Business Review*, Nov./Dec., pp. 60–71.

Stubbart, C.I. (1989) 'Managerial cognition: a missing link in strategic management', *Journal of Management Studies*, Vol. 26, No. 4, pp. 325–47.

Uusitalo, R. (2001) '*Homo entreprenaurus*', *Applied Economics*, Vol. 33, pp. 1631–8.

Weaver, K.M., Dickson, P.H., Gibson, B. and Turner, A. (2002) 'Being uncertain: the relationship beteween entrepreneurial orientation and environmental uncertainty', *Journal of Enterprising Culture*, Vol. 10, No. 2, pp. 87–106.

Wickham, P.A. (2003) 'The representativeness heuristic in judgements involving entrepreneurial success and failure', *Management Decision*, Vol. 41, No. 3, pp. 156–67.

Wright, R. (2000) *Nonzero: History, Evolution and Human Cooperation*. London: Abacus.

Zacharakis, A.L. and Shepherd, D.A. (2001) 'The nature of information and overconfidence on venture capitalists decision making', *Journal of Business Venturing*, Vol. 16, No. 4, pp. 311–32.

Selected case material

CASE 4.1

7 November 2005

Management training for the young

STEPHEN OVERELL

Shortly after mastering the potty, but before they can count to 20, pupils at the Grange Primary School in Derbyshire savour their first taste of life in the corporate fast lane. From the age of three – yes, three – all 400 children become involved in running one of the enterprises that together form 'Grangetown', a model town.

At the school's 'healthy eating shop', for example, children between seven and 11 take on a variety of management tasks. They must research a product base, survey changing customer needs and understand inventory and stock control. Formed with a £250 ($441) loan (now repaid), the shop turns a £100 profit every six weeks. Mercantilism is tempered by social responsibility, however: all profits are ploughed back into Grangetown.

'The national curriculum is still stuck in the 19th-century model of receiving knowledge passively,' says Richard Gerver, the school's headteacher. 'I'm just not sure we are set up to create dynamic, problem-solving, independently minded young people.'

Similar doubts were aired at a conference in London last week organised by the Qualifications and Curriculum Authority (QCA), a state body that oversees the qualifications system, which sought to ask employers which skills they thought would be most valuable in the future.

For Jeff Jennings, director of the Centre for Development at BMW UK, the British arm of the German carmaker, the skills of writing, reading and arithmetic are more important than ever for his industry's future. But the future of both technicians and sales staff depends on other skills, too: a facility with information technology, strong listening and communication abilities, an aptitude for collaboration, deductive reasoning and interpersonal skills, such as reading body language and emotional intelligence.

Schools, he argues, tend to foster 'content sponges', not entrepreneurs. 'If you can't work in a team as a child, you won't be able to as an adult,' he claims.

Naturally, the industrialisation of education inspires terror among some. The fear that what were once known as 'the liberal arts' are being enslaved by 'the servile arts' (occupational learning) is an old one. T.S. Eliot wrote: 'There is no doubt that in our headlong rush to educate everybody, we are lowering our standards . . . destroying our ancient edifices to make ready the ground upon which the barbarian nomads of the future will encamp in their mechanised caravans.'

Yet the QCA is keen to stress that its interest in innovative experiments in schools is not aimed at making them more 'vocational' – a loaded term in Britain. Rather, it is asking if there is more that schools can do to teach academic subjects in ways that will serve employers' long-term skill requirements better.

'Literacy and numeracy standards are absolutely vital,' says David Burrows, director of education for Microsoft, the software company. 'But schools need an appreciation of what the economy is going to need – things like problem-solving, critical thinking, how to – contextualise information, learning to learn.'

▶

CASE 4.1 CONT.

The analysis of future skills needs in western economies is an uncertain task. It involves both attempting to understand the ways that information technology will transform the nature of jobs inside organisations; and also identifying which occupations are most likely to grow or diminish as a result.

According to *The New Division of Labour*, in which Frank Levy and Richard Murnane, two American academics, examine how IT affects work, computers are increasingly taking over work governed by 'rules-based logic'. If a job involves following a set of 'if–then–do' rules, then it is programmable, and a candidate for either computer substitution or offshoring.

The skills most important to the future as nations move up the value chain, the authors argue, will be in two areas: 'expert thinking' – advanced problem-solving and pattern recognition; and 'complex communication' – human interactions involving persuasion, collaboration and negotiation.

The effect of advancing IT in factories and offices is that more of the jobs humans do revolve around interpersonal interactions and sophisticated intellectual work. Technology thus tilts the labour market decisively against the less well-educated.

Take bank cashiers, for example. Automated teller machines now dispense cash and enable simple account administration. But smaller numbers of cashiers are still necessary to sort out complicated queries and push new products.

Given this effect, it is unsurprising that the biggest growth has been in jobs that require significant training or education – managers, professionals, technical and administrative staff. Low-skills service jobs have also grown, hence rising social polarisation – but not at the speed of higher level jobs.

The authors write: 'Between 1969 and 1999 the number of adults employed as service workers [in America] grew from 11.6 per cent to 13.9 per cent of the adult workforce, but managers, administrators, professional workers and technicians taken together – the highest paid categories – grew from 23 per cent to 33 per cent.'

The pattern has been similar in the UK, too. The biggest single occupational category is now managers and professionals – a development anticipated by Karl Marx in the 19th century. And it is high-paying jobs that have grown fastest over the past 25 years.

The UK government's most recent National Skills Survey found that of ten different measures of generic skill used at work, nine showed a rise in requirements. These included literacy, numeracy, technical know-how, problem-solving, checking, planning and various forms of communication. The sole exception was physical strength and stamina. About one-quarter of jobs today require a degree.

Of course, not everyone will become a manager, or would want to. But what is the best way to educate children to prosper in this likely world of work?

Mr Levy, a professor of urban economics at the Massachusetts Institute of Technology, argues against treating expert thinking and complex communication as new subjects in the curriculum.

'Kids still need to know rule-based subjects like algebra,' he says. 'But solving problems has two parts. First, there is modelling a situation and knowing which rules to apply to solve it; and then there is executing a solution. It is knowing which rules to apply that will retain its labour market value.'

Using analogies, project-based collaborations, emphasising the underlying relationships between facts, and cutting back on multiple-choice tests should help develop skills of critical thinking and social capital. However, Mr Levy admits his suggestions for the classroom are as yet tentative.

But, as always, the risk of such innovations is that they may be perceived as yet another flaky fad. After all, languages, literature and maths will never date in the way more 'practical' skills will. Alison Wolf, professor of management and professional development at Kings College, London, has argued in her book *Does Education Matter?*, for example, that traditional academic disciplines are the best preparation for the workplace.

This is also the approach in Germany, which has a long history of high quality adult vocational development. But, notes Gerhard Bosch, vice-president of the Institute Arbeit and Technik, based in Dusseldorf, Germany, for schoolchildren, the state believes 'raising academic achievement prior to entry into the labour force is the best answer to growing social polarisation'.

Source: Stephen Overell, 'Management training for the young', *Financial Times*, 7 November 2005, p. 10. Copyright © 2005 Stephen Overell.

CASE 4.2

28 January 2006

TBA

EMMA CRICHTON-MILLER

It's a sunny Saturday in a garden after a lazy lunch. We are a group of old friends, from our late 30s to early 50s, sprawled on the grass, keeping half an eye on small children trampling the flower beds. The subject turns to work and suddenly we're alert. Rather than a relaxed account of careers rising to high tide, apprehension crackles.

A mixed bunch of professionals, we are all gripped by the same question: how are we going to earn a living for the next 20 or 30 years? Most of us are arts graduates who spurned vocational degrees the first time around to pursue strong personal interests – in art or literature, drama, history or anthropology. Our subsequent careers are a patchwork of passionately pursued projects – either in academe or the media or as film-makers and writers. Mostly we avoided the more obviously lucrative professions available then to arts graduates in PR and advertising – partly, it is true, out of youthful high-mindedness

(clearly misguided!) – but partly because the lure of the next assignment and the pleasures of growing expertise were irresistible. Now, however, the time for play is over.

For some, there is a sense of guilt, at having contributed perhaps less usefully to society than our education might have allowed us to. Certainly I feel the eyes of public-service driven ancestors – all those doctors and priests and teachers – bearing down on me sternly. The shift in values over our adult lifetime from the ego-driven 1980s to the public service culture of New Labour has perhaps exacerbated this crisis of conscience. And for many the increasing casualisation of the workplace and the whole ghastly mess of pension provision are issues that are beginning to bite in the early hours of the morning.

First one person and then another admits that more traditionally vocational professions have recently taken on a new allure. Various reasons are offered: it could be a desire for

89

CASE 4.2 CONT.

financial security and predictability of employment, the quest for job satisfaction, or the unearthing of a latent ambition never before fully expressed. This is not idle chat. It transpires that every one of us has seriously investigated the possibilities.

I inform everyone that to become a solicitor you need to do a graduate diploma in law (£6,000–£7,000), then take a legal practice course (£5,000–£9,000) and then spend two years under a very modestly remunerative training contract. A friend explains how you can move from the diploma to a Bar vocational course, then into pupillage (and temporary penury) to become a barrister. Can he, with a mortgage and three children, afford it?

Another tells the story of a friend who, although she had already trained as a barrister, has shifted in her late 30s from family law to clinical psychology, taking first a conversion degree course in psychology, then completing three years of a PhD, all along volunteering in various mental health institutions, before fulfilling a further probationary period. And she has three children.

Between us we come up with a journalist who retrained as a midwife; a wine merchant who has become a barrister; a solicitor who has become a social worker; a graduate mother who retrained in her late 40s as a barrister; a doctor who moved into equity finance; and a television producer who has become a primary school teacher. Far from downsizing, these people have achieved the kind of substantial career redirection that is fairly common for people in their 20s, still working out what it is they really want to do, but has up until now been rarer for people in their later 40s and 50s.

There are of course significant material reasons why our age group might consider undertaking expensive and time-consuming professional re-education. As the government keeps reminding us, the notion of a 'job for life' is redundant and today's buzz phrase is 'employability for life'. As our energy declines and creative ideas no longer flow to order, a vocational qualification seems a comfortingly clear signal of competence. The fact that we seem likely to be pressed to work until we are 68 or later is a strong incentive to choose a career that will still provide both work and job satisfaction well on into our 60s.

Other, more purely psychological, reasons also play a part. Many people describe a subtle shift in values as they reach the end of their 30s or have children. Others see this moment as their last chance to realise an ambition that maybe their parents, a forbidding teacher or financial circumstances had blocked earlier. Some simply want a new challenge.

Over her professional lifetime, Professor Susan Cartwright of the Manchester Business School has seen an increase in major career change. She herself moved from the insurance industry into organisational psychology when her daughter was small, as the high pay and many travel opportunities of her first career seemed less appealing in her 30s. 'There are so many professions that benefit from having people not straight from university – and organisations should acknowledge that,' she says.

If businesses have been reluctant to offer sabbaticals and some institutions of higher education slow to accommodate the needs of mature students, other universities and colleges have stepped in. The backbone of mature study is the Open University. About half of its students are taking courses explicitly with the intention of changing career and, over the last five years, its careers service has expanded rapidly to help students achieve this. Other universities also offer correspondence and distance learning opportunities, and there has been an expansion in the provision of graduate level conversion degree programmes in vocational subjects such as law and psychology, with reasonable flexibility about completion times and on-site attendance.

Teaching has been actively recruiting older, experienced candidates on to PGCE programmes, with the additional incentive that your fees are paid for you, and even the Law Society, which supervises the professional training of solicitors, admits that the average age of people qualifying is now 28 – requiring a fair constituency of the over-35s.

Medicine is inevitably a harder nut to crack, given the length of time it takes to qualify. Even Kings College's fast track four-year medical degree programme for non-medical graduates rarely sees candidates much over 30.

All this opportunity cannot disguise the fact, however, that once you start probing your own financial and emotional readiness, the loss of earnings and achieved status may just be unsustainable. As Simon Broomer, director of the careers advice service Career Balance puts it: 'The educational door may increasingly be open but if you can't go through it, you can't go through it.' He is very cautious about encouraging major change. Often people have a romanticised view of life on the other side and underestimate the value of the skills and experience they have already acquired. Often a deep dissatisfaction can be resolved either by a change in the sector where they are using their skills, or by the development of new skills within the same sector. You might write novels rather than journalism, teach adults rather than children or move, within the same company, from accounts to personnel.

For Edward French the shift happened early enough, in his early 30s, for him to sustain the financial shock. He had resigned from a high-earning job in the City when a friend suggested family law, which immediately appealed. He used his savings to finance the two years of law course and Bar school and the 16-month period of pupillage, during which he earned very little. 'You have to be confident of your own abilities. You shouldn't try to become a barrister unless it's absolutely what you've got to do.' He feels, however, that family law is particularly suitable for older candidates. 'You've got to represent clients in very difficult and emotional circumstances, so it helps to have some maturity,' he says. He counts among his colleagues a former architect, an erstwhile archaeologist, an ex-midwife and a one-time psychiatric nurse. For another barrister I spoke to, who made the change in his early 40s and is doing his pupillage now, the most difficult part is the financial strain on his family. Alongside this is the vow of humility you have to take when you give up being the boss of your own business, used to managing others, and become the lowest of the low in the pecking order.

For Hannah Stephens, the trigger for change as she entered her 40s was her children. Stephens, who had been a senior television drama producer running a successful team, said 'there was no single Road to Damascus moment'. She had been well paid and allowed to work four days a week to accommodate her children's needs. 'But I had got more involved with and interested in my children's education and was increasingly frustrated at not being able to help them.'

She was so inspired by her interview for the PGCE at the Institute of Education that, although she was offered a very good job the same day she learnt her application had been accepted, she chose the course. Stephens' husband was also a teacher and he was able to support the family while she did her PGCE. She acknowledges that it was a huge bonus that she had achieved a certain level of security for her family before embarking on this new career. 'I learnt something new every day. I was so much more purposeful about studying than the first time around. You only have nine months and you have to come out of it with the right qualification.'

Her fees were paid by the local authority and she received a bursary of £6,000. Curiously, now in her first year as a qualified teacher, teaching at a primary school near her home, she has less time to be with her children. 'I work very long hours. I get up before them and I am not there when they get home from school. I am driven. But it's good to feel driven about something that you feel really matters.'

Max Whitby had already had several careers – as a prolific BBC television producer making science programmes, as a pioneer of interactive television, as the director of an independent production company, as the founder of a science-based company – when a niggling envy of pure science drove him in his late 40s to embark on a Masters in Research in Nanomaterials at Imperial College. 'However absorbing the individual projects, I increasingly felt that I was outside the greenhouse looking in,' he says. Although Whitby had three science A levels, he had read philosophy at university. Normally a good first or upper second class degree in chemistry or physics is a requirement of the course, 'But this is frontier territory, intellectually like the Wild West, and because everybody has got only part of the background, I was able to persuade them to take me.'

Throughout the first year Whitby took emergency maths lessons from a friend, plumbed the expertise of his fellow students in quantum mechanics, chemistry and molecular biology and recorded every lecture on his iPod. 'I loved my first year. I was twice the age of my fellow students but you make up in

guile for the lack of computational power. Occasionally I've hit a brick wall and that is daunting.' At first Whitby's intention had been to take a sabbatical, partly funded by his company. However, having earned a distinction in his Masters and made a potentially exciting discovery, he has now embarked on a PhD and has established a further company for the exploitation of his research findings. Whitby admits that anyone making such a huge change of direction faces all kinds of risks and uncertainties 'but it is also an opportunity to fit in another life'.

For Robert Montagu that other life had been waiting all along. He had been a successful entrepreneur, businessman, audio-visual producer, writer, consultant and father to four children when, aged 50, he started to retrain as a psychologist. 'It was something I had always wanted to do since I was a child. I had had a dysfunctional family life and, when I got to boarding school, I started helping others to help myself. I would practise family therapy illegitimately with groups of up to 10 boys who had problems with severe sexual bullying in the school.'

Montagu took a four-year postgraduate course in systemic family psychotherapy, offered by the KCC Foundation in Vauxhall, partly because their criteria for entry were more flexible. 'I embarked on the course thinking I would use it in business practice. It was only when I started that I realised I was going to change career.' While studying, Montagu practised for three years with the Wandsworth social team, where they had no other therapeutic services. 'This was incredible experience. We handled hundreds of very difficult cases, in a very multi-ethnic environment, and had to work closely with social services.'

After graduating with a distinction, he got a job with the Hertfordshire Health Trust, was promoted rapidly and has just taken a senior position at the Brent Centre for Young People. 'I feel very much at home in my work, very much supported by my colleagues', but Montagu acknowledges that it has been very tough on his wife. They had always lived together in the country. Now Montagu works long hours in London and returns exhausted. However his wife, a sculptor, said: 'We have always both believed in continual growth.'

Montagu's example is confirmed by Julie Evans, director of the conversion degree programme in psychology at the London Metropolitan University. Besides the many students in their early 20s, her next largest group of students are those aged anywhere from late 30s through to 50. She interviews intensively to identify those who have really thought through the whole process from academic qualification to final career transformation and so has an almost invisible dropout rate. What older students lack in brain speed,

they compensate for with clarity of purpose, time management skills and commitment.

Months on from our lazy summer lunch, we are still exchanging notes. One friend is about to embark on the law diploma, another has been offered a job so appealing within her own field that she has gone for it but says the soul-searching has at least enabled her to put other nagging thoughts to rest. I have been too busy to think. But it is still January, and along with the rest of the world, I say maybe this will be the year I make that leap for another life. As the government's anti-age discrimination legislation is made law this October, it could be that many more of us, creeping into middle age, decide that rather than endure the declining satisfactions of our first career, we go for broke and build a second.

Source: Emma Crichton-Miller, 'TBA', *Financial Times*, 28 January 2006, p. 1. Copyright © 2006 Emma Crichton-Miller.

Discussion point

1. To what extent might the different cognitive skills of entrepreneurs (a) be present at birth; (b) develop through schooling; (c) develop through professional experience in later life?

CHAPTER 5

Taking the entrepreneurial option

Chapter overview

This chapter is concerned with developing a picture of the entrepreneur as an individual. It considers the type of people who choose an entrepreneurial path, the characteristics that successful entrepreneurs bring to the job and the skills they use. The chapter concludes by emphasising the importance of understanding the entrepreneur in a social setting and the influences exerted by the culture in which they operate.

5.1 Who becomes an entrepreneur?

Key learning outcome

A recognition of the different type of people who take up an entrepreneurial career.

The discussion in Chapter 1 should make it clear that we should be very wary of trying to answer the question 'who becomes an entrepreneur?' by looking for a certain type of personality or trying to identify innate characteristics. In these terms, *anyone* can become an entrepreneur. A more fruitful approach is to look at the broader life experience and events which encourage a person to make a move into entrepreneurship. A number of general life stories or 'biographies' can be identified.

The inventor

The *inventor* is someone who has developed an innovation and who has decided to make a career out of presenting that innovation to the market. It may be a new product or it may be an idea for a new service. It may be high-tech or it may be based on a traditional technology.

The inventor often draws on technical experience of a particular industry in order to make his or her invention. However, the invention may be derived from a technology quite unrelated to the industry in which they work. It may be based on technical expertise they have gained as the result of a hobby. Alternatively, the invention may result from a 'grey' research programme carried out unofficially within the inventor's employer organisation or it may be the product of a private 'garden shed' development programme.

It is an unfortunate fact of life that, in general, many such 'inventors' have a poor track record in building successful businesses. This is not because their ideas are not good: their innovations are often quite valuable. More often, it is due to the fact that no new product, regardless of how many benefits it might potentially bring to the customer, will manufacture and promote itself. Successful entrepreneurship calls upon a wide range of management skills, not just an ability to innovate. The entrepreneur must establish a market potential for their innovation and lead an organisation which can deliver it profitably. They must sell the product to customers and sell the venture to investors. Inventors can often be so impressed with the technical side of their innovation (often justifiably) that they neglect the other tasks that must be undertaken. An example of an inventor who combined technical insight with consummate business skills is James Dyson, who built up not one but two highly successful businesses to market innovative products.

The unfulfilled manager

Life as a professional manager in an established organisation brings many rewards. It offers a stable income, intellectual stimulation, status and a degree of security. For many people, though, this is still not enough. The organisation may not offer them a vehicle for all their ambitions: for example, the desire to make a mark on the world, to leave a lasting achievement, to stretch their existing managerial talents to their limit and to develop new ones. It may simply not let them do things *their* way. Such a manager, confident in their abilities and unsatisfied in their ambitions, may decide to embark on an entrepreneurial career.

The question they often face is 'doing what?' The desire and the ability to perform entrepreneurially means nothing if a suitable opportunity has not been spotted and an innovation to take advantage of it developed. In a sense, the unsatisfied manager faces the opposite problem to the inventor: entrepreneurial ability but nothing to apply it to. If they are to be successful they must put effort into identifying and clarifying a business idea and developing an understanding of its market potential. This can often be resolved by working as part of an entrepreneurial team with an inventor who dreams up the initial idea.

The displaced manager

The increasing pace of technological and economic change means that managers are likely to make an increasing number of career changes during their professional lives. Restructuring trends such as 'downsizing' and 'delayering' mean that unemployment among professional groups is increasing in many parts of the world. This increases the pressure on managers to work for themselves and one possibility is to undertake an entrepreneurial route. The severance package which may be offered by their organisations (often supplemented with training and support) can sometimes facilitate this possibility.

Many managers approach redundancy positively, seeing it as an opportunity to achieve things they could not within the organisation. In effect, they recognise themselves as unfulfilled managers and feel grateful for the push they have been given. Others, however, may not adopt such a positive approach. They may see the uncertainties looming larger than the possibilities. Making entrepreneurship successful is very difficult, if not impossible, unless it is approached with enthusiasm. If a person does not find the prospect of an entrepreneurial career attractive then such a career is plainly wrong for them. However, one should not underestimate the power of a few early successes to change attitudes and to alter a manager's perception of possibilities.

The young professional

Increasingly, young, highly educated people, often with formal management qualifications, are skipping the experience of working for an established organisation and moving directly to work on establishing their own ventures. Despite some very high-profile success stories, not least with internet ventures, such entrepreneurs are often met with suspicion. There may be a concern that whatever their 'theoretical' knowledge, they lack experience in the realities of business life. While youthful enthusiasm *may* hide a lack of real acumen, the young entrepreneur should not be dismissed out of hand.

In the mature economies of the western world, young entrepreneurs have been disproportionally important in leading new industries, particularly in high-tech areas such as computing, information technology and business services. The fast-growing emergent economies of the Pacific Rim and the developing world have populations which are generally much younger in profile than those of the West. Entrepreneurs may *have* to be younger if sufficient entrepreneurial talent is to be available to drive the economy's growth. The post-communist world of eastern and central Europe is undergoing a radical economic and social restructuring. To a great extent it is young people who are taking the lead and making the adaptations necessary to take advantage of the new possibilities these changes are offering. Delmar and Davidsson (2000) found that some 2 per cent of the Swedish population were considering starting their own business. After exploring a number of social and personal factors they found that sex was the dominant indicator of entrepreneurial intention and age an important secondary factor.

The excluded

Some people turn to an entrepreneurial career because nothing else is open to them. The dynamism and entrepreneurial vigour of displaced communities and ethnic and religious minorities is well documented. This is not because such people are 'inherently' entrepreneurial; rather it is because, for a variety of social, cultural, political and historical reasons, they have not been invited to join the wider economic community. They do not form part of the established network of individuals and organisations. As a result they may form their own internal networks, trading among themselves and, perhaps, with their ancestral countries.

Ethnic entrepreneurship can be very important within a national economy. Small communities often make a contribution to the overall entrepreneurial vigour of a country in a way which is quite disproportionate to their number. Nevertheless, one of the main challenges faced by ethnic entrepreneurs is making the move from running a small business to starting a full-blown entrepreneurial venture. This is because to achieve its growth potential the entrepreneurial venture must spread its network of relationships quite widely, and this often involves going beyond the confines of the small community in which it starts. In a sense, this goes against the reason for the business coming into existence in the first place. In making the move, the ethnic entrepreneur may face risks that the non-ethnic entrepreneur does not.

There is growing evidence that, after a time, say three or four generations, small business managers from ethnic minorities are increasingly willing to make the move to entrepreneurism. In doing so they add another spur to the wider economy.

In a far-reaching study, Blanchflower and Oswald (1998) have investigated the factors that lie behind the drive to become an entrepreneur. The basis of their research was information on the National Child Development Study (NCDS), a database recording biographical information, psychometric and personality test data on all individuals born in Great Britain between 3 and 9 March 1958. Taking a broad view of entrepreneurship, that is, starting one's own business, the researchers attempted to identify the factors that predisposed individuals to take this career option. They found no correlation between personality factors, important life events and entrepreneurial inclination. This is a finding that reinforces this book's proposition that successful entrepreneurship is not personality dependent. The one thing they did find to be important was receiving a lump sum of money, say in the form of a legacy, which allowed individuals to make the initial investment in a start-up. The authors then develop an econometric model of entrepreneurial labour economics. This finding confirms the importance of access to initial capital as a key event in the entrepreneurial process.

This is not to say that one cannot become an entrepreneur if one does not receive a legacy. But it does emphasise the importance of building a good relationship with investors. This is an issue that will be explored further in Chapter 20.

Miner (1997) suggests that four primary types of individual become entrepreneurs. These are:

- The *personal achiever* – the individual who is driven to succeed and chooses the entrepreneurial option as the best means of doing this. The personal achiever is characterised by clear objectives, hard work and dedication.
- The *emphatic supersalesperson* – this type is characterised by a well-developed ability to understand customer needs, to empathise with them and to communicate their offerings to them effectively. They are motivated to become entrepreneurs by their ability to deliver sales.
- The *real manager* – the entrepreneur who is motivated by having an organisation large enough to put demands on their managerial abilities. They are motivated to build their own organisations because of the lack of extant organisations that can offer them the challenges they seek.
- The *expert-idea generator* – an individual who is motivated by the entrepreneurial option because it offers them a platform to develop and market an innovation they have created and to achieve the satisfaction of seeing it become reality.

Miner considers appropriate routes into entrepreneurship and some of the pitfalls along the way for each type.

5.2 Characteristics of the successful entrepreneur

Although there does not seem to be a single 'entrepreneurial type' there is a great deal of consistency in the way in which entrepreneurs approach their task. Some of the characteristics that are exhibited by the successful entrepreneur are discussed below. However, we should

Key learning outcome

A recognition of the characteristics exhibited by successful entrepreneurs.

be careful to draw a distinction between personality 'characteristics' and the character somebody displays when working. The former are regarded as innate, a permanent part of the make-up of their personality. The latter is just the way they approach a particular set of tasks. This is just as much a product of their commitment, interest and motivation to the tasks in hand, as it is a predisposition.

Hard work

Entrepreneurs put a lot of physical and mental effort into developing their ventures. They often work long and antisocial hours. After all, an entrepreneur is their own most valuable asset. That said, balancing the needs of the venture with other life commitments such as family and friends is one of the great challenges which faces the entrepreneur.

Self-starting

Entrepreneurs do not need to be told what to do. They identify tasks for themselves and then follow them through without looking for encouragement or direction from others.

Setting of personal goals

Entrepreneurs tend to set themselves clear, and demanding, goals. They benchmark their achievements against these personal goals. As a result, entrepreneurs tend to work to internal standards rather than look to others for assessment of their performance.

Resilience

Not everything goes right all the time. In fact, failure may be experienced more often than success. Entrepreneurs must not only pick themselves up after things have gone wrong but also learn positively from the experience and use that learning to increase the chances of success the next time around.

Confidence

Entrepreneurs must demonstrate that they not only believe in themselves but also in the venture they are pursuing. After all, if they don't, who will? However, note the issue of *over* confidence discussed in section 4.3.

Receptiveness to new ideas

So, entrepreneurs must not be *overly* confident. They must recognise their own limitations and the possibilities that they have to improve their skills. They must be willing to revise their ideas in the light of new experience. One of the main reasons that banks and venture capitalists give for *not* supporting a business proposal is that entrepreneurs were *too* sure of themselves to be receptive to good advice when it was offered.

Assertiveness

Entrepreneurs are usually clear as to what they want to gain from a situation and are not frightened to express their wishes. Being assertive does not mean being aggressive. Nor does it mean adopting a position and refusing to budge. Assertiveness means a commitment to *outcomes*, not *means*. True assertiveness relies on mutual understanding and is founded on good communication skills.

Information seeking

Entrepreneurs are not, on average, any more intelligent than any other group. They are, however, characterised by *inquisitiveness*. They are never satisfied by the information they have at any one time and constantly seek more. Good entrepreneurs tend to question rather more than they make statements when communicating.

Eager to learn

Good entrepreneurs are always aware that they could do things better. They are aware of both the skills they have and their limitations, and are always receptive to a chance to improve their skills and to develop new ones.

Attuned to opportunity

The good entrepreneur is constantly searching for new opportunities. In effect, this means that they are never really satisfied with the way things are at any moment in time. The entrepreneur uses this sense of dissatisfaction to make sure they never become complacent.

Receptive to change

The entrepreneur is always willing to embrace change in a positive fashion, that is, to actively embrace the possibilities presented by change rather than resist them.

Commitment to others

Good entrepreneurs are not selfish. They cannot afford to be. They recognise the value that other people bring to their ventures and the importance of motivating those people to make the best effort they can on its behalf. This means showing a commitment to them. Motivation demands an investment in understanding how people think. Leadership is not just about giving people jobs to do; it is also about offering them the support they need in order to do those jobs.

Comfort with power

Entrepreneurs can become very powerful figures. They can have a great impact on the lives of other people. Power can be one of the great motivators for the entrepreneur. Effective entrepreneurs are *aware* of the power they possess and recognise it as an asset. They are not afraid to use it and never let themselves be intimidated by it. However, the *true* entrepreneur uses power responsibly, as a means to an end and not as an end in itself.

These are essential characteristics. How they become manifest is, of course, subject to political and economic conditions. They are recognised and judged in a social setting subject to social norms and expectations. How these characteristics are developing in social systems that have undergone major changes (such as the post-communist bloc of central and eastern Europe) is of particular interest. Green *et al.* (1996) and Kuznetsov *et al.* (2000) offer studies of the emergence of entrepreneurial characteristics in Russia.

5.3 Entrepreneurial skills

Key learning outcome

A recognition of the skills that enhance entrepreneurial performance.

A skill is simply knowledge which is demonstrated by action. It is an ability to perform in a certain way. An entrepreneur is someone who has a good business idea and can turn that idea into reality. To be successful, an entrepreneur must not only identify an opportunity but also understand it in great depth. They must be able to spot a gap in the market and recognise what new product or service will fill that gap. They must know what features it will have and why they will appeal to the customer. The entrepreneur must also know how to inform the customer about it and how to deliver the new offering. All this calls for an intimate knowledge of a particular sector of industry. Turning an idea into reality calls upon two sorts of skill. General management skills are required to organise the physical and financial resources needed to run the venture and people management skills are needed to obtain the necessary support from others for the venture to succeed.

Some important general management business skills include:

- *strategy skills* – an ability to consider the business as a whole, to understand how it fits within its marketplace, how it can organise itself to deliver value to its customers, and the ways in which it does this better than its competitors;
- *planning skills* – an ability to consider what the future might offer, how it will impact on the business and what needs to be done to prepare for it now;
- *marketing skills* – an ability to see past the firm's offerings and their features, to be able to see *how* they satisfy the customer's needs and *why* the customer finds them attractive;
- *financial skills* – an ability to manage money; to be able not only to keep track of expenditure and to monitor cash flow, but also to assess investments in terms of their potential and their risks;
- *project management skills* – an ability to organise projects, to set specific objectives, to set schedules and to ensure that the necessary resources are in the right place at the right time;
- *time management skills* – an ability to use time productively, to be able to prioritise important jobs and to get things done to schedule.

Businesses are made by people. A business can only be successful if the people who make it up are properly directed and are committed to make an effort on its behalf. An entrepreneurial venture also needs the support of people from outside the organisation such as customers, suppliers and investors. To be effective, an entrepreneur needs to demonstrate a wide variety of skills in the way he or she deals with other people. Some of the more important skills we might include under this heading are:

- *Leadership skills* – an ability to inspire people to work in a specific way and to undertake the tasks that are necessary for the success of the venture. Leadership is about more than merely directing people; it is also about supporting them and helping them to achieve the goals they have been set.
- *Motivation skills* – an ability to enthuse people and get them to give their full commitment to the tasks in hand. Being able to motivate demands an understanding of what drives people and what they expect from their jobs. It should not be forgotten that, for the entrepreneur, an ability to motivate oneself is as important as an ability to motivate others.
- *Delegation skills* – an ability to allocate tasks to different people. Effective delegation involves more than instructing. It demands a full understanding of the skills that people possess, how they use them and how they might be developed to fulfil future needs.
- *Communication skills* – an ability to use spoken and written language to express ideas and inform others. Good communication is about more than just passing information. It is about using language to influence people's actions.
- *Negotiation skills* – an ability to understand what is wanted from a situation, what is motivating others in that situation and recognise the possibilities of maximising the outcomes for all parties. Being a good negotiator is more about being able to identify win–win scenarios and communicate them, than it is about being able to 'bargain hard'.

All these different people skills are interrelated. Good leadership demands being able to motivate. Effective delegation requires an ability to communicate. The skills needed to deal with people are not innate, they must be learnt. Leadership is as much an acquired skill as is an ability to plan effectively. The ability to motivate and to negotiate can be learnt in the same way as project management techniques.

Entrepreneurial performance results from a combination of *industry knowledge*, *general management skills*, *people skills* and *personal motivation* (Figure 5.1). The successful

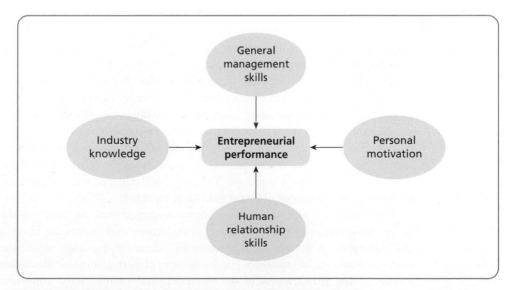

Figure 5.1 Factors influencing entrepreneurial performance

entrepreneur must not only use these skills but learn to use them and learn from using them. Entrepreneurs should constantly audit their abilities in these areas, recognise their strengths and shortcomings, and plan how to develop these skills for the future.

5.4 The supply of entrepreneurs

Key learning outcome

An understanding of the forces which encourage and inhibit entrepreneurship.

If we look at any of the world's economies we will see a certain number of entrepreneurs operating within them. The exact number will depend on how we define entrepreneurship, but their importance to the economy within which they operate will be evident. They will be responsible for providing economic efficiency and bringing new innovations to the market. In mature economies, such as western Europe and North America, they are responsible for most new job creation. In the former communist bloc, the emergence of an entrepreneurial class is a necessary prelude to establishing a market-driven economic order. The question is, what governs the number of entrepreneurs who will emerge at any given time? The answer to this macroeconomic question lies in an understanding of the factors that lead any one individual to pursue an entrepreneurial career.

If we assume that entrepreneurs are born, or that entrepreneurship is the result of inherent personality characteristics, then the supply of entrepreneurs must be fixed. The number will depend on the number of people who are impelled to pursue the entrepreneurial option by virtue of their inherent characteristics, which are likely to be stable over long periods. This might reflect deep-rooted cultural factors but it will be largely independent of external influences. On the other hand, if we assume that entrepreneurs are managers who have freely decided to become entrepreneurs, then the number of entrepreneurs at any one time will be sensitive to a variety of external factors. A simple approach to explaining this uses a model in which there are two pools of labour: a *conventional* labour pool in which people take up paid employment, and an *entrepreneurial* pool in which people are acting as entrepreneurs. Such a model assumes that there is a clear definition of what constitutes entrepreneurship and that it is distinct from 'ordinary' labour. The assumption that there is a clear dividing line between the entrepreneurial and the non-entrepreneurial, is obviously artificial. However, it does serve to make the model simpler. It can be relaxed and more complex models can be developed to reflect a finer-grained reality more closely. These more complex models still work on the same basic premise. Managers are assumed to make a choice between the two options: a 'conventional' career versus an 'entrepreneurial' one (Figure 5.2). The process of moving from the conventional labour pool to the entrepreneurial pool is known as *start-up*. The reverse process of moving from the entrepreneurial pool back to the conventional labour pool is *fall-out*. The choice will depend on the relative attractiveness of the two options as perceived by the individual manager.

Two forces are said to work driving the manager from the conventional labour pool to the entrepreneurial: pull factors and push factors. *Pull factors* are those which encourage managers to become entrepreneurs by virtue of the *attractiveness* of the entrepreneurial option. Pull factors might be thought of as the 'come on in, the water is lovely!' aspects of the attractiveness of the entrepreneurial option. Some important pull factors include:

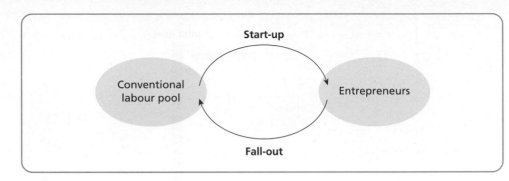

Figure 5.2 The dynamics of entrepreneurial supply

- the financial rewards of entrepreneurship;
- the freedom to work for oneself;
- the sense of achievement to be gained from running one's own venture;
- the freedom to pursue a personal innovation;
- a desire to gain the social standing achieved by entrepreneurs.

Push factors, on the other hand, are those which encourage entrepreneurship by making the conventional option *less attractive*. These might be thought of as the 'get out, the kitchen is too hot!' aspects propelling individuals from conventional employment. Push factors include:

- the limitations of financial rewards from conventional jobs;
- being unemployed in the established economy;
- job insecurity;
- career limitations and setbacks in a conventional job;
- the inability to pursue a personal innovation in a conventional job;
- being a 'misfit' in an established organisation.

The number of entrepreneurs operating at any one time will depend on the strength of the pull and push forces. If the forces are strong, then a large number of entrepreneurs will emerge. However, the supply of entrepreneurs will still be limited if *inhibitors* are operating. Inhibitors are factors which prevent the potential entrepreneur from following an entrepreneurial route, no matter how attractive an option it might appear. Some important inhibitors include:

- an inability to secure start-up capital;
- the high cost of start-up capital;
- the risks presented by the business environment;
- legal restrictions on business activity;
- a lack of training for entrepreneurs;
- a feeling that the role of entrepreneur has a poor image;
- a lack of suitable human resources;
- personal inertia in following through business ideas.

Kouriloff (2000) takes a multi-disciplinary approach to investigating barriers to entrepreneurship, drawing ideas from economics, sociology and psychology, and gives a good

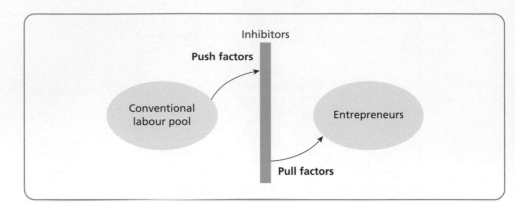

Figure 5.3 Factors in entrepreneurial supply

account of methodologies for exploring the issue. Politicians and economic policy makers increasingly put the elimination of inhibitors to entrepreneurism at the top of their agenda. This is because they recognise the importance of increasing the number of entrepreneurs within the economy to stimulate growth. Figure 5.3 indicates the type of factors operating on managers considering a move to entrepreneurship.

It will be appreciated that life experiences and situations will have an impact on the decision to make the move into entrepreneurship. A study of business start-ups in Western Australia by Mazzarol *et al.* (1999) revealed that gender, employment by government and redundancy had an impact on an individual's desire to start a small business. A host of other factors including age, marital and family status and history of family business were less important. A substantive number of studies have examined factors that support, or hinder, the move to entrepreneurship on a national basis. Nations or regions examined include Australia (Mazzarol *et al.*, 1999; Schaper, 1999), Central Europe (Fitzgerald, 2002), China (Tan, 1996; Zapalska and Edwards, 2001), the Czech Republic (Benacek, 1995), Greece (Maggina, 1992), Korea and the USA (Lee and Oysteryoung, 2001), Hungary and the Ukraine (Danis and Shipilov, 2002), Papua New Guinea (Schaper, 2002), Poland (Zapalska, 1997), Russia (Puffer *et al.*, 2001), southern and east Africa (Trulsson, 2002) and South Africa (Ahwireng-Obeng and Piaray, 1999).

Labour economists and psychologists studying the factors that are influential in encouraging entrepreneurship often use models based on sophisticated econometric and statistical methodologies. A full discussion of these is not possible in this book. The student who has an interest in these approaches is referred to the Mazzarol study above, the Blanchflower and Oswald study discussed in section 5.1 and also a study on business start-up in the UK by Galt and Moenning (1996). Details are given in the 'Suggestions for further reading' at the end of this chapter.

5.5 Influences on the move to entrepreneurship

Whatever the forces acting on the labour market to encourage entrepreneurship, the decision to become an entrepreneur is an individual and personal one. We need to understand the factors involved in driving and shaping that decision in order to understand entrepreneurs. We are all active in an economy because we seek the rewards it brings. However, an economy is part of a wider pattern of social life and, although money is important, we seek more than purely financial rewards from the world in which we live. The decision to pursue an entrepreneurial career reflects a choice about the possibility of achieving satisfaction for a variety of economic and social needs.

We might classify the needs of individuals under three broad headings:

- *Economic needs* – these include the requirement to earn a particular amount of money and the need for that income to be stable and predictable. The amount desired will reflect the need for economic survival, existing commitments such as the home and family, and the pursuit of personal interests.
- *Social needs* – these represent the desire a person has to be a part of, and to fit into, a wider group and their desire to be recognised and respected within that group. The satisfaction of social needs is reflected in the creation and maintenance of friendships and other social relationships.
- *Developmental needs* – these relate to the desire a person has to achieve personal goals and to grow intellectually or spiritually.

A manager seeking to satisfy these needs is faced with a number of possibilities. There may be a choice between two or more conventional career options as well as the possibility of pursuing an entrepreneurial career. The entrepreneurial career itself may present itself in a number of ways. The manager's decision on which path to take will be based on the potential each option has to satisfy the needs they perceive for themselves (Table 5.1). If the entrepreneurial route is seen to offer the best means of satisfying them then this will be chosen. However, making the move between different options will be sensitive to four factors: *knowledge* of entrepreneurial options open, the *possibility* for achieving them, the *risks* they present, and *valence* – the way in which the potential entrepreneur is willing to play off different needs against each other. Figure 5.4 represents a model of the factors involved in making the move to entrepreneurship.

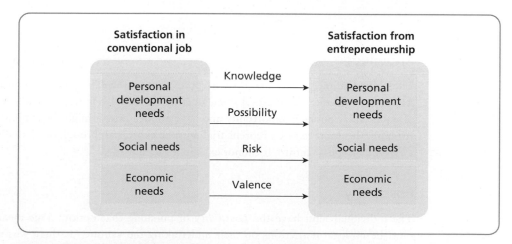

Figure 5.4 A model of the move to entrepreneurship

Table 5.1 The potential of entrepreneurial and conventional careers to satisfy economic, social and personal development needs

	Entrepreneurial career	Conventional career
Economic needs	Can offer the possibility of high financial rewards in the long term	Financial rewards typically lower, but secure and predictable
	However, income may be low in early stages and risks are high	Risks are relatively low
Social needs	Entrepreneur creates organisational change	Established organisation usually provides good stage for making social relationships
	A great deal of freedom to create and control network of social relationships	Manager may have only limited scope to control potential of social relationships formed
	Social status of the entrepreneur usually high	Social status of manager variable
Personal development needs	Entrepreneur in control of own destiny	Good potential to pursue personal development
	Possibility of creating an 'entire new world'	However, the direction of personal development may need to be compromised to overall organisational objectives and values
	Venture may be powerful vehicle for personal development and expression of personal values	Career options limited and subject to internal competition
	However, this is dependent on success of venture	

Knowledge

The individual must *know* that the entrepreneurial option exists and they must be *aware* of its *potential*. In the case of establishing an entrepreneurial venture, the manager must know of a particular business opportunity and have an idea how it might be exploited profitably. After all, the desire to be entrepreneurial must be expressed through the actuality of running a *specific* business venture. It cannot exist in a vacuum.

Possibility

The individual must have the *possibility* of pursuing that option. This means that there must be no legal restrictions on their undertaking the venture (as there was in the former communist bloc, for example). They must also have access to the necessary resources:

start-up funding, human resources and access to the established network. Finally, they must have (or at least feel that they have) the necessary experience and skills in order to make a success of the venture.

Risk

The entrepreneur may have a detailed knowledge of a business opportunity and access to the resources necessary to initiate it. However, the entrepreneur will make the move only if the *risks* are seen as being acceptable. The entrepreneur must be comfortable with the level of risk the venture will entail, and they must be sure that the potential rewards are such that it is worth taking the risk. It is useful to distinguish between the *actual* level of risk in the venture and the level of risk that is *perceived* by the entrepreneur. These may be quite different. Entrepreneurs can often be overconfident and underassess risk. In addition to convincing themselves, entrepreneurs must convince any investors asked to back the venture that the risks are of an acceptable level.

Valence

The conventional career option and the option to start an entrepreneurial venture do not offer separate opportunities to satisfy economic, social and developmental needs, rather they offer a different *mix* of opportunities. The final factor which will influence the option selected is *valence*, that is, the way we are attracted to different options.

Different people are willing to play off different needs against one another in different ways. Whereas many people 'play safe' and give priority to economic needs, by no means everyone does so. Some people prioritise social needs. Thus they may continue to work in an organisation they enjoy, with people they like, even though the option to move to a higher-paid job elsewhere is available to them. The artist starving in a garret or the religious aesthete is pursuing the need for personal development even though it is causing them economic hardship. Similarly, the entrepreneur may be so drawn to the possibilities of personal development offered by the entrepreneurial option, that they will pursue it even though it carries greater economic risks and perhaps, for the foreseeable future, a lower income than a conventional managerial career that is available to them.

An interesting example of valence in action is revealed by Khandwalla in a series of studies of Indian managers and entrepreneurs. Khandwalla (1984, 1985) defines a pioneering-innovative motive which leads individuals to 'make path-breaking achievements through the accomplishment of unique tasks'. This pioneering-innovative drive encourages individuals to pursue an entrepreneurial career even if the financial and personal risks are perceived to be very high.

A decisional model of the motivation to start a business might emphasise the balance of reasoning about the advantages and disadvantages of that move compared to alternatives. Both positive and negative reasons might be articulated for both (Figure 5.5).

The decision requires that a wide range of factors be taken into consideration. Such a decision is termed a *multi-criteria* problem. A lot of experimental work has looked at how individuals compare and integrate the various criteria to arrive at a decision. The findings indicate that decision makers do not usually judge each reason independently to produce a simple, balanced answer. They often weigh different reasons, giving prominence to some and

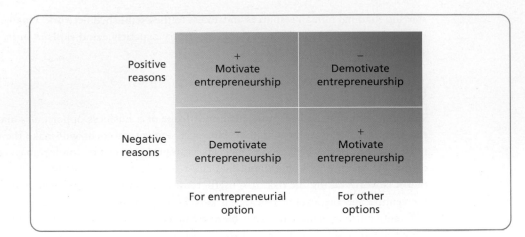

Figure 5.5 The balance of reasons for starting a new venture

downplaying others. Different reasons may interact with each other to change the overall priority given to each. So, while it is true to say that a nascent entrepreneur will initiate a venture if the positives of doing so outweigh the negatives compared with the positives and negatives of the alternatives, how this judgement takes place may be quite complex. Feldman and Bolino (2000) use Schein's model of 'career anchors' to evaluate the motivations entrepreneurs have. Formal utility-based models of the decision to start a venture are developed by Campbell (1992), Katz (1992), Amundson (1995) and Eisenhauer (1995).

5.6 The initiation decision

Key learning outcome

An understanding of the factors that influence the decision to initiate a venture and how these factors might be modelled.

Starting a new business, working independently and facing the risks this presents – *venture initiation* – is clearly a major decision for individuals pursuing the entrepreneurial option. Economists, social psychologists and cognitive psychologists have started to take a great deal of interest in this particular decision and have explored both the motivations for it and the cognitive processes that underpin it.

Herron and Sapienza (1992) emphasise the primacy of the individual in the initiation. They go on to use ideas drawn from behavioural psychology and organisation theory to develop a model of the initiation decision. The primary inputs to the model are the individual's values, personal traits and socio-economic context along with acquired skills, aptitudes and training. In combination, these lead to the individual having certain levels of aspiration that may or may not be met by their current circumstances. If the aspirations are not met, the individual will be dissatisfied and will start to explore alternatives. If the entrepreneurial option is attractive, then the individual will start to search for business opportunities. Once one or more opportunities have been identified, then the individual will evaluate those opportunities and estimate their value, and make a judgement about the opportunity's *equilibrium –*

the balance of rewards (*inducements*) against necessary costs in terms of monetary outlay, opportunities forgone and personal effort (contributions). If this equilibrium is satisfactory, then the venture is initiated. Mazzarol *et al.* (1999) develop a model that looks at the interaction of environmental factors (social networks, capital availability, political support, information availability) with personality factors (personal traits, social background, ethnicity and gender) to model the intentionality that is proximal to the initiation decision. Morrison (2000) suggests that the factors usually suggested as being influential in the initiation decision cannot be regarded separately, but must be considered holistically and the 'construct' of entrepreneurial opportunity should be thought of as a symbiotic relationship between entrepreneurial motivation and culture. Shaver *et al.* (2001) suggest a research approach and methodology for inquiring into an individual's reasons for starting a business. Their approach is based on *attribution theory*, a field of social psychology that examines how individuals attribute events to causes and objects to classes.

5.7 The initiation process

> **Key learning outcome**
>
> An appreciation of the tasks involved in initiating a venture and the question of how consistent different entrepreneurs are in their approach.

Actually initiating a business may be the start of the venture's existence, but it is the end of a particular process as far as the entrepreneur is concerned. The nascent entrepreneur must have first engaged in a number of 'pre-launch preparation' tasks such as gathering and processing information, identifying a new opportunity, imagining (and perhaps designing) an innovation to take advantage of it, evaluation and valuation of the opportunity, initial contact with key supporters, acquisition of start-up capital, and legal and contractual arrangements. Some of these tasks are independent of each other and may be conducted at the same time; some may have to wait until other tasks have been completed.

A number of studies have examined whether the initiation process is relatively consistent or varies across different ventures (Carter *et al.*, 1996). Alsos and Kolvereid (1998) examined how these tasks were organised by novice, serial and portfolio entrepreneurs, and found significant differences. Van Auken (2000) evaluated the relationship between start-up activity and the size of initial investment in ventures. A positive correlation was observed: the higher the investment, the greater the extent of, and detail in, start-up preparations. Pre-launch preparations in relation to the acqusition of investment capital have been studied by Van Auken (2000) and Kellye and Tullous (2002). Galbraith (1982) suggested a four-stage model of the product development phase for high-tech ventures: (1) a proof-in-principle stage in which the technology is demonstrated to have potential; (2) a prototype stage in which a working form of the technology is developed; (3) a model shop stage in which early production runs are undertaken; and finally, (4) the start-up stage where the product is produced in commercial quantities and delivered to the market. Kazanjian and Drazin (1990) extended this model into the post-start-up phase and considered (1) conception and development; (2) commercialisation; (3) early growth; and (4) stability in market phases. Complementing this, Hansen and Bird (1997) distinguished between ventures that develop and sell before taking on employees and those that take on employees, then develop and sell.

Summary of key ideas

- A wide variety of people can become entrepreneurs. Common backgrounds include inventors with new business ideas; managers unfulfilled by working in established organisations; displaced managers; and people excluded from the established economy.

- Whatever their background, successful entrepreneurs are characterised by being hard working and self-starting; setting high personal goals; having resilience and confidence in their abilities; being receptive to new ideas and being assertive in presenting them; being attuned to new opportunities, receptive to change and eager to learn; and being confident with power and demonstrating a commitment to others.

- Effective entrepreneurs use a variety of formal management skills combined with industry knowledge and personal motivation.

- The way entrepreneurs manage their ventures is dependent on the culture in which they operate. Effective entrepreneurs are sensitive to cultural values.

- The supply of entrepreneurs is determined by three sets of factors: *pull factors* which promote entrepreneurship as a positive option; *push factors* which drive people out of the established economy; and *inhibitors* which prevent the entrepreneurial option's being taken up.

- Managers make the move to entrepreneurship after considering the way the option for an entrepreneurial career can satisfy *economic*, *social* and *self-development* needs.

- The initiation decision has come under continued scrutiny and is being explored from economic, social psychological and cognitive psychological perspectives. A number of models have been proposed.

- The pre-initiation phase is one that demands a number of activities on the part of the entrepreneur. Consistencies in the pattern of these activities across different types of entrepreneur are the subject of a growing number of studies. The extent of activity does seem to be correlated with the level of initial investment the venture requires.

Research themes

Cognitive scripts and incubation

Mitchell *et al*. (2000) describe the use of 'cognitive scripts' to establish entrepreneurs' willingness to establish a new venture, their perceptions of their ability to drive those ventures and the availability of critical resources. Identify entrepreneurs (nascent and/or practising) for whom incubation with an organisation or business sector (both formal and informal) has been important and entrepreneurs for whom it has been less important (i.e. entrepreneurs entering a sector in which they have prior managerial experience or not). Following Mitchell *et al.*'s methodology, establish the cognitive scripts for the entrepreneurs prior to start-up or in the early stages of the venture. How important a factor is incubation experience as revealed by the scripts? What are the implications for the development of formal incubation systems?

Entrepreneurs' motivations for starting a new venture

The model developed in this chapter suggests that individuals are motivated to start a venture because of the utility they see in that option compared with alternatives. This utility is determined over the options' different abilities to satisfy economic, social and self-development needs. Even if this balance is favourable to moving to entrepreneurship, then knowledge, possibility, risk and valence can act as inhibitors or encouragements to the move. An empirical test of this model might take the following form. Develop a questionnaire inquiring into what the entrepreneur sees (saw) as the positive and negative factors encouraging or discouraging the entrepreneurial option. Think of these questions as lying in the following grid:

Choice made (or planned)	Reasons for choice of option	
	Positives (encouragements)	Negatives (discouragements)
Entrepreneurial option		
Alternative option(s)		

Encourage the entrepreneur to put in at least five reasons for each option. Have the entrepreneur rank these in order of importance so that valence can be tested. The survey sample might include a range of entrepreneur types, from nascent, through novice to more experienced singular, serial and portfolio entrepreneurs. Code the responses into the ability of the option to satisfy a particular level of need or its role in the knowledge, possibility, risk and valence factors. By way of analysis, compare the coded responses with the model outlined. Does the model provide a good framework for describing entrepreneurial motivation? How does it compare across different sorts of entrepreneur? Are nascent entrepreneurs more naive about what entrepreneurship can offer than practising entrepreneurs? Is Maslow's (1943) prediction that the prioritisation of needs is in the order economic, social and self-development borne out?

Key readings

Two classic statements of entrepreneurial drive and character that fit with many people's intuitive perceptions and make good starting points for discussion are:

McClelland, D.C. (1987) 'Characteristics of successful entrepreneurs', *Journal of Creative Behaviour*, Vol. 21, No. 3, pp. 219–33.

McClelland, D.C. and Burnham, D.H. (1976) 'Power is the great motivator', *Harvard Business Review*, Mar./Apr., pp. 100–10.

Suggestions for further reading

Ahwireng-Obeng, F. and Piaray, D. (1999) 'Institutional obstacles to South African entrepreneurship', *South African Journal of Business Management*, Vol. 30, No. 3, pp. 78–85.

Alsos, G.A. and Kolvereid, L. (1998) 'The business gestation process of novice, serial and parallel business founders', *Entrepreneurship Theory and Practice*, Summer, pp. 101–14.

Amundson, N.E. (1995) 'An interactive model of career decision-making', *Journal of Employment Counselling*, Vol. 32, No. 1, pp. 11–21.

Benacek, V. (1995) 'Small business and private entrepreneurship during transition: the case of the Czech Republic', *Eastern Europen Economics*, Vol. 33, No. 2, pp. 38–73.

Blanchflower, D.G. and Oswald, A.J. (1998) 'What makes an entrepreneur?', *Journal of Labour Economics*, Vol. 16, No. 1, pp. 26–60.

Busenitz, L.W. and Lau, C.M. (1996) 'A cross-cultural cognitive model of new venture creation', *Entrepreneurship Theory and Practice*, Vol. 20, No. 4, pp. 25–39.

Campbell, C.A. (1992) 'A decision theory model for entrepreneurial acts', *Entrepreneurship Theory and Practice*, Fall, pp. 21–7.

Carter, N., Gartner, W.B. and Reynolds, P.D. (1996) 'Exploring start-up event sequences', *Journal of Business Venturing*, Vol. 11, No. 3, pp. 151–66.

Casson, M. (1994) 'Enterprise culture and institutional change in eastern Europe', in Buckley, P.J. and Ghauri, P.N. (eds) *The Economics of Change in East and Central Europe*. London: Academic Press.

Danis, W.M. and Shipilov, A.V. (2002) 'A comparison of entrepreneurship development in two post-communist countries: the cases of Hungary and Ukraine', *Journal of Developmental Entrepreneurship*, Vol. 7, No. 1, pp. 67–94.

Delmar, F. and Davidsson, P. (2000) 'Where do they come from? Prevalence and characteristics of nascent entrepreneurs', *Entrepreneurship and Regional Development*, Vol. 12, No. 1, pp. 1–23.

Diochon, M., Menzies, T. and Gasse, Y. (2005) 'Exploring the relationship between start-up activities and new venture emergence: a longitudinal study of Canadian nascent entrepreneurs', *International Journal of Management and Enterprise Development*, Vol. 2, No. 3/4 , pp. 1–11.

Drucker, P.F. (1985) 'The discipline of innovation', *Harvard Business Review*, May/June, pp. 67–72.

Eisenhauer, J.G. (1995) 'The entrepreneurial decision: economic theory and empirical evidence', *Entrepreneurship Theory and Practice*, Summer, pp. 67–79.

El-Namaki, M.S.S. (1988) 'Encouraging entrepreneurs in developing countries', *Long Range Planning*, Vol. 21, No. 4, pp. 98–106.

Feldman, D.C. and Bolino, M.C. (2000) 'Career patterns of the self-employed: career motivations and career outcomes', *Journal of Small Business Management*, July, pp. 53–67.

Fitzgerald, E.M. (2002) 'Identifying variables of entrepreneurship, privatization and competitive skills in central Europe: a survey design', *CR*, Vol. 12, No. 1, pp. 53–65.

Galbraith, J. (1982) 'The stages of growth', *Journal of Business Strategy*, Vol. 3, No. 1, pp. 70–9.

Gallagher, C. and Miller, P. (1991) 'New fast-growing companies create jobs', *Long Range Planning*, Vol. 24, No. 1, pp. 96–101.

Galt, V. and Moenning, C. (1996) 'An analysis of self-employment using UK census of population data', *International Journal of Entrepreneurial Behaviour and Research*, Vol. 2, No. 3, pp. 82–8.

Gilad, B. and Levine, P. (1986) 'A behavioural model of entrepreneurial supply', *Journal of Small Business Management*, Oct., pp. 45–53.

Green, R., David, J., Dent, M. and Tyshkovsky, A. (1996) 'The Russian entrepreneur: a study of psychological characteristics', *International Journal of Entrepreneurial Behaviour and Research*, Vol. 2, No. 1, pp. 49–58.

Hansen, E.L. and Bird, B.J. (1997) 'The stages model of high-tech venture founding: tried but true?' *Entrepreneurship Theory and Practice*, Vol. 22, No. 2, pp. 111–22.

Herron, L. and Sapienza, H.J. (1992) 'The entrepreneur and the initiation of new venture launch activities', *Entrepreneurship Theory and Practice*, Fall, pp. 49–55.

Jones-Evans, D. (1996) 'Technical entrepreneurship, strategy and experience', *International Small Business Journal*, Vol. 14, No. 3, pp. 15–39.

Katz, J.K. (1992) 'A psychosocial cognitive model of employment status choice', *Entrepreneurship Theory and Practice*, Fall, pp. 29–37.

Kazanjian, R. and Drazin, R. (1990) 'A stage contingent model of design and growth for technology based new ventures', *Journal of Business Venturing*, Vol. 5, pp. 137–50.

Kellye, J. and Tullous, R. (2002) 'Behaviours of pre-venture entrepreneurs and perceptions of their financial needs', *Journal of Small Business Management*, Vol. 40, No. 3, pp. 233–48.

Khandwalla, P.N. (1984) 'Pioneering-innovative (PI) management', *International Studies of Management and Organisation*, Vol. XIV, No. 2/3, pp. 99–132.

Khandwalla, P.N. (1985) 'Pioneering-innovative management: a basis for excellence', *Organization Studies*, Vol. 6, No. 2, pp. 161–83.

Kouriloff, M. (2000) 'Exploring perceptions of *a priori* barriers to entrepreneurship: a multidisciplinary approach', *Entrepreneurship Theory and Practice*, Winter, pp. 59–79.

Kuznetsov, A., McDonald, F. and Kuznetsov, O. (2000) 'Entrepreneurial qualities: a case from Russia', *Journal of Small Business Management*, Vol. 38, No. 1, pp. 219–33.

Lee, S.S. and Oysteryoung, J.S. (2001) 'A comparison of the determinants for business start-ups in the US and Korea', *Journal of Small Business Management*, Vol. 39, No. 2, pp. 195–200.

Maggina, A.G. (1992) 'SMEs in Greece: towards 1992 and beyond', *Journal of Small Business Management*, Vol. 30, No. 3, pp. 87–90.

Maslow, A.H. (1943) 'A theory of human motivation', *Psychological Review*, July, pp. 370–96.

Mazzarol, T., Volery, T., Doss, N. and Thien, V. (1999) 'Factors influencing small business start-ups', *International Journal of Entrepreneurial Behaviour and Research*, Vol. 5, No. 2, pp. 48–63.

Miner, J.B. (1997) 'The expanded horizon for achieving entrepreneurial success', *Organizational Dynamics*, Winter, pp. 54–67.

Mitchell, R.K., Smith, B., Seawright, K.W. and Morse, E.A. (2000) 'Cross-cultural cognitions and the venture creation decision', *Academy of Management Journal*, Vol. 43, No. 5, pp. 974–93.

Morrison, A. (2000) 'Entrepreneurship: what triggers it?', *International Journal of Entrepreneurial Behaviour and Research*, Vol. 6, No. 2, pp. 59–71.

Olson, S.F. and Currie, H.M. (1992) 'Female entrepreneurs: personal value systems and business strategies in a male dominated industry', *Journal of Small Business Management*, Jan., pp. 49–57.

Phizacklea, A. and Ram, M. (1995) 'Ethnic entrepreneurship in comparative perspective', *International Journal of Entrepreneurial Behaviour and Research*, Vol. 1, No. 1, pp. 48–58.

Rotefoss, B. and Kolvereid, L. (2005) 'Aspiring, nascent and fledgling entrepreneurs: an investigation of the business start-up process', *Entrepreneurship and Regional Development*, Vol. 17, No. 2 , pp. 109–27.

Puffer, S.M., McCarthy, D.J. and Peterson, O.C. (2001) 'Navigating the hostile maze: a framework for Russian entrepreneurship', *Academy of Management Executive*, Vol. 15, No. 4, pp. 24–36.

Schaper, M. (1999) 'Australia's aboriginal entrepreneurs: challenges for the future', *Journal of Small Business Management*, Vol. 37, No. 3, pp. 88–93.

Schaper, M. (2002) 'The future prospects for entrepreneurship in Papua New Guinea', *Journal of Small Business Management*, Vol. 40, No. 1, pp. 78–83.

Shaver, K.G., Gartner, W.B., Crosby, E. Bakalarova, K. and Gatewood, E.J. (2001) 'Attributions about entrepreneurship: a framework and process for analysing reasons for starting a business', *Entrepreneurship Theory and Practice*, Winter, pp. 5–32.

Tan, J. (1996) 'Characteristics of regulatory environment and impact on entrepreneurial strategic orientations: an empirical study of Chinese private entrepreneurs', *Entrepreneurship Theory and Practice*, Vol. 21, No. 1, pp. 31–44.

Trulsson, P. (2002) 'Constraints of growth-orientated enterprises in the southern and eastern African region', *Journal of Developmental Entrepreneurship*, Vol. 7, No. 3, pp. 331–9.

Van Auken, H.E. (2000) 'Pre-launch preparations and the acquisition of start-up capital by small firms', *Journal of Developmental Entrepreneurship*, Vol. 5, No. 2, pp. 169–82.

Williams, A. (1985) 'Stress and the entrepreneurial role', *International Small Business Journal*, Vol. 3, No. 4, pp. 11–25.

Witt, P. (2004) 'Entrepreneurial networks and the success of start-ups', *Entrepreneurship and Regional Development*, Vol. 16, No. 5, pp. 391–412.

Zapalska, A. (1997) 'Profiles of Polish entrepreneurship', *Journal of Small Business Management*, April, pp. 111–17.

Zapalska, A.M. and Edwards, W. (2001) 'Chinese entrepreneurship in a cultural and economic perspective', *Journal of Small Business Management*, Vol. 39, No. 3, pp. 286–92.

Selected case material

CASE 5.1

1 February 2006

Why buy-out terms mean you should watch your back

JONATHAN GUTHRIE

You're a big executive. But you're out of shape for a boardroom punch-up. For private equity investors, however, it's a full-time job. They may chuck you off the buy-out without compunction. Just be grateful they don't fling you from a multi-storey car park too, like Michael Caine did to that heavy in *Get Carter*.

I mention this only because John Chisholm, chairman of Qinetiq, the defence research company, stands to make £26m when the business floats. That is not a bad reward for four years' work and a £129,000 investment. But there is an envious ring to current criticism. Stock market investors rejected the mooted float in 2002. Since then, Mr Chisholm has revamped the group with Carlyle, a private equity firm that bought a stake via an auction.

Mr Chisholm's success must make itchy-soled executives more tempted than ever to take the shilling of private equity firms. It falls to me, the Ancient Mariner, to beckon with a wizened finger and recount two cautionary tales of buy-outs where crew members were forced to walk the plank.

Let's talk first to my acquaintance 'Bill'. You may not recognise him pictured as a silhouette and with his voice disguised. But all the legal wrangling has made him shy. He joined a management team that was buying out a manufacturer for £6m, 'assuming I would walk away wealthy'. Instead, he got 'two years of hell and personal debts of £100,000'.

Bill borrowed £35,000 to buy a 10 per cent stake in the company, which he joined as finance director from outside. The private equity backer suggested Bill would make more than a million at exit. It engineered his dismissal four months later when real cash flows fell short of the independent predictions used for the business plan. Bill says: 'I was the scapegoat for forecasts I had not even prepared.' He was entitled to reclaim his investment, or the value of his shares, whichever was lower. When he tried, he says the company wrote off assets previously valued at £700,000, making the shares worthless. When he took the business to court, it went into administration.

Another contact we'll call 'Ted' had a similar experience. He bought out the services company he had run for many years for £8m with colleagues and a private equity firm. He says:

CASE 5.1 CONT.

'Our backers described it as a medium-term investment, but at the celebration lunch they were already talking about a three-year exit.'

Trading was disappointing. The non-executive chairman supplied by the private equity firm asked Ted to step down to a secondary role, and then to leave. Ted had paid £100,000 for a 20 per cent stake. He got back £50,000 for half his shares when he was demoted. But an 'adjustment for poor performance' meant the remaining 10 per cent stake shrank to 2 per cent after he left. 'I walked away after 20 years service with six month's salary and statutory redundancy,' says Ted.

I have not bounced Bill and Ted's complaints off the relevant private equity firms. This is not because I am lazy. No one enjoys doing that self-righteous Roger Cook thing more than I do, except Roger Cook. But I can guess what the private equity people might justifiably say: that the services of Bill and Ted were far from excellent and that they were replaced for the good of the businesses.

Besides, the arguable details of these disputes matter little. More importantly, both cases point to the existence of an army of disgruntled and disappointed former members of buy-out teams. As with failed entrepreneurs, we hear little from them, because they have nothing to celebrate publicly. Andrew Morris, chief executive of the National Exhibition Centre, is a better advertisement for private equity. He made £61m for his family and a 'few bob' for himself through the £245m sale of Earls Court and Olympia in 2004. The Morrises had bought the exhibitions business in 1999 for £183m with private equity backing, installing Mr Morris as chief executive.

Mr Morris says: 'The world of private equity is very exciting and I had a great experience.'

But he warns: 'Pressure is heavy, the pace is stressful and it does not suit everyone. You have to concentrate hard on returns because people have invested heavily in you.'

A private equity man once told me he operated to a rule of thirds: he made acceptable profits if one-third of his deals flew, even if one-third were mediocre and one-third flopped. By that reckoning there would have been more than 1,000 such flops in the UK in the past five years, as there have been over 3,000 buy-outs. And buy-out directors also have to realise investors may defenestrate them to 'refresh the team', even if the company performs acceptably. 'If backers lose confidence, they act decisively,' says Peter Linthwaite of the BVCA, which represents private equity firms.

The balance of risk for executives in these transactions is not at all bad, since they get the opportunity to become millionaires. The downside only looks horrifyingly steep for those whose chance of upside has passed. Would-be buy-out managers should examine the articles of the company critically, says Alan Jones of Averta, an employment law firm. These will set out how directors will be dealt with if they leave. Terms may be poor for a 'bad leaver', typically someone who goes after a disagreement, but better for a 'good leaver'.

However, as Mr Jones points out, under many buy-out contracts you are only likely to depart as a 'good leaver' if men in sombre suits carry you out in a pine box. And that is a fate only marginally preferable to being propelled off the top of a Gateshead car park by Michael Caine.

Source: Jonathan Guthrie, 'Why buy-out terms mean you should watch your back', *Financial Times*, 1 February 2006, p. 14. Copyright © 2006 The Financial Times Limited.

21 December 2005

A venture born of ignorance

ANDREW WARD

When Roger Andresen abandoned a well-paid job with Nortel Networks three years ago to pursue his entrepreneurial ambitions, he could have drawn from his mechanical engineering background to set up a technology company.

Instead, he opted to start a business that would help tackle American ignorance of geography. Mr Andresen's company, A Broader View, produces puzzles and games designed to teach people about countries of the world.

He got the idea after reading a survey in *National Geographic* magazine that showed how little Americans knew about other countries. Among the nationalities surveyed, only Mexicans performed worse.

As a keen traveller who has visited 44 countries ranging from Kenya to Costa Rica, Mr Andresen was horrified by the findings and had an idea about how to change them. 'I remembered learning the states of the US with a wooden puzzle and wondered if anyone had produced something similar for the whole world,' he recalls.

To find the answer, Mr Andresen attended a New York toy fair disguised as a buyer. He went from stall to stall asking suppliers whether they offered a world map puzzle. By the end of the day, he was convinced that no such product existed in the US.

Mr Andresen's next step was to test demand. He spent several days on the streets of Atlanta, his home city, quizzing people about geography and asking two additional questions: 'Would you like to improve your geography skills?' and 'Would you pay $20 for an educational aid to help you do it?' Nearly everyone answered yes to the first question and 83 per cent to the second. The research gave Mr Andresen the confidence to resign from Nortel and borrow $50,000 from his family to develop the product. Colleagues at Nortel were supportive. 'They understood the appeal of the American Dream – to think of a new idea and take it to market,' he says.

Mr Andresen had developed a passion for travel and geography as a student, when his father's job with NorthWest Airlines allowed him to fly anywhere in the world for free. 'I would turn up at the airport with my bags packed not knowing where I was going and get on whichever flight had seats available,' he recalls.

His global travel exposed him to places that few Americans could name let alone locate on a map. 'For most Americans, their idea of travel is to cross the state line,' he says. 'I wanted to do something to open people's eyes to the world beyond America.'

Mr Andresen used some of his start-up capital to buy licences from map companies and design the puzzle. Next came the search for a manufacturer and then the process of customising the production line, which cost $8,000. An initial order was placed for 10,000 puzzles – the minimum required to make a profit. But he soon regretted having been so ambitious.

'My advice to any entrepreneur would be: "Don't do your first product run economically",' he says. 'There are always going to be glitches in the first run, leaving you with stock you are not happy with.'

His mistake had been to dedicate a separate jigsaw piece to every country in the world. 'I started getting e-mails complaining that the puzzle was too complicated,' he recalls. The problem was solved in future editions by grouping together smaller nations. Simpler puzzles limited to a single continent were also introduced. But first he had to sell the flawed products.

'The first two years were difficult and slow,' he says. 'There were times when I almost gave up. It took six months to sell the first 10,000. Now we're selling 10,000 a month.'

Mr Andresen had little experience of marketing before leaving Nortel. 'I used to think: "If you make a good product, people will come",' he says. 'It didn't take long to learn how important marketing was but it took 10 different formulas to get it right.'

First, Mr Andresen had to decide who his customers were. 'I found over time that my market was not children but parents and educators,' he explains. 'A kid is not going to say: "Buy me a geography puzzle". But a mother will buy it for her children.'

Advertising in newspapers and magazines was the most obvious means of reaching potential customers but it was not the most efficient. 'I have not had a single print advertisement give a return on investment,' he says. 'So, we refocused on marketing to retailers. If you get buyers excited about your product, they do the marketing for you.'

Mr Andresen's puzzles are sold in about 900 stores, with a retail price of $14.95. About 80 per cent of sales are made in the US and the rest in Canada, South Africa, Australia and New Zealand. He is looking for distribution channels in Europe but the main goal is gaining access to large US retail chains.

'At the moment, we are mostly in mom and pop stores and small chains,' he says. 'What would put us over the edge would be distribution through a big chain, such as Wal-Mart or Toys R Us,' he says.

Borders is stocking the Global Puzzle on a trial basis and the product is being tested by Wal-Mart in Atlanta. 'Wal-Mart is famous for its ability to make or break a small company,' says Mr Andresen. 'You need to ramp up production to meet its needs. If the product does well you are an instant success. If it fails you are left with massive over-capacity.'

The company's greatest marketing success has been through an international geography quiz on its website. More than 1.5m people from 192 countries have taken part, with the results used to rank countries according to geographical knowledge. The quiz has promoted sales through the website and attracted worldwide media attention.

Last year, A Broader View generated $500,000 of sales, with a 20 per cent profit margin. Revenues were up about 15 per cent in the first 10 months of this year – but more than half of annual sales are made in the two months before Christmas.

'We are doing great now but it is still a constant struggle,' he says. 'We pay ourselves what we need to live and reinvest the rest. Once you start having lots of money in your bank account it is easy to let expenses run out of control. Managing expenses is critical to an emerging company.'

Costs are kept to a minimum by outsourcing almost every part of the business – from manufacturing in China to warehousing and shipping in Wisconsin. The company's headquarters is Mr Andresen's home office in Atlanta and the only full-time employees are his brother, who manages sales, and a webmaster.

Several offers have been made to buy the business. A sale could happen eventually, concedes Mr Andresen, but only under strict conditions. 'Increasing awareness of geogra-phy was the motivation behind A Broader View,' he says. 'That mission must remain at the heart of the business.'

Source: Andrew Ward, 'A venture born of ignorance', *Financial Times*, 21 December 2005, p. 9. Copyright © 2005 The Financial Times Limited.

 ## Discussion point

1. Compare and contrast the issues in taking the entrepreneurial option between a new start-up and a management buyout.

Part 2 The entrepreneur in the macroeconomic environment

CHAPTER 6

The economic function of the entrepreneur

Chapter overview

Entrepreneurs are, first and foremost, economic actors. The tasks they undertake, their social context and who they are as people are of course important. But we are primarily interested in these aspects because of the economic impact of entrepreneurial activity. This chapter is concerned with providing an overview of economic thinking about, and insights into, the entrepreneur and how it has developed.

The first section considers the way in which the entrepreneur is recognised and how the effects they have are accounted for in different schools of economic thinking. It might be argued that the inability of the core neo-classical school of economics to address the issue of entrepreneurship is one of the main drivers for the development of alternative schools of thinking within economics generally.

The second section considers how the economic picture of the entrepreneur is related, in broad terms, to their social and moral role within society.

The final section considers how new developments in the economics of information can inform our understanding of entrepreneurs and their relation with other stakeholders in the venture. In looking at the broader implications of entrepreneurial activity, we are invited into a series of (often quite specialist) debates within a number of social science fields. A single chapter cannot do full justice to the concerns. By necessity, this chapter will raise more issues than it resolves. The aim is not a comprehensive account; it is to introduce the key issues and a flavour of the debates as reference points for the student of entrepreneurship. Further readings are suggested for the student who wishes to explore these issues in proper depth.

6.1 The entrepreneur in economic theory

Economics is (or at least aspires to be) the most 'scientific' of the social sciences. Yet this does not preclude a wide variety of approaches and differing theoretical perspectives within the field. To some extent, these different schools of economic thinking arise because of concerns with, and a relaxation of, one or more of the fundamental assumptions (inevitably challenged as being unrealistic) of the core neo-classical school of economic thinking. Part of their motivation is to account for the very existence of the entrepreneur as a distinct type of economic actor (an issue first raised in section 1.4). The schools considered here are not an exhaustive list. Some commentators may divide them up differently. There is debate about how the different schools might be linked or integrated. However, what follows does provide a broad account of different economic perspectives that concern themselves with entrepreneurship and its effects.

The neo-classical school

Economics has a long heritage. Its origins can be traced back to thinking in the fifth century BCE. This was not just in the Mediterranean with the classical Greek philosophers, but also in China (the social phjilosophy of K'ung Fu-tzu, known in the Latin world as Confucius) and India (the political insights of Kautilya, an advisor to the great Buddhist emperor Ashoka).

Classical economics proper is really a product of the late seventeenth and eighteenth centuries, the industrial revolution and the insights of Enlightenment thinkers. Classical economics introduced concerns still familiar to modern economists: markets, supply and demand, productivity, prices and profits. Economics in its modern form is, however, more recent and can be traced to the mid- to late nineteenth century and what is referred to as the *marginalist revolution*. The marginalists sought to resolve a long-standing problem in classical economics: that the use value (usefulness) and the exchange value (price) of a good were often unrelated. The resolution came in recognising that exchange value was related to *marginal utility* – the additional benefit a buyer gains when adding goods to his or her existing stock of that good, not the absolute usefulness of the good. The dominance of this insight combined with traditional concerns justifies post-marginalist economics being referred to as *neo-classical economics – new* classical economics. The idea of marginal utility immediately suggested the use of mathematical functions to model demand and especially the use of calculus as a mathematical technique. This is sometimes referred to as economics' 'mathematical turn', as an extensive use of mathematics is a feature of much modern economic thinking.

Neo-classical economics does not challenge the assumptions made by classical economics. Indeed, it might be argued that it attempts to develop more sophisticated insights from them. These assumptions have been expressed in various ways. The following summary is intended to represent the fount from which many strands of economic thinking emerge. It should be noted that not all these assumptions are *formally* required as some may be derived from others, but it is useful to be explicit here.

Two assumptions are about the way sell–buy transactions work:

1.1 Supply and demand for goods is a function of their price.

1.2 Markets are costless to set up and run: transactions are 'free' and 'frictionless'.

A further four are about the nature of human beings:

2.1 All individuals in an economy are rational and aim to maximise their personal satisfaction (utility) from the goods they might obtain.

2.2 All individuals are perfectly efficient processors of information.

2.3 All individuals know all there is to know, know what others know and know that others know what they know . . . ad infinitum. This is referred to as *common knowledge*.

2.4 Humans demonstrate marginal utility; that is, an individual's demand for a particular good (and hence the price they are willing to pay to gain an extra unit of that good) will decline as his or her possession of that good increases.

Four are about the nature of industries:

3.1 Within an industry, all goods are *homogeneous*; that is, the goods from one firm within an industry can be swapped for those of another firm within the same industry without the buyer noticing a difference (the goods have exactly the same utility).

3.2 Within an industry there are an infinite number of firms.

3.3 Between industries all goods are *heterogeneous*; that is, no two goods from different industries can be switched in any way, they do entirely different jobs as far as the buyer is concerned.

3.4 It is costless for the buyer to swap between suppliers within the same industry.

Five assumptions are about the nature of the firm:

4.1 Every firm is independent of every other firm (no contact between them when making decisions).

4.2 Every firm makes one, and only one, product.

4.3 Individual firms are 'atomic': they have no internal structure (of interest). This assumption really claims that all transactions are through the market mechanism. All the firm's resources (including labour) are provided through market exchanges.

4.4 A firm entering an industry does not face any costs in excess of those faced by firms already within the industry.

4.5 A firm leaving an industry can sell the assets it has been using without loss.

Taken together, it can be demonstrated that an economy based on these assumptions will, *inter alia*, have open, efficient markets (supply and demand will be equalised), resources will be used in the most efficient way possible and total wealth will be maximised. Individual firms will take a market-determined price for their product and will increase production until marginal revenues equal marginal costs. These assumptions are clearly unrealistic. They do not paint a convincing picture of the world as we know it and many critiques of neo-classical economics are based on pointing this out. The term *Homo œconomicus* (economic man) is sometimes used with a hint of sarcasm to suggest that economists are talking about a species different from *Homo sapiens*. However, the realism of the assumptions is not really at issue. What matters is: do they lead to theories that provide a good description of the way in which the world works? The best answer is: in broad terms, yes. Classical economic theory does lead to a successful generalised picture of human exchange relationships. But there is a lot of detail that cannot be accounted for. There are such things as markets and they do seem to optimise the use of resources (as political experiments in eliminating markets quickly demonstrate). Economies with open and free markets tend to be wealthier and grow faster. However, neo-classical economics cannot explain the existence of entrepreneurs as a distinct class of economic actor. The reason is transparent: entrepreneurs are human beings, and neo-classical theory collects together all human beings under one set of assumptions. So all human beings are the same. It is pointless to talk about *any* distinct set of human beings. We are, if you like, *all* entrepreneurs. It is worthwhile here to reflect back on section 1.3, where we faced difficulties in attempting to distinguish entrepreneurs from other sorts of economic actor such as managers and investors. Yet we intuitively see entrepreneurs as a distinct class, different from 'ordinary' managers and, more importantly, we recognise that they have a distinct role to play in making economies work. One motivation for diversions from neo-classical economics is to try to take account of this.

Austrian School economics

Shortly after the neo-classical school's inception, a group of economists seceded from it. This new school got its name from the fact that many of its leading thinkers, such as Carl Menger (1840–1921), Friedrich von Wieser (1851–1926) and Eugen BohmBawerk (1851–1914) were based in Vienna. Major contributions to the school's thinking include those by von Mises (1949), Hayek (1948) and Kirzner (1979, 1982, 1985, 1997). The central critique of classical thinking was not so much about its assumptions as with the conclusion that economies were in equilibrium and so essentially timeless. A neo-classical economy cannot go anywhere: its equilibrium 'freezes' it into a perfected end-state from which 'it' cannot depart (even if 'it' wanted to, which 'it' would not). Neo-classical economics does not really have any use for the notion of time. In the real world, of course, economies change constantly. Innovations come along. Economies tend to grow in value over time, with many ups and downs along the way. Austrian School economics should be regarded as a broad church of differing economic ideas rather than as a single approach. However, enough commonality (especially in disagreements with the neo-classical school) justifies the different ideas' being united under a single heading.

The key idea in Austrian economics is that competition is an ongoing *process* rather than a *force* that sustains an economy at a static equilibrium. Economies, it suggests, are inevitably out of equilibrium. This equilibrium was a perfected end-point towards which the economy might progress over time, but it never got there, because the equilibrium itself was constantly shifting. Conception of human nature was also different. Rather than the perfected, satisfied, information processor, humans are seen as essentially unsatisfied and limited in their intellectual capacity. We are not content, we can imagine better worlds and we do seek changes to achieve them. In an important respect, Austrian School economics brings the individual (and individual attitudes) back into economics and it emphasises the exchanges individuals make rather than the equilibrating outcomes of large numbers of impersonal exchanges.

If competition is a process driven by individuals then the role of the entrepreneur becomes clear. Economies are out of equilibrium, leaving some individuals unsatisfied. The entrepreneur emerges because of the opportunity to offer goods and services that satisfy these outstanding needs. In doing so, the entrepreneur moves the economy a little closer to equilibrium, increasing its value. It is from this additional value that the entrepreneur gains his or her rewards. Of course, the entrepreneur is not aware of this in a grand sense. Entrepreneurs rarely think at such a level. Rather, they are motivated by the possibility of addressing their own needs through the entrepreneurial option. Another way of thinking about this is that entrepreneurs must seek out and exploit information about new opportunities that is not being used (a neo-classical economy uses all possible information). However, this knowledge is not perfect. There is always an element of uncertainty in what to offer, where and when. Entrepreneurs make decisions at a local level, seeking out proximal opportunities in their immediate environment. No one entrepreneur could be aware of all the opportunities that an economy might present. This is why there is room for a great number of entrepreneurs. Even acting collectively, though, they can never deliver an unattainable equilibrium. So entrepreneurial activity creates, it does not exclude, possibilities for future entrepreneurs. The Italian economist Attilio da Empoli (1904–48) made an important, and largely independent, contribution to this line of thinking with his 1926 work (translated to English, 1931) *The Theory of Economic Equilibrium*. Interestingly, da Empoli's views (as recounted by Wagner, 2001) argue that 'competition' should not be regarded as an adjective (a tag we apply to an organisation denoting its *type*) but as a verb (what the firm *does*).

Heterogeneous demand theory

One of the assumptions in neo-classical economics is that of product homogeneity within industries and product heterogeneity between industries (assumptions 3.1 and 3.3 above). This implies that the products offered by all firms within an industry are perfect replacements for each other and so are effectively identical as far as the buyer is concerned. Products from different industries are totally different and cannot replace each other in any way. Because there are only a finite number of industries, there are a finite number of products. A number of economists have taken issue with these assumptions (Chamberlin, 1933; Robinson, 1933; Smith, 1956; Alderson, 1957, 1965; McCarthy, 1960; Myers, 1996 are of particular note). *Heterogeneous demand theory* points out that firms within a particular industry do not offer homogeneous products at a market dictated price. Rather, they actively *market* products by distinguishing them to appeal to particular groups of buyers, often with the intention of sustaining a price premium over market norms. So the products supplied by a particular industry may vary greatly. Think about automobiles, travel or beauty products, for example. These are clearly not commodities. From the perspective of a particular buyer, different products within these categories are not perfectly substitutable. The driver of a Porsche may not feel like swapping with the owner of a small family car. A six-month cruise has different appeal from a weekend break. A premium branded beauty lotion makes different claims from an own-label product from a discount store. Differentiating products (either by adding features and/or by branding) aims to reduce the product's substitutability with other products – not to the level found between products from different industries, but certainly to the level where buyers will actively choose between them. Ultimately each producer's product is different from that of any competitor: a situation commonly encountered, especially among branded consumer goods. In a sense, each producer seeks a monopoly. This is not as strict a monopoly as found when a single supplier dominates an industry, because buyers can ultimately go somewhere else and new producers can move in. It is just that they decide not to. For this reason, Chamberlin (1933) labelled such a situation *monopolistic competition*. Similar ideas were developed in the German tradition by von Stackelberg (1933) and in the Italian tradition by da Empoli (1931) (see Keppler, 2001). Smith (1956) suggested that differences between products offered within an industry depended on five things specific to the supplier: *knowledge of markets*, *production process*, the firm's wider *resources*, *product research and development capabilities*, and *quality control standards*.

Differential demand theory suggests that the entrepreneur is fundamentally a *marketer*. He or she looks for what particular groups of buyers want from a product, identifies how existing products fail them and innovates new products that will serve them better. The entrepreneur does not just invent. He or she *positions* products within a market to maximise their difference from competing products and to appeal to targeted buyer groups. To sustain this, the entrepreneur must innovate within and manage effectively the five factors Smith points out.

Differential advantage theory

Heterogeneous demand theory offers an explanation as to why firms differentiate their products but it leaves us with a rather static picture. Once all firms have differentiated to their (and their buyers') satisfaction, why should they make any changes? It says nothing about the *process* of competition in a *dynamic* sense. Clark (1940) developed heterogeneous demand theory and initiated a strand of economic thinking known as *differential advantage theory*.

Clark's notion of *generic competition* has three fundamental aspects. First, buyers and seller do not associate randomly; rather they seek to pair up on a more permanent basis with specific firms seeking to serve the needs of specific buyer groups. Second, firms are limited in their ability to increase prices because, ultimately, buyers can go elsewhere if they feel prices are too high. Third – and this is the aspect that adds dynamism – firms are rivals for buyer's purchases and constantly seek to improve products to make them more attractive than those of competitors. The way in which such rivalry takes place depends on several factors, such as the number of firms relative to the number of buyers, how easy it is to make products different and how much it costs a firm to enter and exit a market. The heterogeneous demand thinkers were, in general, suspicious of differentiated products. It was initially seen as just another attempt to create monopolies. It was even suggested, as monopolies reduce total social welfare, product differentiation should be restricted by law. Clark, on the other hand, asked what exactly does a society *want* from competition, given that the abstract notion of welfare maximisation is not attainable? Clark emphasised the importance of people being able to get the products they wanted, firms surviving and innovating new products, economic growth, job creation and freedom for entrepreneurs to start new ventures. If these were being achieved to a society's satisfaction (a political and moral judgement, not just an economic one), then we should be happy with the competition we have.

Clark also made the point that firms are not profit maximisers in the classical sense. They certainly sought profits and would normally seek to increase them if they could. But not so at any cost. Firms might sacrifice short-term profits for a variety of reasons, including the need to reduce uncertainty, reinvestment for growth or to take on wider community responsibility. Alderson (1957, 1965) developed Clark's ideas with a particular emphasis on growth. What concerned managers most, he suggested, was the survival of the firm rather than profit maximisation. Gaining profits was a way to achieve this, but was not an end in itself. Profits were gained so as to preserve the firm's ability to maintain its differences from competitors, to keep buyers coming back and to grow the business.

The differential advantage approach resonates with the way in which entrepreneurs actually manage their businesses. Entrepreneurs do innovate to make their offerings different to competitors. They are interested in building and maintaining a buying community. Survival is often an explicit objective (especially in the early stages of the venture's life). Entrepreneurs are usually longer-term growth rather than immediate-profit orientated.

Industrial organisational economics

Different firms, and different industries, make different levels of profits. This is something neo-classical economics cannot explain. Industrial organisational economics (IOE) is essentially based on the idea that *excess* profits (those above and beyond those necessary to keep a firm in business) arise due to *market imperfections*. Market imperfections occur when classical assumptions fail to occur. Important instances are when there are only a small number of suppliers, giving rise to monopoly, costs associated with entering and exiting a new market, economies of scale, product differentiation and buyers substituting products from one industry with those of another. IOE represents an approach that is important in management thinking. It has been highly influential in the development of business strategy theory.

The school has had three main stages of development. The first stage, initiated largely by Bain (1968) suggested that any firm was in a position where its competitive context presented a different mix of market imperfections. This market *structure* presented opportunities for managers to exploit these imperfections. But they could only do this if they built up the right sort of resources and ran the firm in a particular way, so-called managerial *conduct*. If they did so, then the firm's *performance* would be maximised. This *structure–conduct–performance* relationship is specific to each firm.

The second stage is particularly associated with the work of Porter (1980, 1985). Porter inverted Bain's idea. Rather than firms finding themselves in a structural position and then having to adjust their conduct to improve performance, Porter suggested that managers might actively seek out unexploited structures (market positions) that, given current conduct, or conduct that might be developed, would lead to superior performance. Put metaphorically: Bain suggests that if you are feeling cold, put on a coat; Porter suggests moving to somewhere warmer. Porter has been eloquent and effective in communicating his ideas. His books are among the very few economics texts that have mass-market appeal. Part of the attraction is that he talks in ways managers can readily understand and presents issues that they feel empowered to manage. A central suggestion is the idea of 'five forces' that dictate an industry's abilities to make profits: *industry competition*: the way in which firms compete with each other (especially on price); *entry barriers*: the costs faced by new firms when they enter a market in excess of those already present; *power* relative to suppliers and buyers: the ability to dictate terms to suppliers and the inability of buyers to go elsewhere; and availability of *substitutes*: the possibility of the buyer switching to an alternative product from a different industry. Given these factors, a firm will, ideally, seek out a position where competition is not on price, new entrants are restricted, power can be gained over suppliers and buyers, and few substitutes are available. In effect, the firm seeks out a (competitive) monopoly position. Porter's monopoly concept is much richer and more detailed than that provided by the neo-classical school, which limits it to market share dominance.

The third stage in the development of IOE reflects a change in both perspective and methodology. The change in perspective has been from the (implicit) assumption of the static, 'given' nature of structural market imperfections that surround a firm or sector to a recognition that such imperfections are dynamic and result from interacting decision making by competitors, buyers and suppliers. The shift in methodology has been from studies based on cross-sectional analysis of a number of industries to game-theoretical analysis of *single* industries. This is sometimes referred to as *new* industrial organisational economics to distinguish it from the 'old' organisational industrial economics of Bain and Porter. Ghemawat is a leading thinker in the field and has produced a good account of it (Ghemawat, 1997). Game theory is quite mathematical, but in essence it concerns itself with situations in which managers make decisions knowing that managers in competing firms will make further decisions in response to their decisions, and so on (see section 20.4). New industrial organisational economics is particularly powerful when dealing with competition between small numbers of firms in oligopolistic situations.

The role of the entrepreneur is seen slightly differently at each stage of IOE. In the first stage, the entrepreneur is someone who perceives an opportunity to acquire, mould and manage resources in a way that supports the right conduct given the structural imperfections in the markets in which his or her venture is situated. The second stage suggests that entrepreneurs recognise their conduct possibilities and seek out the opportunities presented by available market imperfections. These are, it might be argued, the ends of a spectrum of possibilities. In practice, entrepreneurs might undertake a mix of these options. New industrial organisational economics does not dissent from this. Rather, it adds the idea of the entrepreneur being not just a decision maker, but also a predictor of competitors' (and others') decisions and a refiner of strategic approach given their likely responses.

Resource-based theory

Thus far, relaxing one or more of the core assumptions of the neo-classical model has allowed a far more realistic picture of economic activity in general and competition in particular to be painted. However, all of the schools considered share a feature in common. They do not concern themselves, overtly at least, with what goes on *inside* the firm. Their main emphasis is with the context in which the firm operates. They do not explicitly challenge the notion of firms' being atomic. *Resource-based theory* (and the *competence-based* and *resource-advantage* theories below) share an emphasis on internal aspects of the firm as determinants of performance.

The central claims of resource-based theory, initiated by the work of Penrose (1959), are that: (a) resources are not inputs to production but collectively provide services that *support* production (resource *bundles*); (b) different firms have different resources available to them (resource *heterogeneity*); and (c) that there is some difficulty in transferring resources between firms (resource *immobility*). Resource heterogeneity suggests that some firms may perform better than competitors if their resources (strictly the services available from those resources) are better able to serve the competed market. Heterogeneity can be maintained only if the better-performing firm retains its resource base *and* competitors cannot imitate it. Imitation may be restricted by a number of mechanisms. A critical resource may be unique (sole access to a critical input, unique managerial talent or exclusive access to a distribution channel). It may be legally bound (a patent or copyright). More subtly, the causal relationship between a complex resource bundle and the resulting performance may not be clear (why, and in what way, does organisational 'culture' enhance performance? Wilcox-King and Zeithaml (2001) explore this issue). Further, resources differ in the ease with which they may be traded. Tangible assets such as production machinery may easily be sold. But organisational learning and a firm's reputation cannot be traded (other than by buying the entire organisation). A competitor may be able to buy *tradable resources* quickly in the marketplace. But *non-tradable resources* can only be built up (accumulated) over time. And time is all that a better-resourced competitor needs in order to gain, and maintain, a winning edge.

Dierickx and Cool (1989) propose that this winning edge can be sustained if non-tradable resources have one or more of five properties. They must be: (a) difficult to build up quickly (a good reputation, for example, cannot be built overnight); (b) easier to add to than to start, so a firm with them can move forward faster than a competitor trying to obtain them (for example, a firm that already has a strong brand name finds it easier to extend that brand to new products than to start a brand from scratch); (c) the resources work better when combined with existing resources (marketing works better for a firm that has good research and development capabilities than one that does not); (d) the resource can be maintained through further investment (for example, training of staff in good distributors to keep them committed); and (e) why the resource works is ambiguous (why, for example, does an 'entrepreneurial attitude' help a firm?).

The examples here will make it clear that the proponents of the resource-based theory take a broad view of what constitutes a resource. Barney (1991), for example, defines resources as:

> All assets, capabilities, organizational processes, firm attributes, information, knowledge, etc. controlled by a firm to conceive of and implement strategies that improve its efficiency and effectiveness.

Managers may recognise all these things as resources and may try to manage them. The problem is that such a broad conceptualisation of resources runs the risk of making resource-based theory self-fulfilling. It predicts that resources lead to performance, but when presented with a firm with unique resources (and all have some unique resources) that is performing well, it is not difficult to retrospectively account for its performance through some description of its resource uniqueness. Comparisons between firms do not help, because each firm is, by assumption, unique. If it falls into this trap, the theory can be no more than rhetoric. This critique aside, resource-based theory does suggest a particular role for the entrepreneur. When faced with an opportunity, he or she must access and acquire relevant resources and then co-ordinate and configure them in a particularly appropriate way so that *collectively* they deliver value in a unique and inimitable manner. And this goes beyond just gaining the right assets and using them efficiently. It includes the management of operational process and 'higher-order processes' such as organisational learning and culture and network relationships (see section 12.5). Alvarez and Barney (2002) provide a general reviews of resource-based theory in entrepreneurship. Bergmann-Lichenstein and Brush (2001) study how resource bundles develop over time in an entrepreneurial business.

Competence-based theory

Competence-based theory shares many features with the resource-based theory but it has a slightly different emphasis and defines a 'competence' more narrowly than resource-based theory does 'resource'. This approach has developed largely within the field of strategic management. It is nascent in early works within the field (e.g. Selznick, 1957; Andrews, 1971) and has been an undercurrent since. The approach places less emphasis on resource inimitability (which it sees as essentially static) and more on the dynamic replenishment of quickly erodible advantages. Put metaphorically, if resource-based theory sees the winners as those who reach mountain peaks before others, competence-based theory sees them keeping ahead in a (never-ending) race that they could fall back in and lose at any time.

Prahalad and Hamel (1990) suggest that competitiveness ultimately comes from producing better (more demanded) products more quickly. Such products should be *unanticipated* by competitors. Once competitors see such products are in demand, they will imitate them. But by the time they do, the succeeding firm will have the next round of unanticipated winners in place. To keep ahead, a firm uses its *core competences*. A core competence is anything that: (a) allows access to a wide variety of markets; (b) offers real and perceivable benefits to buyers; (c) is difficult (expensive) for competitors to imitate; and (d) is extendable to other product/markets in the future.

There is a temptation to define core competences in a broad way and, as with resource-based theory, run the risk of making the theory tautological. But given the characteristics of core competences, a more limited list of proximal capabilities seems relevant. In particular, core competences deliver an ability to source, process and act on information about opportunities in the marketplace (know what buyers want), develop new products quickly and effectively, produce those products profitably, and distribute them cost-effectively to a high number of buyers *better than competitors*. Foss (1997) gives a full account of resource- and competence-based thinking within strategic management). Yu (2001) discusses small-firm performance from a capabilities perspective. Jones and Tilley (2003) provide a thorough account of competences and competitive advantage in small businesses.

In a sense, competence-based theory offers more hope to the entrepreneur than resource-based theory. Given the characteristics of inimitable resource bundles suggested by resource-based theory, it would seem that advantages lie with incumbents rather than with entrepreneurs who try to enter a new market. This is because the bundles are better managed in an incremental way than by trying to invent them quickly. While core competences must be managed incrementally, they may, on the other hand be obtained through a radical and unanticipated innovation. The entrepreneur's responsibility, then, is to recognise what core competences are necessary to exploit a particular opportunity, to innovate in their achievement and to sustain them.

Transaction cost economics

The theories considered so far have prioritised the role of the firm's external environment (heterogeneous demand theory, differential advantage theory, industrial organisation economics) or the firm's internal aspects (resource-based theory, competence-based theory) as determinants of performance. However, none addresses (directly at least) a central issue that neo-classical economics could not explain: why do firms exist at all? The problem is this. A firm is an economic organisation within which market mechanisms are inhibited. A firm *is* a firm (an organisation) because it has some permanence. The resources a firm has are not traded within it (attempts to introduce internal markets within firms (see, for example,

Cowen and Parker, 1997) do so to generate information, not real trading opportunities). The members of the firm agree to long-term contracts (though what constitutes 'long' varies enormously) that will not be buffeted by market forces. After all, a contract of employment has some duration. The members of the firm do not offer their services in a spot market every day. Why should such institutional arrangements exist at all? This is an issue: because markets generate price information they are the best mechanism for allocating resources to where they can best be used (a neo-classical notion, but none of the theories we have considered so far seriously challenges this). Internally, firms lack this information. This is why one of the main tasks of strategic management theory is to develop guides (portfolio methods) that tell managers how resources should be shared among the numerous projects available to the firm in the absence of clear price guidance. So why do firms exist when they should be less effective than the market nexus?

Transaction cost economics addresses this issue directly. Its origins can be traced to Coase (1937), but its full fruition in organisation studies has come largely from the work of Williamson (1996 gives a good summary of his numerous contributions). The fundamental idea of transaction cost economics is that market transactions have a cost associated with them that is additional to the value of the good exchanged. Prosaically, when we pay a price for a good, that price must include the cost of the transaction, not just the final value of the good. Markets are not 'free' and 'frictionless' (assumption 1.2 in the neo-classical model). This additional cost arises from the need to search out suppliers and then negotiate, maintain and enforce contracts with them. Williamson (1994) defines it fully thus:

> [The] ex ante *costs of drafting, negotiating and* safeguarding *an agreement [to transact] and more especially the* ex post *costs of maladaption and adjustment that arise when contract execution is misaligned as a result of gaps, errors, omissions and unanticipated disturbances.*

The key point here is that if a contract is not made, or fully specified, then there could be a cost if the transaction does not result in what the buyer expected (either because of genuine misunderstanding or fraudulent behaviour on the part of the supplier). Such contracts could potentially exist wherever there are technologically separable boundaries between inputs. However, if the cost of establishing and sustaining such contracts become too high, then there is a temptation to forgo the market and bring the production of such components 'in-house', i.e. within an organisational structure, where the transaction is agreed on a long-term basis and can be fully monitored using organisational mechanisms. Price information is lost, but the cost of this (in reduced decision-making capability) is less than the value gained from reducing contract costs. In the transactional cost view, the entrepreneur is responsible for bringing together a set of transactions within an organisation. He or she will look for transactions where the marginal cost of contracting is greater than the marginal cost of using an organisational lock-in to ensure transaction integrity – in short, make-or-buy and sell-or-add-more-value decisions. What would encourage an entrepreneur to bring an activity into the venture? Transactional cost economics predicts that priority would be given to transactions that: (a) would have a high cost if they went wrong; (b) had a high probability of going wrong; and (c) were difficult or costly to police (using market mechanisms). Entrepreneurs who were more acute in judging these factors and managing the organisational changes necessary to absorb the transactions would be more successful.

Evolutionary economics

'Evolution' is a commonly encountered word. It entered the modern consciousness as a result of the work of Charles Darwin in the nineteenth century, through which he suggested a mechanism – *natural selection* – that led to changes in the form of living organisms over millions of years. Living things are adapted to their environments. Their body forms, biochemistry and behaviour are right for the type of life they live. Natural selection explains this in the following way. First, given any population of the same type of organism (a species), individuals within that species will vary (to some degree) in their ability to gain essential resources (food, water, the chance to reproduce). Given this variation, some individuals within the species will be more successful than others. Second, living organisms reproduce themselves. Genetic mechanisms allow the organism to make (potentially many) copies of itself. Given the chance, the number of individuals (the population) would increase exponentially. However, this copying is not perfect. Reproduction generates further variation. Third, the resources the organism needs are limited (or quickly become so as population increases). Given limited resources, the organisms with variations that allow them to gain resources better will tend to survive and reproduce further. Those without those variations will not, and will not live to see copies of themselves in the next generation. Natural selection not only keeps the population in check, but also ensures that each generation will have individuals slightly different (better adapted) than the previous generation.

This digression into evolutionary theory is necessary because it provides the founding metaphor for evolutionary economics. It uses the natural selection model to explain the variety of, survival of and changes within economic populations. As with the Austrian School, evolutionary economics represents a broad church of ideas rather than a single theory. But what they all have in common is a set of assumptions:

- Individual entities within an economy come in particular types, but that there is some variation between individuals within those types.
- The entities reproduce themselves in a sequence of generations.
- Variation between entities leads to different abilities to reproduce into the next generation.
- Selective forces eliminate those (types or forms) that are less well able to reproduce themselves.

Different strands within evolutionary economics differ in what they see as entities, the nature of the variation they exhibit, the way in which the entities 'reproduce' themselves and the source of selective forces. What constitutes an entity? Is it an individual (for example, an entrepreneur), a firm, a network of firms, an industry or a whole economic system? How should variation between individuals be described? In terms of personal capabilities, market position, resource endowments or performance? What do we mean by reproduction? Economic entities clearly do not reproduce in the same way living organisms do. Is it just surviving (i.e. still being present in the next generation or time period? Is it represented by business growth? Is it spawning new products and entering new markets? And what are the selective forces? They must be linked to the (in)ability to gain the resources necessary for survival. But, as seen in the discussion of resource-advantage theory, the meaning of resources is not precise. Does it mean external resources (customers' money, investment capital) or does it mean internal resources (inimitable resources, core competences)? Any combination of these factors could, in principle, lead to a distinct evolutionary theory, although the theories would not necessarily exclude each other.

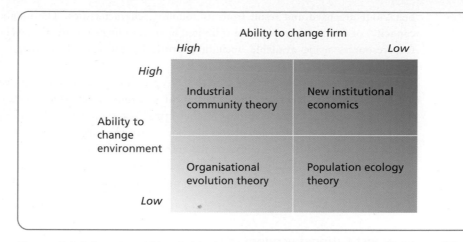

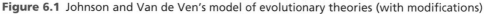

Figure 6.1 Johnson and Van de Ven's model of evolutionary theories (with modifications)

It is at this point that any evolutionary view of entrepreneurship faces a decision: how close to the Darwinian metaphor does it wish to stick? Living organisms can change neither themselves nor their environment. They are passive markers of evolutionary change, not active participants within it. Further, Darwinian evolution suggests no overall design or direction of progress. Evolution is blind and acts at instants. Here the metaphor starts to break down. Can the entities in an economic system (individuals or collections of individuals) not make sense of their world and actively participate in it, or even change it? Do they not change themselves in response to new information? Do they not have goals that suggest progress? After all, in Darwinian evolution individuals do not adapt, *succeeding generations* do. Individuals are fixedly adapted from the moment they are born. This can lead to confusion. An example of this is Nelson and Winter (1982) who infer that adaption is 'all regular and predictable behaviour patterns of firms' (p. 14) and that these should be regarded as the equivalent of 'genes' in evolutionary biology. An animal cannot change its genes, but a firm can be unpredictable and change its behaviour patterns. Johnson and Van de Ven (2002) suggest that 'evolutionary' theories of organisations fall into one of four types depending on the extent to which they allow for (a) individual organisations to change themselves – *organisational inertia* and (b) the extent to which the individuals can change their environment – *environment exogenicity*. This scheme is illustrated in Figure 6.1.

Given that each of these approaches uses (some might suggest misuses) the evolutionary metaphor in quite different ways, it is worth considering them and their implications for understanding entrepreneurship.

Population ecology theory

Ecology is the study of systems of interacting living organisms using the Darwinian paradigm. Because it suggests that economic entities (usually taken as firms) can change neither themselves nor their environment, it represents the closest reading of the Darwinian metaphor. Hence, the word 'ecology' in population ecology theory is (analogously) literal. Firms within a sector are homogeneous and are, at best, able to choose which markets to enter and whether to co-operate with each other. But, in essence, a firm's form, strategy and behaviour are fixed and result from its founding characteristics. The number (and total capacity) of firms within the sector is limited by its *carrying capacity*: the level of (competed for) resources made available, including, critically, the capital customers will provide through purchases.

Clearly, within this model the role of the entrepreneur is quite limited. Aside from imparting some founding character, the entrepreneur can only select which markets to operate within and whether to co-operate with other firms. The success or failure of businesses is a result of there being sufficient, or too limited, a carrying capacity within the sector. This is not something under the control of the entrepreneur. However, the survival, or not, of individual firms is not really the concern of the theory; rather, the theory is concerned with the structure of *populations* of firms within industries. A leading early work in this area is that of Hannan and Freeman (1977).

New institutional economics

New institutional theory, like population ecology theory, maintains that firms are limited in the degree to which they are able to modify their internal constitution, but does suggest that firms can modify their environments. Firms are not supposed to modify their environment in any way they wish, of course. Rather, the theory supposes that firms act individually, or collectively, to modify their *legitimacy*. The origins of new institutional economics can be traced back to the work of Hamilton (1932) and Commons (1924). A modern exponent of the view is Hodgson (1993). Within institutional economics, the term 'institution' has wider meaning than that of 'organisation'. According to Hamilton (1932) an institution is:

> A *way of thought or action of some prevalence and permanence which is embedded in a group or the customs of a people . . . [and which fixes] the confines of and imposes form upon the activities of human beings.*

In these terms, an institution is akin to the anthropological concept of 'culture'. It is a social phenomenon that defines the latitude of what individuals are allowed to do, specifies what they should do and tells them what they cannot do. Although there are several shades of interpretation within this framework, an organisation's resources are regarded as cultural capabilities, not just productive assets. An entrepreneur moving into a new sector (or establishing an entirely new one) will not so much adapt the firm to fit with new opportunities, but seek to build legitimacy with stakeholders such as investors, customers, employees and suppliers and beyond to government and society as a whole. One way of creating legitimacy is for the entrepreneur to present his or herself as an 'outsider' who is challenging (and perhaps being repressed by) an 'old guard' of established businesses that seek to maintain their dominance and hence their ability to exploit their customers, and so is worthy of support. This is certainly a common narrative in press and biographical accounts of entrepreneurs. Ultimately the entrepreneur is not just a creator of firms but also the architect of a new institutional system of beliefs and values.

Organisational evolution theory

Organisational evolutionary theory regards the unit of evolution as the individual firm, rather than the industry of population ecology. The environment is a given, managers cannot change it in any way. But firms can, and do, change themselves. This is consistent with the heterogeneous demand, resource and capability perspectives discussed above. Where it parts company is in the way it views the process of firms' achieving the right resources or capabilities. Those outside the evolutionary framework (discussed above) imply that making an organisation right for the opportunities it exploits is a matter of *design*. The entrepreneur (in particular) constructs the organisation to some sort of strategic blueprint. Organisational evolutionary theories deny the possibility of such a design being available in advance. Rather, entrepreneurs learn to structure their organisations and enhance their strategies in a gradual – *incremental* – way as a result of learning that arises from success and failure feedback. Quinn (1978) gives a good account of this manner of strategy formation. In this view, entrepreneurs are repositories and facilitators of *organisational learning*. An effective entrepreneur is not one who, from the outset, is able to plan a particularly effective organisational end form, but one who is able to make an organisation responsive to new information and reactive towards new opportunities.

Different strands of organisational evolution theory allow for and prioritise the evolution of different aspects of the organisation. The most extensive allow for the entrepreneur to modify the organisation along a large number of dimensions simultaneously, thus making organisational learning a challenging and complex task. Nelson and Winter's *Evolutionary Theory of Economic Change* (1982) is seminal in this area. Organisational evolution theory removes the need for design in organisational structuring just as Darwin's theory of evolution removed the need for an external designer of living organisms, but, unlike conventional evolutionary theory, it makes the individual firm not adapted but *adaptable* in a way that living organisms are not. Because firms can change, selection is between organisations that can learn and those that cannot learn to modify themselves in light of changing environmental (resource-providing) conditions.

Industrial community theory

Industrial community theory is the most general evolutionary theory in that it allows for firms to change both themselves and their environments. This approach gives the richest picture of how entrepreneurs compete, but with some loss of theoretical specificity. Firms are regarded as heterogeneous. Every firm is individual and firms may vary in terms of their industry position and/or their internal capabilities. In this respect, the industrial community view is similar to the organisational evolution view. However, the approach shares the perspective of the new institutional view that firms can actively adapt their environments. They do this by forming mutually supporting coalitions or communities of businesses that have an interest in supporting each other. This network of relationships provides conduits along which pass key resources such as productive labour, financing and information. A clear exposition of this perspective is given by Van de Ven and Garud (1989). Within this view, one of the entrepreneur's key roles is to build and maintain this network of relationships, which is critical to resource provision.

Economic sociology

Thus far, all of the perspectives on the role of the entrepreneur have been drawn largely from the economic tradition within the social sciences. Economic sociology casts its net wider to include traditions within sociological thinking as well. This tradition has a long history. The works of pioneering social theorists such as Max Weber (1864–1920), Emile Durkheim (1858–1917) and Karl Polyani (1886–1964) are frequently cited. More recent contributors include Talcot Parsons (1902–79), N.J. Smelser (b. 1930) and Granovetter (see Granovetter, 1985). Its more radical strands are influenced by the work of Karl Marx (1818–83). One of the key claims within the economic sociology view is that economics (both neo-classical and the views derived from it) cannot account for the realities of organisational life because it takes as its starting point the assumption that human beings are (essentially) self-interested and (to a greater or lesser degree) rational. It ignores the role of socialisation and the influence of social structures on human behaviour. In general terms, these are the mechanisms that govern human behaviour and inculcate cultural and moral norms within a society. Some argue these social forces impede pure competitive behaviour and this must be accounted for. Entrepreneurs sometimes seem to hold off on intense competition if they feel such would break social taboos. Others argue that socialisation may actually increase competitive behaviour as some types of socialisation provide legitimacy for aggressive business actions. The society sets harsher rules for the game. All economic sociologists agree, though, that sociology (with its theoretical approaches and methodology) brings these forces back into perspective. This view places much emphasis on social relationships, group and organisational cultural values and the role of trust. Within this view, the entrepreneur is not just a manager of a business organisation. He or she is one who is both subject to, and in turn creates, cultural norms through business practice. Examples of study of entrepreneurship within this sociological perspective are those by Mumby-Croft and Hackley (1997) and by Zafirovski (1999).

It might be argued that all of the things these different schools of economic thinking say about the entrepreneur are true, but that each discusses a different aspect of the entrepreneur. Further, integrating the perspective of different schools might provide a more complete picture. There have been many attempts in this direction (see, for example, Cockburn *et al.*, 2000; Makadok, 2001). Of particular interest currently is integration of industrial organisational economic and resource-based perspectives. There are, however, three caveats when considering integration. First, many proponents of the different schools would argue that they have no intention of creating a complete picture; rather they are prioritising the *fundamental* aspect of entrepreneurs' activity. Integration subsumes this issue of priority. Second, integrating different perspectives suggests a more complex role for the entrepreneur and this creates methodological problems in testing the predictions of such integrations. Third, different perspectives are often based on different theoretical assumptions. Theoretically sound integration demands the coherence of such assumptions, which may not always be the case.

6.2 Entrepreneurship: wealth, utility and welfare

Entrepreneurs, wealth creation and distribution

The world is getting richer. The western world (western Europe plus North America) is the global economic powerhouse (over 70 per cent of total world economic output). Global prosperity has been added to greatly by the growth (albeit with a recent stall) in Southeast Asia, China and, to a lesser degree, India, and (with some recent economic crises) Latin America.

Key learning outcome

An introduction to some of the broader moral and political issues surrounding entrepreneurship. An appreciation of the economic notions of *wealth maximisation*, *wealth distribution* and *individual utility maximisation*. A recognition of the political and moral stances that are critical of these notions and the distinction between *utility* and *human welfare*. An insight into the debate about whether economic behaviour is determined by our evolutionary heritage or by more immediate social factors, and an introduction to the issue of what determines the morality of an action: *motives* for the act, the act *itself* or the *consequences* of the act.

Some growth has occurred in sub-Saharan Africa, especially Southern Africa, though generally economic growth in Africa is a cause for concern. The question of what drives this increase in global wealth is an issue that engenders not just economic but also political and moral debate. We may attribute this increase in wealth (wholly, or in part) to one or more of three economic institutions: *entrepreneurial activity* (in smaller firms), large, *established corporations* or *government*.

While the contribution to wealth creation of private enterprise seems transparent, the role of government is questionable. Most economists would now agree that while government plays an important part in regulating business (setting out the playing field, as it were), managing macroeconomic stability (keeping the playing field level) and redistributing wealth (sharing the rewards for the game), it is not primarily a *generator* of wealth. Rather, government must be regarded as a cost, properly paid for (via taxation) for the services it delivers. The failure of the communist system in central and eastern Europe (and parts of the emerging world), which prioritised government over enterprise, adds weight to this argument. The role of global corporations (of particular concern to the environmental and anti-globalisation lobbies) is important. Undoubtedly, they have a critical function in maintaining wealth levels and driving investment into the developing world. This said, most economists would agree that entrepreneurs create a significant degree of *new* wealth, not least because entrepreneurs challenge the 'old order' by introducing new and innovative products, by driving competition and by challenging monopolies. The answers to these debates lie in economics.

The trend towards an increasingly formal mathematical language for economics has led some economists to regret its emergence from, and particularly its distinction from, its historical form, *political economics*. Political economics was concerned not only with the resource allocation consequences of economic transactions and the arrangement of economic institutions that maximise wealth (the key concerns of modern economics), but also their political implications, ethical justification and moral necessity. Historically, these domains were not seen as essentially distinct. Modern economics, its critics argue, takes for granted the priority of (and, without challenge, the ethical superiority of) individual wealth maximisation, rather than the distribution of wealth.

Pareto optimality is a good example of this trend in modern economics. *Pareto optimality* is a criterion introduced into many mathematical models. It is achieved when an economy is in a state where total wealth is maximised *and* the wealth of any one individual cannot be increased without reducing the wealth of another individual. Pareto optimality is essentially a mathematical formulation about the properties of an economy in equilibrium, when demand equals supply and all markets clear. This criterion does not foreclose the possibility that one individual is very rich but all others are very poor. Pareto optimality says a lot about the total wealth of an economy but nothing about how such wealth ought to be distributed within that economy. It can be argued that Pareto optimality is simply a description of the final state of an economy (with certain assumptions allowed). It is not a recommendation that that is how a society *should be*. However, it does imply that any attempt to spread that individual's wealth more evenly (say through government intervention via taxation) will actually reduce the overall wealth of the system and it is hard to disentangle this proposition from political and moral judgements. So be it, critics argue. Better a poorer, but more equitable world! We would prefer to be less well off in a just world than slightly richer in an unjust world.

Such choices take us beyond the formal domain of economics into political and ethical debates. An excellent account of these is provided by Little (2002). These are choices about the kind of world we want. Socialism has traditionally argued that equality is an end in itself, an end that should have priority over wealth creation. Libertarians (who believe in the right of individuals to make choices (and so create free markets) unencumbered by governmental intervention) would argue that, while a more equitable world may be preferable to some, its cost in terms of the restriction of individual liberty is a cost too much. Eco-radicals would claim that conventional economic thinking devalues the natural world because it fails (as they see it) to take account of things for which there are no markets and hence no price. Some feminists criticise conventional economics because it does not account for the value of women who work as home-keepers, only for men who sell their labour in a conventional labour market (again, there are no conventional markets within family life).

The philosopher John Rawls (1971) has presented an alternative to the notion of Pareto optimality. He suggests that an economic system is morally optimal if it fulfils three conditions. First, each individual should have a right to the greatest liberty compatible with a like liberty for all others; second, individuals should, ideally, have equal access to opportunities; and third, this liberty itself should be restricted only if it improves the welfare of the worst off to a level not above that of the second worst off. Government intervention may be necessary to see these three things happen. Hausman and McPherson (1996) provide a general discussion of the moral implications of different avenues of economic analysis.

Entrepreneurs and social welfare

An idea that is fundamental to economics is that of *utility*. Utility can be defined (somewhat redundantly) as being the *usefulness* of a resource or situation or the degree of satisfaction it brings. Modern economics regards utility as the thing rational decision makers *maximise*. The revealed preference school of economics thinks of utility as being revealed through the preferences of decision makers. Many philosophers find this circularity unsatisfactory. Utility, they argue, must be defined in its own terms as the difference it makes to the quality of individual and collective lives. They would argue for a primarily moral, as opposed to economic, foundation of utility. Some would prefer that the term utility were left to economics and let moral philosophers talk about *welfare* instead. Welfare is difficult to define and moral philosophers still debate its exact meaning (for the interested student, Sumner (1996) provides an accessible account of this debate). Some argue that welfare is a property of the external objects that humans consume. Others argue that it is internal to the human mind and is the *effect* that consumption has. But most agree it means more than *just* wealth or possessions. Most would agree that issues such as the quality of life, intellectual and political freedom and opportunity are also important. The economist Amartya Sen recently won the Nobel Prize for his work in this area. His superbly written books (such as *Inequality*

Re-examined (1995) and *Development as Freedom* (1999)) make complex ideas in welfare economics understandable and are highly recommended further reading.

The responsibility of entrepreneurs to create *welfare*, rather than just *wealth*, is of course a view that one might take a number of different positions on, depending not least on one's political and ethical perspective and the resulting belief as to what constitutes welfare. Perspectives range from the idea that entrepreneurs' social responsibilities are prior to and should take priority over economic interest, to the suggestion that entrepreneurs are responsible purely for creating commercially successful business organisations and rewarding investors and have only minimal (if any) wider social responsibility, other than their compliance with legal and basic social norms (the issue of social responsibility will be considered further in section 9.5).

The role of business organisations, not least entrepreneurial organisations, as the harbingers of change, as social entities and in relation to their ethical responsibilities to stakeholders other than investors is an area of growing interest. Some economists suggest we must be wary of the idea of compromise over welfare values. Just because we are aware of our own welfare, it does not mean that the collective welfare of a group of individuals is easy to achieve. A number of so-called impossibility theorems suggest that it is not possible to achieve a collective agreement between democratic individuals (all are equal and no one's welfare is given priority over another's) as to what is the best compromise (so-called unanimity) in welfare delivery given that small changes in welfare are unimportant. Put prosaically, democracy cannot deliver a result that pleases everybody. But, as Winston Churchill would have added, democracy is the worst system of government except for all the rest!

The determinacy of entrepreneurial behaviour

The debate over the moral rectitude of different economic systems is leavened by debate over the extent to which human behaviour is determined by evolutionary imperatives. Social scientists are divided over the contrary views that human behaviour is (largely) consequential on cognitive-psychological patterns established early in our evolutionary history or is much more recent and results from immediate social drivers. This debate was raised in the discussion of evolutionary psychology in section 3.2. It is worth noting that the debate is not just one about scientific evidence; it is very much one about the political and moral implications of the beliefs that such views (might?) engender.

While we may regard entrepreneurial behaviour as being something essentially modern (in evolutionary terms) and motivated by the particular opportunities that modern economies present to aspiring individuals, it seems entrepreneurial opportunities may have a deep history. The notion of a 'caveman' (though our ancestors rarely lived in caves) chipping away at a stone tool for his own use, perhaps as part of a small family group, is appealing. However, modern palaeological research suggests that our ancestors were very sophisticated in their social arrangements. Even deep in the Palaeolithic era (the Old Stone Age, roughly half a million years ago, when we should talk about our predecessor species, *Homo erectus*) there is archaeological evidence that tools were not produced by all. Rather, they were the product of specialists who worked at 'factory sites'. Toolmakers presumably exchanged the tools they produced for food gathered by 'specialist' hunters. The numerous innovations in stone tools that feature as we move to the invention of agriculture some ten thousand years ago can then be properly regarded as entrepreneurial innovations, encouraged as tool producers competed with each other. This suggests that not only are our economic arrange-ments a consequence of an evolutionarily endowed psychology, but that our psychology is a product of an evolutionary drive for economically motivated social organisation. Ofek (2001) explores this issue at length.

Moral judgements about entrepreneurs

What does all this mean for modern entrepreneurs, the way in which we regard them and the role we see as proper from them? There is no doubt that task differentiation is economically efficient, that specialism creates wealth. It also seems clear that many aspects of our psychology have evolved to maintain economically valuable relationships (this is a point that we shall return to when we discuss game theory in section 20.4). But we should be cautious in concluding that just because a certain mode of behaviour has an evolutionary imperative we must accept it without question or must regard such behaviour as economically or morally correct. We are not slaves to our behavioural inheritance; our behaviour is flexible and we use it to make our way in the world. Our judgement of the ethical content of what entre-preneurs, specifically, do (and, more generally, what *all* ethical agents do) is not confined to consideration of the actions they take. Our judgement is also based on the *motivation* that agents have when acting and the *consequences* of those acts. Different moral theories are based on differing emphasis on each of these factors. Moral theories that emphasise the motivation of acts are *motivist* theories. We are taking a motivist position if, for example, we judge a business more harshly if it pollutes in an attempt to maximise profits than if it had created exactly the same pollution (and caused exactly the same environmental damage) as a result of an accident that it had tried to avoid. Ethical theories based purely on the act itself are referred to as *deontological* theories. A deontological theory says that some act or other is moral (or otherwise) as a result of the act itself, nothing else. Someone who insists that it is wrong *in any circumstances* to test a new medical product on animals is taking a deonto-logical position. Such a position would insist that no matter what benefits it might bring, testing products on animals is, in itself, inherently and simply wrong. A *consequentialist* position prioritises not the motivation for an act, or even the act itself, but the *consequences* of that act. We may feel it is wrong for a business based in the West to employ (exploit?) 'cheap' labour in a developing country, even if high local wage rates (but low compared with the home country) are paid. If we are swayed by the argument that the employees are better of with the pay on offer than they would be without it, and so the firm is acting ethically, then we are taking a consequentialist position.

All of these positions have problems. Motivist theories are based on the belief that we can actually observe (or at least feel the consequences of) someone else's motivation. (Can we? Why should we judge exactly the same act and consequences to ourselves differently if we suddenly find someone's historical motivation to be different from what we believed to be the case?). Deontological theories are inflexible. We tend to ameliorate our judgement in light of the circumstances in which people act (which we do: given any moral rule we can usually find circumstances in which it will not, or should not, hold). Consequentialism assumes that we can predict all the consequences of an act and attribute back to it the future effects it causes (the cause and effect relationship is not that simple, nor is predicting the future).

This book is not the place in which to pursue these concerns too far. Rather, the aim of this section is to raise awareness of them as an issue and to recognise the difficulty in making simple (or simplistic) ethical judgements about entrepreneurs and about what moral philosophers refer to as *aretaic* issues: what entrepreneurs *must* do, *could* do and *ought* to do. We shall return to the issue of the discretionary responsibilities of entrepreneurs in section 9.5, where our concerns will be more limited, and address the personal motivations of the entrepreneur and the tactical adoption of different ethical values.

6.3 Entrepreneurship and information

> ### Key learning outcome
>
> A recognition of the basic ideas of *information economics*, a qualitative understanding of the concept of *informational asymmetry* and *principle–agent contracts* under conditions of *moral hazard, adverse selection* and *signalling*, and an appreciation of the way these insights contribute to an understanding of entrepreneurship and the entrepreneurial process, particularly entrepreneur–investor relationships.

In section 6.1 the fundamental assumptions of neo-classical economics were discussed. These include the belief that individuals are rational and utility maximising, that individuals are perfectly efficient in processing information and that information is freely available. By 'freely available' it is meant that gaining information has no cost, that all individuals know all that there is to be known and all individuals know what every other individual knows. Formally, economists refer to these four features as information being *frictionless, perfect, symmetric* and *common*. Clearly, these assumptions are unrealistic. Information does have a cost, no individual can possibly know all that there is to be known and different individuals know different things. We rarely know, exactly, what others know. Nascent entrepreneurs all too quickly become aware of the cost of (even basic) market research. If all that was to be known were known, there would be nothing for entrepreneurs to innovate about, and if entrepreneurs knew, and knew only, exactly what their competitors know (and vice versa), there would be no point in the entrepreneur's competing at all.

So what happens if we drop the assumptions that information is frictionless, perfect and symmetric? What happens is perhaps the most important revolution in economics of the twentieth century: a field known as *information economics*. The impact of this discipline on economic thinking and discovery cannot be overstated. The interested student is referred to the review by Stiglitz (2000) for a good, accessible account of how this subject has developed and how it has led to an entirely new series of economic perspectives.

Relaxing assumptions about perfect information allows economics to develop a much more realistic picture of the world. This has had considerable importance for economic considerations of entrepreneurship. Like much of modern economics, information economics is highly mathematical. It was born at a time when economics was well into its mathematical turn. Although its understanding requires only some knowledge of (albeit at times quite advanced) algebra, it is impenetrable to the mathematically uninitiated. This is unfortunate because it offers a great deal to the understanding of entrepreneurship. This section develops a non-mathematical overview of the main ideas in information economics and the entrepreneurial situations in which it might be applied. The more mathematically confident student who wishes to explore the subject in depth might try a standard work in the field. Macho-Stadler and David Perez-Castrillo (2001) is excellent.

Informational economics has a number of connections to another revolutionary twentieth-century development in economics: *game theory*. Some aspects of game theory and its significance to entrepreneurship will be discussed in section 20.4.

Types of informational asymmetry

Information economics takes as its starting point a simple model of the interaction between two economic actors: the *principal*, the individual (or organisation) who wants a project undertaking and contracts an *agent*, an individual (or organisation) who undertakes that project on behalf of the principal; that is, *accepts* the contract. In our context, this represents the investor and the entrepreneur accepting investment to progress the venture. Both of these parties anticipate the way the world will turn out due to events outside either's control in the expectation that both will gain some benefit (utility) from working together. Both face risk or uncertainty. Neither can fully anticipate the events that will occur (their information is not perfect) though they might or might not know the probability with which certain things will happen. This is actually equivalent to saying that not all information is available. We will assume that both are *utility maximising*, that is, both wish to maximise what they gain from the arrangement. After the contract is fulfilled and the events have occurred, both the principal and the agent gain separate outcomes that have a value (or loss) to them. This basic model is depicted in Figure 6.2. This model may appear quite simple compared to real-world economic arrangements, but most real-world situations can be reduced (with some assumptions) to a set of such interactions.

Now we can introduce the idea that information not only is not *perfect* but also is *asymmetric*, that is, the principal and the agent know *different* things – they do not share *common* knowledge of issues relevant to the project. This is particularly significant when the agent knows something the principal does not. There are four basic variations on this theme. In the first, when the agent undertakes some project, the principal is not able to observe what the agent does. The agent can put in a level of effort that only he can observe. (It is traditional in information economics to refer to the principal as 'she' and the agent as 'he'.) In the second, the agent discovers something of relevance to the project that the principal does not know *after* the contract is completed, but before the project (venture) is started. Both of these situations are referred to as *moral hazard*. They may look different but in fact they are variations on a theme. Their mathematical treatment is the same. In the third, the agent knows

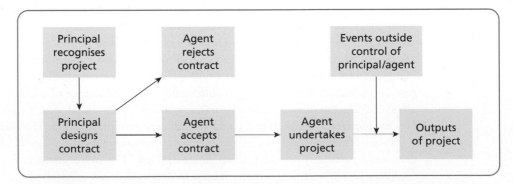

Figure 6.2 The contractual arrangement between the principal and the agent

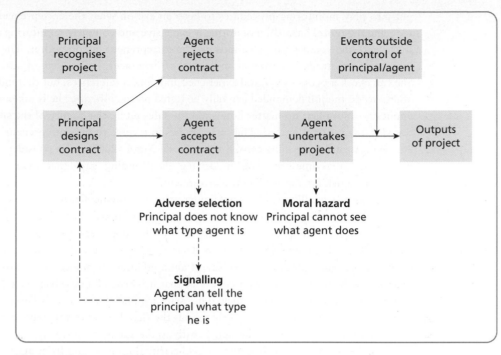

Figure 6.3 Types of informational asymmetry

something that the principal does not know, but this time *before* the contract is agreed. This problem is known as *adverse selection*. In adverse selection, we are usually concerned with the agent (but not the principal) having information on his abilities, or the type of agent he is, that is not shared with the principal. In the fourth, like the third, the agent knows something that the principal does not know but this time decides to inform the principal of what he knows. This is known as *signalling*. Note here that signalling is not the agent simply telling the principal what he knows, as this would just reduce the problem to a classical one of symmetrical information. These four variations are depicted in Figure 6.3.

In each of these situations, the problem is one of how the principal designs an agreement – a *contract* – that will maximise her outcomes given that the contract must be attractive to the agent (given that he can find other projects to dedicate his effort to). Solving this contracting problem under various conditions of informational asymmetry is the central concern of information economics, and its relevance to entrepreneurship will be immediately evident. Remember the original meaning of the word 'entrepreneur': an individual who takes on a contract on behalf of an investor. In practice, an entrepreneur may play the role of either principal or agent depending on the situation. A venture capitalist offering money as an investment in a venture is acting as a principal to the agent entrepreneur. A customer accepting a supply contract from an entrepreneur is in a similar position. An entrepreneur acts as a principal if she contracts the efforts of employees or services from a supplier.

Moral hazard is now recognised as an important feature of venture capitalist–entrepreneur relationships. The venture capitalist must trust the entrepreneur to put in the highest amount of effort on behalf of the venture. Although the venture capitalist may put into play monitoring procedures to keep an eye on what the entrepreneur is doing (so reducing the moral hazard), monitoring is expensive and complete monitoring is impossible. In the end, the venture capitalist must let the entrepreneur get on with it. The entrepreneur who contracts in services from an individual or firm faces the problem of adverse selection. She can check a person's CV and experience and obtain references, but that individual's real ability to do the job demanded can only be tested on the job, after he is taken on. The same applies to a supplier: no matter how good the sales pitch, the quality of the supplier is only tested if a contract is agreed. The same applies in reverse to the entrepreneur as a supplier. An application of this idea can be found in de Meza (2002), who considers the role that informational asymmetry plays in driving the 'funding gap' that many entrepreneurs experience when attempting to raise investment.

The use of signalling is of growing interest in management theory, finance and beyond. Put simply, signalling occurs when an agent tells a principal that he is of a particular type (say, an entrepreneur telling an investor 'I am a good entrepreneur and my business will be successful'). Signalling must go beyond simply stating 'I am of this particular type'. Why should he be believed? Anyone can say, 'I am a going to be a successful entrepreneur'. No matter how heartfelt, there is no guarantee that it is true. To be effective, a signal must be unambiguous (no point if the principal misreads it), and if it is to be believed it must be the case that only an agent of the type that sends the signal 'I am of this type' can send it. One way to ensure this is to make the signal costly to the agent in some way.

A good example of signalling that should clarify this comes not from management theory but from animal behaviour. Alcock (1993), an ethologist (a biologist who studies animal behaviour), noticed something apparently odd about the behaviour of gazelles being hunted by lions on the Serengeti plains of Africa. Lions hunt, kill and eat gazelles that graze in herds. When a lion approaches a herd of gazelles we would expect the gazelles to run away. And indeed they often do. But before they do so, some of the gazelles jump up and down vigorously – behaviour known as 'stotting'. This is odd, because the animal is wasting energy and time that would be better dedicated to making its escape. Why they do this becomes clear only when we appreciate the 'cost–benefit' analysis that both gazelles and lions undertake (unconsciously, of course – it is an evolved behaviour due to natural selection). The lion needs to eat in order to survive, but the more they must chase a gazelle in order to make a kill, the more energy they waste (and so must hunt more to replenish it). The frequency of lion kills is quite low. A lion may have to make several chases before succeeding. The gazelle is also interested in conserving energy. Running away from a lion consumes a lot of energy that must be replaced by more grazing. So the lion will prefer to hunt the weaker and sicker animals in the herd, as they are more easily caught. Hence the healthy gazelle can gain (not be hunted) by signalling to the lion 'Don't hunt me – I'm healthy and fit. Try another member of the herd.' Of course, a gazelle cannot say this directly to a lion, and even if one could, why should the lion believe it? It is in the interest of weak animals to lie. But, by stotting, the gazelle is, in effect, saying 'Look! I am fit and healthy – *and I can prove it* – I am so confident that I can outrun you, I am prepared to waste time and energy now, and still beat you. So pick on someone else.' A weaker animal cannot take this risk. So the lion 'decides' it is better to hunt a gazelle that does not stott – exactly the effect the healthy gazelle wanted. Healthy gazelles are often so confident that their signal has been seen and properly read that they do not bother to run even when the lion charges at the herd. The parallels to entrepreneurship will soon become clear.

Contracts under informational asymmetry

We will assume that the contract offered by the principal is one that is rational to her (she maximises her utility) and is just attractive enough to attract a rational (also utility maximising) agent. That is, it is just valuable enough to attract him from the alternatives he has available. To understand the agent's behaviour we must also assume that his effort presents a cost (a disutility) to him that reduces his reward. So he will maximise his returns based not only on what he might gain, but also in terms of how much effort it will cost him to gain it. This disutility of effort is not a suggestion that people are inherently lazy, rather that even a very hard-working person will try to spread his effort in an attempt to maximise his income – less effort on this project might mean that another (with additional rewards) can be taken on as well. Under conditions of symmetric information it is relatively straightforward for the principal to design such a contract. It is simply a fixed sum, just large enough to attract the agent from taking up any alternative project on offer. As the principal knows what type of agent the agent is, can observe (and so police) the effort he puts in, and know what will result from that effort, this maximises the principal's return given that the project goes ahead. Under conditions of moral hazard, adverse selection and signalling, however, contract design is not nearly so straightforward. We will avoid the mathematics of the contract design, save to say that the optimisation problems they present are technically difficult to solve and further simplifying assumptions are often necessary in order to resolve them.

If moral hazard is present, the contract offered must be one in which the payoff to the agent is dependent on his effort. If it is not, then he will simply put in the lowest amount of effort possible. His effort will make no difference to what he gains as a reward and the less effort he puts in, the less that effort costs. So he must be rewarded for putting in a higher effort. This cannot, of course, be based on the principal *seeing* what he does, because the terms of the moral hazard problem are that she cannot see (monitor) what he does. So they must be based on the outcomes of the project: the value it creates. However, the project's outcomes are not just based on the agent's efforts, they are also based on (unpredictable) events outside the control of the agent or principal (this is a very realistic assumption). Both parties face a *risk*. Making the reward to the agent dependent on the outcome of the project is, then, a way for the principal to offset risk – to 'sell' some of it – to the agent. So, technically, the contract rewards the agent not for his *effort* but for the the *probability* that his effort will produce a good result. This result fits with the observed nature of contracts between investors and entrepreneurs. Contracts through which the investor agrees to put a sufficiently large fixed sum of capital into the venture to allow the entrepreneur to take an amount as personal income whatever the business performance, would be exceptional. Indeed, it would negate the agent as an entrepreneur. He would simply be an employee. Entrepreneurs must accept some of the risk and be rewarded based on performance. Of course, an entrepreneur might put in minimal effort and still be lucky with the success of the venture. But success here is less probable than success achieved with high effort. The entrepreneur must assume that higher effort brings (more likely) rewards.

Adverse selection (where an agent may be one of several types and the principal cannot find out which in advance) presents a different contracting problem. The solution here is for the principal to offer not one but a *menu* of contracts each offering a different reward based on the type of agent at which it is aimed. Of course, only the agent knows what type he is. The trick is for the principal to arrange incentives so that the agent will take the contract that is best for his type. The principal is inclined to offer the 'better' (to her eyes) agent the most rewarding contract and a less attractive contract to an agent who is not of the best type. To prevent all agents (whatever their type) simply taking the best contract, she must introduce incentives for an agent who takes on a contract that fits his type and penalties for an agent that takes on a contract that does not fit his type (something only he knows). The contracts must be *self-selecting*. Such contract types are common in insurance.

For example, an insurance company offering cover does not know the type of customer being sold to: whether the person buying the cover is a 'good' customer (one who will make an effort to protect himself from the risks present), and is less likely to make a claim, or is a 'poor' customer (one who thinks 'I have insurance so I may as well take a few risks'), who is more likely to make a claim. A solution offered by many insurance companies is to offer a reducing rate of insurance charge – a 'no-claims bonus' – for customers who do not make a claim for an increasing period. So at any one time, a customer has a choice between two contracts: making a claim and losing a no-claims bonus, and not making a claim so as to retain it. Such menus of contracts can apply in sophisticated financing deals for entrepreneurial ventures where the risk is offset (in effect, insured against) through a variety of complex financial deals involving mixtures of investment (equity) and loan financing.

Entrepreneurs and venture capitalists find themselves in an exactly parallel situation to that of gazelles and lions when it comes to signalling. (Like all good analogies this should not be pushed too far, though some entrepreneurs may nod sagely at it!) Venture capitalists want to invest in the best entrepreneurs. Entrepreneurs want to tell venture capitalists 'I am the best – invest in me'. So entrepreneurs must signal this to venture capitalists but in a way that they *could only do* if indeed they are the best. The signal must have a cost. There are many ways in which entrepreneurs can send such costly signals. They may offer the investor a higher than market normal return (this is important in market flotations). The entrepreneur may spend a lot of money calling in consultants and market researchers to back up the claims in the business plan. Certo *et al.* (2001) consider how board structure at initial public offerings may signal confidence in future performance. The most usual way, though, is for the entrepreneur to put their own money into the deal. Prasad *et al.* (2000) develop a formal model of the entrepreneur's own contribution as a decision signal. The investor may demand this more as a *signal* than as a substantive contribution. The cost (both in terms of opportunity and risk) to the entrepreneur is then transparent. I once put the question, 'Given a particular total level of investment, what percentage do you expect to be contributed by the entrepreneur personally?', to a venture capitalist. She thought deeply and then replied: 'I don't think about percentages. I want just enough so it *hurts*!' Lee (2001) considers the change of a business name to include 'dotcom' as a signal to investors. She finds that investors reward the firm with an increased stock price, especially if the name change is accompanied with announcements on changes in strategic direction (though this was before the burst of the dotcom bubble; I suspect a similar study might have different findings now).

Summary of key ideas

- The entrepreneur is, first and foremost, an agent of economic activity.

- The neo-classical school of economics has little room or use for the idea of entrepreneurs as a distinct class of economic agent.

- Alternative schools of economic thinking do see entrepreneurs as distinct. Important schools include the:
  - Austrian School
  - heterogeneous demand theory
  - differential advantage theory
  - industrial organisational economics
  - resource-based perspective
  - competence-based perspective
  - transaction cost economics
  - evolutionary theories
  - economic sociology.

- These schools often highlight particular (and sometimes complementary) aspects of entrepreneurial activity.

- Economics makes assumptions about the nature of man and his social responsibilities. Many find these assumptions not only wrong but also offensive if they are taken as recommendations about how people should behave (a libertarian position). Socialist, eco-radical and feminist ideologies are particularly critical of this view.

- Whether (or to what extent) the behaviour of entrepreneurs is 'hard wired' and determined by evolutionary forces or is learnt within a social and cultural setting is controversial.

- Ethical judgements about entrepreneurs are sensitive to whether we are taking a *motivist*, a *deontological* or a *consequentialist* position on moral value.

- Classical economics assumes that all parties to a contract have the same knowledge. This assumption is not sustainable with real entrepreneur–investor (agent–principal) agreements.

- Informational economics has revolutionised thinking about contracts when one party knows something the other does not – *information asymmetry*.

- Information asymmetry leads to one of three situations: *moral hazard*, *adverse selection* and *signalling*.

- Theory suggests that each of these situations is best resolved by different types of contract that share risk between the investor and the entrepreneur. Such contract types are observed in the real world.

Research themes

This chapter has raised a number of issues that cut across a wide range of social science disciplines. Debate on these issues is increasingly technical. However, there are a number of interesting research projects the specialist (or generalist?) in entrepreneurship might tackle.

Entrepreneur's folk-economics

Most economics is theory led. These theories are then tested by empirical observation. The term 'folk-economics' refers not to economists' views of economics, but to 'ordinary' people's (i.e. those with no formal training in economics) beliefs and attitudes. Entrepreneurs are usually such. The project might devise a survey to test entrepreneurs' own beliefs about what their economic functions, effects and responsibilities are. Relevant propositions might be devised by considering the different schools of economic thinking and distilling out some key ideas. These can then be put to practising entrepreneurs (or people who hope to become entrepreneurs) and their agreement with the proposition tested (agree strongly to disagree strongly). A surveying technique such as Delphi analysis would be useful here. By way of analysis, the way agreement corresponds to the different schools of economic thinking could be established. Do entrepreneurs' folk-economic beliefs match strongly with any one school? Do they cut across schools? Do all entrepreneurs think their economic role to be the same?

Entrepreneurs and moral judgements about them

The study of corporate responsibility (and its impact on financial performance) is a fast growing area of research. But it has, traditionally, concerned itself with a largely *deontological* view of moral value: it looks at the *acts* entrepreneurs take (such as expression of belief in social responsibility; the employment of minorities and provision of child-care facilities). This rather ignores the motivist and consequentialist aspects of moral judgement. An interesting project would be to take some descriptions of entrepreneurial ventures that raise moral issues and contain information on the entrepreneur's motives, what they actually did and the consequences of their actions (*Financial Times* articles are a good source; you may want to construct short case studies yourself so you are sure all the issues are covered). Select a small group of people, let them read the article/cases and then lead a brainstorming session on the issues, with subjects indicating their views about the ethical issues in the situation and why they hold those beliefs (be careful not to bias the debate). Afterwards analyse the results, coding statements as making moral judgements on a motivist, deontological or consequentialist basis. Are judgements usually based on a single basis or on more than one? Which, if any, dominates? A good conclusion would be to highlight the implications in terms of what moral criteria future studies of corporate responsibility and performance should include.

Entrepreneur–investor contracts under informational asymmetry

Informational economics is a (mathematically) technical area. The more mathematically confident student may wish to look into this (Macho-Stadler and Perez-Castrillo, 2001, is a good start). However, there are still some useful contributions that depend only on qualitative descriptions of contract types and do not require a high degree of mathematical understanding or analysis. Get some good descriptions of entrepreneur–investor deals (venture capital deals are particularly useful). These may be obtained from *Financial Times* articles and published case studies. Gompers and Lerner (2002) give a good account of some deals; follow their references through. By way of analysis, ascertain the nature of the informational asymmetry between the entrepreneur (agent) and the investor (principal) (for example, are they moral hazard or adverse selection?) and see what sort of contract would be predicted. Does the deal reflect this type of contract? How are risks being shared? How are details such as monitoring and compensation used to resolve the asymmetry? Did the entrepreneur resort to signalling? If so, how did this signal reassure the investor and why was it expensive to the entrepreneur? A solid methodological justification for such case-based studies is offered by Ghemawat (1997).

 ## Key readings

The literature on economic approaches to entrepreneurship is extensive and often quite technical. Two accessible readings that make an interesting contrast (one old, one new; one taking a positioning perspective, the other a resource-based perspective) are:

Alvarez, S.A. and Busenitz, L.W. (2001) 'The entrepreneurship of resource-based theory', *Journal of Management*, Vol. 27, pp. 755–75.

Smith, C.C. (1956) 'Product differentiation and market segmentation as alternative marketing strategies', *Journal of Marketing*, Vol. 21, pp. 3–8.

Suggestions for further reading

Alchian, A.A. (1950) 'Uncertainty, evolution and economics', *Journal of Political Economy*, Vol. 58, pp. 211–21.

Alcock, J. (1993) *Animal Behavior: An Evolutionary Approach*. Sunderland, MA: Sinauer.

Alderson, W. (1957) *Marketing Behaviour and Executive Action*. Homewood, IL: Irwin.

Alderson, W. (1965) *Dynamic Marketing Behaviour*. Homewood, IL: Irwin.

Alvarez, S.A. and Barney, J.B. (2002) 'Resource-based theory and the entrepreneurial firm', in Hitt, M.A., Ireland, R.D., Camp, S.M. and Sexton, D.L. (eds) *Strategic Entrepreneurship: Creating a New Mindset*. Oxford: Blackwell.

Andrews, K.R. (1971) *The Concept of Corporate Strategy*. Homewood, IL: Irwin.

Bain, J.S. (1968) *Industrial Organisation* (2nd edn). New York: Wiley.

Barney, J. (1991) 'Firm resources and sustainable competitive advantage', *Journal of Management*, Vol. 17, No. 1, pp. 99–120.

Ben-Nur, A. and Putterman, L. (1998) *Economics, Values and Organization*. Cambridge: Cambridge University Press.

Bergmann-Lichenstein, B.M. and Brush, C.G. (2001) 'How do "resource bundles" develop and change in new ventures? A dynamic model and longitudinal exploration', *Entrepreneurship Theory and Practice*, Vol. 25, No. 3, pp. 37–58.

Certo, S.T., Daily, C.M. and Dalton, D.R. (2001) 'Signalling firm value through board structure: an investigation of initial public offerings', *Entrepreneurship Theory and Practice*, Winter, pp. 33–50.

Chamberlin, E. (1933) *The Theory of Monopolistic Competition*. Cambridge, MA: Harvard University Press.

Clark, J.M. (1940) 'Towrds a concept of workable compctition', *American Economic Review*, Vol. 30, pp. 241–56.

Coase, R.H. (1937) 'The nature of the firm', *Economica*, Vol. 4, pp. 368–405.

Cockburn, I.M., Henderson, R.M. and Stern, S. (2000) 'Untangling the origins of competitive advantage', *Strategic Management Journal*, Vol. 21, pp. 1123–45.

Commons, J.R. (1924) *Legal Foundations of Capitalism*. New York: Macmillan.

Cooper, A.C. (2002) 'Networks, alliances and entrepreneurship', in Hitt, M.A., Ireland, R.D., Camp, S.M. and Sexton, D.L. (eds) *Strategic Entrepreneurship: Creating a New Mindset*. Oxford: Blackwell.

Cowen, T. and Parker, D. (1997) *Markets in the Firm: A Market-Process Approach to Management*, Institute of Economic Affairs Hobart Paper No. 134.

Da Empoli, A. (1931) *Theory of Economic Equilibrium: A Study in Marginal and Ultramarginal Phenomena*. Chicago: Christiano & Catenacci.

De Meza, D. (2002) 'Overlending', *Economic Journal*, Vol. 112, pp. F17–F31.

Dierickx, I. and Cool, K. (1989) 'Asset stock accumulation and the sustainability of competitive advantage', *Management Service*, Vol. 35, pp. 1504–11.

Foss, N.J. (ed.) (1997) *Resources, Firms and Strategies: A Reader in the Resource-based Perspective*. Oxford: Oxford University Press.

Ferguson, P.R. and Ferguson, G.J. (1998) *Industrial Economics: Issues and Perspectives* (2nd edn). Basingstoke: Palgrave.

Ghemawat, P. (1997) *Games Businesses Play: Cases and Models*. Cambridge, MA: MIT Press.

Granovetter, M. (1985) 'Economic action and social structure: the problem of embeddedness', *American Journal of Sociology*, Vol. 91, No. 3, pp. 481–510.

Gompers, P. and Lerner, J. (2002) *The Venture Capital Cycle*. Cambridge, MA: MIT Press.

Hamilton, W.H. (1932) 'Institution', in Seligman, E.R.A. and Johnson, A. (eds) *Encyclopaedia of the Social Sciences*, Vol. 8. Guildford, CT: Dushkin.

Hannan, M.T. and Freeman, J. (1977) 'The population ecology of organisations', *American Journal of Sociology*, Vol. 82, No. 5, pp. 929–64.

Hausman, D.M. and McPherson, M.S. (1996) *Economic Analysis and Moral Philosophy*. Cambridge: Cambridge University Press.

Hayek, F.A. (1948) *Individualism and Economic Order*. Chicago: University of Chicago Press.

Hodgson, G.M. (1993) *Economics and Evolution*. Ann Arbor, MI: University of Michigan Press.

Hunt, S.D. (2000) *A General Theory of Competition*. Thousand Oaks, CA: Sage.

Johnson, S. and Van de Ven, A.H. (2002) 'A framework for entrepreneurial strategy', in Hitt, M.A., Ireland, R.D., Camp, S.M. and Sexton, D.L. (eds) *Strategic Entrepreneurship: Creating a New Mindset*. Oxford: Blackwell.

Jones, O. and Tilley, F. (2003) *Competitive Advantage in SMEs*. London: Wiley.

Keppler, J.H. (2001) 'Attilio da Empoli's contribution to monopolistic competition theory', *Journal of Economic Studies*, Vol. 28, No. 4/5, pp. 305–23.

Kirzner, I.M. (1973) *Competition and Entrepreneurship*. Chicago: University of Chicago Press.

Kirzner, I.M. (1979) *Perception, Opportunity, and Profit: Studies in the Theory of Entrepreneurship*. Chicago: University of Chicago Press.

Kirzner, I.M. (1982) 'Uncertainty, discovery and human action', in Kirzner, I.M. (ed.) *Method, Process and Austrian Economics: Essays in Honor of Ludwig von Mises*. Lexington, MA: Lexington Books.

Kirzner, I.M. (1985) *Discovery and the Capitalist Process*. Chicago: University of Chicago Press.

Kirzner, I.M. (1997) *How Markets Work: Disequilibrium, Entrepreneurship and Discovery*, Institute of Economic Affairs Hobart Paper No. 133.

Lee, P.M. (2001) 'What's in a name? The effects of '.com' name changes on stock prices and trading activity', *Strategic Management Journal*, Vol. 22, pp. 793–804.

Little, I.M. (2002) *Ethics, Economics and Politics*. Oxford: Oxford University Press.

Lydall, H. (1998) *A Critique of Orthodox Economics: An Alternative Model*. London: Macmillan.

Macho-Stadler, I. and Perez-Castrillo, J.D. (2001) *An Introduction to the Economics of Information: Incentives and Contracts* (2nd edn). Oxford: Oxford University Press.

Makadok, R. (2001) 'Towards a synthesis of the resource-based and dynamic capability views of rent creation', *Strategic Management Journal*, Vol. 22, pp. 387–401.

McCarthy, E.J. (1960) *Basic Marketing: A Managerial Approach*. Homewood, IL: Irwin.

McDaniel, B.A. (2005) 'A contemporary view of Joseph A. Schumpeter's theory of the entrepreneur', *Journal of Economic Issues*, Vol. 39, No. 2, pp. 485–489.

Minniti, M. and Bygrave, W. (1999) 'The microfoundations of entrepreneurship', *Entrepreneurship Theory and Practice*, Vol. 23, No. 4, pp. 41–52.

Mumby-Croft, R. and Hackley, C.E. (1997) 'The social construction of market entrepreneurship: a case analysis in the UK fishing industry', *Marketing Education Review*, Vol. 7, No. 3, pp. 87–94.

Myers, J.H. (1996) *Segmentation and Positioning Strategies for Marketing Decisions*. Chicago: American Marketing Association.

Nelson, R.R. and Winter, S.G. (1982) *An Evolutionary Theory of Economic Change*. Cambridge, MA: Belknap Press.

Ofek, H. (2001) *Second Nature: Economic Origins of Human Evolution*, Cambridge: Cambridge University Press.

Penrose, E.T. (1959) *The Theory of the Growth of the Firm*. London: Basil Blackburn & Mott.

Porter, M.E. (1980) *Competitive Advantage*. New York: Free Press.

Porter, M.E. (1985) *Competitive Strategy*. New York: Free Press.

Powell, T.C. (2001) 'Competitive advantage: logical and philosophical considerations', *Strategic Management Journal*, Vol. 22, pp. 875–88.

Prahalad, C.K. and Hamel, G. (1990) 'The core competencies of the corporation', *Harvard Business Review*, May/June, pp. 79–91.

Prasad, D., Bruton, G.D. and Vozikis, G. (2000) 'Signalling value to business angels: the proportion of the entrepreneur's net wealth invested in a new venture as a decision signal', *Venture Capital*, Vol. 2, No. 3, pp. 167–82.

Quinn, J.B. (1978) 'Strategic change: Logical Incrementalism', *Sloan Management Review*, Fall, pp. 1–21.

Rawls, J. (1971) *A Theory of Justice*. Cambridge, MA: Belknap Press.

Robinson, J. (1933) *The Economics of Imperfect Competition*. London: Macmillan.

Rosen, S. (1997) 'Austrian and neo-classical economics: any gains from trade?', *Journal of Economic Perspectives*, Vol. 11, No. 4, pp. 139–52.

Sandler, T. (2001) *Economic Concepts for the Social Sciences*. Cambridge: Cambridge University Press.

Selznick, P. (1957) *Leadership in Administration*. New York: Harper & Row.

Sen, A. (1995) *Inequality Re-examined*. Oxford: Clarendon Press.

Sen, A. (1999) *Development as Freedom*. Oxford: Oxford University Press.

Smith, C.C. (1956) 'Product differentiation and market segmentation as alternative marketing strategies', *Journal of Marketing*, Vol. 21, pp. 3–8.

Stiglitz, J.E. (2000) 'The contribution of the economics of information to twentieth century economics', *Quarterly Journal of Economics*, November, pp. 1441–78.

Sumner, L.W. (1996) *Welfare, Happiness and Ethics*. Oxford: Oxford University Press.

Van de Ven, A.H. and Garud, R. (1989) 'A framework for understanding the emergence of new industries', *Research on Technological Innovation, Management and Policy*, Vol. 4, pp. 195–225.

Von Mises, L. (1949) *Human Action: A Treatise on Economics*. New Haven, CT: Yale University Press.

von Stackelberg, H. (1933) *Marktform und Gleichgewicht*. Vienna: Springer.

Wagner, R.E. (2001) 'Competition as a rivalrous process: Attilio da Empoli and the years of high theory that might have been', *Journal of Economic Studies*, Vol. 28, No. 4/5, pp. 337–45.

Wilcox-King, A. and Zeithaml, C.P. (2001) 'Competencies and firm performance: examining the causal ambiguity paradox', *Strategic Management Journal*, Vol. 22, pp. 75–99.

Williamson, O.E. (1994) 'Transaction cost economics and organization theory', in Smelser, N.J. and Swedberg, R. (eds) *The Handbook of Economic Sociology*. Princeton, NJ: Princeton University Press, pp. 77–107.

Williamson, O.E. (1996) *The Mechanisms of Governance*. Oxford: Oxford University Press.

Yu, A.F. (2001) 'Towards a capabilities perspective of the small firm', *International Journal of Management Reviews*, Vol. 3, No. 3, pp. 185–97.

Zafirovski, M. (1999) 'Probing into the social layers of entrepreneurship: outlines of the sociology of enterprise', *Entrepreneurship and Regional Development*, Vol. 11, No. 4, pp. 351–71.

Selected case material

CASE 6.1

21 December 2005 **FT**

An alternative energy supply swimming against the tide

KEVIN ALLISON

This winter, a team of engineers at Verdant Power, a small clean energy start-up, will spend hours huddled in a used shipping container on a small sliver of land between Manhattan and Queens, counting fish as they swim by in New York's East River.

Such is the lot of a small but dedicated band of entrepreneurs who are trying to sell the world – and Wall Street – on the benefits of tidal power.

'We are going to spend in excess of $1m just watching the fish,' says Ronald Smith, Verdant's chief executive. The study, run by Verdant with help from the state of New York and several research and development groups, is designed to assuage the concerns of some environmentalists, who fear the company's experimental underwater turbines could harm local fish populations.

Verdant says it has gone to great lengths to make sure its turbines are fish-friendly.

If all goes according to plan, Verdant could install up to 200 turbines in the tidal estuary that separates Manhattan and Queens over the next 12 to 18 months, in the biggest-ever field test of tidal turbine technologies in the US. There, acting like submerged windmills, the turbines will harness the natural ebb and flow of tidal currents to provide power to a local supermarket and a nearby parking garage.

Verdant is looking for $15m to help fund commercial-scale production of its turbines. But industry experts say it faces an uphill struggle.

Thanks to sky-high energy prices and growing concerns about global warming, clean energy has had something of a coming-out party this year. New Energy Finance, a clean energy consultancy, estimates that worldwide investment in clean energy will total about $42bn for 2005.

CASE 6.1 CONT.

But while demand for green technologies, from hybrid cars to wind turbines, is soaring, investment in tidal power has lagged behind.

'The technology is not yet proven but the nature of the sector is such that it requires debt financing,' says Michael Liebreich, chief executive at New Energy Finance. The problem is that debt financiers are put off by the risks of investing in untested technologies.

'There is a financing "valley of death" between the moment when you think you have a promising technology and the moment when it is sufficiently proven to be project financed,' says Mr Liebreich.

'That sort of valley of death can generally only be bridged by some sort of long-term visionary capital, either with governmental support or on the balance sheet of a very substantial and long-term-oriented corporation.'

But visionaries seem to be in short supply after the US left tidal power off the list of technologies eligible for the renewable energy production tax credit, a subsidy widely credited with sparking recent interest in wind farms and solar power.

New Energy Finance estimates that the tax credit, along with various state incentives, together account for up to 65 per cent of the cost of a typical wind power project, with the tax credit alone accounting for more than half. Without such support, tidal power projects have struggled to gain traction.

In the UK, government support has brought Marine Current Turbines, a rival tidal power group, to the verge of completing a field test of its turbines off the coast of Devon in England's southwest, but the technology has yet to be commercialised. In the long run, the success of companies such as Verdant will hinge on whether they attract the investment needed to lower the cost of tidal systems to the point where they become economically competitive with wind and solar power projects. But that will be difficult without a higher public profile and greater political support.

Roger Bedard at the Electric Power Research Institute, an energy industry research and development group that is working with Verdant on the East River projects, says political uncertainty has clouded the outlook for renewable energy in the US.

'In Europe, the incentives are spelled out but no one will invest in the US because the future is so uncertain,' he says.

Mr Bedard says a recent EPRI study showed that if tidal turbines could be produced on a commercial scale, tidal power systems could be more efficient than on-shore wind power in certain areas.

One reason is predictability. Whereas wind patterns change from day to day or hour to hour, tidal flows are directly related to the position of the sun and the moon and can be calculated years in advance.

Still, large numbers of tidal turbines would be required to produce the same amount of power as an average wind turbine. 'They need to have a whole farm of these things,' says Bruno Mejean, senior vice-president of structured finance at Nord LB, the German bank. 'The economies of scale aren't there yet.'

'It's the last of the big energy sources we haven't looked at,' Mr Bedard says, 'and I think it's time.'

Source: Kevin Allison, 'An alternative energy supply swimming against the tide', *Financial Times*, 21 December 2005, p. 9. Copyright © 2005 The Financial Times Limited.

CASE 6.2

4 February 2006 **FT**

Breaking the mould in Notting Hill and beyond

LAURA COHN

In the heart of London's Notting Hill, behind a modest grey gate and a traditional mews house, hides a building that is part minimalist marvel, part family home.

A collaboration between UK property entrepreneur Johnny Sandelson and London-based architect Seth Stein, it is an unusual L-shaped building, dominated by a long glass wall, framed in fresh white paint. Its courtyard provides the contrast with two tables – a big one for adults, and a small one for children – surrounded by a smattering of brightly coloured toys. 'A good house is one you enjoy living in and looks beautiful,' says father-of-three Sandelson.

From the street, it's hard to imagine something so modern existing in an area best known for rows of terraced Victorians. After passing through the nondescript gate and walking down a cobblestone footpath, visitors first come upon the original brown stone mews house, which is now home to an office and wine cellar. Aside from Sandelson's 1972 white Alpha Romeo in the drive, the scene is decidedly historic.

From there, though, things get much more new world. To the left of the mews house, is that long expanse of glass, with massive glass doors revealing an open kitchen and a living room at the short part of the 'L'. Well-groomed plants dot the wooden deck and part of the roof.

Sandelson, who was born in Holland Park and studied history at the University of Buckingham, has long had a passion for modern architecture. His wife Mary, a writer, claims that she knew from the moment she met him that some day he would have to build his own home.

Property has also been a lucrative profession. Sandelson started his own development business by borrowing against a flat he inherited in Chelsea and using the £100,000 to buy a place in central London. Since then, he's invested in more than 1,000 residential and commercial schemes, mostly in his hometown, and launched GuestInvest, a hotel with buy-to-let rooms. 'You should back what you know,' he explains, echoing the well-known philosophy of investment guru Warren Buffett.

He picked the site of his own home, which used to host four or five mews houses that once served as stables, for the same reason. 'It's a neighbourhood I've always felt comfortable with,' he explains.

But, working with Stein, Sandelson was determined to do something unexpected – modern but also fun – with the space. Walking along the length of the courtyard, he points to an example: a discreet square of dark wooden panels hides a small swimming pool. He installed it for the kids, but admits to using it himself once in a while.

Another example: the shape of the building, along with its floor-to-ceiling glass doors and windows, means that inhabitants can see what's happening elsewhere on the ground floor at all times. As if to emphasise the point, Sandelson sits down on his living room couch and waves through the glass to his 2-year-old son, Sacha, in the kitchen. The toddler, sporting messy blonde curls and tiny Ugg boots, comes bounding in to join the tour.

▶

CASE 6.2 CONT.

In a way, the living room is a microcosm of the entire residence. At first glance, it seems entirely minimalist. A high ceiling crowns the space. Three leather couches – two deep chocolate brown and one white – form a horseshoe around a brown shag carpet. A spartan gas fireplace interrupts a blank white wall. On an adjoining wall, four large square paintings are solid blocks of blue, yellow, red and orange. But on the next wall, behind the centre couch, a large white built-in shelf is full of family photos and books on Picasso, Persian art and 20th century architecture. Further breaking up the formality, Sandelson's 7-year-old daughter, Florence, cruises in on roller skates to offer up chocolate cookies.

The first floor is accessed from the living room, up stairs constructed from American walnut beneath a wall that's been painted red. These lead to a narrow 120 ft corridor that branches off into several of the home's six bedrooms. The master bedroom covers 800 sq ft and includes a bathroom with a skylight over a long limestone countertop with his-and-hers sinks. (Sandelson notes that the counter is higher than usual to accommodate his 6 ft 3 in frame.) Even the shower continues the house's theme of transparency, incorporating a small window overlooking the foliage outside. 'It's nice in London to be able to see green,' says Sandelson, who also has a Stein-designed weekend home in Cornwall.

After passing through his daughter's room, which is filled with delightfully anti-minimalist Barbie pink furniture, he moves to the second floor. This level includes his wife's office and another bedroom for his nine-year-old son Jacob.

The aim, Sandelson explains, was to create a light-filled, airy home that also incorporates distinct spaces for each member of his clan; a place for adults and children; work and play. He commissioned Stein, with whom he'd worked on a number of projects, because he was a 'family architect' as well as a modernist, and the house was completed in 2000.

Sandelson, whose Blackberry is virtually glued to his hand, says he tries to bring the same spirit of innovation to his business, both in his residential developments and in GuestInvest, a scheme in which companies and individuals 'buy' a hotel room to use for up to 52 nights a year and rent out for the rest, taking 50 per cent of the income. The second hotel in the chain, Nest, will be located near Paddington station and is scheduled to open in 2007. He expects to bring the concept to foreign cities, including Madrid and Mumbai, next.

It all sounds fairly glamourous for a man who started his professional career at commercial surveyor Nelson Bakewell, measuring warehouses full of baked beans and making photocopies. But, as his own home shows, Sandelson's come a long way since then.

Source: Laura Cohn, 'Breaking the mould in Notting Hill and beyond', *Financial Times*, 4 February 2006, p. 13. Copyright © 2006 Laura Cohn.

Discussion point

1. Compare and contrast the economic function of an 'innovating' entrepreneur with that of a 'trading' entrepreneur. Is it possible to make such a clear-cut distinction in the modern business world?

CHAPTER 7

Entrepreneurship and economic development

Chapter overview

Economic development, its achievement and its consequences, is one of the most important issues facing the world today. This chapter considers the role of the entrepreneur, entrepreneurship and the entrepreneurial process in delivering economic development. This chapter also consider the role of specific cultural factors on entrepreneurial inclination and performance.

7.1 Entrepreneurship, economic performance and economic growth

Since the early eighteenth century and the start of the industrial revolution an inevitable trend (albeit with some ups and downs along the way) has been for the world to get richer. Development and production technology and social organisation have advanced to enhance productivity. We are all much wealthier than our grandparents, and they more than their grandparents. Generally speaking, economic growth is regarded as a good thing. It brings wealth, improved health, better education, longevity, lower rates of child mortality, and, perhaps indirectly, more democracy, greater sexual equality and enriched prospects for personal development.

The branch of economics that addresses how and why this happens is called *developmental economics*. Developmental economics has three, intertwined, branches: a theoretical branch that considers why productivity grows and how this leads to wealth creation; an empirical branch, which calls upon econometric techniques to develop an insight into how input factors (such as technology, the number of entrepreneurs, access to resources, and so on) are connected (correlated) with economic growth; and a policy branch that sets out to advise local, government and supranational-agencies (such as the World Bank and International Monetary Fund) on the best policies to adopt if economic growth is to be achieved. Developmental economics is concerned with economic systems at many levels of analysis: it might concern a neighbourhood, a city, a region, a nation state, a collective of nation states or the entire global economic system. It may also focus on the development of a specific cultural or religious group, aim to address differential development within a particular region – say rural versus urban – or target the development of a specific industrial sector – manufacturing or retailing, for example.

For a long period, developmental economics was somewhat neglected, but there has been a resurgence of interest recently. This is for a number of reasons. First, the collapse of the centrally planned economies of the former Soviet Union (and along with them, some economies in the developing world) has presented a challenge to policy makers on how those countries can best enter the global economy. Second, the failure of much of sub-Saharan Africa to join in the general trend of economic growth – Africa 'left behind' – has led to another policy challenge, for both national governments in the West and supra-national agencies. Third, the general desirability of economic growth has been challenged because of its supposed cost in terms of environmental degradation, 'increasing' inequality and the ravages of 'globalisation' (although it must be said that those who most object to economic growth are those who have most benefited from it already).

This chapter cannot address all the issues associated with economic development. Its concern is limited to the role of the entrepreneur and the entrepreneurial process in economic growth. What, then, is the entrepreneurs' role? In fact there is no simple, agreed answer to this question. This will be for, by now, familiar reasons. First, there is a lack of agreement as to what consititutes an entrepreneur. Second, social-economic systems are extremely complex. It is difficult to disentangle what is cause and what is effect and how they are connected. Third, in laying claim to being a cause of economic growth, the entrepreneur 'competes' (conceptually of course) with other forms of economic organisation (government, the large capitalist bureaucracy, social networks) as the prime driver of economic growth.

Two extreme positions can be discounted at once. The idea that entrepreneurs are not necessary at all (as espoused by extreme forms of central planning) does not hold for the simple reason that central planning does not work. Without any entrepreneurs at all, economic growth is extremely sluggish and even negative. The centrally planned economies of the former Soviet Union collapsed under their own contradictions. The only remaining centrally planned economies – Cuba, Turkmenistan and North Korea – are hardly great advertisments for economic advancement. At the opposite pole, an extreme free market liberalism, in which the entrepreneurial model is the only form of economic organisation advocated, does not seem to work either (although its proponents often suggest it has not ever really been tried). The tendency here is for a powerful economic elite (sometimes called a plutocracy) to emerge and seek, not entrepreneurial competition, but monopolistic exploitation. Without some form of government to set out and enforce the rules as it were, entrepreneurship is discouraged. It would seem, therefore, that entrepreneurs are essential for economic growth, but that they operate within, and contribute to, an economic system with other actors involved.

What, then, of the entrepreneurs' role? The difficulty in defining the role of the entrepreneur has already been considered in section 1.3. It is useful, however, to revisit those ideas with a specific emphasis on the way in which developmental economists see the entrepreneur. As with most branches of economics, developmental economics traces its origins to the classical (and Austrian) traditions. As noted, classical economics has difficulty with the entrepreneur. Entrepreneurship, and economic development, are inherently dynamic economic concepts, they have meaning only in the sense that an economic system can change over time, whereas the classical model is essentially static. At most, the classical model makes entrepreneurship synonymous with 'management', hardly a discriminating perspective.

Moving away from this static picture, different economists with an interest in development issues have suggested different role for the entrepreneur. Joseph Schumpeter (1934) and Isreal Kirzner (1973) emphasised the role of the entrepreneur in identifying unexploited opportunities. Frank Knight (1921) suggested that entrepreneurs' key role was one of accepting risk. John Harris (1973) proposes that entrepreneurs increase the probability that a particular (economic-growth-delivering) project will in fact be undertaken. Harvey Leibenstein (1968) emphasised the importance of entrepreneurs in creating markets where markets are lacking (technically, to correct market imperfections). The industrial organisational economic perspective (see section 6.1) focuses on the role of entrepreneurs in undermining and policing monopolies that tend to reduce social welfare.

Econometric studies tend to show a correlation among the level of entrepreneurial activity, national wealth and economic growth. Such studies are difficult and may be challenged on two counts. First, there is the issue of defining entrepreneurs. Many use self-employment as a criterion. But self-employment is not necessarily the same as entrepreneurship (as defined above). Further, self-employment rates are often distorted by taxation policies that offer an advantage in claiming self-employment when, in a different region, the same job would be classified as employment. This said, such studies are revealing something, especially when compared with more obvious explanations of national wealth. The possession of natural resources that can be sold on world markets, for instance, would be expected to be a major factor in determining national wealth and economic growth. Not so. Countries with vast natural resources can often be quite impoverished (Russia, Nigeria) whereas those with very modest natural resources can be quite rich (Switzerland, Iceland, Luxemburg).

The second issue is one of causality. Are regions wealthy (and with growing wealth) because entrepreneurs operate? Or do entrepreneurs emerge because the region is wealthy and of growing wealth? Econometrics is good at identifying *correlations*, but identifying the direction of causality is much more difficult.

To the extent that developmental economics is achieving a consensus (and, if truth be told, on many issues the consensus is limited), it is that a major factor on the path to economic growth is not the elimination of government but the role of government in delivering effective, stable, honest economic governance.

7.2 National governance and entrepreneurship

Key learning outcome

Recognition of the role of open, effective, open and honest national governance in the stimulation of a vigorous entrepreneurial sector.

Thinkers have argued for over two and a half thousand years as to what the proper role of government should be. The debate is very much leavened by the fact that more than any other institution in society, government is in a position to define its own role. Looking around the world, it is clear that governments have interpreted their role (rights as well as responsibilities) in many different ways. Even with the liberal democratic West, government in the USA differs from government in England, which differs from government in France, Italy and Scandinavia in many subtle (and unsubtle) ways.

It is becoming increasingly apparent that good governance is a necessary (though perhaps not sufficient) condition for the emergence of a vibrant entrepreneurial class. There are a number of aspect to such governance, to which we now turn.

Legalising entrepreneurship

First and foremost, entrepreneurship must be legal. Centrally planned economies past and present made the entrepreneur a criminal – though not monolithically; Hungary, for example, was far more receptive to (discrete) entrepreneurs than was, say, Czechoslovakia. Even in regions where entrepreneurs are quite legal, legislation (for example, bankruptcy laws) still sends signals as to what is acceptable and what is not.

Size of the public sector

Even in the 'liberal' democracies of Europe, the public sector still accounts for between 40 and 50 per cent of all national wealth spending. A high level of public spending discourages entrepreneurs in two ways. First, the public sector must be paid for, and that means taxation. High levels of taxation are likely to demotivate entrepreneurship. Second, if the public sector is delivering a service (over which it usually claims monopology rights), then the entrepreneur cannot. Entrepreneurs are 'crowded out'. One solution (or at least compromise) that many governments are attempting is to put public services out to competitive tender in order to encourage entrepreneurs in.

Tariffs and trade barriers

The world is increasingly global in terms of goods and service distribution and capital flows (but not so much in labour flows). Increasingly, entrepreneurs see the world, not just their local region, as their market. Tariffs and trade barriers (in effect additional taxes on imports) reduce the size of entrepreneurs' markets, limiting their opportunities. Most politicians recognise this and the World Trade Organisation has been set up to reduce trade barriers. Some argue that entrepreneurs actually benefit from trade barriers as they protect them while they establish a foothold in a local market and that the economic strength of the West is a consequence of its protecting itself in the early stages of its economic growth. This position is highly controversial and this is not the place to debate it, save to say that if one group of entrepreneurs is 'protected', then another is likely to suffer as the locked out region retaliates with tariffs of its own. Further, there is no real evidence that those industries that were protected in their early stages fare any better (look, for example, at shipbuilding, textiles and car manufacturing in the UK.)

Taxation policies

Taxation has been noted above in relation to the size of the public sector. But the issue of the impact of taxation on economic activity is complex. The economist Arthur Laffer famously pointed out that if taxation levels were 0 per cent, then government revenues would be zero. Similarly, if they were 100 per cent on all economic activity, government revenues would also be zero – because no one would have any incentive to do anything. So, he suggested, government revenues against taxation level were represented by a upturned U-shaped curve (see Figure 7.1). If taxation levels were too high, government could have its cake and eat it – reduce taxation (electorally popular), stimulate economic activity – not least entrepreneurial activity – and increase government revenues. This idea, more than any other, stimulated the

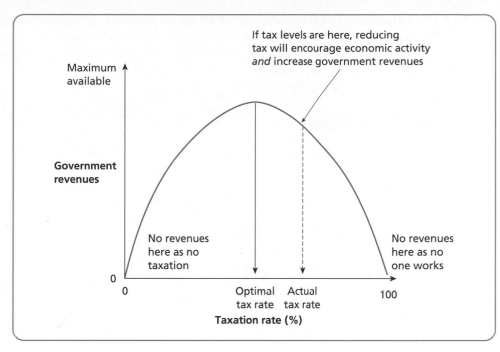

Figure 7.1 The Laffer curve

'supply-side revolution' in the economic policies of Ronald Reagan and in the USA and Margaret Thatcher in the UK.

The extent to which Laffer's ideas are legitimate is, even to this day, controversial. Taxation brings in a number of other issues. Who or what should be taxed? Individual earnings, companies, purchase of goods and services, inter-company transactions? There is no easy answer. Taxing individuals acts as a discouragement to economic activity. Too high a taxation level will drive entrepreneurial activity underground into the grey or even black economy, at its best reducing tax revenues and distorting entrepreneurs' strategic priorities. Taxing goods and services reduces transaction volumes. What government spends its tax revenues on also matters. Spending on entrepreneurial incubation will benefit entrepreneurs directly. Disbursement to consumers will increase their spending power and so indirectly create opportunities for (some) entrepreneurs. Subsidies to incumbent firms, on the other hand, will create barriers to entry for new entrepreneurs.

The post-communist Baltic states are experimenting with a flat-tax rate: company profits are not taxed at all, and all economic transactions are taxed at exactly the same rate, with some apparent success in terms of economic growth.

Inward investment policies

Money is money! The capital that entrepreneurs need to invest in start-up and growth need not originate within their own nation state. It can come from abroad. The recent spectacular economic growth in China, for example, is fuelled to a large extent by inward investment. However, some governments (claiming concern over 'uncontrollable' capital flows or 'theft' of national assets) impose regulation on inward investment either directly, or indirectly (for example, by insisting that the controlling owner be a local business). The inevitable result is that capital is restricted and becomes harder for entrepreneurs to get hold of. This pushes up the price of capital and so discourages entrepreneurs from initiating projects that might otherwise be economically viable.

Finance supply

Even within the local capital system, governments control the supply of capital, either directly, by restrictive legislation over the banking sector, or indirectly by implementing policies that lead to high inflation or (and this is related) high interest rates. High interest rates and inflation increase the cost of capital and discourage entrepreneurship. They also push down the value of the local currency, which may encourage exporting entrepreneurs but makes life hard for those that have to import factors.

Legislative environment

It is in the nature of governments to legislate. Legislation provides their primary means of governing. Generally speaking, entrepreneurs find legislation a burden. 'Red tape' takes time, costs money and restricts activity. And it is a distorting burden. Entrepreneurs usually find it harder to deal with than do large, established players, who have the resources to manage legislation, find an economy of scale in dealing with it and (often) are in a powerful position to lobby against legislation they do not like.

The level and impact of legislation vary enormously. If the legislative burden is too great, entrepreneurial activity will be driven into the grey and black sectors. Even if in the 'white' sector, it can influence an entrepreneur's strategy quite fundamentally. For example, in some parts of the world (India is a prime example), firms with more than a certain number of employees are not allowed to make redundancies without government approval. This takes time and is costly. Entrepreneurs respond simply by keeping their firms just below the number of employees at which this legislation kicks in. Restricting the growth of the business becomes an explicit strategic objective.

Customs and excise policy

Perhaps the oldest way for governments to raise capital is to put a duty (a tax) on goods entering (and sometimes leaving) their realm. It is mentioned in the Bible. Customs duties act as a brake on economic activity. They limit the effective size of the entrepreneur's market (for goods the entrepreneur wishes to sell outside the realm) and increase costs (on goods the entrepreneur wishes to bring into the realm). Further, high levels of customs duty encourage smuggling. Some might argue that smugglers are in fact entrepreneurs. Perhaps so, but they are entrepreneurs with highly distorted strategic priorities (not getting caught rather than growing the business).

Ethnic and religious discrimination

Although ethnic and religious discrimination is rarely an explicit policy of governments, it is one which some governments may encourage or exploit for reasons of populism. And it is the ethnic groups that are most entrepreneurial that are most likely to be targeted. The history of such discrimination is both tragic and terrible. The experience Jewish people throughout history is one of the most notable and appalling. Sometimes it is more subtle: the Ibo of Nigeria, Chinese in Southeast Asia, the Lebanese in West Africa for example.

Corruption

If there is one single feature of bad governance that is certain to discourage entrepreneurial activity it is government corruption. Corruption is a matter of degree. In the West, a government official taking a free holiday in (supposed) return for a small favour may make big news. In other parts of the world, corruption is so rife and endemic that the governments are simply labelled kleptocratic – 'rule by thieves'.

Corruption distorts entrepreneurial activity in several ways and at several levels. First, bribes are usually charged on transactions or in return for government permission (to set up a business, for example). Second, the money taken in the form of bribes is more likely to find its way into a safe foreign bank account. In both cases, the bribe acts exactly as a tax does: increasing costs, reducing the volume of transactions and reducing incentives. The chance that it will find its way to investing in local business is slim. Third, corruption distorts behaviour. Kleptocracies usually have a small, rich 'in' elite and an 'out', impoverished mass of citizens. An individual with entrepreneurial flair will find it more rewarding to dedicate their energies to breaking into the elite than to innovating and creating new enterprises.

For all of these reasons, good governance and the rule of fair, effective law are now seen as the single priority for economic development policy making. The stimulation of a vibrant entrepreneurial sector is not the only objective, but it is a critical one.

7.3 National culture and entrepreneurial inclination

Key learning outcome

Recognition that the behaviour of entrepreneurs is influenced by, but not determined by, a wide range of cultural and social factors.

Entrepreneurs are not robots blindly fulfilling an economic function. They cannot pursue opportunities or strive for economic efficiency without exhibiting some concern for wider issues. Entrepreneurs are human beings operating within societies which define, and are to an extent defined by, cultures. The analysis of culture falls properly within the domain of anthropology. The insights gained by anthropologists are of increasing interest to those who study business behaviour and performance. One of the driving forces behind this growth in interest has been the impressive economic growth achieved by countries in various parts of the world. Of particular interest at present are the 'tiger' economies of the Pacific Rim. The contribution that a range of structural, social and cultural factors have made to their success is widely debated.

This debate has been rekindled by the recent meltdown in many economies in the region. If cultural factors are called upon to explain long-term success, how might they be called upon to explain short-term collapse? How do 'cultural' and 'economic' fundamentals act together? Many observers are now suggesting that culture means little in the face of primary economic realities.

An analysis of culture is not a straightforward matter since a culture is not something that can be placed under a microscope. It is something we construct in order to explain the world rather than something we experience directly. There is a gulf between those who think that a culture can be examined as an objective reality and those who think it must be interpreted as something that impresses on our experience at a personal level. There is a debate (often quite heated) within the social sciences community as to the extent to which cultural differences are important. At one extreme there are those who see a much diminished role for culture. It is, at most, the 'icing on the cake' of an underlying psychic unity for mankind. Such an argument is often based on the fact that human beings are all descended from a relatively recent common ancestor and there has been no time for any fundamental evolutionary distinction between different human beings to take place. At the other extreme are those who argue that culture is all and that human beings are largely determined by their cultures: human nature is culture specific. Most social scientists take an intermediate position.

Clearly, culture plays a role in entrepreneurial behaviour. An American entrepreneur tends to act differently from a Japanese one, who, in turn, behaves differently from a Peruvian one. There are not only great differences *between* these cultures which influence the way that entrepreneurs work, there is also a wide variety of ways in which *individual* entrepreneurs work *within* these cultures. Culture is expressed in both the value *judgements* an individual makes and the value *system* of their wider community. What is at issue is the extent to which these differences reflect deep cultural factors or 'mere' social and economic local contingencies. George and Zahra (2002) explore this issue, and Busenitz and Lau (1996) develop a cognitive model of the effects of culture on new venture creation.

Mitchell *et al*. (2002) examine three questions related to the link between entrepreneurship and national culture using a cognitive approach: Are entrepreneurs different in their cognition? Are these cognitions universal among entrepreneurs? And do they vary across national culture? They conclude that entrepreneurs (as a group) have a cognition distinct from non-entrepreneurs, and that this cognition is largely universal, but that there is some variation in some factors across different national cultures.

Mitchell *et al*. (2000) undertook a cross-cultural study of entrepreneurial cognition based on the existence of three types of *cognitive script*. A cognitive script is a knowledge structure that a decision maker has access to. The types of script in this study were specified as:

- *arrangement scripts* relating to knowledge of contacts, relationships, and asset and resource availability;
- *ability scripts* relating to the individual's assessment of their own technical and general managerial abilities;
- *willingness scripts* relating to the individual's commitment to starting or developing the venture and including knowledge of business opportunities, tolerance of ambiguity and confidence in success.

While recognising the study's limitations, the authors conclude that such scripts do account for variations in the start-up decision, that the scripts do vary (to a degree) by culture, and that cultural effects moderate the impact of the scripts on the start-up decision. Another study, by Hartenian and Gudmundson (2000), evaluates the benefits of cultural diversity within small firms and considers whether it should be an explicit objective for the entrepreneur.

There is not scope within this book to consider all these issues in the depth they deserve. We must be content to note that entrepreneurs are necessarily the product of their cultures and that their cultures mould and influence their actions. What follows is meant to give a flavour of the *factors* which are significant to understanding entrepreneurship in a cultural setting and how they might be approached.

Language

The exact number of languages in the world is debated and depends on where the boundary between languages and dialects is drawn. Most experts agree on a figure of around 6,500. These are collected into about ten or so major language families that share vocabulary and grammatical characteristics and that experts assume emerged from a common ancestral language. Different languages within a family are not necessarily mutually understandable (English and German, for example are from the same *sub*-family). Language is a logistical issue in entrepreneurship as language differences limit communication, prevent contracts being drawn up and so inhibit trade. However, the opportunity to trade between different language groups is often strong enough to encourage the formation of 'pidgins' and 'creoles' that provide a basic common language. These were important in European trade with the Caribbean during the seventeenth century, for example, and have been observed in many parts of the world. The growth of global lingua franca such as English reflects the benefits of a common tongue for entrepreneurs working on a global scale. Such logistical issues are evident. What is more controversial is the suggestion by some social scientists that language creates a human's entire picture of the world (the *Sapir–Whorf* hypothesis) and so is fundamental to explaining cultural experience and differences. Thus, the argument might go, entrepreneurship is facilitated by the presence of words for concepts such as 'risk', 'opportunity', 'investment'. Speakers of languages that do not have such words should not be expected to think about entrepreneurship (if they have such a word) in the same way as a speaker of English (or other European language that has equivalent words) might do.

Religious beliefs

Religious belief is an important factor in shaping a culture. It leads to a view of the world which influences the individual's approach to entrepreneurship. The sociologist Max Weber famously associated the industrial revolution in western Europe and the USA with the attitudes engendered by Protestant religious beliefs known as the 'Protestant work ethic'. Modern commentators speculate on the influence of Confucian 'discipline' to the success of Asian economies. Islamic belief disallows (or at least limits) the setting of interest rates. Such prohibitions on usury were a common part of Christian belief until quite recently. Modern economics sees interest rates not so much as a powerful lender exploiting a weaker borrower, but as something fundamental to setting the price of money and directing it to where it will work hardest. The Islamic banking system has adopted an alternative system of monetary charges to achieve this. Some religious systems set in place quite rigid social stratifications that dictate the class and even job that an individual may take up. Modernisation is providing one means for enterprising individuals to break out of this structure. In India, many entrepreneurs have emerged from the Jain community because their strict vegetarianism and historical refusal to work with animal products excluded them from most conventional occupations, hence they turned to trading. Refer to Devashis (2000) and Choudhury (2001) for excellent reviews of venture capital in India and the Islamic world, respectively.

Personal relationships

The type and scope of personal relationships that a culture encourages will be a critical factor in the way entrepreneurial behaviour is expressed. An important study by the Dutch sociologist of business, Geert Hofstede (1980a), analysed human relationships along four dimensions:

- *Power distance* – the degree of authority that people expect between managers and subordinates, and their willingness to accept that power is not distributed equally.
- *Uncertainty avoidance* – in essence, this is the desire to be in a situation where uncertainty is minimised. Its opposite is a willingness to take risks.
- *Collectivity* – the need to feel that one is part of a group and that one's actions are sanctioned by that wider group. Its opposite is a desire to exhibit individualistic behaviour.
- *Masculinity* – the degree to which the culture emphasises 'masculine' values such as the acquisition of money, prioritising the material over the spiritual, a lack of concern versus a caring attitude, and so forth.

According to Hofstede's study, these four factors give a good account of how attitudes towards personal relationships give rise to different styles of entrepreneurial behaviour over a wide range of national cultures. Hayton *et al*. (2002) provide a review of 21 studies of how entrepreneurial characteristics vary across national cultures using Hofstede's (and other) frameworks. They offer a useful discussion of the methodological difficulties in establishing the link between culture and entrepreneurship and suggest directions for future study.

Attitude towards innovation

Innovation lies at the heart of entrepreneurship, yet to believe in innovation we have to see the world in a certain way. We have to believe in a future that will be *different* from the present. We have to believe that we can act so as to *influence* the world and change it by our actions. Further, if we are to be encouraged to innovate, we must believe that it is appropriate that we are *rewarded* for our efforts in developing innovation.

Many west Europeans will regard these things as 'obvious'. However, they are beliefs which are sensitive to culture. While a west European sees the future as something which brings uncertainties 'towards' them, many cultures, some in West Africa for example, have a different perspective. They draw a distinction between a 'potential time' which is full of things that *must* happen and a 'no-time' of things which might or might not happen. The potential time is *here and now*, a part of the present, whereas no-time is not really a part of time at all. From this perspective, there really is no such thing as the 'future' in the western sense.

Even if we believe in a future, we may not believe that we can influence it. Physical science has often emphasised that the future is *determined*. Marxism is founded on a belief that the world evolves along a predestined path. If an innovation occurs, it occurs because it was meant to occur. Hence, it is not the result of personal inventiveness which might *not* have occurred, and if this is so, why then should we reward the innovator? Hence innovations belong to the world at large, not the individual entrepreneur. Mark Casson (1994) has suggested that such a cultural perspective might be significant to the development of entrepreneurship in the post-communist world.

Networks

A network is the framework of individual and organisational relationships which form the stage upon which entrepreneurial performance is played. It is composed of personal and social contacts as well as economic relationships. A network is shaped by the culture in which it is formed.

The network does not just provide a route for people to sell things to each other. It is a conduit for information. A well-developed network is crucial if entrepreneurial behaviour is to express itself. It defines the terrain in which new business opportunities might be identified and assessed, and it provides a means by which contracts are agreed and risk might be evaluated and shared. It offers an escape route for people who do not think their investments are safe. This occurs not only through formal structures such as stock markets but also through informal confidences and relationships. The structure and functioning of such networks is sensitive to a wide range of cultural factors. The extent to which cultural values strengthen links (so locking individuals together), the scope of linkage they allow (within family group or outside family group), the conditions under which links may be broken (and the penalties for initiating breakage), and the ease with which new links may be formed (new relationships built) are all, to a degree, culturally determined.

It is neither possible nor particularly useful to draw hard and fast rules about managing within a particular culture. However, the idea that a culture provides a perspective within which individuals work might suggest an approach. The entrepreneur must recognise that an individual's response to a particular situation will to some extent be shaped by cultural influences. This will affect the way they can be led and motivated. However, the entrepreneur must not forget that individuals are individuals with their own characteristics, and do not necessarily behave with a collective consciousness. Entrepreneurs will also recognise that their own decision making is the product of their cultural experiences. Recognition of these things is becoming increasingly important as the opportunities for entrepreneurial ventures become ever more international. In the global arena, the effective entrepreneur learns to use cultural differences to advantage rather than be impeded by them.

Entrepreneurs who have built global concerns such as Rupert Murdoch (News International) and the late 'Tiny' Rowland (Lonhro) are renowned for their ability not just to manage people within one culture but to manage across cultures.

Summary of key ideas

- Entrepreneurs and the entrepreneurial process are recognised as playing a critical role in the economic development of regions and nations.

- There is lack of clarity as to the entrepreneur's exact role due to:
  - disagreement as to what, exactly, constitutes an entrepreneur;
  - the function of the entrepreneur in an economic system (different economists prioritise recognising opportunities, taking risks, providing managerial expertise, creating markets, policing monopoly);
  - knowledge about how entrepreneurs interact with other aspects of the economic system: government, existing commercial bureaucracies, social networks;

– difficulty in identifying the direction of causality: do entrepreneurs create wealth, or does wealth encourage entrepreneurship?

- Entrepreneurs thrive best where there is good, effective and open governance in relation to:
  – providing a supportive legislative environment;
  – restraint on the size of the public sector;
  – low and non-distorting taxation;
  – support for open and free international trade;
  – non-discrimination against ethnic and religious minorities;
  – a zero-tolerance attitude towards corruption.

- The influence of culture on entrepreneurial inclination should not be overstated (it seems to be a pan-human phenomenon). However, cultural nuances are provided by:
  – differing cognitive scripts;
  – language and religious beliefs;
  – different attitudes towards interpersonal relationships;
  – attitudes towards innovation;
  – the existence of different types of social networks.

Research themes

Entrepreneurship and government economic development policy at an international level

Select a sample of countries around the world (do not think just about the better known countries). This sample might include a representative mix of nations at various stages of economic development and regional location. Find government-sponsored websites that are dedicated to economic development. Select those that represent a reasonably clear statement of economic development policy, goals and strategy.

Undertake a content analysis with an emphasis on how the terms 'entrepreneur' and 'entrepreneurship' are related, regarded and prioritised within that statement of development goals. Consider how the terms are represented at both a local and international level; look also at how the concepts are linked to ideas such as inward investment. Compare and contrast the findings. Is there any pattern across regional and/or stage of economic development level?

How do your findings correlate with key economic indicators such as gross domestic product (GDP), per-capita GDP (GDP divided by population) and overall economic growth rate. You should find these on the government website you are investigating, but if possible use an independent standardised source (see below).

P.S. Don't forget to reflect on how the fact that the sites you have visited may not have been in the nations' own language may have skewed your findings.

Economic status, growth and venture capital structure

An interesting issue is how the structure of the venture capital industry – the main buyer of entrepreneurs' services – relates to economic development.

Obtain information on GDP, per-capita GDP and GDP growth rate from a reliable source (see below). A good way to represent this information is to use a bubble plot with GDP along the horizontal axis (all converted to the same US dollars – don't forget that comparing GDPs involves assumptions about exchange rates, but that should not complicate this project greatly), GDP growth along the vertical axis and the bubble itself representing population size.

Undertake a comparative analysis of the venture capital industries in each selected country. This should be to a standardised procedure with quantitative figures (e.g. number and size of deals, number of firms), and semi-quantitative (e.g. industry ownership structure) and qualitative (e.g. relationship with government, management culture, etc.) factors considered. The more factors considered the better, but be prepared to discuss how comparisons between factors are being made.

How does the venture-capital industry size, structure and complexity map against the bubble diagram? Again, think carefully about the criteria you are using to compare industries at the national level. What conclusions can you draw? Don't forget to comment on the fact that many venture capital firms operate internationally and not just in their own national arena.

A useful starting resource for this project is the list of reviews of national venture capital industries in section 20.1.

For both of these projects there are a number of sources of statistics on national economies on the internet. Ask your learning resource centre or library about the sources that your school or university subscribes to.

Key readings

A classic statement of the problem of integrating ideas on entrepreneurship with theories of economic development is:

Leff, N.H. (1979) 'Entrepreneurship and economic development: the problem revisited', *Journal of Economic Literature*, Vol. 17, pp. 46–64.

A slightly more conceptual paper, but one with a good conceptual and historical perspective, is:

Brouer, M.T. (2002) 'Weber, Schumpeter and Knight on entrepreneurship and economic development', *Journal of Evolutionary Economics*, Vol. 12, pp. 83–105.

Suggestions for further reading

Acs, Z.J. and Storey, D.J. (2004) 'Entrepreneurship and economic development', *Regional Studies*, Vol. 38, No. 8, pp. 871–7.

Aderson, R.B. (2002) 'Entrepreneurship and aboriginal Canadians: a case study in economic development', *Journal of Developmental Entrepreneurship*, Vol. 7, No. 1, pp. 45–65.

Ahwireng-Obeng, F. and Piaray, D. (1999) 'Institutional obstacles to South African entrepreneurship', *South African Journal of Business Management*, Vol. 30, No. 3, pp. 78–85.

Allen, D.N. and Hayward, D.J. (1990) 'The role of new venture formation/entrepreneurship in regional economic development: a review', *Economic Development Quarterly*, Vol. 4, No. 1, pp. 55–63.

Audretsch, D. and Keilbach, M. (2005) 'Entrepreneurship, capital and regional growth', *Annals of Regional Science*, Vol. 39, No. 3, pp. 457–69.

Benacek, V. (1995) 'Small business and private entrepreneurship during transition: the case of the Czech Republic', *Eastern European Economics*, Vol. 33, No. 2, pp. 38–73.

Bradford, W.D. and Osborne, A.E. (1976) 'The entrepreneurial decision and black economic development', *American Economic Review*, Vol. 66, No. 2, pp. 316–19.

Brookes, O. (1986) 'Economic development through entrepreneurship: Incubators and the incubation process', *Economic Development Review*, Vol. 4, No. 2, pp. 24–9.

Busenitz, L.W. and Lau, C.M. (1996) 'A cross-cultural cognitive model of new venture creation', *Entrepreneurship Theory and Practice*, Vol. 20, No. 4, pp. 25–39.

Casson, M. (1994) 'Enterprise culture and institutional change in eastern Europe', in Buckley, P.J. and Ghauri, P.N. (eds) *The Economics of Change in East and Central Europe*. London: Academic Press.

Choudhury, M.A. (2001) 'Islamic venture capital', *Journal of Economic Studies*, Vol. 28, No. 1, pp. 14–33.

Dandridge, T.C. and Dzieczizak, I. (1992) 'New private enterprise in the new Poland: heritage of the past and challenges for the future', *Journal of Small Business Management*, April, pp. 104–9.

Daneke, G.A. (1989) 'Technological entrepreneurship as a focal point oof economic development policy: a conceptual re-assessment', *Policy Studies Journal*, Vol. 17, No. 3, pp. 643–55.

Danis, W.M. and Shipilov, A.V. (2002) 'A comparison of entrepreneurship development in two post-communist countries: the cases of Hungary and Ukraine', *Journal of Developmental Entrepreneurship*, Vol. 7, No. 1, pp. 67–94.

Devashis, M. (2000) 'The venture capital industry in India', *Journal of Small Business Management*, Vol. 38, No. 2, pp. 67–79.

Falcus, M. (1998) 'Entrepreneurship and economic development in Hong Kong', *Business History*, Vol. 40, No. 3, pp. 163–5.

Fitzgerald, E.M. (2002) 'Identifying variables of entrepreneurship, privatization and competitive skills in central Europe: a survey design', *CR*, Vol. 12, No. 1, pp. 53–65.

Fleming, W.J. (1979) 'The cultural determinants of entrepreneurship and economic development: a case study of Mendoza Province, Argentina, 1861–1914', *Journal of Economic History*, Vol. 39, No. 1, pp. 211–24.

George, G. and Zahra, S.A. (2002) 'Culture and its consequences for entrepreneurship', *Entrepreneurship Theory and Practice*, Summer, pp. 5–8.

Green, R., David, J., Dent, M. and Tyshkovsky, A. (1996) 'The Russian entrepreneur: a study of psychological characteristics', *International Journal of Entrepreneurial Behaviour and Research*, Vol. 2, No. 1, pp. 49–58.

Harper, D.A. (2003) *Foundations of Entrepreneurship and Economic Development*. London: Routledge.

Hartenian, L.S. and Gudmundson, D.E. (2000) 'Cultural diversity in small business: implications for firm performance', *Journal of Developmental Entrepreneurship*, Vol. 5, No. 3, pp. 209–19.

Hayton, J.C., George, G. and Zahra, S. (2002) 'National culture and entrepreneurship: a review of behavioural research', *Entrepreneurship Theory and Practice*, Summer, pp. 33–52.

Hisrich, R.D. and Brush, C. (1986) 'Characteristics of the minority entrepreneur', *Journal of Small Business Management*, Oct., pp. 1–8.

Hofstede, G. (1980a) *Culture's Consequences: International Differences in Work-related Values*, London: Sage.

Hofstede, G. (1980b) 'Motivation, leadership and organisation: do American theories apply abroad?' *Organisational Dynamics*, Summer, pp. 42–63.

Huff, W.G. (1989) 'Entrepreneurship and economic development in less developed countries', *Business History*, Vol. 31, No. 4, pp. 86–97.

Karlsson, C. and Dahlberg, R. (2003) 'Entrepreneurship, firm growth and regional development in the new economic geography', *Small Business Economics*, Vol. 21, No. 2, pp. 73–6.

Kirzner, I.M. (1973) *Competition and Entrepreneurship*. Chicago: University of Chicago Press.

Kiselev, D. (1990) 'New forms of entrepreneurship in the USSR', *Journal of Small Business Management*, July, pp. 76–80.

Knight, F. (1921) *Risk, Uncertainty and Profit*. London: London School of Economics and Political Science. Reissued 1965, New York: Harper & Row.

Kuznetsov, A., McDonald, F. and Kuznetsov, O. (2000) 'Entrepreneurial qualities: a case from Russia', *Journal of Small Business Management*, Vol. 38, No. 1, pp. 101–7.

Lee, S.S. and Oysteryoung, J.S. (2001) 'A comparison of the determinants for business start-up in the US and Korea', *Journal of Small Business Management*, Vol. 39, No. 2, pp. 195–200.

Leibenstein, H. (1968) 'Entrepreneurship and development', *American Economic Review*, Vol. 58, pp. 72–83.

MacKenzie, L.R. (1992) 'Fostering entrepreneurship as a rural economic development strategy', *Economic Development Review*, Vol. 10, No. 4, pp. 55–63.

Maggina, A.G. (1992) 'SMEs in Greece: towards 1992 and beyond', *Journal of Small Business Management*, Vol. 30, No. 3, pp. 87–90.

Martinez, B. (2005) 'Equilibrium entrepreneurship rate, economic development and growth: evidence from Spanish regions', *Entrepreneurship and Regional Development*, Vol. 17, No. 2, pp. 145–61.

Mitchell, R.K., Smith, B., Seawright, K.W. and Morse, E.A. (2000) 'Cross-cultural cognitions and the venture creation decision', *Academy of Management Journal*, Vol. 43, No. 5, pp. 974–93.

Mitchell, R.K., Smith, J.B., Morse, E.A., Seawright, K.W., Peredo, A.M. and McKenzie, B. (2002) 'Are entrepreneurial cognitions universal? Assessing entrepreneurial cognitions across cultures', *Entrepreneurship Theory and Practice*, Summer, pp. 9–32.

Morden, T. (1995) 'International culture and management', *Management Decision*, Vol. 33, No. 2, pp. 16–21.

Nijkamp, P. and Stough, R.R. (2002) 'Special issue on entrepreneurship and regional economic development', *Annals of Regional Science*, Vol. 36, No. 3, pp. 369–71.

Puffer, S.M., McCarthy, D.J. and Peterson, O.C. (2001) 'Navigating the hostile maze: a framework for Russian entrepreneurship', *Academy of Management Executive*, Vol. 15, No. 4, pp. 24–36.

Sage, G. (1993) 'Entrepreneurship as an economic development strategy', *Economic Development Review*, Vol. 11, No. 2, pp. 66–7.

Schaper, M. (1999) 'Australia's aboriginal entrepreneurs: challenges for the future', *Journal of Small Business Management*, Vol. 37, No. 3, pp. 88–93.

Schaper, M. (2002) 'The future prospects for entrepreneurship in Papua New Guinea', *Journal of Small Business Management*, Vol. 40, No. 1, pp. 78–83.

Schloss, H.H. (1969) 'The concept of entrepreneurship and economic development', *Journal of Economic Issues*, Vol. 2, pp. 228–32.

Schumpeter, J.A. (1934) *The Theory of Economic Development*. Cambridge, MA: Harvard University Press.

Sui, Wai-Sum and Martin, R.G. (1992) 'Successful entrepreneurship in Hong Kong', *Long Range Planning*, Vol. 25, No. 6, pp. 87–93.

Tan, J. (1996) 'Characteristics of regulatory environment and impact on entrepreneurial strategic orientations: an empirical study of Chinese private entrepreneurs', *Entrepreneurship Theory and Practice*, Vol. 21, No. 1, pp. 31–44.

Trulsson, P. (2002) 'Constraints of growth-orientated enterprises in the southern and eastern African region', *Journal of Developmental Entrepreneurship*, Vol. 7, No. 3, pp. 331–9.

Wallace, S.L. (1999) 'Social entrepreneurship: the role of social purpose enterprises in facilitating community economic development', *Journal of Developmental Entrepreneurship*, Vol. 4, No. 2, pp. 153–74.

Wennekers, S., van Wennekers, A., Thurik, R. and Small, P. (2005) 'Nascent entrepreneurship and the level of economic development', *Business Economics*, Vol. 23, No. 3, pp. 293–310.

Wrenn, C. (2004) 'Entrepreneurship and economic development: a framework for policy', *International Journal of Entrepreneurship and Innovation Management*, Vol. 4, No. 1, p. 1.

Yu, T.F. (1987) 'Adaptive entrepreneurship and the economic development of Hong Kong', *World Development*, Vol. 26, No. 5, pp. 897–911.

Zapalska, A. (1997) 'Profiles of Polish entrepreneurship', *Journal of Small Business Management*, April, pp. 111–17.

Zapalska, A. and Edwards, W. (2001) 'Chinese entrepreneurship in a cultural and economic perspective', *Journal of Small Business Management*, Vol. 39, No. 3, pp. 286–92.

Zapalska, A., Brozik, D. and Shuklian, S. (2005) 'Economic system of Islam anmd its effect on growth and development of entrepreneurship', *Problems and perspectives in management*, Vol. 1, No. 5, pp. 5–10.

Selected case material

CASE 7.1

18 January 2006

How start-ups are helping countries to catch up

JONATHAN MOULES

Alejandro Pitashny raised more than a few eyebrows when he left a comfortable job at Deutsche Bank in London to return to his native Argentina to start a business during the worst moment of the country's financial crisis.

Four years later, the strategy appears to be paying off. José, which Mr Pitashny created with two former school friends, exports luxury tea and herbal infusions to Britain, the US, continental Europe, the Middle East and Asia. Although sales were just $100,000 in 2004, they grew by about 500 per cent last year.

That someone could forge such an entrepreneurial success in one of the world's middle-income countries is not surprising to the authors of the Global Entrepreneurship Monitor, the world's largest analysis of start-up activity, which published its seventh annual survey this month.

More than 150 academics, from 35 countries across five continents, helped compile the data, dividing the world into middle-income and high-income economies based on their per capita gross domestic product and economic growth rate.

They found that middle-income countries had a larger share of individuals engaged in a business venture with high growth potential as well as higher percentages of people starting businesses than in high-income countries.

The survey, jointly led by Babson College in the US and London Business School, also noted a direct link between per capita growth rates in middle-income countries and the level of innovative entrepreneurial activity in these countries.

Where Mr Pitashny is less typical of the GEM survey is in his use of technology, or lack of it. Probably the biggest innovation at José is its use of hand-tied muslin sacks rather than conventional bags to hold its tea.

The GEM research found that entrepreneurs often help drive new technology adoption in middle-income economies. This, in turn, is helping to close the per capita income gap between middle- and high-income countries, according to Maria Minniti, GEM research director and associate professor of economics and entrepreneurship at Babson College.

These technologies might not be cutting edge, Ms Minniti adds. But middle-income countries can get more out of them because they are starting from scratch.

'China is growing by importing technology and combining it with its competitive advantage, which is cheap labour,' she says. 'A large proportion of the catch-up effect by such countries is due to entrepreneurship. The technologies they deploy are not new to the world but they are new locally and that is good enough to create this catch-up effect.'

Entrepreneurship does not have to be innovative to benefit an economy since the mere competitive threat of a new business can help drive down prices and raise quality of service, Ms Minniti notes. 'Whether you are talking about the American guys in the garage who create a new kind of computer or the African woman who creates another basket-weaving business, entrepreneurship is good for an economy.'

However, she adds that the ideal for economies is to foster high-growth companies, which tend to be more innovative by nature. It is not enough just to have a large number of start-up businesses.

Venezuela, where one-quarter of the working population is running start-ups, has the highest rate of start-up activity in the world. But most of these businesses will not survive six months.

Federico Fernández, who compiled the GEM data for Venezuela, says: 'The Venezuelan spirit has always been to look around and do something. But this has been driven by the bad economic situation and it does not produce economic growth.'

Entrepreneurs in middle-income countries can also lack the government support enjoyed in richer nations. Mr Pitashny at José recalls being laughed out of the Chamber of Tea and Coffee Producers in Buenos Aires after asking for help setting up. 'To do business in Argentina is to overcome constant problems,' he says.

Early-stage entrepreneurs in high-income countries are more likely to become established business owners than those in poorer countries, according to GEM. This was linked to the finding that people in richer countries tended to start opportunity-inspired businesses after spotting a gap in the market rather than necessity-based companies, needed to put food on the table.

GEM's data showed that countries with a higher share of opportunity-driven entrepreneurship have a lower share of early-stage business failures than countries with a high share of necessity-driven entrepreneurship. Entrepreneurs are good for rich nations but chiefly if they introduce cutting-edge technologies, says GEM. 'For these countries, it is all about innovation,' Ms Minniti says.

An example of this is Olivia Lum, recently named south-east Asia's richest businesswoman by *Forbes* magazine. Although Ms Lum was raised as an orphan in a tin-roofed hut in Malaysia, she made money in prosperous Singapore by spotting an opportunity in the water treatment industry.

The challenge for the rich nations is to create effective capital markets to supply the money needed for research and development of new ideas, according to GEM. The good news is that the amount of venture capital investment in high-technology companies increased in 2004, the first time it had done so since the dotcom bubble burst in 2000.

However, North America continues to have a significant lead in the use of venture capital. There, 84.1 per cent of venture capital is invested in high-tech companies, compared with just 20 per cent in Europe.

Bill Bygrave, a professor at Babson and a member of the GEM co-ordination team, admits that venture capital funding is a necessary but not unique requirement for the growth of high-tech companies. 'Venture capital accelerates commercialisation – it doesn't fund inventions,' he says. Mr Bygrave adds that the gap in investment between Europe and the US is worrying. 'I just don't see that gap closing.'

It is not just differences in the total amounts of money invested. The average amount of venture capital pumped into an American company was $8.7m in 2004, compared with $2.7m for European companies and $537,000 for those in Japan.

US companies took 61 per cent of the total venture capital invested in Europe, Japan and the US combined but only accounted for 27 per cent of the total. This implies US venture capitalists were more selective about where they invested but poured more money into companies that they backed.

Mr Bygrave claims this is a sign that European investors are more 'gun shy' than their US counterparts, who show less risk aversion and are more willing to return to the stock market after a crash. 'When the dotcom bubble burst in 2000, you could almost hear the sniggering in Europe at all the money they felt had been wasted in the US.

'However, on the 10th anniversary of Netscape's IPO [initial public offering] last August, the market capitalisation of just four of the largest internet companies – Google, Yahoo!, eBay and Amazon – exceeded all the venture capital money that had gone into the dotcom market.'

Aversion to risk and fear of failure may be the greatest threat to developing high-growth innovative companies in richer nations – for example, in Europe.

Source: Jonathan Moules, 'How start-ups are helping countries to catch up', *Financial Times*, 18 January 2006, p. 11. Copyright © 2006 The Financial Times Limited.

CASE 7.2

24 January 2006

What China could learn from India's slow and quiet rise

YASHENG HUANG

In an article published in 2003 called 'Can India overtake China?' Tarun Khanna of Harvard Business School and I argued that India's domestic corporate sector – strengthened by the country's rule of law, its democratic processes and relatively healthy financial system – was a source of substantial competitive advantage over China. At that time, the notion that India might be more competitive than China was greeted with wide derision.

Two years later, India appears to have permanently broken out of its leisurely 'Hindu rate of growth' – an annual gross domestic product increase of about 2 to 3 per cent – and its performance is beginning to approach the east Asian level. From April to June 2005, India's GDP grew at 8.1 per cent, compared with 7.6 per cent in the same period the year before. More impressively, India is achieving this result with just half of China's level of domestic investment in new factories and equipment, and only 10 per cent of China's foreign direct investment. While China's GDP growth in the last two years remained high, in 2003 and 2004 it was investing close to 50 per cent of its GDP in domestic plant and equipment – roughly equivalent to India's

CASE 7.2 CONT.

entire GDP. That is higher than any other country, exceeding even China's own exalted levels in the era of central planning. The evidence is as clear as ever: China's growth stems from massive accumulation of resources, while India's growth comes from increasing efficiency.

The microeconomic evidence also casts India in a better light. While India's stock market has soared in recent years, the opposite has happened in China. In 2001, the Shanghai Stock Market index reached 2,200 points; by 2005, half the wealth had been wiped out. In April 2005, the Shanghai index stood at 1,135 points. This sharp deterioration occurred against a backdrop of GDP growth exceeding 9 per cent a year. It is difficult to find another country with this strange combination of superb macroeconomic performance and dismal microeconomic performance. It is a matter of time before the two patterns converge.

Why, then, is India gaining strength? Economists and analysts have habitually derided India's inability to attract FDI. This single-minded obsession with FDI is as strange as it is harmful. Academic studies have not produced convincing evidence that FDI is the best path to economic development compared with responsible economic policies, investment in education and sound legal and financial institutions. In fact, one can easily think of counterexamples. Brazil was a darling of foreign investors in the 1960s but ultimately let them down. Japan, Korea and Taiwan received little FDI in the 1960s and 1970s but became among the world's most successful economies.

An economic litmus test is not whether a country can attract a lot of FDI but whether it has a business environment that nurtures entrepreneurship, supports healthy competition and is relatively free of heavy-handed political intervention. In this regard, India has done a better job than China. From India

emerged a group of world-class companies ranging from Infosys in software, Ranbaxy in pharmaceuticals, Bajaj Auto in automobile components and Mahindra in car assembly. This did not happen by accident.

Although it has many flaws, India's financial system did not discriminate against small private companies the way the Chinese financial system did. Infosys benefited from this system. It was founded by seven entrepreneurs with few political connections who nevertheless managed, without significant hard assets, to obtain capital from Indian banks and the stock-market in the early 1990s. It is unimaginable that a Chinese bank would lend to a Chinese equivalent of an Infosys.

With few exceptions, the world-class manufacturing facilities for which China is famous are products of FDI, not of indigenous Chinese companies. Yes, 'Made in China' labels are still more ubiquitous than 'Made in India' ones; but what is made in China is not necessarily made by China. Soon, 'Made in India' will be synonymous with 'Made by India' and Indians will not just get the wage benefits of globalisation but will also keep the profits – unlike so many cases in China.

Pessimism about India has often been proved wrong. Take, for example, the view that India lacks Chinese-level infrastructure and therefore cannot compete with China. This is another 'China myth' – that the country grew thanks largely to its heavy investment in infrastructure. This is a fundamentally flawed reading of its growth story. In the 1980s, China had poor infrastructure but turned in a superb economic performance. China built its infrastructure after – rather than before – many years of economic growth and accumulation of financial resources. The 'China miracle' happened not because it had glittering skyscrapers and modern highways but because bold economic liberalisation and institutional reforms – especially agricultural reforms in the early 1980s – created competition and nurtured private entrepreneurship.

For both China and India, there is a hidden downside in the obsession with world-class infrastructure. As developing countries, if they invest more in infrastructure, they invest less in other things. Typically, basic education, especially in rural areas, falls victim to massive investment projects which produce tangible and immediate results. China made a costly mistake in the 1990s: it created many world-class facilities but badly underinvested in education. Chinese researchers reveal that a staggering percentage of rural children could not finish secondary education and many rural primary schools closed due to lack of funds. India, meanwhile, has quietly but persistently improved its educational provisions, especially in the rural areas. For sustainable economic development, the quality and quantity of human capital will matter far more than those of physical capital. India seems to have the right policy priorities and if China does not invest in rural education soon, it may lose its true competitive edge over India – a well-educated, skilled workforce that drives manufacturing success.

Unless China embarks on bold institutional reforms, India may very well outperform it in the next 20 years. But, hopefully, the biggest beneficiary of the rise of India will be China itself. It will be forced to examine the imperfections of its own economic model and to abandon its sense of complacency acquired in the 1990s. China was light years ahead of India in economic liberalisation in the 1980s. Today it lags behind in critical aspects, such as reform that would permit more foreign investment and domestic private entry in the financial sector. The time to act is now.

Source: Yasheng Huang, 'What China could learn from India's slow and quiet rise', first published in the *Financial Times*, 24 January 2006, p. 17. Copyright © 2006 Yasheng Huang.

Discussion points

1. If you were a policy maker for entrepreneurship development in a middle-income country, what would be your three key policy moves to support entrepreneurship?

2. How do you see the partnership between government and entrepreneurs in attracting foreign direct investment (FDI)?

CHAPTER 8

Not-for-profit and public entrepreneurship

Chapter overview

Entrepreneurship in the domain where the profit motive, and indeed the chance to make profits, is non-existent or very limited is an area of rapidly growing interest. Referred to as social entrepreneurship, it concerns the adoption of an entrepreneurial approach by managers in the not-for-profit (e.g. charities, non-governmental organisations, faith organisations) and public sectors.

This chapter considers the potential of and limitations to applying ideas developed in the study of for-profit (commercial) entrepreneurship to social entrepreneurship, It considers the question of whether the social entrepreneur can be thought of as an entrepreneur proper and, if so, how he or she might be distinguished from the commercial entrepreneur. The chapter concludes that the 'pure' commercial entrepreneur and 'pure' social entrepreneur should be thought of as ends of a spectrum rather than as distinct, non-overlapping types.

8.1 The conceptual challenge of social entrepreneurship

Key learning outcome

An appreciation of critical reasons why the study of traditional 'commercial' entrepreneurship has found difficulties in reconciling the idea of the not-for-profit and public sector – the 'social' – entrepreneur; how and why this integration is occurring; and the conceptual and managerial opportunities it presents.

The social entrepreneur – an entrepreneur who works with the objective of creating positive social change rather than 'mere' profit – seems to be an actor whose time has come. Hopes are high. A leading British politician said recently: 'Just as business entrepreneurs have helped cure the British economic disease [the low growth, high inflation and high unemployment of the 1970s], so social entrepreneurs can help cure Britain's social malaise.'

Traditionally, entrepreneurship, as an activity, has been intimately associated with the world of business and making profits. However, the picture of entrepreneurship we have developed so far has insights that can go beyond purely profit-motivated activity. In particular, we have seen that:

- entrepreneurship is a style of management;
- entrepreneurs are managers who are very effective at pursuing opportunity and creating change;

Figure 8.1 The hierarchy of entrepreneurship in its wider social context

- entrepreneurship is a social as well as an economic activity; and
- the motivations of the entrepreneur are varied and go beyond a desire to make money; they also involve a desire to create a new and better world.

From this it is clear that we might take a much wider view of 'entrepreneurship' and consider many activities outside the world of business as 'entrepreneurial'. For example, a great cultural, artistic or political endeavour could be entrepreneurial. It is not uncommon to hear talk of 'entrepreneurial' artists or politicians. This is not meant to imply that such people are simply interested in making money out of being artists or politicians (though, of course, many do); rather, it is to imply that such people approach their careers with drive, ambition and a clear vision of what they want to achieve. In order to fulfil their ambitions they are willing to develop and use entrepreneurial skills such as effective communication and leadership.

A hierarchy of entrepreneurial activities functioning in different social areas can be constructed as shown in Figure 8.1. At the core is what we conventionally understand to be entrepreneurship, namely managing the profit-making venture. At the next level is management of non-profit-making organisations such as charities. Above this we might place endeavours in the social and cultural arena such as sporting and artistic ventures. At the top of the hierarchy there are activities aimed at creating wholesale social change such as political activity. These levels are not completely separate, of course, and there will be some overlap.

Even though we can recognise entrepreneurship in these wider social arenas it is wise to keep management of the profit-making venture as the central concern for entrepreneurship. If we fail to do so, the subject could become so wide as to be in danger of losing its coherence as a field of study. Therefore, this book will concentrate on profit-motivated activities. However, this does not mean that insights gained from the management of the profit venture cannot be used to help achieve success in not-for-profit ventures, or, conversely, that an understanding of success outside the business sphere cannot be used to illuminate the ways in which entrepreneurship might be improved within that sector.

In a narrow sense, many not-for-profit activities may still demand a managerial approach. They often involve managing money. Thus the charity still has to attract financial resources to distribute to its clients; sport may involve financial sponsorship; artists must still sell their creations; political parties must attract money from supporters if they are to function. All these activities can call upon insights from other business areas such as marketing and human resource management. In a broader sense, though, entrepreneurship, perhaps more than many other management disciplines, goes beyond the mere management of money. Money is just a means to an end for the entrepreneur, and the end is the creation of a better world. We may offer a description of entrepreneurship at a fundamental level by claiming that it is about

creating and managing vision and communicating that vision to other people. It is about demonstrating leadership, motivating people and being effective in getting people to accept change.

This description reflects entrepreneurship as a management skill practised and perfected in a human setting. As such, it can play a crucial part in driving any venture forward, whether that venture be in the business, social, cultural or political domain.

The previous chapters have emphasised the difficulty in defining 'the entrepreneur' as an economic and social actor. As discussed, different (complementary) approaches place different emphasis on the economic, managerial and psychological aspects of entrepreneurial behaviour and effect. Despite this eclecticism, it remains difficult to disentangle the entrepreneur from the manager. Two things that all economic approaches seem to agree on, whether they take a classical, Austrian or competitive monopoly stance (see the review in Chapter 6) are that, firstly, the entrepreneur is motivated by creating new profits by the exploitation on new opportunities, and that consequently, the entrepreneur acts in a commercial setting where those profits can be accumulated.

This creates a great tension within the discipline of entrepreneurship studies. As has been discussed in Chapter 5, the motivations of the entrepreneur are many, and although making a profit may be requisite to the survival of the entrepreneur's organisation, it is far from being their sole motivation. Economic approaches are quite myopic to the distinction between the entrepreneur and the manager. Managers work in many areas that are not purely commercial: the public sector, charities, non-governmental organisations, religious organisations and aid agencies are notable examples. The tension, then, is this: if entrepreneurs are managers, and if not all managers work for profit-motivated organisations and institutions, are economic approaches to the study of entrepreneurship that emphasise profit guilty of excluding many types of entrepreneur – the title *social* entrepreneur is becoming established – from the feast?

This issue resolves itself into four questions. First, how widely would we wish to cast the net in applying the term 'entrepreneur'? This is not just a matter of flattery. It draws in the question of how the resources used to both support and study entrepreneurship are used. Second, given that the net is cast quite wide, how would we distinguish between the classical 'commercial' and the 'social' entrepreneur? This leads on to the third question: in what ways might for-profit and social entrepreneurs differ in their economic, managerial and psychological aspects? Fourth, how might the two types of entrepreneur learn from, and support each other (if they wished to)?

8.2 Is the social entrepreneur really an entrepreneur?

Ultimately, including or excluding the social entrepreneur is a question of definitions and how we wish to use words. As has been pointed out at several times previously, the word 'entrepreneur' lacks strict definition and different people use it in different ways. At one extreme lies those that would argue that entrepreneurship is about pursuing the profit motive and making money, and so the term should be restricted to the classical entrepreneur. Such a position is less frequently advocated in the modern study of entrepreneurship. In great part, this trend has resulted from both a widening interest in entrepreneurship with academics trained in non-economic fields of the social sciences entering into the study of entrepreneurship (see, for example, Zafirovski, 1999; Bygrave and Minniti, 2000; and Downing, 2005, for discussions of this development) and also (and this works in concert) from the development of 'third way' political philosophies that emphasise the importance of the development of social capital as well as financial. This is happening throughout the world. Such philosophies seek to reconcile the dynamic engine of economic growth provided by the free market enterprise system with concerns over social stability engendered by collectivising political policies. With these two concerns in place, the idea of the 'social' entrepreneur becomes an attractive proposition. A third factor is the growing number of people from the not-for-profit and public sector entering business schools and seeking to add an entrepreneurial flair to their management style.

Mort *et al.* (2003), for example, define social entrepreneurship as the 'entrepreneurship leading to the establishment of new social enterprises and the continued innovation within existing ones', and develop this as:

> [A] *multidimensional construct involving the expression of entrepreneurially virtuous behaviour to achieve the social mission, a coherent unity of purpose and action in the face of moral complexity, the ability to recognise social-value creating opportunities and key decision making characteristics of innovativeness, proactiveness and risk-taking.*

Should social entrepreneurs be excluded from the study of entrepreneurship? I see no reason why they should. As has been made clear, entrepreneurship is, first and foremost, a style of management. And it is certainly a style that is seen in many areas outside the purely commercial. If someone manages in an entrepreneurial way, there is no reason not to go the whole hog and refer to them as an entrepreneur.

8.3 Distinguishing the social entrepreneur from the classical entrepreneur

Given that the social entrepreneur is as much an entrepreneur as the classical, how, then, to distinguish them? Seven aspects are critical in the distinction:

- personal motivation
- sector of activity
- organisational form created
- strategies adopted
- definition of, and relationship with, stakeholders
- interaction with wider social environment
- ethical reflections.

Table 8.1 Distinguishing the social entrepreneur from the commercial entrepreneur

	Pure 'classic' entrepreneur	Pure 'social' entrepreneur
Personal motivation	Maximise personal wealth	Maximisation of 'social value'
Sector of activity	Commercial	Not-for-profit/public
Organisational form created	Traditional business hierarchy with entrepreneur taking leadership role	Non-traditional organisational form with an emphasis on egalitarianism rather than efficiency
Strategies adopted	Focused on competition and maximising return to entrepreneur/investors	Avoid competition; focused on creating and delivering social value
Definition of, and relationship with, stakeholders	Relationship with investors considered critical; relationship with customers seen as means to end	Stakeholders defined over wide and broadly defined groups
Interaction with wider social environment	Aspires to no wider social legitimacy	Seeks broad based social legitimacy with wide group of parties
Ethical reflections	Self-interested; not altruistic. Ethically neutral or unethical?	Altruistic at expense of self-interest. Ethical?

Table 8.1 summarises how the commercial and social entrepreneur might (or might be seen to) differ on each of these criteria.

Humans have an innate tendency to classify things. When it comes to the natural world, this is usually a matter of facts (although these might be disputed). When it comes to classifying people, though, values, philosophical stances and personal perspectives come into play. Classifications of people always run the risk of caricature. This can be overcome by recognising that the 'pure' entrepreneurial forms described in Table 8.1 represent the ends of a spectrum rather than distinct types.

Real entrepreneurs – be they commercial or social – fall somewhere along that continunm. For instance, few commercial entrepreneurs are interested solely in maximising personal wealth; they seek other rewards both for themselves and for others. Such non-pecuniary rewards may also be sought (legitimately) by social entrepreneurs. The commercial entrepreneur may aspire towards profit, but social entrepreneurs cannot ignore the need for effective financial management of their resources. The boundaries between the commercial, not-for-profit and public sectors are becoming increasingly blurred. For a spirited discussion of this blurring of 'social' and 'commercial' entrepreneurship, see Oppenheim (2005) on

Fairtrade brands. Business organisations are seeking non-traditional structures as a source of competitive advantage as the not-for-profit and public sectors investigate what they can learn from the efficiency offered by traditional business organisational forms.

One of the main themes in modern strategic thinking is that of the balanced scorecard approach, which encourages managers to think about a wide range of stakeholders as not-for-profit organisations are encouraged to think of their clients as customers. As discussed in Chapter 2, one economic sociological perspective on the (for-profit) entrepreneur sees him or her as a seeker of social legitimacy as well as of capital.

This leaves the issue of ethical reflection. Are social entrepreneurs more ethical than their commercial counterparts? This is a complex question that has already been touched upon in section 6.2. It brings into focus a number of issues: whether humans are altruistic or not, whether the motivations of the entrepreneur, the actions they take or the effects of their actions should be emphasised in moral debate, and so on. It also touches on the issue of corporate social responsibility. There are no simple answers, and this book cannot do justice to the intricacies in the debates concerned. At the end of the day, it is a matter of personal values. Nonetheless, few would say that commercial entrepreneurship is entirely bad in all its effects, nor social entrepreneurship entirely good (see, for example, Rieff (2005) on the 1985 Live Aid project to raise money for Ethiopia).

In summary, all entrepreneurs, commercial or social, lie along a continuum of motivation, strategy, organisational building and social effect. This is not to decry from what social entrepreneurs, or indeed commercial entrepreneurs, do, or try to do. What is does mean is that there is no need for a science of social entrepreneurship distinct from that of commercial entrepreneurship. The same tools can be used; just the emphasis is different.

Summary of key ideas

- As style of management, there is no reason why the concepts of entrepreneur and entrepreneurship should be restricted to the for-profit sector.

- The 'social' entrepreneur can be distinguished from the 'commercial' entrepreneur along a number of dimensions including:
  - personal motivation
  - sector of activity
  - organisational form created
  - strategies adopted
  - definition of, and relationship with, stakeholders
  - interaction with wider social environment
  - ethical reflections.

- However, these dimensions represent continua rather than all-or-nothing categories.

- Different sorts of commercial, social and public entrepreneur can be characterised by the stakeholder group to which they give priority in delivering rewards, focusing communication and creating strategy.

Research themes

Growth in interest in social entrepreneurship

Using an internet search engine, assess by year (say starting in 1990) how many articles include the term 'social entrepreneur' (in the article title as well as the text). Break your analysis down into different sources, say: newspapers, general magazines, business magazines and academic articles. Sample some (you will not be able to do them all, I promise!). Think about your sampling regime.

Analyse your findings. What is the pattern of growth? Who is driving the debate about social entrepreneurship – and in what terms?

Review and commentary

Undertake a review of the academic literature on social entrepreneurship. The readings suggested below are an excellent start. Develop a commentary on the theme: 'Strategic management techniques developed for commercial entrepreneurs are concerned primarily with generating profits and so are not effective for guiding the social entrepreneur'. Develop arguments to support and/or criticise this proposition.

An alternative project would be to organise a tutorial group into two groups, one briefed to support the argument, the other to challenge it and organise a debate. Deliver a summarising commentary of your own at the end. (You may even wish to video the debate as a formal project submission.)

Key readings

Two readings that explore the meaning of the term 'social entrepreneur' and its relationship to conventional 'for-profit' entrepreneurship. Both consider future developments and possible research agendas.

Mort, G.S., Weerawardena, J. and Carnegie, K. (2003) 'Social entrepreneurship: towards conceptualisation', *International Journal of Non-profit and Voluntary Sector Marketing*, Vol. 8, No. 1, pp. 76–88.

Roberts, D. and Woods, C. (2005) 'Changing the world on a shoestring: the concept of social entrepreneurship', *University of Auckland Business Review*, Autumn, pp. 45–51.

Suggestions for further reading

Barendsen, L. and Gardner, H. (2004) 'Is the social entrepreneur a new type of leader?', *Leader to Leader*, No. 34, pp. 43–50.

Boyett, I. (1977) 'The public sector entrepreneur – a definition', *International Journal of Entrepreneurial Behaviour and Research*, Vol. 3, No. 2, pp. 77–92.

Bygrave, W. and Minniti, M. (2000) 'The social dynamics of entrepreneurship', *Entrepreneurship: Theory and Practice*, Vol. 24, No. 3, pp. 25–36.

Downing, S. (2005) 'The social construction of entrepreneurship: narrative and dramatic processes in the coproduction of organizations and identities', *Entrepreneurship: Theory and Practice*, Vol. 29, No. 2, pp. 185–204.

Hibber, S.A., Hogg, G. and Quinn, T. (2002) 'Consumer response to social entrepreneurship: the case of the *Big Issue* in Scotland', *International Journal of Non-profit and Voluntary Sector Marketing*, Vol. 7, No. 3, pp. 288–301.

Hibber, S.A., Hogg, G. and Quinn, T. (2005) 'Social entrepreneurship: undestanding consumer motives for buying the *Big Issue*', *Journal of Consumer Behaviour*, Vol. 4, No. 3, pp. 159–72.

Johnson, V.R. (2002) 'Competition, conflict and entrepreneurial public managers: the legacy of reinventing government', *Public Administration Quarterly*, Vol. 26, No. 1/2, pp. 9–34.

Lasprogata, G.A. and Cotten, M.N. (2003) 'Contemplating "enterprise": the business and legal challenges of social entrepreneurship', *American Business Law Journal*, Vol. 41, pp. 67–113.

Oppenheim, P. (2005) 'Fairtrade fat cats: guilt-stricken consumers are boosting supermarkets' profits', *The Spectator*, 5 Nov., p. 28.

Pepin, J. (2005) 'Venture capitalists and entrepreneurs become venture philanthropists', *International Journal of Non-profit and Voluntary Sector Marketing*, Vol. 10, No. 3, pp. 165–73.

Rieff, D. (2005) 'Dangerous pity', *Prospect Magazine*, No. 112, July, p. 34.

Thompson, J., Alvy, G. and Lees, A. (2000) 'Social entrepreneurship: a new look at the people and the potential', *Management Decision*, Vol. 38, No. 5, pp. 328–38.

Turner, D. and Martin, S. (2005) 'Social entrepreneurs and social inclusion: building local capacity or delivering national priorities', *International Journal of Public Administration*, Vol. 28, No. 9/10, pp. 797–806.

Wempe, J. (2005) 'Ethical entrepreneurship and fair trade', *Journal of Business Ethics*, Vol. 60, No. 3, pp. 211–20.

Zafirovski, M. (1999) 'Probing into the social layers of entrepreneurship: outlines of the sociology of enterprise', *Entrepreneurship and Regional Development*, Vol. 11, pp. 351–71.

Selected case material

CASE 8.1

31 January 2006

Private providers offered fresh opportunities in health shake-up

NICHOLAS TIMMINS

Private sector and not-for-profit providers of care will be given fresh opportunities under the government's white paper on care outside hospitals.

Boots, Bupa, Care UK, Netcare, BMI, United Health, Nuffield, Alliance Medical and many others are likely to become providers to the National Health Service, both in the high street and in the new 'super surgeries', diagnostic centres and community hospitals. Some may also become commissioners of care for the NHS, operating on contract to primary care trusts.

There will also be new entrants in the growing market, including groupings of NHS and enterpreneurial GPs, which will be able to set up in business with financial help and advice from the 'social entrepreneurs' unit in the Department of Health.

Big hospitals face a challenge. As services are moved out, they and their staff will have to adapt, with the likelihood of mergers, reconfigurations and, in some cases, potential closures.

Bernard Ribeiro, president of the Royal College of Surgeons, warned that 'patient convenience must not be promoted at the expense of patient safety', a point underlined by the Healthcare Commission, the NHS inspectorate, which said patients needed the same assurances on quality and standards whether treated in a hospital clinic or super-market surgery.

The private finance initiative will also have to adapt. Some £5bn worth of PFI hospitals have been built or are under construction. Another £6bn are out to tender and a further £6bn have had their strategic outline case approved.

As the *Financial Times* revealed last week, all plans for 'major capital procurement' will have to be reviewed to ensure they are compatible with a future in which resources and activity will move into primary and community settings.

'Positive endorsement of major capital proposals will happen only where this compatibility clearly exists,' the White Paper says.

Patricia Hewitt, the health secretary, said that after this 'reappraisal' it was still estimated that the PFI programme going forward would be bigger than those so far built or under construction – an 'estimated' £7bn to £9bn. But this is still a 25 to 40 per cent reduction on plans for the future.

Stephen Ratcliffe, chief executive of the Major Contractors Group, said PFI providers would be seriously concerned if the big projects nearing financial close, including Birmingham, Leicester and Barts in London – a decision on which is expected this week – were pulled or reconfigured.

He said many contractors were more comfortable with schemes in the £300m range than the £700m to £1.1bn 'mega projects' such as Barts, Birmingham, Leicester and the abandoned St Mary's, Paddington, rebuild.

Ms Hewitt said it was 'an interesting question' whether NHS hospitals and foundation trusts would expand into primary and community care.

'That will need to be judged on a case-by-case basis to ensure we are getting the best services for patients,' she said. It was 'not necessarily true' that there would be hospital closures, she added.

Source: Nicholas Timmins, 'Private providers offered fresh opportunities in health shake-up', *Financial Times*, 31 January 2006, p. 3. Copyright © 2006 The Financial Times Limited.

CASE 8.2

30 January 2006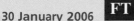

Course choices that help MBAs make the world a better place

ANDREW BAXTER

The teaching of social enterprise or entrepreneurship as an option in MBA programmes is putting down new roots in Europe and broadening its focus in its original home, the US.

Old assumptions – in particular, that the only way for people to be 'do-gooders' was through a career at a non-profit organisation – are being challenged by 21st century realities.

Thus the narrow definition of social enterprise within MBA programmes – preparing students who may always have had an interest in the non-profit sector to join or return to it with their management antennae switched on – is being subsumed into something much bigger: recognition that the chance to make the world a better place can come from many vantage points and at any time in a student's career.

In this new world, people and organisations can make a positive social impact via all sorts of organisations in the non-profit, private and public sectors, and social responsibility has become a byword in many organisations.

Confusingly, perhaps, this broader definition of the environment that business schools seek to address is called social enterprise or social entrepreneurship almost interchangeably. Even so, what is clear is that, as Herman 'Dutch' Leonard, co-chair of Harvard Business School's Social Enterprise Initiative, puts it: 'Most schools have a more expansive picture these days of what they are offering.'

For many of the US schools offering social enterprise electives in their MBAs, the more restricted definition – preparing more effective managers for the non-profit sector – was the starting point. Columbia's Social Enterprise Programme, for example, has its roots in an earlier Public and Non-profit Management Programme, established in 1981.

Ray Horton, director of the Social Enterprise programme, says its antecedent operated on the premise that any student interested in serving the public good would seek a career in a non-profit organisation or a government agency.

'While we shepherded many bright and talented students off to work in the social sector, we were overlooking the majority of MBA students who could contribute to society in meaningful ways through their positions in the public sector,' says Prof. Horton.

This is not to say that schools have lost interest in preparing MBA students for senior roles in the non-profit sector. Allen Grossman, a key member of HBS's social enterprise faculty,

▶

CASE 8.2 CONT.

teaches two courses, on entrepreneurship in the social sector and effective leadership of a social enterprise, which build on his own experiences running a non-profit organisation, Outward Bound USA, in the 1990s.

'In the business world there was a huge amount of theory for practitioners,' says Prof. Grossman, 'but it didn't exist in the not-for-profit world, except scantily. Historically people would say 'run this place like a business and everything will be fine'. That's no more rational than telling someone to run a plant in China the same way as in New Jersey.'

The crux of the issue for non-profits, he says, is the 'double bottom line' – the need to avoid losses in conventional terms and the broader imperative to improve the lives of intended beneficiaries. 'If you are terribly successful financially as a non-profit, are you successful? No, not necessarily. So what is success and what does it look like? What does high performance look like and how do you achieve it?'

The double bottom line of profitability and social impact has now – to a large extent, and varying from sector to sector – entered the mainstream of business, and business schools are responding. Thomas Cooley, dean of NYU Stern School of Business, says thinking about how business can be a positive force for social change is a key role for the school, and one that has become part of its identity.

'People don't often appreciate what an incredibly powerful, transformative thing [business] can be, how it can lift people out of the mire of poverty and on to the ladder of success.' So it is important, he says, to train business people to be socially responsible and develop new ways to bring out their socially-responsive instincts.

Judging by the outcomes at Harvard Business School [HBS], which created its Social Enterprise Initiative in 1993, the schools that have introduced such electives are succeeding in their triple role of training people directly for a career in the non-profit sector, of imparting knowledge to those who want some way of participating in activities that have a social impact, and of instilling a sense of citizenship in those who spend the rest of their careers in the private sector.

Professor Leonard notes how a commitment to the non-profit sector increases as the careers of alumni develop. One illustration of the importance for alumni of social enterprise, he says, is their funding for the Service Leadership Fellows Programme, enabling new HBS MBA graduates to spend a year gaining management experience at a non-profit organisation or public agency.

Similarly, NYU Stern has benefited from the launch in 2004 of the Steward Satter Social Entrepreneurship Programme, supported by alumnus Stewart Satter. The programme oversees curriculum development and provides management help and $500,000 a year in seed funding to social entrepreneurs.

Professor Grossman at HBS notes that, in contrast to 20 years ago when career aspirations were simpler, students almost without exception will have multiple careers. 'Many of them aspire to go into the social sector at some point in their career, so this is a real opportunity for them to learn about it.' Recent alumni surveys suggest that, at any given time, more than one-third of HBS MBA alumni are actively serving on non-profit boards.

European schools have a much shorter history in this field, but the very few schools that have added social entrepreneurship electives to their MBA programmes have started with a broad interpretation of the theme and a desire to be different. 'As a professor thinking about doing a course, the first thing you do is try not to reinvent the wheel,' says Johanna Mair, the Iese Business School professor who designed its social entrepreneurship course. The Spanish school claims it was the first in Europe to have such a course in its MBA.

Prof Mair is encouraged by the take-up for the course, which is held in the second year of the MBA after students have grasped the functional basics. Numbers have risen from 22 in the first year for the course to 45 in the third, a quarter of all students doing the MBA and including a broad international mix as well as students with conventional finance or marketing ambitions.

The course has a strong strategic angle, she says, examining the implications of the social entrepreneurship phenomenon for established companies. 'The main object is not to turn them all into social entrepreneurs,' she says. 'But it does aim to put a seed in their minds, so that when they are in marketing or finance positions, they see the possibilities of working together with social entrepreneurs.'

Iese's debut was followed in the autumn of 2004 by Saïd Business School in Oxford, the first school in the UK to have social entrepreneurship electives in its MBA. The Skoll Foundation, which was set up by Jeff Skoll, the first president of eBay, to advance the cause of social entrepreneurship, has provided £4.4m for the creation of a Centre for Social Entrepreneurship and for five Skoll Scholars to take part in the school's one-year full-time MBA.

Rowena Young, director of the centre, sees an increasing need for entrepreneurial approaches to social problems, and says the centre is designed to help bring legitimacy to the whole field of social entrepreneurship, partly by laying down a knowledge base through a research programme and partly by promoting enhanced leadership through giving people the management education they need to be effective.

The arrival of the first Skoll Scholars was preceded in March 2004 by the school's first annual Skoll World Forum on Social Entrepreneurship, underlining how the school wants to be seen as a hub for discussion of social entrepreneurship. The next forum is to be held on 29–31 March this year.

'The forum is hugely popular, it's the largest event in the school,' says Ms Young. 'That and the uptake of the electives have demonstrated that there really is strong demand for this.'

In the first year, 54 students or one-third of the cohort took one or more of the three social entrepreneurship electives. Ms Young says that students who take all three, choose wisely from other electives with some social context, and pick relevant topics for their two practical business projects can tailor half their MBA to social entrepreneurship, without compromising the core modules of the Oxford MBA.

Perhaps the most encouraging aspect of all these programmes is the activity around them. As with Saïd's World Forum, these are among the busiest and most popular at their respective schools – from the Oxford Social Entrepreneurship Network to the US student clubs and student-run venture funds and competitions. These ensure that social enterprise initiatives have an impact on many more students than those who take the electives.

Source: Andrew Baxter, 'Course choices that help MBAs make the world a better place', *Financial Times*, 30 January 2006, p. 6. Copyright © 2006 The Financial Times Limited.

Discussion points

1. 'Only government can create opportunities for not-for-profit entrepreneurs.' Discuss.

2. 'Not-for-profit entrepreneurs need different skills to profit motivated entrepreneurs.' Discuss.

CHAPTER 9

Success, stakeholders and social responsibility

Chapter overview

Entrepreneurship is about success. This chapter is concerned with
defining success and the ways in which it can be measured. Business success is
considered not only in financial terms but also in a broader social context. The
issue of social corporate responsibility is considered. The chapter concludes with
an exploration of the converse of success: failure. Failure is not seen as completely
negative but rather is viewed as an experience which is occasionally necessary and
which presents an opportunity for the organisation and the entrepreneur to learn.

9.1 Defining success

Key learning outcome

An understanding of what
entrepreneurial success actually
means.

Entrepreneurs aim to be successful. It is the possibility of success
that drives them on and success is the measure of their achievement. Success is, however, quite a difficult concept to define
because it is multifaceted. Both individuals and organisations
enjoy success. It may be measured by hard and fast 'numbers' but
also by 'softer', qualitative criteria. Success is something which is
both visible in public and experienced at a personal level.

Success can be best understood in terms of four interacting aspects:

- the performance of the venture;
- the people who have expectations from the venture;
- the nature of those expectations; and
- actual outcomes relative to expectations.

The performance of the venture is indicated by a variety of quantitative measures. These
relate to its financial performance and the presence it creates for itself in the marketplace.
The indicators can be absolute and compared with the performance of competitors. Such
performance measures relate to the organisation as a whole. However, an organisation is
made up of individual people, and success, if it is to be meaningful, must be experienced by

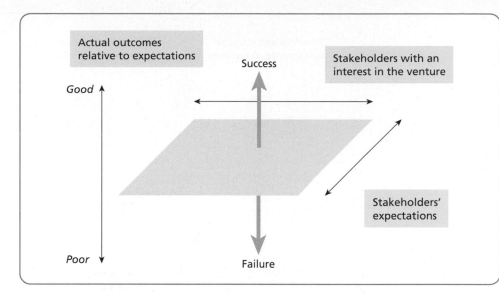

Figure 9.1 A model of entrepreneurial success

those individuals as well as by the organisation. Organisational success is a means to the end of *personal* success. The organisation creates the resources which interested individuals can use to improve their lives. The individuals who have an interest in the performance of the venture are its *stakeholders*. Thus the success of a venture must be considered in relation to the expectations that its stakeholders have for it (see Figure 9.1).

The entrepreneurial venture has six groups of stakeholders, each of which has its own interest and expectations from the venture. The *entrepreneur* (and their dependants) expects the venture to be a vehicle for personal ambitions; *employees* expect reward for their efforts and personal development; *suppliers* expect the venture to be a good customer; *customers* expect the venture to be a good supplier; *investors* expect the venture to generate a return on the investment they have made; and the *local community* expects the venture to make a positive contribution to the quality of local life.

The performance of the venture as an organisation provides the means by which individual stakeholders can fulfil their own goals. Personal goals are manifest at three levels:

- the *economic* – monetary rewards;
- the *social* – fulfilling relationships with other people; and
- the *self-developmental* – the achievement of personal intellectual and spiritual satisfaction and growth.

Success experienced at a personal level is not absolute. Success is recognised by comparing actual outcomes with prior *expectations*. At a minimum, success is achieved if outcomes meet expectations, and success is assured if expectations are exceeded. If expectations are not met, however, then a sense of failure will ensue.

Different stakeholders will hold different expectations. They will look to the organisation to fulfil different types of goals. The investor may be interested only in the venture's offering financial returns whereas the customers and suppliers will want financial rewards, but they

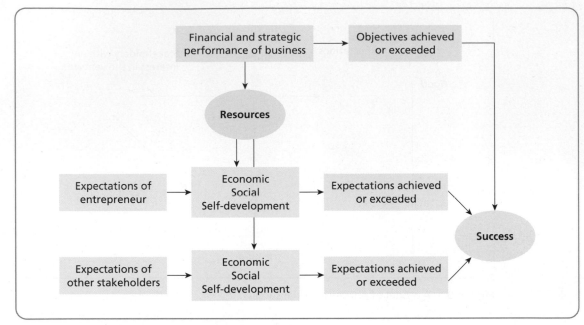

Figure 9.2 The dynamics of entrepreneurial success

may also hope to build rewarding social relationships with people in the organisation. Employees will expect a salary but this will only be their minimum expectation. They will also expect the venture to provide a route for self-development. The venture will be central to the personal development of the entrepreneur.

Success, then, is not a simple thing. The organisation's financial and strategic performance is only part of the picture. Success is achieved if the organisation uses its performance to meet, or better to *exceed*, the financial, social and personal growth expectations of the people who have an interest in it. The success of a venture depends on how its performance helps stakeholders to achieve their individual goals, and the way that different people judge the success of the venture will depend on how well these expectations are met (Figure 9.2). What are the chances that a business will be successful? Nucci (1999) found that for US small businesses, some 20 per cent are terminated by the end of the first year, with 60 per cent gone by the end of the fifth. These do not all represent financial failure. Those actually filing for bancruptcy are quite low. Dennis and Fernald (2001) examine the probability of a new venture's success based on US business statistics. They find that the probability of a venture's success is quite high, but that the probability of a venture's providing an entrepreneur with a substantially increased income over conventional alternatives is quite low.

9.2 Success factors for the new venture

A venture is successful if it meets the aspirations of its stakeholders. In order to do this it must survive and prosper in the marketplace. It must attract resources, reward its stakeholders for their contributions and be financially secure. Every venture is different, but a common set of factors lies behind every successful business.

The venture exploits a significant opportunity

The opportunity spotted by the entrepreneur is real and significant. The venture is faced with the possibility of delivering sufficient value to a large enough number of customers to make the business viable in terms of income and profits.

The opportunity the venture aims to exploit is well defined

The venture must be clear as to why it exists. It must understand the nature of the opportunity it aims to exploit. This may be codified in the form of a *mission statement* (discussed further in Chapter 17). The danger is not just that the business may fail to find a sufficiently large opportunity for its innovation but also that in pursuing too many opportunities, and opportunities that are not right for the business, the venture will dilute its resources across too many fronts and fail to focus its efforts on creating a sustainable competitive advantage in the areas where it has real potential to be competitive.

The innovation on which the venture is based is valuable

The innovation behind the venture, that is, its new way of doing things, must be effective and different from the way existing businesses operate. It must be appropriate to exploit the opportunity identified. Recognising an opportunity, and innovating to exploit it, can only occur if the entrepreneur thoroughly understands the market and the customers who make it up. All new ideas, no matter how good, must be scrutinised in the light of what the market *really* wants.

The entrepreneur brings the right skills to the venture

The entrepreneur possesses the right knowledge and skills to build the venture to exploit the opportunity. These include knowledge of the industry sector they are working in, familiarity with its products and markets, general management skills, and people skills such as communication and leadership. The entrepreneur must not only have these skills but also be active in refining and developing them. The effective entrepreneur learns how to learn.

The business has the right people

Entrepreneurs rarely work alone. They draw other people into their ventures to work with them. The business as a whole must have the right people working for it. Entrepreneurs do not need to employ copies of themselves; rather, they need people with skills and knowledge to complement their own. The business will need specialists and technical experts as well as people to actually make the product or deliver the service the business offers. It will need general managers and people able to build relationships outside the firm. The people who make up the organisation will be linked in a suitable framework of communication links and responsibilities, both formal and informal. As the business grows, identifying and recruiting the right people to support its growth is a task of primary importance for the entrepreneur.

The organisation has a learning culture and its people a positive attitude

The new venture is in a weak position compared with established players in the marketplace. It is young and relatively inexperienced. It has not had a chance to build up the expertise or relationships that its established counterparts have. It will not have access to their resource levels. The entrepreneurial organisation must turn this on its head and make the disadvantage an advantage. The entrepreneurial venture must use the fact that it is new to do things in a fresh and innovative way. It must recognise its inexperience as an opportunity to learn a better way of doing things. This can only be achieved if the organisation has a positive culture which seeks ways of developing and which regards change as an opportunity. Adversity must be met as a learning experience. Culture comes down to the attitudes of the people who make up the organisation. They must be motivated to perform on behalf of the venture. The entrepreneur is responsible for establishing a culture in the organisation through leadership and example.

Effective use of the network

Successful entrepreneurs, and the people who work with them, use the network in which the organisation finds itself to good effect. They look upon suppliers and customers not as competitors for resources but as partners. They recognise that entrepreneurship is not a zero-sum game. If all parties in the network recognise that they can benefit from the success of the venture – and it is down to the entrepreneur to convince them that they can – then the network will make resources and information available to the venture and will be prepared to share some of its risks.

Financial resources are available

The venture can pursue its opportunity only if it has access to the right resources. Financial resources are critical because the business must make essential investments in productive assets, pay its staff and reimburse suppliers. In the early stages, expenditure will be higher than income. The business is very likely to have a negative *cash flow*. The business must have the resources at hand to cover expenditure in this period. Once the business starts to grow, it will need to attract new resources to support that growth. Again, cash flow may be negative while this is occurring. The entrepreneur must be an effective resource manager. They must attract financial resources from investors and then make them work as hard as possible to progress the venture.

The venture has clear goals and its expectations are understood

A venture can be successful only if it is seen to be successful. This means that it must set clear and unambiguous objectives to provide a benchmark against which performance can be measured. Success can only be understood in relation to the expectations that stakeholders have for the venture. These expectations must be explicit. This will be critical in the case of investors, who will be very definite about the return they expect. The business must be sure of what its customers want if it expects them to buy its offerings. Understanding expectations is also important in dealing with employees since it is the starting point for motivating them. The entrepreneur must learn to recognise and manage the expectations of all the venture's stakeholders.

9.3 Measuring success and setting objectives

> ### Key learning outcome
>
> An understanding of the criteria used to set objectives for the entrepreneurial venture and to monitor its performance.

Ultimately, success is personal. The entrepreneurial venture is a vehicle for individual success as much as for organisational success. If it is to be an effective vehicle, the venture must be successful as a business. The performance of the venture is subject to a variety of measures including:

- *absolute financial performance* – e.g. sales, profits;
- *financial performance ratios* – e.g. profit margin, return on capital employed;
- *financial liquidity ratios* – e.g. debt cover, interest cover;
- *absolute stock market performance* – e.g. share price, market capitalisation;
- *stock market ratios* – e.g. earnings per share, dividend yield;
- *market presence* – e.g. market share, market position;
- *growth* – e.g. increase in sales, increase in profits;
- *innovation* – e.g. rate of new product introduction;
- *customer assessment* – e.g. customer service level, customer rating.

These performance indicators are quantitative and are fairly easy to measure. They provide definite goals for the venture to attain. They are *strategic* goals in that they relate to the business as a whole and refer to the position it develops in its external market as well as to purely internal criteria. An entrepreneurial venture is distinguished from a small business by the ambition of its strategic goals.

The specifics of the objectives set for the venture will depend on the type of business it is, the market in which it is operating and the stage of its development. They will be used by management to define objectives, evaluate strategic options and benchmark performance. Different businesses will set objectives in different ways: they will vary in specificity; they may be for the organisation as a whole or they may define the responsibilities of particular individuals; they may be based on agreement and consensus or they may be 'imposed' on the organisation by the entrepreneur. The way the entrepreneur defines and sets goals, and uses them to motivate and monitor performance, is an important aspect of leadership strategy.

The objectives of the firm may not be an entirely internal concern. Financial and market performance measures may form part of the agreement made with investors. They provide manageable and explicit proxies for the success of the business and indicate the returns it can hope to generate. They provide a sound and unambiguous basis for monitoring its development. They may also be used in communication with suppliers and customers to indicate the potential of the business and to elicit their support.

Key learning outcome

An appreciation of how entrepreneurial success impacts on social responsibility.

An entrepreneurial venture touches the lives of many people. All its stakeholders have an interest in its success since this success provides the means by which they can fulfil their personal goals. People have expectations about what an entrepreneurial business can achieve and how it should undertake its business. Some of these expectations are formal, others are informal. Some are explicit, others implicit. Some result from binding contracts, others from trust that has been accumulated. Entrepreneurs perform on a social stage and in creating an entire new world they must take responsibility for its ethical content as well as for its new value (this develops a theme established in section 6.2). The moral dimension of their activity cannot be ignored.

The idea of *corporate social responsibility* is one that has come to the fore of business thinking in recent years. The reasons for this interest are many, but the following factors are important. The first is a move from the 'patrician' management of the 1950s and 1960s where managers were relatively free to spend profits as they wished (and often did so to the advantage of non-investor stakeholders) to the more investor-driven management of the 1980s and 1990s, where managers are expected to concentrate on maximising investor returns. Second, concerns with environmental and development issues are growing, with the rise of non-governmental organisations (NGOs) to lobby for them, particularly with government legislators. Third, there is a belief that 'globalisation' is taking power from governments and passing it to (particularly multinational) business.

The idea of corporate social responsibility goes beyond simply defining the responsibility of the entrepreneur in terms of stakeholder expectations. After all, a profit-maximising firm may still develop rewarding relationships with stakeholders simply as a means to that profit maximisation, in which case (non-investor) stakeholder rewards are an implicit, *means-to-an-end* aspect of strategic objective setting. Advocates of social corporate responsibility generally demand that social and environmental concerns should be an explicit, *end-in-themselves* aspect of strategic objective setting along with an interest in profit creation. This issue is highly controversial. There are, broadly, four positions. At one end, there are those who reject the idea of corporate social responsibility entirely (for example, Friedman, 1962; Henderson, 2001). Rejectors argue that maximising investor return is the only real responsibility that businesses have. This position is often caricatured as a mixture of greed and complacency about world issues. This is unfair. What rejectors are claiming is that profit maximisation is the best way to ensure that resources are used in the best possible way, given individuals' freedom to choose what they want. At the other end of the spectrum are those who believe that corporate social responsibility (imposed by government if necessary) is a way to limit the power of, and even punish, business (again, especially the large multinational). This belief centres on the idea that 'business has been given too free a rein for too long; it is time it paid back'. The middle ground is occupied by those who do not particularly want to see business punished but believe that corporate social responsibility improves collective social welfare, even if it does impose some costs on business (Hutton *et al.*, 1997; De George, 1999). Finally, there are those who argue that it is actually good for businesses to adopt corporate social responsibility and that it can improve profitability (a win–win scenario) (Nash, 1995). This latter view has come to dominate among many business academics.

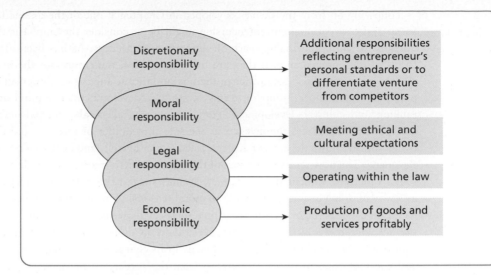

Figure 9.3 Levels of entrepreneurial responsibility

A central theme running through these four positions is the relationship between adopting standards of corporate social responsibility and resulting performance. This is an issue that can, in principle, be evaluated empirically, and is explored in the next section. It should not be forgotten that there is no real agreement between different advocates as to what, exactly, corporate social responsibility is. Avishai (1994) develops a historical account of the development of the concept. Joyner *et al*. (2002) summarises definitions of related concepts as follows:

- *Values* are the core set of beliefs and principles deemed to be desirable by a particular group.
- *Ethics* are the conception of which actions are right or wrong, what individuals should seek to do or avoid, with *business ethics* as a specific set of such views relating to business practice.
- *Corporate social responsibility* is the categories of economic, legal, ethical and discretionary activities of a business entity adapted to the values and expectations of wider society.

This section concludes with an overview of models of corporate social responsibility in strategic objective setting. An early model was developed by Carroll (1979). He suggests a four-dimensional approach to understanding corporate social responsibility, as shown in Figure 9.3.

The first dimension: the people to whom the venture has a social responsibility

Potentially, the entrepreneurial venture has a social responsibility towards all those who are affected by its activities, that is, its *stakeholder groups*. Stakeholders may be members of distinct groups but they are also individuals. The venture has responsibilities towards both individuals and organisations or groups.

Following on from the themes developed in Chapter 8, one of the distinctions between social and conventional entrepreneurship might be to consider the emphasis that different domains of entrepreneurship place on different stakeholders. As has been made clear, all forms of entrepreneurship, if they are to be successful, must consider the interests of all stakeholders, but this does not mean there is no latitude for the entrepreneur to prioritise particular stakeholder groups in terms of strategy development, communication, reward ranking and cultural development. For example, the classical principal–agent model of entrepreneurship places the investor as the sole stakeholder of interest, and the manager-owner model allows the entrepreneur to place him or herself (and dependants) at the head of the queue. The now received wisdom of the customer-first 'marketing' model is that the customer's interests come first (although cynics may suggest this is for instrumental – it works as a way of doing business – rather than moral reasons). The 'Fairtrade' model suggests that its *raison d'être* is the interest of the supplier (especially weaker, poorer suppliers, perhaps in the developing world). The 'cooperative' model (a dying organisational form, although some forms of franchise have taken on many of its characteristics) places emphasis on joint and equitable ownership by employees. Charities target specific groups within the community (these groups may include animals, the environment and social goods) as their critical responsibility. In the public sector, local government intrapreneurship sees the local community as its customer. At an intra- and international level, non-governmental organisational entre/intrapreneurship emphasises the interests of local groups around the world.

The various foci for the different forms of entrepreneurship are summarised in Figure 9.4.

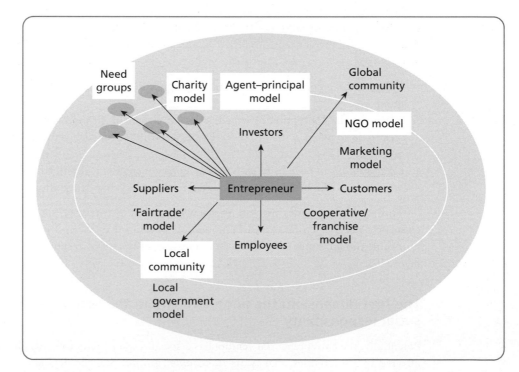

Figure 9.4 Stakeholder focus for different forms of social and commercial entrepreneurship

The second dimension: the levels of social responsibility accepted

The business may accept various types of social responsibility. These may be described as *economic*, *legal*, *moral* and *discretionary*.

Economic responsibility

Economic *responsibility* refers to the basic function of the firm and demands that it produce goods or services and sell them at a profit. This is a minimum level of responsibility. The firm must do this merely to survive within its market. Beyond this basic responsibility, however, the business will recognise a number of other responsibilities.

Legal responsibility

The firm's *legal responsibility* constrains it to operate within the law. The law under which a business operates is defined by the state. Different laws will dictate the way the business operates financially and the way it sets up contracts with other organisations and with individuals. Important examples of laws affecting business are tax and accounting laws and employment laws. A business will be subject to both *criminal* and *civil* law. If the criminal law is broken, the state will act as prosecutor. If a civil law is breached, then it is up to the injured party to bring an action.

Moral responsibilities

A business is a social organisation which operates within a framework of cultural norms. The society within which it exists has ethical standards which it believes must be upheld. These provide rules and norms which create constraints for behaviour. These constitute the firm's *moral responsibilities* and they are difficult to define. They are the unwritten rules about what should be done and what should not be done, and they may not be noticed at all until an individual or organisation breaks them. Although a society will not necessarily articulate its ethics and moral standards, those standards still form an important part of people's expectations, and those affected will react strongly if they are not adhered to.

Discretionary responsibilities

Economic, legal and moral responsibilities comprise the standard constraints operating on the actions of the business. In addition, the entrepreneur may decide to accept *discretionary responsibilities*. Discretionary responsibilities are ones the entrepreneur accepts for their venture even though it is not generally expected that businesses will accept them. They are responsibilities that go above and beyond the norm. Discretionary responsibilities may relate to the way the business treats its employees, the standards it sets for its products or the way it manages the impact of its activities on the environment. They may reflect beliefs and standards which are held dear by the entrepreneur. They may be used to distinguish the business from competitors.

The third dimension: the issues that form part of the venture's social responsibility

There are a variety of issues that the entrepreneur can accept as part of the venture's social responsibility. Minimum standards in the treatment of employees, occupational health and safety, and product liability will usually be the subject of legal regulation. Entrepreneurs frequently take a positive attitude towards wider social issues such as the treatment of the environment, relationships with developing nations, and ethnic and sexual discrimination. Occasionally, they may also take a stand on much broader issues relating to social trends such as the growth in 'consumerism'.

The fourth dimension: the venture's approach to its social responsibility

The business faces a choice in the way in which it approaches its social responsibilities. It may be *defensive*. This means that the business decides that its social responsibilities are a liability and that they hinder its performance. It may then try to avoid them and to minimise their impact. This may boost short-term profits but it can easily lead to a reaction by stakeholders, especially, but not exclusively, its employees and customers. The business must then put its efforts into defending its actions which can lead to a vicious, and expensive, circle. The more the firm seeks to avoid its responsibilities the stronger can be the reaction by stakeholders, so more effort must be put into the defence. This can easily result in a debilitating 'bunker' mentality within the business whereby it feels that its stakeholders are an enemy, rather than partners.

Alternatively, the business may decide not to go looking for social responsibilities but will accept them when confronted by them. In this it is *reactive*. The business does not see social responsibilities either as a source of advantage or as a problem, they are just something else that has to be managed. Accepting social responsibility is probably less expensive than defending against it in the long run, but in being reactive the business is allowing itself to be confronted by uncertainties that it would otherwise be able to control.

A third option is for the business to be *positive* towards its social responsibilities. It can choose to regard them not as liabilities but as opportunities and use them as a source of competitive advantage. Adopting a positive attitude towards social responsibilities brings them under control. They can be made part of the venture's strategy. They can be used to motivate employees and to build a strong relationship with customers and suppliers, or they can be used to address the wider concerns of investors and so gain their support. A positive approach to its social responsibilities can be made into a success factor for the entrepreneurial business.

Social responsibilities constrain the actions of a business. They often define what it *cannot* do rather than what it can. This does not mean that social responsibilities are bad for business. They provide a sound, and shared, set of rules within which the business community can operate. They ensure that the benefits of business activity are distributed in a way which is seen to be fair and equitable. This sustains the motivation of all stakeholders in the venture. Businesses are rarely penalised for meeting their social responsibilities positively. On the other hand, they will be punished if they are seen to evade their responsibilities. This ensures that ventures which set high standards are not penalised by being undercut by those that have lower standards.

Taking on discretionary responsibilities and being proactive with them may be a strategic move. If this meets with the approval of customers and other stakeholders, it can provide a means by which the business can make itself different from competitors and gain an advantage in the marketplace. In recognition of this fact, the entrepreneur may specify the business's social responsibilities in its mission statement.

Using discretionary responsibilities to give the business an edge need not conflict with the personal values of the entrepreneur. The entrepreneur can improve the world with those values only if the business is successful. The social responsibilities the venture accepts, and how it defines them, are not merely 'add-ons' to the entrepreneur's vision, they lie at its core. They are the character of the new world that the entrepreneur seeks to build.

Paine (1994) suggests two basic approaches to social responsibility: first, a *legal compliance strategy* in which the firm adheres to the strict letter of the law, thus avoiding costly legal penalties; and, second, an *integrity strategy*, in which the firm aspires to meet the spirit of the law, fulfilling what it sees as the intention of legislators. This framework is applied to a study of ten US ventures by Joyner *et al.* (2002). The study found that entrepreneurs were often willing to go beyond mere legal compliance.

A matrix model of corporate social responsibility was developed by Martin (2002). The vertical axis of the 2 × 2 matrix is split between 'civil foundation' on the bottom and 'frontier' on the top. The civil foundation is instrumental in that it provides a basal level of social responsibility that all firms are expected to abide by. Adherence may be by choice guided by social and cultural norms or due to legal imposition. The frontier represents behaviour that is intrinsic, in that managers act on their own initiative to adopt particular social responsibility standards above and beyond those expected of the sector as a whole. The horizontal axis is split between 'strategic adherence', in which adopting these higher standards actually increases returns to shareholders (and so is intrinsically motivated) and 'structural adherence', in which case shareholder value is reduced but society as a whole (arguably) benefits. This last category represents a barrier to social responsibility, as adherence may lead to punishment (selling of stock) by shareholders, threatening managers' rewards and, potentially, the independence of the business. A decision tree model for choices about social responsibility was suggested by Bagley (2003). The first node asks if the action is legal. If it is not, it should not be undertaken. If it is, then the next node asks if the action is in line with maximising shareholder value. If it is, then the next node asks if the action is ethical (do other stakeholders benefit?). If so, it should be undertaken. If not, then it should not. If the action does not maximise shareholder value, then the next node asks if it would be ethical *not* to undertake the action (is the imputed cost to stakeholders acceptable given the increased return to investors?). If the answer is yes, then the action should not be undertaken. If the answer is no, then the action should be considered, but investors must be informed of its consequences.

A study by Bucar and Hisrich (2001) explores whether entrepreneurs or (non-entrepreneur) business managers in Britain hold (or aspire to) higher ethical standards. He finds no significant difference between the two groups.

The contributions to Ben-Ner and Putterman (1998) are recommended for those interested in the debate about how economic priorities establish social norms, and how social norms influence economic behaviour.

9.5 Social responsibility and business performance

Key learning outcome

An appreciation of the issue of, and the difficulty in determining if, the adoption of levels of social responsibility above those required of the sector as a whole leads to an improvement in, or has a detrimental effect on, shareholder value.

Does the adoption of discretionary levels of corporate social responsibility result in an improvement or a reduction in total shareholder (investor) value? Arguments may be offered for both positions. On the one hand, a firm adopting higher levels of corporate social responsibility may develop an enhanced reputation, attracting new customers for whom such values are important. Increased sales lead to increased performance. On the other hand, introducing social and environmental objectives into the business will, at the very least, complicate managers' tasks and increase the need for co-ordination, thus raising costs. At worst, it might limit the most efficient use of resources and force the business to ignore certain new opportunities. Both of these will reduce shareholder value. The total change in shareholder value will reflect the balance of these positive and negative forces. The resulting balance is, in principle, observable. It simply requires that the correlation between adoption of social responsibility and performance be measured. However, there are several reasons why this is not as straightforward as it seems.

First of all, there needs to be an accepted definition of what corporate social responsibility is. As noted above, there is not. Different commentators prioritise different issues. Second, what do we mean when we say that a firm is adopting a particular social responsibility? The bottom line must be how much of its resources are being dedicated to delivering on this responsibility. Conventional accounting does not report on such things, not least because they are difficult to audit. Third, there is the issue of which actions are judged to be socially responsible. Do we regard them as such because they have the right motives, or because they are moral in themselves, or because they have beneficial outcomes? This is an issue explored in section 6.2, where motivist, deontological and consequentialist approaches to judging morality were discussed. Different perspectives will change the judgement of the ethical quality of a particular action. Is a firm really being ethical if it adopts corporate social responsibility because it will actually increase its profits? Is protecting the environment, for example, moral in itself, no matter what other costs it incurs? Is a firm that employs low-cost labour in the developing world right to argue that it is in fact acting with social responsibility because it is providing jobs that otherwise would not be there?

Finally we have the issue of what constitutes performance. If this is limited to financial performance (and measuring even this is not unproblematical), then it might be argued that other benefits (and costs) are being ignored. If social and environmental factors are accounted for, how are these to be measured in financial terms when there are not fully formed markets to price them. One group's (personal) estimation of the value created will differ from another's whose (again personal) values and valuations are different.

If a 'balanced scorecard' approach is taken, then *ipso facto*, firms adopting social responsibility will perform better. A number of studies have attempted to address and circumvent these issues, and research in this area is growing rapidly. A review by McWilliams and Siegel (2000) suggests that there are two sorts of study. The first looks at short-run profits after adoption of social responsibility standards, assessing, for example, the effect on share price of announcements of new standards or of failures (an example being the study by Clinebell and Clinebell, 1994). The second looks at long-run profitability by taking a cross-sectional analysis of company accounts and comparing social responsibility adoption with profits over a relatively long period (an example being the study by Waddock and Graves, 1997).

The findings have been mixed. For example, Aupperle *et al.* (1985) found no relationship between social responsibility and performance. Waddock and Graves (1997) found that profitability correlated positively with financial performance a year later. McGuire *et al.* (1988) found that performance prior to the adoption of social responsibility was important (suggesting that more successful firms were willing to adopt it), but that subsequent performance was not improved. McWilliams and Siegel themselves suggest that earlier studies are at fault because they do not take into account the effect of investment in research and development on corporate performance. Once this is taken into account, they suggest, social responsibility is largely neutral in terms of performance. Of course, a mixed picture might be expected. The demand for a general rule: 'Does undertaking socially responsible action X lead to an improved (or reduced) performance?' is probably a demand too much. Contingent factors such as the business sector, the expectations of customers, the actions of competitors and the prominence of particular social issues at the time are likely to have a significant impact and be highly variable.

How does this add up as far as the entrepreneur is concerned? Should they seek to aspire to a higher level of social responsibility? There is no clear answer. Taking on discretionary responsibilities and being proactive with them may be a strategic move. If this meets with the approval of customers and other stakeholders, it can provide a means by which the business can make itself different from competitors and gain an advantage in the marketplace (though, for some, this may negate the ethical character of the move). In recognition of this fact, the entrepreneur may specify the business's social responsibilities in its mission statement. Using discretionary responsibilities to give the business an edge need not conflict with the personal values of the entrepreneur. The entrepreneur can improve the world with those values only if the business is successful. The social responsibilities the venture accepts, and how it defines them, are not merely 'add-ons' to the entrepreneur's vision, they lie at its core. They are the character of the new world the entrepreneur seeks to build.

9.6 Understanding failure

Key learning outcome

An understanding of what business failure actually means.

Entrepreneurs are always faced with the possibility of failure. No matter how much they believe that their innovation offers new value to customers and regardless of how confident they are that they can build a business to deliver it, they will ultimately be tested by the market. However many success factors they think are present, they may be found wanting in some respects. Uncertainty and risk are always present. Statistics of business failure are widely reported and they are usually quite frightening. Yet 'failure' is not a simple notion. It implies the absence of success and, like success, it can only be understood in relation to people's goals and expectations. Failure happens when expectations are not met. It is a question of degree and means different things to different stakeholders.

From the perspective of the entrepreneur, at least eight degrees of 'failure' can be identified based on the performance of the business and the way the entrepreneur retains control of it. These are listed in order of increasing severity below.

1 The business continues to exist as a legal entity under the control of the entrepreneur

(a) The business performs well financially but does not meet the social and self-development needs of the entrepreneur

To most outsiders the business may appear to be a success. It may be performing well financially and making an impact on its market. It may be providing for the economic needs of the entrepreneur and their dependants but this does not necessarily mean it is meeting higher needs. The work necessary to keep the business running may be disrupting the entrepreneur's social life. The entrepreneur may have had unrealistic expectations about how the venture would satisfy their self-development needs. If the entrepreneur feels that they have failed in this respect, they will be demotivated, and this can have an impact on their personal performance.

(b) The business fails to achieve set strategic objectives

The business may meet the financial targets that have been set for it by the entrepreneur and its investors but even so may fail to meet the strategic targets, such as market share, growth and innovation rate set for it. This may not be of immediate concern if profits are being generated. However, it may warn of challenges ahead and potential problems with the long-term performance of the business. Much will depend on how sensitive business performance is to the strategy adopted and how flexible that strategy is.

(c) The business fails to perform as well as was planned but is financially secure

The venture may not meet the financial objectives set for it by the entrepreneur and investors but still remain financially secure. The objectives may have been quite ambitious, setting income targets which were very comfortable in relation to necessary expenditure. Although the business may not be in immediate danger, investors may feel disappointed in the returns they will receive. Planned investments may have to be forgone. The entrepreneur may be called upon to address the business's strategy and revise its plans to improve performance in the future.

(d) The business fails to perform as well as was planned and needs additional financial support

The financial performance of the business may be so weak that income cannot cover necessary expenditure. Cash flow problems will be encountered and it is likely that the business will not survive without a further injection of cash. This is likely to come from investors, but additional support may also be gleaned by agreeing special terms with customers and suppliers. In this instance the entrepreneur is likely to be called upon to address the direction of the business and the way it is being run.

If financial performance falls below a certain level, and the commitments of the business exceed its ability to meet them, then investors and creditors may lose confidence altogether. A change in management may be called for. A number of scenarios are possible.

2 The business continues to exist as an independent entity but the entrepreneur loses control

(a) The business is taken over as a going concern by new management

The business that an entrepreneur creates is separate to them in that it has its own legal and organisational identity. It is possible that the business can continue and prosper even if the entrepreneur is no longer involved in its running. The entrepreneur may leave the business for a variety of reasons. Though successful, the entrepreneur may feel that the business does not offer them sufficient challenges or they may feel that managing it does not fulfil them (as in 1(a) above). They may sell their interest to a new manager or management team and move on to do something else. If this is what the entrepreneur wants to do then it must be counted as a success. The entrepreneur may, however, be called upon to leave the business against their wishes.

If the business is not performing, its backers may decide that their interests are best served by bringing in new management with different ideas and different ways of doing things. The ability of the investors to oust the resident entrepreneur will depend on how much of the business they own, their ability to liquidate their investment and the contracts they have with the entrepreneur.

(b) The business is taken over with restructuring

As in scenario 2(a), the entrepreneur is called upon to leave. However, rather than run the business much as it was, the new management team may feel that performance can only be improved if the business undergoes a fundamental restructuring. This can involve changing its employees and making major acquisitions and divestments of assets.

3 The business does not continue to exist as an independent entity

(a) The business is taken over as a going concern and absorbed into another company

One business may be acquired by another through a takeover. It may retain some of its original character, and a modified legal status, by becoming a subsidiary of the parent. It loses its separate identity and all legal character if it is merged with the parent. In this case its employees move to work for the parent and its assets are combined with the parent's assets.

A takeover, or merger, may take place at the behest of the entrepreneur who wishes to sell their interest and move on to something else. It may also be instigated by investors who have lost confidence in the entrepreneur and the venture and wish to cut their losses by liquidating their investment. The entrepreneur may, or may not, retain an involvement by becoming a manager for the new parent.

(b) The business is broken up and its assets disposed of

Takeover and mergers take place if there is a belief that the venture has some potential, even if a completely new management approach is called for. If there is no confidence even in this,

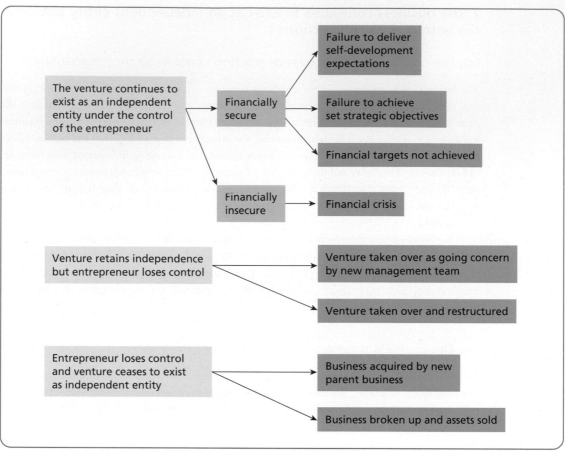

Figure 9.5 Levels of entrepreneurial failure

then the business may be broken up and its assets sold off. The proceeds are used to reimburse stakeholders. Creditors and outstanding loans take priority. The investors, i.e. the owners of the venture, are only entitled to anything left after all creditors have been paid (Figure 9.5).

Managing failure

Failure is a fact of business life. It is the possibility of failing that makes success meaningful. Failure is not always a disaster and it does not inevitably mean the end of the venture. Failure is part of the learning process. Minor failures can be positive indicators of how things might be done better. Such failures should not be ignored. They must be addressed before they become the seeds of larger failures. Success and failure exist relative to *expectations*. Failure occurs when expectations are not met. Managing success, and managing failure, has a lot to do with managing people's expectations for the venture: keeping those expectations positive, but at the same time keeping them realistic.

Summary of key ideas

- The success of the entrepreneurial venture must be understood through three dimensions: the *stakeholders* who have an interest in the venture; their *expectations* of the venture; and actual *outcomes* relative to those expectations.

- The most effective entrepreneurs define objectives for success in relation to *all* the venture's stakeholders (not just its investors) and operate with a keen sense of social responsibility.

- Many successful entrepreneurs have demanded that their businesses operate with a higher level of social responsibility than other businesses operating in their sectors.

- The issue of corporate social responsibility is complex and of growing interest. There is no clear picture as to whether, in general, accepting higher levels of responsibility increases or decreases shareholder value.

- In many ways, different types of entrepreneurship (social versus conventional) might be seen as different prioritisations of stakeholders within a general entrepreneurship framework.

- Failure has many degrees and is an integral part of venturing. Good entrepreneurs learn from failure.

Research theme

Entrepreneurs' perceptions of success

Section 9.1 developed a model of entrepreneurial success based on the venture's ability to satisfy economic, social and developmental needs, the stakeholders involved in the venture and their expectations relative to outcomes. This framework provides a basis for exploring entrepreneurs' belief in and attitudes towards success. Select a poll of entrepreneurs. These may be nascent, novice, singular or portfolio. It would be interesting to correlate beliefs across these different types of entrepreneur. Conduct a survey with the sample group, ascertaining:

- their general thoughts about success;
- whom they feel has a role in success, and who has a priority for rewards from the venture's success;
- what needs success aims to satisfy (have the entrepreneur prioritise economic, social and developmental needs);
- how the entrepreneur sees the role of expectations and how they should be managed (e.g. should the entrepreneur over-promise at the start to get stakeholders on board, or under-promise so that stakeholders will be satisfied with actual outcomes?).

For the analysis, categorise the entrepreneurs in terms of their priorities with regard to the needs that their ventures must satisfy (e.g. economic over social and developmental) and their priorities with stakeholders (e.g. investors over employees). Do entrepreneurs fall into neat 'rationalist' (self-priority – economic needs) and 'humanist' (other stakeholder – broader needs) categories, or are they more dispersed? How do the categories identified match with the entrepreneurs' development stage? How do the categories match with the entrepreneurs' management of expectations?

Key readings

The classic paper that considers different levels of organisational responsibility (and used as the basis for the discussion here) is:

Carroll, A.B. (1979) 'A three-dimensional model of corporate performance', *Academy of Management Review*, Vol. 4, No. 4, pp. 497–505.

The original is still worth reading for its clarity and expansion on ideas.

A more recent review that considers current thinking on issues relating to small business and entrepreneurial performance (not just what we measure, but how) is:

Garengo, P., Biazzo, S. and Bititchi, U.S. (2005) 'Performance measurement systems in SMEs: a review for a research agenda', *International Journal of Management Reviews*, Vol. 7, No. 1, pp. 25–47.

Suggestions for further reading

Atkinson, A.A., Waterhouse, J.H. and Wells, R.B. (1997) 'A stakeholder approach to strategic performance measurement', *Sloan Management Review*, Spring, pp. 25–37.

Aupperle, K., Carroll, A. and Hatfield, J. (1985) 'An empirical examination of the relationship between corporate social responsibility and profitability', *Academy of Management Journal*, Vol. 28, No. 2, pp. 446–63.

Avishai, B. (1994) 'What is business's social compact', *Harvard Business Review*, Vol. 72, No. 1, pp. 38–48.

Bagley, C.E. (2003) 'The ethical leader's decision tree', *Harvard Business Review*, Feb., pp. 18–19.

Ben-Ner, A. and Putterman, L. (eds) (1998) *Economics, Values, and Organization*, Cambridge: Cambridge University Press.

Bucar, B. and Hisrich, R.D. (2001) 'Ethics of business managers vs entrepreneurs', *Journal of Developmental Entrepreneurship*, Vol. 6, No. 1, pp. 59–72.

Buchholz, R.A. and Rosenthal, S.B. (2005) 'The spirit of entrepreneurship and the qualities of moral decision making: towards a unifying framework', *Journal of Business Ethics*, Vol. 60, No. 3, pp. 307–15.

Brown, D.M. and Laverick, S. (1994) 'Measuring corporate performance', *Long Range Planning*, Vol. 27, No. 4, pp. 89–98.

Carroll, A.B. (1979) 'A three-dimensional model of corporate performance', *Academy of Management Review*, Vol. 4, No. 4, pp. 497–505.

Clinebell, S.K. and Clinebell, J.M. (1994) 'The effects of advance notice of plant closures on firm value', *Journal of Management*, Vol. 20, pp. 553–64.

Dawson, S., Breen, J. and Satyen, L. (2002) 'The ethical outlook of micro-business operators', *Journal of Small Business Management*, Vol. 40, No. 4, pp. 302–13.

De George, R. (1999) *Business Ethics*. Upper Saddle River, NJ: Prentice Hall.

Dennis, W.J. and Fernald, L.W. (2001) 'The chances of financial success (and loss) from small business ownership', *Entrepreneurship Theory and Practice*, Fall, pp. 75–83.

Dollinger, M.J. (1984) 'Measuring effectiveness in entrepreneurial organisations', *International Small Business Journal*, Vol. 3, No. 1, pp. 10–20.

Douma, S. (1991) 'Success and failure in new ventures', *Long Range Planning*, Vol. 24, No. 2, pp. 54–60.

Fisscher, O., Frenkel, D. Lurie, Y and Nijhof, A. (2005) 'Stretching the frontiers: exploring the relationship between entrepreneurship and ethics', *Journal of Business Ethics*, Vol. 60, No. 3, pp. 207–9.

Friedman, M. (1962) *Capitalism and Freedom*. Chicago: University of Chicago Press.

Griffiths, B., Sirco, R.A., Barry, N. and Field, F. (2001) *Capitalism, Morality and Markets*, London: Institute of Economic Affairs.

Harrison, E.F. and Pelletier, M.A. (1995) 'A paradigm for strategic decision success', *Management Decision*, Vol. 33, No. 7, pp. 53–9.

Harrison, E.F. and Pelletier, M.A. (2000) 'Levels of strategic decision success', *Management Decision*, Vol. 38, No. 2, pp. 107–17.

Henderson, D. (2001) *Misguided Virtue: False Notions of Corporate Social Responsibility*. London: Institute of Economic Affairs.

Hutton, W. (ed.) (1997) *Stakeholding and its Critics*, Choice in Welfare No. 36. London: Institute of Economic Affairs.

Joyner, B.E., Payne, D. and Raiborn, C.A. (2002) 'Building values, business ethics and corporate social responsibility into the developing organisation', *Journal of Developmental Entrepreneurship*, Vol. 7, No. 1, pp. 113–31.

Kaplan, R.S. and Norton, D.P. (1996) 'Linking the balanced scorecard to strategy', *California Management Review*, Vol. 39, No. 1, pp. 53–79.

Longenecker, C.O., Simonetti, J.L. and Sharkey, T.W. (1999) 'Why organizations fail: the view from the front line', *Management Decision*, Vol. 37, No. 6, pp. 503–13.

Martin, R.L. (2002) 'The virtue matrix: calculating the return on corporate social responsibility', *Harvard Business Review*, Mar., pp. 68–75.

McGuire, J., Sundgren, A. and Schneeweis, T. (1988) 'Corporate social responsibility and firm financial performance', *Academy of Management Journal*, Vol. 31, No. 4, pp. 854–72.

McWilliams, A. and Siegel, D. (2000) 'Corporate social responsibility and financial perform-ance: correlation or misspecification?', *Strategic Management Journal*, Vol. 21, pp. 603–9.

Mole, K. (2000) 'Business advisers impact on SMEs', Middlesex University Discussion Paper Series: Business and Management. Available at: http://mubs.mdx.ac.uk/research/Discussion_Papers/Business_and_Management/dpapmsno_4.pdf.

Nash, L. (1995) 'The real truth about corporate values', *Public Relations Strategist*, Summer.

Nucci, A. (1999) 'The demography of business closings', *Small Business Economics*, Vol. 12, No. 1, pp. 25–9.

Osborne, R.L. (1993) 'Why entrepreneurs fail: how to avoid the traps', *Management Decision*, Vol. 31, No. 1, pp. 18–21.

Osborne, R.L. (1995) 'The essence of entrepreneurial success', *Management Decision*, Vol. 33, No. 7, pp. 4–9.

Paine, L.S. (1994) 'Managing for organisational integrity', *Harvard Business Review*, Mar./Apr., pp. 106–17.

Porter, M. and Kramer, M.R. (2002) 'The competitive advantage of corporate philanthropy', *Harvard Business Review*, Dec., pp. 56–69.

Routamaa, V. and Vesalainen, J. (1987) 'Types of entrepreneur and strategic level goal setting', *International Small Business Journal*, Vol. 5, No. 3, pp. 19–29.

Sacks, J. (ed.) (1998) *Morals and Markets*, Institute of Economic Affairs Occasional Paper No. 108. London: Institute of Economic Affairs.

Seglod, E. (1995) 'New ventures: the Swedish experience', *Long Range Planning*, Vol. 28, No. 4, pp. 45–53.

Smallbone, D. (1990) 'Success and failure in new business start-ups', *International Small Business Journal*, Vol. 8, No. 2, pp. 34–47.

Throsby, C.D. (2001) *Economics and Culture*. Cambridge: Cambridge University Press.

Waddock, S. and Graves, S. (1997) 'The corporate social performance–financial performance link', *Strategic Management Journal*, Vol. 18, No. 4, pp. 303–19.

Watson, J. and Everett, J. (1993) 'Defining small business failure', *International Small Business Journal*, Vol. 11, No. 3, pp. 35–48.

Watson, K., Hogarth-Scott, S. and Wilson, N. (1998) 'Small business start-ups: success factors and support implications', *International Journal of Entrepreneurial Behaviour and Research*, Vol. 4, No. 3, pp. 217–38.

Selected case material

> ### CASE 9.1
>
> 27 January 2006
>
> ## The polluter pays: how environmental disaster is straining China's social fabric
>
> **FIONA HARVEY AND RICHARD MCGREGOR**
>
> A week after scrambling to handle a discharge of tonnes of poisonous metals into a local river on which millions rely for drinking water, Jiang Yimin, the chief of the environment protection bureau in Hunan, south-central China, was adamant. Further spillages would be prevented, he vowed to visitors.
>
> In Mr Jiang's sights were 50 to 60 small factories producing indium, a metallic element used in the manufacture of semi-conductors and liquid-crystal display screens, near the Xiang River, about an hour by road from the provincial capital, Changsha. 'I am signing the order to close them today!' he declared.
>
> Moments later, however, Mr Jiang's assistant phoned the local environmental officials to request they show visitors the bureau's work in the area, only to be rebuffed. Permission would have to come from the county government first. It was a telling reminder that the authority of even senior officials such as Mr Jiang means little on the ground.
>
> Once upon a time China's environmental problems would scarcely have mattered beyond its borders. But the country's high-speed growth and energy-intensive development model, combined with ineffective local enforcement of anti-pollution rules, has transformed its national shortcomings into a global problem.
>
> For Beijing, meanwhile, facing increasingly well-organised and often violent protests by villagers whose land has been ruined by pollution from factories built with local government support, the environment is the cause of an ever more pressing challenge to the nation's social cohesion and industrial dynamism.
>
> Joshua Muldavin, a professor of human geography at Sarah Lawrence College in the US who has spent 20 years in rural China, mostly working on environmental issues, believes the government may already have paid an irrevocable price. 'China's fabulous growth since the 1980s was achieved through environmental destruction and social and economic polarisation which now threaten its continuation,' he says. 'There is an emerging pattern of rural unrest that challenges the very legitimacy of the Chinese state and the development path on which it has embarked.'
>
> Figures released by the Chinese government's official Xinhua news agency at the end of December found that the drinking water of 300m people, nearly one-quarter of the population, was contaminated, often by harmful chemicals. About 90 per cent of China's cities also suffer from polluted water and more than 100 cities suffered serious water shortages last year.
>
> In the last 15 years, China has hurried to establish an extensive system of environmental laws and regulations, many of them modelled on those of the west. Unlike the US, the only country that produces more greenhouse gases than China, Beijing's leaders have put the environment at the heart of their rhetoric about economic development.
>
> China's latest five-year economic blueprint lays out an ambitious plan to improve energy efficiency and enshrines in policy-making the

▶

CASE 9.1 CONT.

concept of 'green GDP' (gross domestic product) – adjusting growth figures to take account of the impact of economic activity on the environment. In theory, the work of all government officials will be judged against those yardsticks. China also has precise targets to more than double the use of natural gas, renewables and nuclear power in its primary energy mix, in an effort to wean itself off over-reliance on coal.

Such pronouncements win praise from foreign energy experts but, as Mr Jiang in Hunan could testify, the situation on the ground is very different.

The area around the Xiang River bears the ravages not just of recent spillages of toxic metals but of three to four decades of pollution from a zinc smelter, the largest in China, and assorted related factories. The landscape is littered with scores of large and small factories – the oldest built in the fifties, the newest last month – separated by rancid pools of water and small vegetable patches. The villagers say they try to sell the produce because they dare not eat it themselves.

Huddled around a mudbrick home behind a levee bank, villagers laugh sardonically when told that the environment bureau in Changsha is about to crack down on the indium plants. They are cynical about the media, too: they have conducted many interviews for local television stations but have yet to see one aired.

'We can't drink water from the river; we can't drink it from the pools on the ground, and not even from underground,' says Ma Shaomin. He hospitably rustles up some tea but then adds: 'We always offer tea, but no visitors will drink it when they come here.'

The 50 or 60 indium factories under scrutiny from Mr Jiang are mostly new, built in 2003 amid a frenzy of ramshackle construction by entrepreneurs untrammelled by official oversight at a time when the price of the metal began soaring on world markets.

The price of indium has risen about eight-fold from just above $100/kg in 2003 to nearly $900 earlier this year. Some of the latest rises are due to the closure of indium manufacturers in southern China last December after another toxic spill.

Mr Jiang admits that many county officials have shares in the factories and their huge profits, which makes his job of closing them down even harder. 'They are playing guerrilla games with us,' adds his assistant, saying the plants will close briefly, before reopening nearby, often in the shells of old abandoned factories.

Elizabeth Economy of the Council on Foreign Relations, who is the author of *The River Runs Black*, a book on China's environment, says the weakest link in anti-pollution policy is poor local enforcement but that the problem goes deeper. 'The root cause of China's environmental problem is a fundamental unwillingness on the part of both Beijing and local governments to reform the political and economic system in a way that would make doing the right thing environmentally an attractive proposition,' she says.

Energy and water are cheap, so factories simply pay low pollution fines or use the cheapest waste water treatment technologies. Corruption is endemic, she says.

Zhang Jianyu, of the Beijing office of Environmental Defence, a consultancy, agrees the issue is more complex than the conventional analysis, which blames the problem on the gap between the central government's state-of-the-art laws and poor local enforcement. Whenever he sees a new law, he says: 'I go straight to the penalties section to see whether they are severe enough.' Mostly, they are not, with penalties for even the worst breaches of anti-pollution rules rarely costing companies more than Rmb200,000 ($25,000).

China's Clean Air Act, for example, devolves responsibility for issuing permits to factories to local officials, who for the most part have an interest in keeping factories open, as they are benchmarked according to economic growth in the area.

The State Environmental Protection Administration, central government's highest anti-pollution body, by contrast, remains a weak and understaffed actor in the Beijing bureaucracy, with just 250 staff and a budget of Rmb300m. Its US equivalent has 18,000 staff and $6bn, according to Mr Zhang.

Nevertheless, it was Sepa that was held responsible after the most recent environmental crisis, the spill of toxic benzene from a petrochemical plant into the Songhua River late last year, which forced local authorities to cut off water to millions of residents in Harbin, north-east China. The Sepa minister was sacked for his handling of the issue, something that Mr Zhang compared to 'imprisoning the policeman because he could not catch the thief'.

Even the attempt to introduce 'green GDP', much admired overseas, looks less heroic when seen through the prism of Chinese domestic politics. The idea is now being piloted in 10 provinces but already the National Bureau of Statistics has said that it has not been able to find a formula for it. That isolates Sepa as it attempts to push the scheme through.

However, China's ability to solve its environmental problems, while also influencing policies in the rest of the world, should not be underestimated, according to Peter Sharratt of WSP Environmental, a consultancy.

Mr Sharratt cites the current worldwide shortage of wind turbines, which has driven up prices and constrained the growth of renewable energy in many countries. If the manufacturing of some of these products, and other technologies such as solar panels, were to be undertaken in China at low cost and also

used there, it could prompt a massive take-up of renewable energy.

The Chinese government is also collaborating with the European Union to build coal-fired power stations that will pioneer a drastic reduction in carbon dioxide emissions. The emissions will then be buried, ensuring that they do not contribute to climate change.

This is a vital issue. China has abundant coal and it is the country's default source of energy. Even by 2020, with a huge take-up in renewables, natural gas and nuclear energy, coal is expected to provide about 60 to 70 per cent of China's electricity needs.

John Ashton is the chief executive of Third Generation Environmentalism, a consultancy, and a former British diplomat who served as political adviser to Chris Patten, then Hong Kong governor, during the territory's handover. He says the EU-backed power station will have a huge impact. 'Coal is an extremely important fuel for China, and for other countries like India, as it is much cheaper than oil and often more readily available.'

Funding for environmental projects in China is becoming more readily available from sources such as the World Bank, which last month signed some of the biggest deals yet struck under a mechanism of the Kyoto protocol that funds greenhouse gas emissions reductions in developing nations. Two Chinese chemical companies will receive nearly $1bn in return for reducing emissions by 19m tonnes a year.

For the residents living around the polluted Xiang River in Hunan, change cannot come fast enough. They point up the hill to a collection of small houses, which they call 'widow's village' because most of the men have died of cancer-related diseases.

Even small improvements can win praise in such a degraded environment. Yao Yunxian, dean of the department of environmental supervision at Changsha Institute of Environmental

CASE 9.1 CONT.

Technology, has his own benchmark for measuring advances in the quality of the water in the Xiang.

In some parts of the river, he says, the water used to turn many different colours from all the different kinds of pollution. With large numbers of factories shut down by the authorities and a reduction in discharges, 'the water colour has started to turn black recently'.

That, he reckons, is progress.

Source: Fiona Harvey and Richard McGregor, 'The polluter pays: how environmental disaster is straining China's social fabric', *Financial Times*, 27 January 2006, p. 17. Copyright © 2006 The Financial Times Limited.

CASE 9.2

31 January 2006 **FT**

New Bosnia chief makes boosting economy priority

STEFAN WAGSTYL

The international community's new high representative in Bosnia, who starts work tomorrow, plans to make boosting the economy a priority.

Christian Schwarz-Schilling, a veteran German politician and businessman with long experience of the Balkans, intends to start his stint in Sarajevo with a visit next month to Germany's Cebit technology fair at the head of a group of Bosnian entrepreneurs. 'We have to create conditions for normal business to grow in Bosnia,' he said.

Mr Schwarz-Schilling, who takes over from Britain's Lord Ashdown, said his aim was to promote reforms that would create normal political and economic conditions in Bosnia. '[I want to continue reforms] to bring the population to the point of taking real ownership of their institutions and not relying on the high representative as a governor to do this job.'

The US, the European Union, Russia and other countries and agencies, which have supervised Bosnia's progress since the end of its civil war in 1995, are now pushing for a change of status in Sarajevo with plans to end the high representative's role and transfer power to local politicians. Under this plan, the EU's special representative would become the senior international figure in Sarajevo and act like a powerful ambassador, having influence but no executive powers.

Mr Schwarz-Schilling said this change could take place 'at least three months' after the October general election. But that would not end Mr Schwarz-Schilling's personal role, as he is also the EU envoy, and would remain in Sarajevo in that role.

Mr Schwarz-Schilling, 75, served for 10 years in Chancellor Helmut Kohl's government. Afterwards, he worked in Bosnia in the 1990s as a mediator between the hostile Bosnian Serb, Muslim and Croat communities.

Lord Ashdown has been an assertive figure in Bosnia, forcing local politicians to accept his will in the drive to create Bosnian state institutions above the institutions of the two entities into which Bosnia is divided – the Bosnian Serb Republic and the Muslim/Croat Federation. Lord Ashdown also pushed Bosnian leaders to accept reforms needed for talks with the EU on a stabilisation and association agreement, the entry level of co-operation that could one day lead to EU membership.

Mr Schwarz-Schilling is expected to be a more conciliatory high representative, who will try to cajole Bosnians into making the emerging institutions work. He declined to comment on Lord Ashdown's approach directly but he pointed to his own record as a mediator and said: 'The diplomacy [that has determined the shape of Bosnia since the 1995 Dayton peace agreement] has been a top-down approach. It is important that I have done ten years of bottom-up work as a mediator.'

Mr Schwarz-Schilling dismissed suggestions his age might undermine his effectiveness.

The new high representative's other responsibilities include assisting in the hunt for fugitive alleged war criminals headed by Radovan Karadzic, the former Bosnian Serb leader, and Ratko Mladic, his army chief. 'This is tremendously important. You can't really create confidence in the justice system unless you can solve this problem,' said Mr Schwarz-Schilling.

Source: Stefan Wagstyl, 'New Bosnia chief makes boosting economy priority', *Financial Times*, 31 January 2006, p. 9. Copyright © 2006 The Financial Times Limited.

Discussion points

1. Analyse Case 9.1 using the models of business responsibility developed in the chapter.

2. What are the responsibilities of entrepreneurs in building a nation or region after a major conflict?

CHAPTER 10

The entrepreneurial process

Chapter overview

This chapter is concerned with developing a model of the process by which entrepreneurs create new wealth. It suggests that entrepreneurship, in the first instance, is driven by a desire for creating change on the part of the entrepreneur. This desire for change leads the entrepreneur to bring together three contingencies – opportunity, resources and organisation – in an innovative and dynamic way.

The chapter also considers the limits of entrepreneurship and whether it extends beyond the profit-making domain to the management of artistic, social and cultural endeavours.

10.1 Making a difference: entrepreneurship and the drive for change

Key learning outcome

An understanding of the changes that entrepreneurship drives and the differences entrepreneurs make.

Entrepreneurship is about bringing about change and making a *difference*. The world is not the same after the entrepreneur has finished with it. In a narrower sense, entrepreneurship is about exploiting innovation in order to create value, which cannot always be measured in purely financial terms. Innovation in this sense goes beyond just invention. It means doing something in a way that is new, different and better.

The entrepreneur is concerned with identifying the *potential* for change for the better. He or she exists in a state of tension between the *actual* and the *possible*, that is, between what *is* and what *might be* (see Figure 10.1). This tension is manifest in three dimensions: the *financial*, the *personal* and the *social*.

The financial dimension: the potential to create new value

Entrepreneurship is an economic activity. It is concerned, first and foremost, with building stable, profitable businesses which must survive in a competitive environment. If they are to

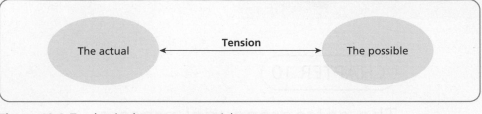

Figure 10.1 Tension in the entrepreneurial process

thrive and prosper they must add more value and deliver that value to buyers more effectively than their competitors. The new world created by the entrepreneur must be a more valuable one than that which existed previously. The opportunity exploited and the innovation present must create additional value if the venture is to be successful in the long term since it is this additional value that entrepreneurs use to attract and reward the venture's key stakeholders.

A point worth noting here is that in creating *new* value, entrepreneurship is not a 'zero-sum game'. Even though business is competitive, it is not inevitable that if an entrepreneur wins then someone else must lose. Entrepreneurship often presents win–win scenarios. As discussed in section 6.2, entrepreneurial activity increases the overall value of economies. Entrepreneurs do more than just shift existing wealth around. The new value that the entrepreneur creates can be shared in a variety of ways.

The personal dimension: the potential to achieve personal goals

Entrepreneurs are motivated by a number of factors, and although making money may motivate some, it is not the only factor, nor necessarily the most important. A sense of achievement, of having created something, or of 'making an entire new world' is often a much more significant driving factor. The entrepreneurial venture can be an entrepreneur's way of leaving their mark on the world.

Entrepreneurs may also be motivated by the challenge that the competitive environment presents, namely a chance for them to pit their wits against the wider world. Driving their own ventures also gives entrepreneurs a chance to design their own working environment and instils a sense of control. In order to understand entrepreneurial motivation it is essential to recognise that, for many entrepreneurs, what matters is not the *final destination* of the business they build up, but the *journey* – the process of creating the business.

The social dimension: the potential for structural change

Entrepreneurs operate within a wider society. In making an 'entire new world' they must, of course, have an impact on that society. They provide the society with new products and access to new services. They provide fellow citizens with jobs. They help make the economic system competitive. This may be good for the economic system as a whole, but not for the less dynamic, less efficient competitors they will drive to the wall.

All of this gives the entrepreneur power to drive changes in the structure of a society. The kind of world that an entrepreneur envisages, perhaps the possibility of a better world, can be an important factor in motivating the entrepreneur. It also means that the entrepreneur must (and often eagerly decides to) operate with some degree of social responsibility, sometimes in excess of that shown by their incumbent competitors. The kind of world that the entrepreneur would like to see is often a part of their *vision* for their firm and for the future. This vision may be enshrined in the mission that the organisation sets itself.

10.2 The entrepreneurial process: opportunity, organisation and resources

> ### Key learning outcome
>
> An understanding of the factors in the process of entrepreneurial value creation.

Every entrepreneurial venture is different, with its own history. Its successes are the result of it having faced and addressed specific issues in its own way. Nonetheless, it is useful to consider the process of entrepreneurship in a generalised way since this gives us a framework for understanding how entrepreneurship creates new wealth in several terms and for making sense of the detail in particular ventures. It also provides us with a guide for decision making when planning new ventures.

The approach to the entrepreneurial process that will be described here is based on four interacting *contingencies*. The entrepreneur is responsible for bringing these together to create new value. A contingency is simply something which *must* be present in the process but can make an appearance in an endless variety of ways. The four contingencies in the entrepreneurial process are the *entrepreneur*, a market *opportunity*, a business *organisation* and *resources* to be invested (Figure 10.2).

The entrepreneur

The entrepreneur is the individual who lies at the heart of the entrepreneurial process, that is, the manager who drives the whole process forward. Entrepreneurs often act singly but in many instances *entrepreneurial teams* are important. Different members of the team may take on different roles and share responsibilities. They may be from the same family, for example the Benetton siblings from northern Italy who revolutionised the manufacture of textiles, or alternatively, they may be from an existing management team who have joined together to initiate their own venture, perhaps through a management buyout.

Opportunity

An opportunity is the gap left in a market by those who currently serve it. It represents the potential to serve customers better than they are being served at present. The entrepreneur is responsible for scanning the business landscape for unexploited opportunities or possibilities that something important might be done both *differently* from the way it is done at the moment and, critically, *better* than it is done at the moment. The improved way of doing it is the innovation that the entrepreneur presents to the market. If customers agree with the entrepreneur that it is an improvement on what exists already and if the entrepreneur can supply the innovation effectively and profitably then new value can be created.

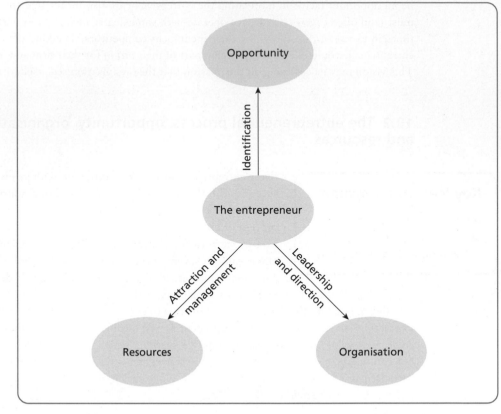

Figure 10.2 The entrepreneurial process: opportunity, resources and organisation

Organisation

In order to supply the innovation to the market, the activities of a number of different people must be co-ordinated. This is the function of the organisation that the entrepreneur creates. Organisations can take on a variety of forms depending on a number of factors, such as their size, their rate of growth, the industry they operate in, the types of product or service they deliver, the age of the organisation and the culture that it adopts.

Entrepreneurial organisations are characterised by strong, often charismatic, leadership from the entrepreneur. They may have less formal structures and systems than their more bureaucratic, established counterparts. In many respects the entrepreneurial organisation is still learning, but rather than judge this to be a handicap the business turns it into a strength by being receptive to new ideas and responsive to the need for change.

Current thinking on entrepreneurial organisations tends not to draw a hard and fast distinction between those inside the organisation and those who are on the outside. It has been found more productive to think in terms of the organisation in a wider sense as being a *network* of relationships between individuals, with the entrepreneur sitting at the centre. This network stretches beyond just the individuals who make up the formal company, to include people and organisations outside the venture such as customers, suppliers and investors. The relationships that make up the network are very diverse. Some are defined by contracts, whereas others are defined by open markets; some are formal and some informal; some are based on self-interest, whereas others are maintained by altruism; some are driven by short-term considerations, and others by long-term interests.

In the network view, then, the organisation is a fluid, defined by a *nexus of relationships*. Its boundaries are permeable. The idea of a network provides a powerful insight into how entrepreneurial ventures establish themselves, how they locate themselves competitively, and how they sustain their position in their market by adding value to people's lives.

Resources

The final contingency in the entrepreneurial process is resources. This includes the money that is invested in the venture, the people who contribute their efforts, knowledge and skills to it, and *physical assets* such as productive equipment and machinery, buildings and vehicles. Resources also include *intangible assets* such as brand names, company reputation and customer goodwill. All these features can be subject to *investment*. One of the key functions of the entrepreneur is to attract investment to the venture and to use it to build up a set of assets which allow the venture to supply its innovation competitively and profitably.

The entrepreneur plays a critical role in identifying opportunity, building and leading the organisation, and attracting and managing resources. The three external contingencies quickly develop a momentum of their own and become independent of the entrepreneur at the centre. As the organisation grows, it develops processes and systems, and the people within it adopt distinct roles. The entrepreneur must delegate responsibility within the organisation and specialist functions may take over some aspects of the entrepreneur's role. For example, the marketing department may identify opportunities and innovate the firm's offerings to take advantage of them; the finance department may assume responsibility for attracting investment. In this way, entrepreneurial ventures quickly take on a life of their own. They become quite distinct from the entrepreneur who established them. Consequently, the entrepreneur must constantly address the question of their own role within the organisation.

10.3 The entrepreneurial process: action and the dynamics of success

> ### Key learning outcome
>
> A recognition that entrepreneurship is a dynamic process in which success fuels success.

The entrepreneurial process results from the *actions* of the entrepreneur. It can only occur if the entrepreneur acts to develop an innovation and promote it to customers. The entrepreneurial process is *dynamic*. Success comes from the contingencies of the entrepreneur, the opportunity, the organisation and resources coming together and supporting each other over time. The entrepreneur must constantly focus the organisation on to the opportunity that has been identified. They must mould the resources to hand to give the organisation its shape and to ensure that those resources are appropriate for pursuing the particular opportunity. These interactions are the fundamental elements of the entrepreneurial process and together they constitute the foundations of the *strategy* adopted by the venture.

Table 10.1 An outline of organisational assets, structure, process and culture for three global entrepreneurial businesses

Organisation	McDonald's	The Body Shop	Microsoft
Opportunity pursued	Desire for fast, convenient, consistent meals	Desire for toiletries in convenient packaging; a concern for the environment	Desire to process information
Assets	Brand name, outlets, locations, people	Brand name, outlets, locations, people	People, knowledge, patents, brand name
Structure	Series of production/ retail outlets	Series of retail outlets	Project teams based at one location
Process	Production and distribution standardised at outlets. Central financing and marketing	Production centralised. Distribution through outlets. Promotion largely by store presence	Product development, production, distribution and marketing centralised
Culture	Positive attitude, concern for quality, customer focus	Attitude of concern. Emphasis on wider social responsibility for organisation	Innovative and creative 'technophilia'. Emphasis on managerial informality

Opportunity–organisation fit

The nature of the opportunity that is being pursued defines the shape that the organisation must adopt. Every organisation built by an entrepreneur is different. Organisations are complex affairs and there are a variety of ways in which they might be described and understood. The essential features are the *assets* of the organisation, that is, the things which it possesses; its *structure*, namely how it arranges communication links (both formal and informal) within itself; its *processes*: how it *adds value* to its inputs to create its *outputs*; and its *culture*, that is, the attitudes, beliefs and outlooks that influence the way people behave within the organisation (see Table 10.1).

Assets, structure, process and culture are not separate parts of an organisation. They are merely different perspectives we may adopt in describing it. These four perspectives on the organisation form a unified whole which must be appropriate for the opportunity that the organisation is pursuing. The organisation must be shaped to *fit* the market gap that defines the opportunity.

Resource–organisation configuration

Resources are the things that are used to pursue opportunity. They include *people*, *money* and *productive assets*. In a sense, an organisation is 'just' a collection of resources, although this does not exhaust possibilities for its description. The *configuration* of the resources is the way in which a particular mix of resources is brought together and blended to form the organisation's assets, structure, process and (through the attitude of the people who make it up) its culture.

Resource–opportunity focus

The entrepreneur must decide what resources will make up the organisation; for example, its mix of capital, how this will be converted into productive assets, and the nature and skills of the people who will make it up are all matters to be decided by the entrepreneur in the first instance. If the organisation is to develop the assets, structure, process and culture that will enable it to fit with its opportunity then the resource mix must be correctly balanced.

Entrepreneurs must be active in attracting resources such as suitably qualified employees, financial backing in the form of investors' money, and the support of customers and suppliers. Even so, they usually find that they do not have access to the same level of resources as established players in a market and, because their risks may be higher, they will find the resources to be more expensive. If they are to compete successfully then entrepreneurs must make the resources they can get hold of work much harder than perhaps many established players do. The entrepreneur must be single-minded and *focus* those resources definitely and unambiguously on to the opportunity that has been identified since the performance of the entrepreneurial organisation depends on how well the contingencies of opportunity, organisation and resources are linked together (Figure 10.3).

Learning organisations

These three aspects of the entrepreneurial process – making the organisation *fit* the opportunity it aims to exploit, *configuring* the resources to shape the organisation and *focusing* the

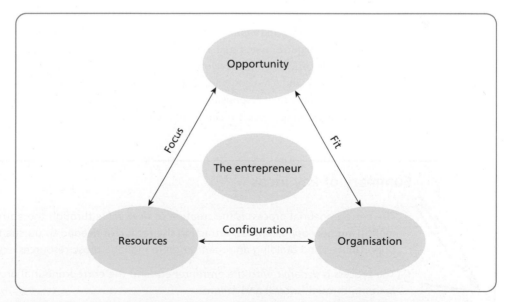

Figure 10.3 The entrepreneurial process: focus, fit and configuration

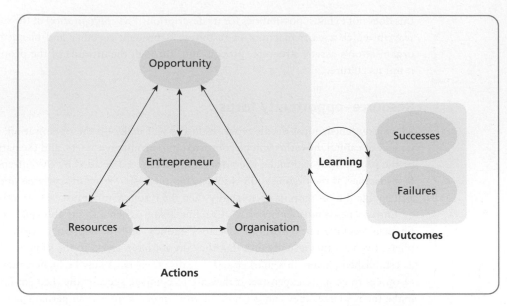

Figure 10.4 The entrepreneurial organisation constantly learns from its successes and failures

resources in pursuit of the opportunity – are not reflected in separate spheres of activity. They merely provide different perspectives on the same underlying management process. However, they do illuminate the essence of the entrepreneur's task and the direction their leadership must take. That leadership must be applied *constantly* since organisations are fluid things and, left to themselves, they can lose their shape and sense of direction. Furthermore, the entrepreneurial organisation must be a *learning* organisation. That is, it must not only *respond* to opportunities and challenges but also *reflect* on the outcomes that result from that response and *modify* future responses in the light of experience. The venture cannot afford to acquire assets and set up structures and systems which are incapable of evolving as the organisation develops. Assets and structures must be modified as the organisation grows and changes and, critically, learns from its successes and failures. The entrepreneur must take responsibility for stimulating the firm to change in the light of experience. This learning process is shown in Figure 10.4.

Summary of key ideas

- The entrepreneurial process is the creation of *new value* through the entrepreneur identifying new *opportunities*, attracting the *resources* needed to pursue those opportunities and building an *organisation* to manage those resources.

- The process is *dynamic* with the entrepreneur and the entrepreneurial organisation learning through *success* and *failure*.

Research themes

Theorising about processes

The entrepreneurial process is one of the core aspects of entrepreneurial research. Consider the model of the entrepreneurial process developed in this chapter, in terms of its theoretical and methodological foundations. What paradigm does it represent? What methodologies would be appropriate for validating and developing the model? Could the model be integrated into other paradigmatic approaches? In particular, ask whether it might be used as an interpretive framework for non-positivistic approaches. Could it be used to make sense of cognitive maps of entrepreneurs' perceptions of the issues they face in developing their ventures such as opportunity identification, resource acquisition, organisation creation and competition? Primary information may be gained from interviews with practising entrepreneurs.

Types of entrepreneur and the entrepreneurial process

Chapter 2 discussed various types of entrepreneur. A distinction was made between singular, sequential and portfolio entrepreneurs. Use the contingency model developed in this chapter to propose generic issues in the development of singular, sequential and portfolio ventures, emphasising the contingencies of the entrepreneur, opportunity, resources, organisation, fit, focus and configuration as a guide. Use case studies of each type of venture as a source of information to develop real examples of the issues identified. How do they differ for each type of venture? What are the implications for each type of venture? Are the issues generic across each type of venture? How might these affect the need for external support for different types of venture?

Key readings

Two highly influential studies that helped to establish the notion of an 'entrepreneurial process' that make good preparatory reading are:

Bhave, M.P. (1994) 'A process model of entrepreneurial venture creation', *Journal of Business Venturing*, Vol. 9, No. 3, pp. 223–42.

Gartner, W.B. (1985) 'A conceptual framework for describing the phenomenon of new venture creation', *Academy of Management Review*, Vol. 10, No. 4, pp. 696–706.

Suggestions for further reading

Batstone, S. and Pheby, J. (1996) 'Entrepreneurship and decision-making: the contribution of G.L.S. Shackle', *International Journal of Entrepreneurial Behaviour and Research*, Vol. 2, No. 2, pp. 34–51.

Bouchiki, H. (1993) 'A constructivist framework for understanding entrepreneurial performance', *Organisation Studies*, Vol. 14, No. 4, pp. 549–70.

Brockner, J., Higgins, E.A. and Low, M.B. (2004) 'Regulatory focus theory and the entrepreneurial process', *Journal of Business Venturing*, Vol. 19, No. 2, pp. 203–20.

Fayolle, A. (2002) 'Insights to research on the entrepreneurial process from a study on perceptions of entrepreneurship and entrepreneurs', *Journal of Enterprising Culture*, Vol. 10, No. 4, pp. 257–75.

Hill, R. (1982) 'The entrepreneur: an artist masquerading as a businessman?', *International Management*, Vol. 37, No. 2, pp. 21–6.

Jones, M.V. and Coviello, N.E. (2005) 'Internationalisation: conceptualising an entrepreneurial process of behavior in time', *Journal of International Business Studies*, Vol. 36, No. 3, pp. 284–303.

Kodithuwakku, S.S. and Rosa, P. (2002) 'The entrepreneurial process and economic success in a constrained environment', *Journal of Business Venturing*, Vol. 17, No. 5, pp. 431–65.

Lessem, R. (1978) 'Towards the interstices of management: developing the social entrepreneur', *Management Education and Development*, Vol. 9, pp. 178–88.

Selected case material

CASE 10.1

25 January 2006

A shot of rum turns crisis into opportunity

ANDY WEBB-VIDAL

When Alberto Vollmer appeared with Hugo Chávez earlier this month on the Venezuelan president's Sunday television show, viewers could have been forgiven for thinking someone had handed out the wrong script.

At first glance, the president's supporters might have considered the tall and fair-haired Mr Vollmer as just the sort of 'rancid oligarch' that the rumbustious Mr Chávez regularly insists is plotting the overthrow of his leftist 'revolution' for the poor.

But, instead of grilling a hapless victim, Mr Chávez heaped praise on Mr Vollmer as a model entrepreneur. It would seem that Mr Chávez shares common ground with the high priests of Harvard Business School.

And for good reason: Mr Vollmer's management of Ron Santa Teresa, a rum company, is exemplary, both in turning round a near-bankrupt enterprise and in piloting it through a sea of social and political obstacles that would have left many businesses adrift.

Today, Venezuela's Santa Teresa produces one of the world's finest premium rums, unique in its distilling method, regularly winning medals for flavour.

Mr Vollmer, 37, has strong feelings about the social role of an entrepreneur. 'It is the responsibility of those with most talent, wealth and vision to safeguard society's health.' He warns: 'To not pay attention to this reality can lead to enormous costs in the long term.'

The road to success for Mr Vollmer has been an unusual one. After college in France and training as a civil engineer he worked for four years in a Caracas barrio, or slum, helping the poor to build homes. He eschewed the rum business that had been passed down through four generations to his father.

The Santa Teresa hacienda, or estate, located in a lush valley 60 km west of the capital, was founded in 1796. It was acquired by Mr Vollmer's great-great grandfather, a German adventurer. Santa Teresa began to produce rum in 1896, and modernised its distillery through the 20th century. In the 1970s it expanded its portfolio of rums and forged an alliance with a local whisky distributor.

But the company suffered in Venezuela's volatile economy. Currency fluctuations led to financial problems, whisky imports crimped the rum market and Santa Teresa faced tougher competition. Ron Cacique and Pampero, the two main competitors, were taken over by Seagram and United Distillers, respectively. (Diageo later took over United Distillers.)

In an attempt to hold its position, Santa Teresa sold 20 per cent of its shares to Allied Domecq. But after a clash of management styles and a succession of chief executive officers, Santa Teresa had lost its sense of direction.

It was not until he entered the Santa Teresa distillery in 1996 as a bottling supervisor that Mr Vollmer realised the source of the family's wealth was on the rocks. The banks were calling in overdue loans, and some board members were plotting. 'It was in bad shape,' recalls Mr Vollmer.

Mr Vollmer and his brother, Henrique, decided to propose a management takeover plan to their father, who was then Venezuela's ambassador to the Vatican. 'We got on the first plane to Rome and we said to him: "If the company is to be saved we need a major restructuring, and soon",' recalls Mr Vollmer. 'He agreed.'

In 1999 the board granted Mr Vollmer full decision-making powers, and he began a painful restructuring. 'It was a critical moment. We had lost two-thirds of our capital and we had $25m in overdue debts,' he says. 'The company didn't know if it was a producer or an importer.' Mr Vollmer fended off threats to call in the receivers and restructured outstanding loans. Crucially, he also refocused the mission of the company.

'The aim was to refocus on our core product – rum – and dignify the brand,' he adds. Most of the company's 260 products were eliminated, leaving only 17. Mr Vollmer says: 'We focused on them and grew by 25 per cent in three months.'

While Santa Teresa's sales since 1998 have steadily risen, to a projected $39m this year, its margins have been transformed. After several years in the red, the company recorded a profit of just over $1m in 2001. This year Mr Vollmer forecasts it will reach almost $5m.

The world rum market accounts for about 60m cases per year, but Santa Teresa's strategy is to aim for the top quartile of the market, specifically drinkers who favour premium rums. Rum used to be seen as a commodity favoured by sailors, and in Venezuela the drink of prestige is still whisky. But trends are changing.

Exports are expanding. From only 2 per cent of total sales five years ago, export revenue is forecast to reach 15 per cent this year.

Turning around Santa Teresa's finances, however, has been only half the challenge. Venezuela under Mr Chávez, in power for the past seven years, has been gripped by political turmoil, presenting perhaps the toughest business environment in the Americas bar Cuba.

'We survived the restructuring. But immediately a new front opened up: the social one,' says Mr Vollmer. 'In February 2000, only 15 days after completing the debt restructuring with the banks, we were invaded.'

CASE 10.1 CONT.

About 250 local families took over 30 hectares of the 3,000 ha estate, demanding housing. The land invasion was organised by a former soldier and comrade-in-arms from Mr Chávez's military days. Encouraged by the government, there has been a surge in land invasions in recent years.

Enter Mr Vollmer's experience in the Caracas slum. 'We had to rethink our ideas. I had learnt a lot about the problems in the barrios. It was clear: if we didn't invest heavily in the social area, we were not going to survive.'

Mr Vollmer and his closest managers offered to donate the land, on the condition that the company design a housing project. Today, the area has about 100 plots with family homes.

Mr Vollmer, however, argued that what was needed was not philanthropy, but sustainable development. 'We completed the housing project but realised that we had to invest in the community to avoid this happening again.' Santa Teresa has experimented with local tourism to develop the adjacent town, blighted by unemployment, and sponsored sport and medical facilities.

Perhaps the biggest test came in 2003, when members of a local gang attacked one of Santa Teresa's security guards. Mr Vollmer's response was again enlightened: he proposed to two of the youngsters that either they work for three months without pay or they would be handed over to the police. The whole 20-strong gang turned up to work.

The idea was christened Project Alcatraz, and adjusted to allow the youths to work in the morning and attend social values classes in the afternoon. Since Alcatraz's inception, four gangs have passed through – and the local incidence of crime has fallen by 35 per cent.

Pedro Gallardo, 32, who spent 18 months in Project Alcatraz, says: 'Alcatraz has been fantastic. Your wallet wouldn't be safe in your pocket when I was around. I have learnt to be less of a rebel.'

Alcatraz has now been expanded to include a housing construction workshop. 'It is an issue of turning a crisis into an opportunity,' says Mr Vollmer, who adds that while Santa Teresa invests about 2 per cent of its profits in the social projects, it has attracted about three times that amount from other sources.

The Andean Development Corporation, or CAF, was the first institution to back Project Alcatraz. Ana Botero, CAF's director for cultural and community development, says it is a model that should be replicated elsewhere. Mr Vollmer has already been invited by Colombia to advise on its programme to return guerrilla fighters to civilian life.

Experts are also convinced that the model adopted by Santa Teresa is not just prudent politics, but also the most appropriate blueprint for business success in places with multiple problems such as Venezuela.

'The management of Santa Teresa has wisely recognised that its viability and profitability are dependent not only on its ability to produce a superior product, but also to generate social value for its surrounding community,' says Professor James Austin of Harvard Business School's Social Enterprise Initiative. 'Generating business and social value synergistically is the new paradigm for success throughout Latin America.'

Mr Vollmer is certain Mr Chávez would agree.

Source: Andy Webb-Vidal, 'A shot of rum turns crisis into opportunity', *Financial Times*, 25 January 2006, p. 11. Copyright © 2006 The Financial Times Limited.

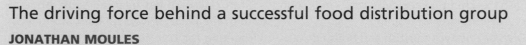

CASE 10.2

21 January 2006   FT

The driving force behind a successful food distribution group

JONATHAN MOULES

When Mustafa Kiamil has a problem, he does something about it.

In 1989, Jenny's Burgers, his family's fast food restaurant chain, had trouble getting regular supplies of tinned and fresh produce, so he set up his own catering delivery business.

Sixteen years later, JJ Fast Food Distribution is operating from a six acre purpose-built site in an Enfield industrial park, delivering tinned and frozen food across a 100 mile radius.

Among its claims to fame, JJ is the largest distributor of chips in London.

The business model has some similarities to that of the Ryanair, the budget airline. JJ's fleet of 200 delivery lorries consist of just two brands, making maintenance simple. The lorries are serviced and refuelled on site, minimising the time they spend off the road. JJ's on-site 68,000 litre fuel store also means the company is less exposed to the fluctuations in petrol prices.

Efficiencies in vehicle operations alone adds another 6 per cent to the bottom line, according to Mr Kiamil, who was named this year's Credit Suisse Entrepreneur of the Year. 'We have just taken a very old industry and done it differently.'

Recently his problem became finding truck drivers. Changes in the rules for heavy goods vehicle (HGV) licences limited the number of hours drivers were allowed to be on the road.

The subsequent reduction in earning capacity has dissuaded many British workers from becoming truck drivers, encouraged existing drivers to change careers and made competition between companies that need drivers more intense, according to Mr Kiamil.

'It became unfashionable to be a driver. Those that would work were spoilt for choice, wanted double the money and would change companies at the drop of a hat.'

As a result, Mr Kiamil started looking outside the UK for staff. The expansion of the European Union last May opened up the opportunity of employing Polish workers, many of whom had an equivalent of an HGV licence, earned during national service in the army.

His Polish workers had an excellent work ethic. Some even worked for him while building their own businesses. But there were problems with JJ bringing people over.

Firstly, there was the language barrier. A key way that JJ tries to differentiate from its competition is through politeness with customers and friendly service, so the Polish drivers needed good conversational English as well as being able to communicate with the operational team back at headquarters.

Secondly, Mr Kiamil was concerned about experience on the road.

'We knew that their driving licences were correct but they often get them purely by joining the army and it didn't mean that they had driven a truck.

'A lot of our competitors saw they had their driving licences and just put them in a truck. As far as we were concerned, if they had driven before it was on the other side of the road and they might have just been behind a wheel of a tractor.

'We said if we are going to do this, let's do it properly.' As a result, Mr Kiamil ensured that every Polish driver received a half-day's

▶

CASE 10.2 CONT.

English teaching every Saturday and four weeks of lorry driving training.

Divisions between British and Polish drivers was also a concern, so the most experienced of JJ's existing hauliers were assigned an eastern European recruit to ride in their cab until they knew the ropes. He also insisted that the Polish drivers earned the same wage as the rest of the staff.

'We didn't want to make them feel exploited. They earned the same as other drivers throughout the training. But it was made clear that, if they didn't make the grade, then we would put them on as a driver's mate permanently and they would earn an appropriate salary.

'As time went on, they found out that other companies didn't do that and so that earned us a lot of loyalty from our drivers.'

JJ started with a handful of Polish drivers and is now up to 70, more than a third of the team.

The intensive language courses have now stopped. 'We found that we can be a little more selective about who we employ, so we now only take Polish workers who already speak English.'

Staff retention has been an issue. About a third of the Polish drivers go back after a year of working for JJ to the family they have left behind, often having earned enough money to build a better home back in Poland.

This is not necessarily a problem, Mr Kiamil says, since often those that leave will send a brother or a cousin to replace them. This is encouraged by Mr Kiamil.

'I know it sounds old-fashioned but work is about people dealing with people,' he says.

'If somebody brings in a member of their family with a recommendation, they tend to make good employees who stay with the company.'

Not all JJ's Polish staff return home. The company has had its first marriage between a Polish driver and one of the British staff.

As Mr Kiamil notes: 'This is a family business.'

Source: Jonathan Moules, 'The driving force behind a successful food distribution group', *Financial Times*, 21 January 2006, p. 20. Copyright © 2006 The Financial Times Limited.

Discussion point

1. Apply the model of the entrepreneurial process to (a) the turnaround of a Venezuelan drinks company and (b) a food distribution group.

CHAPTER 11

The nature of business opportunity

Chapter overview

This chapter presents an examination of the starting point for the entrepreneurial process, that is, the business opportunity. Entrepreneurs are motivated by the pursuit of opportunity. An analogy is developed through which a business opportunity can be pictured as a gap in the landscape created by existing business activities. The different types of innovation that can fill that gap, and so offer a means of exploiting opportunity, are considered. It is recognised that exploiting opportunities creates new wealth which can be distributed to the venture's stakeholders.

11.1 The landscape of business opportunity

Key learning outcome

An understanding of what comprises a business opportunity.

All living systems have *needs*. At a minimum, animals need food and oxygen, plants need sunlight and water. Human beings are different from many living organisms in that we are not content simply to survive using the things nature places to hand. We build highly structured societies and within these societies we join together to create *organisations*. Human organisations take on a variety of forms. However, they all exist to co-ordinate *tasks*. This co-ordination allows people to specialise their activities and to collaborate in the production of a wide variety of *goods* (a word taken to mean both physical products and services). Goods have *utility* because they can satisfy human needs. The products produced in the modern world can be used to satisfy a much more sophisticated range of human wants and needs, and to satisfy them more proficiently, than can the raw materials to be found in nature.

An organisation is an arrangement of *relationships* in that it exists in the spaces between people. Organisations exist to address human needs. Their effectiveness in doing this is a function of the form adopted by the organisation and the way it works. As the number of people involved increases, so too do the ways of organising them. In fact, the possibilities quickly become astronomical. This leads to a simple conclusion: whatever the organisational arrangement is at the moment, there is probably a *better* way of doing things. Even if, by chance, we did find the optimum arrangement, it would not stay so for long. The world is not static. Technological progress would quickly change the rules.

Ideas from classical economics suggest that the optimal (that is, the most productive) organisation is one in which individuals work to maximise their own satisfaction from the goods available and freely exchange those goods between themselves. Such behaviour is said to be *economically rational*. While this provides a powerful framework for thinking about economic relationships, it is clearly only an approximation. People gain satisfaction from a variety of things, not all are exchanged through markets (how much does a beautiful sunset, or a personal sense of achievement cost?). Nor is it obviously the case that individuals will maximise their own utility without any consideration towards their fellows. We can, and often do, act from altruistic motives.

Even if we *wanted* to act rationally, we probably could not. We simply do not have access to the information we would need to make decisions on purely rational lines. If all the information *were* available, individuals would still be limited in their ability to process and analyse it. In response to this, some economists talk of *satisficing* behaviour. That is, individuals aim to make the best decision available given a desire to address a wider sphere of concerns than purely economic self-satisfaction and taking into account limitations in knowledge.

An opportunity, then, is the possibility to do things both *differently* from and *better* than how they are being done at the moment. In economic terms, *differently* means an innovation has been made. This might take the form of offering a new product or of organising the company in a different way. *Better* means the product offers a *utility*, in terms of an ability to satisfy human needs, that existing products do not. The new organisational form must be more *productive*, i.e. more efficient at using resources than existing organisational forms. Yet the decisions as to what is different and whether it is better are not made by economic robots. Both entrepreneurs and the consumers who buy what they offer are social beings who engage in satisficing behaviour. They must also base their decisions on the knowledge they have to hand, and their ability to use it. Furthermore, they make their decisions while following the rules they have laid down for themselves and the rules of the culture that shapes their lives.

We may think of business opportunity as being rather like a *landscape* representing the possibilities open to us. As we look across the landscape we will see open ground, untouched and full of new potential. We may see areas which are built up, leaving few new opportunities to be exploited. We will see other areas which are built up but where the buildings are old and decrepit, waiting to be pulled down and for something new built in their places. Effective entrepreneurs know the landscape in which they are operating. They know where the spaces are and how they fit between the built-up areas. They know which buildings can be pulled down and which are best left standing. Critically, they know where to move in and start building.

11.2 Innovation and the exploitation of opportunity

A business opportunity is the *chance* to do something differently and better. An innovation is a *way* of doing something differently and better. Thus an innovation is a *means* of exploiting a business opportunity. Innovation has a definite meaning in economics. All goods (whether physical products or services) are regarded as being made up of three factors: *natural raw materials*, *physical and mental labour*, and *capital* (money). An innovation is a new combination of these three things. Entrepreneurs, as innovators, are people who create new combinations of these factors and then present them to the market for assessment by consumers. This is a technical conceptualisation of what innovation is about. It does not give the practising entrepreneur much of a guide to what innovation to make, or how to make it, but it should warn that innovation is a much broader concept than just *inventing* new products. It also involves bringing them to market. Some important areas in which valuable innovations might be made are discussed below.

New products

One of the most common forms of innovation is the creation of a new product. This may exploit an established technology or it may be the outcome of a whole new technology. The new product may offer a radically new way of doing something or it may simply be an improvement on an existing theme. David Packard built a scientific instrumentation and information processing business empire, Hewlett-Packard, based on advanced scientific developments. Frank Purdue (founder of the major US food business Purdue Chickens), on the other hand, built his business by innovating in an industry whose basic product was centuries, if not millennia, old: the farmed chicken. Whatever the basis of innovation, the new product must offer the customer an *advantage* if it is to be successful: a better way of performing a task, or of solving a problem, or a better quality product.

Products are not simply a physical tool for achieving particular ends. They can also have a role to play in satisfying *emotional* needs. *Branding* is an important aspect of this. A brand name reassures the consumer, draws ready-made associations for them and provides a means of making a personal statement. The possibility of innovations being made through branding should not be overlooked. The British entrepreneur Richard Branson, for example, has been active in using the Virgin brand name on a wide variety of product areas following its initial success in the music industry. To date, it has been used to create a point of difference on, among other things, record labels, soft drinks and personal finance products.

New services

A service is an *act* which is offered to undertake a particular task or solve a particular problem. Services are open to the possibility of new ideas and innovation just as much as physical products. For example, the American entrepreneur Frederick Smith created the multi-million dollar international business Federal Express by realising a better way of moving parcels between people.

Like physical products, services can be supported by the effective use of branding. In fact, it is beneficial to stop thinking about 'products' and 'services' as distinct types of business and to recognise that *all* offerings have product and service aspects. This is important because it is possible to innovate by adding a 'customer service' component to a physical product to make it more attractive to the user. Similarly, developments in product technology allow new service concepts to be innovated.

New production techniques

Innovation can be made in the way in which a product is manufactured. Again, this might be by developing an existing technology or by adopting a new technological approach. A new production technique provides a sound basis for success if it can be made to offer the end user new benefits. It must either allow them to obtain the product at lower cost, or to be offered a product of higher or more consistent quality, or to be given a better service in the supply of the product. An important example here is Rupert Murdoch's drive for change in the way newspapers were produced in the 1980s. Production is not just about technology. Increasingly, new production 'philosophies' such as just-in-time (JIT) supply and total quality management (TQM) are providing platforms for profitable innovation.

New operating practices

Services are delivered by operating practices which are, to some extent, routinised. These routines provide a great deal of potential for entrepreneurial innovation. Ray Kroc, the founder of McDonald's, for example, noted the advantages to be gained in standardising fast-food preparation. As with innovations in the production of physical products, innovation in service delivery must address customer needs and offer them improved benefits, for example easier access to the service, a higher quality service, a more consistent service, a faster service, a less disruptive service.

New ways of delivering the product or service to the customer

Customers can only use products and services they can access. Consequently, getting distribution right is an essential element in business success. It is also something which offers a great deal of potential for innovation. This may involve the *route* taken (the path the product takes from the producer to the user), or the *means* of managing its journey.

A common innovation is to take a more direct route by cutting out distributors or intermediaries. A number of successful entrepreneurial ventures have been established on the basis of getting goods directly to the customer. This may be an indirect way into high street retailing, for example Richard Thalheimer in the USA with the Sharper Image catalogue or the Littlewoods chain in the UK (however, the closure of Littlewood's Index stores in 2005 is a good example of Shumpetarian 'creative destruction' in action). Another approach is to focus on the distribution chain and specialise in a particular range of goods. This type of 'category busting' focus has allowed Charles Lazarus to build the toy retail outlet Toys 'Я' Us into a worldwide concern.

New means of informing the customer about the product

People will only use a product or service if they *know* about it. Demand will not exist if the offering is not properly promoted to them. Promotion consists of two parts: a *message*, what is said, and a *means*, the route by which that message is delivered. Both the message and the means present latitude for inventiveness in the way they are approached. Communicating with customers can be expensive, and entrepreneurs, especially when their ventures are in an early stage, rarely have the resources to invest in high-profile advertising and public relations campaigns. They are therefore encouraged to develop new means of promoting their products.

Many entrepreneurs have proved to be particularly skilful at getting 'free' publicity. Anita and Gordon Roddick, for example, have used very little formal advertising for their toiletries retailer The Body Shop. However, the approach adopted by the organisation, and its stated corporate values, have made sure that The Body Shop has featured prominently in the widespread commentary on corporate responsibility that has regularly appeared in the media. As a result, awareness of their organisation is high and consumer attitudes towards it are positive.

New ways of managing relationships within the organisation

Any organisation has a wide variety of communication channels running through it. The performance of the organisation will depend to a great extent on the effectiveness of its internal communication channels. These communication channels are guided (formally at least) by the organisation's *structure*. The structure of the organisation offers considerable scope for value-creating innovations. Of particular note here is the development of the *franchise* as an organisational form. This structure, which combines the advantages of small business ownership with the power of integrated global organisation, has been a major factor in the growth of many entrepreneurial ventures, including The Body Shop retail chain, the Holiday Inn hotel group and the McDonald's fast-food chain.

New ways of managing relationships between organisations

Organisations sit in a complex web of relationships. The way in which organisations communicate and relate to each other is very important. Many entrepreneurial organisations have made innovation in the way in which they work with other organisations (particularly customers) into a key part of their strategy. The business services sector has been particularly active in this respect.

The advertising agency Saatchi and Saatchi, founded by the brothers Charles and Maurice Saatchi in 1970, did not build its success solely on the back of making good advertisements. The brothers also realised that managing the relationship with the client was important. An advertising agency is, in a sense, a supplier of a service like any other, but its 'product' is highly complex and expensive, and its potential to generate business for the client is unpredictable. Thus advertising is a high-risk activity. The brothers realised that if advertising were to be managed properly, the agency had to become an integral part of the management team within the client organisation. It had not just to create advertisements but also to work with the management team at resolving the issues generated by advertising, as well as help the team to exploit the potential of its advertising. In effect, the brothers broke down the barrier between their organisation and their customers.

Multiple innovation

An entrepreneurial venture does not have to restrict itself to just one innovation or even one type of innovation. Success can be built on a *combination* of innovations: for example, a new product delivered in a new way with a new message.

11.3 High- and low-innovation entrepreneurship

Key learning outcome

An understanding of the distinction between high- and low-innovation approaches to exploiting business opportunities.

Even though innovation has been defined as a key characteristic of entrepreneurship and has been used as one of the factors that distinguishes the entrepreneurial venture from the small business, particular entrepreneurial ventures differ in terms of the degree of innovation they adopt. Manimala (1999), in a major study of entrepreneurship in India, has drawn a distinction between what he refers to as *high* and *low pioneering-innovativeness* (PI) entrepreneurship. These two types can be distinguished on the basis of a variety of strategic characteristics, the selection of which reflects the innovation discovered, the business opportunity and resources available and the personal preferences of the entrepreneur. These characteristics are summarised (with modification) in Table 11.1.

11.4 Opportunity and entrepreneurial motivation

Key learning outcome

An understanding of how the effective entrepreneur is motivated by business opportunity.

An opportunity, then, is a gap in a market or the possibility of doing something both differently and better; and an innovation presents a means of filling that market gap, that is, a way of pursuing the opportunity. Such definitions, while they capture the *nature* of opportunity and innovation from both an economic and a managerial perspective, do little to relate the *way* in which opportunity figures in the working life of the entrepreneur. Opportunity *motivates* entrepreneurs. Therefore, it is the thing that attracts their attention and draws their actions. But good entrepreneurs are not blindly subject to opportunities; they take control of them. It is important to understand how entrepreneurs should relate to business opportunities and allow themselves to be motivated by them.

Entrepreneurs are attuned to opportunity

Entrepreneurs are always on the lookout for opportunities. They scan the business landscape looking for new ways of creating value. As we have seen, this value can take the form of new wealth, a chance to pursue an agenda of personal development or to create social change. Opportunities are the 'raw material' out of which the entrepreneur creates an 'entire new world'. To be motivated by opportunity entails the recognition that the current situation does not represent the best way of doing things; that the status quo does not exhaust possibilities. While this may be a spur to move forward, it could also create motivational problems. If we are too conscious of *what might be*, do we not become disillusioned with *what is*? Can the entrepreneur ever get to where they are going?

There is no simple answer to this question. There are certainly some entrepreneurs who are driven forward because they are not satisfied with the present. However, many, while not losing their motivation for what might be, are still able to enjoy what is. Some gain satisfaction, not from reaching the end-points of their activity, but in the *journey* itself. Others make

Table 11.1 High and low pioneering-innovativeness (PI) entrepreneurial strategies

Strategic characteristics	Low PI entrepreneurship	High PI entrepreneurship
Idea management	Tend to rely on local contacts and ideas from existing products	Tend to be more inventive and obtain ideas from a wider source, perhaps internationally
	Strategic vision starts limited but may evolve over time	Strategic vision ambitious from the start
	Stick to and repeat earlier successes	Eager for new ideas
Management of autonomy	Prefer to manage autonomy by working with close-knit team	Will appoint individuals with relevant expertise even if personal knowledge of them is limited
	Develop own expertise through experience	Will develop expertise through employment opportunities and formal training
Management of competition	Tend to stick to what is tried and trusted. Avoid competing when experience is limited	Will undertake, new, higher-risk competitive moves
	Tend to build good working relationship with limited number of key customers (say, as subcontractor)	Greater drive to bring new customers on board. Emphasis on product, quality and service
Growth strategy	Desire for growth but rely on clear and unhindered market opportunity to achieve growth	Desire for growth but more willing to actively compete for market space
	Unlikely to make risky diversification moves	More likely to make risky diversification moves
Human resource management	Tend to rely on known, experienced workers	Experts brought on board as and when needed
	More likely to rely on directions and routines as a means of control	More likely to rely on strategy, culture to exert control
Risk management	Limit risk taking. Tried and trusted route	More likely to manage risk through information, e.g. market researching
	Seeking of institutional and governmental support for expansion moves	Also keen for institutional and governmental support, but more willing to make unsupported risky moves
Network development	Mainly local. Keen to use informal as much as formal networks	Broader base and range of networking. Use local base for further expansion. Also use informal networks, but more adept at managing formal networks

sure they create space for themselves to take pride in what they have achieved, as well as looking forward to what they might achieve. Entrepreneurs must be aware of their motivation. As well as knowing *what* they want to achieve they must be aware of *why* they want to achieve it and why they will enjoy the *process* of achieving it.

Opportunity must take priority over innovation

It is easy to get excited about a new idea. However, an innovation, no matter how good it is, should be secondary to the market opportunity that it aims to exploit. The best ideas are those which are inspired by a clear need in the marketplace rather than those that result from uninformed invention. Many innovations which have been 'pushed' by new product or service possibilities rather than 'pulled' by unsatisfied customer needs have gone on to be successful. However, without a clear understanding of why customers buy and what they are looking for, this can be a very hit-or-miss process. Mistakes are punished quickly and they can be expensive. Failure is certainly demotivating, but this is not to suggest that new product ideas should necessarily be rejected. It does mean that they provide the inspiration to assess their market potential, not to rush the idea straight into the market.

Identifying real opportunities demands knowledge

One of the misconceptions that many people entertain about entrepreneurs is that they are the 'wanderers' of the business world. The notion that they drift between industries, opportunistically picking off the best ideas missed by less astute and responsive 'residents', is widely held. This idea can be traced to the view that the entrepreneur is a 'special' type of person. If they are entrepreneurial by character, then they will be entrepreneurs wherever they find themselves. So they can move at will between different areas of business taking their ability with them. Such an idea is not only wrong, it is also dangerous because it fails to recognise the knowledge and experience that entrepreneurs must have if they are to be successful in the industries within which they operate.

Some important elements of this knowledge include knowledge of:

- the technology behind the product or service supplied;
- how the product or service is produced;
- customers' needs and the buying behaviour they adopt;
- distributors and distribution channels;
- the human skills utilised within the industry;
- how the product or service might be promoted to the customer;
- competitors: who they are, the way they act and react.

This knowledge is necessary if good business opportunities are to be identified and properly assessed. Acquisition of this knowledge requires exposure to the relevant industry, an active learning attitude and time. Most entrepreneurs are actually experienced in a particular industry sector and confine their activities to that sector. Many have acquired this experience by working as a manager in an existing organisation. This 'incubation' period can be important to the development of entrepreneurial talent.

However, industry-specific knowledge does not produce entrepreneurs on its own. It must be supplemented with general business skills and people skills. If an entrepreneur with these skills were to be transplanted between industries, these skills would still be valuable but they would be unlikely to come into their own until the entrepreneur had learnt enough about the new business area to be confident in making good decisions. It is interesting to note that entrepreneurs who do move between industries demonstrate a skill in drawing out and using the expertise that exists within those different industries. Richard Branson, for example, is renowned for his ability to work effectively with industry specialists.

11.5 The opportunity to create wealth

> **Key learning outcome**
>
> An appreciation of the role of wealth creation in the entrepreneurial process.

Entrepreneurs can often become well-known public figures. They are of public interest because they have been *successful*, and this success has often made them wealthy. Their success is of interest in its own right, but their wealth may give them a good deal of social (and perhaps political) power. So while entrepreneurship, and the desire to be an entrepreneur, cannot usually be reduced to a simple desire to make money, it must not be forgotten that making money *is* an important element in the entrepreneurial process.

Business success, and the accumulation of wealth this brings, creates a number of possibilities for the entrepreneur and their ventures to dispose of that wealth.

Reinvestment

If the entrepreneur wishes to grow their business then that growth will demand continued investment. Some of this may be provided by external investors but it will also be expected, and may well be financially advantageous, that the business reinvest some of the profits it has generated.

Rewarding stakeholders

The entrepreneurial venture is made up of more than just the entrepreneur. Entrepreneurs exist in a tight network of relationships with a number of other internal and external stakeholders who are asked to give their support to the venture. They may be asked to take risks on its behalf. In return, they will expect to be properly rewarded. Financial success offers the potential for the entrepreneur to reward them, not just financially but in other ways as well.

Investment in other ventures

If reinvestment within the venture has taken place, and the stakeholders have been rewarded for their contributions, and there are still funds left over, then alternative investments might be considered. The entrepreneur may start an entirely new venture (an option which can be particularly tempting to serial entrepreneurs when their business has matured and they feel that its initial excitement has gone). Another option is that of providing investment support to another entrepreneur. Successful, established entrepreneurs will often act as 'business angels' and offer their knowledge and experience, as well as spare capital, to young ventures.

Personal reward

Some of the value created by the entrepreneur and their venture (though by no means *all* of it) can be taken and used for personal consumption. Funding a comfortable lifestyle is part of this. It may be regarded by the entrepreneur as a just reward for taking risks and putting in the effort that the success has demanded. Some entrepreneurs may also be quite keen to put their money into altruistic projects: for example, they may sponsor the arts or support social programmes. This may reflect their desire to make a mark on the world outside the business sphere, which is part of their desire to leave the world different from the way in which they found it.

Keeping the score

For many entrepreneurs, money is not important in itself. It is just a way of quantifying what they have achieved; a way of keeping the score on their performance, as it were. The money value of their venture is a measure of how good their insight was, how effective their decision making was, and how well they put their ideas into practice.

As far as the entrepreneur is concerned, money is more usually a *means* rather than an *end* in itself. That we notice the entrepreneurs who are highly rewarded for their efforts should not blind us to the fact that this reward is more often than not the result of a great deal of hard work and it is a reward that is far from inevitable.

11.6 The opportunity to distribute wealth

Key learning outcome

A recognition of who expects to be rewarded from the entrepreneurial venture.

No entrepreneur works in a vacuum. The venture they create touches the lives of many people. To drive their venture forward, the entrepreneur calls upon the support of a number of different groups. In return for their support, these groups expect to be rewarded from the success of the venture. People who have a part to play in the entrepreneurial venture generally are called *stakeholders*. The key stakeholder groups are *employees*, *investors*, *suppliers*, *customers*, the *local community* and *government*.

Employees

Employees are the individuals who contribute physical and mental labour to the business. The business's success depends on their efforts on its behalf and therefore upon their motivation. Employees usually have some kind of formal contract and are rewarded by being paid a salary. This is usually agreed in advance and is independent of the performance of the venture, although an element may be performance related. Employees may also be offered the possibility of owning a part of the firm through share schemes.

People do not work just for money. The firm they work for provides them with a stage on which to develop social relationships. It also offers them the possibility of personal development. When someone joins an organisation they are making a personal investment in its future and the organisation is investing in their future. Changing jobs is time consuming and can be expensive. Those who decide to work for an entrepreneurial venture are exposing themselves to the risk of that venture, even if they are being paid a fixed salary.

Investors

Investors are the people who provide the entrepreneur with the necessary money to start the venture and keep it running. There are two main sorts of investor. *Stockholders* are people who buy a part of the firm, its *stock*, and so are entitled to a share of any profits it makes. Stockholders are the true owners of the firm. The entrepreneur managing the venture may, or may not, be a major shareholder in it. *Lenders* are people who offer money to the venture on the basis of its being a *loan*. They do not actually own a part of the firm. All investors expect a return from their investment. The actual amount of expected return will depend on the risk the venture is facing and the other investments that are available at the time. The return the stockholder receives will vary depending on how the business performs. Lenders, on the other hand, expect a rate of return which is agreed independently of how the business performs before the investment is made. Lenders usually take priority for payment over stockholders, whose returns are paid only once the business has met its other financial commitments. Lenders consequently face a lower level of risk. However, there is still the possibility that the venture might become insolvent and not be able to pay back its loans.

Suppliers

Suppliers are the individuals and organisations who provide the business with the materials, productive assets and information it needs to produce its outputs. Suppliers are paid for providing these *inputs*. The business may only make contact with a supplier through spot purchases made in an open market, or contact may be more direct and defined by a formal contract, perhaps a long-term supply contract.

Suppliers are in business to sell what they produce and so they have an interest in the performance of their customers. Supplying them may involve an investment in developing a new product or providing back-up support. A new venture may call upon the support of its suppliers, perhaps by asking for special payment terms to ease its cash flow in the early days. Information and advice about end-user markets may be provided. The chance to build a partnership with suppliers should never be overlooked.

Customers

As with suppliers, customers may need to make an investment in using a particular supplier. Changing suppliers may involve *switching costs*. These include the cost of finding a new supplier, taking a risk with goods of unknown quality, and the expenses incurred in changing over to new inputs. When customers decide to use the products offered by a new venture rather than one with an established track record, they may be exposing themselves to some risk. (This is something the entrepreneur needs to take into account when devising a selling strategy.) The entrepreneur's business may sell to its customers on an open market but, as with suppliers, the possibility of building a longer-term partnership should always be considered.

The local community

Businesses have physical locations. The way that they operate may affect the people who live and other businesses which operate nearby. A business has a number of responsibilities to this local community, for example in not polluting their shared environment. Some of these responsibilities are defined in national or local laws, others are not defined in a legal or formal sense but are expected on the basis that the firm will act in an *ethical* way.

Corporate responsibility is a political and cultural as well as an economic issue. If the firm is international and operates across borders then the way it behaves in one region may influence the way it is perceived in another. For example, a number of well-known sports shoes manufacturers were criticised recently for paying Indian workers less than $0.5 for manufacturing shoes that retailed for over $200 in the USA. Whatever the fair 'market' price of labour in India, the firm's managers had to react to the damage this criticism did to the brand names they were trying to market in the West.

Government

A major part of a government's responsibility is to ensure that businesses can operate in an environment which has political and economic stability, and in which the rule of law operates so contracts can be both made and enforced. The government may also provide central services such as education and health care which the workforce draws upon. These services cost money to provide and so the government taxes individuals and businesses. In general, governments aim to support entrepreneurial businesses because they have an interest in their success. Entrepreneurs bring economic prosperity, provide social stability and generate tax revenue.

Distribution of rewards

All the stakeholders shown in Figure 11.1 expect some reward from the entrepreneurial venture. By working together they can maximise its success. Even so, the new wealth created by the entrepreneur is finite. It can only be shared so far. The entrepreneur must decide how to distribute the wealth among the various stakeholders. To some extent the entrepreneur's

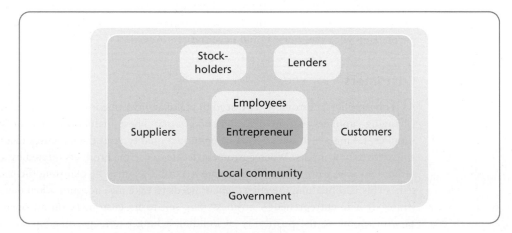

Figure 11.1 Stakeholders in the entrepreneurial venture

hands are tied since the sharing of the profits is, in part, determined by external markets. Legal requirements and binding contracts also play a part in deciding what goes where.

However, the entrepreneur has *some* freedom to decide who gets what. Customers can be rewarded for their loyalty. Higher payments may be used to motivate employees. Profits can be used to support projects in the local community. Distributing the rewards created by the venture is a great responsibility. Using this latitude for rewarding stakeholders creatively is important to the future success of the venture. If rewards are distributed in a way which is seen as fair and proper then they can motivate all involved in the venture. However, a distribution which is seen as illegitimate is a sure way to cause ill feeling.

11.7 Entrepreneurship: risk, ambiguity and uncertainty

Key learning outcome

An understanding of the role that knowledge of business opportunities plays in defining the types of decision an entrepreneur must make.

Entrepreneurs are often characterised as risk takers. Although, as argued in Chapter 1, it is properly investors, not entrepreneurs, who take risks, it is certainly true that entrepreneurs *manage* risk and make decisions in relation to it. Strictly speaking, though, decisions made in the face of risk constitute only one type of decision that an entrepreneur makes. Modern decision theory clearly distinguishes among decisions made under conditions of risk, of uncertainty and of ambiguity. All these decision types are based on knowledge of three information sets:

- The set of *states of the world*. These are the eventualities that the world may throw up in the future. They are outside the active control of an entrepreneur. An entrepreneur cannot control (or can influence in only a very limited way) factors such as overall demand for a new product, the actions of competitors, government interventions or broader world events. Such states of the world are regarded as discrete: we can distinguish one situation from another. Generally speaking, this is theoretically sound, but in practice it may be difficult to distinguish closely related or fine-grained states such as a competitor launching one product or launching a closely related one.
- The set of *acts*. These are the choices that the entrepreneur can make and has control over. For example, an entrepreneur may decide to launch one product or another, or invest in production machinery rather than advertising and so on. Acts are made in anticipation of the state of the world that will obtain. An act results from a particular decision. As with states of the world, acts are regarded as discrete and distinguishable, at least in principle.
- The set of *outcomes*. Outcomes result from the intersection of an act with a state of the world. They are the payoff expected to happen if the entrepreneur does 'this' and 'that' occurs. So the entrepreneur may invest in developing an export market in the expectation that demand in that market will grow. If it does so, then extra revenue will result. If it does not do so, however, then a lower return will be obtained. The entrepreneur may have invested in developing a new product for the domestic market, but decided not to do so because a launch by a competitor was expected, a launch that would have reduced demand for the new offering. It may turn out that the competitor does not go through with the expected launch, and so the investment in the domestic market would have given a better return than the export drive.

Decisions, then, are made on the basis of knowledge about states, acts and outcomes. Different levels of knowledge about each of these lead to different types of decision:

- Decisions under *certainty*. A decision under certainty is one where the actual state of the world that will occur is known definitely – for example, placing a bet on the sun rising tomorrow. In this case, the decision maker simply selects the act that gives the highest returns. These returns will definitely be obtained. As might be imagined, such decisions under certainty occur very rarely in business life.

- Decisions under *risk*. A decision under risk is one where the states that might occur are known, but it is not known for definite which one will occur. What is known is the *probability* with which each state might occur. Decisions of this type occur in gambling – for example, betting that a tossed coin will come up heads or that a thrown die will land with six uppermost. The probability of a head is 1 in 2, that of throwing a six, 1 in 6. A rational decision maker will adjust the bet so that their expected payoff is maximised. The probabilities involved in such gambling games is known because the frequency with which the events will occur is known. There may be situations where frequencies are not known but where expert judgement can ascribe a probability – for example, a weather forecaster suggesting that the chance of rain tomorrow is 20 per cent, or a doctor suggesting that a particular treatment has a 90 per cent chance of being successful. Strictly speaking, risk is present only if such probabilities are known.

- Decisions under *uncertainty*. In fact, despite the widespread use of the word 'risk' in business, decisions under risk are quite rare in business life (they may occur with stock market investments, for example). They are rare because, while a manager may have a good knowledge of what might happen, he or she does not usually have detailed knowledge of the actual probabilities of what will happen. For example, a competitor may or may not launch a new product (states of the world); but what is the probability of this? If this is not known at all, the decision is said to be one under *uncertainty*. Under conditions of uncertainty, decision makers may adopt a number of guiding rules depending on whether they wish to maximise their minimum return, or minimise the maximum loss they might make.

- Decisions under *ambiguity*. Of course, an experienced manager might suggest that they have a 'feel' for whether or not the competitor will launch. This judgement will be based on knowledge of the market and of the way the competitor has acted in the past. The manager may resist putting a definite figure on the probability of the launch, but will be prepared to make a decision based on their intuition that the launch is very likely, moderately likely or unlikely. Decisions under ambiguity lie between those under uncertainty and risk. There is no definite probability for the things that might happen (risk), but the situation is not one of complete uncertainty either. Normative rules for decision making under ambiguity are far from clear and are the subject of research in field of the decision theory.

- Decisions under *ignorance*. Ignorance represents the opposite end of the spectrum to certainty. In this situation, not only are probabilities not known, but even what might happen is not known. Without even this foresight, it is difficult to make any decision at all.

Most managerial, and entrepreneurial, decisions are decisions under *ambiguity* rather than under risk. With this distinction in mind, it can be argued that what entrepreneurs actually do is not take on risk but act to convert uncertainty (and ignorance) into risk (via ambiguity) by using their judgement to analyse and clarify the eventualities (states) that might occur, estimate their probabilities and then identify the acts that will maximise payoffs given these eventualities. This is a service that entrepreneurs offer to investors. Investors will take on risk, but they will not take on uncertainty.

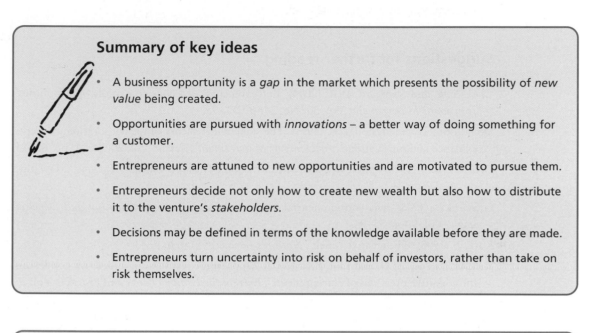

Summary of key ideas

- A business opportunity is a *gap* in the market which presents the possibility of *new value* being created.

- Opportunities are pursued with *innovations* – a better way of doing something for a customer.

- Entrepreneurs are attuned to new opportunities and are motivated to pursue them.

- Entrepreneurs decide not only how to create new wealth but also how to distribute it to the venture's *stakeholders*.

- Decisions may be defined in terms of the knowledge available before they are made.

- Entrepreneurs turn uncertainty into risk on behalf of investors, rather than take on risk themselves.

Research themes

High- and low pioneering-innovativeness (PI) entrepreneurial strategies

Manimala's scheme for distinguishing between high- and low-innovativeness entrepreneurship is described in section 11.3. This distinguishes between the two types on a categorical and heuristic basis (see also section 18.6). Using either case study descriptions of a series of entrepreneurial ventures or information obtained from primary surveys (at least 20 ventures in either case), evaluate them in terms of the criteria described. On the basis of these criteria, does Manimala's scheme clearly divide the ventures into high- and low-PI categories? Are there any other factors that discriminate between them? Might more categories or intermediate categories be needed?

Key readings

An interesting study that draws out the different ways in which entrepreneurs and 'administrators' identify and respond to opportunities is:

Cave, F. and Minty, A. (2004) 'How do entrepreneurs view opportunities: rose tinted spectacles or the real option lens?' *Journal of Private Equity*, Vol. 7, No. 3, pp. 60–7.

A formal framework for guiding and supporting entrepreneurial creativity is described in:

Dutta, D.K. and Crossan, M.M. (2005) 'The nature of entrepreneurial opportunities: understanding the 4L organizational learning framework', *Entrepreneurship: Theory and Practice*, Vol. 29, No. 4, pp. 425–49.

Suggestions for further reading

Choi, Y.R. and Shepherd, D.A. (2004) 'Entrepreneurs' decisions to exploit opportunities', *Journal of Management*, Vol. 30, No. 3, pp. 377–95.

Donaldson, T. and Preston, L.E. (1995) 'The stakeholder theory of the corporation: concepts, evidence and implications', *Academy of Management Review*, Vol. 20, No. 1, pp. 65–91.

Drucker, P.F. (1985) 'The discipline of innovation', *Harvard Business Review*, May/June, pp. 67–72.

Gray, H.L. (1978) 'The entrepreneurial innovator', *Management Education and Development*, Vol. 9, pp. 85–92.

Katz, J. (1990) 'The creative touch', *Nation's Business*, March, p. 43.

Keh, H.T., Foo, M.D. and Lim, B.C. (2002) 'Opportunity evaluation under risk conditions: the cognitive processes of entrepreneurs', *Entrepreneurship: Theory and Practice*, Vol. 27, No. 2, pp. 125–48.

Manimala, M.J. (1999) *Entrepreneurial Policies and Strategies*. New Delhi: Sage.

Vandekerckhove, W. and Dentchev, N. (2005) 'A network perspective on stakeholder management: facilitating entrepreneurs in the discovery of opportunities', *Journal of Business Ethics*, Vol. 60, No. 3, pp. 221–32.

Selected case material

CASE 11.1

7 February 2006

How and why giveaways are changing the rules of business

MICHAEL SCHRAGE

A simple lyric explains the dynamic driving so much innovation in today's post-industrial marketplace: 'The best things in life are free.'

Never in history has so much innovation been offered to so many for so little. The world's most exciting businesses – technology, transport, media, medicine and finance – are increasingly defined by the word 'free'. Whereas Wal-Mart, the world's largest retailer, promises 'everyday low prices', entrepreneurs and ultra-competitive incumbents develop business models predicated on providing more for free. It is a difficult proposition to beat.

Google charges users nothing to search the internet; neither does Yahoo! nor Microsoft MSN. E-mail? Instant messaging? Blogging? Free. Skype, the Luxembourg-based company that is now a multibillion-dollar division of eBay, offers free VOIP – Voice Over Internet Protocols – telephone calls worldwide. San Francisco-based Craigslist provides free online classified advertising around the world.

In America, the Progressive insurance group gives comparison-minded shoppers free vehicle insurance quotes from its competitors. Innumerable financial service companies offer clients free tax advice, online bill payments and investment research. Michael O'Leary, Ryanair's colourful founder, predicts his discount carrier may soon offer free tickets to his cost-conscious euro-flyers.

Of course, Milton Friedman, the Nobel economist, is right: just as 'there's no such thing as a free lunch', there is also no such thing as a 'free innovation'. These 'free' offerings are all creatures of creative subsidy. Free

search engines have keyword-driven advertisers. Financial companies use cash flow from profitable core businesses to cost-effectively support alluringly 'free' money management services. Ryanair counts on the lucrative introduction of in-flight gambling to make its 'free tickets' scenario a commercial reality. Innovative companies increasingly recognise that innovative subsidy transforms the pace at which markets embrace innovation. 'Free' inherently reduces customer risk in exploring the new or improved – and bestows competitive advantage. To the extent that business models can be defined as the artful mix of 'what companies profitably charge for' versus 'what they give away free', successful innovators are branding and bundling ever-cleverer subsidies into their market offerings. The right 'free' fuels growth and profit. Technology has successfully upgraded King Gillette's classic 'razor and blades' business model.

All this freedom poses provocative challenges for global regulators and economic development champions. One company's clever cross-subsidy is another's anti-competitive predatory pricing. Ingenious subsidies inevitably invite invasive scrutiny. Look at Airbus and Boeing. American and European trust-busters certainly frowned on Microsoft's successful bid to bundle 'free' internet browsers into its dominant Windows operating system. Yet bundling 'free' e-mail and other 'free' online services into Yahoo! and Google search engines was deemed legitimate. In trade competition, not all 'frees' are created equal. Europe's proposed 'Google-killer', the Quaero search engine initiative, for example, is itself

CASE 11.1 CONT.

a *créature de subvention*. 'Free' competition with Google, Microsoft and Yahoo could prove expensive. However, regulators might argue that the ever-growing suites of cross-subsidised 'free' digital innovations proffered by these companies unfairly compete. That is, these search engineers could take cash from their most profitable keyword advertising and use it to offer 'free' Quaero-like multimedia searches. Good for cost-conscious searchers, yes; not so great for state-supported competitors.

The simple reality is that technology will continue eroding entry barriers to provocative cross-subsidy. The more digital or virtual a process, product or service, the faster and easier crafting clever subsidies become. Scale matters, too. Global scale facilitates global subsidies. Just as advertisers subsidise free Google searches, marketers can easily download advertising-supported 'free' songs, videos and games into iPods, Sony PSPs and Nokia phones. Internet-based telephone calls similarly lend themselves to sponsorship: 'This free call from your brother in New York is brought to you by Tesco . . . please press #1 to accept . . .' While that prospect will not thrill traditional telecommunications companies, consumers might appreciate the 'free' choice.

Opportunities to add 'free' value that matters in a networked world are expanding exponentially. Why wouldn't Ikea, the Swedish furniture giant with a reputation for horrible DIY documentation, want to post free instructional videos on its websites to make it less risky to buy its unassembled wares? By definition, successful companies are better positioned to subsidise such 'free' innovation to deter potential rivals. Competing against 'free' is hard. Consequently, complaints of unfair competition will multiply as innovative subsidy facilitates technical innovation.

The emerging 'economics of free' thus creates policy quandaries for emerging economies. Do developing countries want to enjoy and exploit the economic benefits of 'free' telecommunications and information for their citizenry and workforce? Or are 'free' search and e-mail services merely post-industrial counterparts to the agricultural subsidies undermining a nation's ability to grow its own digital entrepreneurs? Might China or a South American coalition complain to the World Trade Organisation that a Yahoo! and Google were effectively dumping their services in ways that unfairly hurt indigenous industrial development?

Certainly, the 'free' market paradigm is finding its way into the business plans of local Asian and Indian innovators in telecommunications, microfinance and other sectors. The work of C.K. Prahalad, the US-based management expert, on profitably bringing innovation to the bottom of the pyramid has inspired even established incumbents such as Unilever and Procter & Gamble to redefine 'free' promotion in emerging markets.

The rise and intricate complexity of government subsidies in public life is increasingly provoking political controversy. Similarly, the private sector's growing dependence on cross-subsidy as an innovation edge seems guaranteed to provoke a regulatory and litigatory backlash. Ironically, free markets create markets for 'free' that conjure the spectre of unfair and anti-competitive subsidy. That conflict is inherently unavoidable. But while 'free' has its costs, this century's economic reality is that the surest sign of dynamic innovation is a sector where everyone – producer and consumer alike – eagerly awaits what is offered for 'free'.

Source: Michael Schrage, 'How and why giveaways are changing the rules of business', *Financial Times*, 7 February 2006, p. 19. Copyright © 2006 Michael Schrage.

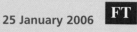

CASE 11.2   25 January 2006   FT

The geeks have inherited the earth – and it is hell for efficiency

JONATHAN GUTHRIE

I have new e-mail. I also have a headache. There are 2,965 unread e-mails in my inbox. I face a career choice. I can become a full-time e-mail administrator. Or I can carry on working as a business journalist, blithely letting unread correspondence mount up in ever-deeper digital drifts.

Moore's Law states that the power of semi-conductors increases by roughly 50 per cent every year. But this gives rise to another tenet, which I call the 'For God's Sake No More Law'. This states that the efficiency of human communication declines in inverse proportion to growth in the number of messages and channels for their transmission.

Eli Noam of Columbia University wrote perceptively in the *Financial Times* last week about the brake that slow regulation applies to the speeding vehicle of technology. But I believe much of the efficiency gains that IT claims to offer are illusory in the first place because of an inherent friction. This is the input of time and money needed simply to keep up with the demands of new technology.

E-mail is a good example. If I conscientiously nurse-maided the attention-seeking brat that is my inbox, I would do no work. The FT's filter already routes such spam as penis enlargement promotions and solicitations from West African fraudsters to a quarantine centre I never visit. Most items in my inbox relate at least peripherally to my job. I receive 70–80 e-mails daily, reading maybe six or seven that look like individual correspondence. Even so, I regularly fail to spot personal e-mails whose contents I should read. Many of these disappear when I speed-delete the bulk of my unread messages once a fortnight.

I assume many other busy people adopt a similarly slipshod approach. Anyone who conscientiously dealt with every e-mail they received would cost their employer thousands of pounds a year in lost productivity. Rare messages with a legitimate purpose are swept away in the tide of e-mail generated by the lazy and insecure. To the solipsist, e-mailing the entire staff of a multinational law firm to ask whether anyone knows a plumber in Hemel Hempstead does not seem like an imposition. For someone who is underemployed, or fears social contact, spending 40 minutes setting out an idea in an e-mail is preferable to explaining it in a five-minute conversation. E-mail has meanwhile given skivers a perfect means of gossiping with friends while apparently remaining hard at work.

John Caudwell, the mobile phones magnate, banned staff from e-mailing each other last year. But even this most exacting of bosses found it impossible to enforce the prohibition.

E-mail is just one of several exciting new means of failing to communicate that the technology revolution has given us. There are also the voicemail oubliettes belonging to anyone with the typical endowment of two landlines and a mobile. Usually the recorded message will inform callers their contact will be back after the Christmas break, even if it is already Easter. Then there are text messages. To my incredulous fury, someone from public relations recently sent me one of these. Who did he think I was? Vicky Pollard? I would have texted a withering response had I known how to do so.

I work remotely for the FT and I reckon I spend more than 5 per cent of my time fixing

CASE 11.2 CONT.

computer faults or learning to use new systems. A help desk in London provides me with advice and equipment. None of this costs me anything because I am an employee. But I dread to think what burden IT imposes on the small ventures around me in the serviced office block we share. Keeping abreast of technology helps IT entrepreneurs spot new opportunities. But for most new businesses, it feels like time wasted. Yet if they fall behind, they risk appearing as old-fashioned as if they illustrated sales presentations with magic lantern slides.

Enough. I propose a buyers' strike of at least a year. Technology companies would have to postpone the launch of new computers, software or communications devices. IT geeks could realise long-cherished ambitions to backpack around the world or perform in Grateful Dead tribute bands. IT users could get to grips with systems that were temporarily free from the threat of obsolescence, maybe even using them to generate extra business.

Since my chances of arresting technological advances driven by remorseless global competition are pretty low, I have a more modest plan B. It is to launch a Slow Business movement. The Slow Food movement aims to replace burgers and fries with traditional fare cooked and eaten at a leisurely rate. Slow Business would swap frenetic, energy-sapping activity for the unhurried realisation of strategy. Slow businesses would delight customers sufficiently to make their waits worthwhile.

Slow Business, you might think, would be commercial suicide. Think again. Companies with some of its key characteristics are already among us. Banks that take three days to clear a cheque are some of the UK's most successful organisations. A motorist can drive a cheap Ford Fiesta away from a dealer as soon as he has paid for it, but Ford's upmarket Aston Martin subsidiary makes him wait up to 18 months for a Vantage V8. Generic cookers are installed the day after purchase, but Aga does nicely from ranges it delivers in six weeks.

An important trait of disciples of Slow Business would be answering 'urgent' e-mails with handwritten notes dispatched after a few weeks of reflection. This would generally conclude the correspondence, because the problem bugging the e-mailer would meanwhile have resolved itself. Please e-mail me if you want to discuss this further. I promise to reply. Eventually.

Source: Jonathan Guthrie, 'The geeks have inherited the earth – and it is hell for efficiency', *Financial Times*, 25 January 2006, p. 16. Copyright © 2006 The Financial Times Limited.

Discussion point

1. What are the similarities and differences between the business opportunity presented by (a) a 'giveaway' business model and (b) changing technology?

CHAPTER 12

Resources in the entrepreneurial venture

Chapter overview

People, money and operational assets are the essential ingredients of the entrepreneurial venture. This chapter explores each of these resource types and the management issues they raise for the entrepreneur. Why investment in such resources leads to risk for the backers of the venture is considered. The concept of resource stretch and leverage is applied to develop an understanding of how entrepreneurs can work their resources harder than established competitors.

12.1 Resources available to the entrepreneur

Key learning outcome

An understanding of the nature and type of resources that the entrepreneur uses to build the venture.

Resources are the things that a business uses to pursue its ends. They are the inputs that the business converts to create the outputs it delivers to its customers. They are the substance out of which the business is made. In broad terms, there are three sorts of resource that entrepreneurs can call upon to build their ventures. These are:

- *financial resources* – resources which take the form of, or can be readily converted to, cash;
- *human resources* – people and the efforts, knowledge, skill and insights they contribute to the success of the venture;
- *operating resources* – the facilities which allow people to do their jobs: such as buildings, vehicles, office equipment, machinery and raw materials, etc.

The entrepreneurial venture is built from an innovative combination of financial, operating and human resources (Figure 12.1). Thus when Frederick Smith founded the US parcel air carrier Federal Express he needed to bring together people – a board of directors, pilots, operational staff, etc. – along with a fully operational airline which was able to give national coverage. This demanded an investment of the order of $100 million.

Regardless of the form they take, all resources have a number of characteristics in common. Resources are *consumed*; they are converted to the products which customers buy, and there is competition to get hold of resources. A number of businesses, entrepreneurial and

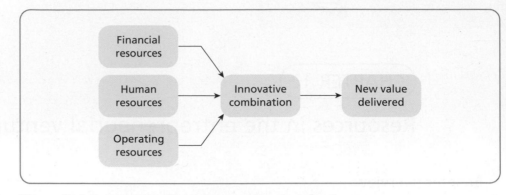

Figure 12.1 Entrepreneurship and the combination of resources

otherwise, will be trying to acquire a particular resource; consequently, managers are willing to pay for resources. Third, resources have a cost.

The cost of a resource is an indication of how it might be used by a business to create new value. Resources are bought and sold by businesses and their cost is determined by the market created for that resource. Resources with the potential to create a lot of new value will be expensive. This cost is not the same as the *value* of the resource to a *particular* business since the value of a resource lies in the way a business will use it, how innovative it will be with the resource and how hard it will make the resource work.

One type of resource can be converted into another. This process normally involves selling a resource, thereby converting it into cash, and then using this cash to buy something new. However, in some cases, resources may be exchanged directly through 'asset swaps'. In places where financial markets are not well developed, such as in parts of the developing world and the former communist bloc, 'bartering' may be important. Not all markets for resources are equally accessible. Some markets are more developed than others. The ease with which a particular resource can be converted back into ready cash is called its liquidity: *liquid* resources are easily converted back, *illiquid* resources are converted back only with difficulty.

Entrepreneurs must be active in acquiring resources for their ventures. The paths through which resources are obtained and exchanged make up the network in which the business is located. In the long run, the entrepreneur only has access to the same resources as any other business. Competitiveness in the marketplace cannot normally be sustained on the basis of having access to unique resource inputs. If an input is valuable, other businesses will eventually find a way to get hold of it or of something like it. What entrepreneurs must do to be competitive is *combine* the resources they have access to in a unique and valuable way – that is, *innovate* with them and then make those resources work harder than their competitors do. It is this which ultimately enables the entrepreneur to deliver new value to the customer.

12.2 Financial resources

Financial resources are those which take a monetary form. Cash is the most liquid form of resource because it can be used readily to buy other resources. The following are all financial resources which have a role to play in the entrepreneurial venture:

> ## Key learning outcome
>
> An appreciation of the financial resources available for use by the entrepreneur.

- *Cash in hand.* This is money to which the business has immediate access. It may be spent at very short notice. Cash in hand may be held either as money, i.e. petty cash, or it may be stored in a bank's current account or other direct access account.
- *Overdraft facilities.* Such facilities represent an agreement with a bank to withdraw more than is actually held in the venture's current account. An overdraft is a short-term loan which the business can call upon, although it is normally quite expensive to service and so tends to be saved for emergencies.
- *Loans.* Loans represent money provided by backers, either institutional or private, which the business arranges to pay back in an agreed way over a fixed period of time at an agreed rate of interest. The payback expected is usually independent of the performance of the business. Loans may be secured against physical assets of the business which can be sold off to secure repayment. This reduces the risk of the loan to the backer.
- *Outstanding debtors.* This represents cash owed to the business by individuals and firms which have received goods and services from it. Many debtors will expect a period of grace before paying and it may not be easy to call in outstanding debt quickly. Outstanding debtors are one of the main reasons that cash flow may be negative in the early stages of the venture's life.
- *Investment capital.* This is money provided to the business by investors in return for a part-ownership or share in it. Investors are the true owners of the business. They are rewarded from the profits the business generates. The return they receive will be dependent on the performance of the business.
- *Investment in other businesses.* Many businesses hold investments in other businesses. These investments may be in unrelated businesses but they are more often in suppliers or customers. If more than half of a firm is owned, then it becomes a *subsidiary* of the holding firm. Investments can be made through personal or institutional agreements, or via publicly traded shares. A firm does not normally exist solely to make investments in other firms. Individual and institutional investors are quite capable of doing this for themselves. However, strategic investments in customers and suppliers may be an important part of the dynamics of the network in which the business is located. For this reason, such investments tend to represent long-term commitments, and although they can be sold to generate cash, doing so is not routine.

All financial resources have a cost. This cost takes one of two forms. The *cost of capital* is the cost encountered when obtaining the money: it is the direct charge faced for having an overdraft; the interest on loans; the return expected by investors, and so forth. In addition to this direct cost, there is an *opportunity cost*. Opportunity cost is the potential return that is lost by not putting the money to some alternative use. For example, cash in hand and outstanding debts lose the interest that might be gained by putting the money into an interest-yielding account.

Financial resources are the most liquid, and thus the most flexible, resources to which the venture has access. However, they are also the least productive. Cash, of itself, does not create new value. Money is valuable only if it is put to work. This means that it must be converted to other, less liquid, resources. The entrepreneur must strike a balance. A decision must be made between how liquid the business is to be, how much flexibility it must have to meet short-term and unexpected financial commitments, and the extent to which the firm's financial resources are to be tied up in productive assets.

Such decisions are critical to the success of the venture. If insufficient investment is made then the business will not be in a position to achieve its full potential. If it becomes too illiquid, it may be knocked off course by short-term financial problems which, in the long run, the business would be more than able to solve. Managing the *cash flow* of the business is central to maintaining this liquidity balance. The financial resources to which an entrepreneur can gain access will depend on how well developed the economy they are working in is and the type of capital markets available. In the mature economies of western Europe and the USA, capital is usually provided by explicit and open institutional systems such as banks, venture capital businesses and stock markets. In other parts of the world, provision of financial resources may be through less formal networks. Displaced communities often create financial support networks around the extended family. One of the main challenges to developing entrepreneurism in the former communist bloc is the setting up of supportive and trusted financial institutions.

12.3 Operating resources

> ### Key learning outcome
>
> An appreciation of the operational resources available for use by the entrepreneur.

Operating resources are those which are actually used by the business to deliver its outputs to the marketplace. Key categories of operating resources include:

- *premises* – the buildings in which the business operates. This includes offices, production facilities and the outlets through which services are provided;
- *motor vehicles* – any vehicles which are used by the organisation to undertake its business such as cars for sales representatives and vans and lorries used to transport goods, make deliveries and provide services;
- *production machinery* – machinery which is used to manufacture the products which the business sells;
- *raw materials* – the inputs that are converted into the products that the business sells;
- *storage facilities* – premises and equipment used to store finished goods until they are sold;
- *office equipment* – items used in the administration of the business such as office furniture, word processors, information processing and communication equipment.

Operating resources represent the capacity of the business to offer its innovation to the marketplace. They may be owned by the business, or they may be rented as they are needed. Either way, they represent a commitment. Liquid financial resources are readily converted into operating resources, but operating resources are not easily converted back into money. The markets for second-hand business assets are not always well developed. Even if they are, operating resources depreciate quickly and a loss may be made on selling.

In order to use operating resources effectively it is important that entrepreneurs make themselves fully conversant with any technical aspects relating to the resources; legal issues and implications relating to their use (including health and safety regulations); suppliers and the supply situation; and the applicable costs (both for outright purchase and for leasing). It is in this area that partnerships with suppliers can be rewarding, especially if the operating resources are technical or require ongoing support in their use.

The commitment to investment in operating resource capacity must be made in the light of expected demand for the business's offerings. If capacity is insufficient, then business that might otherwise have been obtained will be lost. If it is in excess of demand, then unnecessary, and unprofitable, expenditure will be undertaken. It is often difficult to alter operating capacity in the light of short-term fluctuations in demand. This results in *fixed costs*, that is, costs which are independent of the amount of outputs the firm offers. Critically, fixed costs must be faced *whatever* the business's sales. Fixed costs can have a debilitating effect on cash flow. The entrepreneur must make the decision about commitment to operating capacity in the light of an assessment of the sales and operating profits that will be generated by the business's offering, that is, on the basis of an accurate *forecast* of demand. Even good demand forecasting cannot remove all uncertainty and therefore the entrepreneur must be active in offsetting as much fixed cost as possible, especially in the early stages of the venture. This may mean renting rather than buying operating resources. It can also mean that some work is delegated to other established firms. In the early stages of the venture, managing cash flow and controlling fixed costs may be more important than short-term profitability. It may be better to subcontract work to other firms rather than to make an irreversible commitment to extra capacity, even if this means short-term profits are lost.

12.4 Human resources

> ### Key learning outcome
>
> An appreciation of the human resources available for use by the entrepreneur.

People are the critical element in the success of a new venture. Financial and operating resources are not unique and they cannot, in themselves, confer an advantage to the business. To do so they must be *used* in a unique and innovative way by the people who make up the venture. The people who take part in the venture offer their labour towards it. This can take a variety of forms:

- *productive labour* – a direct contribution towards generating the outputs of the business, its physical products or the service it offers;
- *technical expertise* – a contribution of knowledge specific to the product or service offered by the business. This may be in support of existing products, or associated with the development of new ones;
- *provision of business services* – a contribution of expertise in general business services, for example in legal affairs or accounting;
- *functional organisational skills* – the provision of decision-making insights and organising skills in functional areas such as production, operations planning, marketing research and sales management;
- *communication skills* – offering skills in communicating with, and gaining the commitment of, external organisations and individuals. This includes marketing and sales directed towards customers, and financial management directed towards investors;
- *strategic and leadership skills* – the contribution of insight and direction for the business as a whole. This involves generating a vision for the business, converting this into an effective strategy and plan for action, communicating this to the organisation and then leading the business in pursuit of the vision.

The entrepreneur represents the starting point of the entrepreneurial venture. He or she is the business's first, and most valuable, human resource. Entrepreneurs, if they are to be successful, must learn to use themselves as a resource, and use themselves effectively. This means analysing what they are good at, and what they are not so good at, and identifying skill gaps. The extent to which the entrepreneur can afford to specialise their contribution to their venture will depend on the size of the venture and the number of people who are working for it. If it is moderately large and has a specialist workforce then the entrepreneur will be able to concentrate on developing vision and a strategy for the venture and providing leadership to it. If it is quite small then the entrepreneur will have to take on functional and administrative tasks as well. Even so, the entrepreneur must be conscious of how the human resource requirements of the business will develop in the future by deciding what skill profile is right for their business and what type of people will be needed to contribute those skills. But employing people with the right skills is not enough; those people must be directed to use their skills. They must also be motivated if they are to make a dedicated and effective contribution to the business. This calls for vision and leadership on the part of the entrepreneur.

Human resources represent a source of fixed costs for the business. The possibility of taking on, and letting go of, people in response to short-term demand fluctuations is limited by contractual obligations, social responsibility and the need to invest in training. Further, motivation can only be built on the back of some sense of security. Hence, making a commitment to human resources involves the same type of decisions as making a commitment to operating resources, namely: what will be needed, to what capacity, over what period, must the resource be in-house or can it be hired when needed? However, people are still people even if they are also resources, and such decisions must be made with sensitivity.

12.5 Organisational process and learning as resources

Key learning outcome

Recognition of organisational learning and process as resources critical to the venture's success. Appreciation of the importance of uniqueness, inimitability and non-tradability as characteristics of resources that confer competitive advantage.

The idea that resources are key to the success of a venture was introduced in section 6.1 with a discussion of the resource- and competence-based views of business performance. It was noted there that what constitutes a resource in these perspectives is quite broad. This section develops a framework for understanding resources in their wider context and examines further the ideas of resource imitability and tradability as the basis for gaining a sustainable competitive advantage.

The broad definition of resources is at once both an opportunity and a challenge. The opportunity lies in the flexibility of the resource-based perspective to account for a wide spectrum of resource–performance links. The challenge lies in maintaining the theoretical and methodological soundness of the approach given that it can easily become tautological (a circular argument of the form: performance is the result of unique resources, so a high-performing business is such because of its unique resources; and these are freely defined), and the causal link between resources and performance is, in any case, ambiguous. To be rigorous, the approach must be strict in its definition of what constitutes a resource, develop a hypothesis linking that resource causally to performance and then test that hypothesis empirically.

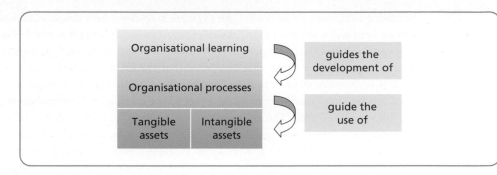

Figure 12.2 Three levels of organisational resource

An immediate move is to distinguish different types of resource. Clearly, the notion of a resource must be broader than simply physical assets. The resource-based view makes it evident that it is not assets *per se* that are important, but what the entrepreneur *does* with them. So resources must include the organisational processes that manipulate and utilise assets. However, these processes are not static. They must adapt and develop as the venture gets bigger, and its competitive position and situation change. At this level, organisational learning must be counted as a resource. This is depicted in Figure 12.2. The hypothesis is that organisational learning develops organisational processes that then control the use of assets.

Assets and processes are (in principle at least) directly observable. Organisational learning is not usually directly observable, but its effect can be gauged by observing changes in the organisational processes. Assets may be divided into three categories. Tangible assets have physical form. Intangible assets do not have physical form, but are nonetheless valuable to the business. Examples here would be patents and brand names. This distinction is made in accounting practice as tangible assets are recorded on the balance sheet but intangible assets are not usually recorded (though some moves have been made in accounting to value such assets). Intellectual assets refer to specific knowledge of technology or products held within the business that directly informs its activities.

What connects the idea of a resource to that of competitive advantage? In short, a resource confers a competitive advantage if it fulfils three criteria:

- That resource can be used in some way to deliver value to buyers.
- That resource is unique to the venture.
- Competitors find it hard to imitate or acquire that resource.

The issue of resource access is linked to the idea that some resources may be traded with or can be imitated by competitors. Four types of resource can be distinguished on the basis that they can be copied (imitated) or bought and sold (are tradable) within a market. Tradable resources are those that can be 'packaged up' and sold within a market whereas non-tradable resources cannot be detached from the firm using them and so cannot be traded within a market. Imitable resources are those that can easily be copied by competitors. Inimitable resources are not easy to copy because they have legal protection or they take time to build up or they have causal ambiguity and their link to performance is not clear. *Commodity* resources are those that are both tradable and can easily be copied. General factory equipment and offices are an example. *Exchangeable* resources are those that cannot be traded but can easily be copied. An example here might be a unique organisational structure or staff skills and training. *Tradable* resources are those that are not easy to copy but that can be traded freely – patents, copyrights and brand names, for example. Finally, *competitive* resources are those that can be neither traded nor copied. Examples here might include the entrepreneur's visionary leadership, a culture that encourages and rewards the discovery and exploitation of new opportunities, or an effective approach to integrating new organisational learning. The most secure competitive advantage is that built on competitive resources. Tradable resources might also be a platform for a time, but being tradable, other entrepreneurs might well set up to establish ventures trading in them, limiting their long-term appeal. Many universities have set up science parks with the explicit intention of trading in scientific and technological ideas and the patents protecting them. A brand is valuable only if competitors (often larger and better resourced) do not compete with their own brands more strongly.

12.6 Resources, investment and risk

Key learning outcome

An understanding of how and why investing in resources creates risk for the entrepreneurial venture.

In one sense, a business is 'just' the financial, operating and human resources that comprise it. Only when these things are combined can the business generate new value and deliver it to customers. Resources have a value and there is competition to get hold of them. A business is *not* being competitive when it converts input resources into outputs of higher value. It is being competitive only if it is creating more value than its *competitors* can do. Thus resources are used to pursue opportunities and exploiting those opportunities creates new value. The profit created by an entrepreneurial venture is the difference between the cost of the resources that make it up and the value it creates. This is the *return* obtained from investing the resources. Although profits are important for survival and growth, the performance of an entrepreneurial venture cannot be reduced to a simple consideration of the profits it generates. Profits must be considered in relation to two other factors: *opportunity cost* and *risk*.

Resources are bought and sold in markets and so they have a price. This price is not the same as the cost of *using* a resource. The true cost incurred when a resource is used is the value of the opportunity *missed* because the resource is consumed and so cannot be used in an alternative way. This is the *opportunity cost*. If the entrepreneur uses the business's resources in the most productive way possible then the value created will be higher than that which might have been generated by an alternative investment and so the opportunity cost will be less than the value created. If, on the other hand, the resources are not used in the most productive way possible, then some alternative investment could potentially give a better return. The opportunity cost will be greater than the value created. Opportunity cost is a fundamental factor in measuring performance. This is because investors are not concerned in the first instance with the *profit* made by a venture but with the *return* they might get if they put their money to an alternative use.

The second factor in considering how well an entrepreneur is using resources is *risk*. We cannot predict the future with absolute accuracy so there is always a degree of uncertainty about what will happen. This uncertainty creates risk. No matter what return is anticipated,

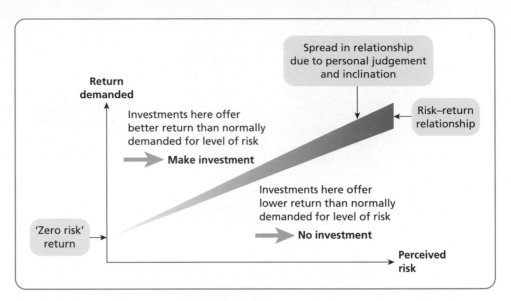

Figure 12.3 The risk–return relationship for investment in an entrepreneurial venture

there is always the possibility that some unforeseen event will lead to that return being lower. Customers may not find the offering as attractive as was expected. Marketing and distribution may prove to be more expensive than was budgeted for. Competitors may be more responsive than was assumed to be the case. Investors make an assessment of the risk that a venture will face. If the risk is high then they will expect to be compensated by a higher rate of return. If they perceive that it is low then they will be happy with a lower return. Consequently there is a payoff between risk and return. The exact way in which expected return is related to risk is quite complex and is a function of the dynamics of the market for capital. The risk–return relationship for investment in an entrepreneurial venture is shown in Figure 12.3. In practice, institutional investors will aim to hold a *portfolio*, that is, a collection of investments with different levels of risk and return. The objective here is to reduce the overall level of risk for the portfolio.

Risk occurs because resources must be *committed* to a venture. Once money is converted into operating and human resources it is either too difficult or too expensive, or both, to convert it back. Therefore, once resources have been brought together and shaped to pursue a particular opportunity, there is no going back if a better opportunity demanding a different shaping of the resources is identified later. In this way, entrepreneurial innovation demands an irreversible commitment of resources (Figure 12.4). The opportunity cost must be faced and it is the investor in the venture who must absorb this cost, not the entrepreneur (although the entrepreneur may be an investor as well).

In summary, if an entrepreneur identifies an opportunity that might be exploited through an innovative way of using resources and then asks investors to back a venture pursuing that opportunity, two fundamental questions will come to the investor's mind: how do the returns anticipated compare with the alternative investments available, and what will be the risks? The decision to support the venture or not will depend on the answers to these questions. It should not be forgotten that although investors are people who put *financial*

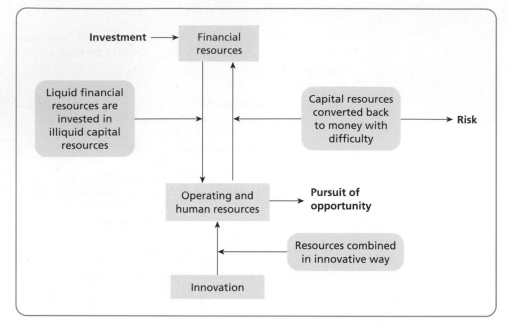

Figure 12.4 Resource commitment in the entrepreneurial venture

resources into a venture, individuals who work for a business are also making a *personal* investment in it. They expect to be rewarded for their efforts and to be given an opportunity to develop. They also face opportunity costs in not being able to offer their efforts elsewhere, and face the risk of the venture not being successful. Similarly, non-financial commitments may also be made by customers and suppliers who build a relationship with the venture. In this way, risk is spread out through the network in which the venture is located.

12.7 Stretch and leverage of entrepreneurial resources

Key learning outcome

An understanding of the way in which entrepreneurs often compete – and win – against better resourced incumbent competitors through superior exploitation – 'stretch and leverage' – of critical resources.

As has been noted earlier, entrepreneurs and their success do appear to be paradoxical. After all, they do not have the same level of resources as established competitors, they lack the internal success factors incumbents have access to (such as costs, established customer relationships) and they do have to pay more for the resources they obtain (paying for the risk premium they present). See Mosakowski (2002) for a recent discussion. The answer to this paradox seems to be that entrepreneurs work their resources harder than do established businesses. The question is, in what way does this working take place? In an influential paper, Hamel and Prahalad (1993) suggested that ten processes could describe the way that resources were worked. They suggest that 'competitiveness is born in the gap between a company's resources and its managers' goals'. Their concern in the article cited was with business in general, not just entrepreneurship, but it seems that entrepreneurs are 'stretchers and leveragers' of resources *par excellence*. The ten processes Hamel and Prahalad discuss are as follows:

- *Convergence*. This refers to the creation of a gap between resources and the aspirations of the venture that will act as a driver of competitive advantage. It reflects 'loyalty' to the entrepreneur's vision.
- *Focus*. Here, focus refers specifically to a dedication to create and maintain a competitive advantage, and once established, to move on to enhance it and create the next competitive advantage. The entrepreneur must never become complacent about competitive advantage.
- *Extraction*. New information is coming into the business all the time. Extraction is the process whereby that information is used as the basis of learning about the opportunities available to the venture and how the venture might enhance its competitive position. That learning must be open and honest, even if it conflicts with long-held and established ideas.
- *Borrowing*. This refers to gaining information from all available sources, both inside and outside the business. Effective entrepreneurs use meetings with customers as an opportunity to gain new insights as well as an opportunity to sell.
- *Blending*. As the venture grows, the people who make it up will tend to specialise in specific areas. This provides the opportunity to improve efficiency. However, individuals can still learn from each other and learn to blend their skills in new and valuable combinations. This is especially important for the entrepreneur, whose role can become detached from the cutting edge of the business as it grows.
- *Balancing*. This implies that excellence in one area is not undermined by mediocrity in another. Excellence must be balanced across all areas of the business. The entrepreneur must ensure that examples of excellence in one area provide lessons for, and are shared with, other areas of the business.
- *Recycling*. Competitive advantage should be regarded as a resource for the whole organisation, not just some part of it. It should be recycled around the whole venture. This can be particularly important for serial entrepreneurs who wish to transfer competitive advantage in one business to another independent start-up or acquisition.
- *Co-option*. This refers to the effectiveness with which the entrepreneur draws other organisations into the venture's network to provide money, skills and information to the venture. It demands an understanding of the structure of the network, what different parties are gaining from the network and the role they play in sustaining the venture.
- *Shielding*. Competitive advantage is comparative: it is an advantage *over* competitors. The effective entrepreneur is aware of competitors' (relative) weaknesses, how to use their own venture's strengths to attack those weaknesses and how to do so in a way that limits (resource-richer) competitors' abilities to counterattack.
- *Recovery*. This relates to the venture's overall agility and its ability to turn information on market opportunities into profitable offerings faster than competitors do. It impacts on every stage in the venture's operations: its ability to obtain information, product development, production, and delivery and distribution.

Necessarily, these ten processes are interlinked. One cannot be managed in the absence of, or without reference to, the others. The entrepreneur will not necessarily see them in these distinct terms, but will take them on board in a holistic manner and regard them simply as an integrated aspect of their management practice. However, there is value in considering them separately as a basis for creating strategy out of vision. The stretch and leverage model provides a managerial perspective on a game-theoretical economic model developed by Hirshleifer (2001), who suggests that, under certain conditions, the resource-weaker competitor may win against the resource richer because it can use its resources to tax the stronger more than the stronger can tax it. This is discussed in more detail in section 21.1.

Summary of key ideas

- Entrepreneurs must attract resources to their ventures in order to pursue business opportunities.

- Resources occur at three levels: assets, organisational processes and organisational learning.

- Resources are distinguished by the degree to which they can be traded and the ease with which they might be imitated.

- Competitive advantage is most securely based on competitve assets that are difficult to trade and cannot be imitated easily.

- Assets are *valuable* and are traded in *markets*.

- The entrepreneur must *compete* with other businesses to get hold of resources by offering a good return from using them.

- Dedicating resources to a particular venture exposes investors to *risk*, namely the possibility that the return gained will be less than expected.

- Entrepreneurs stretch and leverage their resources to make them work harder in the face of resource-richer competitors.

Research themes

Do entrepreneurs stretch and leverage resources?

This study adopts a case-study methodology. Obtain descriptions of a series of entrepreneurial ventures (case studies are a good source). Ideally they should compare the entrepreneurial firm with a conventional incumbent in the same sector. Otherwise you may find information from a primary research survey. Can you find evidence of the stretch and leverage processes described by Hamel and Prahalad in entrepreneurial businesses? If so, do entrepreneurs recognise these processes in their own management? One way to do this would be to use a survey instrument to outline each process in terms of a short (up to 50 word) scenario and ask entrepreneurs to describe how they would respond to each of these challenges (don't just use the Hamel and Prahalad terms; they will probably not mean much to practising entrepreneurs). For example, a test for co-option might be:

When you (or one of your people) make a sales call, is your primary objective to:

(a)   *gain a sale*

(b)   *obtain information on new opportunities and competitors' activities*

(c)   *both of the above*

or for balancing:

A manager in your business proves to be very effective in dealing with customers. Is your first priority to:

(a)   *keep him/her in the front line with customers*

(b)   *promote him/her to lead others working with customers*

(c)   *give him/her a wider leadership role and be a champion for the customer within the business*

and so on in this style. Code the responses and look for evidence of the Hamel and Prahalad stretch and leverage processes.

Resources and industry structure

The resource-based perspective can be made to make predictions about the performance of individual firms and the structures of the industries in which they are located. Obtain some good descriptions of businesses in a variety of sectors. This may be obtained directly from a survey instrument or published information. Characterise the sectors in terms of the resources they use as discussed in section 12.2. Attempt to identify sectors that are largely based on commodity resources and those for which competitive resources are more prevalent (other resource types may be included if the sample is large enough). Be prepared to set up strict criteria for judging the inclusion of resources under each type. Categorise them in terms of assets, organisational process and organisational learning. Check if they are tradable and if they are imitable. The best practice is to have someone independently check the categorisation. It can be hypothesised that sectors based on competitive resources will have:

- higher overall profitability;
- a greater range of profitabilities (as competitive resources sort the winners from losers); and
- higher growth performance for winners

when compared to sectors based on commodity resources. Test these predictions using financial data for the sectors. To be statistically robust, at least 25 firms of each resource type should be included.

 ## Key readings

Two papers that are not specifically about entrepreneurship, but their insights have had an enormous impact on thinking about entrepreneurship and the ways in which entrepreneurs manage resources:

Hamel, G. and Prahalad, C.K. (1993) 'Strategy as stretch and leverage', *Harvard Business Review*, Mar./Apr. pp. 75–84.

Wernerfelt, B. (1984) 'A resource based view of the firm', *Strategic Management Journal*, Vol. 5, pp. 171–80.

Suggestions for further reading

Alvarez, S.A. and Barney, J.B. (2002) 'Resource-based theory and the entrepreneurial firm', in Hitt, M.A., Ireland, R.D., Camp, S.M. and Sexton, D.L. (eds) *Strategic Entrepreneurship: Creating a New Mindset*. Oxford: Blackwell.

Alvarez, S.A. and Busenitz, L.W. (2001) 'The entrepreneurship of resource-based theory', *Journal of Management*, Vol. 27, pp. 755–75.

Amit, R. and Schoemaker, P.J.H. (1993) 'Strategic assets and organisational rent', *Strategic Management Journal*, Vol. 14, pp. 33–46.

Bergmann-Lichenstein, B.M. and Brush, C.G. (2001) 'How do "resource bundles" develop and change in new ventures? A dynamic model and longitudinal exploration', *Entrepreneurship Theory and Practice*, Spring, pp. 37–58.

Collis, D.J. (1994) 'How valuable are organisational capabilities?', *Strategic Management Journal*, Vol. 15, pp. 143–52.

Foss, N.J. (ed.) (1997) *Resources, Firms and Strategies: A Reader in the Resource-based Perspective*. Oxford: Oxford University Press.

Hall, R. (1992) 'The strategic analysis of intangible resources', *Strategic Management Journal*, Vol. 13, pp. 135–44.

Hamel, G. and Prahalad, C.K. (1993) 'Strategy as stretch and leverage', *Harvard Business Review*, Mar./Apr. pp. 75–84.

Hirshleifer, J. (2001) 'The paradox of power', in *The Dark Side of the Force: Economic Foundations of Conflict Theory*. Cambridge: Cambridge University Press.

Makadok, R. (2001) 'Towards a synthesis of the resource-based and dynamic capability views of rent creation', *Strategic Management Journal*, Vol. 22, pp. 387–401.

Mosakowski, E. (2002) 'Overcoming resource disadvantages in entrepreneurial firms: when less is more', in Hitt, M.A., Ireland, R.D., Camp, S.M. and Sexton, D.L. (eds) *Strategic Entrepreneurship: Creating a New Mindset*. Oxford: Blackwell.

Peteraf, M.A. (1993) 'The cornerstones of competitive advantage: a resource based view', *Strategic Management Journal*, Vol. 14, pp. 179–91.

Wernerfelt, B. (1984) 'A resource based view of the firm', *Strategic Management Journal*, Vol. 5, pp. 171–80.

Wernerfelt, B. (1995) 'The resource based view of the firm: ten years after', *Strategic Management Journal*, Vol. 16, pp. 171–4.

Wilcox-King, A. and Zeithaml, C.P. (2001) 'Competencies and firm performance: examining the causal ambiguity paradox', *Strategic Management Journal*, Vol. 22, pp. 75–99.

Yu, A.F. (2001) 'Towards a capabilities perspective of the small firm', *International Journal of Management Reviews*, Vol. 3, No. 3, pp. 185–97.

Selected case material

CASE 12.1

26 January 2006

When language gives and industry the edge

ANDREW JACK

The hours are long and the time difference tough but, shuttling between their offices in Cambridge and Ahmedabad, Sunil and Prashant Shah co-ordinate a fledgling company that is riding India's fast-growing pharmaceuticals wave.

Since April 2005, cheap travel, telephony and cameras in their laboratories have allowed the two entrepreneurs to build Oxygen Healthcare into a business marketed from the UK to European and North American biotech clients, with their contract chemistry conducted in Gujarat.

But if they claim that the enthusiasm and flexibility of their Indian workforce helps them turn around projects quickly and effectively, they have already had to modify an initial business plan which was based on the expectations of low wages for top quality employees.

'It's really difficult to get experienced people to move,' says Prashant Shah. 'You have to give them a 30 to 40 per cent pay rise. That's an indication that a lot of companies are investing and increasing their capacity.'

For many years, India was best known in the medical world for its thriving generic industry, and the manufacture of the active pharmaceutical ingredients from which drugs are formulated.

One company, Hetero, last month signed a sub-licensing agreement with Roche of Switzerland to produce Tamiflu, the antiviral drug experiencing soaring demand on the back of fears of a flu pandemic. The contract implicitly endorsed the Indian company's technical skills. Cipla, based in Mumbai, one of the country's largest producers by sales, has made a name for itself not only domestically, but as a leading supplier of affordable anti-retroviral drugs for HIV sufferers across the developing world. It has helped reduce the prices of the large companies that first patented Aids medicines.

'Take a look around you at our products,' says Yusuf Hamied, the chairman, gesturing towards glass cabinets stretched around a large meeting room in the corporate headquarters lined with its own-brand versions of well-known medicines.

But a short drive away into Mumbai's suburbs, in its smart new office block, Nicholas Piramal is taking a radically different strategic approach. The company's core pharmaceuticals business is contract manufacturing for western drugs companies but, increasingly, it is undertaking original research too.

It argues that Indian companies cannot only mimic but develop their own innovative drugs at a fraction of western prices, by exploiting the country's genetic diversity and lower costs for research, development and manufacturing alike. It has several in the pipeline, and in a sign of new-found confidence, recently acquired a UK business.

Ranbaxy may be suing GlaxoSmithKline (GSK) over patents in the west, but it has also signed a contract with the same multinational to carry out research and development at home. The Indian company is also working with the Medicines for Malaria Venture to produce a new synthetic drug.

CASE 12.1 CONT.

'More and more companies are trying to put their footprint in India,' says Simon Friend, head of the pharmaceuticals group at PwC. 'Compared with China, India has the edge by four to five years because of the language and the infrastructure.'

One of the big triggers for change has been intellectual property. In the early 1970s, many multinational drugs companies left India when it introduced new patent laws that only granted protection for processes, not for the original products or compounds on which drugs were based. That created a vast copycat industry.

As a condition of joining the World Trade Organisation, however, India agreed to introduce legislation in 2005 that provides tougher patent protection on products too, and which could threaten the generic producers.

Separately, regulatory changes have helped break down other protectionist barriers, making it easier to conduct clinical trials in the country – albeit accompanied by ethical guidelines being introduced to limit past abuses.

GSK has been among the first to exploit the shifting trends. Itself the largest single pharmaceutical company in India, which it sees as a market with considerable growth, it has outsourced back office functions to India and begun collaborative research with Ranbaxy.

It is also looking more and more to conduct clinical trials in India. The company insists that this has nothing to do with simple cost cutting, arguing that the facilities are excellent and that many doctors are British trained.

'India has 8,000 to 10,000 manufacturers, 18,000 distributors and 250,000 pharmacies,' says Shailesh Gadre, head of the Indian office of IMS, the market research company. 'It is a very complex system. A company that gets in early will have a very good advantage.' He says that with sales – partly because of the absence of higher margin branded drugs – at $5bn last year, India still represents only a little more than 1 per cent of global pharmaceutical sales. These figures represent the retail market, which makes up the vast bulk of sales.

But revenue grew by 8 per cent in 2005, and Mr Gadre predicts it will increase by about 10 per cent a year for the coming five years. He points out that, by 2010, 450m Indians will have western middle-class incomes. Demand for western-style chronic treatments – for the cardiovascular and central nervous systems, for instance – are already on the rise.

However, he cautions that India remains a country of vast contrasts, with widespread poverty, a very modest state-supported health care system, and private insurance which remains its infancy. That creates considerable tensions and uncertainties.

Others warn that it will be some time yet before western companies are confident about intellectual protection. Nearly 9,000 patents filed between 1995 and 2005 remain in the 'mailbox' awaiting consideration, with none yet granted, and there are reports of inconsistent work by India's different regional patent offices.

Mr Shah is confident but realistic about India's pharmaceutical future. He admits that significant problems of corruption, basic infrastructure and work culture remain. 'We're at least five years away from a blockbuster drug coming from grass roots companies,' he says.

CASE 12.2

Entrepreneur fires broad attack on manufacturers

PETER MARSH

British manufacturers have failed to invest enough in marketing and given too much management control to accountants, according to Edward Atkin, one of the country's most successful engineering entrepreneurs of the past decade.

In a speech tonight in London, Mr Atkin, who created a personal fortune of about £225m when he sold his babies' bottles company last year, will also criticise the government for lack of foresight over manufacturing generally and in particular for neglecting the country's transport infrastructure, as a result providing huge handicaps for industrial companies.

'Government now, far from being supportive, each year piles more and more cost, complication and restriction on industry. We are probably the first generation since the invention of the wheel which, in spite of great technical advances, cannot look forward to ever greater ease of access to all parts of our country,' Mr Atkin will say.

Until recently Mr Atkin was the managing director and majority owner of Avent, one of the world's biggest makers of babies' bottles and which bases all its manufacturing in a high-tech plant in Suffolk.

He sold Avent to a venture capital company for £300m, of which £225m (minus advisers' fees) came to Mr Atkin and his family. The entrepreneur is now weighing up several ideas about ways in which to invest some of the cash in innovative businesses.

Avent has sales from babies' bottles and other infant feeding products such as breast pumps of just over £80m a year. It is thought to account for about a sixth of global revenues from such items and has 80 per cent of its sales coming from outside the UK.

In a speech to the Institution of Electrical Engineers Mr Atkin will say that most successful manufacturers require a stable investment climate and an interest in making world-beating products.

These factors are more likely to be in place if the businesses are owned privately, and also have people with an interest in engineering at the helm, rather than accountants.

'As soon as financial criteria become the main method used for evaluating investment opportunities, the company is almost certainly doomed,' Mr Atkin will say.

He will say that companies subject to the control of investors through a stock market flotation are more likely than private entrepreneurs to be swayed by short-term financial considerations, which are likely to deflect them from decisions linked to building up a global brand on the back of innovative and competitive products.

'It is impossible to forecast variables like volumes, competitive pricing, raw material costs, interest rates or currencies three or five years out,' Mr Atkin will say. 'What is very easy, however, is to appreciate that speeding up a process, reducing waste, eliminating direct labour and improving tolerances and reliability will enhance both the products and their manufacture, as well as the experience of the enduser. These benefits will be long-term and valid, irrespective of the output, exchange rate, raw material costs and all the other variables.'

CASE 12.2 CONT.

Among the few recent success stories in UK manufacturing, according to Mr Atkin, are excavator maker JCB and the Dyson vacuum cleaner producer, which are both privately owned, while the Rolls-Royce aero-engine producer is, he says, an exception among quoted UK manufacturers to have been a consistently strong performer on global markets. Avent was privately owned for all the 33 years in which Mr Atkin was in charge.

These four companies, Mr Atkin will say, have understood the importance of marketing their products on a worldwide basis – something that leads to a culture of continuous development of products so these can be improved to meet the new requirements of customers.

Turning to other examples, Mr Atkin will say that successful manufacturers such as US semiconductor maker Intel, and BMW and Toyota, two of the world's biggest car producers, have made as a centre of their businesses 'an unbroken trend of consistent [product] development, decade after decade'.

This is a culture, Mr Atkin will say, that makes it relatively easy to build up strong teams of engineering and marketing experts within the company that will stay for long periods. It also makes it easier to establish long-term brand loyalty.

Source: Peter Marsh, 'Entrepreneur fires broad attack on manufacturers', *Financial Times*, 17 January 2006, p. 5. Copyright © 2006 The Financial Times Limited.

Discussion points

1. What 'generic' resources might an entrepreneurial business in India possess? (Think other than just financial resources.)

2. In what sense(s) is 'marketing' a resource within an entrepreneurial business?

CHAPTER 13

The entrepreneurial venture and the entrepreneurial organisation

Chapter overview

The fundamental task of the entrepreneur is to create or to change an organisation. This chapter explores what is meant by 'organisation'. The first section explores the way in which entrepreneurs (and other managers) use metaphors (either consciously or unconsciously) to create a picture of the organisations they manage. The second section looks at how entrepreneurs use organisations to control the resources that make up the venture. The third and fourth sections develop a broader view of organisation and view the entrepreneur as operating within a network of resources. The final section considers how this can provide an insight into developing a practical entrepreneurial strategy.

13.1 The concept of organisation

Key learning outcome

An appreciation of how different ideas of organisation aid understanding of the entrepreneurial approach to management.

The notion of organisation is fundamental to management thinking. An organisation is what a manager works for, and organising it is what they do. The entrepreneur may create a new organisation or develop an existing one. Whichever of these options they choose, they create a new organisational world. Organising resources is the means to the end of creating new value. If entrepreneurship is to be understood then the nature of organisation needs to be appreciated.

There are a number of ways in which we can approach the concept of organisation. We cannot see any organisation directly; all that we can observe is individuals taking actions. We call upon the idea of organisation to explain why those actions are co-ordinated and directed towards some common goal. If we wish to understand how an organisation co-ordinates those actions, we must create a picture of the organisation using *metaphors*. Thus, we can think of the organisation both as an *entity*, an object in its own right, and as a *process*, a way of doing things. The type of metaphor used is important because it influences the way in which management challenges are perceived and approached. It underlies the entrepreneur's management style. There are three types of metaphor. *Active* metaphors are created consciously and explicitly as a strategy for developing understanding. An example here is the use of ideas from evolutionary biology to create a model of populations of organisations, which was discussed in section 6.1. *Dormant* metaphors are those that are clear when we think about them, but we do not often do so. An example here would be the use of the word 'organisation' itself. Its root is clearly related to that of 'organ' and 'organism', suggesting a biological metaphor. Another example is the use of the word 'corporate', which is derived from *corpus*, the Latin word for body (we also talk of a corpus of knowledge). Finally, *extinct* metaphors are those that are so deeply embedded in our thinking that we only rarely challenge them. Examples here are to 'see' an opportunity (we don't *actually* see it) or for a business to 'feel' its way forward (a business cannot actually 'feel' anything). All three types of metaphor are common in business. The student who knows a little geology might recognise the words 'active', 'dormant' and 'extinct' as referring to different types of volcano. We are using a metaphor to understand metaphors! Gareth Morgan (1986) provides an extensive and critical study of how we understand organisation through metaphor.

Some conceptualisations of organisation which are important to understanding entrepreneurship are described below.

The organisation as a co-ordinator of actions

People do not work in isolation in an organisation. They get together to co-ordinate and share tasks. Differentiating tasks allows a group of people to achieve complex ends that individuals working on their own could not hope to achieve. An organisation is a framework for co-ordinating tasks. It provides direction, routines and regularities for disparate activities. An organisation has goals which are what the people working together in the organisation aim to achieve as a group. The organisation acts to align and direct the actions of individuals towards the achievement of those goals.

Entrepreneurs are powerful figures within their own organisations. Indeed, the organisation is the vehicle through which they achieve their ambitions, it extends their scope and allows them to do things that they could not do as an individual. The organisation is the tool that entrepreneurs use to create their entire new world. They use their influence and leadership to shape the organisation and to direct it towards where they wish to go.

The organisation as an independent agent

An agent is simply something that acts in its own right. Regarding the organisation as an agent means that we give it a character quite separate from that of the people who make it up. The organisation takes actions on its own behalf and has its own distinguishing properties. Thus we can talk about the organisation 'having' a strategy which it uses to pursue 'its' goals. We can talk about the assets 'it' owns and the culture 'it' adopts. This conceptualisation is important from a social and legal perspective. The business organisation is regarded as a legal entity in its own right, quite separate from the identities of its owners and managers. The firm has rights and responsibilities which are distinct from those of its managers.

Recognising the organisation as an independent agent is important because it reminds us that the organisations created by entrepreneurs have an existence independent of their creators.

The organisation as a network of contracts

Organisations are made up of people who contribute their labour to the organisation on the basis that they will receive something in return. The organisation is the means that people use to pursue their own ends. The idea that the organisation is a network of contracts is based on the notion that people work together within a framework of agreements defining the contribution that each individual will make to the organisation as a whole, and what they can expect from the organisation in return. These agreements are referred to as *contracts*.

Organisational contracts take a variety of forms. They may be quite formal and be legally recognised, for example a contract of employment. Frequently, however, a major part of the contract will not be formalised. Many of the commitments and responsibilities that people feel towards their organisation and those they feel it has towards them are unwritten. They are based on ill-defined expectations as to how people should work together and act towards one another. These aspects of the contract may not even be recognised until they are broken by one party. Organisations are built on *trust* and the nature of the contracts that hold the organisation together are a major factor in defining its culture.

The idea of the organisation as a network of contracts is important because it reminds us that individuals do not completely subsume their own interests to those of the organisation; rather, the organisation is the means by which they pursue their own goals. They will pursue the organisation's interests only if they align with their own. This concept of the organisation also highlights the fact that the individual's relationship with their organisation goes beyond the written legal contract. It is also defined by trust and unspoken expectations. Individuals will only be motivated to contribute to the organisation if those expectations are met, and their trust is not broken.

The organisation as a collection of resources

Organisations are created from resources including capital (money), people and productive assets such as buildings and machinery. The resource-based view of the firm sees it in terms of the collection of resources that make it up. The organisation is built from resources that can be bought and sold through open markets. What makes a particular firm unique is the *combination* of resources that comprise it. Innovation is simply finding new combinations of resources.

Having access to appropriate resources and using them both creatively and efficiently is central to entrepreneurial success. It should not be forgotten that people are the key resource since only they can make capital and productive resources work in new and different ways.

The idea of the firm as a collection of resources reminds us that the entrepreneur must be an effective manager of resources, which means being a manager of people as much as a manager of assets and processes.

The organisation as a system

A system is a co-ordinated body of things, or elements, arranged in a pattern of permanent or semi-permanent relationships. The notion that the business organisation is a system develops from the idea that a firm takes resource inputs and attempts to convert them into outputs of higher value. The greater the value that is added, the more productive the system.

The elements of the organisational system are the people who make it up and the manner in which they are grouped. The actions that people take are defined by the pattern of relationships that exist between them. Permanent relationships and consistent actions lead to regular routines and programmes. The systems view of organisation explains the way organisations develop and evolve by drawing on ideas such as feedback loops and control mechanisms.

The idea that the organisation is a system is valuable because it emphasises the dynamic nature of the organisation. It is what the organisation *does* that matters. It also draws attention to the fact that routines take on a life of their own as the system develops its own momentum. Control mechanisms freeze the organisation's way of doing things. This is valuable. They lock in the organisation's source of competitive advantage. However, in order to remain innovative, the entrepreneurial organisation must avoid inertia, which requires a continual assessment of the way it does things and a willingness to challenge existing routines if necessary. Entrepreneurial businesses achieve success by being more flexible and responsive to environmental signals than established firms. New contributions to systems thinking from areas such as chaos theory and non-equilibrium dynamics are providing a valuable perspective on the way that entrepreneurial businesses function and how they succeed.

The organisation as a processor of information

Information is a critical part of business success since information, properly used, leads to knowledge, and knowledge can lead to competitive success. The organisation can be thought of as a device for processing information, for example information on what needs the customer has, what products will satisfy those needs, how they can be prepared and delivered efficiently, how their benefits can be communicated to customers, and so on. In this view, the performance of the firm is determined by the quality of the information it has and how well it uses it. Further, by co-ordinating the intelligence of the people who constitute it, the organisation as a whole can exhibit intelligence. It not only uses information, but can constantly learn how to use information better.

Innovation is at the heart of entrepreneurship and innovation must be based on knowledge. The idea of the organisation as an information processor highlights the fact that the success of the entrepreneurial organisation lies not just in its innovation but also in the way it *uses* that innovation and learns to go on using it. The entrepreneurial organisation achieves flexibility and responsiveness through its willingness to learn about its customers and itself.

These different perspectives on the organisation are not mutually exclusive; indeed, to some extent they are complementary. None of the perspectives gives a complete picture of what the entrepreneurial firm is about; rather, each gives a different set of insights into what the firm is, how it performs its tasks, the relation it has to the people who make it up and what the basis of its success might be. If entrepreneurs are to fully understand their business then they must learn to use all these perspectives to gain a complete view.

13.2 Organisation and the control of resources

Entrepreneurs use resources to achieve their aims in that they combine resources in a way which is innovative and offers new value to customers. This *is* the pursuit of opportunity.

Resources are brought together under the control of an organisation. The power of entrepreneurs to control resources directly is limited because there is only so much that they can do as individuals. Therefore, entrepreneurs must shape the organisation they build and use the organisation to configure the resources to which they have access. As the organisation grows and increases in complexity, tasks must be delegated down the organisational hierarchy. Controlling the resources in the organisation means controlling the actions of the people in the organisation who use them. If entrepreneurs are to be effective in leading and directing their organisation then they must understand how the resources that make it up can be controlled.

Entrepreneurs must make a decision as to what they will control themselves and what control they will pass on to others. The balance of this decision will depend on the size and complexity of the organisation, the type and expertise of the people who make it up, the type of resources with which the organisation is working and the strategy it adopts. This decision must be subject to constant revision as the organisation grows, develops and changes. Even if an entrepreneur has delegated the management of resources to other people within the organisation, this does not mean that he or she has given up *all* control over them. A number of control mechanisms are retained (see Figure 13.1).

Directed action

The entrepreneur may retain control by directing that specific tasks are undertaken. The course to be followed will be instructed in detail. The actions are likely to be short term, or repetitive, with well-defined outcomes. By directing specific actions the entrepreneur is using others to undertake tasks that they would perform themself but lack the time to do so.

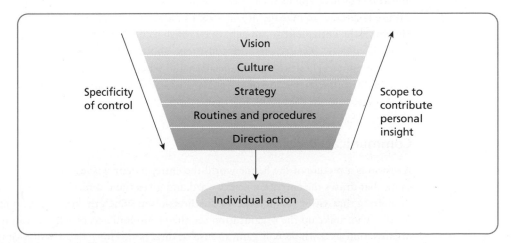

Figure 13.1 Factors influencing individual action in the entrepreneurial venture

Routines and procedures

Routines and procedures are used to establish patterns of action to be repeated. No direct control is exercised, but people are expected to follow the course of actions set down. The actions defined by the routine may be specified either in outline or in detail. The possibility of deviating from the pattern or modifying it will vary depending on the degree of control desired and the need to constrain the outcomes of the actions. When the organisation is too complex to be controlled by directed action, the entrepreneur may concentrate on controlling through procedures.

Organisational strategy

A strategy is a framework for thinking about, and guiding the actions of, individuals within the organisation. The organisation's strategy will be directed towards the achievement of specific goals. It will define the major areas of resource deployment (usually through *budgeting*) and outline the main programmes of activity. The strategy may be imposed by the entrepreneur, or it may be developed through discussion and consensus. People within the organisation might be given a great deal of latitude to develop their own projects of action within the strategy. They will, however, be expected to be guided by the strategy, work towards its goals and operate within its resource constraints. A strategy, even if well defined, offers a greater scope for interpretation than does a routine.

Organisational culture

The concept of organisational culture is an important one. A culture is the pattern of beliefs, perspectives and attitudes which shape the actions of the people within the organisation. An organisation's culture is largely unwritten. Its existence may not even be recognised until someone acts outside its norms. Culture is important in creating motivation and setting attitudes. It can be a critical aspect of competitiveness. For example, a positive attitude towards customer service, constantly seeking innovation or greeting change positively are all determined by culture. Things such as these cannot be enforced through rules and procedures, so culture is difficult to manage. It is a state of mind rather than a resource to be manipulated. However, the entrepreneur can help to establish a culture in their organisation by leading by example and by being clear and consistent about what is expected from people, what behaviour is acceptable to the organisation and what is not. Peters and Waterman (1982), in their highly influential study of US business, *In Search of Excellence*, identified culture as a critical factor in the success of an organisation.

Communicated vision

A vision is a picture of the better world the entrepreneur wishes to create. The vision is the thing that draws the entrepreneur forward and gives them direction. The entrepreneur can, by sharing that vision, communicate the direction in which the organisation must go. If the people who make up the organisation see the vision and accept what it can offer, then the organisation as a whole will gain a sense of direction. However, a vision only specifies an end, not a means. It indicates where the organisation can go, not the path it must take.

A vision leaves open the potential for a wide range of possibilities and courses of action. Different courses must be judged in terms of how effective they will be in leading the organisation towards the vision.

The hierarchy of resource control devices

These means of controlling resources form a hierarchy, as shown in Figure 13.1. As it is ascended, the entrepreneur becomes less specific in their direction. Their control becomes less direct and immediate. On the other hand, they give the people who work with them more latitude to use their own talent and insights and so enable them to make a more substantial contribution to the business. The exact mix of controls used will depend on the size of the organisation, the people who make it up, the tasks in hand and the entrepreneur's personal style. The controls adopted, and the way they are used, will form the basis of the entrepreneur's leadership strategy.

13.3 Markets and hierarchies

Key learning outcome

An appreciation of the distinction between the market and the hierarchy as forms of organisation.

The business world is full of organisations which offer goods and services to each other and to individual consumers. These goods and services are traded in *markets*. Organisations and markets represent different ways in which individuals can arrange exchanges between themselves.

A market consists of a range of sellers offering their goods to a number of buyers. It is characterised by short-term contracts centred on exchanged products, as shown in Figure 13.2. Buyers

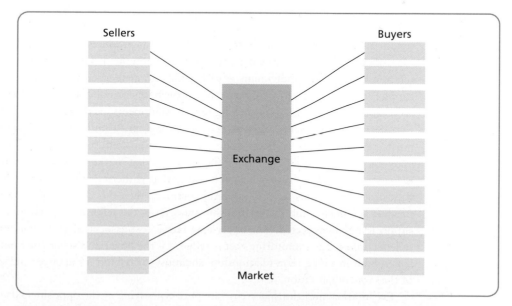

Figure 13.2 The market as a form of organising exchange

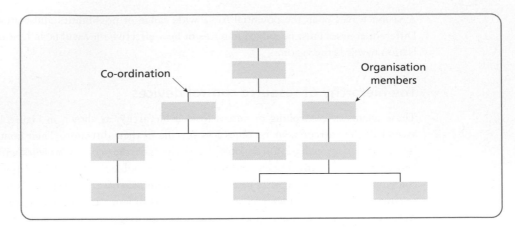

Figure 13.3 Hierarchical organisation

are free to select the seller they wish to buy from. The seller must offer goods at a price dictated by the market. Classical economics assumes that the goods of one supplier are much the same as the goods of any other, although, in practice, sellers may be able to differentiate their products from those of competitors. If this differentiation offers advantages to the buyer, then the seller may be able to sustain a price higher than the market norm. In a market, the relationship between the buyer and seller is centred on the product exchanged between them. The seller has no obligation other than to supply the product specified, and the buyer has no obligation other than to pay for it. The relationship is short term, with the buyer being free to go to another supplier in the future.

Markets are not the only means that people use to organise exchange. They also form organisations such as business firms. Organisations are sometimes referred to as non-market *hierarchies*, indicating the way in which the individuals who make them assign responsibilities. In a hierarchy, individuals still supply a product, their *labour*, to the organisation. Different parts of the hierarchy will supply products and services to other parts and to the organisation as a whole. The factory may pass on its products to the marketing department for example, or the accounts department may supply financial services. In a hierarchy the relationship between individuals goes beyond the mere product or service they agree to supply. It has a long-term character based on both formal and informal criteria. A hierarchical organisation is based on long-term commitments, as depicted in Figure 13.3.

A hierarchy represents a loss of economic freedom. Within an organisation, individuals must use each other's services. They cannot shop around in the market for a better deal. Why, then, do organisations form? The answer is that markets do not come for free. There is a cost associated with assessing what is available: gathering information may be expensive. If, instead, individuals set up long-term contracts, then this cost is reduced. Further, if the product is complex and the relationship short term, the seller may be tempted to cheat and supply less than expected. The buyer may face a cost associated with *monitoring* what the seller supplies. The monitoring cost is reduced if the buyer and seller *trust* one other. Trust is best built in a long-term relationship, and most easily built if the buyer and seller are parts of the same organisation.

The 'market' and the 'hierarchy' are pure types lying at the opposite ends of a spectrum of organisational types. Organisations in the real world lie somewhere in between. They have some of the characteristics of a hierarchy, with relationships based on long-term agreements and formal contracts, and some of the characteristics of markets in which individuals come and go, offering their labour and services on a competitive basis. This is true not only within organisations but also between them. Organisations do not just rely on markets, they set up contracts and make long-term commitments to each other. The network provides a more realistic model of how entrepreneurial ventures actually operate than either of the pure types of the market and the hierarchy.

This observation has led to the development of a powerful economic approach to understanding both why organisations form and the shape they take. This approach is known as *transaction cost economics*, introduced in Chapter 6. The fundamental idea behind transaction cost economics is that some market exchanges have costs associated with them. These costs arise because, with some transactions, one party may believe that there is a chance that the other party will renege on the deal. This means that they must invest in setting up binding contracts and then policing them. If these contract costs become too high, then it may be better for the parties to work together within an organisational setting, so locking their interests together. There is a cost associated with this move in that the efficiency that the market might have provided is lost. However, if this loss is lower than the expected transaction cost, setting up the organisational structure will still be the more efficient option. Oliver Williamson has been at the forefront of the development of the transaction cost perspective, and a full exploration of the insights of this approach can be found in his 1985 book *The Economic Institutions of Capitalism* and his 1991 article.

It is often the case that entrepreneurs prefer to work within an organisational setting rather than 'expose' themselves to market uncertainties. One area of resistance that is often encountered is entrepreneurs' unwillingness to share the secrets of their innovation with outsiders, whom they fear might 'steal' it. Another is they might doubt the commitment of external investors (particularly banks and venture capitalists) to the broader aims of the venture, asserting that they are 'only out for themselves'. As a result of these concerns, entrepreneurs try to bring as many transactions within their organisation as possible. However real such concerns may be, the entrepreneur must be aware of the costs, both direct and in terms of loss of flexibility, in adopting organisation-based rather than market-based solutions.

13.4 Networks

Key learning outcome

An understanding of the concept of the network and its role in the entrepreneurial process.

Individuals use both organisations and markets to facilitate exchanges between themselves. Markets offer a freedom to choose whereas permanent hierarchies emerge when trust is important. Real-life organisations possess some characteristics of both markets and hierarchies. A business organisation has a definite character. It is an agent with legal rights and responsibilities, it has a name. People will know whether they work for it or not. It will have some sort of internal structure.

A business organisation does not exist in isolation. It will be in contact with a whole range of other organisations. Some of these relationships will be established through the market but others may have a longer-term, contractual nature. Businesses set up contracts with suppliers. They may agree to work with a distributor to develop a new market together. An organisation providing investment capital to the venture may be invited to offer advice and support. An entrepreneur may call upon an expert friend to offer advice on marketing. An old business associate may provide an introduction to a new customer. Rather than think about an organisation as closed and sitting in a market, it is better to think of it as being located within a *network* of relationships with other organisations and individuals. In this view the firm does not have a definite boundary. The individuals who make it, and the organisations it comes into contact with, merge into one another. The network is built from relationships which possess both hierarchical and market characteristics. These relationships will be established on the basis of market-led decisions, formal contracts, expectations and trust.

When a new venture is established it must locate itself in a network. This means that it must work to establish a new set of relationships with suppliers, customers, investors and any others who might offer support. The new venture will need to compete with established players. This means that it must break into and modify the network of relationships that *they* have established. A tight network is one in which relationships are established and the parties to them are largely satisfied with these relationships. A loose network is one in which relationships are distant and easily modified. A tight network will be hard to break into; a loose one will be easier. Once a firm is located in a tight network it will find it easier to protect its business from new challengers.

Understanding the nature of the network is important to the success of the entrepreneurial venture. Managing the network will be a crucial part of the strategy for the venture. In particular, the entrepreneur must make decisions in relation to the following questions:

- What is the existing network of relationships into which the new venture must break?
- What is the nature of the relationships that make up the network? Is the network tight or loose? Are the relationships based on formal contracts or on trust?
- How can the new venture actually break into this network of relationships? (Who must be contacted? In what way? What must they be offered?)
- How can the network be used to provide support to the venture?
- What resources (capital, people, productive assets) will the network provide?
- How can risk be shared through the network?
- How can relationships in the network provide a basis for sustaining competitive advantage?

The process of developing answers to these questions will be explored in Part 5 of this book.

In short, a network is a kind of glue which holds a business community together. An entrepreneur initiating a new venture must be active in breaking into a network. Once this has been achieved, the network can be called upon to support them (see Figure 13.4). Thompson (2003) provides a theoretical account of networks and their analysis.

Key learning outcome

An understanding of how the network may be used to increase the power of the entrepreneurial organisation.

13.5 The extended organisation and the hollow organisation

The idea that an organisation is wider than that part of it which is legally defined as the firm provides the entrepreneur with an

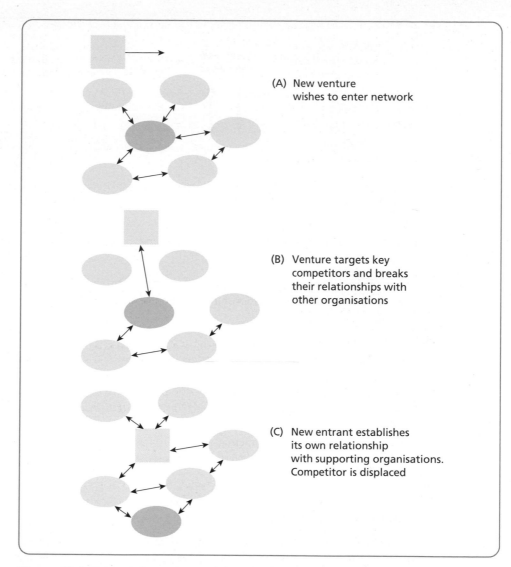

Figure 13.4 Network formation and the entrepreneurial start-up

opportunity. The network offers entrepreneurs the possibility of moving beyond the limits of their own organisation and achieving a great deal more than they could in isolation. Two types of organisation in particular use the potential of the network.

The extended organisation

The extended organisation is one which uses the resources of other organisations in its network to achieve its goals (Figure 13.5). Access to these resources is gained by building long-term, supportive and mutually beneficial relationships. Particularly important are suppliers who provide the venture with the inputs it needs, associated organisations in the same

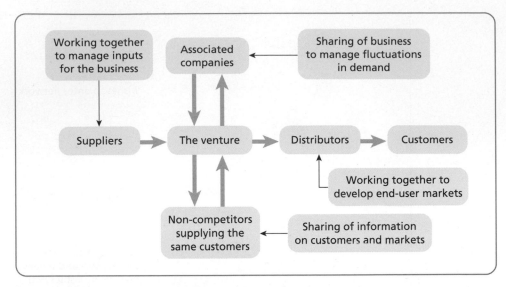

Figure 13.5 Co-operative relationships in the entrepreneurial network

business who can help manage fluctuations in demand, and distributors who can get the firm's goods or services to its customers. Distributors need not be limited to the functions of storing and transporting goods. They can also be active partners in developing a new market and add their support to achieving and sustaining a strong competitive position. The business may also develop a productive relationship with other businesses that supply the same customers with non-competing products. Here information on customers and their needs can be exchanged and market research costs shared. It may also be possible to share selling and distribution costs.

The hollow organisation

The hollow organisation is one which exists not so much to do things itself but to bring other organisations together. In effect it creates value by building a new network or making an existing one more efficient (Figure 13.6). The formal organisation is kept as small as possible – it may only be a single office – and it sticks to its essential or *core* activities. A common example of a hollow organisation is one which simply 'markets' products. It will buy these products from the company which manufactures them. It will use independent distributors to get the product to customers. It may call upon the services of separate market research and advertising agencies. It may even contract-in its sales team. The hollow organisation does not manufacture, distribute or advertise goods or services. It simply exists to bring together the organisations that perform these functions. It is rewarded from the value it creates by co-ordinating their activities.

An excellent example of what can be achieved by adopting a hollow organisational strategy is that of Naxos Records, a venture founded by the Hong Kong-based German entrepreneur Klaus Heymann. This is a business which has established a market-leading

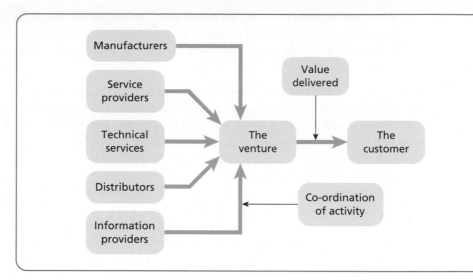

Figure 13.6 The hollow organisation

position in the low-cost classical CD market. Yet the core organisation does little itself except co-ordinate the production and marketing of the product. Musicians and orchestras (often from eastern Europe) are commissioned as they are needed. Recording facilities are hired in. Production and packaging of the CD are outsourced (usually in the Far East), and distribution is via independent retailers.

Factors affecting the choice of organisational form

Both the extended organisation and the hollow organisation are attractive options for the entrepreneur. There are a number of reasons for this:

- they are easy to set up;
- the initial investment needed is small and entry costs are low;
- they allow the entrepreneur to concentrate on their core skills;
- they are flexible and can be easily modified;
- fixed costs are minimised;
- they allow the entrepreneur access to the resources of other organisations;
- growth is relatively easy to manage.

Competition to set up extended and hollow organisations can be quite intense because they are both such attractive options for starting new ventures. If they are to be successful, entrepreneurs must be quite sure of the strategy they are adopting. In particular they must be confident about:

- where the business will be located in the value-addition chain;
- the value they are adding, i.e. why customers will benefit from what the business has to offer;

- why the product they are offering is different from what is already on offer;
- how they will manage the relationships on which the business will depend;
- how they will sustain those relationships in the face of competitors trying to break the relationships it has established.

These are important ideas which will be developed further in Part 5 of this book.

The internet has made a great impact on the world of business. Internet ventures such as the book retailer Amazon and the computer supplier Dell have been high-profile stock market successes. The merger of the media company Time Warner with the online service provider America On-Line (AOL) created great interest and initially a considerable mark-up on the stock-market value of the separate companies.

The internet is primarily a communication system, albeit one of great sophistication and reach. The reason that it is creating such high expectations is the way it is enabling information to be stored and accessed by organisations and the facility it offers to pass information between them. Advocates of the potential competitive advantages that the internet is offering to business are keen to draw a distinction between what is referred to as *e-commerce*, the use of the internet as an adjunct to selling and promotional activities, and *e-business*, the use of the internet to enhance the performance of the organisation's entire operational stance. E-business goes beyond just selling. It is concerned with managing the business's whole value-addition chain and creating an active, two-way dialogue with the customer, not just sending a message to them.

Strategically, the internet is encouraging the development of hollow organisations. This is because it is so powerful in co-ordinating in an efficient and relatively low-cost way the activities of otherwise separate organisations. Many new internet start-ups are concerned not so much with manufacturing or even direct service delivery as with providing a facility that brings traditional suppliers and potential consumers together. Customers appreciate the power of the internet in terms not only of making purchase easy but also of its ability to provide information, making the purchase decision more informed. Suppliers recognise the potential to create new business through a relatively low-cost route. However, many also appreciate the tendency of the internet to make buyer price comparison easier, and so competition keener.

The key challenge for the internet-based hollow organisation is not so much gaining entry, which is quite straightforward, as gaining long-term competitive advantage. Low entry costs are attractive for entrepreneurs, and investors, because they reduce risk. However, they also mean that competitors find it easy to follow. Achieving competitive advantage is more difficult. Internet distributors, like any other distributor, cannot significantly alter the final product or service the consumer uses. Internet distributors have lower costs than traditional distributors, but costs can only be reduced so far. In any case, offering the buyer a lower price reduces the venture's profits. Ultimately, successful internet ventures will be those which build a relationship with customers based on range of offerings, quality of service and reputation supported by a trusted brand. The internet may be changing the business world, but it is not changing its fundamental rules.

Summary of key ideas

- The entrepreneur must bring the resources they use together in the form of an *organisation*.

- Organisations are best understood through the use of *metaphors*: the things they are like.

- The *open market* and the *closed hierarchy* are pure forms of organisation.

- The entrepreneurial organisation is best thought of as a *network* of relationships defined through markets and formal hierarchies. The network lies somewhere between the two pure forms.

- Entrepreneurs can create new value by building *extended* or *hollow* organisations which co-ordinate the activities of other organisations.

Research themes

The role of networks in internet ventures

The internet has provided a number of opportunities for entrepreneurs. As a technology it has particularly facilitated the development of ventures based on networked and hollow organisational forms. Good case studies of many internet-based ventures are now available. Using such case studies (the more the better), identify networked organisational forms in which the venture itself has only a low resource base but is active in co-ordinating and focusing the activities of other (established and probably much larger) organisations. What is the structure of network linkages? To what extent does the venture prioritise relationships with these other organisations? How does the venture manage that relationship, and, in particular, how does it establish and maintain unique access to that organisation and keep competitors out? How does the venture add value as far as customers are concerned? What are the implications for the venture gaining sustainable competitive advantage (refer to Chapter 25 for ideas here)? Select case studies of internet ventures that have been both successful and not. Be prepared to compare the venture with established competitors using a more traditional organisational form. What does this suggest about the possibilities, strengths and limitations of the networked organisational form? What are the key success factors for success with the organisational form?

Key readings

A seminal proposal about the role of networks in the entrepreneurial process is:

Birley, S. (1985) 'The role of networks in the entrepreneurial process', *Journal of Business Venturing*, Vol. 1, pp. 107–17.

And an interesting application of the idea to the process of entrepreneurial organisation creation is:

Larson, A. (1993) 'A network model of organisation formation', *Entrepreneurship Theory and Practice*, Vol. 12, No. 2, pp. 5–15.

Suggestions for further reading

Anderson, J.C., Håkansson, H. and Johanson, J. (1994) 'Dyadic business relationships within a business network context', *Journal of Marketing*, Vol. 58, pp. 1–15.

Anderson, P. (1992) 'Analysing distribution channel dynamics: loose and tight couplings in distribution networks', *European Journal of Marketing*, Vol. 26, No. 2, pp. 47–68.

Birley, S., Cromie, S. and Myers, A. (1991) 'Entrepreneurial networks: their emergence in Ireland and overseas', *International Small Business Journal*, Vol. 9, No. 4, pp. 56–74.

Boisot, M.H. (1986) 'Markets and hierarchies in a cultural perspective', *Organisation Studies*, Vol. 7, No. 2, pp. 135–58.

Cheung, S.N.S. (1998) 'The transaction cost paradigm', *Economic Inquiry*, Vol. 36, No. 4, pp. 514–21.

Falemo, B. (1989) 'The firm's external persons: entrepreneurs or network actors?' *Entrepreneurship and Regional Development*, Vol. 1, No. 2, pp. 167–77.

Jarillo, J.C. (1988) 'On strategic networks', *Strategic Management Journal*, Vol. 9, pp. 31–41.

Jones, G.R. and Hill, C.W.L. (1988) 'Transaction cost analysis of strategy–structure choice', *Strategic Management Journal*, Vol. 9, pp. 159–72.

Larson, A. (1992) 'Network dyads in entrepreneurial settings: a study of the governance of exchange relationships', *Administrative Science Quarterly*, Vol. 37, pp. 76–104.

Larson, A. (1993) 'A network model of organisation formation', *Entrepreneurship Theory and Practice*, Vol. 12, No. 2, pp. 5–15.

Morgan, G. (1986) *Images of Organisation*. London: Sage.

Perry, M. (1996) 'Network intermediaries and their effectiveness', *International Small Business Journal*, Vol. 14, No. 4, pp. 72–9.

Peters, T. and Waterman Jr, R.H. (1982) *In Search of Excellence*. New York: Harper & Row.

Szarka, J. (1990) 'Networking and small firms', *International Small Business Journal*, Vol. 8, No. 2, pp. 10–22.

Thompson, G.F. (2003) *Between Hierarchies and Markets: The Logic and Limits of Network Forms of Organisation*. Oxford: Oxford University Press.

Tyosvold, D. and Weicker, D. (1993) 'Co-operative and competitive networking by entrepreneurs: a critical indent study', *Journal of Small Business Management*, Jan., pp. 11–21.

Williamson, O. (1985) *The Economic Institutions of Capitalism*. New York: Free Press.

Williamson, O. (1991) 'Comparative economic organization: the analysis of discrete structural alternatives', *Administrative Science Quarterly*, Vol. 36, pp. 269–96.

Selected case material

CASE 13.1

25 January 2006

The security of mutual support

PAUL TYRELL

The founder

John Horton, 59, worked as a software engin-eer at GEC and a technical director at Acorn Computer before co-founding Net-tel, the company that eventually became Clearswift. He stood aside as chief executive after com-pleting his first round of venture capital investment and is now company secretary. He also oversees government-grade, high-security projects.

The story of how I came to meet Richard Anton starts with an American entrepreneur, Andy Demari, who collaborated with Net-tel on various projects in the early days. He put me in touch with an ex-colleague of his from Olivetti [the Italian computer maker], who had become a fund manager for Pino, a small Milan-based venture capital firm. Pino was interested but could not handle the size of deal we needed on its own and suggested Amadeus as a lead investor.

As it turned out, I knew the head of Amadeus already. It was Hermann Hauser, the founder of Acorn Computer, which invented the ARM chip (used in most of the world's mobile phones and personal digital assist ants). I had worked closely with him for five to six years and knew he was incredibly bright. As far as I was concerned, any company he was involved with would have to be good.

Richard and I met up in Cambridge and I immediately found him supportive. He had invested in other software companies in the past, knew a lot about the industry and was very sharp. He led us through the process of shaping up for investment without taking advantage of our ignorance in any way. Ultimately, the Amadeus investment com-mittee could have vetoed the deal, but we really felt the company was on our side during the due diligence.

There were three investors in the first round, which brought in about £6.5m. Until then, I was the chief executive – the other co-founders had moved on. But my background was that of a technical director and we really needed a professional chief executive, as well as extra support in sales and marketing.

Amadeus felt we needed a large option pool to beef up our management team. I disagreed – Richard was effectively asking us to dilute ourselves for our employees, and that was new territory for me. However, he eventually persuaded me. We lined up Don Taylor (previously a director at the software firm Oracle) as our chief executive before the funding round was finished, and he helped us to focus and develop the company significantly.

A similar disagreement concerned the marketing spend necessary to consolidate our acquisition of Content Technologies in 2002. However, overall our relationship has been quite smooth – Richard has simply tempered my aggressive entrepreneurialism. He has joined us at trade shows, making himself visible to potential customers as well as investors, and today we participate in business-school seminars run by Amadeus about the relationships between VCs and entrepreneurs.

CASE 13.1 CONT.

The backer

Richard Anton, 41, has extensive experience in private equity and high technology. From 1994 to 1996 he was an early-stage investor for Apax Partners, the private equity firm. He then served as director of business development and finance at two of his investments in the software industry, Autonomy and Neurodynamics. He joined Amadeus in 1998.

I was interested in John Horton from our first meeting, primarily because he had a credible background in technology. I was already interested in the space in which he was operating – Autonomy had looked at e-mail filtering and I had tracked developments in the technology ever since I worked for Autonomy.

John had a plan to move his business into full-service content security – indeed, he had made some early moves to achieve that. And I thought it had a lot of potential. I was aware of the new types of threat emerging and of the potential for e-mail to be a vector for those threats.

I could see opportunities in both in-bound and out-bound filtering. We could license technology to service providers so they could do the filtering themselves, or we could sell direct to [business] customers. Overall, Net-Tel struck me as a treasure chest of good technology that had not yet been fully exploited commercially.

John is strong technically and understands the defence market extremely well. He is the stable core of the business – the memory bank. He is also very reliable – when something different needs doing, he'll pick it up. But perhaps his most impressive quality is that he is supportive to the professional management team I helped to bring in. Often founders act as, or are perceived to be, back-seat drivers. By contrast, John understood he had to pass on the baton. He is able to review the strengths and weaknesses of the business completely objectively, as if he were both executive and non-executive.

What I brought to the partnership was experience of commercial positioning, finance and management recruitment.

At the beginning I visited the company regularly and made a point of meeting customers and potential industry partners to validate the proposition with them. I was closely involved in the acquisition of Content Technologies.

I also involved myself in all issues of management succession – for example, Andy Demari, our initial chairman, was suitable for the early days post-investment, but he has his own business to run on the west coast of the US. We replaced him with Carl Symon, who ran IBM in the UK during the 1990s and is currently on the board of three FTSE companies. We needed that heavyweight experience for the next period of growth.

John and I disagreed over the size of the option pool necessary to bring in people like Carl, but only because he didn't know what the market norms really were. We resolved things by going through a kind of budget, writing down on a whiteboard all the significant heads we had to hire and totalling the equity they would expect to receive.

Since the second funding round, my involvement has been more hands-off, but I'm still a non-executive director and always attend board meetings. The team is in place to realise Clearswift's potential – the company went through a loss-making period while it absorbed the Content Technologies acquisition, but is now in a position to prepare for an initial public offering.

Source: Paul Tyrell, 'The security of mutual support', *Financial Times*, 25 January 2006, p. 16. Copyright © 2006 The Financial Times Limited.

6 February 2006 FT

Biotechnology chief lauds Scottish skills

ANDREW BOLGER

Scotland's flourishing life sciences sector could attract millions of pounds of research work that currently goes to the US, according to the founder of Biocon, India's biggest biotechnology company.

Kiran Mazumdar-Shaw, chairman and managing director of the Bangalore-based company, said Scotland was well placed to take over drug discovery and clinical development work from US companies.

There are more than 550 life sciences organisations in Scotland, employing more than 26,500 people, according to Scottish Enterprise.

Scotland is home to 15 per cent of the UK's life sciences companies, and has more than 50 academic institutions and 80 companies engaged in drug discovery. There are also more than 100 Scottish-based medical devices companies.

Interviewed by the *Financial Times* on a visit to Scotland, Ms Shaw said: 'Last year we spent $2m (£1.14m) in this area and in future years that will grow to tens of millions of dollars – work that I think I could very easily shift here. There is a lot of pre-clinical toxicology that needs to be done. India has some gaps that Scotland could fill very easily.'

Although India enjoys a considerable cost advantage, Ms Shaw explained that some products needed global trials. 'You can easily do development work outside the US as long as you conform with FDA [Food and Drug Administration] standards,' she said.

The entrepreneur, whose company has a market capitalisation of $1.1bn, was speaking after attending her first meeting of the international advisory board of Scottish Enterprise.

The board is part of the government-funded development body's 'globalscot' network, a group of 900 senior business leaders based overseas who try to help Scottish companies and the economy.

Ms Shaw was introduced to the network by John Shaw, her Scottish husband, who was chairman and managing director in India of Madura Coats, the textiles group, from 1991 to 1998. He has since joined Biocon.

Ms Shaw said it had been 'an eye-opener' for her to discover the strength of Scotland's skills base, which meant work could be done more quickly than in the US.

She was also excited by Scotland's potential as a base for epidemiological studies, because of the links between government, universities and life sciences companies.

The Scottish executive has announced it will invest £4.4m to study the ways genetic and lifestyle factors cause heart disease, osteoporosis and mental illness.

Generation Scotland, the programme being run in conjunction with the universities of Aberdeen, Dundee, Edinburgh, Glasgow and the National Health Service, wants to recruit up to 50,000 Scottish volunteers for the research. The findings will help identify groups at high risk of developing inherited conditions and allow early treatments with new drugs.

Andy Kerr, health minister, said: 'We have the potential to develop novel therapies which not only help patients but also help the Scottish biotechnology economy.'

Source: Andrew Bolger, 'Biotechnology chief lauds Scottish skills', *Financial Times*, 6 February 2006, p. 4. Copyright 2006 The Financial Times Limited.

Discussion point

1. In what ways are Richard Anton and Kiran Mazumdar-Shaw trying to create entrepreneurial organisations?

CHAPTER 14

Intrapreneurship

Chapter overview

Intrapreneurship is something of a holy grail for management: the promise of entrepreneurial dynamism, agility and adeptness in exploiting opportunities combined with the stability, market power and low risk of the established business. However, there are problems in combining the two.

14.1 The nature of intrapreneurship

Key learning outcome

An appreciation of the potential and role of intrapreneurship in established organisations.

In recognising the power of the entrepreneurial organisation, it is important not to be too dismissive of what the established 'non-entrepreneurial' organisation has to offer its stakeholders. After all, an established business is only established because it has enjoyed success. The entrepreneurial organisation and the established organisation both have advantages. The entrepreneurial shows an acceptance of (even a need for) change and an ability to exploit new opportunity. The established demonstrates an ability to consolidate around success, manage risk and control resource flows.

A combination of the two, that is, an organisation which recognised the basis of its success and was able to manage it to reduce risk and yet at the same time was flexible to the shifting needs of its stakeholders, remained attuned to new market opportunities and responsive to the need for change, would suggest itself as an ideal type of business. The *intrapreneur* provides a means of achieving the established–entrepreneurial synthesis.

The intrapreneur is a role defined by Pinchot (1985) in his book, *Intrapreneuring*. In essence, the intrapreneur is an entrepreneur who works within the confines of an established organisation. The intrapreneur's role would parallel that of the entrepreneur. In particular he or she would be responsible for developing and communicating organisational vision; identifying new opportunities for the organisation; generating innovative strategic options; creating and offering an organisation-wide perspective; facilitating and encouraging change within the organisation; challenging existing ways of doing things and breaking down bureaucratic inertia. This role has also been described as that of a 'change master' (Kanter, 1985).

Intrapreneurial activity can be directed at four levels within and outside the organisation. These differ in the impact they will have on the organisation and its surroundings, their effect on the venture's stakeholders, the resources they will require and the level of risk they entail.

- *The management of specific projects.* All businesses engage in new projects of some type. Projects such as new product development, the exploitation of a new market opportunity (perhaps international through exporting or strategic alliance), the integration of a new technology into the firm's operations or the acquiring of new funding are especially important to the maturing entrepreneurial venture that wants to keep its competitive edge. Such projects may be best managed in an entrepreneurial way that cuts across conventional organisational boundaries. They may be made the responsibility of a particular cross-disciplinary team that operates with intrapreneurial flair. Ahuja and Lampert (2001) develop a model of how intrapreneurism helps large firms to achieve breakthrough inventions.

- *The setting up of new business units.* As the venture becomes larger, new and distinct business functions and units come into their own. A particular part of the business may operate best if it has a distinct character and a degree of independence. The setting up of new business units is a demanding project. Not only must the structural and external strategic issues be considered, but there are also the resourcing issues (including human), and the relationship with the parent business to be taken into account. Again, an intrapreneurial team, the members of which may have a future role in the new unit, may best manage this sort of project.

- *Reinvigorating the whole organisation.* The success of entrepreneurial ventures is largely based on their flexibility and responsiveness to new and unmet customer demands. Such flexibility can be lost as the business grows and its attention is drawn to internal concerns. Reintroducing the inventive spirit back into the business may be a radical process. Making the organisation entrepreneurial again is clearly an intrapreneurial project. An intrapreneur must lead such a project with entrepreneurial vision for the organisation's future, with an entrepreneurial approach to using power, leadership and motivation and an ability to overcome organisational resistance to change.

- *Reinventing the business's industry.* Entrepreneurs make a difference. The world is not the same after they have built their venture. The most successful entrepreneurs do not just enter a market: they reinvent the industry in which they operate by introducing new technology, delivering new products or operating in a new, more effective way. There is no reason why the maturing entrepreneurial venture should not hold on to this ambition. A business can win by playing to the rules well; but it can also win by changing the rules to suit itself. Clearly though, such a project is wide in its scope and challenging to implement. It demands an eye on the future, strategic vision, comfort with risk and an ability to lead people forward. It is at this level that intrapreneurship meets up with and becomes entrepreneurship.

Intrapreneurism offers an exciting option for the consolidating entrepreneurial venture. It promises a way to build on success while retaining the original dynamism of the venture. It suggests a way to reduce risk while still pursuing fleeting opportunities. However, any organisational form which promises such high rewards must also present some challenges. There are limitations to intrapreneurship, a point developed by Ross (1987).

14.2 The challenges to intrapreneurship

> **Key learning outcome**
>
> A recognition that the potential for intrapreneurship may be limited.

Existing managers' comfort

Allowing a role for the intrapreneur to develop demands that the existing senior managers must create space for the intrapreneur to operate. That means letting go of some degree of control. Existing senior (and not so senior) managers may not feel comfortable with this. In effect, allowing the intrapreneur to operate means that senior managers must give up, or at least share a part of their power at a core rather than a peripheral level. After all, as Young (1999) points out, intrapreneurial management is about breaking rules. And this means the rules that existing managers see as their role to protect and may even have created in the first place.

Decision-making control

Entrepreneurs exist to challenge orthodoxies. They seek a better way of doing things. They must be dissatisfied with the status quo. This same dissatisfaction must also motivate the intrapreneur. Unlike the entrepreneur, however, the intrapreneur must operate within some sort of organisational decision-making framework. If they did not, then they would not actually be working for the organisation at all. The question here is to what extent the intrapreneur can be allowed to challenge existing decision-making procedures and to what extent they must be bound by them. A balance must be created between allowing the intrapreneur freedom to make their own moves and the need to keep the business on a constant strategic path.

Internal politics

The intrapreneur must question the existing order and drive change within the organisation. For many individuals and groups within the organisation, such change will present a challenge. As a result, the intrapreneur is likely to meet resistance, both active and passive, to the ideas they bring along. An ability to predict and understand that resistance, and developing the leadership skills necessary to overcome it, present a considerable challenge to the manager. Intrapreneurs are a rare breed. Tom Peters (1989) has suggested that intrapreneurs must be able to 'thrive on chaos'.

Rewards for the intrapreneur

The intrapreneur, if they are to be effective, must bring along the same type and level of skills that entrepreneurs themselves offer. The question is, can the organisation *really* offer the intrapreneur the rewards (economic, social and developmental) they might come to expect in return for using them? In short, if someone is an effective intrapreneur, how long will it be before the temptation of full-blown entrepreneurship is felt and they move off to start a venture of their own?

Clearly, intrapreneurship presents itself as a spectrum which, as a style of management, acts to connect 'conventional' management with entrepreneurial management. It offers a way to bring the advantages of both types of management together. In this it is a compromise. The entrepreneur can only facilitate intrapreneurship within the business by recognising the nature of this compromise and making decisions in relation to it. The central question relates to how much latitude the venture's strategy gives individuals to make their own decisions. The question is not just strategic. An entrepreneur must decide to what extent they will be willing to accept dissent from the intrapreneur. Will it be received as a challenge? How does active dissent fit with the leadership strategy the entrepreneur has nurtured?

Entrepreneurs must also ask how the reward structure they have set up encourages and discourages individual decision making. What does the individual get in return for venturing on behalf of the business? What sanctions come into force if things go wrong? The entrepreneur must remember that such rewards and sanctions are not always formal and explicit. Further, the entrepreneur must recognise the level of resistance that agents driving change meet from the organisation and accept responsibility for helping the intrapreneur to overcome this. No less than any other member of the organisation, the intrapreneur needs support, encouragement and leadership.

Summary of key ideas

- Intrapreneurship – the entrepreneur in the established organisation – would seem to offer a great prize: the possibility of entrepreneurial dynamism with the stability and market power of the proven firm.

- Intrapreneurs can operate at several levels:
  - managing specific projects;
  - setting up new business units;
  - reinvigorating the organisation;
  - reinventing industries.

- However, the potential for intrapreneurship is limited by:
  - existing managers' comfort with rule-breaking intrapreneurs;
  - keeping the intrapreneur aligned with the organisation's strategy;
  - the ability to provide the effective intrapreneur with sufficient rewards (financial and developmental).

Research themes

Defining the intrapreneur

Refer back to the discussion of defining the entrepreneur in Chapter 1. Consider the two studies undertaken by Gartner (1988, 1990) to ascertain the definitions of the entrepreneur that various people (politicians, managers, experts) suggested and how the responses were analysed.

Repeat the study (or at least using a similar methodology) focusing in on the terms 'entrepreneur' and 'intrapreneur'. You may find human resource and development managers within established firms to be a good response group. (You will find that by using e-mail your study will not be as expensive to conduct as Gartner's!)

Compare your findings to those of Gartner. Is there a greater consensus on what an intrapreneur is? How is the intrapreneur distinguished from the entrepreneur?

Conceptualising the intrapreneur

Review the discussion about economic approaches to the entrepreneur in Chapter 7. To what extent can the points made from various economic perspectives be said to apply to the intrapreneur as much as to the entrepreneur? Can any of them distinguish the intrapreneur from the entrepreneur? Attempt to relate your conclusions in the form of some diagram or conceptual map.

 ## Key readings

Two contrasing readings, the first emphasising the opportunity of intrapreneurship, the second emphasising its limitations, are:

Stopford, J.M. (1994) 'Creating corporate entrepreneurship', *Strategic Management Journal*, Vol. 15, pp. 521–36.

Wesley Morse, C. (1986) 'The delusion of intrapreneurship', *Long Range Planning*, Vol. 19, No. 6, pp. 92–5.

Suggestions for further reading

Ahuja, G. and Lampert, C.M. (2001) 'Entrepreneurship in the large corporation: a longitudinal study of how established firms create breakthrough inventions', *Strategic Management Journal*, Vol. 22, pp. 521–43.

Coulson-Thomas, C. (1999) 'Individuals and enterprise: developing intrapreneurs for the new millennium', *Industrial and Commercial Training*, Vol. 31, No. 7.

Gartner, W.B. (1998) '"Who is an entrepreneur?" is the wrong question', *American Journal of Small Business*, Spring, pp. 11–32.

Gartner, W.B. (1990) 'What are we talking about when we talk about entrepreneurship?', *Journal of Business Venturing*, Vol. 5, pp. 15–28.

Jennings, R., Cox, C. and Cooper, G.L. (1994) *Business Elites: The Psychology of Entrepreneurs and Intrapreneurs*. New York: Routledge.

Johnson, D. (2001) 'What is innovation and entrepreneurship? Lessons for larger organizations', *Industrial and Commercial Training*, Vol. 13, No. 4, pp. 135–40.

Kanter, R.M. (1985) *The Change Masters*. London: Unwin Hyman.

Koon, P.A. (2000) 'Developing corporate intrapreneurs', *Engineering Management Journal*, Vol. 12, No. 2, pp. 3–7.

Moon, M.J. (1999) 'The pursuit of managerial entrepreneurship: does organization matter?', *Public Administration Review*, Vol. 59, No. 1, pp. 31–43.

Morris, M.H. and Jones, F.F. (1999) 'Entrepreneurhip in established organizations: the case of the public sector', *Entrepreneurship: Theory and Practice*, Vol. 24, No. 1, pp. 71–91.

Pearson, G.J. (1989) 'Promoting entrepreneurship in large companies', *Long Range Planning*, Vol. 22, No. 3, pp. 87–97.

Peters, T. (1989) *Thriving on chaos*. London: Macmillan.

Pinchot, III, G. (1985) *Intrapreneuring*. New York: Harper & Row.

Prassad, L. (1993) 'The etiology of organizational politics: implications for the intrapreneur', *SAM Advanced Management Journal*, Vol. 58, No. 3, pp. 35–41.

Robinson, M. (2001) 'The ten commandments of intrapreneurs', *New Zealand Management*, Vol. 48, No. 11, pp. 95–7.

Ross, J. (1987) 'Corporations and entrepreneurs: paradox and opportunity', *Business Horizons*, July/Aug., pp. 76–80.

Stopford, J.M. (1994) 'Creating corporate entrepreneurship', *Strategic Management Journal*, Vol. 15, pp. 521–36.

Wesley Morse, C. (1986) 'The delusion of intrapreneurship', *Long Range Planning*, Vol. 19, No. 6, pp. 92–5.

Young, A.P. (1999) 'Rule breaking and a new opportunistic managerialism', *Management Decision*, Vol. 37, No. 7, pp. 582–8.

Selected case material

CASE 14.1   25 July 2005   **FT**

Smart companies take an 'intrapreneurial' spirit

PAUL TYRELL

How do large companies such as Apple Computer continue to innovate and respond rapidly to new opportunities, as if they were start-ups?

Apple seemed to produce the iPod out of thin air in 2001 – at the time, a personal digital music player was not regarded as the obvious progeny of a personal computer manufacturer. Yet the company has since re-entered the FT Global 500 ranking of the world's largest companies after a four-year absence.

The iPod now accounts for one-third of Apple's revenues and its 'halo effect' has contributed to a 35 per cent increase in sales of the company's Macintosh computers over the past year.

The iconic music player has also given critical mass to an entirely new market – the selling of digital music online. Even with his expertise in marketing, Steve Jobs, Apple chief executive, could never have predicted such success. Yet he was prepared for it in part thanks to a company culture in which innovative opportunities are spotted, nurtured and championed in an entrepreneurial manner – in short, a culture that is 'intrapreneurial'.

The term has its roots in an *Economist* article of 1976 by its then-deputy editor, Norman Macrae. Among other things, Mr Macrae argued that 'dynamic corporations of the future should simultaneously be trying alternative ways of doing things in competition with themselves.'

In a follow-up article, published in 1982, he suggested large organisations should form internal markets in which groups of staff would compete for modules of work and proportionate remuneration, rather than simply being paid for attendance.

The term 'intrapreneur' was coined at about the same time by a husband-and-wife team, Gifford and Elizabeth Pinchot, who cited Macrae's 1976 article as their inspiration.

Both entrepreneurs and business consultants, the Pinchots suggested individuals could act like entrepreneurs within a large organisation to the benefit of both employee and employer, provided they were willing to risk something of value to themselves – a portion of their salary, for example. Such intrapreneurs could exchange a completed project for a cash bonus or capital to invest internally in future projects.

The idea of setting up semi-autonomous units dedicated to innovation had a famous precedent.

Lockheed Martin, the US aerospace company, set up its 'Advanced Development Projects Unit', nicknamed 'Skunk Works', during the Second World War. A small facility, it was given huge resources and top personnel to develop cutting-edge technology in secret.

Some of the world's most famous military aircraft – such as the SR-71 Blackbird, the high-speed and radar-resistant reconnaissance aircraft – emerged from its hangars. Still operating from an Air Force base in California, Skunk Works is now a registered trademark and a widely used term for any secret innovation-led project.

During the 1970s, similar units were set up inside many organisations to think 'disruptively' – to look at products or markets outside their usual offering.

One of the most famous was 'Project Chess', the twelve-man team at IBM that developed the first personal computer in 1981. Similarly, after the Macintosh computer was launched in 1984, Steve Jobs described its development as an 'intrapreneurial venture' within Apple – since the machine would compete with the Apple II, previously the company's core product.

Today the term intrapreneurship encompasses two main concepts: first, 'corporate venturing', which usually describes the search for spin-off opportunities; and second, the fostering of an entrepreneurial culture in large organisations, with the main objective of innovation.

The first of these has a dismal track record. Recent research by Ashridge and London business schools concluded that less than 5 per cent of corporate venturing units created new businesses that were taken up by a parent company.

Nevertheless, Julian Birkinshaw, a professor at London Business School, suggests that in certain conditions large companies can create value by acting like venture capitalists.

These include 'harvest venturing', where surplus resources are used in commercial ventures, and 'ecosystem venturing', where the company supports entrepreneurial moves

▶

CASE 14.1 CONT.

among its stakeholders – investing in its suppliers, for example, to ensure that components are always available.

Evidence suggests that an 'intrapreneurial' culture may be more powerful. Professor Birkinshaw says that companies now treat the generation of ideas as a vital task.

'If you went back 50 years and asked someone on the production line who was responsible for quality, they'd point to the quality assurance guy at the end of the line,' he says. 'Now quality is everyone's responsibility. Similarly, when you ask someone in a large organisation today who is responsible for new ideas, the venturing laboratory is no longer a satisfactory solution. You need to get everybody alert to opportunities and acting on them.'

Corporations should aim to be 'ambidextrous', Prof. Birkinshaw says. In other words, 'good at both traditional, boring, efficiency-oriented functions and at spotting and acting on sexy new ideas'.

A sales manager, for example, may sell to a specific group of clients, but through their awareness of others they may identify an entirely untapped group, or even a new line of business. In such a situation, the successful company will have a culture that supports them – one that is 'empowering as well as aggressively performance-oriented'.

Moreover, such a company is more likely to have a culture that supports learning, says Dylan Jones-Evans, director of the newly formed National Entrepreneurship Observatory for Wales.

Professor Jones-Evans was part of a team that recently surveyed the 120 most innovative companies in South Korea, as classified by the government. He found that the most successful were those that continually tried to learn from their competitors and other external sources of information about their markets.

'As organisations grow out of their entrepreneurial stage, many suffer from what we call founders' disease,' he says. 'They develop their core competence to such an extent that it becomes all they concentrate on. As a result, they're left behind by the dynamic environment around them.'

Recent research by Clark Gilbert, a professor at Harvard Business School, suggests the best innovations result from thinking about external forces.

'Intrapreneurial' ventures should be 'opportunity-based rather than resource-based', he says, explaining that most large organisations try unsuccessfully to develop new ideas from their existing resources and competencies, rather than look outside for ideas. 'The problem in so many existing markets is that product lines have already overshot what most consumers can absorb,' he adds.

In such an environment, companies should be aiming for 'disruptive' ideas of the sort described by economist Joseph Schumpeter when, in 1934, he described the 'creative destruction' of established businesses by entrepreneurs.

'We find big firms are interested in disruption only when they think it will overlap or attack their business,' says Prof. Gilbert. 'Yet it always leads to growth in the overall market. The personal computer did disrupt the mainframe but it caused the total market for hardware to grow.

'Easyjet is disrupting the airline industry but it's also bringing growth in the consumption of air travel. Often, big firms are so worried about cannibalising that they fail to realise they're poised on the edge of huge growth opportunities.'

Source: Paul Tyrell, 'Smart companies take an "intrapreneurial" spirit', *Financial Times*, 25 July 2005, p. 11. Copyright © 2005 The Financial Times Limited.

9 August 2004   FT

CASE 14.2

Know the limits of corporate venturing

JULIAN BIRKINSHAW AND ANDREW CAMPBELL

With growth back on the agenda after a period of austerity and cost cutting, it is worth reflecting on the lessons arising from similar periods in the past.

In the late 1990s, more than three-quarters of companies in the Fortune 100 and an equivalent number of FTSE 100 companies set up corporate venturing units as part of their search for growth. For example, BAT, the tobacco company, set up two units: Imagination, to search for new ideas, and Evolution, to develop the ideas into new businesses. While these units helped the company explore a number of areas, they failed to develop any significant new businesses.

Recent research into corporate venturing units and corporate incubators by both Ashridge and London business schools concluded that less than 5 per cent of corporate venturing units created new businesses that were taken up by the parent company. Moreover, many failed to make any positive contribution.

So why do corporate venturing units fail to help their parent companies find new legs? There are three reasons.

First, early stage venturing is a tough job, even for professional, independent venture capital (VC) companies. Many VC companies earn less than their cost of capital unless they are fortunate enough to invest in one of the rare big winners. Angels, another form of independent investor in early stage ventures, also frequently fail to earn a good return on their investments. Without some advantage, corporate venturers are unlikely to beat these odds.

Second, corporate venturers rarely have an advantage over the professionals. Those business opportunities where the company does have a clear advantage are normally dealt with through the strategic planning process. At BAT, for instance, acquisitions of tobacco companies in new regions would not be allocated to a corporate venturing unit. Instead, BAT's venturing focused on areas such as e-commerce, where its sources of advantage were questionable.

Further, individuals in a corporate venturing unit rarely match their independent competitors. They may include some of the most entrepreneurial managers in the company, but they do not usually have the accumulated experience of seasoned venture capitalists.

Third, the new ventures that start up within a corporate venturing unit often attract little attention or commitment from the core of the company. Because they are developed within a separate unit, they are not part of the strategic planning discussions that drive resource allocation.

When the parent company is short of resources, either because of an economic downturn or because the new activities begin to compete with existing businesses, the new ventures lose out. Since it takes longer to nurture a new venture than most business cycles, competition for resources is almost inevitable.

These obstacles to corporate venturing appear to be insurmountable. In our research, we could find no examples of new legs being developed from a venturing unit that passed the test of being 'significant, permanent new businesses' – meaning that they are profitable, are part of the parent company's portfolio and amount to 20 per cent of sales or $1bn in value. Even when the research was extended

▶

back to venturing units set up in the 1970s or 1980s, none of them spawned a new business that passed our significance and permanence tests. Corporate venturing units do not, it appears, deliver growth.

Managements looking for new growth have two routes: strategic planning (thinking through the options and choosing one or more with reasonable chances of success), or opportunistic investments (reacting to events or external proposals when they appear sufficiently promising).

In a separate strand of research, we assembled a database of companies that had created new businesses that passed the significance and permanence tests. In only one of these cases did the new business begin its life in a corporate venturing unit or corporate incubator. Two-thirds were the result of carefully considered strategic decisions and one-third were more opportunistic.

So, if corporate venturing does not create new businesses, does it have any place within large companies? The answer is yes. The techniques of corporate venturing can be harnessed for four purposes:

- **Harvest venturing** – This is appropriate when some corporate resources, such as technology, managerial skills, brands and even fixed assets, are surplus to requirements. It uses the techniques of venturing to convert existing corporate resources into commercial ventures, and then into cash.

  Lucent New Ventures Group was an example of harvest venturing before it was sold to Coller Capital. Set up to exploit Lucent's technology, the unit evaluated over 300 opportunities, started 35 ventures and drew in $350m (£192m) of external venture capital.

- **Ecosystem venturing** – This is appropriate when the success of a business unit depends on a community of connected businesses, such as suppliers, agents, distributors, franchisees, technology entrepreneurs or manufacturers of complementary products.

  If this ecosystem is short of venture capital funds there is an opportunity for the company to act as a support to entrepreneurs in the community. The benefit to the company is the vibrancy of the community and the impact this has on its core businesses, rather than the prospect of capital gain from the investments.

  Intel Capital and Microsoft both use corporate venturing to stimulate their ecosystems. Intel Capital's early investments were made in suppliers, often to guarantee availability of components. As the component industry matured, Intel switched to investing in software companies and supercomputer makers to promote the use of Intel technology.

- **Innovation venturing** – This is appropriate when an existing function within a business unit, normally research or new product development, is underperforming because there is insufficient energy directed towards innovation. There must also be some belief that entrepreneurial energy is latent inside the company and can be fostered by stimulating 'intrapreneurs' or by tapping into external entrepreneurs.

  A unit with a venturing approach is set up to take on part of the function that is underperforming. By providing the right conditions, internal or external managers with entrepreneurial instincts will take more risks and invest more energy in developing new technologies or ways of working. Shell's GameChanger programme was set up in 1996 to increase innovation in the technical function of Shell's exploration business. The idea was to take 10 per cent of the technical budget and spend it in a 'venturing' way. This new approach to innovation was taken up by other divisions in Shell and is viewed as having produced a step-change in some areas.

- **Private equity venturing** – This is appropriate under rather limited circumstances. It is equivalent to a diversification into the private equity business, so the company needs to believe that it has better access to a flow of good deals than independent private equity companies. Also, managers must be confident that the deal flow they are tapping into is in the early stages of an upswing. To make money in the cycle of boom and bust, managers need to invest early and exit before the shakeout.

Nokia Venture Partners was set up to make minority investments in wireless internet projects. As one of the partners explained: 'We do not do strategic investments [for Nokia] but the reason we exist is strategic for Nokia.'

Managers planning any kind of venturing unit need to be clear about which type they are setting up and why. 'New leg venturing' and units with mixed objectives do not work. Unless managers are clear about which of the four types they want, they will not build the necessary business model or skills to be successful. Companies wanting to do more than one kind of venturing need more than one type of venturing unit.

Source: Julian Birkinshaw and Andrew Campbell, 'Know the limits of corporate venturing', *Financial Times*, 9 August 2004, p. 11. Copyright © 2004 The Financial Times Limited.

Discussion points

1. Sketch the outline of a compensation and reward package for an 'intrapreneur'. (Think in terms of fixed salary, performance bonuses and non-financial rewards.)

2. What parallels and distinctions might be drawn between the intrapreneur as innovator and the intrapreneur as the establisher of new business units? How might these two roles be compared with those of the traditional entrepreneur?

CHAPTER 15

The changing role of the entrepreneur in the consolidated organisation

Chapter overview

This chapter is concerned with an exploration of the way in which the entrepreneur's role changes as the organisation's rate of growth slows and it consolidates its position in the marketplace. The role of the entrepreneur is compared and contrasted with that of the chief executive. It is considered why, despite its many strengths, entrepreneurial control may not always be right for the mature venture. The chapter concludes with a consideration of the responsibility of the entrepreneur to plan to pass on control to others after they have departed the organisation.

15.1 The entrepreneur versus the chief executive

Key learning outcome

An appreciation of the differences between the roles of the entrepreneur and the chief executive officer.

The vast majority of organisations offer a role for a single, most senior manager. This position has a number of titles. In for-profit businesses it is often the *managing director* or *president*. Generically, the role is referred to as the *chief executive officer* (CEO). Whereas all organisations have a chief executive officer of some description, not all are led by someone we would recognise as an entrepreneur.

So, while the entrepreneur *may* be a chief executive officer, the chief executive officer is not *necessarily* an entrepreneur. Clearly, both roles present considerable management challenges. Both demand vision, an ability to develop strategic insights and provide leadership. That said, the two roles are distinct in a number of ways.

Internal co-ordination versus external promotion

The resource-based view of the organisation (see section 26.7 below) emphasises the role that managers have in bringing in the resources that are critical to the success of the venture: capital, information, people and the goodwill of customers. The entrepreneur, especially when the venture is at an early stage and has limited management resources, will take on the responsibility for bringing in most of these things. He or she will be the venture's salesperson, its finance expert, its recruitment specialist and so on.

The chief executive of even a moderately large organisation will not have direct responsibility for doing these things. He or she may not even have responsibility for *delegating* them, at least directly. What they will have responsibility for is setting up *management structures* within the organisation which will enable these tasks to be co-ordinated and carried out in a way that is effective and is responsive to the overall strategic direction chosen by the business. They may also recognise a need to manage the organisation's *culture*. The chief executive is, responsible not so much for acquiring resources as for making sure that those which are acquired are used at a strategic level, in the best possible way.

In these terms, the entrepreneur provides a bridge between the small business manager and the chief executive of a large firm. In growing the venture, the entrepreneur transforms the role of acquiring resources into that of creating and maintaining structures to manage resources. The role changes from one of *external* promotion (that is, managing the venture in its wider *network*) to one of *internal* co-ordination.

Managing continuity versus driving change

As related in section 6.1, entrepreneurs are interested in driving change. So too are chief executives. In a fast-changing world, organisations must change if they are to survive and prosper. The management of change is now properly recognised as one of the key responsibilities of senior management, in whatever sector their organisation is operating. Entrepreneurs and chief executives are both interested in changing their organisations in response to the opportunities presented to them.

However, there is a difference in the *degree* of change that entrepreneurs wish to see and that which chief executives would normally wish to occur. Entrepreneurs are interested in *radical* change. The entrepreneur's vision is created out of a tension between what is and what might be. For that vision to be powerful, the difference between what is and what might be achieved must be great. Chief executives, on the other hand, are more likely to be interested in slower and more measured *incremental* change. This is understandable. After all, their organisations have proved their success, at least historically. They must be doing something right! Incremental change can build on that success: strengths are managed in while weaknesses are managed out. Radical change threatens to throw away the strengths as well as address the weaknesses.

Management by 'right' versus management by appointment

The third feature that distinguishes entrepreneurs from chief executives is the basis on which they obtain authority to manage the business and the influence this has on the power base they develop. As noted in section 1.6, *authority* and *power* are quite different things. Power is an ability to influence the course of actions within the organisation. Authority merely offers the potential to influence the organisation by virtue of a position within it. Authority is an *invitation* to power, not power itself.

Chief executives obtain their authority to run the business by virtue of appointment to the position. They may arrive at this position as a result of internal promotion or by being recruited into the organisation. The appointment process is governed by established organisational procedures. The views not only of internal managers but also of important investors may be sought. Once in this position, the power of the chief executive arises from the way they control resources and systems and the leadership they offer.

Entrepreneurs also gain authority from the position they occupy, their management of resources and systems, and the leadership they give to the organisation. However, an entrepreneur has an additional source of authority providing not only authority to run the business, but also a *right* to run it. Whereas the chief executive is employed by the organisation, the organisation is perceived to 'belong to' the entrepreneur. This perceived right can be derived from the entrepreneur's ownership of the business. However, owning the organisation they lead is not a necessary characteristic of the entrepreneur. The business is actually owned by those who invest in it. More important is the entrepreneur's historical relationship to founding the organisation and their association with *building* it up.

This difference is important not only for the way the entrepreneur actually manages the organisation but also for the way in which they are exposed as a result of its performance. While we would expect a chief executive to be ousted if the organisation fails to perform, we can still be surprised when an entrepreneur who is seen to have created the organisation is handed the same fate.

Of course, these three criteria do not create hard and fast categories. We are dealing with fuzzy concepts in the same way as we were when we discussed the distinction between the small business and the entrepreneurial venture in section 2.1. Whom we regard as an entrepreneur and whom we see as 'merely' a chief executive is a matter of judgement based on a consideration of the balance between all three criteria.

As with the distinction between the small business manager and the entrepreneur, we should not rush to make a judgement as to who is, or is not, an entrepreneur. We should not look towards the individual to assess whether they are an entrepreneur or not; rather, we should look at what and how they manage in terms of the balance between internal and external co-ordination, the change they seek to create and the way authority is ascribed to them, i.e. the basis of their power (Figure 15.1).

15.2 The dangers of entrepreneurial control in the mature organisation

Key learning outcome

An appreciation of some of the limitations of an entrepreneurial style of management in the mature venture.

Entrepreneurial management has a lot to offer. The entrepreneur's vision offers the potential for leadership. That vision and leadership can be used to give the venture direction. It provides an impetus for the changes that are necessary if a venture is to survive and prosper in a rapidly changing world. However, as a *style* of management, entrepreneurship is merely one style among many, and while entrepreneurship is a very powerful style of management it, like any other style, has its limitations.

Entrepreneurial management is concerned with the *whole* organisation. In the early stages of the venture this allows the entrepreneur to manage the organisation in an integrated way. The entrepreneur can put balanced emphasis on attracting all the resources the organisation requires: money, people,

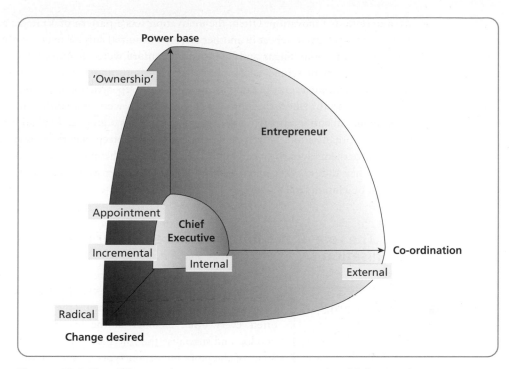

Figure 15.1 The difference between an entrepreneur and a chief executive

customers and knowledge. Unfortunately, this may lead the entrepreneur to underestimate the value of the management of particular functions. They may be quite dismissive of the need for a dedicated approach to marketing or finance or human resource management as the venture grows and matures (relate this to the heuristics described in section 18.6 below). This can lead the entrepreneur to underestimate the contribution that specialists can make to the venture. Having made a success of the venture themselves they can become suspicious of the need for 'experts'. As a result, the entrepreneur may find it difficult to give specialist managers sufficient room to make the decisions they need to make.

Further, entrepreneurial management is concerned with driving change. This is a key and positive aspect of the entrepreneur's approach. It is only from change that new value can be created. However, it is often the case that the entrepreneur exhibits a greater desire for change than do other stakeholders. The entrepreneur may still be seeking new ways to push the venture forward while investors and employees seek consolidation and stability. As a result, there may be a conflict over the type of investments undertaken by the mature venture. A number of high-profile run-ins occurred between highly successful entrepreneurs and institutional investors at the end of the 1980s in both the USA and the UK as the financial climate became more difficult. For example, both Anita and Gordon Roddick, founders of The Body Shop and Alan Sugar, founder of Amstrad, became involved in expensive share buy-backs to increase their personal control of their enterprises.

This touches on a wider issue. All organisations develop an *inertia* or resistance to change. Entrepreneurs and the organisations they create are not immune to this. While the entrepreneurial organisation is founded on an innovation, there is no guarantee that it will be innovative in its innovation. Often, the innovation sets a pattern of strategic activity which the venture attempts to repeat in another sector. The initial success may not always translate to other sectors. Alan Sugar and his Amstrad venture were phenomenally successful with a formula which presented uncomplicated, easy-to-use and low-cost hi-fi systems to the general public. However, the same formula was not repeated so successfully with business computers, a sector where the customer-buying criteria were quite different.

All in all, an entrepreneurial style of management has a great and valuable role to play in the mature organisation. However, it is essential that entrepreneurs recognise that the way they involve themselves with, and apply their talents to, the mature organisation differ from the way they did so when the organisation was in a fast-growing state. This is a theme explored by Hamm (2002).

15.3 The role of the founding entrepreneur in the mature organisation

> ### Key learning outcome
>
> An appreciation of the types of role the entrepreneur can undertake in the mature organisation.

The role of the entrepreneur must change as the venture develops. Growth offers founding entrepreneurs the same opportunity as it offers every other member of the organisation: the chance to develop and specialise the role they play within the organisation. Some of the more important types of specialisation are described below (see also Figure 15.2).

Chief executive

The most obvious role for the entrepreneur to play is that of chief executive. In this the entrepreneur has a clearly defined position at the head of the organisation. He or she retains the power to make and influence key decisions about the way the business should be

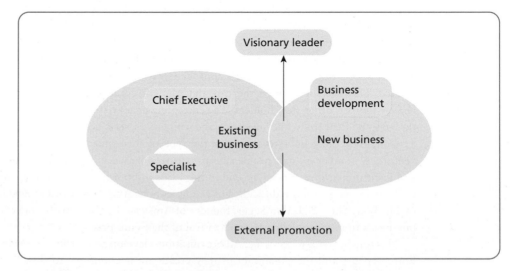

Figure 15.2 The roles of the entrepreneur in the mature organisation

conducted. The chief executive role is, of course, one which the entrepreneur can drift into by virtue of always being at the head of the business. However, the points made in the previous section about the differences between the way the entrepreneur leads the growing business and the way that the chief executive manages the mature business must be considered here in relation to the evolution of that role.

Visionary leader

As discussed in section 13.2, the entrepreneur has a variety of means at their disposal when it comes to influencing the direction the organisation takes and the way it manages its resources. Entrepreneurs do not have to direct every decision personally. They can use indirect means of communicating vision, directing strategy and controlling the organisation's culture. This means that the entrepreneur can specialise the role they play along the leadership dimension. By taking on the role of a visionary leader, the entrepreneur avoids making decisions personally. Rather, they create an environment which brings out the best in the organisation's people by motivating them and giving them an overall sense of direction. This is the kind of role played by the Virgin chief, Richard Branson, who, while providing leadership to his organisation, leaves most of the decision making to his professional managers.

Manager of business development

Entrepreneurs sometimes find it difficult to let go of the entrepreneurial approach they have developed. They do not find the chief executive role a comfortable one. Yet they can still recognise the need for a consolidatory approach to the management of the mature venture. They may resolve this dilemma by concentrating on the development of new business, a task which is well suited to an entrepreneurial style. The entrepreneur then delegates management of the established business to another manager. If the business is made up of a number of independent business units then this arrangement can be made explicit. The entrepreneur can leave the running of the business units to their managers and can concentrate on making new acquisitions, for example. On the other hand, if the business is a single, coherent organisation then the arrangement may be more implicit and be based on internal delegation. An example here might be Rupert Murdoch with his News International and BSkyB business ventures. While taking a very active interest in the established business, Murdoch is most active at the cutting edge of his growing empire.

Technical specialist

Sometimes the entrepreneur may decide to give up the chief executive position altogether and take on what, at face value, appears to be a subordinate role within the organisation. In this role they will specialise in some way, perhaps in managing product development or marketing. Though uncommon, this sometimes occurs in high-technology organisations which have been founded by technical experts. An example of this is Martin Woods, a physicist, who while based at the Cavendish Laboratories founded the successful Oxford Instruments Company, a major manufacturer of components for hospital scanners. Once the venture had passed the stage where product innovation was the most important thing, and marketing and financial management became of greater importance, Dr Woods passed on the day-to-day running of the company to marketing and finance professionals and moved back to the laboratory as the company's research and development director.

Promoter of the venture

The entrepreneurial venture must continue to attract the support of external stakeholders, not least customers and financial backers. The entrepreneur may take on the role of figure-head and work at promoting the organisation to these stakeholders. An important example of this kind of approach is that of Anita and Gordon Roddick and The Body Shop organisation. The conventional chief executive role is largely played by Gordon while Anita Roddick represents the organisation in the media, promotes it to existing and new franchise holders and seeks out new ingredient suppliers in the developing world.

Entrepreneur in an alternative venture

Entrepreneurs can, of course, decide that the consolidated organisation has little to offer them. They may decide to liquidate their holding and use the resources to start another venture. This is precisely what the serial entrepreneurs Howard Hodgeson of Hodgeson Holdings and James Dyson have done in the past.

15.4 Succession in the entrepreneurial business

Key learning outcome

A recognition of the importance of managing leadership succession when the entrepreneur leaves the venture.

The average life of a business is probably about the same as the working life of a manager. However, this average can be misleading. It includes a lot of businesses which last only a few years, and a few which have existed for hundreds. The successful entrepreneurial venture should be expected to last a lot longer than the career span of the founding entrepreneur. This longevity raises the issue of *succession*.

Succession creates a number of issues for the venture. Even though the business has an existence independent of the entrepreneur, the entrepreneur is more than an 'optional extra'. He or she is an integral part of the organisation. The loss of the entrepreneur represents the loss of one of its key resources. The entrepreneur must be replaced. How the entrepreneur is to be replaced, by whom, when, and in what way, represent critical decision areas for the business.

As Harris and Ogbonna (1999) make clear, founding entrepreneurs leave a *strategic* as well as a personal legacy. Reuber and Fischer (1999) develop a perspective on founder contribution that emphasises that the founder's knowledge and experience is not so much a 'stock' but a continual 'stream' that flows into the organisation.

The need for continuity . . .

All organisations need some continuity. The entrepreneur, especially if they are a motivating leader, offers a reference point about which the organisation can cohere. After the entrepreneur has gone that coherence may be lost. As a result the business risks losing focus and direction.

. . . and for change

On the other hand, all organisations must recognise the need for change in response to a rapidly changing environment. Founding entrepreneurs, while they may be effective managers of subsequent change, may also impart an inertia to the business which makes some changes difficult. Bringing a new leader presents an opportunity which, if used properly, offers the chance to effect necessary and beneficial changes in the way the business is run.

Choosing a successor

Change at the top is a contingency which may be planned for. The entrepreneur may not like to think in terms of ending their relationship with the venture but they owe it to all the other stakeholders to consider the possibility and prepare for it. A major part of this is identifying a successor. It is important here for the entrepreneur to recognise the opportunity for change. The business will have moved a long way from its foundation. The characteristics the entrepreneur originally brought to the venture may not be the same ones that it needs from a chief executive now. In choosing a successor, the entrepreneur must look for someone who is right for the business, not someone who is a copy of themselves.

The entrepreneur should also look for advice in choosing a successor. The opinions of other managers and key outsiders (particularly investors) may be valuable and influential. A successor may be sought within the business or they may be brought from outside. There are a number of questions that must be asked about any candidate for succession:

- Do they have the necessary technical knowledge of the business sector?
- Do they have the right business skills?
- Do they have the ability to manage and develop the relationships the entrepreneur has established?
- Do they have an ability to lead the business?
- How will the leadership style offered compare with that of the outgoing entrepreneur?
- Do they have the ability to take on the entrepreneur's vision and continue to communicate it?
- Do they have the ability to provide a sense of continuity?
- Yet are they also capable of offering a new perspective?
- Will they be acceptable to all the stakeholders in the venture?

A 1992 issue of the *Journal of Accountancy* (Vol. 174, No. 4, p. 24) offers a comprehensive checklist for managing family succession. Fox *et al.* (1996) consider the management of these issues.

Mentoring

The entrepreneur may be replaced as the head of the business. However, this is only a transfer of title. Being made the new chief executive offers a promise only of *authority*, that is, the potential to create change, not of *power*, which is an ability to create change. (Consider the points made in section 1.6.) Exercising power demands not only a position but also influence over the organisation's resources. This means not just tangible resources but also the intangibles of generating vision and control of the symbolic dimensions of organisational life.

Mentoring may offer a means by which these things may be transferred. The entrepreneur selects a successor well ahead of the time when succession actually need take place and the successor is then trained to take over. This process involves the transfer of knowledge, education and support and a passing on of power. The successor is made *visible* as a successor. The organisation is made to recognise the successor as its future leader. The entrepreneur educates his or her successor not only in the details of the business but also in terms of how it may be led and controlled. The actual transfer of power may be gradual, with the successor given responsibility for distinct aspects of the business over time.

Remember the business

Choosing a successor is not easy. It demands that the entrepreneur admit to being mortal. It may also be tempting for the entrepreneur to favour a relative as successor if a relative wishes to take over. Many family members do not wish to take up the reins, though (Stavrou, 1999). Morris *et al.* (1996) detail some of the challenges that family successors meet on taking over the business. While the offspring of entrepreneurs often show great business acumen and leadership ability, there is no reason why they *must* do so. Entrepreneurship is learnt, not inherited. Keeping a business within the family may be appropriate (especially if it is privately owned). However, the entrepreneur has a responsibility to *all* the organisation's stakeholders. The entrepreneur should always remember the business and select a successor who is able to manage it as effectively as they themselves could.

Succession is an important issue and it is one which good entrepreneurs address openly, rationally and honestly. Successful entrepreneurs build entire new worlds. There is no reason why that new world should not continue after they have left it. The businesses they leave are testaments to the differences they have made.

Summary of key ideas

- The roles of the entrepreneur and the chief executive are subtly different, although they overlap in many ways. The entrepreneur is more interested in creating change, and may be more willing to take risks than the role of chief executive properly calls for. This can expose the mature venture to unnecessary risk.

- Consolidation gives entrepreneurs an opportunity to specialise their roles within their organisations.

- Effective entrepreneurs manage the process of *succession* (the handing over of power within the venture) positively and effectively when it is time for them to move on.

Research themes

Entrepreneurs' management of the succession process

Use a case study approach to explore and describe the way that entrepreneurs manage their succession. Use published information supplemented by personal interviews. You may need to spend some time building up trust with the subject organisation if this type of study is to be effective. In particular, inquire into the entrepreneur's feelings about the succession, the concerns of key stakeholders such as employees and investors, the managerial issues that were identified and the approach taken to dealing with them. How far in advance was succession planned for? To what extent was mentoring used to groom a successor? Did the entrepreneur back out quickly or was the handover a more gradual process? Use the ideas developed in this chapter to guide the inquiry. What went right with the process and what went wrong? How would key players handle things differently if they had the chance to do them again? If more than one study is conducted, then comparisons and contrasts may be made. Are there any generalisations that might be made about how the process should be managed?

Key readings

Two good papers that deal with the legacy of the entrepreneur in the consolidating and consolidated organisation are:

Harris, L.C. and Ogbonna, E. (1999) 'The strategic legacy of company founders', *Long Range Planning*, Vol. 32, No. 3, p. 333.

Reuber, A.R. and Fischer, E. (1999) 'Understanding the consequences of founders' experience', *Journal of Small Business Management*, Vol. 37, No. 2, pp. 30–45.

Suggestions for further reading

Fox, M., Nilakant, V. and Hamilton, R.T. (1996) 'Managing succession in family-owned businesses', *International Small Business Journal*, Vol. 15, No. 1, pp. 15–25.

Gabarro, J.J. (1985) 'When a new manager takes charge', *Harvard Business Review*, May/June, pp. 110–23.

Hamm, J. (2002) 'Why entrepreneurs don't scale', *Harvard Business Review*, Dec., pp. 110–15.

Harris, L.C. and Ogbonna, E. (1999) 'The strategic legacy of company founders', *Long Range Planning*, Vol. 32, No. 3, p. 333.

Kransdorff, A. (1996) 'Succession planning in a fast-changing world', *Management Decision*, Vol. 34, No. 2, pp. 30–4.

Morris, M.H., Williams, R.W. and Nell, D. (1996) 'Factors influencing family business succession', *International Journal of Entrepreneurial Behaviour and Research*, Vol. 2, No. 3, pp. 68–81.

Reuber, A.R. and Fischer, E. (1999) 'Understanding the consequences of founders' experience', *Journal of Small Business Management*, Vol. 37, No. 2, pp. 30–45.

Slatter, S., Ransley, R. and Woods, E. (1988) 'USM chief executives: do they fit the entrepreneurial stereotype?' *International Small Business Journal*, Vol. 6, No. 3, pp. 10–23.

Stavrou, E.T. (1999) 'Succession in family businesses: exploring the effects of demographic factors on offspring's intentions to join and take over the business', *Journal of Small Business Management*, Vol. 37, No. 3, pp. 43–61.

Wills, G. (1992) 'Enabling managerial growth and ownership succession', *Management Decision*, Vol. 30, No. 1, pp. 10–26.

Selected case material

CASE 15.1

4 February 2006 FT

An ambitious man of steel

PETER MARSH

Lakshmi Mittal will be relaxing today in his luxurious London home, eight days after launching an €18.6bn (£12.7bn) hostile bid by his Mittal Steel company for Luxembourg-based Arcelor in an effort to build a huge steelmaker with an output three times larger than its three closest rivals combined. The move sparked a furious reaction from Guy Dollé, Arcelor's chief executive, who has portrayed the Indian billionaire as a man not to be trusted, and from political leaders in France and Luxembourg, who have urged resistance. The 55-year-old responded with a hectic charm offensive as he toured European capitals in his Gulf Stream jet to press his case.

'This is the biggest battle Lakshmi has faced but he won't be put off,' says a former employee. 'He's tough and savvy but he's dealt with politicians before and normally comes out on top.' Nonetheless, the extent of the furore has surprised the quietly spoken Mr Mittal, who – up to a $4.5bn deal 15 months ago to buy the US's International Steel Group and make his company the world's biggest steelmaker – has generally shunned publicity. Although share prices in both the Netherlands-based Mittal and Arcelor have risen, denoting some enthusiasm for the transaction, steel experts are divided as to the wisdom of uniting Mittal with the world's second biggest steelmaker, a company with a differing style and traditions. 'This deal looks like a giant bet,' says Georges Ugeux, chairman of Galileo Global Advisors, a New York financial group.

The inherent riskiness of the move fits in with the thrust of Mr Mittal's 30-year love affair with steel – an industry only recently rehabilitated (partly thanks to China's surging demand) from its image as a business graveyard. Mr Mittal's forays in the field started in his 20s, when he began work in a steel company started by Mohan Mittal, his father, in 1952 in Calcutta. Since then, Lakshmi Mittal has built up through acquisitions a global business spanning four continents and 220,000 employees. A highlight was a 1995 move to buy for $700m a virtually derelict steel plant in Kazakhstan that his company transformed into one of the world's most efficient steel mills. He later added plants in countries as removed as the US and South Africa, and developed a particular knack for taking over formerly communist-run operations including in Poland, the Czech Republic and Ukraine; and he has a minority share in a leading Chinese steel maker. Mittal is 88 per cent owned by Mr Mittal and his family – making him one of the world's richest men, worth roughly $18bn.

The entrepreneur's family comes from the Marwari merchant caste in Rajasthan in north-west India, known for its trading and deal-making mentality. Some of this style was illustrated at a private dinner Mr Mittal hosted for Mr Dollé at his London home on January 13, two weeks before the formal bid for Arcelor. Mr Dollé was taken aback when Mr Mittal asked him over a pre-meal drink whether he would be open to a merger. The Frenchman said No, and the conversation turned to other things.

Schooled in continental European business formalities, Mr Dollé later criticised Mr Mittal for breaking what he saw as 'the unwritten rules' of commercial conduct. But to Mr Mittal such informal conversations are part of business life. 'Mr Mittal is urbane and diplomatic but there's a streak in him of the hustler,' says someone who knows him well. 'He has an agenda and he expects an outcome from every meeting.'

Part of the style is that while Mr Mittal knows what is on the agenda, others may not. 'Mr Mittal is confident and forthright and you feel good when you are around him, but he is sometimes difficult to pin down,' says Rodney Mott, a leading US steel executive and former chief executive of ISG, who worked briefly for Mr Mittal until last April before leaving over a disagreement. Mr Mott – who says he bears Mr Mittal 'no grudges' – says of Mr Mittal's style: 'There's an element of "command-and-control" about him and he can be intimidating.' A contrasting view comes from Wilbur Ross, a US billionaire financier who, as former chairman of ISG, has become a non-executive of the Mittal board since the takeover. Mr Ross says that – even though Mr Mittal owns such a huge part of the company, a stake that would be diluted to just over half should the Arcelor takeover go through – 'he is a lot less dictatorial as a chief executive' than many others he knows in conventional US companies.

In India, Mr Mittal is widely feted – at least in public – as a business hero whose endeavours have highlighted the talent in one of the word's fastest expanding economies. The applause has grown in the past year as Mr Mittal announced plans for a $9bn steel plant in eastern India, his first investment in his homeland. 'If you look at his ambition and persistence, it blows your mind,' says Vikram Kirloskar, chairman of Kirloskar Systems, an Indian industrial group. 'I'm a huge admirer,' says Lord Paul, an India-born businessman who chairs the London-based Caparo engineering group. Under the surface, however, some in the Indian business community consider Mr Mittal with disdain, particularly over stories of his lavish lifestyle – illustrated by his extravagant London home, bought for a reputed £70m, and the six-day wedding party for his daughter two years ago in Paris. Mohan Mittal, too, is said to have warned his eldest son about the potential dangers of growing too fast and sailing too close to the wind. Lakshmi is considered less close to his father than his two younger brothers – Pramod and Vinod – who together run

CASE 15.1 CONT.

Mumbai-based Global Steel, a relatively small steel company. Like Mittal, Global Steel has evolved from Mohan's original steel business but its record, in contrast, looks pedestrian.

As financial experts ponder the merits of the Arcelor bid, it is worth recalling Mr Mittal's difficult period in the late 1990s when steel prices were low. Back then, a relatively small part of Mr Mittal's empire was in a publicly quoted arm and the rest was in a private group whose finances were opaque. The private and public parts of the empire were united in a single company that was formally registered only last year, taking in ISG. 'Everyone knew Mr Mittal was in trouble around 2000,' says one steel industry expert. Fortunately for the steel magnate, external events came to his rescue, in the shape of China's sudden jump in demand, laying the foundations for his company's future growth. As Mr Mittal ponders the likely outcome of his bid for Arcelor he will no doubt consider that – like all hustlers the world over – he will need some extra luck in the future if he is to come out on top.

Source: Peter Marsh, 'An ambitious man of steel', *Financial Times*, 4 February 2006, p. 11. Copyright © 2006 The Financial Times Limited.

CASE 15.2

23 February 2005

Rakuten head hits out over accounting rules

MICHIYO NAKAMOTO AND DAVID PILLING WITH ADDITIONAL REPORTING BY BARNEY JOPSON

Hiroshi Mikitani, one of Japan's best-known entrepreneurs, intends to launch an aggressive campaign to convince regulators to change how they account for goodwill, saying that current plans discourage Japanese companies from building up strength through acquisitions.

Under changes to Japanese accounting standards being introduced from April next year, companies will be required to amortise goodwill over two to 20 years.

Mr Mikitani, chairman of Rakuten, Japan's largest internet shopping mall, said Japanese regulators were 'stupid' because they did not understand the needs of emerging business.

He said Japan should adopt US-style regulations allowing companies to keep the goodwill of acquired companies as an asset, without having to depreciate it and depress profits.

'We are going to lobby,' he told the FT. 'It's going to be very disadvantageous for high-growth companies like us. In the US, you can keep [goodwill] as an asset for ever.'

Rakuten suffered an extraordinary loss of ¥52bn ($499m) in the year to March 2004, reflecting the impact of writing off goodwill related to two acquisitions it made that year. Mr Mikitani has generally chosen to amortise goodwill in a single year and has been fairly successful in persuading investors to ignore the short-term negative effect on stated profits.

'The accounting community don't understand and think we are doing things too aggressively,' Mr Mikitani said. 'But this is a matter of judgement for our investors.'

Takaaki Niimi at accountants Ernst & Young Shin-Nihon said it was 'selfish' to argue that amortisation presented a heavy burden.

If a company acquired an asset that generated future revenues, it should also have a cost, he said. Just as companies must depreciate physical assets, they should have to amortise goodwill.

'Amortisation is more reasonable [than impairment],' Mr Niimi said. Under next year's new rules, companies will also be liable for an impairment charge should the value of their brand deteriorate rapidly.

Even someone of Mr Mikitani's influence will struggle to overturn the regulator's decision to enforce the amortisation of goodwill on a systematic basis, Mr Niimi said. Regulators were fully aware of arguments in favour of the US method before they decided on the change and were unlikely to alter their opinion now, he said.

Source: Barney Jopson, Michiyo Nakamoto and David Pilling, 'Rakuten head hits out over accounting rules', *Financial Times*, 23 February 2005, p. 34. Copyright © 2005 The Financial Times Limited.

Discussion points

1. Write a job description for Lakshmi Mittal.

2. How does Hiroshi Mikitani's political lobbying fit with his role as an entrepreneur?

CHAPTER 16

Entrepreneurial vision

Chapter overview

The presence of a powerful, motivating personal vision is one of the defining characteristics of entrepreneurial management. This chapter is concerned with exploring the concept of vision and understanding how it can be used by the entrepreneur to give the venture a sense of direction and purpose. It also addresses how vision can be refined, articulated and communicated to make it into an effective managerial tool.

16.1 What is entrepreneurial vision?

Key learning outcome

An appreciation of the power of entrepreneurial vision and of the value it offers to the venture.

Entrepreneurs are managers. They manage more than just an organisation; they manage the creation of a 'new world'. This new world offers the possibility that value will be generated and made available to the venture's stakeholders. This value can only be created through change: change in the way things are *done*, change in *organisations* and change in *relationships*. Entrepreneurs rarely stumble upon success. It is more usually a reward for directing their actions in an appropriate way towards some opportunity. Effective entrepreneurs know where they are going, and why. They are focused on the achievement of specific goals.

The entrepreneur's vision is a picture of the new world they wish to create. It is a picture into which the entrepreneur fits an understanding of why people will be better off, the source of the new value that will be created, and the relationships that will exist. This picture is a very positive one and the entrepreneur is drawn towards it. They are motivated to make their vision into reality. Vision exists in the tension between what *is* and what *might* be. A vision includes an understanding of the rewards that are to be earned by creating the new world and why people will be attracted to them. Vision specifies a *destination* rather than a route to get there. It is created out of possibilities, not certainties.

Entrepreneurial visions have detail. This detail may be extensive, as if the picture were painted with fine brush strokes. Alternatively, the detail may be limited and the picture drawn from broad strokes. The details may be in sharp focus and thoroughly defined, or they may be quite vague, calling for further clarification. Whatever the shape of the details, the different parts of the vision will fit together to form a coherent whole. To the entrepreneur the vision pulling the venture forward will have an existence of its own, a unity quite separate from its component parts.

A vision is a mental image in that it is something the entrepreneur carries around in their head. This does not mean it is insubstantial; indeed, far from it. It is a very powerful tool for the management of the venture. In particular:

- it provides a sense of direction by being the 'light at the end of the tunnel';
- it helps the entrepreneur to define their goals;
- it provides the entrepreneur with a sense of encouragement when the going gets tough;
- it guides the generation of strategy for the venture;
- it gives the venture a moral content and helps to define social responsibilities;
- it can be used to communicate what the entrepreneur wishes to achieve;
- it can be used to attract people to the venture and motivate them to support it;
- it plays a crucial role in supporting the entrepreneur's communication and leadership strategy.

Vision is an important tool for the entrepreneur. It defines where the entrepreneur wants to go, sheds light on why they want to be there and provides signposts for how they might get there. If it is to be an effective tool, vision must be used actively. However, vision must be properly shaped and nurtured. It must be refined and tested. A vision which is unachievable, or which is based on wrong assumptions, or which points in the wrong direction, will easily lead the venture astray. The entrepreneur must learn to challenge vision. It must be defined and shaped so that it is appropriate, viable and achievable, before it can be put to use.

16.2 Developing and shaping vision

Key learning outcome

An understanding of how entrepreneurial vision can be developed and shaped by the entrepreneur to make it into an effective tool for the management of the venture.

Vision is the starting point for giving shape and direction to the venture. Some sense of vision must exist before strategy development and planning can start. If it is to lead the business in the right direction, vision must be properly examined, refined and evaluated.

Vision develops from the idea that things might be different from, and better than, they are currently. A vision might 'present' itself to the entrepreneur quite suddenly, or it might emerge slowly, taking shape as the entrepreneur explores an opportunity and recognises its possibilities. No matter how it comes about, vision is something which is constructed personally. It is, first and foremost, a communication with oneself. Communicating with oneself follows similar rules to communicating with anyone else. The objectives behind making the communication should be understood and it must be thought through and properly articulated. If vision is to be used effectively as a force for self-motivation and as a guide to setting goals, developing strategy and attracting support, then the entrepreneur must become aware of their vision, isolate it, communicate it to themselves, and refine it.

The vision will be a picture of the new world the entrepreneur seeks to create. It is constructed personally and will vary from entrepreneur to entrepreneur. Whatever form it takes,

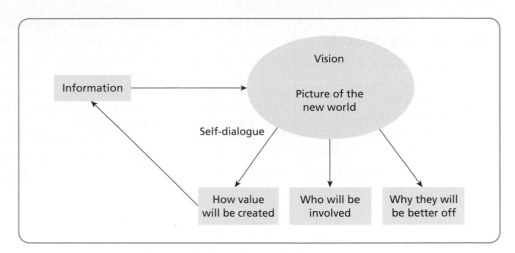

Figure 16.1 Shaping entrepreneurial vision

the entrepreneur must learn to question the vision. At first, the entrepreneur's vision will be ill defined, with its details out of focus. Questioning it helps bring it into focus. Some important questions to ask are:

- What will be the *source* of the value to be created in the new world?
- Who will be *involved* in this new world (i.e. who are the stakeholders)?
- Why will those involved be *better off* in the new world than they are at present?
- In what way will they *gain* (financially, socially, through personal development)?
- What financial reward will be received *personally* for creating the new world?
- What new *relationships* will need to be developed?
- What is the *nature* of the relationships that will be built in the new world?
- Why will this new world fulfil, or offer the potential to fulfil, personal *self-development* goals?

In short, entrepreneurs must understand *why* their vision offers a picture of a more valuable world and how it will reward them and the other stakeholders involved in the venture. To do this they must understand their personal motivation and the motivations of the other stakeholders. This questioning must be a *continual* process. Vision must be constantly refined and kept in focus. While it should provide a consistent and constant sense of direction, it should be kept flexible. Its shape may change as the entrepreneur's understanding of their personal motivations and the motivations of others evolves. To keep it fresh, entrepreneurs should constantly renegotiate their vision with themselves. Vision should always pull entrepreneurs forward. It should never hold them back (Figure 16.1).

16.3 Communicating and sharing vision

The entrepreneur's vision gives their venture direction and motivates them to progress the business. Vision is, in the first instance, a personal picture of the new world that the entrepreneur seeks to create. If it is to be used to attract other people to the venture then this new world must be communicated to them. They must be invited to share in what it can offer. Communication is not just about relating information. It is also about eliciting *action* on the part of the receiver. It is not so much about getting people to know things as about getting them to *do* things. Effective entrepreneurs understand how their vision can be used to motivate others as much as it can be used to motivate themselves.

The first stage must be to understand why other people will find the vision attractive. The entrepreneur must identify what the new world will offer stakeholders, both as individuals and as groups. The questions the entrepreneur must ask in relation to the stakeholders are:

- What benefits will they gain if the new world comes into being?
- How will they be better able to address their economic, social and self-development needs in the new world than they can in the existing one?
- Will they be attracted by the moral and discretionary social responsibility entailed in the vision and the specific issues that it addresses?
- What risks will the new world present to them?
- How credible will they find the possibility of achieving the new world?
- How will they view the journey they must take to get to the new world?

Finding the answers to these questions is part of the process the entrepreneur must go through in shaping and refining their vision. The answers will influence the way they communicate it to others. Some important approaches to communicating vision are as follows.

'I have a dream . . .'

Entrepreneurs using this approach are explicit about their vision. They describe the better world just as they see it. The vision is presented as a coherent whole. Its parts fit together to create a unified picture. Entrepreneurs expect other people to find it as attractive as they do and to be drawn towards it.

Talking specific goals

Alternatively, entrepreneurs can break down their vision into a series of specific goals, relating, for example, to economic outcomes, to the value that will be gained, to the relationships that will be created, and to the moral content of the new world. Each of these is communicated separately or in particular combinations. The choice of what is communicated will depend on to whom the vision is being communicated, when it is being communicated, in what situation and with what intention.

Talking strategy

Here entrepreneurs do not talk so much about *ends* as about *means*. Strategy relates to the approach that the business will take to achieving its goals and the tasks that must be undertaken in order to create the new world. In this, entrepreneurs are reliant on the fact that people will be attracted to the journey as well as to the destination.

Story-telling

In using a story-telling approach entrepreneurs think of their vision as a stage on which the venture is played out. The stakeholders are actors who play parts on that stage. Entrepreneurs give their vision a dynamic form by describing scenarios and telling stories about what might happen. The communication takes shape by relating future events and the roles that people can play in them. Entrepreneurs aim to motivate people by attracting them to their roles within the story.

A study by O'Connor (2002) of high-technology start-ups suggests that entrepreneurs create a range of narratives to draw stakeholders into the venture. O'Connor identifies six basic narrative types in three categories. The themes of these narratives are as follows:

1. Personal stories
   (a) Founding stories – autobiographical accounts of why the venture was started.
   (b) Vision stories – stories about innovation and breakthroughs.
2. Generic stories
   (a) Marketing stories – stories about the superiority of the venture compared with competitors.
   (b) Strategy stories – stories about the history of the venture and its future trajectory.
3. Situational stories
   (a) Historical stories – stories about the development of the venture's industry.
   (b) Conventional stories – stories about beliefs and attitudes of industry players and customers.

Lounsbury and Glynn (2001) propose a framework for what they refer to as 'cultural' entrepreneurship in which story-telling acts to mediate between the resources the entrepreneur has actually acquired and subsequent resources brought into the venture through its success as a way of creating a new identity for the venture and building legitimacy with key stakeholders.

Why things can be better

With this approach the entrepreneur emphasises what is wrong with the world as it is rather than what will be better in the new world. The aim is to push people forward using their sense of dissatisfaction, rather than to pull them forward by using the attractions of new possibilities. While it may rid people of their complacency, too much emphasis on this approach runs the risk of simply sounding negative and being demotivating, especially if no positive alternative appears to be offered.

What's in it for you

In this approach entrepreneurs focus on the particular benefits that will be gained by the recipient of the communication. The vision is broken down and 'packaged' for the individual. Tailoring the vision in this way is a good way of ensuring the commitment of a particular person. If overused, however, the recipient may feel that their commitment is being bought. This approach to communication runs the danger of giving the impression that the entrepreneur regards the recipient as being mercenary and motivated purely by personal gain.

Selecting a communication strategy

The above approaches to communicating vision are not mutually exclusive. They are individual strands that can be brought together to make up an overall communication strategy for the entrepreneur's vision. By using a diverse approach to communicating this vision, the entrepreneur keeps it relevant, avoids being repetitive and keeps the message fresh to recipients. The particular strategy adopted will depend on a number of factors. Some of the more important include:

- the nature of the vision being shared (how complex is it? how much detail does it have?);
- the entrepreneur's leadership style (is it collaborative, democratic, authoritarian?);
- the stakeholders to whom the vision is being communicated (who are they? how many?);
- the nature of the commitment desired from them;
- the stakeholders' particular needs and motivations (economic, social, self-development);
- the stakeholders' relationship to the entrepreneur;
- the situation of the communication (formal or informal, one-to-one, one-to-many, etc.);
- the medium through which the communication is transmitted (face-to-face, verbal, written, etc.).

An ability to articulate the vision and communicate it to different stakeholders in a way that is appropriate to them and in a way that is right for the situation is the basis on which the entrepreneur builds their leadership and power.

16.4 Entrepreneurship and strategic foresight

> ### Key learning outcome
>
> An appreciation of the concept of strategic foresight and recognition of its role in entrepreneurial success.

The notion of entrepreneurial vision suggests that the entrepreneur is anticipating a new, better world. The achievement of that world reflects on both the entrepreneur's ability to engage with and make changes in the world and to anticipate those things the entrepreneur cannot change (the business environment in its wider sense). The entrepreneur must mould the raw stuff of the world. There is potential to shape it into different forms, but the stuff itself does not change. The success of a vision (or success in delivering that vision) is, to a degree, dependent on the entrepreneur's having foresight about how the world will be in the future. This aspect of an entrepreneur's abilities is of growing interest in the entrepreneurship research field and is the subject of a book edited by Tsoukas and Shepherd (2003). Gibb and Scott (1985) define strategic foresight (which they term 'strategic awareness') in terms of it being the ability to assess the total impact of a particular change or decision; to be able to project into the future the effects and consequences of a particular action and to think about these in strategic terms. Slaughter (1995) characterises strategic foresight as 'a process that attempts to broaden the boundaries of perception in four ways':

- by assessing the implications of present actions, decisions, etc. (consequent assessment);
- by detecting and avoiding problems before they occur (early warning and guidance);
- by considering the present implications of possible future events (proactive strategy formulation);
- by envisioning aspects of desired futures (normative scenarios).

Strategic foresight is a competence both of the individual entrepreneur and of the organisation, as the entrepreneur imparts that foresight into the venture's decision making. Such a competence is a potential source of competitive advantage as it allows the venture to anticipate future opportunities and to adopt the means to exploit both them and the risk issues that will arise in their exploitation in a way that is superior to competitors who lack the foresight. Hamel and Prahalad (1994) refer to a 'highly visible vision of the future', a 'strategic intent' as a source of competitive advantage. A study by Ensley *et al.* (2000) indicates that such entrepreneurial vision does contribute positively to the performance of a venture. Strategic foresight might also be considered to be a part of a broader responsibility of the entrepreneur in turning ambiguity (which cannot be quantified, and so cannot be insured against) into risk (which can). Schoemaker (1997) suggests that strategic vision enables an organisation to differentiate itself through foresight. It is not, however, the remit of the entrepreneur alone; rather, it is effective only if organisation members share the vision. Schoemaker suggests a four-stage process for ensuring that foresight is in fact shared. Kandampully and Duddy (1999) argue for a specific role of strategic foresight in anticipating the value of service delivery to create and maintain lifetime customer loyalty.

Traditional decision theory places restrictions on the knowledge that one can have about the future. One may know (or not) what eventualities will occur and be able to refine eventualities with varying degrees of precision. Further, one may have knowledge of the likelihood that particular eventualities will take place. Fuller *et al.* (2003) look beyond conventional decision theory and take a more interpretive approach and regard strategic foresight as a personal competence of the entrepreneur, which is not necessarily reducible to conventional decision theoretical concepts. The notion of strategic foresight is an idea that has a long history. As far back as 1934, Schumpeter noted in his characterisation of entrepreneurship as 'creative destruction' that some individuals can see the future in a way which afterwards proves to be true, even if it cannot be established at the time.

Summary of key ideas

- Entrepreneurs are managers with a *vision*.
- A vision is a picture of the *new and better world* that the entrepreneur wishes to create.
- Vision can be refined and articulated as a *management tool*.
- Vision can be used as the basis of a powerful *leadership strategy*.
- Visionary leadership demands *communication* of the vision in a way which draws stakeholders towards the venture and *motivates* them to work for its success.
- Strategic foresight is a skill in or capability for anticipating the future and predicting the long-term effects of decisions made now. Effective strategic foresight may play a role in entrepreneurial success.

Research themes

Entrepreneurial vision: articulation and communication

As noted, vision can be moulded into an effective managerial and leadership tool. This chapter has developed models of how vision is articulated and communicated. Does this match up with how entrepreneurs articulate and communicate vision in practice? Obtain a series of communications by entrepreneurs that record their communication of vision. Sources might include business plans, case studies, newspaper articles (the *Financial Times* is a good source), public communications to employees, statements in accounts or media interviews. These sources may be supplemented by primary research asking entrepreneurs to describe their vision for their businesses. How do entrepreneurs develop and shape their vision? How much detail does the vision have? What latitude are they leaving for negotiation about the vision? How are they communicating it? Does the pattern of communication meet with the criteria described in section 16.3?

Key readings

Two papers that emphasise that vision is not a mystery but a practical management tool, and go on to develop a practical agenda for its use are:

Lipton, M. (1996) 'Demystifying the development of organisational vision', *Sloan Management Review*, Summer, pp. 83–92.

Stewart, J.M. (1993) 'Future state visioning – a powerful leadership process', *Long Range Planning*, Vol. 26, No. 6, pp. 89–98.

Suggestions for further reading

Boyce, M.E. (1996) 'Organisational story and storytelling: a critical review', *Journal of Organisational Change Management*, Vol. 9, No. 5, pp. 5–26.

Campbell, A. and Yeung, S. (1991) 'Vision, mission and strategic intent', *Long Range Planning*, Vol. 24, No. 4, pp. 145–7.

Ensley, M.D., Carland, J.W. and Carland, J.C. (2000) 'Investigating the existence of the lead entrepreneur', *Journal of Small Business Management*, October, pp. 59–77.

Filion, L.J. (1991) 'Vision and relations: elements for an entrepreneurial meta-model', *International Small Business Journal*, Vol. 9, No. 1, pp. 15–31.

Fuller, E., Argyle, P. and Moran, P. (2003) 'Entrepreneurial foresight: a case study in reflexivity, experiments, sensitivity and reorganisation', in Tsoukas, H. and Shepherd, J. (eds) *Developing Strategic Foresight in the Knowledge Economy: Probing the Future*. Oxford: Blackwell.

Gibb, A.A. and Scott, M.G. (1985) 'Strategic awareness, personal commitment and the process of planning in the small business', *Journal of Management Studies*, Vol. 22, No. 6, pp. 597–625.

Gratton, L. (1996) 'Implementing a strategic vision – key factors for success', *Long Range Planning*, Vol. 29, No. 3, pp. 290–303.

Hamel, G. and Prahalad, C.K. (1994) *Competing for the Future*. Boston, MA: Harvard Business School Press.

Kandampully, J. and Duddy, R. (1999) 'Competitive advantage through anticipation, innovation and relationships', *Management Decision*, Vol. 37, No. 1, pp. 51–6.

Lounsbury, M. and Glynn, M.A. (2001) 'Cultural entrepreneurship: stories, legitimacy and the acquisition of resources', *Strategic Management Journal*, Vol. 22, pp. 545–64.

O'Connor, E. (2002) 'Storied business: typology, intertextuality and traffic in entrepreneurial narrative', *Journal of Business*, Vol. 39, No. 1, pp. 36–54.

Schoemaker, P.J.H. (1997) 'Disciplined imagination: from scenarios to strategic options (preparing for the future: developing strategic flexibility from a competence-based perspective)', *International Studies in Management and Organisation*, Vol. 27, No. 2, pp. 43–70.

Schumpeter, J.A. (1934) *The Theory of Economic Development. An Inquiry into Profits, Capital, Credit, Interest and the Business Cycle*. Cambridge, MA: Harvard University Press.

Shirley, S. (1989) 'Corporate strategy and entrepreneurial vision', *Long Range Planning*, Vol. 22, No. 6, pp. 107–10.

Slaughter, R.A. (1995) *The Foresight Principle: Cultural Revovery in the 21st Century*. London: Adamantine Press.

Tsoukas, H. and Shepherd, J. (eds) (2003) *Developing Strategic Foresight in the Knowledge Economy: Probing the Future*. Oxford: Blackwell.

Westley, F. and Mintzberg, H. (1989) 'Visionary leadership and strategic management', *Strategic Management Journal*, Vol. 10, pp. 17–32.

Selected case material

Expansion boosts area's prosperity

WILLIAM HALL

Associated British Ports (ABP), the UK's biggest port operator, dominates the Humber. It owns the ports of Hull, Grimsby, Immingham and Goole and is the statutory harbour authority for more than 80 miles of waterway from the Spurn light float to Gainsborough on the Trent and Skelton on the Ouse.

The Humber harbour master is an ABP employee and so are the more than 100 pilots who oversee the 35,000 shipping movements a year in one of the UK's busiest estuaries.

Not much can happen on the Humber without ABP's consent. Two out of ABP's five main board port directors are stationed on the Humber and it has invested more than £140m in expanding its Humber presence over the last five years.

ABP is pushing ahead in Immingham with a £44.5m deep water coal terminal and a £35m roll-on, roll-off (ro-ro) terminal for DFDS, one of Europe's biggest ferry companies.

Across the river at Hull, ABP plans to double the size of the Hull Container Terminal (HCT), the biggest container terminal on the Humber, by investing up to £40m in a new riverside facility.

ABP has already invested £14m in a riverside berth at Hull for P&O's 60,600 tonne super-ferries which can carry 400 freight units, 250 cars and 1,360 passengers.

However, all ABP's 11 other ro-ro berths at Hull remain inside the enclosed docks and can handle only much smaller ferries.

But ABP is not the only player on the Humber. During the past four years Simon Group has stolen a march by investing £60m in four ro-ro berths a few miles upstream from Immingham at its Humber Sea terminal (HST). Unlike ABP's existing ro-ro facilities, HST's berths jut out into the river which means that ferries do not have to pass through lock gates and can be turned round more quickly.

Tim Chadwick, Simon's chairman, says that plans are well advanced to build two more ro-ro berths and the group has recently bought another 70 acres of land, giving it access to about 335 acres of storage facilities. Simon has already received a number of takeover approaches from city investors who sense the potential of the Humber's newest port which is no more than 200 miles from almost all the UK's big cities.

It will be another year at least before ABP's riverside ro-ro berths, capable of handling the next generation of bigger North Sea ferries, come on stream and already Simon has poached Cobelfret, one of ABP's bigger customers. Cobelfret has signed a 20-year lease with Simon, which now claims to be handling 350,000 units a year plus a considerable amount of car traffic.

Next door to Simon, Able UK, headed by Peter Stephenson, an entrepreneur from the north-east of England, is developing the 674 acre Killingholme ports facility. For the moment it is specialising in offering storage facilities for customers using the Humber Sea Terminal and Immingham port.

But it is possible that it might eventually decide to compete with Simon and ABP by building is own ro-ro or container ship berths on the river.

PD Ports, which owns Tees and Hartlepool, the Humber's main competitor, is also very active on the Humber. It operates the Hull Container Terminal on a lease from ABP and also operates the port of Keadby on the Trent and the Port of Howden on the Ouse. Both ports can take vessels up to 3,000 dwt, are 60 miles inland from the sea and adjacent to motorways much closer to the final customer.

RMS Europe, the subject of a £13m management buyout, handles 1.8m tonnes a year of cargo through its inland ports at Goole, and Flixborough and Gunness on the Trent. It is capitalising on its shipping ties with Duisburg, Europe's largest inland port on the Rhine, and its closeness to the UK motorway network.

The development of the Humber ports over the last 250 years reflects the ebb and flows of competition which have favoured one port over another at varying times. Hull, which opened its first enclosed dock in 1774, was for a long time the most important port on the Humber, and remains the regional capital.

Its early growth was fuelled by the whaling industry, and continued with the arrival of the railways and the growth of the deep sea fishing industry which was employing 10,000 by the turn of the last century.

However, by the 1850s, Hull's fishing industry was starting to face competition from Grimsby, which was closer to the North Sea.

Its role as the main port for Yorkshire was also threatened by the opening of the Aire and Calder canal which connected Goole with Leeds and Yorkshire's fast-growing textile, steel and coal industries.

The subsequent collapse of these industries took their toll on all three ports and they have had to reinvent themselves. Coal exports have been replaced by coal imports, oil products are now the biggest cargoes and nearly a quarter of the UK's forest products comes through the Humber ports.

Although Grimsby's current fleet of 11 trawlers is a shadow of the 500 that used to land their catch, it still has the UK's biggest fish market. It has also become the biggest port in the north of England for vehicle imports and exports.

Hull has reinvented itself as a leading ferry and container port, while Goole is rediscovering its strengths as the UK's premier inland port, just 2km from the M62 motorway, the main east–west road artery across the north of England.

There are plans for a Goole intermodal terminal which could trigger renewed growth in barge traffic along the Aire and Calder canal and up to Leeds and the rest of Yorkshire's industrial heartland. However, the success of the Humber ports has been driven by the newest port – Immingham – which opened less than a century ago. It is closest to the Humber's deep water channel and was built to accommodate much bigger vessels than were common a century ago.

By the 1960s Immingham had overtaken Hull as the Humber's biggest port and it is now the UK's largest east coast ro-ro port with more than 60 sailings and 350 freight trains a week.

During the last decade its traffic has grown by 34 per cent, or more than three times as fast as the UK port sector. However, the growing size of ships means that Immingham's enclosed docks are no longer as attractive as they were.

This is the reason ABP is rapidly expanding its deep water Humber International Terminal on the river and three ro-ro berths for DFDS – both of which are outside its enclosed Immingham dock system – to accommodate future growth, and make sure that its customers stay to do business.

Source: William Hall, 'Expansion boosts area's prosperity', *Financial Times*, 23 February 2005, p. 2. Copyright © 2005 The Financial Times Limited.

28 February 2005   **FT**

Breaking with tradition in Italian business

ADRIAN MICHAELS

Clessidra is a new name in Italian financial circles but, when rumours of forthcoming deals are aired in the media, the private equity fund is already frequently mentioned as a potential acquirer.

Claudio Sposito, the fund's chief executive and chairman, shrugs with bemusement at the unsought publicity. The recurrence of the fund's name shows only, he believes, how few groups there are like his in the Italian market, and therefore the lack of competition.

The Clessidra fund closed last month, having accumulated €800m (£550m) since it started raising money in October 2003. Mr Sposito says Clessidra is the largest Italian fund focused solely on the domestic market.

He has attracted many big names as investors. A third of the money was put up by non-Italian groups, such as ABN Amro, Lehman Brothers and big US retirement funds including Calpers and the New York State Common Retirement Fund.

Inside Italy, investors include the largest banks, such as Banca Intesa, Unicredito, Mediobanca and Capitalia; insurers such as Generali; and industrial groups such as Telecom Italia. 'It's the first time that Italian institutions have given this kind of support to an initiative of this nature,' Mr Sposito says.

They are presumably attracted in part by the track record and connections of the seven-partner team. Mr Sposito spent ten years at Morgan Stanley and was then chief executive of Fininvest, the business group managing the interests of the family of Silvio Berlusconi, the prime minister.

The main draw, though, must be the investment opportunities. Mr Sposito's goal is to find eight to 10 deals of €40m–€100m each, or to contribute that amount as part of a syndicate taking control of a medium-sized company. Clessidra has already made investments in companies in gas transmission, business infrastructure and gaming. The Italian economy may be the world's sixth largest, Mr Sposito says, but it is predominantly powered by family-owned, small and medium-sized companies, many with their aged founders still at the helm.

Some blame the country's slow growth on the reluctance of controlling families to go outside the domestic market, or to cede control by looking beyond bank loans for funding. Clessidra is positioned to spot investment opportunities as that structure changes. Some traditional, family-run companies will try to expand and hand control to non-family managers.

Mr Sposito says: 'It is obviously true that you see families changing their attitudes. The succession issue is becoming more and more important, as the founders are pretty old and the family may not want to continue the business.'

The family companies have traditionally funded their growth through bank debt. 'The model was "small is beautiful",' Mr Sposito says. 'But many companies have seen that model under stress from China, from currency movements.'

In Mr Sposito's view, companies that might be interested in relocating production to lower-cost countries, for example, need to be of a certain size. This would force small entrepreneurs to consolidate.

Bank debt starts to lose its cost-effectiveness and availability as companies grow. Some equity is needed as well. Meanwhile control and ownership, which are easier to maintain when companies are small, become harder to manage. Larger families, or combined families, have additional issues to overcome.

Clessidra hopes to come in once companies have already struggled with many of these issues, when the entrepreneur who started the business has introduced a class of managers.

The fund, as is common with private equity, is interested only in making investments in companies that it then controls, implying a family has already come to terms with giving up control. The medium-sized companies that are undergoing change are one rich source of investments. Others come from the break-up of large companies, the continuing programme of privatisations and the fragmentation of utility companies.

Public equity markets as a source of funding are also undeveloped. There are only about 250 public companies in Italy. 'In the US and UK,' Mr Sposito says, 'entrepreneurs develop companies and at some point float them or sell them and move on. In Italy there is a lot of emotional attention paid to the concepts of ownership, control and management.'

As a result, 'equity is a scarce resource,' Mr Sposito says. 'The stock market has not developed yet the right level of attention for small cap companies and there are not enough specialised funds that follow small or medium-sized companies.

'Most mutual funds tend to track the index of largest companies. You can track that by tracking 15 companies, so small cap companies are neglected in terms of research, coverage, trading and therefore valuation.'

A low valuation makes the market a less attractive source of capital but there are changes coming in the public markets, too. The Milan stock exchange has been launching new indices, giving emphasis to small and medium-sized companies that have, for example, transparent and independent corporate governance regimes more familiar to US or UK investors.

The aim is to attract more attention to the best companies around, bringing in more liquidity and coverage, and making it worthwhile for companies to alter their governance.

By the time Clessidra has made the rest of its investments in three or four years, both the public and private equity markets could have undergone a fundamental transformation.

Source: Adrian Michaels, 'Breaking with tradition in Italian business', *Financial Times*, 28 February 2005, p. 8. Copyright © 2005 The Financial Times Limited.

Discussion points

1. Discuss Peter Stephenson's vision for ABP.

2. Discuss Claudio Sposito's vision for Clessidra.

The entrepreneurial mission

Chapter overview

This chapter is concerned with the development of a mission for the entrepreneurial venture. A mission is a formal statement defining the purpose of the venture and what it aims to achieve. It is a powerful communication tool which can both guide internal decision making and relate the venture to external supporters. After establishing how a formal mission can actually help the venture, a prescriptive framework for generating, articulating and communicating the venture's mission is developed.

17.1 Why a well-defined mission can help the venture

Key learning outcome

An appreciation of the value of a formal mission for the venture.

A mission is a formal statement as to the purpose of the venture. It defines the *nature* of the venture, *what* it aims to achieve and *how* it aims to achieve it. It provides entrepreneurs with a way to codify their vision, to be clear about the difference they will make. Recent surveys indicate that some 80 per cent of all major businesses have a mission or value statement of some kind. Developing a formalised mission can be valuable to the entrepreneurial venture for a number of reasons.

It articulates the entrepreneur's vision

Developing a mission offers entrepreneurs a chance to articulate and give form to their vision. This helps them to refine and shape their vision, and it facilitates communication of the vision to the venture's stakeholders.

It encourages analysis of the venture

The process of developing a mission demands that entrepreneurs and those who work with them stand back and think about their venture in some detail. If the mission is to be meaningful, then that analysis must be made in a detached way. Entrepreneurs must be able to subject their own vision to impartial scrutiny and consider how realistic and achievable it is.

It will challenge them to consider what they wish to achieve, to audit the resources they have to hand, to identify what additional resources they will need, and to evaluate their own strengths and weaknesses. Developing a mission is a piece of communication with oneself. This process is iterative. Entrepreneurs must negotiate the possibilities of creating new worlds with their ambitions and the actuality of what they can achieve.

It defines the scope of the business

An entrepreneurial venture exists to exploit some opportunity. Opportunities are most successfully exploited if resources are dedicated to them and brought to bear in a focused way. This demands that the opportunity be defined precisely. The business must know which opportunities lie within its grasp and which it must ignore. Often, success depends not only on the venture taking advantage of a big enough opportunity but also on it not being tempted to spread its efforts too widely. The mission helps to distinguish between those opportunities which 'belong' to the venture and those which do not.

It provides a guide for setting objectives

A mission is usually *qualitative*. It does not dictate specific quantitative outcomes. This is the role of *objectives*. The mission provides a starting point for defining specific objectives, for testing their suitability for the venture and for ordering of their priorities.

It clarifies strategic options

A mission defines what the venture aims to achieve. In this it offers guidance on what paths might be taken. The mission provides a starting point for developing *strategic options*, for evaluating their consistency in delivering objectives and for judging their resource demands.

It facilitates communication about the venture to potential investors

Attracting the support of investors is crucial to the success of the new venture. This is not simply a matter of presenting a series of facts to them, rather it demands that the facts be communicated in a way that makes the possibilities of the venture look convincing. One of the potential investor's first questions will almost certainly be 'What is the business about?' The mission provides the entrepreneur with a clear, succinct and unambiguous answer to this question. First impressions do matter: a well-rehearsed, articulate and confident answer gets the relationship off to a good start. Answering in this way efficiently locates the venture positively in the investor's mind. This facilitates commitment and encourages further inquiry about the opportunity that the venture aims to exploit and the rewards it may offer. It also suggests that the entrepreneur has thought about the business in a professional way, that is, has defined its scope and is focused on its goals.

It draws together disparate internal stakeholder groups

The different stakeholders who make up the business may not agree what the business is about. They may disagree on the goals it should have, how it should go about achieving them and how they will benefit if they are achieved. Organisations are frequently *political* and the mission can be used to provide a common point of reference around which to draw internal stakeholders together. It can guide arbitration when conflicts occur. A broad qualitative mission may be more useful than specific objectives in this respect. Often, the very detail of objectives reduces flexibility and can provide a focus for discontent and disagreement.

It provides a constant point of reference during periods of change

The organisation driving the entrepreneurial venture will have the potential to achieve growth. Growth is good because it reflects the success of the business and increases its ability to reward stakeholders. It does, however, present the challenge of managing *change*. As the organisation grows and develops, it will be in a state of flux. It will acquire new assets and develop new relationships. Individuals will come and go. New customers will be found, old ones lost. In these turbulent circumstances, the mission can provide the organisation with a fixed point or a recognisable landmark connecting the organisation's past to its future.

It acts as an *aide-mémoire* for customers and suppliers

The mission statement can be communicated to the other key stakeholders in the venture, namely its customers and suppliers. It locates the business in the minds of customers and reminds them of what it offers and the commitment being made to them. It also gives the venture a presence in the minds of suppliers, reminding them of the opportunity it presents and of the need for their commitment to that opportunity. This encourages them to give the venture priority and service.

Empirical studies correlating business performance with the articulation of mission statements have produced mixed results. A seminal study by Pearce and David (1987) found that for large (Fortune 500) companies performance was positively correlated with the comprensiveness of mission statements. Other studies to find a positive relationship include Falsey (1989), Germain and Bixby Cooper (1990), Collins and Porras (1991), Klemm *et al.* (1991) and Rarick and Vitton (1995). Studies more critical of mission statements include Piercy and Morgan (1994) and Simpson (1994). A replication of the Pearce and David study, but looking at small business, undertaken by O'Gorman and Doran (1999) found no correlation between mission comprehensiveness and performance. In studies such as these, care should be taken in attributing (or not) enhanced performance causally to mission articulation. It may be the case that the mission is helping the business, but it could also be the case that the fact that the business is performing well is giving managers the time, resources or inclination to develop a mission. Equally, developing a mission and performance could both be linked to a third, unidentified factor (overall strategic planning capability, for example). All of these studies examined missions in extant, ongoing businesses. No study (to my knowledge) has examined the role of the mission in attracting start-up funding, something I suggest as the critical role for a mission in entrepreneurial ventures. I will pick up on this in the Research Themes section at the end of the chapter.

Key features of the mission

The mission provides the entrepreneur with a powerful management tool. However, if it is to be effective and to contribute positively to the performance of the venture, it must be right for the business, it should encapsulate useful information and it must be properly developed and articulated.

17.2 What a mission statement should include

> **Key learning outcome**
>
> An understanding of what information should be included in the mission statement for an entrepreneurial venture.

A mission statement may define both *what* the business aims to achieve and the *values* it will uphold while going about its business. It relates both what the business does and why its members are proud of what it does. These two parts are often referred to as the *strategic* and the *philosophical* components of the mission statement, respectively. For example, The Body Shop emphasises corporate values in its mission. It claims to:

> *Make compassion, care, harmony and trust the foundation stones of business. Fall in love with new ideas.*

The Scandinavian furniture retailer Ikea, on the other hand, is much more strategic in its approach to defining products, markets and benefits. The company states its 'business idea' in the following terms:

> *We shall offer a wide range of home furnishing, items of good design and function, at prices so low that the majority of people can afford them.*

The strategic component of a mission statement can, potentially, include the following elements:

- *Product/service scope* – this element specifies exactly what the firm will offer to the world. It stipulates the type or range of products or services that the firm will engage in producing and delivering.
- *Customer groups served* – this element stipulates which customers and distinct customer groups will be addressed by the firm.

Both product/service scope and customer groups need to be specified with three things in mind. First is the *total market* in which the business operates. This is the universe in which the business's offerings are located. Second are the markets that the business *currently* serves since these are the base on to which the business must build its growth. Third are the market sectors, or *niches*, that the business *aspires* to serve. These are where the growth will come from since these niches lie between the current business and the total market. These sectors must stretch the business and make its aspirations demanding, yet they must be realistic given the resources to which the business has access and its capabilities. The sectors must also represent distinct segments of the total market within which the firm's innovation can provide a sustainable competitive advantage.

Other elements that might be included in a mission statement are:

- *Benefits offered and customer needs served* – this element specifies the particular needs that the customer groups have and the benefits that the firm's products or services offer to satisfy these needs. Needs (and the benefits that satisfy them) can be defined at a number of levels. Spiritual, social and developmental needs are as important as, and often more important than, economic or functional ones.

- *The innovation on which the business is based and the sources of sustainable competitive advantage* – this element defines the way in which the firm has innovated, how it is using this to exploit the opportunity it faces and how this provides it with a competitive advantage in the marketplace that can be sustained in the face of pressure from competitors.
- *The aspirations of the business* – this element defines what the business aims to achieve. It indicates how its success will be measured. It may refer to financial performance – for example, to be 'profitable' or to 'offer shareholders an attractive return' – or it may refer to market position – for example, to be a 'market leader' or to be 'a significant player'. Care should be taken that the aspirations are *realistic*, specify an achievement which is *meaningful* and provide a real *benchmark* for measuring achievements.

Pearce and David (1987) summarise the above elements slightly differently. Their eight elements are:

- specification of target customers and markets;
- identification of principle products and/or services;
- identification of geographical domain;
- identification of core technologies;
- expression of a commitment to growth, prosperity and survival;
- specification of key elements of company philosophy;
- identification of the company self-concept (including views on key strengths);
- identification of the firm's desired public image.

In addition to the strategic elements, reference may be made to the discretionary responsibilities taken on by the venture, that is, to the *company values* upheld by the business. The philosophical component of the mission statement illuminates the values and moral standards that the organisation will uphold while pursuing its business. This may refer to the way in which the company aims to treat its employees or customers. It may also specify the discretionary social responsibilities that the business will accept (see section 9.4). Values may be included in the mission statement because they reflect the personal principles of the entrepreneur or because the business believes its higher standards will appeal to customers and perhaps investors. These two reasons are not incompatible; indeed, positive values are best upheld by a successful business.

Figure 17.1 shows a schematic representation of the elements in a mission statement for the entrepreneurial venture.

17.3 Developing the mission statement

If it is to help the venture, the mission must be right for it and it must be appropriate given the opportunity it aims to exploit and the innovation it intends to utilise. Further, if it is to be more than just so many words, then it must inform and influence people's decision making. A mission must be relevant to those who make up the venture and they must take ownership of it. These conditions will be met only if the mission is developed in the right way. The mission should stretch the business but be consistent with its ambitions, be realistic in terms

Key learning outcome

An appreciation of the practical ways in which a mission can be developed for the venture.

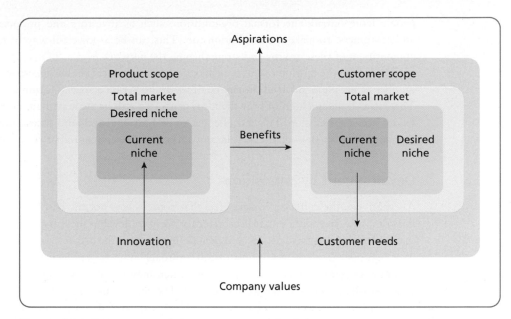

Figure 17.1 Components of the entrepreneurial mission statement

of the opportunity it faces, and be compatible with its capability to exploit that opportunity. The mission must be developed alongside, and be judged in the light of, a strategic audit for the business. An audit of this nature includes:

- consideration of what the entrepreneur wishes to achieve;
- consideration of what other stakeholders aim to achieve and how the venture might help them;
- an assessment of the opportunity the venture aims to exploit;
- an assessment of market conditions;
- an assessment of the challenges and risks that will be encountered in exploiting that opportunity;
- an assessment of the business's capabilities and its competitive advantages;
- an evaluation of the resources the business has access to, future resource requirements and the resource gap this implies;
- an assessment of the structure of, and conditions in, the firm's network.

The entrepreneur must also consider how the mission will be generated. Broadly, there are two approaches.

Development through consensus

The consensus approach involves getting the whole, or as many parts as possible, of the organisation to contribute towards the development of the mission. The aim is to gather information, create ideas and gain as many insights as possible for generating and evaluating the mission. Allowing people to be involved in creating the mission also gives them a feeling of ownership and so a commitment towards it. The entrepreneur may go as far as inviting people from outside the formal organisation, such as investors and important suppliers and customers, to make a contribution too. This can be a powerful way of attracting the commitment of these groups and strengthening the network.

Developing the mission in this way may present a logistical challenge, especially if a large number of people is involved. It may be necessary to set up a special forum for the exercise. There is also the question of how the ideas generated will be evaluated and judged and then fed into the final mission. This must be seen to be a rational and fair process, otherwise there is a danger that people may feel their contribution has been ignored or rejected.

Development by imposition

Alternatively, the entrepreneur may feel that consensus is not the best way to generate the mission. They may decide that it is better for them to develop the mission themselves, or in consultation with a small group, and then to impose it on the organisation as a whole. There may be a number of good reasons for this approach. The entrepreneur may see the mission as an articulation of their personal vision which may not be negotiable in the way that a consensus-building approach would demand. The entrepreneur may be the only person who has sufficient knowledge of the business and its situation to develop a meaningful mission. If the organisation is growing rapidly, it may be difficult to keep reassessing the mission as new people come in. It might also be inappropriate; after all, the mission is meant to be a constant in a time of flux. New people coming on board will be asked to accept the mission as it stands (they may, of course, have been attracted by it in the first place). The entrepreneur may also feel that it suits their leadership strategy to impose the mission on the organisation, that is, to be seen to give direction and to 'lead from the front'.

Choice of approach

Both of these routes for developing a mission have things to offer. The decision as to which is better will depend on the venture, how complex its business is, the way in which it is developing and the leadership style adopted by the entrepreneur. Developing a mission may in fact be one of the key exercises through which the entrepreneur establishes and demonstrates their leadership approach to the venture as a whole.

17.4 Articulating the mission statement

> ### Key learning outcome
>
> An understanding of how the mission for the venture might be phrased.

Once the mission of the venture has been rationalised in terms of the elements in its strategic component and the values the venture wishes to uphold, then it needs to be *articulated* in the form of a definite statement. This statement then *becomes* the mission for the venture. If it is to be a valuable and an effective tool for the management of the venture it must fulfil several conditions. In particular, it must emphasise what is distinct about the venture; it must be informative; it must be clear and unambiguous; it must have impact; and it must be memorable. A balance between each of these requirements must be achieved. One generic format which includes all the elements described in the previous section is as follows:

The [company] aims to use its [competitive advantage] to achieve/maintain [aspirations] in providing [product scope] which offers [benefits] to satisfy the [needs] of [customer scope]. In doing this the company will at all times strive to uphold [values].

The starting point for articulating the mission in this way is to find phrases describing each italicised element. These must be quite short or the mission statement will become too long, therefore it will be difficult to remember and so will lose impact. Single words are best! Not every element need be included, thus if a particular element is obvious, does not really inform or does not distinguish the business from its sector in general then it may be safely dropped. If in doubt, it is probably better to make the mission statement more, rather than less, succinct.

The business will be faced with numerous opportunities to communicate its mission. It may be posted prominently within the organisation. It may form a starting point for setting objectives. It can be included on promotional material sent to customers. It will feature in the business plan presented to investors. However, not all communication need be so formal. The mission need not always be presented as a formal 'statement', it can easily be slipped informally into conversations. It is, after all, only the answer to the question: 'What does your business aim to do?'

Summary of key ideas

- A *mission* is a positive statement which defines what a particular venture is about and what it aims to achieve.

- A well-defined mission helps the venture by encouraging analysis of its situation and capabilities; drawing together its internal stakeholders; and facilitating communication of the venture to external stakeholders.

- The mission statement can include a definition of the venture's market scope, what it aims to do for its stakeholders, its ambitions and its values.

- Entrepreneurs can use development of the venture's mission as part of their leadership strategy.

Research themes

Entrepreneurs' adoption and valuation of formal missions

A number of studies have been conducted into the adoption of formal missions by large businesses. Much less work has been undertaken on their adoption by smaller and entrepreneurial businesses. A survey methodology may be used to complement work in this

▶

area. Select a sample (the larger the better, aim for over 100) of small and entrepreneurial businesses. The sample may be based on discrete sub-samples of businesses based on criteria such as sector, rate of business growth, etc. The survey should aim to establish the following:

- Does the business have a formal mission? If so, what is it?
- How important does the entrepreneur see the mission as a management tool?
- In what way did (does) it prove valuable (as a focus for analysis; as an internal communication tool; as an external communication tool)?
- What is its primary role in the current running of the business?
- To which stakeholders is it communicated? In what way?
- What decisions has the mission contributed to and supported?
- How valuable has it been in attracting key stakeholders?

In addition, code the elements of the mission statement using the framework described in this chapter. What information does the mission include? By way of analysis, correlate the form of the mission statement and its information content with its perceived value for the different types of venture in the selected sample. Summarise the findings with recommendations for the development and use of formal missions in small and entrepreneurial ventures.

 ## Key readings

Two useful papers that review organisational mission and develop practical guidelines for their development are:

Baetz, M.C. and Bart, C.K. (1996) 'Developing mission statements which work', *Long Range Planning*, Vol. 29, No. 4, pp. 526–33.

Wickham, P.A. (1997) 'Developing a mission for an entrepreneurial venture', *Management Decision*, Vol. 35, No. 5, pp. 373–81.

Suggestions for further reading

Calfree, D. (1993) 'Get your mission statement working!', *Management Review*, Vol. 82, pp. 54–7.

Campbell, A. (1989) 'Does your organisation need a mission statement?', *Leadership and Organisational Development Journal*, Vol. 10, No. 3, pp. 3–9.

Campbell, A. and Yeung, S. (1991) 'Creating a sense of mission', *Long Range Planning*, Vol. 24, No. 4, pp. 10–20.

Campbell, A., Devine, M. and Young, D. (1990) *A Sense of Mission*. London: Hutchinson.

Collins, J. and Porras, J. (1991) 'Organizational vision and visionary organizations', *California Management Review*, Vol. 34, No. 1, pp. 30–52.

David, F.R. (1989) 'How companies define their mission', *Long Range Planning*, Vol. 22, No. 3, pp. 90–7.

Falsey, T. (1989) *Corporate Philosophy and Mission Statements*. New York: Quorum Books.

Germain, R. and Bixby Cooper, M. (1990) 'How a customer mission statement affects company performance', *Industrial Marketing Management*, Vol. 19, pp. 47–54.

Klemm, M., Sanderson, S. and Luffman, G. (1991) 'Mission statements: selling corporate values to employees', *Long Range Planning*, Vol. 24, No. 3, pp. 73–8.

O'Gorman, C. and Doran, R. (1999) 'Mission statements in small and medium sized enterprises', *Journal of Small Business Management*, Vol. 37, No. 4, pp. 59–66.

Pearce, J. (1982) 'The company mission as a strategic tool', *Sloan Management Review*, Vol. 38, pp. 15–24.

Pearce, J. and David, F. (1987) 'Corporate mission statements: the bottom line', *Executive*, Vol. 1, pp. 109–16.

Piercy, J. and Morgan, N.A. (1994) 'Mission analysis: an operational approach', *Journal of General Management*, Vol. 19, No. 3, pp. 1–19.

Rarick, C. and Vitton, J. (1995) 'Mission statements make cents', *Journal of Business Strategy*, Vol. 16, pp. 11–12.

Simpson, D. (1994) 'Rethinking vision and mission', *Planning Review*, Vol. 22, p. 911.

Want, J. (1986) 'Corporate mission: the intangible contribution to performance', *Management Review*, Aug., pp. 40–50.

Selected case material

CASE 17.1	23 February 2005 **FT**

Traditionalist embraces change

JON BOONE

Mixing business and pleasure is clearly something that Chris Woodhead relishes. The former chief inspector of schools turned education entrepreneur is weighing up how best to give Peter Hyman, a prime-ministerial speechwriter-turned-teacher at Islington Green School, 'a good kicking' in a newspaper review of Mr Hyman's book about the school that Woodhead controversially declared to be 'failing' in 1997.

Everyone benefits from the marriage of his two roles as campaigner for traditional education and as chairman of Cognita, Britain's fastest growing chain of for-profit private schools, says Mr Woodhead. And as for Mr Hyman, 'I still think Islington Green is failing, whatever Downing Street says.'

When he is not writing articles and making television appearances – 'PR is an important part of the business' – Mr Woodhead's chairmanship of the private equity-backed company takes him 'hurtling around' the country visiting the schools the group has snapped up since its first acquisition in November last year and attending to its 'pipeline' of future purchases in a market dominated by traditional schools run as charities.

▶

CASE 17.1 CONT.

Thus far Mr Woodhead, backed by cash from Englefield, the private equity group, has proved highly skilled at persuading owners, governors and headteachers that they should sell up. He has already acquired 20 schools, by the end of the year he expects to add another 10 and believes the group – already the biggest in the country – will swell to 50.

He insists that it is not just the cash that attracts the owners of small private schools, who have often built their businesses over a lifetime, but his reputation as an 'unashamedly traditional' educationalist. 'They believe, like us, that children should learn to read and write, they should learn the traditional subjects of the curriculum and the job of the teacher is no different in the new millennium, whatever the government might believe, than it was in the 20th or even the 19th century. We don't think the teacher in the 21st century has to be reinvented.'

He is conscious of how a clutch of 50 schools could greatly enhance the already considerable clout he enjoys in educational circles. He can imagine a time in the future – although he insists it is not an immediate priority – when Cognita could desert the A-level system in favour of a new qualification arranged by an exam board set up by top private and state schools.

Despite the rapid growth of the empire, the company itself is being kept deliberately lean, with just three staff managing the business and another three equivalent full-time posts working on the education side. The company will shortly vacate its plush offices in Bibendum, the Terence Conran complex on the trendy Fulham Road. From its new offices in the less glamorous Milton Keynes it aims to keep costs low by reaping economies of scale and boosting the profitability of its schools by increasing their capacity. This has, Mr Woodhead admits, alarmed some parents.

'We are very conscious that they chose the schools that we now own because they are relatively small – and the last thing that we want to do is turn them into great educational factories. But some of the sites have got opportunities for further buildings and the rolls could be increased at some of the schools without the need for more building.'

Ultimately, however, the plan is to sell the company in 'seven-plus years' or even float it on the stock market. This too has caused consternation among some parents, particularly those that work in the City. 'They see the potential downside and ask the same questions I asked when I was first approached by Englefield,' he says. 'I did not want to be used as a frontman for an education company that was solely interested in making as quick and dramatic a profit as possible.

'I understand why some parents wonder if we are only interested in buying up schools for property development when one of our schools in Hertfordshire is on a street surrounded by multi-million pound houses and the site is much more valuable for residential development than it is as a school.

'Like them, I needed to be convinced that Englefield was serious in the sense that it understood my point about quality education being the driver of the profit and it was committed to a reasonable period of time for the investment.'

After leaving Ofsted, the UK schools inspectorate, in 2000 Mr Woodhead helped cook up a similar scheme with Numis, the broker, but failed to raise enough capital for the idea and he started an '18-month conversation' with Englefield that finally convinced him of the company's good intentions.

The final business plan that he developed with Edmund Lazarus, one of the founding partners of Englefield, envisages that parents will be prepared to spend between £6,000 and £9,000 a year on schools, provided they are carefully located in areas where parents are sufficiently wealthy and where 'state education might be problematic'.

Mr Woodhead explains: 'That could be because standards in state schools are low or they are worried about behaviour. Or it could be that there's a selective grammar school and the parents want their children to come to our prep schools to give them a better chance of getting into the grammar school.'

Nor is he interested in competing with the top tier of private schools – where fees can top £20,000 and where there is a 'general desire to make the place as palatial as possible'.

'It's not that we are not offering particular subjects. What we are not doing is investing in luxury resources and fabric. We don't, for instance, need to reinvent the computer suite every other year – yes, technology has to be updated, but I think an awful lot of money can be spent unnecessarily on computers.'

In short, Cognita, he cheerfully accepts, is Tesco to Eton's Harrods. And he is adamant that parents and teachers should not be alarmed by a free-market approach. 'There is no conflict . . . because the better the education that we provide for parents and their children, the more popular the schools will be.'

Indeed, he predicts that the market, which now only has a handful of companies running chains of for-profit schools, will change dramatically over the next 10 years. 'I think we are seeing the beginning of consolidation. It is likely that some charitable-status schools may become for-profit schools. Certainly some charitable schools are talking to us with a view of us acquiring them, or to some form of joint venture.'

They are attracted, he says, by the investment that companies such as Cognita are prepared to make – but he declines to spell out exactly how much Englefield, which has £500m in total funds, is prepared to spend on the company.

'All we can say is we have got access to very significant capital through our backers and our backers are committed given that the business case is right to invest as necessary.'

Mr Woodhead is clearly enjoying both roles. Cutting our interview short, he leaves to take part in a live television debate. Someone might need a good kicking.

Lessons to be learnt in business development from the education industry

In selling its 14 schools to Chris Woodhead's Cognita last month, Asquith Court maintains it found a solution that benefits all parties, including staff and consumers, writes Miranda Green. 'We found a good buyer in Cognita,' says Philip Rhodes, Asquith's chief executive. 'You need to have a long horizon for the schools business, and good educational credentials.' But for his own company, the future – and the serious profits – lie in holding on to and expanding the remaining two thirds of the business: pre-school nurseries. 'Schools are a good business, but very different – and we have long since found that there was a lack of synergy,' Mr Rhodes maintains. He cites different management requirements and different investment and cash flow cycles. Schools, run by individual headteachers, face tough competition for students and typically require constant investment. Nurseries, on the other hand, are often run as chains and require less frequent investment. Asquith now owns and runs 110 separate nurseries, predominantly in south-east England. These cater for about 8,000 children a week, and employ 2,500 people. After Nord Anglia, it is the biggest company in the private nursery business. But the top 10 companies in the sector only run between 12 per cent and 14 per cent of nurseries. This is expected to change, as small nursery businesses sell up to the larger companies. Jeremy Hand, managing director of

▶

West Private Equity, Mr Rhodes's backer, says: 'There are huge, fantastic opportunities here, but scale will drive success in this market. You need to make a profit to keep on developing the business and we hope this strategy will take us, one day, to the public markets.' He adds that he and most of his competitors realised the venture capitalists who backed them had a 'never for ever' attitude.

Source: Jon Boone, 'Traditionalist embraces change', *Financial Times*, 23 February 2005, p. 17. Copyright © 2005 The Financial Times Limited.

CASE 17.2

25 July 2005   **FT**

The chief executive who saved the best for last

DEBORAH BREWSTER

Not many chief executives decide, on the brink of their retirement, that the thing they need to do is to transform the company they founded 43 years ago and double its size overnight. Yet that is what Chip Mason, the 68-year-old founder and chief of Legg Mason, did when he announced his deal of a lifetime last month.

Mr Mason set up a brokerage company aged 25, merged it with another in 1970 and took it public in 1974. Since then, he has built Legg Mason, based in Baltimore, into a highly regarded fund management company and brokerage. The firm's flagship Value Trust has beaten the Standard & Poor's 500 index for 14 years in a row, with Bill Miller, its fund manager, being the only person ever to have managed this.

Under Mr Mason's deal, Legg Mason will abandon its origins and offload its brokerage to Citigroup, acquiring in exchange Citi's $440bn (£252bn) asset management operation. The move doubles Legg Mason's assets under management to about $830bn and turns the low-key company into the fifth biggest investment house in the US.

'It started five or so years ago, with a German bank,' says Mr Mason, who, like many entrepreneurs, operates without layers of support staff and appears to use his office mostly for visitors. Folksy and direct in manner, he sprinkles his conversation with words such as 'neat' and 'baloney'.

'We didn't do the German deal, but I discovered that they and others were questioning whether they ought to be money managers or if they should just be distributors of other people's funds.

'I thought, "we have to pay attention to this because it could change the dynamics of the business". Then the regulators jumped in and added a whole new element . . . saying that being the manager of the money and the distributor had some funny conflicts in it.

'I don't think that view is correct,' says Mr Mason, who makes clear his impatience with what he perceives as overreaching regulators. 'But in the end it doesn't matter. The regulatory wind kept getting stronger. I kept thinking: "This isn't a positive development – we distributed [our funds] almost solely through our own brokerage, so eventually we were going to have to deal with the problem."

'It was clear we were going to have to do something, and 70 per cent of our profits came from asset management, and 20 per cent from brokerage and nine or 10 per cent from capital markets. There you are, you're going to have to go with the 70 per cent. We either needed to separate the broker/dealer into a separate company, or sell it.

'We were moving towards the separation idea and had it all mapped out – but, about five months ago, I got a call from Citi. They said: "Should we consider swapping businesses?" I thought about it, and called them back ten days later and went up there in the next three or four weeks to talk about it. The talks would stop and start. It would fall apart because I'd get cold feet".

'Selling the broker/dealer was traumatic,' admits Mr Mason, who appears to enjoy discussing broking more than asset management. 'I'd spent my whole life in it. Even on the day we announced it, it was very traumatic. I got everyone out of the room because I had to do it alone, call the employees and tell them. For four days, I dreaded that call. I just dreaded it. We'd hired all these people, we'd trained them, we'd worked together all these years, it was very, very hard.'

Mr Mason is one of the highest paid executives in asset management, earning more than $10m last year before taking into account his options. However, given Legg Mason's rapid growth and solid reputation, few have criticised him for that. The group's shares rose 60 per cent in the year before the Citigroup deal, and are up another 25 per cent since, reflecting investors' view that Mr Mason effectively named his price for the brokerage and got the best end of the deal.

Mr Mason says that he plans to retire in the next 'couple of years', and the board is close to naming his successor, which will allow for a transition period. 'We have been grooming people internally, and they [the board] have someone in mind,' he says.

Until then, he will continue to spend his time doing calculations on how to integrate his new empire, and visiting its outposts. He typically works a 12-hour day, he says, with another hour in the evening 'to put the day together'.

'By September/October, we will have a lot of it clear,' he says, sitting in the Legg Mason tower, which dominates downtown Baltimore, having come from a town hall session with most of Citigroup's asset management employees in New York. 'There is naturally uneasiness because they're wondering who will lose their job,' he says. 'We have to get to that, and move on. We can't say no one will lose their job.'

Citigroup's fixed income asset management, which accounts for more than half its total, will be integrated with Legg Mason's fixed income subsidiary, Western Asset Management, which will become the biggest fixed income manager in the world, with almost $500bn – an extraordinary rise from $3bn 20 years ago.

'There is no doubt fixed income will be a lot of work, it's a big bite,' says Mr Mason. 'The equity business will be easier. We will probably put that all into a separate unit and run it like a separate asset manager.

'There was a lot of analysis . . . still is,' says Mr Mason, who carries a calculator with him everywhere he goes and also fills large yellow pads with sums. 'I'm not big on computer print-outs,' he explains. 'If one number is wrong, they make all the others wrong. I do all the calculations myself – add, subtract, multiply and divide. For some people, numbers don't do anything. For me they spell it out very clearly, they tell the story. I like numbers, always have.'

As if the Citigroup deal were not enough, Legg Mason on the same day announced that it would take the plunge into hedge funds, buying one of the oldest fund of funds – Permal – from Italy's Agnelli family. That entailed none of the agonising of the brokerage sale – Mr Mason says he jumped at the offer.

'I didn't want to own a direct hedge fund,' he says. 'I wasn't sure we could manage them from a risk and regulatory point of view. About six or seven years ago, I went to see a hedge fund and spent a day there and I was with them for 30 per cent of what they said and then they lost me. The investment banker who took me in persuaded me to go back and I managed to understand about half what they said, but I just thought I'd be on pins and needles the whole time if I owned this, so I passed.

'What was so neat about Permal was that it was totally outside the US, dealing all over the world with wealthy investors, and it had just

come into the US, which could be its biggest growth potential. When we first got called on it, I said straight away that this is a deal we should do – it gets us in the alternative space, where we need to be. And we wanted one that had relationships with the key managers, which you need some age to do. Permal has been 30-plus years in the market.'

The group, which has $20bn in assets under management, also requires no integration and will be left alone to carry on its business, Mr Mason says.

As for Mr Mason himself, he says he will have more than enough to do after he retires. He is the chairman of Johns Hopkins University and holds several civic and charitable posts in Baltimore. 'I'll put this deal away, and my work will be complete,' he says.

Source: Deborah Brewster, 'The chief executive who saved the best for last', *Financial Times*, 25 July 2005, p. 10. Copyright © 2005 The Financial Times Limited.

Discussion points

1. Develop a mission for Cognita.

2. How would you describe Chip Mason's mission for Legg Mason?

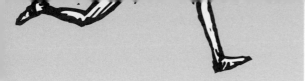

CHAPTER 18

The strategy for the venture

Chapter overview

Strategy is a central concept in modern management practice. This chapter looks at business strategy from the entrepreneurial perspective. The value of a well-considered and well-defined strategy to the venture is advocated, and the way in which entrepreneurs can control strategy development is considered. The chapter concludes by exploring the strategies entrepreneurs can use to initiate their ventures.

18.1 What is a business strategy?

Key learning outcome

An understanding of the key elements of the business strategy for the entrepreneurial venture.

The idea that an organisation has a 'strategy' lies at the centre of much management thinking. A strategy can be defined, broadly, as the actions an organisation takes to pursue its business objectives. Strategy drives *performance* and an effective strategy results in a good performance. An organisation's strategy is multifaceted. It can be viewed from a number of directions depending on which aspects of its actions are of interest. A basic distinction exists among the *content* of a business's strategy, the strategy *process* that the business adopts to maintain that strategy, and the environmental *context* within which the strategy must be made to work. The strategy content relates to what the business actually *does* whereas the strategy process relates to the way the business *decides* what it is going to do. The strategy content has three distinct decision areas: the *products* to be offered, the *markets* to be targeted and the approach taken to *competing*.

Strategy content

Strategy content relates to three things: the final product range, the customers it serves and the advantage it seeks in the marketplace.

The product range

This covers the type and range of products that the firm supplies to its markets (note that the word 'product' is used here in a general sense to include both tangible products and intangible services). The decisions the entrepreneur faces here are:

- What type of products should the business offer?
- What should their features be?
- How will they address customer needs? What benefits will they offer?
- What mix of physical and service elements should be offered with the product?
- If the product is to be successful, in what way(s) must the customer find it more attractive than those of competitors?
- What unit cost is acceptable? How does this relate to price?
- How wide should the product range be? How many product variants will be necessary?

Market scope

The market scope defines the customer groups and market segments that will be addressed by the firm. Key decisions here include:

- How is the total market to be defined?
- What features (e.g. customer types, customer needs, buying behaviour, location) are important for characterising the market and defining its sectors?
- On what group(s) of customers should the business concentrate?
- In what sectors will these customers be?
- Should the firm concentrate its efforts on a narrow group or spread its efforts more widely?
- Why will the group(s) selected find the firm's offerings more attractive than those of competitors?
- What will be the geographical location and spread of the customers (e.g. local, regional, national, international)?

Clearly, decisions on product range and market scope are interlinked. The decisions made with respect to one influence the decisions that must be made for the other. Therefore, it may be better for the entrepreneur to regard themselves as facing a *single* set of decisions about the combined *product–market domain* of the firm.

Competitive approach

Competitive approach refers to the way in which the firm competes within its product–market domain to sustain and develop its business in the face of competitive pressures. This aspect of strategy content reflects the way in which the firm tries to influence the customer to favour their offerings. Important decisions to be made in relation to this approach include:

- How should the product be priced relative to competitors? (Should a discount or premium be offered?)
- What distribution route will be used to get the product to the customer?
- What financial rewards and incentives will be offered to intermediaries and distributors?

- What support (e.g. exclusivity, preferential selling, display) will be expected from distributors?
- How will the customer's buying decision be influenced?
- What message will be sent to consumers about the product?
- How will the message be delivered? (For example, by advertising, by personal selling, or through distributors?)
- Will customers be encouraged to compare the product to the offerings of competitors? (If so, on what basis: price, quality, features, performance?)
- Or will customers be told that the innovation is so great that there is nothing else like it?

The strategy content which the business aspires to achieve must be consistent with the entrepreneur's vision and the mission they have defined for the venture. Decisions about strategy content must be made in the light of an understanding of 'external' conditions such as characteristics of the market, the competitive situation and the way in which different sectors can be served, and in the light of 'internal' concerns such as the mission and goals of the organisation, the resources it has to hand and its capabilities. The strategy content for the venture is the way in which it competes to sustain and develop its product–market domain (Figure 18.1).

The venture will achieve success if it directs its resources in an appropriate way towards delivering a rewarding and sustainable strategy content. The strategy content dictates the investment of resources that the business must undertake. Investments in financial, operating and human resources will all play a part in supporting the strategy content. Consequently, strategy content decisions must be evaluated in terms of the investments that they entail, the rewards that are likely and the risks involved.

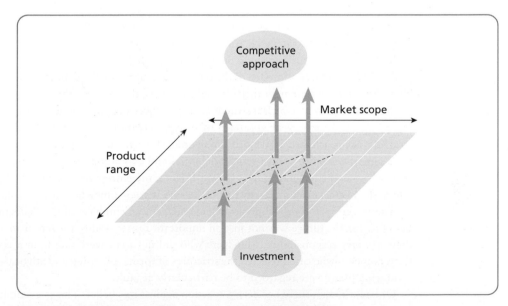

Figure 18.1 Strategy content and product–market domain

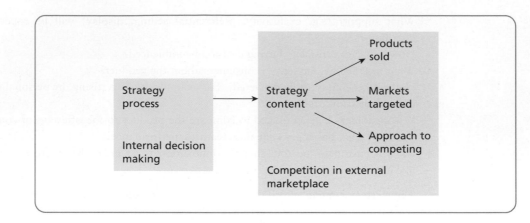

Figure 18.2 Strategy content and strategy process

18.2 Strategy process in the entrepreneurial business

> **Key learning outcome**
>
> An understanding of the ways in which an entrepreneurial business decides which strategies to adopt.

The firm's strategy process is the way in which the business makes decisions about the strategy content it wishes to achieve (Figure 18.2). It is reflected in the way the organisation considers its future, how it selects its goals and the way it decides how to allocate resources in order to achieve them. Strategy process is embedded in the structures, systems and processes that the organisation adopts, as well as its culture and the leadership style of the entrepreneur running it.

One of the most important themes in modern strategic management is the distinction between, and the relative values of, *deliberate* (or *planned*) and *emergent* approaches to strategy creation. A deliberate approach to strategy creation is one in which the entrepreneur sets out to define a strategic policy for the venture in which the future goals and competitive approach of the business are clearly defined and translated into specific objectives. The entrepreneur then sets out to achieve this strategy through an explicit process of implementation in which instructions as to objectives and budgets are passed down the organisation. An emergent approach to strategy creation is one in which future goals and strategic approach are left more ambiguous. Rather, the entrepreneur concentrates on managing the venture's short-term capabilities and exploiting the opportunities that present themselves as the business moves forward. Here, the entrepreneur is not so concerned with where the business is going; they just make sure it goes somewhere interesting.

The traditional approach to strategic management emphasised the deliberate approach. Planning for the future was not just an important responsibility for senior managers; it was their *primary* responsibility. Managers who did not plan were failing in a critical respect. Entrepreneurs who often rejected the strictures of formal planning and advocated action over producing plans were regarded to be particularly at fault.

Of late, though, there has been a reaction against this belief. This is exemplified in Henry Mintzberg's seminal book *The Rise and Fall of Strategic Planning* (1994). The critique of the planning approach is based on two arguments. The first is that empirical observation of business performance does not show a strong correlation with formal planning activity. Many businesses that do not carry out a lot of planning are as successful as those that invest heavily in it. The second argument is that the planning approach is in theory flawed. Planning works only if the future can be predicted with some certainty. This is rarely the case, especially for the fast-growing entrepreneurial venture in a dynamic, unpredictable environment. It also assumes that managers can control everything that the extended organisation does. Experience of organisations suggests that managers (even entrepreneurs with strong leadership skills) cannot control every detail. As a result, emergent approaches to strategy creation should not be dismissed as wrong. They reflect a perfectly good managerial approach to developing at least some businesses given their capabilities and the opportunities the environment offers them.

As with many debates in which opinions are polarised, the resolution of the planning–emergent debate has, to a great extent, resulted in a broader perspective in which both positions are integrated. Drawing a hard and fast distinction between the stages of creating – *formulating* – and putting into practice – *implementing* – a particular strategy is seen as artificial. 'Implementers' who have played no part in the development of a strategy are unlikely to take ownership of it from the 'formulators' who have. A strategy must be modified between the drawing board and taking to the air.

Entrepreneurs make good strategies happen through leadership, not just through planning, and leadership requires listening to people, learning from them and taking their ideas on board. Leadership also means giving people the latitude to make their own decisions and put their own insight into practice. This is the only way that an organisation can learn and be flexible. However, leaving room for an organisation to grow and develop does not mean that the entrepreneur has no view on where it should go. As we discussed in Chapter 16, even if an entrepreneur does not have a definite, highly detailed plan in mind, they should certainly have a vision as to where the venture should be heading. Such a vision may offer a space into which the business might go, rather than a definite destination, but nonetheless it will control its destiny. A cognitive study comparing entrepreneurial intentions with actual outcomes by Jenkins (1997) suggests that many entrepreneurs adopt an emergent approach to strategy creation and are adept at using it.

Eden and Ackermann (1998) have suggested an integrated and participative approach to strategy creation. They suggest that good strategies emerge from an interactive process that they refer to as the 'journey' of strategy, where the word 'journey' is an acronym for 'Jointly, Understanding, Reflecting and Negotiating'. In this process, individuals still have a responsibility for identifying and evaluating strategic options; however, these options are flexible 'opening positions' and can evolve as they are implemented through the 'journey' the strategy takes through the organisation. Making the strategy happen is as important as making it in the first place. In the context of the entrepreneurial venture, this process resonates with the entrepreneur defining, articulating and communicating their vision.

The entrepreneurial approach to management is distinct at the level of strategy process, not content. It is not what an entrepreneur *does* (the business they are in) that matters. What makes a manager entrepreneurial is the *way* they organise the venture and use it to innovate and to deliver value to the customer in a way that existing players cannot.

At any point in time the venture will have a strategy content, that is, a product range being sold to a distinct group of customers with a particular approach taken to attracting those

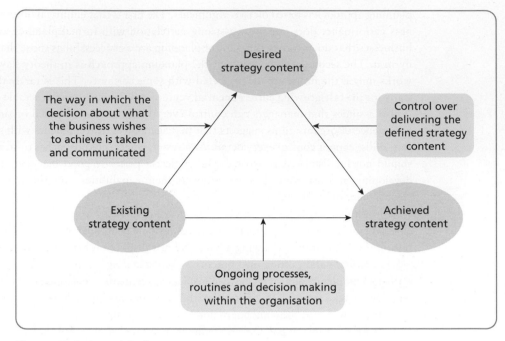

Figure 18.3 A model of strategy process

customers and competing within the marketplace. The strategy content will evolve as the business grows and develops. New products will be introduced, old ones dropped. The competitive approach may alter as the organisation learns and market conditions change. At any moment in time the entrepreneur and other managers in the organisation will have views and expectations about what the business's strategy content should be in the future. This interest may also extend to other stakeholders such as important customers looking for specific new products and influential investors who offer advice on how the business might develop.

The strategy process adopted by the organisation is defined by the way in which decisions about strategy content are taken. As shown in Figure 18.3, it is reflected in the relationship that exists between the *existing* strategy content, the strategy content *desired* by the business for the future and the strategy content that is actually *achieved*. The results of these decisions influence the investments made by the venture.

The link between existing strategy content and the strategy content achieved in the future

The strategy content of the business will evolve over time. The way in which the business modifies its range of products, changes its customer base and develops its competitive approach will be the result of a series of ongoing decisions and actions taken by the people who make up the organisation. These decisions will occur even if the organisation does not have an explicit strategy to guide them. They may be incremental and the result of short-term pragmatic considerations, or they may be made in response to immediate market opportunities. However, this does not mean that these decisions are not controlled. They will be shaped by a wide variety of organisational and environmental factors, including:

- the reporting relationships that define the organisation's structure;
- the mechanisms the organisation adopts to control the allocation of resources;
- the organisation's systems for motivating and rewarding performance;
- the way the organisation manages information and identifies opportunities;
- the organisation's technological competence and any technical developments;
- the organisation's historical performance;
- resource availability within the organisation;
- the organisational culture;
- internal disputes and political infighting within the organisation;
- the expectations and influence of external stakeholders such as customers and investors.

If these features are allowed to control decision making about the evolution of a business's strategy content without reference to an overriding strategic context then the firm's strategy process may, using the terminology of Mintzberg and Waters (1985), be said to be *emergent*.

The link between existing strategy content and desired strategy content

An emergent strategy may establish itself for a number of reasons. However, an entrepreneur is unlikely to be satisfied unless the organisation operates with at least some sense of what it might achieve in the future. After all, the entrepreneur is motivated by the difference between what *is* and what *might be*. The future state desired by the entrepreneur can take a variety of forms. It will vary in several particulars, including:

- the types of detail it contains;
- how specific those details are;
- the latitude the entrepreneur will accept in its achievement;
- the period over which it is to be achieved;
- the way in which it is communicated to other stakeholders;
- the extent to which it is negotiable with other stakeholders.

There are a number of ways in which the organisation can become aware of the desired strategy content.

The entrepreneur's communication of their vision

The entrepreneur can articulate and communicate their vision to the rest of the organisation. This may be sufficiently powerful and attractive to motivate the whole organisation. A vision may (deliberately) lack detail but it should highlight the desirability of achieving certain parts of the strategy content in preference to others.

The definition of a mission

The organisation's mission will specify the key elements of the strategy content. The amount of detail it provides will depend on how the strategic component in the mission is specified. The mission will, at a minimum, be able to provide a test as to which parts of the strategy content are desirable and acceptable. The mission may be developed by a process of consensus or it may be imposed on the organisation by the entrepreneur.

The setting of objectives

The desired strategy content may be defined explicitly by the setting of specific objectives. These may be financial or strategic in nature. They may refer to the organisation as a whole, or they may relate to a particular project or they may fall within the responsibility of an individual. Objectives may be subject to negotiation and agreed through consensus, or alternatively, they may be imposed by the entrepreneur without opportunity for debate. The approach taken depends upon the entrepreneur's personal style and leadership strategy. Quantified objectives provide a means of benchmarking the achievement of a desired strategy content.

Through informal discussion

The identification of a desired strategy content may not occur by a formal process. It may become evident through ongoing discussions about the business and the opportunities offered by the market. These discussions may involve a variety of people both within and perhaps from outside the organisation, and they may take place over a period of time.

The link between desired strategy content and achieved strategy content

This link is manifest in the ability of the entrepreneur to deliver the strategy content they desire for their organisation. Two things may limit this. The first is the potential to achieve that strategy content in the marketplace. If the strategy content is to be delivered, it must be both *achievable* given the market conditions and the competitive forces present, and *feasible* in terms of the resources available to make the necessary investments. The second possible limitation is the degree of control the entrepreneur has over the organisation.

Even though it might be 'their' organisation, entrepreneurs are limited in the extent to which they can control the actions of the people who make up their organisation. They cannot enforce their will over it completely. Some of the organisation's strategy will always be 'emergent'. The way in which entrepreneurs control the organisation and ensure that it delivers the strategy content they desire is dependent on a large number of factors. Some of the more critical include:

- their personal leadership style;
- the consensus they build for the desired strategy;
- their ownership of resources;
- the way in which they control resources;
- the control mechanisms and procedures they have established;
- their technical expertise;
- their access to information and their ability to control that information within the organisation;
- the way they set objectives;

- the way in which they reward achievement of objectives;
- their creation of, and the way they are legitimised by, symbolic devices within the organisation;
- their influence over, and control of, organisational politics;
- the relationship they build with external stakeholders;
- the way they manage *attributions*, that is, the way they associate themselves with success and dissociate themselves from failure within the organisation.

The entrepreneur will be motivated by a distinct picture of how the world should be. That is what their vision *is*. Yet they must always match their desire to achieve particular outcomes with their ability to control what the organisation can actually do both internally and in its marketplace. They must also balance their need to control the organisation with giving the people who make up the organisation latitude to make their own decisions and use their insights and intuitions to further its ends.

18.3 Controlling strategy process in the venture

Key learning outcome

A recognition of the decisions the entrepreneur must make to control the strategy process in their venture.

If the entrepreneur is to maintain control of the organisation and focus it on the opportunities that it seeks to exploit, then they must control its strategy. This demands control of its strategy *process* as well as its strategy *content*. This means controlling the way the organisation identifies options for its future, the way in which these are communicated and shared, the way in which control is maintained over resource investments aimed at achieving the desired outcomes, and the way in which rewards are offered for delivering the outcomes.

The essential decisions that the entrepreneur must make in relation to developing and controlling the strategy process include the following.

Decisions relating to the development of the mission

- By what process will the business mission be developed? (Through consensus or by imposition?)
- How will it be articulated?
- To whom will it be communicated?

Decisions relating to the development of strategy

- Who in the organisation will be invited to contribute to the development of the desired strategy content?
- How will their ideas be evaluated and judged?
- Where will the information needed to develop the strategy content come from?
- Who in the organisation will collect, store and control that information?
- How will the desired strategy content be communicated to the rest of the organisation?
- How will the strategy content be communicated to external stakeholders?

Decisions relating to the control of resources

- What procedure will control how investment decisions are made?
- Who will have responsibility for what level of investment?
- How will new investments be distinguished from routine payments?
- How will budgets be allocated?
- What budgetary control systems will be put in place?
- How will information on budgetary control be stored, manipulated and shared?
- By whom will information on budgetary control be stored, manipulated and shared?

Decisions relating to the way objectives will be set, monitored and rewarded

- How will objectives be set?
- Who will be responsible for setting them?
- For whom will objectives be set? (The organisation, functions, teams, individuals?)
- What will be the nature of the objectives? (Financial or strategic?)
- Will objectives be negotiable? If so, in what way and by whom?
- What information will be needed to monitor objectives?
- How will this information be collected and stored? Who will have access to it?
- What will be the rewards for achieving set objectives? What will be the response if they are not achieved?

These decisions will be influential in giving the organisation its form, structure and systems because they will influence the culture it develops. Consequently, they must be subject to constant revision and review as the business grows and develops. Jenkins (1997) used a causal mapping technique (a way of creating a visual representation of the connection of ideas in an individual's cognition) to compare entrepreneurs' intentions (what they plan to do) and outcomes (what actually happened). He found that the causal maps were consistent with intentions, but not with outcomes. He interprets this to suggest that entrepreneurs may not hold clear, well thought through strategic approaches in their conscious minds. Rather than drive for a particular future, with an *intended and deliberate* strategy combination, many entrepreneurs, it would seem, merely respond flexibly to new opportunities as they come along and capitalise on an *emergent* strategy route.

18.4 Why a well-defined strategy can help the venture

Key learning outcome

An appreciation of the value in generating an explicit strategy for the venture.

Working under an emergent strategy is a far more common feature of managerial life than many textbooks on business planning would have us believe. Developing, assessing and communicating a strategy content represents an *investment*. It takes time, effort and money to achieve a well-defined strategy. Like any investment, it must be assessed in terms of the returns it will bring in the way it will improve organisational performance. If this return is not forthcoming then the organisation may well benefit from allowing its strategy to be emergent.

There are a variety of conditions under which an organisation's strategy tends to become emergent. These include:

- when its expectations are limited, i.e. when the desired strategic content is not very different from the existing one;
- when it is experienced in pursuing its business, i.e. when knowledge of how to achieve a particular strategic content is well established and not subject to extensive discussion;
- when the competitive environment is stable, i.e. when environmental shocks do not occur;
- when the competitive structure is stable, i.e. when competitors do not tend to infringe on each other's business;
- when the rules of competition are established, i.e. when competitor's reactions are predictable;
- when the industry technology is established, i.e. innovations are few and of limited scope;
- when patterns of investment are routinised, i.e. managers do not seek guidance at a strategic level when making investment decisions;
- when the organisation's leadership is weak, i.e. when power to impose a particular strategy content is limited;
- when the organisation is political, i.e. when agreement on a particular strategy content could not be gained.

These conditions tend to be found in mature, established organisations whose decision making has become routinised and even bureaucratised. They are not the typical conditions to be found in a new, fast-growing venture which is innovating and changing the rules of competition within its marketplace. Thus the entrepreneurial venture would be expected to gain in the following ways from investing in developing a strategy and communicating it to stakeholders.

A Stategy . . .

Encourages entrepreneurs to assess and articulate their vision

A strategy represents the way in which the entrepreneur will achieve their vision. The potential to make a vision into reality will be dependent on the possibility of creating a strategy to deliver it. This possibility will be a function of the *achievability* of the strategy in the competitive marketplace and of the *feasibility* of the strategy in terms of the resources available.

Ensures auditing of the organisation and its environment

A strategy is a call to action. If it is to be successful then it must be based on a sound knowledge of the environment in which the organisation finds itself, the conditions within its marketplace, particularly in terms of the competitive pressures it faces, and of its own internal capabilities and competences. Developing a strategy demands that the organisation's capabilities and competences are audited.

Illuminates new possibilities and latitudes

A strategy is developed in response to the dictates of the entrepreneur's vision. However, the process is iterative. Strategy development feeds back to vision. It reinforces the vision's strong parts and asks the entrepreneur to readdress its weaknesses. It clarifies the possibilities the venture faces and the latitude the entrepreneur will accept for the achievement of them.

Provides organisational focus

A strategy provides a central theme around which the members of the organisation can focus their activities. It relates the tasks of the individual to the tasks of the organisation as a whole. A strategy is the stream of actions that make up the organisation. As such it is a unifying principle which gives organisational actions meaning and significance in relation to each other.

Guides the structuring of the organisation

A strategy highlights the tasks necessary for the entrepreneur to achieve their goals. Some of these tasks will be short term, others long term; some will be of a general management nature, others will be specialist; some will be concerned with generating and sustaining external relationships, whereas others will be concerned with internal technical issues. The nature of the tasks that must be undertaken defines the roles that must be filled within the organisation. This in turn guides the entrepreneur in developing a structure for the organisation.

Acts as a guide to decision making

A strategy provides a framework for making decisions. A decision is a response to proffered possibilities. The strategy helps to highlight and evaluate these possibilities. It indicates how significant a particular decision will be, and the impact its outcomes will have. It illuminates the information that will be needed if the decision is to be made confidently. The strategy then enables the various options to be evaluated and the right course of action to be rationalised.

Provides a starting point for the setting of objectives

By specifying the tasks that need to be undertaken in order to achieve desired outcomes, a strategy provides a starting point for defining quantified measurable objectives for both the organisation as a whole, and for the individuals who comprise it.

Acts as a common language for stakeholders

An organisation is characterised by its strategy. The strategy provides the context in which the organisation acts. It is the perspective which enables individuals to make sense of the organisation's actions and their own part in those actions. The organisation's strategy provides a way for its stakeholders to relate to each other: they *interact* through its strategy. Strategy is a common language they can use to talk to each other about the organisation and their relationship to it.

Vision, mission and strategy in the entrepreneurial process

Vision, *mission* and *strategy* are intertwined aspects of a single entrepreneurial perspective (Figure 18.4). Each of these components represents both a different aspect of the world the

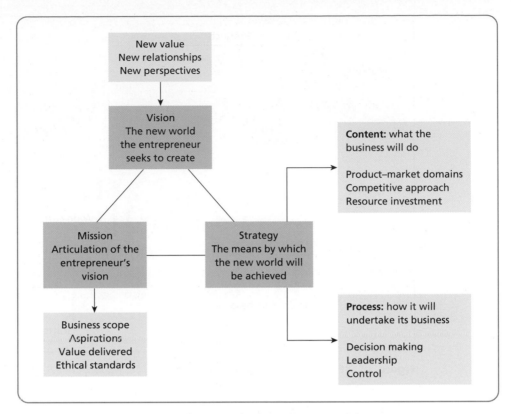

Figure 18.4 Vision, mission and strategy in the entrepreneurial process

entrepreneur seeks to create and the means by which they will create it. Together, they turn the entrepreneur's desire to make a difference in the world into an effective management tool for delivering change. This tool works by reconciling the entrepreneur's vision with actual possibilities and capabilities, by articulating that vision so that it may be communicated to others and by defining the actions necessary to progress the venture.

18.5 An overview of entrepreneurial entry strategies

Key learning outcome

A recognition of the strategies adopted by entrepreneurs to establish their ventures.

A strategy is the pattern of actions that define an organisation. Every entrepreneurial venture is different, and each has its own strategy. However, there are common and recognisable patterns in the way in which businesses compete with one another. These are called *generic strategies*. Entrepreneurial ventures adopt a number of generic strategies in order to establish themselves in the marketplace. These strategies differ in the way in which the venture offers new value to the marketplace and the market they wish to serve (Figure 18.5).

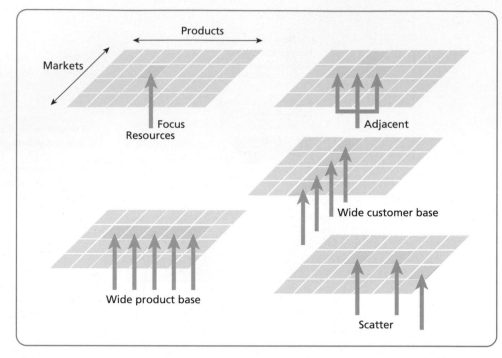

Figure 18.5 Entrepreneurial entry strategies

Product–market domain

The entrepreneur must select the product–market domain in which to establish their venture. This defines the scope of the product they wish to offer to what market segments. The product scope is the range of product categories the firm will provide. Product scope must be understood in terms of the way that customers distinguish among different products in the market. Important factors are product features; product quality; patterns of product usage in terms of place, time and quantity; market positioning; and branding and imagery. The market sectors served are the distinct customer groups addressed by the firm.

Customer groups must be classified in terms of the way their needs both coincide and differ. Important factors for consideration here are demographic and sociographic characteristics, psychographic profile, customer location, buying behaviour and usage patterns. Such analysis is a well-established part of marketing thinking. The entrepreneur has five generic entry strategies in relation to product–market domain. These are:

- *Focused entry* – addressing a single well-defined product–market domain.
- *Product spread* – offering a wide range of products to a single well-defined market.
- *Customer spread* – delivering a single or narrow range of products to a wide base of customers.
- *Adjacency* – offering a wide range of products to a broad customer base. All product–market segments are adjacent in that the characterising features of each segment are continuous or can be related to each other.
- *Scatter* – a variety of different products are offered to a variety of different customers. The segments are not adjacent.

Competitive approach

A competitive approach to market entry refers to the way the venture attracts customers by offering them value that existing competitors do not. Generic strategies in relation to this approach include the following.

Offering a new product or service

The innovative product or service must perform a task for the customer, or solve a problem for them, in a way which is both different from, and better than, existing products.

Offering greater value

The customer is offered a product or service which is comparable to those already in existence, but at a lower price, so offering them greater value for money.

Creating new relationships

The entrepreneur exists in a network of relationships built on trust. Trust both reduces costs and adds value. The entrepreneur can be competitive by creating new relationships between providers and users, and by managing existing relationships better.

Being more flexible

Customers' needs are not fixed. Even if they are in the same market segment, different customers will present a slightly different set of needs. Further, a particular customer's needs are subject to constant change. However, at any one point in time a group of customers must satisfy their needs with the limited range of products and services on offer. The entrepreneur can create new value for the customer by being flexible in terms of what they offer. This may involve modifying the products and services they provide to make them specific to the requirements of the customer or developing a means by which the product can be continually modified in response to customers' requirements.

Being more responsive

As customers' needs change and evolve, existing products serve those needs less effectively. As a result, new opportunities emerge and take shape. The entrepreneur can add value in the marketplace by being attuned to those changes, in terms of recognising the new opportunities as they develop and responding quickly to them by modifying their existing offerings and innovating new ones.

Choice of entry strategy

These two aspects of generic entry strategy, namely product–market domain and the competitive approach, exist in an iterative relationship to each other. The choice of competitive approach will depend on the particular characteristics of a product–market segment. How

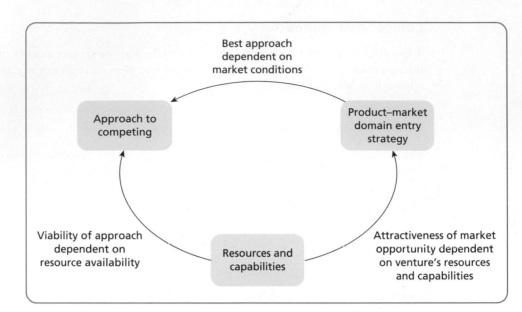

Figure 18.6 The relationship between strategy, resources and capability

that presents itself as an opportunity to the business will depend on the resources it has to hand and its capabilities. Exploiting that opportunity will reward the business with further resources to maintain and expand its presence in its product–market domain. The choice of generic entry strategy depends on the resources and capabilities of the organisation (Figure 18.6).

18.6 Talking strategy: entrepreneurial strategic heuristics

Key learning outcome

A recognition of heuristics as guides to, and indicators of, entrepreneurial decision making.

The discussion of entrepreneurial strategy so far has adopted a formal approach. Entrepreneurial strategy has been described as much from the 'top-down' perspective – that of an outsider looking in – as from the 'bottom up' – of an entrepreneur looking out. This is a legitimate approach. Just as a doctor brings along knowledge and expertise and can diagnose a disease, so the expert in entrepreneurship can recognise strategic approaches that individual entrepreneurs may not themselves recognise. Entrepreneurs do not necessarily, or even usually, have formal knowledge of business strategy creation. An expert in strategy may be able to identify the strategic posturing of the venture even if the venture's managers cannot, or do not see any point in articulating it in formal terms. This is not to say, of course, that they are not implementing the strategy effectively.

This distance between the 'professional strategic expert' and the practising entrepreneur must, however, be closed. The expert must be able to resonate with the way in which the entrepreneur actually makes decisions if they are both to understand the entrepreneur's venture and to articulate support and encouragement effectively. Mitchell (1997) has advocated attention to entrepreneurs' own 'oral histories' as an approach to understanding entre-preneurship. A meaningful way of closing the gap has come from recognising the *heuristics* that entrepreneurs use.

A heuristic is a *decision rule* based on insight and experience. It is called into play when an entrepreneur is required to analyse a situation and make a decision in relation to it. Entrepreneurs are often able to articulate, quite succinctly, the heuristics they use. These fre-quently take the form of punchy aphorisms. They are rarely specific. Rather they are general statements, rules of thumb, that reveal the entrepreneur's attitudes and approaches. These not only provide a practical insight into the approach that the entrepreneur is taking, but can also be used as analytical devices to describe and analyse entrepreneurs and their ventures (a good example of their use is provided by Manimala, 1999).

Table 18.1 describes a series of entrepreneurial strategic heuristics and their opposites, which might be described as counter-heuristics. As will be appreciated, the terms 'heuristic' and 'counter-heuristic' are interchangeable. A heuristic and its counter both have resonance and reflect an equally valid 'common-sense' approach to business. Neither is right or wrong. They must be judged in terms of the entrepreneur's characteristics, the nature of the venture they are pursuing and the success they bring. The list in Table 18.1 is not exhaustive. It is intended to illustrate the heuristic themes entrepreneurs develop and use.

Table 18.1 Examples of entrepreneurial strategic heuristics

Strategic theme	Heuristic	Counter-heuristic
Innovation	Avoid run-of-the mill products	Stick to what is tried and trusted
	Search out new ideas from many sources	Keep an eye on one or two key areas
Flexibility	Keep an open mind to new approaches	Once you have found a good way of doing things – stick to it
	Success only comes from continual improvement	Keep on using a successful formula
Vision	Develop a vision and never compromise it	Let your vision evolve
	Share a vision – but don't negotiate it	Let others contribute to your vision
Start-up strategy	Start small and build	Go for it big time before someone else does
Using external support	All businesses benefit from professional help	Professionals are a poor investment. If they know so much, why aren't they rich?
	Build a partnership with investors	Avoid bringing in investors. They are only interested in what's in it for them
Sharing information	(With non-competitors at least) a good way of reducing costs	Never give anything away. Everyone is a competitor!
	Information is power	It's not what we know that matters – it's what we do

Table 18.1 (*Cont'd*)

Delegation	Leadership is about empowering people to make their own decisions well	It's my job to make all the important decisions
	The only way the business can grow	I don't pass decisions down. Whose business is it anyway!
	We need to push decision making down	I don't delegate. The buck stops here!
Expertise	Developing employee expertise is a priority	The business needs the entrepreneur at the helm
	The most important expert is the entrepreneur	Everyone is an expert in their own way
Entry strategy	Limited, confident start followed by expansion	Make yourself known in the market from day one
Expansion	Grow in sure-footed stages	Build quickly on the innovation
	Establish our presence in as many markets as possible, as early as possible	Exploit our established markets before moving on
Competition	Avoid head-to-head conflicts	An entrepreneur must compete. Hit them where it hurts!
Investment	Less risk using own money	Borrow to grow. Use other people's money
Risk	Avoid risk wherever possible	Risk should be managed, but, at the end of the day, risk is what it is all about
	Entrepreneurs and investors must work together to manage risk and return	Let investors take the risk – I'll have the return!

Summary of key ideas

- A strategy is the means by which the venture will achieve its aims.

- Strategy *content* defines the products the venture will offer, the customer groups to be targeted and the way in which the venture will compete within its markets.

- Strategy *process* defines the way in which the venture will make *decisions* about the strategy content to adopt.

- A well-defined strategy aids the venture by defining the means by which it will achieve its goals in the marketplace.

- A strategy acts as a guide for decision making and provides a common language for the venture's stakeholders.

- Entrepreneurs often express their venture's strategy in the form of *heuristics*.

Research themes

Entrepreneurs' entry strategies

Section 18.5 explored different patterns of entry for entrepreneurs. The entry strategy adopted can easily be accessed by examining the venture's sales literature (a catalogue or price list is ideal, and usually freely available). How does the entry strategy correlate with the initial size of the venture, say in terms of early sales? (Get the business's accounts. Most are available on the internet. Alternatively, a selection of businesses from reports in the *Investors Chronicle* will give financial information and stock market measures such as market capitalisation, which are also appropriate for businesses actively trading shares). Is it the case that businesses with a larger start-up do so on the back of an initial introduction of a range of products or by tackling a range of markets? Or do some businesses become large quite quickly on the basis of a single product–market introduction? Be prepared to set in place strict criteria as to the judgement of the scope of product range and market range. Think about the products and markets strategically. Are the products simply variations on a fundamental product? Are they different products but based on a common technology? Or are they quite diverse products based on different technologies? Are all markets served by the same marketing (sales) effort, or distribution route or do they need different resource bases for their promotion? The paper by Cooper *et al.* (1989) provides a useful methodological template for this type of study.

Entrepreneurs' heuristics

Heuristics are practical decision rules adopted to guide decisions. They are many and varied and, as recounted in Table 18.1, different entrepreneurs may adopt contradictory heuristics. Entrepreneurs may be encouraged to reveal their heuristics. Set up a series of decision situations that entrepreneurs may face. These decisions may relate to resource acquisition, internal management issues, competitive behaviour, business expansion and resource distribution (see above). Outline these using brief descriptions (200–300 words). Identify a pool of nascent and practising entrepreneurs (the more the better – aim for at least 20). Use an interview technique to ascertain what decision the entrepreneur would make in relation to each situation. Then inquire into how the entrepreneur would summarise their decision as a general rule. Code the responses to establish patterns in the heuristics. How consistent are they? Do different entrepreneurs adopt contradictory heuristics? How do the heuristics of nascent and experienced entrepreneurs differ?

Key readings

An accessible but seminal and still highly influential paper drawing a distinction between strategy content and strategy process is:

Mintzberg, H. and Waters, J.A. (1985) 'Of strategies deliberate and emergent', *Strategic Management Journal*, Vol. 6, pp. 257–72.

A slightly more demanding paper that is good not only for its conclusions but also for its insights into methodology is:

McDougall, P. and Robinson, R.B. (1990) 'New venture strategies: an empirical identification of eight "archetypes" of competitive strategies for entry', *Strategic Management Journal*, Vol. 11, pp. 447–67.

Suggestions for further reading

Atkins, M. and Lowe, J. (1994) 'Stakeholders and the strategy formation process in small and medium enterprises', *International Small Business Journal*, Vol. 12, No. 3, pp. 12–24.

Bowman, C. and Ambrosini, V. (1996) 'Tracking patterns of realised strategy', *Journal of General Management*, Vol. 21, No. 3, pp. 59–73.

Calori, R. (1985) 'Effective strategies in emerging industries', *Long Range Planning*, Vol. 18, No. 3, pp. 55–61.

Cooper, A.C., Woo, C.Y. and Dunkelberg, W.C. (1989) 'Entrepreneurship and the initial size of firms', *Journal of Business Venturing*, Vol. 4, No. 5, pp. 317–32.

Eden, C. and Ackermann, F. (1998) *Making Strategy: The Journey of Strategic Management*. London: Sage.

Gallen, T. (1997) 'The cognitive style and strategic decisions of managers', *Management Decision*, Vol. 35, No. 7, pp. 541–51.

Grieve Smith, J. and Fleck, V. (1987) 'Business strategies in small high-technology companies', *Long Range Planning*, Vol. 20, No. 2, pp. 61–8.

Idenburg, P.J. (1993) 'Four styles of strategy development', *Long Range Planning*, Vol. 26, No. 6, pp. 132–7.

Jenkins, M. (1997) 'Entrepreneurial intentions and outcomes: a comparative causal mapping study', *Journal of Management Studies*, Vol. 34, No. 6, pp. 895–920.

Manimala, M.J. (1999) *Entrepreneurial Policies and Strategies: The Innovator's Choice*. New Delhi: Sage.

Miller, D. (1992) 'The generic strategy trap', *Journal of Business Strategy*, Jan./Feb., pp. 37–41.

Mintzberg, H. (1973) 'Strategy making in three modes', *California Management Review*, Vol. XVI, No. 2, pp. 44–53.

Mintzberg, H. (1978) 'Patterns in strategy formation', *Management Science*, Vol. 24, No. 9, pp. 934–48.

Mintzberg, H. (1988) 'Generic strategies: towards a comprehensive framework', *Advances in Strategic Management*, Vol. 5, pp. 1–76.

Mintzberg, H. (1994) *The Rise and Fall of Strategic Planning*. London: Prentice Hall.

Mintzberg, H. and Waters, J.A. (1985) 'Of strategies deliberate and emergent', *Strategic Management Journal*, Vol. 6, pp. 257–72.

Mitchell, R.K. (1997) 'Oral history and expert scripts: demystifying the entrepreneurial experience', *International Journal of Entrepreneurial Behaviour and Research*, Vol. 3, No. 2, pp. 122–39.

Quinn, J.B. (1978) 'Strategic change: logical incrementalism', *Sloan Management Review*, Vol. 20, pp. 7–21.

Selected case material

CASE 18.1

28 July 2005

Dumpy bottles for baby prove a world beater

PETER MARSH

When the history of 20th century technology comes to be written, a footnote may be left for Edward Atkin, inventor of the first babies' bottles that are squat rather than long and thin.

Not only are Mr Atkin's bottles easier for babies to hold, the teats in them are shaped using computer technology to replicate faithfully the contours of a woman's breast, providing further satisfaction for the infant.

Last month, Mr Atkin's diligence in pursuing these ideas earned him and his family about £225m after he sold Cannon Avent, the company he headed for 33 years, to Charterhouse Capital Partners. The pay-out was one of the biggest individual gains from such a buyout in the UK in recent years.

Cannon Avent has become one of the biggest in the world in the field of babies' feeding products, including not just bottles but sterilising equipment and breast pumps. The pumps are used to express milk from women's breasts for use at some later time, ensuring the child can drink natural rather than artificial milk even when the mother is not present.

Total sales of feeding products worldwide are put at about £600m a year, with the share of Mr Atkin's former company about a sixth, with 80 per cent of its sales coming from outside the UK.

Beth Christie, new managing director of the company, which after the acquisition has been renamed Avent, says she is keen to double its sales in the next five years through geographical expansion as well as development of new products.

'I intend to continue the strategy that Edward has put in place,' she says. 'The man is a genius who was amazingly adept at identifying opportunities before anyone else could see them and has left an immense legacy at the company.'

For the past 15 years, Ms Christie has run the US side of Avent's business, which accounts for about 40 per cent of its revenues.

Total sales last year of Avent came to £109m, of which roughly 85 per cent were accounted for by baby products and the rest from automotive parts.

Avent, which does all its manufacturing in the UK, mainly at a high-technology plant in Suffolk, exports 80 per cent of its products on the feeding side of the business, total sales of which have risen nearly twenty-fold since 1989. It sells in 60 countries and last year made a pre-tax profit of £18.5m, representing a high ratio for a UK manufacturer.

Michael Samuel, managing director of Mayborn, a UK-based rival in babies' products that uses the Tommee Tippee brand, has followed Mr Atkin's career for the past 20 years. He says: 'Edward's a very capable guy who has had an engineer's approach to the business but also paid a lot of attention to design. It was his idea to come up with fat bottles – everyone else followed in his wake.'

Mr Atkin – who inherited the business in 1972 from his father – is no longer involved at Avent. He will occupy himself in the future stewarding of the small automotive company that was previously part of Avent, of which he is keeping ownership. Mr Atkin is also looking

CASE 18.1 CONT.

at investing some of his new fortune in other commercial fields.

Malcolm Offord is the Charterhouse partner who agreed the deal to take over Avent.

Apart from Mr Atkin, its other shareholder was 3i, an investment group for which Mr Offord worked 10 years ago. Back then, 3i took a stake of £5m – a sum that it multiplied 13 times through last month's deal.

Mr Atkin kept in close touch with Mr Offord over the years. When the Avent boss decided to sell, he eschewed the normal auction route and offered the company to the Charterhouse partner on a 'take it or leave it' basis with a price already in mind.

Mr Atkin says he agreed the transaction 'in three minutes'.

'We paid a high price for the business but then it is a very good company,' Mr Offord says. 'We are going to change it as little as possible. Mr Atkin is a dying breed of business entrepreneur [in Britain] and the country would be a lot better if we had more like him.'

Avent wants to expand in a number of fields including new types of breast pumps that are easier for women to use and include novel electronic systems to express a given amount of milk in as short a time as possible.

It may also enter areas such as skincare lotions for mothers and babies and equipment to hold nappies and other baby-related items. It also wants to expand in emerging economies such as Brazil and China, where the business of baby products is fairly undeveloped.

In an interview with the FT before the deal took place, Mr Atkin said one of the secrets of his company's growth had been its 50-strong head office in London, which accommodates people from 22 countries, capable of speaking many languages and able to sell products around the world.

Also, he said, babies were essentially the same the world over – which means they lend themselves to a global approach. 'If a product works for a baby in Latvia, it will work for one in Malaysia.'

Source: Peter Marsh, 'Dumpy bottles for baby prove a world beater', *Financial Times*, 28 July 2005, p. 24. Copyright © 2005 The Financial Times Limited.

CASE 18.2

19 July 2005

A business groomed for success

TIM BURT

Ronald Lauder wants to make something clear. Central European Media Enterprises is not for sale.

The son and heir of Estée Lauder, founder of the world's largest privately owned cosmetics company, does not want to cede control of a television business that broadcasts to more than 90m people in eastern Europe.

Several international media groups have cast envious eyes at Central European Media

Enterprises (CME), where Mr Lauder and his family owns 20 per cent of the equity and 71 per cent of the voting power.

News Corp, led by Rupert Murdoch, last year considered a transaction that would have left the US media giant holding a substantial stake in Mr Lauder's company. But the two sides failed to agree terms, according to people familiar with the putative deal.

Mr Lauder, who is also chairman of Estée Lauder International and Clinique Laboratories, now scorns the idea of a tie-up. In comments that might irritate potential suitors, he says: 'The only reason to buy CME is because their own market is not growing. Why would shareholders want to be boarded by a company trying to get out of the mud?'

The CME chairman is a member of that an exclusive club of truly wealthy US entrepreneurs that who have used the family fortune to build a new business, hoping to prove their own industry flair. Others include Edgar Bronfman Jnr, who is now running Warner Music after losing part of his family wealth after following a painful tie-up with Vivendi Universal of France, or and Bennett Dorrance, heir to the Campbell Soup fortune, who now runs one of the largest property real estate developers in the western US.

Mr Lauder's company, which is controlled through a Bermuda-based parent group and holding companies in the Dutch and Netherlands Antilles, has attracted attention because its business defies the sluggish growth and volatile advertising of network television in the US and western Europe.

The business – albeit small in global media terms – boasts underlying profit margins of 30 per cent on sales that rose by 46 per cent last year to $182m. It has emerged as the largest commercial broadcaster in the Czech Republic and has nine television channels in five other central and east European countries.

In a rare interview, given at his London offices, Mr Lauder, 61, admits the 10-year development of CME has cost him up to $100m of his personal fortune. The entrepreneur – one of those larger-than-life investors that populate the media industry – fully expects a payback. But the former US ambassador to Austria, treasurer of the World Jewish Congress and one-time US deputy assistant secretary of defence is prepared to wait. For CME has been a long time in gestation.

'It's something very personal,' he says. 'As a teenager, when most people were going to vacation in the Hamptons or wherever, I was in eastern Europe. My grandparents came from Budapest and Slovakia, and I was in Hungary when the Berlin Wall came down. I realised that it was a once-in-a-lifetime opportunity to change things.'

Mr Lauder, a relative outsider in the media industry, set about acquiring control of or signing partnerships with commercial TV companies in former Soviet satellite states. Several other media groups followed suit. SBS, News Corp and RTL, the television arm of Germany's Bertelsmann group, have all expanded into the region.

Earlier This month, RTL moved into Russia by agreeing to acquire a 30 per cent stake in REN TV, the television and production company. Gerhard Zeiler, RTL chief executive, said the deal underlined its determination to expand in eastern Europe, describing Russia as one of the world's fastest growing advertising markets.

Another industry executive adds: 'We're all dancing around Serbia, where there could be a TV privatisation, and Ukraine has several networks that could be up for grabs.'

The industrial logic is clear. Average spending on television advertising in western Europe is flat, at best. In the past three years, spending has increased by more than 60 per cent in the six markets where CME operates. Economic growth in those countries is higher than in both the US and the European Union. Terrestrial television networks in eastern Europe face less competition from pay-TV rivals and, there are fewer acquisition opportunities for other media groups; and, unlike more developed markets, audiences and advertising are not yet migrating to online media.

CME is planning to launch three new channels in the Czech Republic after buying TV Nova, the country's dominant station, for almost $900m earlier this year.

'If you're going to be in Europe, the east is a very attractive place to be,' according to one executive. 'It is like the western market in the 1970s with only a handful of commercial TV groups carving up a big advertising market.'

Mr Lauder, however, appears to regard CME as much more than a business. Most industry leaders avoid political controversy or grand geo-political statements like the plague. But but not the scion of the Estée Lauder empire.

Mr Lauder, a former Republican contender for mayor of New York, says: 'CME stations all talk about democracy. We give a positive view of America and appeal to the new capitalist-oriented generation now growing in eastern Europe.'

CME, nevertheless, has suffered the body blows associated with the rapid emergence of free market economies in former Soviet-controlled states, often led by local oligarchs. Its strategy was threatened when Vladimir Zelezny, a Czech entrepreneur and CME's one-time partner, seized control of TV Nova in the Czech Republic and cut CME out of the partnership.

'He wanted all the profits and made the decision to try to get everything, encouraged by the government,' says Mr Lauder, who subsequently launched a multi-million-dollar lawsuit to regain control of the business.

Almost three years ago, CME was awarded $358.6m in compensation after an international tribunal upheld a ruling that the Czech government had failed to protect the company against Mr Zelezny's illegal seizure.

The settlement encouraged CME to continue its eastward expansion. But the partnership strategy is risky, as CMR it admitted in a share prospectus linked to TV Nova. In it, the company said admitted it did not have management control of its affiliates in the Slovak Republic or Ukraine and could not 'affirmatively direct the operations'. The prospectus also revealed errors in the group's calculation of earnings per share over the past three years, indicating a 'material weakness' in financial controls.

Controls have been tightened and accounting procedures reviewed following the arrival last year of Michael Garin as chief executive, replacing Fred Klinkhammer, the TV executive who pioneered CME's acquisition strategy. Mr Garin, a founder of Lorimar Telepictures, the company behind the hit television show Dallas, and Knot's Landing, has devolved management control to the stations (Mr Lauder says the former chief executive 'was not one of the great delegators') and invested in local production.

About 40 per cent of the schedule on CME channels is now devoted to locally produced content. That figure will rise following this year's acquisition of TV Nova – re-purchased this year from PPF, the Czech investment company which acquired control following the Zelezny controversy.

Mr Lauder, who handles the delicate negotiations with government leaders in the regions, says the company is now looking at more channels following the TV Nova purchase. He hints that Poland and Russia could be future growth areas, and says argues that CME is well placed to capture those opportunities.

'You can't run a business of this kind sitting in New York or Germany,' he says. 'To global players, eastern Europe is just a dot on the map. But we only play in this region and we get the rewards.'

Source: Tim Burt, 'A business groomed for success',
Financial Times, 19 July 2005, p. 13.
Copyright © 2005 The Financial Times Limited.

 Discussion points

1. What aspects of Avent's strategy engendered its success?

2. What advice would you offer Ronald Lauder in terms of achieving a growth strategy?

CHAPTER 19

The business plan: an entrepreneurial tool

Chapter overview

A business plan is an essential tool for the entrepreneur. This chapter explores the role of the business plan and the kind of information it should include. It considers the way a business plan can help the venture by guiding analysis, creating a synthesis of new insights, communicating the potential of the venture to interested parties, and promoting management action. It also describes the Pyramid Principle: a method of structuring the business plan to produce an effective and influential communication tool. The chapter concludes by looking at the ways in which business planning can increase the flexibility and responsiveness of the venture.

19.1 Planning and performance

Key learning outcome

A recognition of the influence of formal planning activity on the performance of the entrepreneurial venture.

Entrepreneurs, like many other managers, are often called upon to prepare formal, written plans. They may do this of their own accord or it may be at the instigation of external investors such as venture capitalists or banks. The picture of entrepreneurs 'locked away' writing formal business plans sits ill at ease with the image of them as dynamic individuals actively pursuing their business interests. Many entrepreneurs object to preparing plans because they feel their time would be better spent pushing the venture forward. They claim that they already know what is in the plan and that no one else will read it.

This objection highlights an important point in that developing a plan demands time, energy and (often) hard cash. It ties up both the entrepreneur and the business's staff. A business plan represents an *investment* in the venture. It must be justified as an investment, that is, in terms of the return it offers the business. The relationship between formal planning and business performance has been the subject of numerous statistical studies; however, no clear picture has emerged. The correlation between *formal* planning and performance is generally weak so it is not possible to say with certainty that formal planning will improve the performance of a particular business. As a result, there has been something of a reaction against formal planning in recent years, especially in relation to smaller businesses. As noted in the previous chapter, Mintzberg (1994) has offered a profound criticism of at least a narrow approach to planning. However, a recent study by Perry (2001) indicated a negative correlation between planning and failure rates for small businesses in the USA. Formal planning was not found to be a common activity, but businesses that had planned were less likely to fail than those that had not. Schneider (1998) provides a general defence of planning for the smaller business.

However, the poor statistical correlation should not be taken to mean that performance is unaffected by planning. Statistical studies usually compare 'planning activity' (the definition of this varies between studies) against performance measured in financial or growth terms. Inevitably, these studies must reduce a complex organisational phenomenon to simple variables. Planning is not an easily defined, isolated activity. Rather, it is an activity embedded in both the wider strategy process of the organisation and the control strategy of the entrepreneur. Financial performance is important but it is not the only measure of achievement which motivates the entrepreneur. The entrepreneur may compromise financial gains in order to achieve less tangible benefits. They may even *plan* to make this compromise. Intuitively it seems the case that a good plan will lead to an improved performance and, equally, that a bad one will lead the business astray. There is also the problem of distinguishing between the existence of a plan and whether that plan is actually *implemented*.

Statistical studies of planning and performance also face the issue of causation; that is, when two things seem to correlate, how can we be sure which is the cause and which the effect? It may be that the variation in performance observed is not so much due to the mere existence of planning as to the *quality* of the planning. It has even been suggested that planning does not lead to performance, but rather that a good performance allows managers the time and money to indulge in planning.

The planning/performance debate reflects the problems to be encountered in teasing out cause-and-effect relationships in a system as complex and subject to as many variables as an entrepreneurial venture. In short, then, it is impossible to give a straight yes or no answer to questions like: 'Should entrepreneurs produce a formal plan?' or 'Should entrepreneurs formalise the way their organisation plans?' Overgeneralisation is unwise. The decision to engage in formal planning, like most other decisions the entrepreneur faces, must be made in the light of what is best for the individual venture, the way it operates and the specific opportunities it faces. Planning, if it is approached in a way which is right for the venture and is aimed at addressing the right issues, would seem to offer a number of benefits. The remainder of this chapter examines the decision to create a formal plan, explores the ways in which it might benefit the business and suggests ways in which the plan might be structured.

19.2 The role of the business plan

Key learning outcome

An understanding of how the business plan works as a management tool.

The activity of creating a formal business plan consumes both time and resources. If it is to be undertaken, and undertaken well, there must be an appreciation of the way in which the business plan can actually be made to work as a tool for the business. In principle, there are four mechanisms by which a business plan might aid the performance of the venture.

As a tool for analysis

A business plan contains information. Some of this information will be that used as the basis for articulating and refining the entrepreneur's vision, for generating the mission statement and for developing a strategy content and strategy process for the venture. The structure of the business plan provides the entrepreneur with an effective checklist of the information they must gather in order to be sure the direction for their venture is both achievable and rewarding (see Schneider, 1998, for a development of this point). Creating the plan guides and disciplines the entrepreneur in gathering this information. Hills (1985) emphasises that the level of background market research in entrepreneurs' plans is usually quite low, but investment in market research can have a high payoff, not least in making demand planning more effective. Wyckham and Wedley (1990) demonstrate the value of the plan in distinguishing feasible from unfeasible ventures.

As a tool for synthesis

Once data have been gathered and analysed in a formal way then the information generated must be used to provide a direction for the venture. The information must be integrated with, and used to refine, the entrepreneur's vision and used to support the development of a suitable mission and strategy. The planning exercise acts to *synthesise* the entrepreneur's vision with a definite plan of action in a unified way. This synthesis converts the vision into a strategy for the venture, and then into the actions appropriate to pursuing that strategy.

As a tool for communication

The business plan provides a vehicle for communicating the potential of the venture, the opportunities it faces and the way it intends to exploit them in a way which is concise, efficient and effective. This may be of value in communicating with both internal and external stakeholders. The plan may draw internal people together and give them a focus for their activities. The business plan is particularly important as a tool for communicating with potential investors, gaining their interest and attracting them to the venture.

As a call to action

The business plan is a call to action. It provides a detailed list of the activities that must be undertaken, the tasks that must be performed and the outcomes that must be achieved if the entrepreneur is to convert their vision into a new world. The plan may also call upon formal project management techniques such as critical path analysis in order to organise, prioritise and arrange tasks in a way which makes the best use of scarce resources.

The four ways in which the planning exercise contributes to the success drive of the venture do not operate in isolation. They underpin and support each other and the performance of the venture (Figure 19.1). Together they define not only the plan that should be developed for the venture, but also the way the venture should engage in planning.

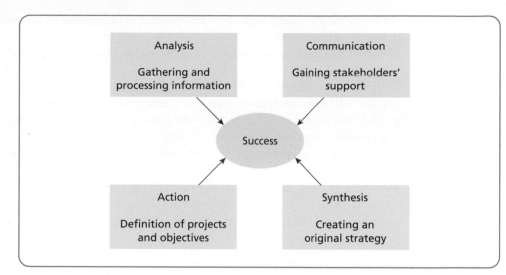

Figure 19.1 Planning: analysis, communication, synthesis and action

19.3 What a business plan should include

There are no hard and fast rules about what a business plan should include since a business plan must be shaped to reflect the needs and requirements of the venture it represents. The entrepreneur and the management team will have their own preferences. The information included will depend on what stage the venture is at: the plan for a new venture may be more exhaustive than the ongoing yearly plan for one which is quite well established. Importantly, the plan will reflect the information required by the audience to whom the plan is directed as well as the action the entrepreneur desires from them. Financial backers may dictate both the format the business plan must take and the information it should include.

The type and scope of information that might be included in a fairly exhaustive business plan are set out below.

Mission

- *The mission for the venture* – the formal mission statement that defines the business, what it is, what it is aiming to deliver, to whom, why it makes a difference and what it aspires to achieve.

Overview of key objectives

- *Financial objectives* – the turnover and profit targets for the period of the plan; the growth desired over the previous period.
- *Strategic objectives* – achievements in the market and gains to be made in market position.

The market environment

- *Background to the market* – i.e. how the market is defined; the size of the market; major market sectors and niches; overall growth rate; key trends and developments in consumer behaviour and buying habits; and technological developments in the product, service delivery and operations.

- *Competitors* – key competitors, their strengths and weaknesses; competitors' strategy and likely reaction to the venture's activity.
- *Competitive conditions* – the basis of competition in the market; the importance of price, product differentiation and branding; the benefits to be gained from positioning.
- *Competitive advantage of the venture* – the important strengths of the venture relative to competitors; sources of competitive advantage.
- *Definition of product offerings* – the products/services that the business will offer to the market.
- *Definition of target markets* – the way in which the market is split into different sectors; the dimensions of the market important for characterising the sectors; and the market sectors that will be priority targets for the business.

Strategy

- *Product strategy* – the way in which the product/service will be differentiated from competitors (e.g. features, quality, price); why this will be attractive to customers.
- *Pricing strategy* – how the product/service will be priced relative to competitors (e.g. offer of a premium, discounting); means of establishing price; promotional pricing and price cutting; pricing policy and margins to be offered to intermediaries.
- *Distribution strategy* – the route by which the product/service will be delivered to the customer; intermediaries (wholesalers, distributors, retailers) who will be partners in distribution; strategy for working with distributors; policy for exporting and international marketing if appropriate.
- *Promotional strategy* – approaches to informing the customer (and intermediaries) about the product/service; advertising message, means and media; sales activity and approach to selling; sales promotions (including price promotions); public relations activity.
- *Networking* – relationship between the organisation and other organisations in the network; use of the network to create and support competitive advantage.

Financial forecasts

- *Income* – revenues from trading activity; structure of the capital provided by investors.
- *Routine expenditure* – expenditure on salaries, raw materials and consumables; payment of interest on debt.
- *Capital expenditure* – major investment in new assets; how these assets will enhance performance.
- *Cash flow* – difference between revenues and expenditure by period; cash flow reflects the liquidity of the business and its ability to fund its activities. If income is more than expenditure then cash flow is positive. If expenditure is more than income then cash flow is negative.

Activity

- *Major projects* – the key projects that will drive the venture forward and deliver the objectives, e.g. new product developments, sales drives, launches with distributors and advertising campaigns.

People

- *Key players in the venture* – the individuals behind the venture; the skills and experience they will contribute to the business; evidence of their achievements; personal profiles and CVs.

The list above reflects a 'traditional' structure of a business plan that is related in many planning guides. However, a list is just an account of what should be included, not necessarily an instruction on the order in which it is presented. Section 19.6 considers a more effective way of structuring the plan. The information included in the business plan will depend on how it is intended to use the plan and to whom it will be communicated. The business need not be restricted to a single version of the plan, and it may prove advantageous to use different formats for different audiences. A detailed and exhaustive 'master' plan may act as a source for the rapid, and informed, production of such specific plans.

19.4 Business planning: analysis and synthesis

> ### Key learning outcome
>
> An appreciation of how business planning facilitates analysis of the venture's potential and a synthesis of its strategy.

Effective planning requires information. Information is all around us but it rarely comes for free. Information has a cost: this may be relatively low – a trip to the local library perhaps – or it may be very expensive – commissioning a major piece of market research, for example. Even if it has no direct cost, gathering and analysing information takes time. Hence information must be gathered with an eye to how it will be used. The benefits to be gained from having the information must justify its cost.

Information is used to manage uncertainty. Having information means that uncertainty is reduced, which in turn reduces the risk of the venture and improves the prospects of its success. Essentially, the entrepreneur is interested in answering the following questions:

- What are the customer's fundamental needs in relation to the product category? (What benefits does the product offer? What problems do customers solve with the product?)
- How does the market currently serve those needs? (What products are offered? What features do they have?)
- In what way(s) does the market fail to serve those needs? (Why are customers left dissatisfied? How often are they left dissatisfied?)
- How might customer needs be better served? (How might the product on offer be improved?)

Marketing, as a discipline, offers a number of techniques to develop these answers. In addition, the entrepreneur must ask:

- How does the better way being advocated add up as a real business opportunity?
- What risks are likely to be present in pursuing such an opportunity?

These final two points are critical. Developing an answer to these questions, and understanding the decisions they involve, will be explored fully through the development of the *strategic window* in Part 5 of this book.

Planning certainly supports strategy development but it is not *equivalent* to it. Mintzberg (1994) observes that planning is about *analysis*; it is about breaking down information to spot opportunities and possibilities. Strategy, on the other hand, is about *synthesis*; it is about bringing the capabilities of the business to bear on the opportunity in a way which is creative and original. Developing answers to the questions listed above is the analysis part of the equation. Reconciling them into a workable, rewarding strategy is the synthesis part. This synthesis must include both the strategy *content* and the *process* to deliver it.

In order to synthesise an original strategy the entrepreneur must address the following questions:

- How will the venture address the needs of the customer? (What is the nature of the opportunity that has been identified?)
- Why will the venture's offerings serve those needs better than those of competitors? (What is the *innovation*? Why is it valuable?)
- How will demand be stimulated? (This involves issues of communication, promotion and distribution.)
- Why can the entrepreneur's business deliver this in a way that competitors cannot? (What will be the *competitive advantage* that the business enjoys? What will it be able to do that its competitors cannot do that is valuable for its customers?)
- What is it about the business that enables them to do this? (What are the *competences* and *capabilities* of the business?)
- Why will competitors be unable to imitate them? (In what way(s) is the competitive advantage *sustainable*?)

Planning helps the business by first demanding an analysis of information about the market, customers and competitors. This information provides a sure basis for decision making. Planning goes on to help the business by synthesis, that is, by integrating the information into a strategy. This strategy gives the venture a shape and a direction. It forms the basis for plans and projects which offer definite actions for the people who make up the venture and those who support it to follow. Thus information is valuable because it links the analysis of opportunity with the synthesis of strategy in a planning framework (Figure 19.2).

19.5 Business planning: action and communication

Key learning outcome

An appreciation of how the business plan may be used as a communication tool and as a call to action.

Communication is not just about passing on information. It is an attempt to elicit a particular *response* from someone. In business, it is not only what we want people to *know* that matters; it is also what we want them to *do*. The ways the business plan functions both as a piece of communication and as a recipe for action are closely interrelated.

The business plan is a communication that relates in a succinct way a precise and unambiguous account of the venture *and* what it aims to achieve. It defines the decisions the entrepreneur has made in relation to the opportunity that has been identified; the way the opportunity will be exploited; the value the entrepreneur aims to create as a result of exploiting it; the resources that will be needed in order to progress the venture; the risks those resources will be exposed to; and the projects the entrepreneur will undertake with the resources they receive.

These decisions are communicated with the intention of gaining support for the venture. The entrepreneur will be particularly interested in communicating with and influencing the following groups of people.

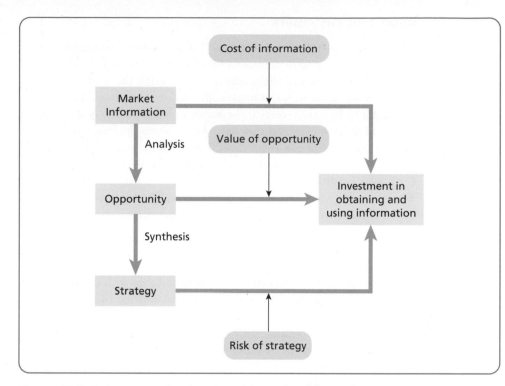

Figure 19.2 Factors governing investment in market information

Investors

The business plan relates not only the potential of the venture and the rewards it offers to investors but also the risks that it entails. It is also an opportunity for the entrepreneur to convince the investor of the skills the entrepreneur has, and to make the investor feel confident that the goods can be delivered. Numerous studies have found that the quality of the business plan and the effectiveness of its communication are critical factors in gaining investors' interest and support. See, for example, the studies by Macmillan *et al*. (1985, 1987), Knight (1994) and Mason and Harrison (1996). This is an issue we shall revisit in Chapter 20.

Employees

Employees make their own investment in the business by committing themselves to it. The business plan can give them confidence in the future of the venture. It will also specify the key projects that need to be undertaken, so defining individual objectives and the way in which the role the individual plays fits with the goals of the organisation as a whole. Jan Carlzon, the entrepreneur who turned around the failing Scandinavian Airline Systems (SAS) in the early 1980s, issued each of the organisation's 20,000 employees with a plan which outlined the vision and strategy he had devised. This plan became known as the 'little red book'.

Employee commitment does not come simply from letting people in on the plan. Letting them get involved in *creating* it in the first place is also a sure way to gain their support.

Important customers

A customer may face a cost in taking on a new supplier. Moving between suppliers demands the time and attention of managers. In some cases there may need to be a direct investment in new equipment so that the products can be used. If the product is new, the customer may have to learn to use it, for example staff may need additional training. The customer may be willing to face these costs if the benefits offered by the new product are high enough. They will resist, however, if they have doubts about the long-term viability of the supplier. Sharing the business plan with them is an effective way of giving them confidence in the entrepreneurial venture and encouraging them to make the necessary commitment. Customers are usually flattered to be asked to become involved with the venture in this way. Therefore, for a new venture, communicating the business plan as well as the product offering can be an important part of the selling strategy.

Major suppliers

Suppliers may also need to make an investment if they wish to supply the venture. This may take the form of dedicated selling and support activity and may even involve developing bespoke products. Although the venture offers the prospect of new business, suppliers will, like the venture's customers, resist making the investment if they harbour doubts about the long-term viability of the venture. Again, the business plan may be used to give them the confidence to make an investment of time and resources on behalf of the venture.

In short, the business plan is a communication tool which can be used by the venture to help build the network of relationships which will be critical to its long-term success.

19.6 Structuring and articulating the business plan: the Pyramid Principle

> ### Key learning outcome
>
> An appreciation of Barbara Minto's Pyramid Principle technique for structuring and articulating in business communication, and how it can be applied to create an influential business plan.

A business plan is not just a repository for facts and statements. It is a business *communication*. And like any form of human communication its impact and influence are determined by *how* things are said as well as *what* is said. The organisation of ideas is as important as the ideas themselves. The structuring of the business plan considered in the section 19.3 places emphasis on the information that must be communicated rather than on the case that the business plan is attempting to make. The impact of the business plan on key decision makers (particularly, but not exclusively, potential investors) will depend on the way in which information is *delivered* as well as the information itself. Effective business communications work with, rather than against, the cognitive processes that human decision makers adopt. The ideas to be explored in this section are based on the work of Barbara Minto (1996), a management consultant who has studied business communication styles and their effectiveness in depth. These ideas are not restricted just to business plans but are effective with any business communication (written or verbal).

(I am not ashamed to admit I use them for structuring academic papers.) Barbara Minto's book *The Pyramid Principle* is highly recommended to those who wish to explore these ideas in more depth.

Minto's central idea is based on discoveries in cognitive psychology about the way in which humans store and manage information and then use it to support decision making. It is clear that we human beings are actually quite inefficient information processors. When presented with a lot of information, we inevitably simplify it. We are, at best, able to store between five and nine pieces of information at any one time. From any one communication we only take away one or two key ideas. Further, we do not store information in our brains in a linear way, one idea after another. Rather, we build hierarchies of information in which facts are connected in a network of linkages. Minto suggests that we can use all of these facts to construct communications that will be more effective and influential.

First, she suggests, we should consider the *one* key message the recipient will take away, what she refers to as the 'key point'. Given that the recipient is likely to take away only one 'big idea', we should aim to control what that is, rather than let the recipient do it for themself. Second, we should order information in a way that builds a hierarchy (a pyramid) of understanding under our control rather than deliver the information linearly and assume that the recipient will order it in the way we would wish. In other words, we should take active control of the process of 'translating' both from the idea network to its written (linear) form and back again.

Minto's ideas provide useful insights into the preparation of effective business plans. First, the key point or 'big idea'. It is important to recognise what we want the recipients of the plan to *do*, rather than what we would wish them to *know*. Communication transfers information, but this is the means to the end of eliciting action, not an objective in itself. What we wish a recipient of a business plan to do depends on who the recipient is. If an investor, then we hope they will provide the investment requested. If a potential employee, then the key point will be 'work for me'; a customer: 'buy from me', and so on. We must then put in place supporting ideas (ideally five to eight) that lay out a case for that big idea. Moving down the pyramid, we should then develop *arguments* that justify the supporting ideas. Finally, at the bottom of the pyramid, we must provide evidence that backs up the arguments.

Table 19.1 illustrates such a structure for a business plan aimed at investors. Six supporting ideas are entered, reflecting the series of questions an investor would wish to see answered. These are the supporting questions I often use, but I would not claim this version is definitive. Other supporting questions may also be appropriate and arguments may be articulated differently.

With this pyramid structure in place, the next step is to construct the business plan around it. The pyramid must be converted into a linear flow of narrative while retaining a feel for the underlying pyramid structure. Minto suggests that using headings and sub-headings to indicate different levels of the pyramid is a good way of doing this, and this approach works for a business plan. The headings should be short and to the point and be used to highlight the pyramid structure. They should not be thought of as informative in their own right. The plan has the overall structure shown in Figure 19.3.

An illustration of the process in action is as follows. The first step is to construct an introduction. The introduction serves two purposes. First, it is an invitation to the recipient to read the plan and to engage them. (Don't forget, the majority of business plans sent to

Table 19.1 Pyramid structure of business plan

Key point
Invest in this venture!

Supporting questions

1. Is there a gap in the market for this product/ service?	2. Does this market have potential?	3. Why will this innovation fill that gap?	4. Can this innovation be delivered profitably and at acceptable risk?	5. Does the venture have a long-term future?	6. Are the proposers the right people to deliver it?
Arguments					
Individuals have these needs in relation to this product category	Assumptions about market definition	This innovation meets customer needs better than anything currently on offer. It offers unique and attractive benefits	Pricing is sufficient to cover unit production costs	Venture has a sustainable competitive advantage	Managerial experience, capabilities and motivation
Current offerings fail to meet these needs satisfactorily	Demand in this sector is high and is likely to grow	This innovation is new and original	Long-term profits will sustain necessary investment	It is delivering something of value; it is doing so in a unique way; competitors can be fended off	
Recent developments in the product category still leave these needs unmet	Market conditions offer potential to new entrants	Technological and organisational capabilities are in place to effect delivery to market	Distribution route is available	Advantage will be gained in terms of costs, strategic assets, innovation capabilities, reputation and/or organisational architecture	
			Promotional plans have been thought through and costed	Options for future expansion have been considered	
			Risk has been assessed and its management considered		
Evidence					
Primary and secondary customer research	Rationale for market definition	Primary and secondary customer research	Costing data and financial projections	Strategic analysis of venture and competitors	Managers' CVs
Competitor analysis	Market research: market size, growth rate and structure	Product testing and trials	Assumptions about output volumes, prices, costs and demand conditions	Explanation as to why competitive advantage will be gained and sustained	Evidence of relevant experience, qualifications, sector knowledge and previous successes
Product evaluation	Existing supply structure	Evidence of technical and organisational capabilities	Competitor costs and investment benchmarks		Evidence supporting leadership abilities
	PEST analysis		Evaluation of promotional plans and distribution routes		
			Scenario analysis		

Main heading: Introduction

Main heading: Supporting question 1
Sub-heading: *Argument 1 – Evidence 1*
Sub-heading: *Argument 2 – Evidence 2*
Sub-heading: *Argument 3 – Evidence 3*
etc.

Main heading: Supporting question 2
Sub-heading: *Argument 1 – Evidence 1*
Sub-heading: *Argument 2 – Evidence 2*
Sub-heading: *Argument 3 – Evidence 3*
etc.

Main heading: Supporting question 3
Sub-heading: *Argument 1 – Evidence 1*
Sub-heading: *Argument 2 – Evidence 2*
Sub-heading: *Argument 3 – Evidence 3*
etc.

Main heading: Summary

Figure 19.3 Organising the pyramid structure

venture capitalists are dismissed without being fully read. If attention is not captured in the first few paragraphs, it never will be.) Second, it may be used to lay out the structure of the case to be made for the venture. As a first move, the introduction should put in place the big idea. A good opening would be:

Introduction

This plan proposes a new business venture that offers a major and attractive investment opportunity.

The next step is to relate the supporting arguments in a succinct manner. (Do not be tempted to overexpand on the ideas at this stage; this will come later.)

It will outline an innovative product (service) that offers unique benefits to customers in a way superior to existing competitors in a market with significant potential. The experienced management team leading the venture is confident that the venture has long-term potential, will be financially sound, and will gain and sustain an advantage over existing competitors.

385

At this stage, it is important that the recipient is guided in developing a mental image of the business concerned. Too often with business plans the reader is left to fit together pieces of information about the business from different parts of the plan. This takes effort that the reader may not be willing to invest. They may simply reject the plan. Even if they do put in that effort, the picture built is not under the proposer's control. A good way to take control is to relate the venture's mission. Articulating the mission was considered in Chapter 17.

The venture's mission

Following this, the venture's key objectives (financial, market, growth) can be related.

Key objectives

With the introduction in place, the plan can then expand, argue for and give evidence to support the claims made. Each supporting idea is dealt with in turn. For example, the first supporting question is, 'Is there a gap in the market for this product?'. Again, following the Pyramid Principle, the opportunity should be taken to map out the structure of the arguments to follow.

The market gap

There is a significant gap in the market for the new product (service). Customer expectations are high and existing products are not meeting requirements. Recent developments in the product category have not significantly delivered on these expectations.

Now sub-headings can be used to detail each argument in turn and provide evidence for it.

Customer needs and expectations

Customers have high expectations about what this product category should offer. In particular, they feel that it should . . .

Now is the opportunity to support these claims with evidence, for example:

This is confirmed by independent market research using focus groups . . .

And then on to the second argument under this supporting question:

Customers' attitudes to products already available

Purchases in this product category are significant [introduce evidence on market size here]. The market is buoyant [introduce evidence on market growth rate here]. While customers do express some satisfaction with current offerings, they have a number of criticisms that add up to a clear opportunity for a new product. Research with focus groups and a telephone survey of a large sample of buyers indicate that the key failings are . . .

And then on to the third argument

Recent developments in the product category

Development of new products in this category is relatively active. X and Y have both launched new products. While these have been relatively successful, they do not address the fundamental failings of the category as seen by customers. Our research indicates . . . [evidence]

Once the first supporting question has been addressed, then the second can be explored in the same way. Then the third.

Another example: the venture's long-term potential (supporting question 5 in Table 19.1):

Long-term profitability and growth

We believe the business will have long-term potential and will be able to hold its position against follower competitors.

Now lay out the arguments:

As has been illustrated, the venture is offering a product with unique benefits to a large number of buyers. These benefits are unique and are not matched by any existing product [may re-summarise evidence here]. This valuable uniqueness is protectable.

Detail the argument on the last point, depending on particular sources of competitive advantage:

This will be achieved by:

- *access to unique and valuable resources;*
- *a lower cost structure;*
- *faster and more effective innovation;*
- *a better reputation than competitors; and/or*
- *performance enhanced through organisational and network architecture.*

(Refer to Chapter 25 for a full discussion of these sources of competitive advantage.)

Once this process is complete, a summary can be used to close the plan and encapsulate its ideas in the mind of the recipient. Aim to repeat the key point and the supporting questions once again:

Summary

This plan has highlighted a major investment opportunity. It demonstrates . . . [lay out supporting questions again].

The objective of the summary is to provide a final reinforcement of the key point, 'Invest in me!', not to summarise everything in the plan. Don't be tempted to go through the arguments and evidence again.

This approach gives a business plan a quite different structure to the 'list structure' discussed in section 19.3. For a start, there is no one section that relates all the market research. Market research is introduced when and where it is needed to back up a claim. So the reader's attention is being drawn to facts that matter, when they matter, rather than as a mass of data, which the reader will not be able to absorb or directly relate to the case for investment being made. Considerations on strategy are integrated with discussion of market opportunity, not separated.

Here are a few points by way of a summary. First, at each stage in the pyramid, summarise the structure below that will follow. Second, it will be recognised that given the number of supporting ideas, arguments and evidence, not much needs to be said at each stage. Do not be tempted to overexpand on points made. If a section is longer than a couple of paragraphs, it is probably better to go back to the pyramid and split the ideas. Third, do not worry too much about repetition. My experience with entrepreneurs introduced to the Pyramid Principle is that they feel they are being repetitious and saying the same thing over and over again. This reflects the fact we value originality. However, the value of a business plan is its effectiveness in engendering support, not its literary qualities. In any case, readers do not find the pyramid structure repetitious, just highly informative and impactful.

19.7 Strategy, planning and flexibility

> ### Key learning outcome
>
> An understanding of how planning may be used to make the business responsive, rather than rigid, in the face of opportunity and uncertainty.

Many entrepreneurs are suspicious of formal planning. They may see the written plan as restrictive, and feel that it reduces their room for manoeuvre. They may be concerned that by defining future actions they limit their options. However, these suspicions are ill founded. If approached in the right way, planning increases, rather than restricts, flexibility. The right sort of strategy can make the business more, not less, responsive.

Focus on ends rather than means

Goals should be given priority over plans. It is what the business aims to achieve that matters. It may be that there is more than one way in which the business can reach its objectives. If so, all the possibilities should be explored. Not all are likely to be equally attractive and one route may be given priority. However, a knowledge of the alternatives allows for contingency plans to be made and an alternative course can be followed if some routes become blocked.

Challenge assumptions

What are the assumptions on which the plan is based? For example, what assumptions have been made in measuring the size of markets and the venture's rate of growth, in determining how attractive the innovation is to customers and in gauging the strengths of competitors? How sensitive is the plan to these assumptions? What will happen if they are wrong? How can the plan be 'immunised' against poor assumptions by building in contingencies for when they are wrong?

Model scenarios

What are the likely outcomes if the plan is implemented? How certain are these outcomes? In the face of uncertainty, what is likely to be the *best* of all possible worlds and what is likely to be the *worst*? What is the *most likely* outcome? Determine what scenarios will result if an *optimistic*, a *pessimistic* and a *realistic* attitude is taken to the outcomes that are expected (particularly in relation to income and expenditure). How will the business fare in the face of each eventuality? How exposed is the business if the pessimistic scenario comes about? Has it (or can it get) the resources to manage the optimistic? Furthermore, have investors been made party to all scenarios, not just the best?

Create strategic flexibility

At the end of the day, a strategy is just a way of doing things. Strategic flexibility is a way of doing things well when faced with uncertainty. It involves actively responding to outcomes and adjusting activity, not just blindly following set plans. Strategic flexibility comes from questioning moves. For example, can the product or service be modified in the light of consumer responses to it (*positive* as well as negative)? If one target market is proving hard to break into, can an alternative one be approached? Can costs be managed in response to demand (for example, how exposed is the business to fixed costs)? If some relationships in the network prove to be less valuable than expected, can new relationships be built quickly?

Leave space to learn

The way in which entrepreneurs and their businesses meet opportunities and respond to challenges is dependent on how they see the world, the knowledge that they have and their range of skills. All these factors must evolve through learning. The entrepreneur must constantly question the business. Are the underlying assumptions still valid? Is this still the best way to do things? Success does not speak for itself and it is important to question why a particular outcome is a success. What was done right? In what way might the business have been even *more* successful? What were the failings? How might they be avoided next time?

Learning is an active process. The good business plan identifies and highlights those areas where learning can take place. In short, a good strategy should be about flexibility, about enabling the business to take advantage of opportunities as they take shape, and to manage the unexpected. It is not about setting a rigid course of action.

Summary of key ideas

- There is no simple correlation between investment in planning and business performance, although there is evidence that planning may be important in small business survival.

- A business plan can help the entrepreneurial venture by:
  - ensuring that a full analysis of the situation and the environment has been undertaken;
  - encouraging the synthesis of insights to generate a vision and a strategy;
  - acting as a call to action;
  - being a medium for communication with both internal and external stakeholders.

- Barbara Minto's Pyramid Principle can be adopted to produce impactful and influential business plans.

- A well-defined business plan will increase the venture's flexibility, not impair it.

- The level of formality in planning will be influenced by the level of investment in the start-up, the involvement of external stakeholders (especially, but not exclusively, investors), the availability and cost of information, external support, and the entrepreneur's personal style.

Research themes

Impact of pyramid structuring

Using the framework in Table 19.1, obtain information for four business plans (aim for 2,000–3,000 word descriptions, a typical length for a business plan). These may be imaginary, based on case studies, or based on real business plans you have access to. For each of the four data sets, construct two different versions of the plan. For the first, deliver information in a pyramid format with the 'big idea' up front and then a supporting idea, its argument and then its evidence, then on to the next supporting idea followed by its argument and evidence, and so on until all supporting ideas have been covered. For the second version, deliver the information linearly, starting with the 'big idea', then all the supporting ideas, then all the arguments, then all the evidence. Take a sample of decision makers (fellow students would be ideal). Split them into two equal groups and offer each group the four plans, two pyramidally structured and two linearly structured. Switch the ordering between the two groups. Have each subject rate the four business plans in terms of their attractiveness as investment opportunities. This could be by ranking, or on a Likert scale (e.g. would definitely invest, may invest, probably would not invest, would definitely not invest, etc.). Compare the ratings across the two different structures. Does pyramid structuring make the plan more attractive?

Information acquisition from business plans

This is a variation on the theme of the project above and might be included with it. Using the described method, create four business plans with linear and pyramid structures. Set up a comprehension test for subjects who have read the plans. This might include questions about the venture's products, its target markets, how it will gain competitive advantage, the capabilities of the management team, and so forth. Centre these on the supporting questions and arguments within them. I suggest about 10 questions in total. A multi-choice format will make analysis easier. If Barbara Minto's reading of cognitive psychology is correct (and there is a lot of evidence to suggest it is), then individuals should achieve better comprehension from the pyramid structure than from the linear. Let the subjects (again, fellow students would be ideal) read the plans (set a time limit, say 15 minutes) and then take the plan away so the subject cannot refer back to it. Then present the comprehension test (again, set a time limit). Analysis should concentrate on the comprehension scores and how they correlate with plan structure. Is the prediction borne out?

 ## Key readings

Now quite old, but nonetheless the debate is still current and the points raised are still valid:

Thurston, P.H. (1983) 'Should smaller companies make formal plans?', *Harvard Business Review*, Sept./Oct., pp. 162–88.

Looking towards a resolution by rethinking the role, form and function of the business plan for the small and entrepreneurial venture:

Ames, M.D. (1994) 'Rethinking the business plan paradigm: bridging the gap between plan and plan execution', *Journal of Small Business Strategy*, Vol. 5, No. 1, pp. 69–76.

Suggestions for further reading

Ackelsburg, R. (1985) 'Small businesses do plan and it pays off', *Long Range Planning*, Vol. 18, No. 5, pp. 61–7.

Allaire, Y. and Firsirotu, M. (1990) 'Strategic plans as contracts', *Long Range Planning*, Vol. 23, No. 1, pp. 102–15.

Bhide, A. (1994) 'How entrepreneurs craft strategy', *Harvard Business Review*, Mar./Apr., pp. 150–61.

Bracker, J.S., Keats, B.W. and Person, J.N. (1988) 'Planning and financial performance among small firms in a growth industry', *Strategic Management Journal*, Vol. 9, pp. 591–603.

Chakravarthy, B.S. and Lorange, P. (1991) 'Adapting strategic planning to the changing needs of a business', *Journal of Organisational Change Management*, Vol. 4, No. 2, pp. 6–18.

Cooper, A.C. (1981) 'Strategic management: new ventures and small business', *Long Range Planning*, Vol. 14, No. 5, pp. 39–45.

Grieve Smith, J. and Fleck, V. (1988) 'Strategies of new biotechnology firms', *Long Range Planning*, Vol. 21, No. 3, pp. 51–8.

Hamel, G. and Prahalad, C.K. (1993) 'Strategy as stretch and leverage', *Harvard Business Review*, Mar./Apr., pp. 75–84.

Harari, O. (1994) 'The hypnotic danger of competitive analysis', *Management Review*, Vol. 83, No. 8, pp. 36–8.

Higgins, J.M. (1996) 'Innovate or evaporate: creative techniques for strategists', *Long Range Planning*, Vol. 29, No. 3, pp. 370–80.

Hills, G.E. (1985) Market analysis and the business plan: venture capitalists' perceptions', *Journal of Small Business Management*, Vol. 23, pp. 38–46.

Hopkins, W.E. and Hopkins, S.A. (1994) 'Want to succeed? Get with the plan!', *Journal of Retail Banking*, Vol. XVI, No. 3, pp. 26–31.

Kim, W.C. and Mauborgne, R. (2000) 'Knowing a winning business idea when you see one', *Harvard Business Review*, Sept./Oct., pp. 129–38.

Knight, R.M. (1994) 'Criteria used by venture capitalists: a cross-cultural analysis', *International Small Business Journal*, Vol. 13, No. 1, pp. 26–37.

Macmillan, I.C., Siegel, R. and Subba Narashima, P.N. (1985) 'Criteria used by venture capitalists to evaluate new venture proposals', *Journal of Business Venturing*, Vol. 1, pp. 119–28.

Macmillan, I.C., Zeeman, L. and Subba Narashima, P.N. (1987) 'Effectiveness of criteria used by venture capitalists in the venture screening process', *Journal of Business Venturing*, Vol. 2, pp. 123–38.

McKiernan, P. and Morris, C. (1994) 'Strategic planning and financial performance in UK SMEs: does formality matter?' *British Journal of Management*, Vol. 5, Special Issue, pp. S31–41.

Mason, C. and Harrison, R. (1996) 'Why "business angels" say no: a case study of opportunities rejected by an informal investor syndicate', *International Small Business Journal*, Vol. 14, No. 2, pp. 35–51.

Minto, B. (1996) *The Pyramid Principle*. London: FT Pitman.

Mintzberg, H. (1994) *The Rise and Fall of Strategic Planning*. London: Prentice Hall.

Perry, S.C. (2001) 'The relationship between written business plans and the failure of small business in the US', *Journal of Small Business Management*, Vol. 39, No. 3, pp. 201–8.

Schneider, T.W. (1998) 'Building a business plan: a good business plan will not ensure success, but the lack of one is a formula for failure', *Journal of Property Management*, Vol. 63, No. 6, pp. 1–2.

Schwenk, C.R. and Shrader, C.B. (1993) 'Effects of formal planning on financial performance in small firms: a meta-analysis', *Entrepreneurial Theory and Practice*, Vol. 17, No. 3, pp. 53–64.

Shuman, J.C., Shaw, J.J. and Sussman, G. (1985) 'Strategic planning in smaller rapid growth companies', *Long Range Planning*, Vol. 18, No. 6, pp. 48–53.

Waalewijn, P. and Segaar, P. (1993) 'Strategic management: the key to profitability in small companies', *Long Range Planning*, Vol. 26, No. 2, pp. 24–30.

Wyckham, R.G. and Wedley, W.C. (1990) 'Factors related to venture feasibility analysis and business plan preparation', *Journal of Small Business Management*, Vol. 28, No. 4, pp. 48–59.

Selected case material

CASE 19.1   20 January 2006

The entrepreneur who wants to give it all away

BEN KING

So you have made half a billion dollars and you have paid for a trip to space. What on earth do you do next? Some might consider politics, others would sit back and enjoy a life of leisure. But for technology entrepreneur and cosmonaut Mark Shuttleworth the next battle was to take on the might of Microsoft on its core territory: the desktop.

He has developed a complete suite of software for personal computers that handles everything from the inner workings to word processing. It is called Ubuntu, named after one of the founding principles of post-apartheid South Africa, the country where he was born. In both the Zulu and Xhosa languages, it means 'humanity to others'.

The project is based on Linux, the free operating system written largely by volunteers and widely used by businesses, governments and other organisations to run servers, the computers that sit at the heart of networks. Ubuntu is meant to take this complex but powerful system and make it easy for non-technical people to use. Hence the project's mission statement: 'Linux for human beings'.

Although the technology behind it may be very different, a computer running Ubuntu looks much like one running Microsoft's Windows. The interface is based on similar menus, icons and windows, and users can surf the internet with the popular Firefox browser, or edit documents and spreadsheets with OpenOffice.

Instead of the largely blue world of Windows XP, Ubuntu is predominantly brown. Some quirky features hint at its African origin, such as the little burst of drumming that rings out when an application opens. Each new version of Ubuntu is known not just by the usual number, but an animal codename, such as Warty Warthog or Breezy Badger.

Less than two years after launch, Ubuntu has established itself as a favourite among the hundreds of different Linux-based operating systems. Ubuntu is top by some distance on a popularity chart for different flavours of Linux compiled by the website, DistroWatch. Exact numbers are hard to come by, but estimates put the number of computers running Ubuntu at up to 6m and doubling every eight months.

Unlike some of the other leading Linux projects, such as Linspire, Novell and Red Hat, Ubuntu is distributed free. Users can download it and use it without paying at all, and Mr Shuttleworth's company, Canonical, will even post a free installation compact disc to anyone who requests it.

This is possible because of Mr Shuttleworth's vast fortune. He made $575m (£327m) selling his internet company, Thawte Consulting, in 1999, and invests about $10m a year in Ubuntu. It is unlikely to make him any money, at least not for several years. Canonical sells support and related services for Ubuntu, but Mr Shuttleworth has no firm idea about when it will make a profit.

He launched the project because he believes he is in the vanguard of a revolution. 'It is very high risk,' he says. 'It is not a sensible business model. But shaping the digital platform of the future is an incredibly interesting position to be in.'

He has certainly created a powerful and effective desktop software package. From its commitment to freedom to its quirky public image, Ubuntu has many appealing features and considerable momentum. However, to continue growing at the current rate, it will need to expand beyond its existing technology-savvy base to embrace people with no prior experience of Linux.

Linux consultant and author Tom Adelstein thinks it is still hard for such people to use. 'From a usability point of view, Ubuntu is ahead of the others, I think. But it is still in the Linux bag – you have to be computer literate to use it. Microsoft is still far ahead on that.' Likewise, many buyers will be put off by the fact that a number of programs, notably games, are not available for Linux systems.

Few of those target users would install an operating system themselves. So a key stage in Ubuntu's growth will be persuading PC makers to sell machines with Ubuntu already installed. Some computer makers already ship PCs with Linux suites such as Linspire.

Smaller PC makers, competing at the lower end of the market, are particularly interested in free software, as it helps them to cut their prices. Small companies account for one-third of the global market, according to research company IDC, and Mr Shuttleworth is soon to visit Taiwan to open negotiations with some of them.

Corporate and government desktops may also be fertile ground for growth. A survey by Forrester, the research company, found that

30 per cent of companies in North America are considering switching some or all of their desktops to Linux.

Among those changing is Google, which has developed its own version of Ubuntu, called Goobuntu. Mr Shuttleworth says he is also in talks with the city government in Munich about creating an edition of Ubuntu for them.

This ability to customise Linux is a big selling point, and Canonical is developing an easy way for corporations to design and maintain specific versions of Ubuntu to suit their exact needs.

Although a stock-market darling such as Google may seem an excellent reference customer, it has an intense rivalry with Microsoft so it is keener than average to try alternatives to Windows. Other organisations will need more convincing reasons to adopt Ubuntu. Being free is clearly an advantage and Linux advocates argue that the security and robustness of Linux products are superior to those of Windows, although these issues are hotly debated.

Mr Shuttleworth has managed to rally one important group around his standard: developers. Canonical has just 50 staff, but Ubuntu has attracted many thousands of engineers at partner companies, as well as volunteers and students, who do most of the work of extending and improving the software.

The Ubuntu community has a reputation for friendliness – which is important when you are not being paid. Also, many developers who dislike the increasing commercialisation of other Linux projects are attracted by Ubuntu's commitment to remaining free.

However, selling Ubuntu beyond the circle of geeky initiates will require a massive marketing and education process, and even Mr Shuttleworth's deep pockets are no match for the budgets of Microsoft and Apple. He hopes that the virtues of a free, open operating system will sell themselves.

'My instinct tells me that free software is going to be a significant force on the desktop,' he says. 'Whether that is an Apple Mac-like force of 3–5 per cent; or whether that is a Linux in the data centre [on servers] force, that is 50 per cent and growing really, really fast – I don't know.'

With no serious business plan, it would be easy to dismiss Ubuntu as the plaything of a whimsical hobbyist that will not go far beyond the geek fraternity. Can a Breezy Badger really be a serious challenge to a titan like Microsoft?

During his interview with the *Financial Times*, Mr Shuttleworth sits across his chair with both legs on the armrest, as if it were a hammock – not something you imagine Larry Ellison, Oracle's chief executive, doing.

But he has an impressive record, and you certainly cannot question his dedication. He is currently on a gruelling three-week world tour in his private jet, promoting Ubuntu and making contacts in Croatia, Pakistan, India, China, Indonesia and Kenya. After that, he plans to 'unwind' by meeting other enthusiasts for free software in, of all places, the war-torn republic of Sierra Leone.

For some, Mr Shuttleworth just seems to be having too much fun to be taken seriously. But Linux has surprised many people before – there is nothing a geek finds more fun than turning a whole industry on its head.

Source: Ben King, 'The entrepreneur who wants to give it all away', *Financial Times*, 20 January 2006, p. 13. Copyright © 2006 The Financial Times Limited.

CASE 19.2

15 September 2005

FT

Mediobanca to target perceptions

ADRIAN MICHAELS

Mediobanca outlined the next phase of its internal revolution this week, in the process driving reforms in the structure of Italian capitalism.

The powerful investment bank, founded after the Second World War, has been the most influential in Italian business for decades. It has been at the centre of a web of cross-shareholdings and directorships in which a few businesses and people used their limited capital to look after each other's interests and maintain their positions. It helped provide crucial stability through numerous upheavals.

Mediobanca, though, was not often seen as a great investment opportunity in its own right by outside investors who thought it could be seen as the sum of the parts of its equity holdings.

But the bank has been trying to change perceptions and focus investor minds on the earnings potential of its banking activities. It had already separated its equity investment portfolio into 'strategic' and 'non-strategic' holdings.

Now it has transferred responsibility for almost all the holdings to its wholesale banking division and said there would be a €1.5bn ($1.8bn) reduction in capital allocated to the equity portfolio.

Only holdings in insurer Generali and RCS, the media group which runs *Corriere della Sera*, one of Italy's most respected newspapers, are not being transferred. Mediobanca owns 14 per cent of both RCS and Generali.

Mediobanca's holdings in a large number of other Italian companies, including Telecom Italia, Pirelli and Fiat, might now be regarded as less stable than in the past, particularly since they are being treated as 'for sale' under new accounting rules.

But investments in companies already classified as non-strategic could go first. They include defence company Finmeccanica and financial groups Mediolanum and Fondiaria SAI.

Alberto Nagel, the bank's co-general manager, said some holdings were still untouchable, including those in TI and Fiat. All the same, analysts saw the announcement as seismic.

Matteo Ramenghi, analyst at UBS, said Mediobanca's first approach to investors last year 'was a very bold statement; this one is more so: it is a push to the evolution of the entire Italian system'.

The Italian market is opening up all the time, but it is still maturing compared with other countries in western Europe or the US. This year has seen some dramatic posturing against the old establishment, as epitomised by Mediobanca.

A group of younger entrepreneurs has been taking large shareholdings in companies which are part of Mediobanca's sphere of influence, including the investment bank itself. Stefano Ricucci is now the largest single shareholder in RCS and has not ruled out a takeover bid.

A number of establishment members have been visibly riled by the challenge which has increased the reputation of the Italian market for volatility and rumour and comes amid a banking scandal which also involves Mr Ricucci among others.

It is curious then that Mediobanca may soon be increasing speculation about the shareholder composition of some important companies.

But the bank sees the step as important in promoting its future shape. In the process it may help to open up Italy's market.

Source: Adrian Michaels, 'Mediobanca to target perceptions', *Financial Times*, 15 September 2005, p. 30. Copyright © 2005 The Financial Times Limited.

Discussion points

1. In what ways might a business plan improve Ubuntu's chances of success?

2. If you were one of the young entrepreneurs mentioned, how would you see a business plan helping you? What key pieces of information would you include in one?

CHAPTER 20

Gaining financial support:
issues and approaches

Chapter overview

Attracting financial support for the venture is one of the
entrepreneur's most important tasks. This chapter considers the supply of
investment capital and how backers go about selecting investment opportunities.
The chapter concludes by advocating that a major factor in successfully attracting
investment is the entrepreneur having an understanding of the questions that
investors need to ask and being prepared to answer them.

20.1 Sources and types of financial investment

Key learning outcome

A recognition of the different
sources of capital available
for investment in the
entrepreneurial venture.

Investment capital is a valuable commodity. As with any other
commodity, markets develop to ensure that supply meets demand.
Although 'capital' is itself an undifferentiated commodity (one
five-pound note is exactly like any five-pound note), a number of
different types of supplier emerge to offer investment capital.
These different types of supplier differentiate themselves not in
what they supply but in the *way* they supply the capital, the *price*
they ask for that capital and the *supplementary services* they offer.

The interaction of supply and demand results in a *price* being set for the capital. This
price is the *rate of return* the supplier (the lender or investor) expects from their investment.
A number of factors influence the cost of the capital being offered. The critical factors are the
risk of the investment (that is, the probability that the return will be less than that anticipated) and the *opportunity cost* (that is, the return that has to be forgone because alternative
investments cannot be made). This *risk–rate of return line* provides one of the key dimensions along which investors differentiate themselves. In principle, this mechanism should
ensure that the amount of capital provided should be equal to that demanded by
entrepreneurs. However, many entrepreneurs complain about a 'funding gap' – an inability
to get hold of capital to support their ventures. Some politicians agree with them and demand
that banks serve them better. However, market failure (due to capital providers' monopoly position, say) is only one explanation. It could also be the case that the entrepreneur's

assessment of the risks of their venture are lower than those of investors, so the entrepreneur thinks the capital on offer is coming with too high a price tag. The issue of entrepreneurs' (over)optimism and its impact on investors is explored further in section 20.4. The funding gap might also arise as a result of informational asymmetry between the entrepreneur and investor (an idea encountered in section 6.3). Whatever its source, the funding gap presents problems to entrepreneurs, investors and the wider world that benefits from entrepreneurial activity. Harris (1995) investigates organisations that are attempting to address the funding gap.

Like in many markets, suppliers in the market for investment capital differentiate themselves. This differentiation is based on the type and level of capital they provide and the level of risk they are prepared to accept. Key suppliers of capital are described below.

Entrepreneur's own capital

The entrepreneur's own capital may derive from personal savings, or it may be a lump sum resulting from a capital gain or a redundancy package, in which case it might be quite a significant amount. The research by Blanchflower and Oswald (1998) quoted in Chapter 5 revealed the importance of inherited money in start-ups. Serial entrepreneurs liquidate their holdings in their ventures once they mature in order to pursue new business ideas. Clearly, the entrepreneur is free to use this capital as they wish.

Informal investors

An entrepreneur may attract investment support on an informal basis from their family and friends. The expectations of what the returns will be, and when they might be gained, are usually set informally or, at most, semi-formally. Harrison and Dibben (1997) study the nature of informal investor decision making and find that in addition to rational evaluation of the business plan, personal trust in the entrepreneur is also important.

Internal capital networks

Many communities, especially those based around a group of people who are displaced and who are, or at least feel, excluded from the wider economic system, show strong entrepreneurial tendencies. This often enlivens and enriches the economy as a whole. Important examples include a variety of Asian groups in Britain, North Africans in France, Chinese expatriates in Southeast Asia, and the Lebanese in West Africa. Such groups often encourage investment among themselves. These communities set up *internal capital networks* which direct capital towards new business opportunities within the community. These networks often have an international character. In emerging economies they provide important conduits for inward investment.

Although often quite informal in a narrow legal sense, these networks are guided by a rich set of cultural rules and expectations. Risk, return and the way in which returns are made are often embedded in complex patterns of ownership and control of ventures.

Retained capital

The profits that a venture generates are, potentially, available to be reinvested in its development. However, such profits belong neither to the venture nor to the entrepreneur; rather they are the property of the *investors* who are backing the venture (this group may, of course, include the entrepreneur). Reinvesting the profits might offer a good investment opportunity, but it is an opportunity which the investor will judge like any other on the basis of risk, return and the possibility of taking the profits and seeking alternative investment opportunities.

Business angels

Business angels are individuals, or small groups of individuals, who offer up their own capital to new ventures. They are usually people who have been successful in business (perhaps as entrepreneurs themselves) and as a result have some money 'to play with'. Investment structure and return expectations vary, but are usually equity based and codified in formal agreements.

Business angels differ from other types of organisational investor in one important respect. They like to get involved in the ventures they are backing, and in addition to capital backing, they offer their skills, insights and experiences. As a result they usually seek investment opportunities in ventures where their knowledge or business skills are appropriate. Business angels are also more likely to select ventures in their own geographical locale. The development of informal venture capital in the UK is considered by Harrison and Mason (1996). Tashiro (1999) presents a good account of business angels in Japan.

Retail banking

Retail or 'high street' banks usually offer investment capital to start-ups and expanding small firms. Support is almost inevitably in the form of loan capital and returns are subject to strict agreement. The bank will expect the entrepreneur to make a personal commitment and may seek collateral to reduce the risk of the deal. The decision-making processes within banks that provide small business funds is explored by Berger and Udell (2002). Brau (2002) investigates the extent to which banks price anticipated owner-manager agency costs in their lending.

Corporate banking

To an extent, the corporate banking sector picks up where retail banking stops. Corporate banks are interested in bigger investment opportunities and may settle for longer-range returns. Loan capital dominates but some equity may also be offered. Deals may be quite complex and involve conversions between the two forms of investment. Again, a significant commitment by the entrepreneur and asset security may be sought.

Venture capital

Venture capital is a critical source of investment for fast-growing entrepreneurial ventures. Venture capital companies usually seek large investment opportunities which are characterised by the potential for a fast, high rate of return. As such, they tend to take on higher degrees of risk than banks. Venture capital companies will rarely involve themselves with investments of less than £250,000 and typically seek annual returns in excess of 50 per cent to be harvested over five years or less. Usually the deals are equity-based and they may be complex. However, a clear *exit strategy*, which enables the returns to the venture capital investment to be liquidated quickly, must be in place. A number of studies (e.g. Zacharakis *et al.*, 1999; Riquelme and Watson, 2002) have explored venture capitalists' judgements on the factors that lead to success and failure in entrepreneurial ventures. Devashis (2000) and Choudhury (2001) provide detailed accounts of the operation of venture capital systems in India and the Islamic world, respectively. Cook (2001) considers small business financing in the developing world.

Public flotation

A public flotation is a means of raising capital by offering shares in the venture to a pool of private investors. These shares can then be bought and sold in an open stock market or, in continental Europe, a *bourse*. There are a variety of stock markets through which capital may be raised. All mature economies have national stock markets, of which London, New York and Tokyo are among the most important internationally. There are a number of *emerging* stock markets which trade stock from companies in the developing world and in the post-command economies of central and eastern Europe (that is, the economies that were under communist control until the late 1980s).

In addition to the stock markets for established companies, there are special stock markets for smaller businesses and for fast-growing ventures. The most important European small-company stock market is the Alternative Investments Market (AIM) based in London. This market has some 265 companies listed and a capitalisation of nearly £6 billion. Other European small business markets include the Nouveau Marché in Paris, Easdaq based in Brussels and the Neuer Markt in Frankfurt. It is planned to link all these markets through a network dubbed EURO.NM. Small and fast-growing business investment in the USA is carried out through a market known as Nasdaq.

Government

Very few governments nowadays fail to see that they have an interest in encouraging enterprise. New businesses create jobs, bring innovation to the market and provide competitive efficiency. Across the world, however, governments differ in the extent to which, and the way in which, they engage in intervention to support the creation and survival of new and fast-growing businesses.

Support is usually given to start-ups when capital for investment is hardest to obtain and when cash flow can be at its tightest. Generally, direct government investment is in decline. However, there are a number of quasi-governmental agencies which can direct grants towards the entrepreneurial start-up. In addition to capital grants, government may offer support in the form of consulting services and training. Examples of this include the Training and Enterprise Councils (TECs) in the UK and the Small Business Administration (SBA) in the USA. In continental Europe (and increasingly also in central and eastern Europe), local chambers of commerce play an important role in this respect. In addition to overt support, governments often give smaller firms a head-start through tax breaks.

Commercial partnerships

An entrepreneurial venture may look towards existing businesses as a source of investment capital. This will usually occur when the established business has a strategic interest in the success of the venture, for example if it is a supplier of a particularly innovative and valuable input. The support demonstrated by IBM for Microsoft in its early days is a case in point. Commercial partnerships can also occur when the venture is developing a technology which will be important to the established firm. The wide range of investments by established pharmaceutical companies in biotechnology start-ups in the 1980s provides an example of this.

There are various arrangements by which the established firm can impose control over its investment in the entrepreneurial venture. At one extreme is complete ownership, and at the other is a simple agreement to use the venture as a favoured supplier. In between there are a variety of forms of *strategic alliance*.

Micro-finance

In broad terms, micro-finance refers to small (often less than £50) loans to individuals or families in the developing world to enable them to start a business. It is proving to be highly successful (for borrowers as well as lenders), and growth in the sector is rapid. Indonesia, for example, claims to have over 600,000 micro-finance institutions. There is considerable difficulty in monitoring the sector. Strictly speaking, the loan should be to start a business, not be for personal use and the lending institution should be registered. However, if a person buys a bicycle to make deliveries, or a mobile telephone to charge for others to make calls, the dividing line between private use and business use is inevitably blurred. Further, many traditional (unregistered) lenders are moving into micro-finance. The success of the sector as an investment opportunity is attracting the attention of larger, established lending institutions. For an up-to-date review of the micro-finance sector, see *The Economist* (2005).

Choice of capital supply

The types and range of investment capital providers operating in an economy depend on the stage of development of that economy and a variety of other political and cultural factors. The choice of capital supplier by the entrepreneur is a decision which must be made in the light of the nature of the venture, its capital requirements, the stage of its development and the risks it faces.

The venture capital industry was originally established in the USA and then more latterly, the UK. It is now becoming a global industry. For the student who is interested in developing a global perspective on venture capital and private equity investment, Table 20.1 summarises recent reviews of the development and state of the venture capital industry in various parts of the world. The list is not exhaustive. Criteria for selection are that the reviews are the most recent, provide a good overview of the private equity sector in the region and, in many cases, are rich in quantitative data.

20.2 How backers select investment opportunities

Investment is a buying and selling process. The entrepreneur is trying to sell the venture as an investment opportunity, and the investor is looking to buy opportunities which offer a good return. As such, a consideration of the marketing-buying behaviour behind investment

Table 20.1 Recent reviews of the restore capital industry worldwide

Region	Authors/year	Article title	Publication
Asia and Pacific Rim	Lockett, A. and Wright, M. (2002)	Venture capital in Asia and the Pacific Rim	*Venture capital*, Vol. 4, No. 3, pp. 183–95
Australia	Ferris, W.D. (2001)	Australia chooses: venture capital and a future Australia	*Australian Journal of Management*, Vol. 26, Special Issue, pp. 45–64
Canada	Best, A. and Mitra, D. (1997)	The venture capital industry in Canada	*Journal of Small Business Management*, Apr.
Central Europe	Wright, M., Karsai, J., Dudzinski, Z. and Morovic, J. (1999)	Transition and active investors: venture capital in Hungary, Poland and Slovakia	*Post-Communist Economics*, Vol. 11, No. 1, pp. 27–46
China	Vaughn, C.M. (2002)	Venture capital in China: developing a regulatory framework	*Columbia Journal of Asian Law*, Vol. 16, No. 1, pp. 227–52
Europe	Bottazzi, L. and Da Rin, M. (2002)	European venture capital	*European Policy*, Apr., pp. 231–69
	Bottazzi, L. Da Rin, M. and Hellmann, T. (2004)	The changing face of the European venture capital industry: facts and analysis	*Journal of Private Equity*, Spring, pp. 26–53
France	Dubocage, E. and Rivaud-Danset, D. (2002)	Government policy on venture capital support in France	*Venture Capital*, Vol. 4, No. 1, pp. 25–43
Germany	Weber, C. and Weber, B. (2005)	Corporate venture capital organizations in Germany	*Venture Capital*, Vol. 7, No. 1, pp. 51–73
Hong Kong	Chu, P. and Hisrich, R.D. (2001)	Venture capital in an industry in transition	*Venture Capital*, Vol. 3, No. 2, pp. 169–82
India	Mitra, D. (2000)	The venture capital industry in India	*Journal of Small Business Management*, Apr., pp. 67–79
Islamic World	Choudhury, M.A. (2001)	Islamic venture capital: a critical examination	*Journal of Economic Studies*, Vol. 28, No. 1, pp. 14–33
Israel	Levenfield, B., Platt, B.S., Schapiro, D. and Tisoni, O. (2005)	Private equity and venture capital in Israel	*International Financial Law Review*, Vol. 24, pp. 31–3
Latin America	Pascual, R. and Kilpatrick, S. (2000)	Venture capital in Latin America	*Corporate Finance*, No. 190, pp. iii–vi
UK	British Venture Capital Association (2003)	Report on investment activity	Available on internet
USA	Green, M.B. (2004)	Venture capital investment in the United States 1995–2002	*The Industrial Geographer*, Vol. 2, No. 1, pp. 2–30

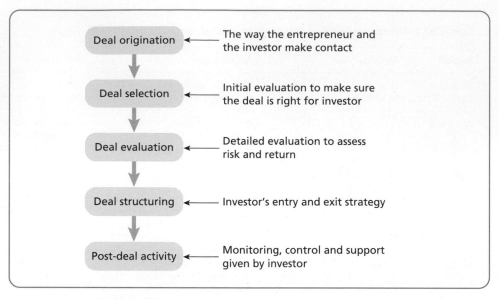

Figure 20.1 A model of investment decision making (adapted from Tyebjee and Bruno, 1984)

Key learning outcome

An appreciation of the process by which investors select investment opportunities.

deals can provide an insight into how that process might be understood and so be managed to be more effective.

Tyebjee and Bruno (1984) have developed a model of the investment process. Although these researchers used the model to understand venture capital investment, it is generic in form and so can be used to understand investment in general. The model is outlined in Figure 20.1.

The model identifies five key stages in the investment process. These are described below.

Stage 1: Deal origination

Deal origination is the process by which the entrepreneur and the investor first become aware of each other. This results from a mix of *searching* activity by the investor and *promotional* activity by the entrepreneur. Few venture capitalists actively search for new opportunities. They wait for the entrepreneur, or often a third party working on behalf of the entrepreneur, to approach them. Similarly, retail and corporate banks place the onus on the entrepreneur to make the first move.

If the business has shares which are available on a market then private and institutional investors will be active in seeking out stock which fits their portfolio and offers them an attractive return. Business angels are often informed about investment opportunities through informal networks of business contacts.

Stage 2: Deal screening

Many investors specialise in certain types of investment. Deal screening reflects the initial evaluation of the proposal to see if it fits with the investor's profile of activities. Important criteria include the amount of investment being sought, the type of technology on which the venture is based, the industry sector of the venture and the venture's stage of growth.

Stage 3: Deal evaluation

If the proposal fits with the investor's portfolio of activities, then a more detailed evaluation of the proposal may be carried out. The objective of this exercise is to compare the returns offered by the venture with the risk that it faces. The key factors to be considered in this evaluation will be the potential for the venture in terms of the innovation it is offering, the conditions in the market it aims to develop and the competitive pressures it will face. If this potential is good then consideration will also be made of the ability of the management team to actually deliver it. The investor will also be interested in any security the entrepreneur can offer, say in the form of readily liquidisable assets.

Stage 4: Deal structuring

Deal structuring concerns the decisions that must be made in relation to how the initial investment will be made and how the investor will see that investment bear fruit. The critical issues in relation to the investment stage will be how much the entrepreneur is seeking and over what period that investment is to be made. Critical to the return stage will be the actual return offered, how long the investor must wait before that return is seen and the form it will take. For example, will it be cash or will it be a share in the company? If it is a stake in the company, can it be liquidated readily?

Stage 5: Post-investment activity

Investors, especially those with a significant interest in the venture, will usually retain a degree of involvement in it. There are two broad areas of post-investment activity: *monitoring* and *control*. Monitoring relates to the procedures which are put in place to enable the investor to evaluate the performance of the business so they can keep track of their investment. Financial reporting by way of a balance sheet and profit and loss account (see section 26.3) provides a legally defined means by which the investor can monitor the business. Important investors may demand more frequent and detailed information, perhaps going beyond purely financial data.

Steiner and Greenwood (1995) examine deal structuring and post-deal investment activities by venture capitalists. They conclude that breaking into the venture capital network is a significant task for the entrepreneur and that relationships are more important than business plans in securing deals. They also find that, in many instances, a deadline imposed by the venture capitalists may be missed by the entrepreneur as a result of delays on the part of the venture capitalists themselves.

Control mechanisms give the investor an active role in the venture and power to influence the entrepreneur's and the venture's management decision making. One common control mechanism is for the investor to be represented on the firm's management team, perhaps as a director. Business angels often offer this not just as a control mechanism but, because of their experience and insights, as a positive contribution to the management of the venture.

Tyebjee and Bruno's five-stage model highlights some of the key areas of information that are needed by the investor before they can make an effective investment decision. Providing that information and answering the investors' questions must form the basis of the entrepreneur's communication strategy towards the investor. This model can be seen in operation in a study by Mason and Harrison (1996) in which they describe in great depth the investment process of one particular group of business angels. The group under study was formed by a retired UK businessman after seeing business angels operate in the USA. Its members, selected on the basis of experience, compatible personalities and commitment, were attracted by an advertisement in the business opportunities column of the *Financial Times*. Deals were initiated by a variety of means, including newspaper advertisements and by independent business brokers. About half of all deals were initiated by the entrepreneur's approaching the group. About one-quarter were initiated by the group approaching an entrepreneur and the remaining one-quarter were the result of introduction by independent agents. All deals were initially offered in the form of a written proposal. Initial screening was undertaken by an individual member of the group. Some 80 per cent of the deals were eliminated at this stage because they did not look financially viable. The remaining 20 per cent were summarised in a standard format and offered to the whole group for comment. If the group felt the deal was worth exploring further (about 10 per cent of all initial proposals), then a project leader was appointed to evaluate the proposal in detail. This was done in conjunction with two other members of the group. This involved background research and a meeting with the investee company. After due consideration, the project team would make a formal presentation and recommendation to the whole group. If, and only if, all members of the group were in favour of the deal, then a formal offer would be made to the investee company. The project team would consider how to structure the deal for entry and exit and would probably offer support in the management of the venture.

As in many areas of management, decision making in practice may differ markedly from the decision-making process that managers claim to follow. In a study of differences in Australian venture capitalist in-use and espoused decision criteria, Shepherd (1999) found that venture capitalists tended to overstate factors that were relatively unimportant to, and understate factors that were in fact important to, their decisions. Morris *et al*. (2000) examine venture capitalists' support for portfolio entrepreneurs in South Africa.

20.3 The questions that investors need answering

Key learning outcome

A recognition of the kind of information that investors need before they can make an investment decision.

In a narrow sense, investors are *rational* in that they seek the best possible return from their capital for a given level of risk. However, such rational behaviour is dependent on investors having information from which to make decisions and on their being able to make those decisions efficiently. Neither of these conditions is ever met fully. There is always an *informational asymmetry* between entrepreneur and investor. Clearly, the entrepreneur knows more about their venture than does the investor. That is why the investor employs the entrepreneur to run the business! Even if investors have all the information necessary to make an investment decision, they are still human beings who suffer the same cognitive limitations that all human beings suffer. Although they may be practised in making investment decisions, those decisions are not necessarily optimal in a precise economic sense. Rather, investors, like all human decision makers, exhibit *satisficing* behaviour; that is, they make the best decision given the information available, their abilities and the influence of cultural factors. Studies of business angels, for example, have revealed that they rarely use formal mathematical methods to determine the return on the investments they make; rather, they seek investments that 'feel right'. A study by Shepherd (1999) draws a distinction between espoused and in-use decision making by venture capitalists. His findings indicate that the decision criteria that venture capitalists *say* they are using may be different from what they *actually* use in practice.

Before an investor makes an investment they will need some information about the venture. Thus the entrepreneur will need to answer a series of questions about it. The key questions are as follows.

Is the venture of the right type?

Many, if not most, investors specialise in certain types of business. Private investors and business angels may confine themselves to industry sectors in which they have knowledge and experience. Some venture capitalists focus on investment opportunities in certain technological areas; for example, biotechnology or information technology. Another important dimension of specialisation is the *stage of development* of the business and the nature of the financing it requires. Of late, venture capitalists have shifted their attention away from new start-ups and have moved to investing in lower-risk management buyouts (MBOs). Banks will support start-ups through their retail arms, but will deal with expansion financing through their corporate operations.

The investor will need to be assured that the venture is in the right area and at the right stage for them.

How much investment is required?

Investors will be interested in the amount of financing required. This will be judged in relation to the business the investor is in, their expertise and the costs they face in monitoring and controlling their investments. Retail banks will offer loans from a few hundred to tens of thousands of pounds. Venture capitalists, on the other hand, are not interested in investments of less than about £250,000, and are only really interested in investments of several million pounds. A market flotation is usually concerned with raising at least £5 million.

The key question is, is the investor really the right source given the level of investment needed?

What return is likely?

The return on investment is the likely financial outcome of making a specific investment. The investor will want to know on what basis this has been calculated. Further, they will ask how reasonable it is given the potential for the venture and of its management team. The decision to invest will be based on an assessment of the returns in relation to the risks and how the investment opportunity compares with others available. However, it should be noted that even for quite large investments, this comparison may be made on an intuitive rather than an explicit basis. Certain investors specialise in different levels of risk. Venture capitalists seek more risk than retail banks. Specialist high-growth markets usually reflect higher-risk investments than mainstream ones.

What is the growth stage of the venture?

Critically, this question relates to what the investment capital is required for. Is it to start a new business or is it to fund the expansion of an established business? Is the venture at an early stage in its growth, requiring capital to fund an aggressive growth strategy, or is the business at a mature stage with the capital to be used to fund incremental growth? How does this impact on the risk entailed and return offered? Is this stage of growth right for the investor?

What projects will the capital be used for?

This question relates to how the capital will be used within the venture. Is it to cover cash flow shortfalls which result from strong growth or is it to be used for a more specific project, such as development of new products, funding a sales drive or marketing campaign, or for entering export markets? Again, the question is how does this impact on risk, return and specialism from the point of view of the investor?

What is the potential for the venture?

The investors will want to know what the venture can be expected to achieve in the future. This will depend on two sets of factors: first, on its *market potential*: that is, how innovative its offering is, how much value this offers the customer in relation to what is already available, and the possibilities and limitations the venture faces in delivering this innovation to the customer. Second, it depends on the quality of the entrepreneur and the management team: that is, the skills and experience of the venture's key people and their ability to deliver the potential that the venture has. The critical question is, will the investor find the venture's potential attractive, and if not, why not?

What are the risks for the venture?

To an investor, the risk of the venture is the probability that it will not deliver the return anticipated. Critical to judging this is an understanding of the assumptions that have been made in estimating the likely return. Some critical areas are assumptions about customer demand, the ability of the business to manage its costs, the ability of the venture to get distributors and other key partners on board, and the reaction of competitors.

The investors' judgement of risk will also depend on their ability to exit the investment by liquidating their holding. An investor will ask exactly how liquid the business is and whether or not the investment can be secured against particular liquidisable assets. How do the risks match up with what the investor will expect?

How does the investor get in?

The investor will wish to know exactly how their investment is to be made. Is it to be a lump sum up-front or will it take the form of a regular series of cash injections? The entrepreneur must ask whether this is the way the investor normally operates.

How does the investor get out?

The investor will want to know how they will see their return. Will it take the form of cash? If so, will it be a single cash payment at some point in the future, or will it be a series of payments over time? Alternatively, will it take the form of a holding of stock in the firm? If so, how can such a holding be liquidated? Loans are usually paid back in cash form whereas an equity holding will mature as a holding in the firm. Venture capitalists with equity holdings will insist on a clear exit strategy which will enable them to convert their equity to cash, either by selling on a market or converting it with the venture.

What post-investment monitoring procedures will be in place?

An investor will want to know the means by which they will be able to keep track of their investment. A business plan will normally be required before an injection of capital is made. The business plan is an excellent way of communicating and of managing the investors' expectations. Regular financial reports will provide key information on the performance of the business and its liquidity (and hence its exposure to risk). The entrepreneur must consider whether the monitoring procedures on offer will be considered adequate by the investor.

What control mechanisms will be available?

Monitoring is of little use unless the investor can use the information gained to influence the behaviour of the venture's management. Investors who hold shares can signal their approval or otherwise by buying and selling their stock in the market. This buying and selling changes the value of the company. The ultimate sanction is for the value of the business to fall to a level where a takeover can happen and a new set of managers be brought in.

Large investors will usually take a more direct route to control. This may be by lobbying the venture's management or by having a representative permanently on the firm's board. The question that must be asked is how the control mechanisms on offer will influence the investor's decision.

Communication skills

Entrepreneurs and investors meet through a process of communication. Communication is a human process involving not only the passage of information but also an attempt to influence behaviour. Entrepreneurs communicate with investors not just because they wish to tell them about their ventures but also because they want the investors to support them.

The process of communication between an entrepreneur and an investor is not just a matter of the *what* of the answers but also the *how*. The entrepreneur can exert a positive influence on investors by understanding the questions they are asking, by ensuring that the answers to those questions have been explored, and, where appropriate, by having hard evidence to back up the answers given.

Venture capitalists reject the vast majority (over 95 per cent) of proposals made to them. Although banks may back a higher proportion of proposals, rejections still greatly outnumber acceptances. Even if the business idea is sound, an investment of time and energy in making sure that proposals and other communications to backers are sympathetic to their information needs, and are well constructed as pieces of communication, will help the investor to make their decision and will reflect positively on the professionalism of the entrepreneur. This will ensure that the venture is in the forefront of the race to obtain capital.

In an entertaining article, Kawasaki (2001) lists the top ten 'lies' of entrepreneurs in their claims to investors. These lies (a strong word, self-delusion may be fairer) are tempting, but examining them reveals why investors will not be impressed. In ranked order, these are as follows.

1. 'Our projections are conservative' – Really? Most entrepreneurs exaggerate.
2. 'A large player estimates our market will be worth (add your own billions here!) by 2005' – So what? Why should I believe them?
3. 'A major buyer will sign a deal next week' – Call me back when you have a signature!
4. 'Key employees are set to join as soon as we get funded' – Well, I'll fund you as soon as they join. People first – then money!
5. 'We have no competition' – So either there is no market – or you haven't looked!
6. 'We want a non-disclosure agreement on our business idea/plans' – Why? If it is so easy to copy, how are you going to maintain a business on the back of it?
7. 'That major competitor is just too slow to present a threat' – Really? How did they get to be big then?
8. 'We are glad the bubble has burst' – So are we, because we are going to charge more for our capital.
9. 'Patents make our business defensible' – No they don't. Patents usually get copied somehow!
10. 'We only need 1 per cent of the market' – Not much ambition, then?

Make sure your business plan does not fall into any of these traps!

20.4 Playing the game: game-theoretical ideas on the entrepreneur–investor relationship

Key learning outcome

To recognise the basic principles of game-theoretical thinking and appreciate the light this can throw on the entrepreneur–investor relationship.

So far our discussion of the entrepreneur–investor relationship has dealt with the practical issues relating to the specifics of that relationship. There is, however, a theoretical perspective on generalised relationships between agents (people or organisations who are free to make decisions) that is of immense power and illuminates the nature of decision making in those relationships greatly. This is called *game theory*. Along with information economics (discussed in section 6.3), game theory has revolutionised economic thinking in the twentieth century. Games might be regarded as rather trivial affairs, distractions after the hard work of making money is done. And so they were by economists (aside from an interest in gambling, which is of economic significance) until mathematicians in the 1950s and 1960s recognised their economic importance. Of note here are John Von Neumann and Oskar Morgenstern with their groundbreaking book *The Theory of Games and Economic Behaviour*. Also important is John F. Nash, whose series of papers demonstrated the central significance of games to economic theory. The central idea of game theory is (beautifully) simple. Unfortunately, the works of Von Neumann, Morgenstern and Nash are of a highly technical nature and not for the mathematically faint-hearted. But this does not prevent a straightforward and (largely) non-mathematical exposition of the key ideas.

A game is formally an interaction between two or more 'players' (agents or decision makers) who can each play one of two or more different 'strategies' (acts or decisions). However, the 'winnings' (payoffs or outcomes) of the game for each player depend on the acts of all other players, not just the act of that particular player. The simplest game is one in which there are two players each able to select one of two acts. Each player selects their act without knowing what the other player has chosen to do and gets their winnings without any other decisions being made (we say the game is instantaneous). Game theory assumes that the players are rational. This means more than just sensible in their decision making. It means that the player will *always* take the action that is expected to maximise their outcomes (winnings) and that they recognise that other players are also rational and will do exactly the same. Although the idea of rationality has come in for criticism by many social scientists, it is not a bad approximation to the realities of economic life. The game can be represented with a 'payoff matrix' like the one shown in Figure 20.2.

The winnings can take any values of course. But if we set them such that a_{21} is greater than a_{11} which is greater than a_{22} which is greater than a_{12} (don't worry, an example will soon make this ordering clear), then we get a special type of game called a *prisoners' dilemma*. The reason this particular game is so called comes from an example offered by Albert Tucker in the 1950s. This example also illustrates why the game is so important in economic thinking.

Consider two people who have been arrested on suspicion of a crime and have been put on trial. At the trial, the judge offers both defendants a deal, on which they must make an immediate decision. This is put to each defendant in private, so they have no knowledge of

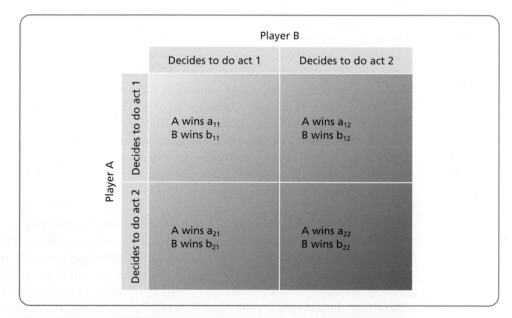

Figure 20.2 Payoff matrix

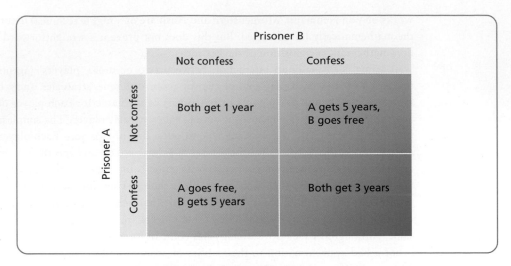

Figure 20.3 Payoff matrix for the prisoners' dilemma

what the other has decided to do. The deal put by the judge is this: 'You may confess to the crime, or not confess to it. If you both confess, then I will be sure of your guilt, but I will appreciate your not having wasted the court's time, so I will give you three years each. If neither of you confesses, then, although the evidence is against you, I will err on the side of caution and just give you one year each. If, however, you confess, but the other defendant does not, then I will, as a reward for your co-operating with the court, release you with a suspended sentence and imprison your accomplice for five years. I am putting this same deal to the other defendant. Do you wish to confess or not?' Such courtroom 'plea-bargaining' deals are not common in European courts but do happen in the USA. The payoff matrix for this situation is shown in Figure 20.3.

What is the rational course of action here, given that imprisonment is not enjoyed and a rational subject would wish to minimise their period of imprisonment? Well, a joint refusal to confess presents the minimum *total* period of incarceration, two years. However, consider the position of prisoner A (prisoner B is in exactly the same position). First, she considers that B has not confessed. In this case, her best strategy is to confess (she will then go free). Then she considers the alternative, that B *has* confessed. If she does not confess, then she will face five years. She can reduce this to three by confessing. In short, whatever the other prisoner has decided, her best option is to confess. Confessing is a strategy that is said to *strongly dominate* not confessing (it is always better than the alternative, whatever the other agent has done). But prisoner B, being in the same position, will go through the same argument and also decide to confess. The result will be that both prisoners will get three years. Yet, by both not confessing, both could have minimised their sentence to one year each.

The prisoners' dilemma actually represents a dilemma in that both prisoners cannot obtain (at least by thinking and acting rationally) the minimum period of imprisonment. Have you ever attended a major sporting event or a rock concert? If so, then you may have personally experienced an example of the prisoners' dilemma. Let's take it that sitting down is preferable to standing at such an event. If everyone sits, then everybody is comfortable. But any one person can gain a better view (an advantage) by standing. But if he does, then those behind must stand to get a better view. Result, everyone stands, even though all would have been more comfortable sitting down.

What has all this to do with entrepreneurs and investors? Quite a lot, because entrepreneurs and investors can often find themselves in a prisoners' dilemma situation, and neither is likely to come to the decision that would best benefit both parties. At least, not without some sort of mechanism to help them reach an optimal agreement. But more on this in a little while. Game theory relies (as any form of mathematical modelling must) on simplifying complex social situations so as to describe them and to discover why people make the decisions they do. This is not really a compromise. The point of game theory is to capture the *essence* of the interaction between players (and their decisions), not its peripheral details. We can always increase the complexity of the model to take account of subtleties, but this can cost in terms of the model's clarity. So we will describe the relationship between an entrepreneur and an investor in somewhat simplified terms, though these will be recognised as being realistic. Cable and Shane (1997) provide a comprehensive review of the entrepreneur–venture capitalist relationship in prisoner's dilemma terms.

Entrepreneurs and investors live in a world of competition. Not with each other, we might argue, because by working together they can both win, but with other entrepreneurs and other investors. Entrepreneurs compete with each other for investors' resources. Investors compete with each other for opportunities to invest in good entrepreneurial opportunities. The dynamic of the competition is the rate of return that entrepreneurs offer investors and the rate of return that investors, in turn, demand. Of course, the cake that entrepreneurs create is only so big. If a higher return is offered to an investor, then the return to the entrepreneur must be that much lower, and vice versa.

When offered an investment opportunity an investor can make one of two decisions: to support that venture or not (there may be subtleties in the agreement, but this is essentially it). This decision will be based on the return that the venture is offering relative to the risk that venture presents and the return that can be obtained elsewhere with other investment opportunities (of varying levels of risk). An entrepreneur presenting their business plan to an investor wants to make a good impression. They want the investment to take place. They also want the investor to see the risks in the venture as being as low as possible so that the return that the investor demands is as low as possible. A business plan is an anticipation. It is a projection of what might happen in the future. The future is not fully predictable. So a business plan offers a good deal of latitude for interpretation of the 'facts' that go into it. Entrepreneurs are keen to put a positive spin on the plan: how innovative the product is, the attractiveness of the market, the positive interest of potential customers, the weakness of competitors, and so on. This optimism is likely to be reflected in cash flow and profit projections. And all it takes is unchallenged optimism; there need be no suggestion that the entrepreneur is being consciously dishonest (though of course they can be). However, the greater such optimism, the less likely it will be that the entrepreneur can actually deliver what the plan says will be delivered. (It is useful here to reconsider some of the points on managing investor expectations made in section 9.1). The entrepreneur can get away with this because they are the expert on the business being presented and the investor must accept what the entrepreneur is saying.

Investors of course recognise this. This is why they challenge business plans rather than accept them at face value. But at the end of the day, the investor must accept (or not) what is being offered. In *simple* terms this means that the entrepreneur also has two options

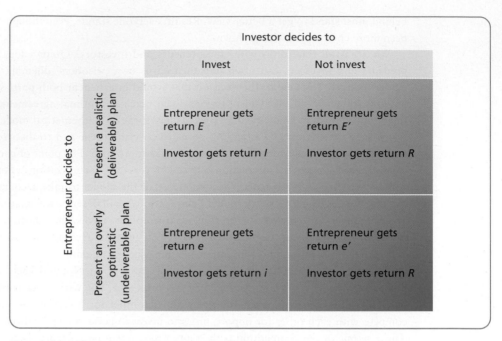

Figure 20.4 Entrepreneur/investor payoff matrix

available: to present a *realistic* plan (which presents risks as higher, but which is deliverable) or to present an overly *optimistic* plan (which minimises present risks but which cannot actually be delivered).

So we have two players, each able to take one of two actions where the 'winnings' (return from investment in the venture) for both depend on what both parties do – we have a formal game. This is depicted in the payoff matrix in Figure 20.4.

Let us consider the winnings in terms of their being returns from investment in the venture. On the one hand, if the investor backs a realistic plan then both parties win, the investor gets a return I and the entrepreneur a return E. If the plan is overly optimistic, however, the entrepreneur gets a return e and the investor a return i. Why does the plan make a difference to the returns? Because of the rate of return the investor will ask for. If the investor backs a plan that understates risks (and they believe that risk assessment), they will ask for a rate of return lower than if they fully recognised the risks. What the venture delivers (we may assume) is independent of what the entrepreneur offers, so the entrepreneur gains by having an overly optimistic plan accepted. On the other hand, if the investor decides not to invest then their return is always R, the return that is obtained from an alternative investment. The entrepreneur goes elsewhere for the investment, but presumably gets a worse deal (presumably the original investor was the preferred investor). In this case, if the plan is overly optimistic then the entrepreneur gets a return E'; if a realistic plan is presented, then the return is e'.

How do these returns stack up? Well, for the entrepreneur the order is:

e is greater than E is greater than e' is greater than E'.

The rationale is that an optimistic plan always costs less in returns demanded by the investor, and the preferred investor is offering a better deal than that offered by any other investor.

For the investor, the returns stack up as:

I is greater than R is greater than i.

The rationale here is that a realistic plan will encourage them to ask for a proper rate of return for the risk. If they decide to invest, then this investment should be better than the alternative investment available. However, if they have a strict portfolio and are asking a market rate of return then any underestimation of risk will lead to a return that is actually lower than that offered by a (market) alternative. (It is worthwhile to refer back to section 12.6 for clarification on this point.)

Although this all sounds rather convoluted, it does represent a scenario that often occurs in practice. The point is that it represents a prisoners' dilemma. To see why, consider the rational choice for the entrepreneur. Whether the investor decides to invest or not (and so the entrepreneur goes elsewhere), a greater personal return is obtained by presenting an overly optimistic plan. In other words, no matter what the investor does, the entrepreneur gets a greater return by presenting a more positive (if undeliverable) plan.

But now consider the rational choice for the investor. They know that the entrepreneur (being rational) will present an overly optimistic plan. In which case, the best option is not to invest, because it will lead to a return that can be improved by going elsewhere. So the entrepreneur and investor do not get together. But then both lose. The entrepreneur has to go to an investor they would prefer not to go to, and the investor misses out on an investment opportunity that they would have found attractive (against alternatives).

Empirical studies confirm this model. De Meza and Southey (1996) develop the model and apply it to bank lending to small businesses. They find that 'overoptimism' by would-be entrepreneurs can explain entrepreneur's reliance on loans (rather than equity), low interest rate margins and credit rationing. However, investors and entrepreneurs do get together. How is the prisoners' dilemma solved for them in practice?

Practical resolution of the dilemma

Human beings are creative. In practice, mechanisms have emerged to deal with a prisoners' dilemma and produce a resolution that allows both parties to make an agreement. We will go on to consider these in detail. Before doing so, it is important to recognise that the word 'emerge' is the right one. There is no suggestion that entrepreneurs or investors have consciously designed these mechanisms with the prisoners' dilemma problem in mind. The dilemma was not formally recognised until the 1950s, and investors and entrepreneurs have been getting together for many centuries. These mechanisms are the result of trial and error. The interesting thing is that the arrangements that have been found to work in practice can be seen through a game-theoretical perspective as means to ensure that a *rational* decision maker will conclude that co-operation (in our example, presenting a realistic business plan) is the best option. This said, game theory is increasingly being called upon to provide practical guidance in designing contracts for real business deals.

A mechanism for resolving a prisoners' dilemma in a social setting is usually composed of five interrelated elements. These are *repetition* (with *reputation*), *negotiation*, *contracting*, *punishment* and *external intervention*. Most practical social mechanisms involve a combination of these elements. They all play a role in sustaining the relationship between entrepreneurs and investors.

Repetition involves the game being played more than once. This would happen if the entrepreneur and the investor work together on more than one venture or if the one venture needs subsequent investment. If this happens, then an entrepreneur who presents an overly optimistic plan and fails to deliver on it is unlikely to get investment next time. So if the entrepreneur and investor have a long-term relationship the entrepreneur will be encouraged to present a realistic plan.

If players are coming into repeated contact, then the *reputation* of a player becomes important. Investors prefer serial entrepreneurs who have a reputation for delivering, to those who have not. But not all entrepreneurs are serial entrepreneurs. Reputation will not be so important to an entrepreneur who is seeking a one-off investment and will not need to call upon that reputation in the future. In which case the other mechanisms become important.

Negotiation is a fundamental part of the entrepreneur–investor relationship. Negotiation involves not just agreeing over how big a slice of the final cake each party will get, but also poring over the plan that the entrepreneur is presenting. Investors are aware that entrepreneurs put a positive spin on their plans. The investor seeks to challenge their optimism. They demand evidence to back up claims. The more independent that information the better. For really big deals, entrepreneurs may call in independent consultants to write and present plans for them, as Frederick Smith did when seeking $90 million to start Federal Express. Investors may themselves call in consultants to check facts for them. Some may demand personality testing for the entrepreneur to make sure they have the potential to deliver the plan (this issue is considered in section 3.2). In game-theoretical terms, all of this is about eliminating the space for the entrepreneur's unguarded optimism, thus ensuring the investor is making a decision on a realistic plan.

But all of this can be costly. It is worth investing in it for large deals, but it is prohibitively expensive for smaller ones. *Contracting* is a mechanism through which investors can, in effect, insure themselves against the possibility that the entrepreneur is presenting an overly optimistic plan. The contract is structured by the investor on the assumption that the entrepreneur knows things that they (the investor) do not. This brings in ideas on the economics of asymmetric information discussed in section 6.3. Formally, the investor's problem is one of *adverse selection*. The contract is so designed that it is in the entrepreneur's interest to present a realistic plan. The investor offers two contracts, one designed on the assumption that the entrepreneur is 'good' and will actually deliver the optimistic plan, the other on the assumption that the entrepreneur is 'poor' and will not deliver. Only the entrepreneur knows whether they are 'good' or 'poor', and so the investor must build in an incentive to ensure that the entrepreneur accepts the plan that is designed for their type. So there must be a reward for delivering on the plan, encouraging the entrepreneur to present one that is realistic. This reward must be additional to the normal returns of the investment (which the entrepreneur will gain whatever they present), or there will be no incentive. Conversely, there might be a cost if they do not deliver. Although this sounds complicated, a contract that actually delivers this is very simple and is almost universal in venture capital and bank investment deals: insist that the entrepreneur puts some of their own money into the venture. This aligns the interests of the investor and the entrepreneur. It makes the entrepreneur an investor as well, an investor who does know whether the entrepreneur is 'good' or 'poor' and has an interest in investing according to their type.

Punishment sounds severe, but all it means is that the entrepreneur is exposed to a cost that reduces the gains they make from presenting an overly optimistic plan to below those they make from presenting a realistic plan. In terms of our game-theoretical model above, this means that there is a cost, c, if the entrepreneur gains E that brings $(E - c)$ down to below e. Rationally, the entrepreneur will then prefer e and so present a realistic plan. Most investment deals include the possibility of some sort of action if the venture is not progressing towards its projected financial targets. This may take the form of a monetary penalty, but the possibilities here are limited. If the venture is not able to pay its promised return, then it is not likely to be able to pay an additional 'fine'. More likely is the possibility of the investor's moving in, replacing the entrepreneur with alternative managers, or, *in extremis*, foreclosing on the deal and having the business broken up with the aim of recovering the investment from the sale of assets. Of course, if the entrepreneur can be shown to be fraudulent in what has been presented to the investors, legislative action is a possibility.

External intervention is a mechanism whereby a third party moves in to ensure that the entrepreneur presents a realistic plan. To some extent, independent consultants can play this role. As noted, either the entrepreneur or the investor, or both, may call in consultants, especially if the deal is a big one. Of course, the legal system within which the entrepreneur and investor are operating sets standards of honesty in their dealings, with the threat of punitive action if these standards are breached. In addition, the general cultural rules within which the parties operate may moderate behaviour. These will not usually be codified in law but may take semi-legal status as guidelines from professional bodies.

As mentioned at the beginning of this section, these mechanisms have not been designed as a specific response to the prisoners' dilemma. They are long-standing parts of the warp and weft of business deals. What the game-theoretical perspective adds is a coherent and unified theory of why these mechanisms work in terms of modifying rational behaviour and ensuring that entrepreneurs and investors can avoid *rationally* deciding not to work together and so both lose. Entrepreneurs often complain about the impositions investors make: the need to invest their own money, the right that investors claim to intervene in the business, and the threat of punitive action if the venture does not perform. The game-theoretical perspective suggests that, however onerous, such mechanisms are necessary to make the entrepreneur–investor relationship happen at all.

Summary of key ideas

- Financial support is a critical factor in the success of the new venture.

- Suppliers of investment capital are differentiated by the *amount* of capital they will supply, the *risks* they will undertake and the way in which they will expect to see their investment *mature*.

- Investors select investment opportunities by *filtering* them for suitability. This filtering process has formal analysis and informal 'intuitive' aspects.

- The vast majority of investment proposals are rejected.

- Effective entrepreneurs approach investors with an understanding of the *questions* for which they will need answers before they decide to support the venture.

- Professional investors are acute to, and dismissive of, extravagent claims in business plans.

- The prisoners' dilemma provides an illuminating game-theoretical model of entrepreneur–investor interactions and can explain why entrepreneurs and investors can sometimes fail to agree to mutually rewarding deals.

Research themes

The entrepreneur–investor relationship is a subject of considerable research. This often involves quite sophisticated finance theory. However, there are a number of valuable projects that might be undertaken that do not demand such technical knowledge.

The nature of the funding gap

Entrepreneurs often complain of a funding gap: their inability to gain investment for start-up or business expansion. It has been proposed that this funding gap is not so much due to market failure as to a lack of communication between entrepreneurs and investors. The framework described in section 20.2 suggests the information that entrepreneurs should be offering to potential investors in relation to the questions that investors need answering.

Conduct a two-stage survey with practising entrepreneurs who have received funding and (ideally) some who have not and with capital providers (ideally different types such as high street banks and venture capitalists). In the first stage, have the investors spontaneously identify the information they require and the entrepreneurs spontaneously indicate the information they feel investors want. How do these compare? Are there any pieces of information which the entrepreneurs do not feel is necessary but which the investors value?

In the second stage, present a list of information categories based on the framework here described. Have the investors indicate their prioritisation of, and valuation of, those categories. Similarly, have the entrepreneurs indicate their views of the priority and value of that information for investors. Again, is there any mismatch between the priority and value ascribed to the information between the two groups? Have entrepreneurs who have received funding a better understanding than those who have not? Summarise by making recommendations as to how entrepreneurs might be better supported in making funding bids.

Entrepreneurs, investors and the prisoners' dilemma

Game-theoretical studies are mathematically challenging, but the prisoners' dilemma model developed in section 20.4 does make some qualitative predictions. As with the study above, identify three groups: entrepreneurs who have received funding, entrepreneurs who have not received funding, and relevant investors. A prisoners' dilemma will arise if the entrepreneur is overstating the potential of the venture and understating its risks and if investors are assuming that they are doing so. Survey the three groups, inquiring into their attitudes towards the communication of potential and risks. With the entrepreneurs, present a series of propositions such as 'it is best to be optimistic in presenting potential returns', 'it is best to be pessimistic when presenting potential returns', 'it is best to understate risks', and so on, and have them state their agreement or otherwise (use a Likert scale: agree strongly, agree a little, . . . , disagree strongly). With the investors, present propositions such as 'entrepreneurs always tend to understate risks', 'entrepreneurs are usually overoptimistic when predicting returns', and so on. Again, have the investors indicate their agreement with these propositions. Do the entrepreneurs' and investors' attitudes suggest that a prisoners' dilemma might occur? Is there any significant difference between the attitudes of the entrepreneurs who were successful in gaining funding and those who were not? If so, summarise by making recommendations as to how the dilemma might be resolved.

Key readings

The following article provides a very clear statement as to the venture capital selection process. It is somewhat idealised, but useful as a starting point for developing more realistic models of the process:

Tyebjee, T.T. and Bruno, A.V. (1984) 'A model of venture capital investment activity', *Management Science*, Vol. 30, No. 9, pp. 1051–66.

A good comparator (based on a case study rather than inductive methodology) is:

Fried, V.H. and Hisrich, R.D. (1994) 'Towards a model of venture capital investment decision making', *Financial Management*, Vol. 23, No. 3, pp. 28–37.

An extremely entertaining but highly insightful and educational paper that always goes down well in tutorials:

Kawasaki, G. (2001) 'The top ten lies of entrepreneurs', *Harvard Business Review*, Jan. pp. 22–3.

Suggestions for further reading

Berger, A.N. and Udell, G.F. (2002) 'Small business credit availability and relationship lending: the importance of bank organisational structure', *Economic Journal*, Vol. 112, pp. F32–F53.

Blanchflower, D.G. and Oswald, A.J. (1998) 'What makes and entrepreneur?' *Journal of Labour Economics*, Vol. 16, No. 1, pp. 26–60.

Boocock, G. and Woods, M. (1997) 'The evaluation criteria used by venture capitalists: evidence from a UK venture fund', *International Small Business Journal*, Vol. 16, No. 1, pp. 36–57.

Brau, J.C. (2002) 'Do banks price owner-manager agency costs? An examination of small business borrowing', *Journal of Small Business Management*, Vol. 40, No. 4, pp. 273–86.

Cable, D.M. and Shane, S. (1997) 'A prisoner's dilemma approach to entrepreneur–venture capitalist relationships', *Academy of Management Review*, Vol. 22, No. 1, pp. 142–176.

Camp, S.M. and Sexton, D.L. (1992) 'Trends in venture capital investment: implications for high-technology firms', *Journal of Small Business Management*, July, pp. 11–19.

Carter, R.B. and Van Auken, H.E. (1994) 'Venture capital firms' preferences for projects in particular stages of development', *Journal of Small Business Management*, Jan. pp. 60–73.

Choudhury, M.A. (2001) 'Islamic venture capital', *Journal of Economic Studies*, Vol. 28, No. 1, pp. 14–33.

Cook, P. (2001) 'Finance and small and medium-sized enterprise in developing countries', *Journal of Developmental Entrepreneurship*, Vol. 6, No. 1, pp. 17–40.

de Meza, D. and Southey, C. (1996) 'The boorower's curse: optimism, finance and entrepreneurship', *Economic Journal*, Vol. 106, pp. 375–86.

Devashis, M. (2000) 'The venture capital industry in India', *Journal of Small Business Management*, Vol. 38, No. 2, pp. 67–79.

Fiet, J.O. (1995) 'Risk avoidance strategies in venture capital markets', *Journal of Management Studies*, Vol. 32, No. 4, pp. 551–74.

Fletcher, M. (1995) 'Decision-making by Scottish bank managers', *International Journal of Entrepreneurial Behaviour and Research*, Vol. 1, No. 2, pp. 37–53.

Fried, V.H. and Hisrich, R.D. (1988) 'Venture capital research: past, present and future', *Entrepreneurship: Theory and Practice*, Fall, pp. 15–28.

Gompers, P. and Lerner, J. (2001) 'The venture capital revolution', *Journal of Economic Perspectives*, Vol. 15, No. 2, pp. 145–68.

Haar, N.E., Starr, J. and Macmillan, I.C. (1988) 'Informal risk capital investors: investment patterns on the east coast of the USA', *Journal of Business Venturing*, Vol. 3, pp. 11–29.

Hall, J. and Hofer, C.W. (1993) 'Venture capitalists' decision criteria in new venture evaluation', *Journal of Business Venturing*, Vol. 8, pp. 25–42.

Harris, S. (1995) 'Managing organizations to address the finance gap', *International Journal of Entrepreneurial Behaviour and Research*, Vol. 1, No. 3, pp. 63–82.

Harrison, R.T. and Dibben, M.R. (1997) 'The role of trust in the informal investor's investment decision: an exploratory analysis', *Entrepreneurship Theory and Practice*, Summer, pp. 63–81.

Harrison, R.T. and Mason, C. (1996) 'Developments in the promotion of informal venture capital in the UK', *International Journal of Entrepreneurial Behaviour and Research*, Vol. 2, No. 2, pp. 6–33.

Hills, G.E. (1985) 'Market analysis and the business plan: venture capitalists' perceptions', *Journal of Small Business Management*, Vol. 23, pp. 38–46.

Kawasaki, G. (2001) 'The top ten lies of entrepreneurs', *Harvard Business Review*, Jan., pp. 22–3.

Kerins, F., Smith, J.K. and Smith, R. (2004) 'Opportunity cost of capital for venture capital investors and entrepreneurs', *Journal of Financial and Quantitative Analysis*, Vol. 39, No. 2, pp. 385–405.

Knight, R.M. (1994) 'Criteria used by venture capitalists: a cross cultural analysis', *International Small Business Journal*, Vol. 13, No. 1, pp. 26–37.

Landström, H. (1993) 'Informal risk capital in Sweden and some international comparisons', *Journal of Business Venturing*, Vol. 8, pp. 525–40.

Macmillan, I.C., Siegel, R. and Subba Narashima, P.N. (1985) 'Criteria used by venture capitalists to evaluate new venture proposals', *Journal of Business Venturing*, Vol. 1, pp. 119–28.

Macmillan, I.C., Zeeman, L. and Subba Narashima, P.N. (1987) 'Effectiveness of criteria used by venture capitalists in the venture screening process', *Journal of Business Venturing*, Vol. 2, pp. 123–38.

Maier, II, J.B. and Walker, D.A. (1987) 'The role of venture capital in financing small business', *Journal of Business Venturing*, Vol. 2, pp. 207–14.

Mason, C. and Harrison, R. (1996) 'Why 'business angels' say no: a case study of opportunities rejected by an informal investor syndicate', *International Small Business Journal*, Vol. 14, No. 2, pp. 35–51.

Morris, M.H., Watling, J.W. and Schindehutte, M. (2000) 'Venture capitalist involvement in portfolio companies: insights from South Africa', *Journal of Small Business Management*, July, pp. 68–77.

Murnighan, J.K. (1994) 'Game theory and organizational behaviour', *Research in Organisational Behavior*, Vol. 16, pp. 83–123.

Murray, G.C. (1992) 'A challenging marketplace for venture capital', *Long Range Planning*, Vol. 25, No. 6, pp. 79–86.

Norton, E. and Tenenbaum, B.H. (1992) 'Factors affecting the structure of US venture capital deals', *Journal of Small Business Management*, July, pp. 20–9.

Ray, D.M. and Turpin, D.V. (1993) 'Venture capital in Japan', *International Small Business Journal*, Vol. 11, No. 4, pp. 39–56.

Rea, R.H. (1989) 'Factors affecting success and failure of seed capital/start-up negotiations', *Journal of Business Venturing*, Vol. 4, pp. 149–58.

Riquelme, H. and Watson, J. (2002) 'Do venture capitalists' implicit theories on new business success/failure have empirical validity?', *International Small Business Journal*, Vol. 20, No. 4, pp. 395–420.

Roberts, E.B. (1991) 'High stakes for high-tech entrepreneurs: understanding venture capital decision making', *Sloan Management Review*, Winter, pp. 9–20.

Rock, A. (1987) 'Strategy v tactics from a venture capitalist', *Harvard Business Review*, Nov./Dec., pp. 63–7.

Schilit, W.K. (1987) 'How to obtain venture capital', *Business Horizons*, May/June, pp. 76–81.

Shepherd, D.A. (1999) 'Venture capitalist's introspections: a comparison of 'in use' and 'espoused' decision policies', *Journal of Small Business Management*, Vol. 37, No. 2, pp. 76–87.

Steiner, L. and Greenwood, R. (1995) 'Venture capitalist relationships in the deal structuring and post-investment stages of new firm creation', *Journal of Management Studies*, Vol. 32, No. 3, pp. 337–57.

Sweeting, R.C. (1991) 'UK venture capital funds and the funding of new technology-based businesses: process and relationships', *Journal of Management Studies*, Vol. 28, No. 6, pp. 601–22.

Tashiro, Y. (1999) 'Business angels in Japan', *Venture Capital*, Vol. 1, No. 3, pp. 259–73.

The Economist (2005) 'The hidden wealth of the poor: a survey of microfinance', 5 Nov.

Tyebjee, T.T. and Bruno, A.V. (1984) 'A model of venture capital investment activity', *Management Science*, Vol. 30, No. 9, pp. 1051–66.

Van Auken, H.E. (2001) 'Financing small technology-based companies: the relationship between familiarity with capital and ability to price and negotiate investment', *Journal of Small Business Management*, Vol. 39, No. 3, pp. 240–58.

Von Neumann, J. and Morgenstern, O. (2001) *Theory of Games and Economic Behavior*. Dusseldorf: Verlag Wirtschaft und Finanzen (first published 1944).

Wright, M. and Robbie, K. (1998) 'Venture capital and private equity: a review and synthesis', *Journal of Business Finance and Accounting*, Vol. 25, No. 5/6, pp. 521–70.

Zacharakis, A.L., Meyer, G.D. and DeCastro, J. (1999) 'Differing perceptions of new venture failure: a matched exploratory study of venture capitalists and entrepreneurs', *Journal of Small Business Management*, Vol. 37, No. 3, pp. 1–14.

Selected case material

CASE 20.1

17 December 2005   **FT**

Inventor taps into funding support

JONATHAN MOULES

The inventor of a device to prevent baths from overflowing, a go-karting enthusiast and an IT business in the west country secured support of up to £150,000 at a funding competition at London's Excel Centre, sponsored by the National Council for Graduate Entrepreneurship.

The budding entrepreneurs were among 20 hopefuls who presented their business plans in a five-minute pitch to a panel of business angels, including Jacqueline Gold, managing director of Ann Summers and Knickerbox, and self-made millionaire and broadcaster Jonathan Jay.

James Barnham, who came up with the idea to prevent baths overflowing when taps are left on, walked away with the promise of £150,000 in funding and the offer of mentoring by two of the panel experts.

Mary Ann Horley, who plans to set up a series of blogs on her website (www.kartlink.com) was praised for her innovative product and has also been offered advice and support.

Charles Radclyffe has run Titan Computing, which provides emergency IT support in Devon, for the past three years. He was told to aim higher than his request for £250,000 in funding.

Although he did not receive any money on the day, he has since entered direct negotiations with the panellists for the money.

Source: Jonathan Moules, 'Inventor taps into funding support', *Financial Times*, 17 December 2005, p. 20. Copyright © 2005 The Financial Times Limited.

CASE 20.2

22 January 2005 FT

'I am sceptical about people who are too smooth'

ALEXANDER JOLLIFFE

Bruce Macfarlane, a director of MMC Ventures, a venture capital syndicate, is paid to sniff out up-and-coming entrepreneurs. And he is seeing more and more of them scrambling for cash to back their new undertakings.

MMC, which invests in small companies needing between £500,000 and £2m to expand, receives about 600 business plans a year and this 'deal flow' is rising. 'It's an indication of the animal spirits in the UK,' he says.

Sifting through this number of investment opportunities is a challenge. But Macfarlane, a former managing director for UK investment banking at Merrill Lynch, says there are normally several characteristics that sort the wheat from the chaff.

'It depends how hungry they are. We look for people who have mortgaged their houses, borrowed from their grandmothers – one guy had mortgaged two flats.'

He also looks for businessmen who are looking to make money by selling their businesses, not by paying themselves fat salaries. 'We want people who are driven by the return on their shares, who see the equity as their retirement prospect. The salaries should be modest. We would certainly be turned off if we saw numbers above £80,000 because you don't want people to be too comfortable.'

Macfarlane concedes that it can be difficult distinguishing between those people who are good at running businesses from those who are just good at doing presentations.

But he argues his past banking experience has helped him. 'Having been in the investment banking world, I'm sceptical about people who are too smooth.'

Another tell-tale sign that puts him off are businesses who garnish their letter heads with the names of the great and the good of the business world without getting them to invest.

'If companies have great names on their boards, but those people have not put any money in, that's a gigantic negative. We don't put anyone on the board who hasn't put cash in.'

MMC employs full-time executives to analyse small companies' business plans.

But it is unusual because it has a network of experienced businesspeople – from lawyers to company directors – who invest in the

▶

423

companies, and these people all pay to be part of MMC's network.

Some of these experienced businesspeople also work as directors of the small companies they invest in and they all pay £10,000 to join the network. Most of these people have other jobs and they feel the entry fee is justified, partly because they get access to MMC's 'deal flow'. The entry fee is also designed to ensure that people are serious about contributing their experience and helping the small companies to grow. 'The syndicate is not stuffed with retired guys whose wives don't want to see them round the house,' says Macfarlane.

In one case an executive got so enthusiastic about a company in which he had invested that he braved a tricky set of connecting flights and flew from Bangalore, where he worked, to Belfast, for an 'off-site' meeting with the management.

The companies that MMC has invested in include Neoss, which has a patented dental implants system. Macfarlane favoured it because he expected strong demand for dentistry. He cites research by Goldman Sachs and Merrill Lynch showing that the worldwide market has been growing recently at about 30 per cent a year.

However, there was little activity in the UK, and MMC expected this to change as Britons followed the trend in countries including Germany and Switzerland to care for their teeth. Macfarlane also believed that Neoss could make good profits without running into competition from big companies in the industry. 'In the US, you don't see politicians with dodgy teeth. And as for competition, we took the view that big companies wouldn't care because they had double digit growth.'

Another stock was SupaPlants, a spinout from Sheffield University that developed a gel that prolongs the life of supermarket herbs.

But investing in small companies, which might have untested products or strategies, can be dangerous. Macfarlane accepts this. 'Early stage investing by definition is highly risky,' he says. 'If you get it wrong, it has the worst returns of all private equity.'

He points to an internet art company that MMC Ventures invested in, which Macfarlane says would have hit serious problems if it had not merged with a competitor. 'It was too ambitious: it was trying to sell new art, online, to people who had never bought art before. It was part of the internet bubble.'

In spite of these risks, MMC is willing to invest in companies that are not generating sales or profits. Macfarlane says he and his colleagues value companies based on their knowledge of comparable businesses, their assessment of the management team and the market opportunity.

'It does come down to our instinct.'

Another possible danger for investors in MMC's £7m fund relates to its fairly limited range of investments. MMC's fund has only done 10 deals so far but Macfarlane says that improving deal flows mean that investors should be exposed to four or five new transactions a year, so they should quickly build diversified portfolios.

Macfarlane is a firm believer that these risks go hand in hand with high returns. He and two colleagues who jointly founded MMC invest their own money in every company which the fund finances. 'If you get it right, early stage investing has the best performance.'

Macfarlane contrasts 'early stage' investing with 'later stage' and 'mature stage'. MMC focuses on the first of these phases, during which companies develop and market their products, expand their sales or manufacturing capacity and secure the working capital needed to fund expansion.

In spite of this, of the ten companies MMC has invested in since April 1999, two have floated on AIM, the junior stock market for small companies.

These successes have helped MMC to ensure that MMC's portfolio companies have produced a gross return of 33.5 per cent a year between 1999 and 30 June 2004.

The return includes tax relief for Enterprise Investment Schemes, tax shelters for investing in small companies. But even excluding these generous tax breaks, the underlying returns are still 23.3 per cent a year between 1999 and July 2004.

As for the queue of small businesses eager to raise funds from MMC Ventures, Macfarlane sees it as evidence that capital to finance small businesses is in short supply as many of these smaller companies will have sought – and failed – to find finance elsewhere.

'The fact that people are finding us tells you that there's a gap in the market. It's far easier to borrow £50m in this country than to raise £500,000.'

Source: Alexander Jolliffe, '"I am sceptical about people who are too smooth"', *Financial Times*, 22 January 2005, p. 27. Copyright © 2005 The Financial Times Limited.

Discussion points

1. Compare and contrast the issues the three ventures described will face in obtaining funding.

2. What would a venture capitalist look for when evaluating the strategy of a prospective investment?

CHAPTER 21

The strategic window: identifying and analysing the gap for the new business

Chapter overview

Entrepreneurs identify and exploit new opportunities. This chapter considers why there will always be gaps in a market that the entrepreneur can exploit, despite the presence of established businesses. The chapter goes on to develop a picture of opportunity as a strategic 'window' through which the new venture must pass.

21.1 Why existing businesses leave gaps in the market

Key learning outcome

An understanding of why an established business environment will always leave opportunities for the entrepreneur.

In principle, established businesses are in a strong position relative to entrepreneurial entrants. This is because they have gained experience in their markets through serving customers; they have experience in operating their businesses; they have established themselves in a secure network of relationships with customers and suppliers; they face lower risks and so their cost of capital is usually lower; they may enjoy lower costs by having developed experience curve economies; and they have an established output volume which gives them economy of scale cost advantage.

Despite these advantages, entrepreneurs do compete effectively against established, even securely entrenched, players. They identify and exploit new opportunities despite the presence of experienced competitors. There is always, it seems, a better way of doing things. There are a variety of reasons why existing businesses leave gaps in the market that the innovative, entrepreneurial venture can exploit.

Established businesses fail to see new opportunities

Opportunities do not present themselves, they have to be actively sought out. A business organisation has not merely a way of *doing* things; it also has a way of *seeing* things. The way in which a business scans the business environment for new opportunities is linked to the systems and processes that make up that organisation. *Organisational inertia*, that is, resistance to change in response to changing circumstances, is a well-documented phenomenon. An established organisation can become complacent. It can look back on its early success and take its market for granted. Its opportunity-scanning systems can become rigid and bureaucratised or caught up in political infighting. It might adopt a particular perspective or 'dominant logic' which leads it to see the world in a certain way. That perspective may not change as the world changes. As a result it may be less attuned to identifying new opportunities in the market than a hungry new entrant. For example, IBM missed the opportunity for software operating systems that would enable Bill Gates's Microsoft to become one of the world's largest companies.

New opportunities are thought to be too small

The value of a new opportunity must be seen as relative to the size of the business which might pursue it. The chance to gain an extra £100,000 of business will mean far more to a business with a turnover of £1 million than to one with a turnover of £100 million. As a result, 'small' opportunities may be ignored, or at least not pursued vigorously, by large, established players. The smaller new entrant will, however, find them attractive. They may prove to be just the foot in the door that they need.

Technological inertia

Opportunities are pursued by innovation. An innovation is founded on some technological approach. However, a technology is simply a way of doing things. It is a means to address a need. An established organisation may regard its business as based on a particular technology rather than the serving of customer needs. It might prefer to rely on the technological approach 'it's good at'. However, new technological approaches to satisfying needs can develop rapidly. Such technological inertia leaves the field open for new entrants to make technological innovation the basis of their business.

For example, the last mechanical typewriter manufacturer closed recently. The typewriter industry had a great deal of expertise in designing, manufacturing and marketing machines which produced documents. The manufacturers were very good at their business. However, they defined themselves in terms of the mechanical technology used by typewriters. They did not think of themselves as providing customers with a document management service. As a result, they were easy prey for a whole generation of entrepreneurs who moved in with electronic word processing products, which provided a much better way to manage documents.

Cultural inertia

Along with its technology, an established business has its own 'way of doing things'. This way of doing things – its culture – influences the way in which it delivers value to its customers. The best way to deliver value to customers will change as the competitive climate evolves. If the business does not change its way of doing things to meet new challenges then it may not be in a position to exploit new opportunities. New entrants may take advantage of this by adopting a culture more appropriate to the altered climate. Thus the Swedish entrepreneur Jan Carlzon turned Scandinavian Airline Systems (SAS) into a great aviation success story by changing its culture from one where the needs of aircraft and airports were managed to one where the needs of customers were given priority.

Internal politics

Managers in established organisations often engage in political infighting. This occurs when individuals and groups do not feel their interests and goals are aligned with those each other or with those of the organisation as a whole. Organisations pursue new opportunities in order to achieve their objectives. Being focused on a new opportunity demands a commitment to objectives. If this is not present then, at best, there will be disagreement on the value that particular opportunities present. At worst, different factions will work against one other. As a result, opportunities will slip by. This will leave the more focused and less political new entrant free to exploit them.

Anti-trust actions by government

Governments are concerned to ensure that monopolies do not distort the workings of an economy. If a firm is felt to be gaining too much dominance in a market, then the government may be tempted to act against its growth. By definition, this action will work against the dominating players and so will favour the new entrant. An example of this is the US Supreme Court's ruling that the giant Microsoft be split into two. The court's ruling is based on the belief that Microsoft's monolithic market power is restricting entrepreneurial entry into the sector and hindering the development of smaller players who are already present.

Government intervention to support the new entrant

In general, governments are acutely aware of the importance, both economic and political, of small and fast-growing new firms in an economy. They are responsible for providing economic efficiency, for bringing innovations to market and for creating new jobs. As a result, governments are tempted to provide support for both the smaller business and the new entrant. This can take the form of tax incentives and more liberal employment laws or it can be more direct and involve cheap loans and credit. Support may also be offered for technical development, education and consulting. Again, this support tips the balance in favour of the new entrant.

Economic perspectives on entrepreneurial gaps

The points made above relate to how businesses function. They are *institutional* effects. In these terms, established businesses leave gaps largely because they lack adeptness in exploiting some opportunities, leaving a space into which entrepreneurs can move. The classical economic perspective suggests that such institutional effects represent a failure of economic efficiency and that the managers of established businesses are not acting fully rationally. If managers of established firms were more effective, then they could devise strategies that would keep out entrepreneurial upstarts.

However, a number of recent mathematical studies are challenging this conventional view. An analysis by Arend (1999) suggests it may not always be the case that incumbents will exploit new opportunities, *even if they are aware of them*. In this study, Arend explores economic interactions in quite a subtle way. The study suggests that, under some circumstances, established businesses may leave gaps for new entrepreneurial entrants (who will become competitors) even though they are aware of the entrepreneurial opportunity that is available and act rationally to exploit it.

Arend's argument is developed using a game-theoretical perspective. Game theory is a branch of mathematics that is concerned with the way in which a set of agents will act to achieve the outcomes they desire given that the actions of one agent will affect the outcomes of all others (see section 20.4). Individual agents must judge the actions (the *strategy*) they adopt, given the likely actions of other agents, knowing that other agents will modify their strategies in response to the actions they take. Game theory has proved to be very important to economics, particularly in describing competitive behaviour.

Reflecting the mathematical rigour of game theory, Arend's article is somewhat technical. However, the basic argument can be stated qualitatively. Classical economics suggests that competing firms have only one optimal strategy if they wish to maximise profits. This conclusion is based on two assumptions, though: first, that all competitors have equal access to the technology that is used to create and deliver the industry's products (a condition economists refer to as *exogenous*); second, that this technology is fixed and does not change over time (technology is *stable*). In general terms, we can regard 'technology' as being the chance to exploit a new opportunity.

If we make the (more realistic) assumptions that technology is changing in a way that promises to make firms more efficient (new opportunities are coming along) and that all firms have equal access to this technology, then something interesting happens. Under these circumstances, firms have not one but two optimal strategies. Even though the technology (opportunity) is offered to the firm by the 'outside' world (firms do not have any research and development costs), they still face a cost in integrating that technology into their operations (that is, investing in exploiting the opportunity). The first strategy a firm can adopt is to ignore the technological advance, not face the cost of integrating it, and so maintain short-term profitability. This is referred to as a *static efficiency strategy*. The second option is to integrate the technology. This increases short-term costs but it offers the promise (with some risks) of increasing long-term profitability. This is referred to as the *dynamic efficiency strategy*. There is no (efficient) middle ground between these strategies. A firm must choose one or the other and both are equally valid attempts to maximise profits.

Using a game-theoretical argument, Arend demonstrates a remarkable result. Under such conditions, incumbent players will, in certain circumstances, ignore technological advances and allow new entrants to take advantage of them, *even if the new entrant eventually displaces them*. In doing so they are still acting rationally. This is because, once locked together in a competitive battle, at no point can the incumbent increase its profitability by switching to the new technology. Further, no such move can increase the total profitability of the two firms. Hence, even if managers were willing to make the move, investors with an interest in both firms would not support it.

While this argument may sound arcane, Arend uses it to make predictions about entrepreneurial entry under different situations of competition and technological change. His empirical evidence bears out the model. The conclusion is that the institutional 'inefficiency' of established players in exploiting new opportunities might not be inefficiency at all. Leaving gaps for entrepreneurs may just be an inevitable (and, for the wider world, a welcome) feature of competitive life.

In a similar vein, Ghemawat (2002) uses game-theoretical methods to explain why entrepreneurial new entrants were more inclined to be innovative than monopolistic incumbents in the telecommunications industry and the steel industry when it came to new product and new production process development, respectively. Another formal analysis, by Hirshleifer (2001), suggests a reason why new entrants can, despite their weakness relative to powerful incumbents, not only survive but also win the competitive battle. Hirshleifer considers a game-theoretical model of two competitors who can each dedicate their resources either to producing a particular good or service or to directly competing with rivals. Like all mathematical models of business interactions, this is based on simplifying assumptions, but these are not unrealistic if we consider an entrepreneur splitting their resources between, say, increasing production capacity or advertising against competitors. The discussion here considers the qualitative implications of the model, not its mathematical detail. Students interested in the detail should follow the reference.

Intuitively, we might argue that the more resource-rich (more powerful) player would be in an advantageous position. However, the model suggests that, at least under certain conditions, the weaker (resource-poorer) player can win. Hirshleifer calls this the 'paradox of power'. The model considers the interaction of the two competitors and asks, if they act rationally, how will they split their resources between 'production' and 'competition'. Given some assumptions (which are not particularly unrealistic), and certain conditions (which are likely to occur in some competitive battles), the model finds that the weaker player can gain more from competing than can the stronger player. In effect, the weaker player is in a position to 'tax' the stronger player through competition at a higher rate than the stronger can 'tax' the weaker, in which case the weaker player will win. Hence the 'paradox'.

Hirshleifer's model is largely theoretical, but it fits with the intuitive notion that entrepreneurs win against stronger competitors because they 'work' their resources harder and in a more agressive way. Hirshleifer's model is important in that it provides a counter to the 'resources equal power' paradigm. It provides a rational explanation of why entrepreneurs can sometimes win. Being theoretical, it is crying out for empirical validation, a point considered in the research theme at the end of this chapter. A somewhat salutory reminder that the entry of an entrepreneur into a market does not imply that if they win, others lose is provided by Bhide (2000). There are scenarios where harmony, rather than strife, may emerge.

A word of warning

The large, established business, despite its inherent advantages, leaves gaps into which the ambitious new entrant can move because the large business often undervalues new opportunities, is complacent about them and is unresponsive owing to internal inertias. While exploiting this, entrepreneurs should never forget that this is a fate that can also await them as their businesses grow.

21.2 The strategic window: a visual metaphor

Metaphors are ever-present in our communication. They represent an attempt to illuminate an idea by drawing attention to something it is like. Understanding is created because we can draw parallels between the two ideas and see how the interconnectedness of themes in one idea might be reflected in the other. Metaphors may be *active*. We can use one deliberately to create effect. For example, we can say that an entrepreneur is like the 'captain of a ship' and the idea of the entrepreneur taking charge and leading a group who share an interest and taking them somewhere new is created. At other times, metaphors may be *dormant*. A dormant metaphor is one that is used frequently and we may not recognise it as a metaphor unless we think about it. As noted in Chapter 13, the word 'organisation' shares its roots with the words 'organism' and 'organic'. This dormant metaphor is reflected in much thinking about organisations. An *extinct* metaphor is one that we use so often that we may never recognise that it is a metaphor. Note the visual metaphor implied in the use of the words 'see', 'draw', 'parallel' and 'reflected' in the sentences above. An active metaphor that can be used to help us picture, and remember the details of, the process of identifying, evaluating and exploiting a new business opportunity is that of the *strategic window*.

The first stage in this metaphor is to picture a solid wall. This represents the competitive environment into which the entrepreneur seeks to enter. The wall is solid because of competition from established businesses. Those businesses are active in delivering products and services to customers in an effective way. The entrepreneur can do nothing new or better and so new value cannot be created. However, as we discussed in the previous section, established businesses leave gaps. There are areas where entrepreneurs *can* do something new and better. These gaps represent windows of opportunity through which the entrepreneur can move. It is through the window that the entrepreneur can see the 'whole new world' that they wish to create. The first task of the entrepreneur is to scan the business environment and find out where the gaps, the windows, are.

Having spotted a window the entrepreneur must measure it. The entrepreneur must be sure that the window – the opportunity – is big enough to justify the investment needed to open it. Opening the window represents the start-up stage of the venture. Moving thorough the window means developing the business and delivering new value to customers.

The final stage is closing the window. The window must be closed because, if it is not, competitors will be able to follow the entrepreneur through and exploit the opportunity themselves. Closing the window refers to building in competitive advantage, in short, ensuring that the venture's customers keep coming back so that competitors are locked out.

This metaphor – opportunity as a window, exploiting that opportunity as moving through the window – is a powerful *aide-mémoire* for analysing, and planning, the process of opportunity identification and exploitation. We now explore each stage in more detail.

Seeing the window: scanning for new opportunities

The solid wall presented by existing players must be scanned to find the windows, that is, to spot the gaps in what the existing players offer to the market. This process demands an active approach to identifying new opportunities and to innovating in response to them.

Locating the window: positioning the new venture

Developing an understanding of where the window is *located* demands an understanding both of the *positioning* of the new offering in the marketplace relative to existing products and services, and of how the venture can position itself in the marketplace relative to existing players to take best advantage of the opportunity presented.

Measuring the window

Measuring the window involves evaluating the opportunity and recognising the potential it offers to create new value. In short, it means finding out how much the opportunity might be worth. This demands getting to grips with the market for the innovation, measuring its size, understanding its dynamics and trends, evaluating the impact the innovation might make in it and ascertaining how much customers might be willing to spend on it. Measuring the window also demands that the entrepreneur develop an understanding of the risks the venture might face.

Opening the window: gaining commitment

Having identified, located and measured the window, the next stage is to *open* it. Opening the window means turning vision into reality, i.e. actually starting the new business. Critical to this stage is the need to get stakeholders to make a commitment to the venture, to attract investors and employees, to develop a new set of relationships and to establish the venture within its network. Once the window is opened, then the entrepreneur can move through it, metaphorically speaking, by starting up the business.

Closing the window: sustaining competitiveness

Once the window has been opened and the entrepreneur has passed through it then the window must be closed again. If it is not, then competitors will follow the entrepreneur through and exploit the opportunity as well. This will reduce the potential of the entrepreneur's business. Closing the window to stop competitors following through means creating a long-term *sustainable competitive advantage* for the business. This provides the basis on which the entrepreneur can build the security and stability of the business and use it to earn long-term rewards.

Each of these stages presents itself to the entrepreneur as a series of *decisions*. Developing the business means addressing those decisions. The following four chapters explore these decisions in detail.

Summary of key ideas

- A business environment is full of opportunities because existing businesses always leave gaps. There is always the potential to create new value. This may be because of both institutional failings on the part of incumbents and game-theoretical interactions between competitors.

- The *strategic window* is a visual metaphor which allows entrepreneurs to make sense of the opportunities they pursue.

- The six stages of the strategic window are: *spotting, locating, measuring, opening, moving through* and *closing*.

Research themes

Note: This chapter introduces the idea of the strategic window metaphor in general terms and Chapters 22 to 25 expand on its different stages. Research ideas specific to each stage are given at the end of each chapter, but the interested student may like to consider the integration of projects from different stages into a wider project dealing with the metaphor in its broader context.

Entrepreneurs' narratives of opportunity identification

Entrepreneurs usually love to tell stories, not least about how they got the inspiration for the venture they started. The strategic window metaphor offers a means of structuring such narratives. Select a pool of entrepreneurs (practising entrepreneurs at the novice or later stage should be prioritised). Using an interview, invite them to discuss freely how they identified a new opportunity, innovated to take advantage of it, evaluated the potential for the innovation, initiated and developed the venture and built in sustainable advantage. This open-ended discussion should be allowed before the entrepreneur is prompted to discuss particular aspects in more detail. How does this narrative fit with the strategic window metaphor? Does the metaphor account for the different stages described for the venture? Is the order of the narrative in line with that of the metaphor? The interview may conclude with the entrepreneur being introduced to the metaphor and being asked if it makes sense of their experience and allows them to describe it better.

Key readings

Abdel's paper emphasises the dynamic nature of competition and the fact that the space for the new competitor does not stay open for long.

Abel, D.F. (1978) 'Strategic windows', *Journal of Marketing*, July, pp. 21–6.

A good, stimulating discussion paper about what makes a good business idea:

Kim, W.C. and Mauborgne, R. (2000) 'Knowing a winning business idea when you see one', *Harvard Business Review*, Sept./Oct., pp. 129–38.

Suggestions for further reading

Arend, R.J. (1999) 'Emergence of entrepreneurs following exogenous technological change', *Strategic Management Journal*, Vol. 20, pp. 31–47.

Bettis, R.A. and Prahalad, C.K. (1995) 'The dominant logic: retrospective and extension', *Strategic Management Journal*, Vol. 16, pp. 5–14.

Bhide, A. (2000) 'David and Goliath, reconsidered', *Harvard Business Review*, Vol. 78, No. 5, pp. 26–7.

Cyert, R.M., Kumar, P. and Williams, J.R. (1993) 'Information, market imperfections and strategy', *Strategic Management Journal*, Vol. 14, pp. 47–58.

Ghemawat, P. (2002) *Games Businesses Play: Cases and Models*. Cambridge, MA: MIT Press.

Hannan, M.T. and Freeman, J. (1984) 'Structural inertia and organisational change', *American Sociological Review*, Vol. 49, pp. 149–64.

Hirshleifer, J. (2001) 'The paradox of power', in *The Dark Side of the Force: Economic Foundations of Conflict Theory*. Cambridge: Cambridge University Press.

Prahalad, C.K. and Bettis, R.A. (1986) 'The dominant logic: a new linkage between diversity and performance', *Strategic Management Journal*, Vol. 7, pp. 485–501.

Yao, D.A. (1988) 'Beyond the reach of the invisible hand: impediments to economic activity, market failures and profitability', *Strategic Management Journal*, Vol. 9, pp. 59–70.

Selected case material

CASE 21.1

17 August 2005

The merino makes a break from the flock for a life of luxury

VIRGINIA MARSH

Open the Icebreaker outdoor clothing catalogue and you will see arty shots of mountains and lakes, and pensive looking men and women dressed in sleek black outfits. Do not expect to find many sheep, even though the Wellington-based company's outdoor clothing uses merino wool.

'Wool is our enemy,' says Jeremy Moon, chief executive. 'It is prickly, itchy and heavy and we didn't like wearing it when we were kids.'

Mr Moon is one of a handful of New Zealand-based entrepreneurs who, in the space of a decade, have helped create a new niche export industry for the country. This has been achieved by remarketing the wool of the merino flocks that inhabit the country's Southern Alps, a traditional product that had been in decline.

'There has been a radical shift, in a relatively short period of time, from merino being a raw material export into it developing high value markets,' says Cheryll Sotheran, director of creative industries at New Zealand Trade & Enterprise, a government agency.

Just 10 years ago, the merino segment had no strategic direction, little knowledge of its customers, limited new product or market development and suffered from a perception that all New Zealand wool was coarse, says Andrew Caughey, international marketing director at the New Zealand Merino Company.

Today, after being repositioned as a distinct fibre, it has become highly prized by international luxury labels such as John Smedley, the British knitwear group, and Loro Piana, the Italian suit and clothing company, which has developed its Zelander range of

CASE 21.1 CONT.

fabrics based on it. At home, it has been intrinsic to the success of new companies such as Icebreaker, which produces only merino clothing.

The idea of merino as a luxury product is not new. With a fibre valued as strong yet light and soft enough to be worn comfortably next to the skin, merino flocks were raised in Spain from the middle ages and for centuries could be exported only by the country's royal family. The fibre's technical qualities, such as durability, elasticity and ease of care, have been known since the 1950s, says Scott Champion, NZ Merino's research and innovation manager.

But, before the recent revival, merino had lost visibility. For decades, the wool industry in New Zealand – the world's second largest wool exporter, after Australia – relied on the International Wool Secretariat, owner of the Woolmark brand, for global marketing and for research and development, funded by a compulsory levy. By the mid-1990s, says John Brakenridge, chief executive of NZ Merino, there was dissatisfaction with this generic, global approach as well as rising concern at the shrinking relevance of wool as the popularity of fleece-based and other synthetic clothing grew. Both the broader New Zealand wool industry, and merino farmers in particular, decided to break away and form their own marketing organisations.

The approach of NZ Merino, the company that evolved from this initiative, has been two-pronged: it has created a separate identity and niche for merino and engineered a better commercial outcome for farmers.

'The idea was to be not production- but market-led and to work from the retail end backwards through the chain and align demand,' says Mr Caughey.

From the technical point of view, Mr Champion says moisture absorption is a key point of differentiation for merino – it soaks up moisture at a higher level and differently from synthetics, so it evaporates more easily.

Mr Moon's Icebreaker received an important early endorsement when Sir Peter Blake, the late yachtsmen, returned from a record-breaking round-the-world voyage saying he planned to throw away all his synthetic underwear after wearing the company's merino alternatives for 43 days.

Sustainability is also at the heart of NZ Merino's work with farmers.

When the organisation was formed, sales were conducted via auctions with volatile prices. Farmers had little idea who the end users were, let alone their requirements. Now, they are grouped into supplier clubs and about 70 per cent of local merino is sold through contracts arranged by NZ Merino. The company – which is owned by farmers and Wrightson, a local agriculture group – has also introduced a rigorous wool-grading system that enables it to match buyers with the most appropriate suppliers.

Looking ahead, Mr Brakenridge says the active outdoor clothing segment, the niche occupied by Icebreaker, is growing fastest. It already consumes about one-quarter of local merino production, up from just 5 per cent five years ago.

Source: Virginia Marsh, 'The merino makes a break from the flock for a life of luxury', *Financial Times*, 17 August 2005, p. 11. Copyright © 2005 The Financial Times Limited.

CASE 21.2

17 August 2005

As new investors rush in, old hands look further afield

JIM PICKARD

The last foray by British property groups to the European mainland – in the 1970s – ended in ignominious retreat.

Consequently, most listed companies and fund managers spent the 1980s and 1990s licking their wounds and sticking to the domestic market they knew best.

Until recently, only a few solitary pioneers such as Freeport and Gerald Ronson's Heron International were very active on the Continent.

But in the past year, some of the most conservative names in the business have reassessed the situation.

Yields in Britain are among the lowest in Europe, with some properties in London's West End selling for outrageous prices – a few have exchanged hands at yields of as little as 3.6 per cent in recent months.

In addition, borrowing rates are higher, giving investors a painful double whammy.

As a result, many managers are inclined to head for other countries despite the operational risks.

Schroders, Insight Investment, Prudential, Henderson and Grosvenor are among the fund managers to have announced big European investments. Capital & Regional, the listed co-investing fund manager, has just set up a German fund.

They have been joined by a throng of other buyers – Irish consortia, private British companies and individual investors as well as various international investors.

Some of these are taking the logic further. Paris and Milan may offer better returns than London, they say, but eastern Europe has even higher yields.

According to research published this week by Savills, the agents, yields in Warsaw and Prague are above 7.5 per cent but they are below 5 per cent in London, Dublin, Madrid, Zurich and Paris.

A few years ago it was mainly US opportunity funds run by Heitman, the real estate investment management firm, that were buying office blocks and shops in central and eastern Europe.

Now, however, the presence of conventional institutions such as Morley, ING or Germany's DIFA is unlikely to raise eyebrows in cities such as Prague.

Invesco Real Estate closed its second Central European Real Property Fund in January and is just completing a second closing, which is expected to take the fund up to €700m (£480m).

Paul Kennedy, Invesco's head of research, says attitudes have changed significantly. 'What is happening is, particularly in core Prague, core Warsaw and core Budapest, these markets have gone from being markets that are targeted by opportunistic investors or brave core investors to the Prudentials of this world.'

The higher yields of central and eastern Europe, say some, reflect certain risks: unemployment is high, prospects for growth in gross domestic product are unclear and property ownership rights can be opaque.

Yet some experts warn that it is no longer easy to make phenomenal returns in central Europe, given that prices have already jumped and competition for deals is fierce. Brenna O'Roarty, head of European research at

CASE 21.2 CONT.

Deutsche Bank Real Estate, asks: 'When you look at certain office markets in Hungary and the Czech Republic and then you look at a less risky market like Sweden, where yields are not that much lower, does it justify the risk?'

As a result, some of the more seasoned operators are starting to comb more obscure markets.

For some, this means secondary or tertiary cities in central Europe.

For others, it means trawling countries that have not yet joined the European Union, such as Romania and Bulgaria, or others, such as Russia and Ukraine, that may never do so.

A host of start-up funds and companies, often aimed at niche markets such as residential property on Bulgaria's Black Sea coastline, have appeared.

The market has seen flotations by Lewis Charles Sofia Property Fund, aimed at Bulgaria, First Croatia Properties, aimed at Croatia, and Dawnay Day Carpathian, which hopes to spend £750m on retail property across eastern Europe.

Grainger Trust, the residential property group, has started a joint venture in the Baltic States.

While most operators still blanche at the thought of Russia's opaque property market, others are keen.

Anton Bilton, a property entrepreneur, has set up a new AIM-listed vehicle called Raven Russia to invest in warehouses.

Invesco's latest fund is authorised to invest in Russia as well as Poland, Hungary and the Czech Republic.

Mr Kennedy, at Invesco, says: 'Russia is a very challenging market but we think there are reasons to go in and invest sensibly. You can still get decent yields of 11 to 12 per cent for decent office buildings.'

Source: Jim Pickard, 'As new investors rush in, old hands look further afield', *Financial Times*, 17 August 2005, p. 22. Copyright © 2005 The Financial Times Limited.

Discussion points

1. In what ways are a new market created by the opening of new markets to an existing product and a new market created by new branding opportunities similar and in what ways are they different?

2. What are the implications for the way in which prospective entrepreneurs evaluate and analyse the market?

CHAPTER 22

Seeing the window: scanning for opportunity

Chapter overview

The first stage in using the strategic window is identifying it. This chapter looks at how new opportunities may be spotted, screened and selected.

22.1 Types of opportunity available

Key learning outcome

An understanding of the types of opportunity that present themselves to the entrepreneur.

An opportunity is the chance to do something in a way which is both different from and better than the way it is done at the moment. It offers the possibility of delivering new value to the customer. In its details, every opportunity is different, but there are some common patterns in the way in which opportunities take shape.

The new product

The new product offers the customer a physical device which provides a new means to satisfy a need or to solve a problem. A new product may be based on existing technology or it might exploit new technological possibilities. It might also represent a chance to add value to an existing product by using an appropriate branding strategy.

The new service

The new service offers the customer an act, or a series of acts, which satisfy a particular need or solve a particular problem. Many new offerings have both 'product' and 'service' dimensions. Robert Worcester, for example, built the enormously successful market research business MORI, founded not so much on the basis that business and politicians wanted a *product* (market information) as on the recognition that they wanted a *service* that would help them make decisions.

New means of production

A new means of producing an existing product is not an opportunity in itself. It will offer an opportunity if it can be used to deliver *additional* value to the customer. This means the product must be produced at lower cost or in a way which allows greater flexibility in the way it is delivered to the customer. For example, Takami Takahashi, the founder of the diversified Japanese multinational Minebea, grew the business from being a small niche player in the ball-bearing market by exploiting its experience in small component manufacturing to offer low-cost products to the electronics, engineering and precision instruments markets.

New distribution route

A new way of getting the product to the customer means that the customer finds it easier, more convenient, or less time consuming to obtain the product or service. This may involve the venture's developing an innovative way of getting the product to the end-user or a new way of working with intermediaries.

Improved service

There is an opportunity to enhance the value of a product to the customer by offering an additional service element with it. This service often involves maintaining the product in some way but it can also be based on supporting the customer in using the product or offering them training in its use. Frederick Smith's inspiration for the US parcel service Federal Express was a recognition of the gap in the market for a business that would be dedicated to providing a high-quality parcel delivery service. This gap was left by existing suppliers, chiefly passenger airlines, which offered a parcel service as a sideline to use up excess weight capacity on aircraft but did not consider it to be an important part of their business, and so did not consider the service element to be important to their customers.

Relationship building

Relationships are built on trust, and trust adds value by reducing the cost needed to monitor contracts. Trust can provide a source of competitive advantage. It can be used to build networks which competitors find it hard to enter. A new opportunity presents itself if relationships which will be mutually beneficial to the entrepreneur and the customer can be built. Rowland 'Tiny' Rowland's ability to develop close and trusting relationships with African leaders was an important factor in the success of the Lonrho empire. The Saatchi brothers did not merely provide an advertising service, they also concentrated on building relationships with their clients.

Opportunities do not have to be 'pure'. It is often the case that a particular opportunity comprises a mixture of the above elements. A new product may demand an additional support service if customers are to find it attractive. Getting the product to them may demand that relationships are formed. The entrepreneur must take an open mind and a creative approach to the way in which opportunities may be exploited.

22.2 Methods of spotting opportunities

Key learning outcome

An appreciation of the methods which might be used to identify new opportunities.

It is often assumed that entrepreneurs are graced with some special kind of insight that enables them to see opportunities and the way in which they might be exploited. While creativity is certainly important, the view that entrepreneurs work purely by inspiration undervalues the extent to which they are rewarded for the hard work involved in actively seeking out and evaluating new opportunities. There are a variety of techniques that can be of help in this search. Some are rather rough and ready whereas others are more formal. Some are so straightforward the entrepreneur may not even realise that they are using them. They may be articulated in the form of a heuristic or rule of thumb. Others are complex and may demand the support of market research experts if they are to be used properly. It is useful to be aware of the ways in which a market may be scanned for new opportunities, and of the techniques available to assist in this process.

Heuristics

Entrepreneurial heuristics have been considered earlier in section 18.6. Heuristics are an integral part of creativity. The heuristics – the word literally means 'serving to find out' – that entrepreneurs call upon to generate business ideas can be seen to involve two types. The first are *analysis* heuristics. These are the cognitive strategies that entrepreneurs adopt in order to gain and integrate new information about the world, to understand the patterns in this information and to spot market gaps. The second are *synthesis* heuristics. Synthesis involves using a cognitive strategy to bring the ideas developed from analysis back together again in a new and creative way, generating a new perspective on customer needs and how they might be addressed. Analysis is about spotting opportunities; synthesis is about creating innovations that might exploit those opportunities. These two sets of heuristics lie at the centre of a process with information as an input and new business opportunities as an output (Figure 22.1). This process is *iterative*. Each cycle refines the insight into the opportunity and makes it clearer. This process may be made explicit but more often it is simply the way in which the entrepreneur has learnt (perhaps even *actively* taught themself) to develop a decision when faced with opportunities and challenges.

Heuristics are ultimately cognitive phenomena and interest in the cognitive basis of opportunity identification is growing. Cognitive models of entrepreneurial creativity are developed by Ardichvili *et al.* (2003) and Gaglio (2004). An international perspective on entrepreneurial opportunity cognition is introduced by Zahra *et al.* (2005).

Problem analysis

Problem analysis starts by identifying the needs that individuals or organisations have and the problems that they face. These needs and problems may be either explicit or implicit. They may or may not be recognised by the subject. The approach begins by asking the question, 'What could be better?' Having identified a problem, the next question is, 'How might this be solved?' An effective, rewarding solution represents the basis of a new opportunity for

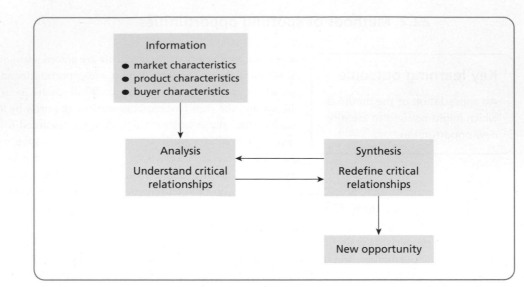

Figure 22.1 Heuristic discovery: information, analysis and synthesis

the entrepreneur. This approach demands a full understanding of customer needs and the technology that might be used to satisfy them.

Customer proposals

A new opportunity may be identified by a customer on the basis of a recognition of their own needs. The customer then offers the opportunity to the entrepreneur. Customer proposals take a variety of forms. At their simplest they are informal suggestions of the 'wouldn't it be great if . . .' type. Alternatively, they can take the form of a very detailed and formal brief, for example, if the customer is an organisation and a large expenditure is involved. Some organisations are active in 'reverse marketing' their needs to potential suppliers. Whatever the means used, an effective entrepreneur is *always* keen to solicit ideas from customers.

Creative groups

An entrepreneur does not have to rely on their own creativity. The best entrepreneurs are active in facilitating and harnessing the creativity of other people too. A creative group consists of a small number of potential customers or product experts who are encouraged to think about their needs in a particular market area and to consider how those needs might be better served. The customers may be the ultimate consumers of the product or service or they may be industrial buyers.

Creative groups need control and leadership and their comments to be properly analysed if they are to be informative. Getting people together in the right environment may also present a logistical challenge. Many market research companies offer specialist services in setting up, running and interpreting such creative group sessions.

Market mapping

Market mapping is a formal technique which involves identifying the dimensions defining a product category. These dimensions are based on the features of the product category. The features will differ depending on the type of product, but indicators such as price, quality and performance are quite common. The characteristics of *buyers* may also be used to provide a more detailed mapping. A map is created of the market by using the feature–buyer dimensions as *co-ordinates*. Products separate out into distinct groups depending on their location on the map. The map defines the *positioning* of the product. The map may be used to identify gaps in the market and to specify the type of product that might be used to fill them.

A variety of statistical techniques are available for sorting out the information and presenting it in a two-dimensional form. Often, though, just an imaginative sketch will do. The map then provides a powerful visual representation of what is in the market, how different offerings are related to each other and, critically, the gaps that are present in it.

Features stretching

Innovation involves offering something new. This means looking for ways in which changes might be made. Features stretching involves identifying the principal features which define a particular product or service and then seeing what happens if they are changed in some way. The trick is to test each feature with a range of suitable adjectives such as 'bigger', 'stronger', 'faster', 'more often', 'more fun' and so on, and see what results from such testing.

Anita Roddick's Body Shop provides a good example. Her initial inspiration was to provide good quality toiletries in packs much *smaller* than those offered by other high street retailers. (Environmentalism came later.)

Features blending

As with features stretching, features blending involves identifying the features which define particular products. Instead of just changing individual features, however, new products are created by blending together features from different products or services. This technique is often used in conjunction with features stretching. Both features stretching and features blending make good team exercises and can prove to be quite good fun. A good example here is Alan Sugar's success with the Amstrad stack hi-fi system which combined the features of CD player, tuner and amplifier in a single unit.

The combined approach

Effective entrepreneurs do not rely on inspiration alone. They actively encourage creativity by thinking methodically about the market areas in which they have expertise. They also encourage other people such as employees, independent technical experts and customers to be creative on their behalf. The techniques described above are not exclusive of each other. They may be used together. Using them in a new way offers the potential to identify new and unexploited opportunities. For example, Richard Branson, the chief executive of the highly diverse Virgin Group, is renowned for his ability to bring out the creative talents in those around him.

22.3 Screening and selecting opportunities

> **Key learning outcome**
>
> An understanding of the decisions to be taken in selecting opportunities.

Not all opportunities are equally valuable. A business with limited resources cannot pursue every opportunity with which it is faced. It must select those opportunities which are going to be the most rewarding. The key decisions in screening and selecting opportunities relate to the size of the opportunity, the investment necessary to exploit it, the rewards that will be gained and the risks likely to be encountered. Specifically, the entrepreneur's decision should be based on the answers to the following questions.

How large is the opportunity?

- How large is the market into which the innovation is to be placed? (What products will it compete with? What is the total value of their sales?)
- What share of the market is likely to be gained? (How competitive will it be against existing products? What percentage of customers can be reached? What fraction will convert to the innovation?)
- What gross margin (revenue minus costs) is likely? (What price can be obtained? What is the unit cost likely to be?)
- Over what period can the opportunity be exploited? (How long will customers be interested? How long before competitors move in?)

What investment will be necessary if the opportunity is to be exploited properly?

- What are the immediate capital requirements? (What investments in people, operating assets and communication will be required to start the business?)
- What will be the long-term and ongoing capital requirements? (What future investments will be necessary to continue exploiting the opportunity?)
- Does the business have access to the capital required?
- If the opportunity is as large as expected, will the business have sufficient capacity?
- If not, can it be expanded or be (profitably) offset to other organisations?
- What human resources will be needed? Are they available?

What is the likely return?

- What profits will be generated? (What will be the rates? What will costs be like?)
- Over what period?
- Is this attractive given the investment necessary? (How does return on investment compare with other investment options? What is the opportunity cost?)

What are the risks?

- How sound are the assumptions about the size of the opportunity? (How accurate were the data on markets? Have *all* competitor products been considered?)

- What if customers do not find the offering as attractive as expected?
- What if competitors are more responsive than expected? (Have all competitors been considered? How could they react in principle? How might they react in practice?)
- To what extent is success dependent on the support and goodwill of intermediaries and other third parties? (How will this goodwill be gained and maintained?)
- How sensitive will the exploitation be to the marketing strategy that has been adopted (particularly in relation to pricing, selling points against competitors, customers targeted)?
- Can adjustments be made to the strategy in the light of experience? How expensive will this be?
- Can additional resources be made available if necessary? (Will these be from internal sources or from investors?)
- What will be the effect on cash flow if revenues are lower than expected?
- What will be the effect on cash flow if costs are higher than expected?
- How should investors be prepared for these eventualities?
- How should future revenues be discounted?
- Under what circumstances might investors wish to make an exit? (Will this be planned or in response to a crisis?)
- If so, how will they do it? (By being paid from profit stream or by selling their holding?)

Opportunities only have meaning in relation to each other. The entrepreneur must select opportunities not in absolute terms but after comparing them with each other. A business (like an investor) will find an opportunity attractive only if it represents the *best* available investment option. Opportunities must be prioritised. They must compete with each other for the business's valuable resources. What matters is not so much cost as *opportunity* cost, that is, not the cost of actually using resources, but the potential returns lost because they were not used elsewhere.

22.4 Entrepreneurial innovation

Key learning outcome

An appreciation of market, technological and capability knowledge as the basis for entrepreneurial innovation.

Innovation lies at the heart of the entrepreneurial process and is a means to the exploitation of opportunity. Economically, innovation is the combining of resources in a new and original way. Entrepreneurially, it is the discovery of a new and better way of doing things. Innovation goes beyond invention. The new way does not stand on its own merits. It will create new value only if it offers customers an improved way to approach tasks and to solve problems. Innovation is not something that happens at some point in time. It is a process. This process of innovation can be described in terms of Figure 22.2.

The first stage is the identification of a new opportunity, a gap in the market competitors are leaving unfilled in their way of doing things. This opportunity must be evaluated. This evaluation consists of both a *qualitative* aspect (Who are the potential customers? What needs do they have? Why are existing products not meeting these?) and a *quantitative* aspect (How much would exploiting the opportunity be worth? What level of investment is appropriate?). The next stage is designing an innovation that will fulfil customer needs. This may

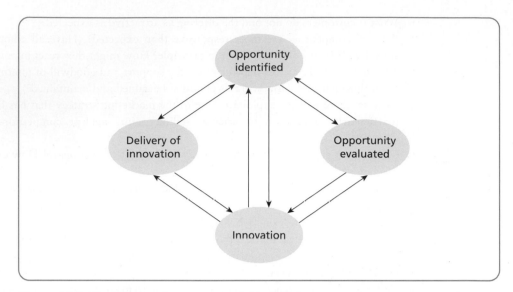

Figure 22.2 The process of entrepreneurial innovation

involve invention, the creation of a new product or service, but it goes beyond this. Innovation also includes an understanding of how a new product can be delivered to customers and how it might be promoted to them. The final stage is the actual delivery of the innovation to customers. Each stage is iterative. Understanding of the opportunity develops as potential innovations are considered. Means of delivery and promotion will be explored as the innovation takes shape. The opportunity and the innovation may be reconsidered in terms of promotional and distribution constraints.

Of course, innovation has many degrees. Any new way of doing things is an innovation. The magnitude may be of any order. One way of understanding the type of innovation an entrepreneurial venture is exploiting is to consider the technological base of the innovation, whether it is established or new, and the venture's ambitions in terms of market impact. Figure 22.3 illustrates the four quadrants that these alternatives define.

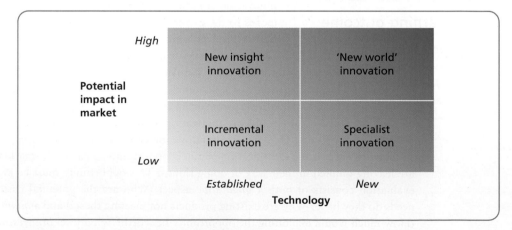

Figure 22.3 Types of entrepreneurial innovation

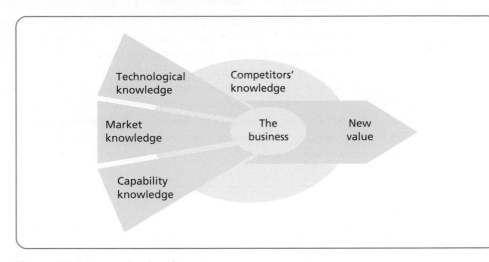

Figure 22.4 Innovation breakout

Incremental innovation is concerned with minor improvements to an existing technology with limited market ambitions. If market ambitions are higher, but still based on modifications to existing technology, and competition will be dependent on a new way of using the technology, then the innovation can be described as *new insight innovation*. If the innovation is based on a new technology, but with limited market ambitions, and competition will be based on an appeal to a narrow group of customers, then the innovation can be described as *specialist innovation*. An innovation founded on a new technology with high market impact ambitions can be called a *'new world' innovation*.

Innovation is a knowledge-based process. A new way of doing things must be based on a new way of seeing things. Successful innovation is founded on knowledge in three areas. *Market knowledge* is concerned with customers, their needs, demands, likely demand growth and what competitors are supplying. *Technological knowledge* relates to the effective development and production of the product or service aimed at the customers. These two areas of knowledge must be brought together with a third knowledge area: *capability knowledge*. This is the venture's understanding of what it does and why it does it well. It includes knowledge of the informational, cost, flexibility and human advantages the venture can call upon to compete effectively. If these three knowledge areas are brought together in a new, inventive and valuable way to drive the innovation process then the venture has the potential to break out of the trap that the industry's 'what we do and how we do it' thinking sets and so create new value (Figure 22.4).

Innovation is not, of course, something that is unique to the entrepreneurial venture. All businesses, no matter how mature, must be active innovators if they hope to maintain their position in the market. There are differences between the way entrepreneurs manage innovation and the way it is progressed in the large, mature firm. Entrepreneurial innovation is driven by vision, the desire to create a new world. Corporate innovation tends to be strategy driven. Although managerial vision may be important, the main driver is the recognition by the business that it must move forward if it is not to be left behind. Entrepreneurial innovation is, as far as the venture is concerned, radical. Its success or otherwise will have a major

449

impact on performance. Corporate innovation is more likely to be marginal. Success will add to the business's performance rather than be fundamental to it. Entrepreneurial innovation usually involves the whole business. The venture's structure and processes will be defined around the need for innovation. A large business is more likely to compartmentalise the management of innovation within a particular function or teams. These different approaches are not hard and fast alternatives. They are ends of a spectrum. Entrepreneurs are particularly good at managing the innovation process. This is one of the main reasons why intrapreneurship (entrepreneurship within an established business) is of such interest. This is an issue to be considered in section 27.3.

Summary of key ideas

- The first stage in the strategic window is *spotting* it.

- Spotting the window means identifying a new opportunity in terms of the possibility of creating new value.

- There are a variety of methods, both formal and informal, by which entrepreneurs can spot new opportunities.

- Entrepreneurs are constantly attuned to new opportunities.

Research themes

The process of opportunity spotting

One of the great mysteries of entrepreneurship is the creative process that leads entrepreneurs to discover new opportunities. This is the subject of much research, especially in the cognitive field. Necessarily, much of this research is based on a technical understanding of cognitive science and the student with this background may wish to follow through some of the references in section 4.1. However, there are opportunities for research in this area that do not demand a high level of theoretical sophistication. Much remains to be done in simply describing and categorising the processes through which entrepreneurs spot new opportunities. Select a sample of entrepreneurs. These may come from a variety of sectors and stages in the venture's life. Use a survey technique to ascertain issues such as:

- Was the entrepreneur opportunity or motivation led (i.e. did they spot a business idea that inspired them to become an entrepreneur, or did they decide to become an entrepreneur and was then active in identifying a business opportunity to pursue)?
- To what extent was the opportunity a 'flash of inspiration' or did the entrepreneur positively work at a problem to gain a 'eureka' insight?
- If the latter, how much effort was put into this process? Was working on the problem separated from the insight by a period of cognitive incubation?

- To what extent was the entrepreneur already experienced in the product/technology/ business sector of the innovation? Was the innovation from a sector outside the entrepreneur's current experience?
- Was organisational incubation important? (Examine the role of both formal incubators such as business schools and informal incubators such as incumbent employers.)
- What other support did friends, family, external experts and support agencies provide?
- What other support would the entrepreneur have liked?

In evaluating the results of the survey, attempt to develop a general model of opportunity identification, taking into account the possible variations in the factors discussed. The more entrepreneurs investigated, the more valuable this study will be. It may be best to focus on a limited number of sectors at first to build up a coherent initial model before moving on to apply it to a wider range of sectors. It is likely that the opportunity spotting process will be sensitive to sector particulars (e.g. high-tech ventures will be different from retailers).

Key readings

A solid theoretical account of entrepreneurial opportunity identification and development. Calling upon Dubin's (1978) approach to theory building, it is somewhat challenging but repays working through.

Ardichvili, A., Cardozo, R. and Sourav, R. (2003) 'A theory of entrepreneurial opportunity identification and development', *Journal of Business Venturing*, Vol. 18, No. 1, pp. 105–23.

For a little relief afterwards:

Saks, N.T. and Gaglio, C.M. (2002) 'Can opportunity identification be taught?', *Journal of Enterprising Culture*, Vol. 10, No. 4, pp. 313–47.

The debate as to whether creativity is innate or can be taught always engenders a lively discussion.

Suggestions for further reading

Ardichvili, A., Cardozo, R. and Sourav, R. (2003) 'A theory of entrepreneurial opportunity identification and development', *Journal of Business Venturing*, Vol. 18, No. 1, pp. 105–23.

Assael, H. and Roscoe, M., Jr, (1976) 'Approaches to market segmentation analysis', *Journal of Marketing*, Oct., pp. 67–76.

Dubin, R. (1978) *Theory Building* (2nd edn). New York: Free Press.

Gaglio, C.M. (2004) 'The role of mental simulations and counterfactual thinking in the opportunity identification process', *Entrepreneurship: Theory and Practice*, Vol. 28, No. 6, pp. 533–52.

Hague, P. (1985) 'The significance of market size', *Industrial Marketing Digest*, Vol. 10, No. 2, pp. 139–46.

Haley, R.I. (1968) 'Benefit segmentation: a decision-orientated research tool', *Journal of Marketing*, July, pp. 30–5.

Johnson, R.M. (1971) 'Market segmentation: a strategic management tool', *Journal of Marketing Research*, Feb., pp. 13–18.

Lindsay, N.J. and Juslin, C. (2002) 'A framework for understanding opportunity recognition', *Journal of Private Equity*, Vol. 6, No. 1, pp. 13–24.

Mattson, B.E. (1985) 'Spotting a market gap for a new product', *Long Range Planning*, Vol. 18, No. 1, pp. 87–93.

Park, J.S. (2005) 'Opportunity recognition and product innovation in entrepreneurial hi-tech start-ups: a new perspective and a supporting case study', *Technovation*, Vol. 25, No. 7, pp. 739–52.

Shane, S. (2000) 'Prior knowledge and the discovery of entrepreneurial opportunities', *Organizational Science*, Vol. 11, No. 4, pp. 448–69.

Ucbasaran, D., Westhead, P., Wright, M. and Binks, M. (2003) 'Does entrepreneurial experience influence opportunity identification?', *Journal of Private Equity*, Vol. 7, No. 1, pp. 7–14.

Zahra, S.A., Korri, J.S. and JiFeng, Y. (2005) 'Cognition and international entrepreneurship: implications for research on international opportunity recognition and exploitation', *International Business Review*, Vol. 14, No. 2, pp. 129–46.

Selected case material

CASE 22.1 14 December 2005 **FT**

Tricks of the truckers' trade

ALICIA CLEGG

As one of the mergers and acquisitions team at Goldman Sachs in London, Sam Gyimah mixed with representatives of Europe's largest companies in comfortable surroundings. When he visits clients today, the discussion is more than likely to take place in an industrial Portakabin.

Not that 29-year-old Mr Gyimah regrets the work-style exchange he made when he left his former employer in 2003 to set up a business specialising in training and recruiting lorry drivers with co-founder Christopher Philp. 'Building a business is simply more fun than

advising,' he says. 'In a large organisation it is only when you become very senior that you get to use your judgement.'

So far the judgment displayed by the pair, who met as students at Oxford, looks sound. They came up with the idea for Clearstone when Mr Philp, who had left McKinsey, the management consultancy, aged 24 to co-found his first business, was wrestling with the day-to-day nightmares of shipping stocks to trade customers.

'Whenever we received a complaint we would trace the problem back and almost always find that it originated with an agency driver hired by one of our sub-contractors,' Mr Philp recalls. 'When we asked why they were using temps, they would tell us that there was a huge shortage of drivers and they just couldn't get permanent staff.'

From a business perspective, this hand-to-mouth reliance on temporary drivers made no sense at all to Mr Philp, who investigated the matter with Mr Gyimah. 'We found firms that were sourcing 20 and even 50 per cent of their workforce through temporary staff,' says Mr Philp.

Soon, they decided they had stumbled on a gap in the logistics market crying out to be filled.

'The existing recruitment firms were locked into a model of supplying temporary staff on an agency basis,' says Mr Philp. 'No one was doing what Michael Page and other firms do in sectors such as accountancy – providing a service dedicated to the recruitment of permanent staff.'

They set up Clearstone to exploit this opportunity and address the root cause of the labour shortage, which the partners attributed to the logistics industry's failure to market lorry driving as a career. The core idea was to run punchy advertising in national newspapers, such as *The Sun* and *The Mirror*, offering low-paid or unemployed workers the opportunity to become licensed drivers of large goods vehicles, and earn substantially higher wages. As well as arranging the training, Clearstone promised to find a permanent job for every driver who qualified with it.

The company got off the ground in mid-2003 with start-up capital of about £1m contributed by a network of private investors. These included several of Mr Gyimah's former bosses at Goldman Sachs, plus a handful of entrepreneurs.

During the first year of operation it fell to Mr Gyimah to manage the business virtually single-handedly while his partner concentrated on preparing his earlier business venture, which was now turning over £70m, for a stock market debut. The flotation of Blueheath took place in July 2004, and the following month Mr Philp came into Clearstone as joint managing director.

In the two and a half years since it was founded, Clearstone has consistently exceeded its business targets, achieving sales of slightly more than £400,000 in its first 12 months. Annualised turnover has now reached £8m, and the company has steadily increased its profits since it broke even in July. The question now is whether the partners, named a fortnight ago as 'entrepreneurs of the future' in the CBI/Real Business Growing Business Awards, can capitalise on the early success.

One challenge that Clearstone may soon have to face is how to fend off new entrants who seek to copy its formula. 'The problem is that the barriers to entering this sector are not high and logistics firms are constantly on the look-out for ways to reduce their procurement costs,' says Sergio Nogueira, a senior executive at Accenture, the consultancy. 'To remain ahead of the game Clearstone will need to keep on adapting its services.'

One step the company has taken is to manage to combine two independent revenue streams generated at different points in the business cycle: training fees from drivers, which are paid in advance, and placement fees paid by employers. In this way, Clearstone's business model neatly overcomes the classic conundrum of how to generate a smooth cash flow for business expansion.

Operationally, the firm is organised for efficiency and sales growth. Housed in a three-storey converted warehouse in north London, the business functions as a call centre and has no branch offices. Would-be applicants who call to enquire about Clearstone's courses are credit checked immediately, via an electronic

▶

453

CASE 22.1 CONT.

link to Lloyds TSB, and those who are unable to afford the tuition fees are offered the chance to take out a loan. Says Mr Philp: 'Because we guarantee permanent jobs to drivers who qualify with us the risk is very low.'

In the next calendar year, Clearstone expects to make net operating profits of about £2m on a projected turnover of £12m. As part of the growth strategy the partners are buying a network of driving schools. The business logic for doing this is that the training division will keep the entire margin from the courses, which they formerly bought in, while the placement division will gain access to all the lorry drivers on the schools' books.

Looking further afield, the partners plan to extend a successful pilot scheme to recruit drivers from eastern Europe.

In an example of red tape offering an opportunity, recent European Union legislation restricting the number of hours lorry drivers can work weekly is expected to boost the company's growth further, by aggravating the shortage of drivers. Further ahead, Clearstone looks set to profit from another European directive that will substantially increase legal training requirements for drivers of large goods vehicles.

It is ironic that Mr Gyimah and Mr Philp, both active figures in Conservative party policy forums and outspoken opponents of red tape, should be poised to benefit so handsomely from EU regulation.

Point this out and the pair seem momentarily discomfited but, with an instinct worthy of a politician, they rebuff any suggestion that it puts them in an awkward position. 'We are not advocating more EU directives,' says Mr Gyimah.

'We deal with legislation as we find it, not as we wish it to be,' adds Mr Philp. 'We just do what we can to help industry.'

Source: Alicia Clegg, 'Tricks of the truckers' trade', *Financial Times*, 14 December 2005, p. 14. Copyright © 2005 The Financial Times Limited.

CASE 22.2

17 November 2005

Way of the web: start-ups map the route as big rivals get Microsoft in their sights

CHRIS NUTTALL

Bill Gates' worst nightmare may be taking shape at Ritual Coffee Roasters, a hip café in San Francisco's Mission district. Amid the lattes, patrons at their laptops are whipping up an internet revolution that could shake Microsoft's software empire. Five years after the dotcom phenomenon burnt itself out, a new version of the web is taking shape.

The Microsoft chairman has recognised the threat. In a memo to staff released last week, he warned that the latest phase of online innovation was likely to be 'very disruptive' to the industry's established powers. 'This next generation of the internet is being shaped by its grassroots adoption and popularisation model,' he added.

Work done on coffee-shop sofas is producing the processes of what is being called Web 2.0. Flickr, a photo-sharing site that earlier this year enjoyed its 15 minutes of fame as the most talked-about company in Silicon Valley, has held meetings around a large table at Ritual. Designers and coders from Rollyo, a 'roll-your-own' customisable search engine, and other start-ups have worked on applications and tested their sites over its free wireless connection. The low-key nature of it all is a mark of how different the new phase of internet invention is from the boom of the late 1990s.

It may not seem a likely setting for a technology shift capable of unseating Microsoft. After all, the software giant had little trouble dispatching Netscape and adapting its own business to the internet when the online medium was born a decade ago. Yet there are differences that could make the latest outbreak more difficult to quell.

Flickr, recently bought by Yahoo, was one of the new breed of companies mentioned by Ray Ozzie, Microsoft chief technical officer, in his own e-mail to colleagues. Alongside larger competitors such as Google and Yahoo!, 'tremendous software-and-services activity is occurring within start-ups and at the grassroots level,' he warned. In his note to staff, Mr Gates compared the significance of the Ozzie memo to his own 'Internet Tidal Wave' warning ten years earlier, when he predicted that the internet was going to change for ever the landscape of computing and that Microsoft risked being swept away if it failed to adapt. Though Microsoft has long used stark warnings like this to shake its developers into action, a groundswell of technological change is clearly under way.

Views about the significance of the Web 2.0 surge of innovation vary greatly. To those who are in the midst of it, it amounts to an entirely new way of producing and delivering software. Google has become the standard-bearer for this new generation of technology: the sophisticated software behind its search engine is accessed over the internet, available as a service supported by advertising – a far cry from Microsoft's way of doing business. Others, while acknowledging the significance of the moment, question how much upheaval it will bring. 'I think this is a genuine revolution as well,' says Charlene Li, analyst with Forrester, the research group. 'But it's with a small "r" rather than a big "R". The web represented a total mind-change, whereas this is a variation on a theme: it's not as earth-shattering to the consumer or business experience.'

Two important developments that have taken place since the dotcom bust help to account for the rise of Web 2.0 and may help to sustain it for longer than the last wave of internet mania. One is the spread of broadband internet access. As pointed out by Mr Ozzie in his memo, high-speed connections have created a big audience for content and applications produced online. The second change has been the internet advertising market created by Google.

By accepting ads from Google's network of advertisers on their own websites, many of the Web 2.0 upstarts have been able to generate immediate revenue from their efforts. Where the dotcommers could only collect 'eyeballs' and dream of one day finding a business model that would work on the web, Google has supplied one on tap. It is this arrival of advertising-supported software, delivered over the web, that has stirred Microsoft into action. Much consumer software, and even some of that used by small businesses, may one day be paid for this way, according to Mr Ozzie.

Against this background, the Web 2.0 crowd has discovered how to create internet services with mass market appeal on a shoestring. The watchwords of this approach: wherever possible, develop 'lightweight' software from

▶

standard technology building-blocks that can be released quickly over the web, then learn from the experience of early users to refine the service. 'In the past, you needed a big development team and a way to distribute the programs – a lot of resources, in other words,' says Ms Li. 'With Web 2.0, you can be talking about just a couple of engineers building something interesting and compelling, because the cost has gone down.'

Joe Kraus, chief executive of a start-up called Jotspot, says the changes have been dramatic for him second time around – he was co-founder and president of Excite, a Yahoo!-type web portal now owned by Interactive Corp. 'The cost of starting a company these days is an order of magnitude lower than it was a decade ago,' he says. 'When I started with Excite, it cost us $3m from the idea to when we had a product in the market. For Jotspot, it has cost me $100,000.'

One reason for the fall in costs is that applications can be speedily constructed with the help of the freely available building blocks of open-source software. They can be joined together with a blend of web tools that are transforming the browser experience to one where applications can look and perform just like programs stored on a computer hard drive.

It is not only start-up companies that are using these techniques. Google has become the champion of many of the standardised, lightweight technologies and its rapid-fire release of services has become a model for product development in the Web 2.0 world.

In earlier versions of the mapping services being offered by Google and Yahoo!, moving around an online street map meant clicking on arrows that caused a fresh page to be loaded. Now, users can drag the map with a mouse continuously along the route they wish to pursue. In internet terms, the map is being generated dynamically within the browser.

Other examples include Writely.com and Mr Kraus's Jotspot Live, which allow people to collaborate online in real time in order to draft a document. Much of this innovation rests on assembling a number of technology components, along with well-tried techniques for building online communities, to create a new breed of service.

Flock, a browser recently accorded the dubious distinction of being the Web 2.0 application with the most 'buzz' surrounding it in Silicon Valley, combines many tools associated with Web 2.0 with Firefox, an open-source browser competitor to Microsoft. It allows easy access to users' blogs and photo-sharing sites, takes in news feeds the user subscribes to and allows online shareable tagging of interesting web pages – more collaborative than bookmark 'favourites'.

'We are excited about social trends and giving the browser back to the user again – I see Flock as a client-side mash-up where users can mix and match applications without being limited to any one vendor,' says Bart Decrem, chief executive of Flock. 'Small entrepreneurs are on a level playing field again.'

Microsoft has found a challenger in Google in a very different arena from the browser wars it engaged in and won 10 years ago when taking on Netscape, says Tim O'Reilly, joint organiser of the Web 2.0 conference first held in October last year that gave the movement its name. Competing with this wave of innovation will not be as straightforward. 'It's a fundamental business challenge Microsoft did not face with Netscape,' says Mr O'Reilly. 'That was a battle still framed across a software application.'

Many of the latest services remain small and fragmented. 'The start-up's advantage is the speed with which it can move and Web 2.0 really extends that strength,' says Mr Kraus. 'Usually these waves [of innovation] produce a few big companies.'

His service aims to break into the corporate software business by offering 'wikis' – encyclopaedic databases built by user contributions – as company intranets, with the bonus of offering quick development of custom applications using Web 2.0 tools.

Tapping into applications like this as services over the web, rather than using them as pieces of software loaded on computers, will be a norm for consumers in ten years' time, he predicts. In the corporate world, online providers such as Salesforce.com say this has already arrived and that Web 2.0 endorses their own models. 'The era of the traditional software "load, update and upgrade" business and technology model is over. [Microsoft] is simply a dinosaur,' Marc Benioff, chief executive, told Salesforce.com staff last week.

Microsoft should not be counted out so fast. Through MSN, its own internet service, it already ranks among the online giants – even if it has struggled to make money from the service – and is in hot pursuit of Google and Yahoo! in the search business. It is also adapting the Web 2.0 toolkit to its own purposes, both by embedding it in its technology and acquiring start-ups: two weeks ago it bought FolderShare, an online file synchronisation service.

'I think the competition that is happening is very healthy,' says Mr O'Reilly. 'It's not just Microsoft and Google, but Google and Yahoo! as well. When Microsoft has good competition, it does great work; when it doesn't, it does lousy work. I'm eagerly awaiting lots of surprises.'

Source: Chris Nuttall, 'Way of the web: start-ups map the route as big rivals get Microsoft in their sights', *Financial Times*, 17 November 2005, p. 17.

Discussion point

1. Using the models developed in the chapter compare and contrast the likely opportunity-spotting processes for the two ventures described.

CHAPTER 23

Locating and measuring the window: positioning the new venture

Chapter overview

The second stage in using the strategic window is to locate it. This means relating the opportunity to the business activity of established firms and understanding it as a gap in what they offer to the market. The idea of positioning provides a powerful conceptual framework for doing this.

23.1 The idea of positioning

Key learning outcome

An appreciation of how the concept of positioning may be used as a guide to entrepreneurial decision making.

The idea of positioning provides a powerful tool to aid entrepreneurial decision making. Positioning provides a framework for *locating* the venture in relation to its competitors. Existing suppliers to a market do not serve its customers as completely as they might. They leave gaps in the market which a new venture can attempt to fill, so gaining a foothold in that market. Identifying the window of opportunity means spotting where these gaps are. A new venture is, at face value, in a weak position relative to established competitors. Even if the established players had not previously spotted the window of opportunity, a new start-up will signal its presence to them. Their greater resources, established network of relationships and lower costs may put them in a much stronger position to exploit the window.

Positioning the venture means locating it in relation to a market gap such that it can exploit that gap in a profitable way. This involves structuring the business so that it can serve the requirements of a particular market niche *better* than existing competitors. An effective positioning means that the business will be able to develop a *competitive advantage* in serving this niche. This makes the niche *defendable* against competitors. It also enables the new venture to move into the market in a way which avoids direct head-on competition with established players. Head-on competition is usually a difficult game for the new venture to play since the playing field is tipped in favour of the established player. At best, head-on competition will prove to be expensive, and at worst, it will result in failure for the new venture.

Positioning relates to a *location*, and location means occupying a *space*. Understanding positioning and using it as a decision-making tool demand an appreciation of the characterisation of the competitive space in which the venture operates. In general, a competitive space is characterised by the ways in which competitors seek to distinguish themselves from each other. Two distinct approaches to positioning provide different and complementary insights. *Strategic positioning* looks at the way in which the business's approach to delivering value to its customers is distinct from that of its competitors. Strategic positioning is concerned with the way in which the business *as a whole* distinguishes itself in a valuable way from competitor businesses. *Market positioning*, on the other hand, looks at the way in which the business's *offerings* to the market are differentiated from those of its competitors. Market positioning is concerned only with the business's products and services. Strategic positioning and market positioning can be used as decision-support tools for the entrepreneurial business.

23.2 Strategic positioning

> **Key learning outcome**
>
> An understanding of the decisions which define the venture's strategic positioning.

Identifying a strategic position is a fundamental element of the strategic planning process. A strategic position is the way the business as a whole is located relative to competitors in the playing field of the market, that is, the *competitive space*. Abell (1980) suggests that this competitive space can be defined along four dimensions: stage in value addition, customer segments addressed, customer needs addressed, and the means of addressing needs.

Stage in value addition

The goods that are bought by consumers, or which are used by those who provide services to them, are usually highly refined. Yet, ultimately, they are all made from raw materials obtained from the earth. However, there may be a lot of businesses that play a role in the process between the extraction of a raw material and the delivery of the final product.

Consider, for example, a home computer that has been purchased from a distributor. That distributor will have purchased the computer from a hardware manufacturer. The manufacturer will have bought a variety of components such as silicon chips, plastic parts and glass screens from component suppliers. Those component suppliers will have made them from refined raw materials obtained from suppliers of pure silicon, plastics and glass. These suppliers will have refined their products from raw commodities obtained from the businesses that collect sand and extract oil from the earth. This process whereby the outputs of one business provide the inputs for the next business along is called the *value addition chain* (Figure 23.1).

An entrepreneur must decide what stage, or stages, in the value addition process they expect their venture to occupy. This resolves itself into questions about the inputs and the outputs of the business. These questions are:

- Will the business make a particular input (which might be a physical product or a service) for itself or will it buy it in?

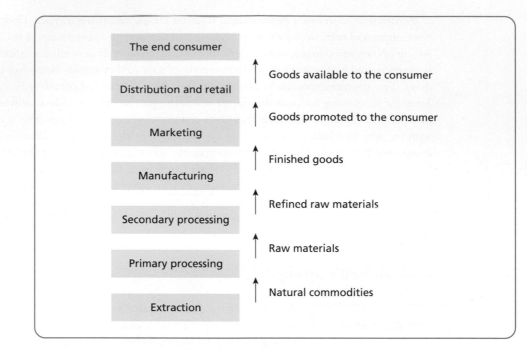

Figure 23.1 Value addition in an industry chain

- Will the business sell on a particular output to another business for further processing or will it try to add that value itself?

The decisions made in response to these questions must be based on an appreciation of the competences of the business, its resources and its competitive advantage relative to both competitors and the businesses adjacent to it in the value addition chain.

Customer segments addressed

It is rare that a business can serve the needs of an *entire* market. The strengths of a particular business lie in the way it can appeal to certain groups of customers. When Richard Branson started the Virgin Airline he concentrated on business passengers who wanted to cross the Atlantic. Alan Sugar, when founding his consumer electronics business Amstrad was explicit about the fact that he was targeting the 'lorry driver and his family' rather than the hi-fi aficionado. Selecting a well-defined customer segment enables the business to focus limited resources, to concentrate its efforts and to defend itself against competitors.

There are a variety of ways in which a customer segment can be defined. Some of the more important include the following:

- *Geographical location* – where the customer is. Many entrepreneurial ventures start out serving a small local community. As they grow they expand to achieve national and even international scope.
- *Industry* – the industrial sector of organisational buyers. In its early stages an entrepreneurial venture may decide to concentrate on selling its product to a particular industry segment.

This option may be attractive because the needs and buying habits of that sector are thoroughly understood by the entrepreneur.

- *Demographics of buyer* – e.g. social class, age, personal attitudes or stage in life cycle. For example, Gerald Ratner revitalised the high street jewellery trade in the UK by targeting young, relatively low-income people.
- *Buying process* – the way the product is bought and the role of influencers and decision makers. Entrepreneurs may concentrate their efforts towards businesses which buy in a certain sort of way. For example, business service firms such as the market research company MORI are adept at negotiating the complex decision-making process that lies behind the buying and use of market research in large organisations.
- *Psychographics* – buyers' attitudes towards the product category. Richard Branson, for example, has moved his Virgin brand into personal financial services on the basis that the brand offers trust in an area where many buyers have suspicions about the existing products on offer.

Customer needs addressed

Consumers and businesses have many, and complex, needs and wants. No single business could hope to serve them all. An entrepreneur must decide exactly which of the customer's needs their venture will exist to serve. Success depends on gaining customer commitment, and the best way to do that is to genuinely serve the needs and to solve the problems that customers have.

Customers may be aware of their needs or they may not have articulated them to themselves, yet these needs can be explicit or implicit. Different needs are not independent of each other, they often interact and must be prioritised. Satisfying one need may mean that others go unsatisfied. The entrepreneur must learn to understand the needs of their customers, to rationalise them and to distinguish them from each other. The entrepreneur must often articulate the needs of customers on their behalf.

Means of addressing needs

Satisfying a need represents an end, and there are a number of means by which that end can be achieved. The need to communicate with someone, for example, can be served by a postage stamp, a telephone, the internet or by going to visit them. Having decided which particular customer needs they will satisfy, the entrepreneur must decide the means, or *technology*, that they will adopt in order to do so. Alan Sugar recognised people's desire to be entertained by listening to music. He provided them with electronic equipment to replay recorded music. He might, conceivably, have served that desire by building concert halls or by providing a service whereby musicians would come and play to people in their homes. For whatever reasons, these were technological alternatives he avoided.

The industry-building entrepreneur is often the one who has recognised a new technological approach for addressing a basic need. Henry Ford recognised that a low-cost motor car was a better way of moving from one place to another than horse and cart. Bill Gates recognised that a computer with the right software could transform the way in which a variety of domestic and office information-processing tasks were performed. Innovation is not just about creating new technology. It is about understanding how a particular technology can be used to address a need in a new and fruitful way.

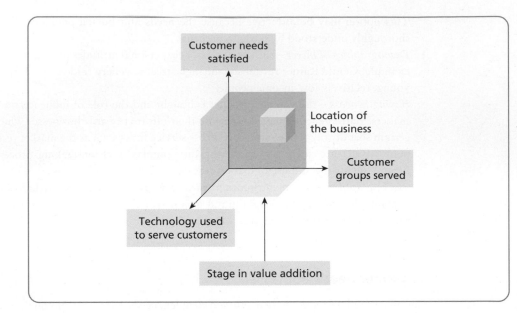

Figure 23.2 The dimensions of strategic positioning

These four dimensions, as shown in Figure 23.2, describe the strategic positioning of a venture or its location in competitive space (see also Day, 1984, p. 21). This is the niche where the new venture sits. It defines who its competitors are and the way in which they are competitors. Of course, merely occupying the niche is not enough. The business must structure itself and adopt operating processes and a culture which allow it to serve that niche effectively.

23.3 Market positioning

Key learning outcome

An understanding of how the idea of market positioning can be used to differentiate the venture's offerings from those of its competitors.

Strategic positioning describes the way the venture is located in a competitive space. *Market positioning* describes the way its outputs, products and services are located in the marketplace relative to those of competitors. Success will be achieved only if the new venture offers customers something which is *different* from and more *attractive* than that offered by existing players. This means it must offer them greater value by being more suited to their needs, or the same level of benefits but at lower cost.

The first stage in market positioning is to develop an understanding of the criteria by which buyers distinguish among the different products on offer and the extent to which they consider them to be substitutable. Some general factors in market positioning are:

- *price* – how the offering is priced relative to competitors;
- *perceived quality* – quality seen as high or low (what matters is perceived value for money, i.e. quality relative to price);

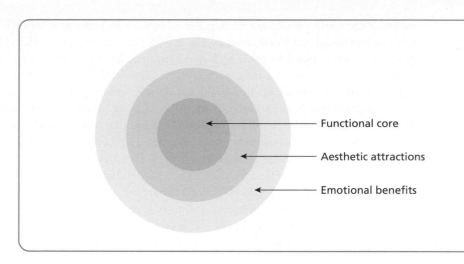

Figure 23.3 Positioning of the venture's product

- *demographic imagery* – upmarket versus downmarket, young versus old; dynamic versus conservative;
- *performance* – high performance or more limited performance;
- *number and type of features* – e.g. advanced versus basic; complex versus simple; hi-tech versus low-tech;
- *branding imagery* – the associations that the branding elicits;
- *service and support* – additional assistance offered in understanding, using and maintaining the product;
- *attitude towards supplier* – positive or negative associations gained from ethical stance of supplier.

Different buyers will prioritise and weight these factors differently.

One way of thinking about positioning is to consider three aspects of the product or service being offered. A product can be positioned using one or more of the three ways in which its consumer relates to it – see Figure 23.3. At the centre is the *functional core*, that is, the features of the product or service which actually deliver its functional benefits. Surrounding this functional core are the aesthetic attractions of the product or service. These include design and branding elements which make the product or service attractive to use. At the outer level are the *emotional benefits*. These are those aspects of the product or service which appeal directly to the consumer's emotional and spiritual needs rather than to their purely functional ones. This may be achieved through branding which allows the consumer the chance to say something about her or himself by being seen to consume the product. It may also be enshrined in the way the product is sourced, or in the values adopted in its production.

The aim of positioning is to reduce the extent to which the customer feels that the product or service is *substitutable* by those of competitors. In effect, this means focusing the offering on the needs of the customer in a unique and effective way. The positioning need not be solely in its functional core. Differentiation can often be achieved very effectively by giving the product or service a unique aspect in its aesthetic attractions and emotional benefits. For example, a £3.99 digital watch may be as good as a Cartier watch for telling the time, but the owner of the Cartier would not think it a good swap. The buyer may see their purchase set into a wider social and moral context. The actual 'physical' products offered by The Body Shop are easily imitated by other high street retailers, but its customers still feel that The Body Shop offers them something more valuable because of its ethical stance. The eponymous chain of jewellers set up by Gerald Ratner revolutionised the UK jewellery retailing sector in the 1980s but did not pretend to be offering products of the highest quality. Nonetheless it was felt to be fun and accessible by its young customers. Charles and Maurice Saatchi of Saatchi and Saatchi reinvented advertising in the 1960s and 1970s by positioning themselves as partners in the management process rather than by just supplying advertisements for clients. The McDonald's chain of fast-food outlets as established by Ray Kroc are not just places to eat; they are an invitation to share the American Dream.

Positioning is a valuable entrepreneurial tool. It guides the entrepreneur in offering the customer something new and valuable and it avoids the need for head-on competition with established (and more powerful) players. Effective positioning is a critical success factor for the new venture.

23.4 The need for information

Key learning outcome

An appreciation of the importance of managing and using market information effectively.

Relevant market information is extremely useful to the entrepreneur. Entrepreneurs are decision makers. They are different from other types of manager because they make the decision to *venture*. Venturing means stepping out into the unknown, and information provides a map of how to move forward into this unknown. Information eliminates uncertainty and so reduces *risk*. However, information on its own is not enough: if it is to be valuable, it must be analysed, understood and acted upon.

Information does not come for free, it has a cost. While the entrepreneur will know many things simply as a result of their experience within an industry, a lot of additional information may need to be gathered actively. Even if the information has no direct cost (for example, information gathered 'free' from a public library), valuable time is used in collecting it. Some information can have a high direct cost; for example, information obtained through formal market research surveys can appear very expensive to the entrepreneur just starting out. However, information represents an *investment* in the business. It is used to increase the performance of the business. The payoff for that investment needs to be appreciated before the information is gathered.

Information can guide action. However, lack of information should not be an excuse for *inaction*. While it may be sensible to hold back on a move until more information is available and that move can be made with more confidence, there are times when the entrepreneur must rely on their instincts and 'go for it'. If they wait too long, someone else may take the move first. While information reduces risk, the entrepreneur cannot expect to eliminate *all* risk and sometimes they must take a step into the dark. The entrepreneur must walk a narrow path between making ill-informed and ill-judged decisions and an inertia caused by the venture's becoming more interested in gathering and analysing information than in taking direct action. The founders of organisation systems thinking, Kast and Rosenzweig, called these two extremes 'extinction by instinct' and 'paralysis by analysis' (1970; also see Langley, 1995).

Strategic management provides a wide variety of tools and conceptual frameworks to aid decision making. A variety of formal methods is available to guide resource allocation and make competitive moves. While the entrepreneur would be foolish to shun the insights that can be gained through such formal analysis of information, they should not be wholly dependent on it. Often it is the overall *pattern*, not the *detail*, that matters. They must learn to develop their intuition and make judgements based on holistic thinking and their own heuristic approach. The successful entrepreneur learns to see the wood before the trees.

23.5 Analysing the market and identifying key issues

Key learning outcome

An appreciation of the importance of analysing and understanding market conditions.

If they are to be successful, entrepreneurs must understand the market in which they are operating. This understanding is important because success depends on their ability to serve that market in a way which is better than that of their competitors.

There are a number of issues about which the entrepreneur must be informed if they are to make effective decisions in relation to their venture. These issues fall into four broad categories. These relate to: (a) the existing market conditions and the opportunity they present, (b) the way in which the entrepreneur might innovate and offer something of value to the market, (c) the way in which the entrepreneur can get the venture started, and (d) the way in which competitors are likely to respond to the venture. Some specific information requirements are:

- *General market conditions* – customers' needs and requirements; the size of potential markets; market growth rate and trends in its development; the structure of customer groups and segments; and customer and consumer buying behaviour.
- *The attractiveness of the innovation* – customers' satisfactions and dissatisfactions with current offerings; customers' reaction to the entrepreneur's new offering; competitor pricing and customers' pricing expectations; and likely volume of demand.
- *The way the new venture can be initiated and positioned in the marketplace* – resource requirements for start-up; resource requirements for the later development of the venture; the structure of the network in which the venture will be located; sources of investment capital; customers and customer groups to be given priority; and means by which the customer might be informed about the new offering.
- *The way in which competitors might react to the new venture* – the nature, type, strengths and weaknesses of competitors; strategies adopted by competitors; and likely actions (strategic and tactical) by way of a response to the entrepreneur's start-up.

Information of this nature is available from a variety of sources. Some of it will be knowledge the entrepreneur already holds about their industry. Some may be obtained from published sources such as market reports and trade publications; such sources are referred to as *secondary* sources. Alternatively, primary research involves a bespoke analysis of a market situation using market research techniques in answer to specific questions.

In many instances the entrepreneur may feel quite informed on these issues. In other instances they may feel that information is lacking and greater certainty is needed. The entrepreneur must never be complacent. The rule must be always to challenge knowledge and assumptions. When deciding upon the degree of precision required for information, two questions must be asked. First, how sensitive will decision making be to the accuracy of the information used as the basis of those decisions? Second, with respect to this, is the cost of gaining the information worth the return it offers?

23.6 Analysing the opportunity

> **Key learning outcome**
>
> An appreciation of the methods by which the 'whys' of the opportunity may be understood.

There are two types of question that must be asked if a business opportunity is to be fully appreciated. Both may be answered by appropriate market research and analysis techniques. The first set of questions relate to the nature of the opportunity, its qualities and the approaches that might be taken to exploiting it. These are the 'who?', 'what?' and 'why?' questions. They are best answered using *qualitative* methods. The second set of questions relate to the value of the opportunity and the effort that should be put into exploiting it. These are the 'how much?' and 'how many?' questions. These are best answered using *quantitative* methods.

Qualitative methods might be used to answer questions of the following sort. Who are the customers? How are they defined as a group? How are they differentiated from non-customers? What needs do these customers have in relation to the product category (in terms of functional, social, emotional and developmental needs)? How do they articulate their needs – explicitly or implicitly? How well do consumers find that current offerings satisfy those needs? In what ways are current offerings unsatisfactory? What are the customers' attitudes towards the product category in general – positive, negative or mixed? Why do non-customers not use the product category? How might they be attracted to it? If the product is not available, how might other types of product be used as a substitute? How does this define a gap for an innovative offering? How do customers go about buying a product? How are they normally informed about the product category? What is their knowledge of the product category? Who influences their decision when making a purchase? Who influences the consumer when they use the product? How is such influence exercised? How do they greet innovations in the product category – positively or with suspicion?

Many entrepreneurs will feel confident in their ability to answer these questions based purely on their experience in a particular industry sector working with customers and a particular product category. However, if the area is new to them, or they feel the innovation they are offering changes the rules, or they just wish to challenge assumptions, then obtaining answers directly from customers and potential users will be a valuable exercise. There are various methods for doing this, ranging from the quite informal (actively listening to customer) to quite formal (focus groups, market surveys, questionnaires). Which are selected will depend on what the entrepreneur wants (needs) to know, how valuable that information will be (increased returns, reduced risks, gaining stakeholder commitments) and the resources available (financial, understanding).

23.7 Analysis and planning formality

Business plans can take a variety of forms and vary greatly in their content and detail. A plan might be just a few ideas on a piece of paper, or it might be a highly formal and detailed document containing a lot of information. That information may have been gathered by external experts such as market researchers and management consultants. What determines the formality of the plan? It must be recognised that the more formal a plan, the higher its cost. This is not just in terms of the entrepreneur's time and energy, but also in terms of the direct cost of obtaining information. A formal plan represents an investment in the venture and must be justified by the return it can offer. An entrepreneur is wise to keep the formality of the plan in line with its role. Six factors would be expected to determine the level of formality of (and hence the necessary investment in) the plan.

- *The cost of start-up.* The higher the level of initial investment in the venture, the more likely that the plan will be formal. This reflects both the inherent risk in higher-cost start-ups and the fact that the proportion of the overall budget spent on planning will decrease.
- *The involvement of external stakeholders.* This is linked to the previous point. If external investors are involved in supporting the venture, they will expect to see a formal, well-evidenced and reassuring plan making a case for the viability of the venture. Other stakeholders, such as key employees and customers, may also need to be convinced with a formal plan.
- *The availability and cost of information.* Before the plan can be written, the information to go into it must be obtained. In some instances, information is readily available. This may be because the entrepreneur is in an incubator organisation (formal or informal), thus making access to information easier and less expensive. In other instances, information may not be readily available or may only be obtained at high cost. Easily accessed, low-cost information will encourage planning formality.
- *Perceptions of business risk and ambiguity.* Decisions are based on information. Risk occurs when the range of things that might happen is known along with the probabilities of the different eventualities. Ambiguity occurs when those probabilities are not known. Formal market research is a way of gauging probabilities more accurately and so turning ambiguity into risk. It can illuminate risky eventualities in a way that allows them to be managed with more certainty, both by entrepreneurs and by investors. The higher the level of perceived risk and ambiguity, the more that formal research will be encouraged.
- *External support with planning activities.* A number of support agencies assist with business planning. Important examples include business schools that run educational programmes involving developing business plans as a learning device. These are often practically orientated and are undertaken on behalf of practising entrepreneurs and governmental schemes that subsidise professional consultants to prepare plans for entrepreneurs. If external support is available, then planning formality will be encouraged.
- *The entrepreneur's personal style.* Formal planning requires knowledge of the principles and methods of business planning. Not all entrepreneurs have this. Further, some entrepreneurs may be suspicious of, and doubt the value of, formal planning. Planning may not fit with their personal analytical style. More formal plans may be produced by those who are comfortable with, and see the value of, such plans.

Summary of key ideas

- The second stage in the strategic window is *locating* it.

- Locating the window means developing a *position* for the new venture and its offerings to the marketplace.

- *Strategic positioning* relates to the way the venture fits in the marketplace in relation to its stage in the value addition chain, the customer groups it serves, the customer needs it addresses, and the technology it adopts to serve its customers.

- *Market positioning* relates to the way the venture's offerings fit in the marketplace in relation to the offerings of competitors.

- Measuring the windows means developing an understanding of the size of the opportunity and what it might be worth.

- A business opportunity is analysed by *qualitative methods* which answer 'what' and 'why' questions and *quantitative methods* which answer 'how much' and 'how many' questions.

- Information can be expensive. Effective entrepreneurs weigh the value of information against the cost of obtaining it. Information is regarded as an *investment* in the business.

- A number of factors drive the extent to which the entrepreneur engages in formal as opposed to informal market analysis and planning.

Research themes

Entrepreneurs' conceptualisation of market positioning

The concepts of strategic and market positioning discussed in this chapter are relatively technical and adopt a language that most entrepreneurs would not be familiar with. This is not to say that entrepreneurs do not have a sensitive and sophisticated intuitive idea of the positioning of their ventures. This may be explored by evoking entrepreneurs' cognitive maps of their competitive environment. An interview technique is best here. The key issues to be ascertained are as follows:

- What products/services do entrepreneurs see as their competitors? A more detailed picture can be gained by having the entrepreneur detail competitor products as close, near or distant competitors (an 'onion ring' picture of the competitive environment).
- On what basis are the entrepreneurs including competitors? Possibilities include the competitors being seen by virtue of their:
  - being in the same industry (if so, check on how the entrepreneur perceives the industry sector);
  - sharing the same technology;

- being available through the same distribution channel;
- being made by the same production process;
- being alternative purchases by customers.

These factors may be used in combination. Explore the entrepreneur's perceptions and identify the two that the entrepreneur believes dominate. Be careful not to lead the entrepreneur down a particular path; make sure it is the entrepreneur's perceptions that are being revealed.

- The entrepreneur may then be introduced to the idea of market mapping. Set out a rectangular space with the two dimensions that are most important in the entrepreneur's classification strategy. Have them plot the location of their own product and those of competitors. Once the entrepreneur is satisfied that this represents their picture of the competitive environment, inquire into how the entrepreneur sees their products' competitive edge over the competitors identified. Does the entrepreneur agree that the map makes their ideas on positioning clear?

- A more sophisticated approach might use more than two dimensions of competitor product discrimination and use a more formal mapping technique (this will take time to analyse and depict, so two interviews are likely to be necessary). A further sophistication would be to have the entrepreneurs connect their view of the performance of their venture's products causally to its (unique, valuable) positioning.

Entrepreneurial entry and innovative positioning

Innovation is intimately associated with entrepreneurship. Consequent upon the view that entrepreneurs are innovators is the belief that entrepreneurs enter new markets in an unoccupied niche with a product that is different from those being offered by existing suppliers. But how true is this? The concept of market positioning offers a way of testing the proposition.

Obtain details on a number of entrepreneurial start-ups with good, detailed information on the new product (service) the entrepreneur is offering and those already available. Create market maps of the product category using the descriptive criteria described above (additional criteria might be introduced). The more criteria introduced, the more incisive will be the findings. However, if more than two criteria are introduced, more sophisticated mapping techniques will be needed. How distinct is the entrepreneur's offering? Do entrepreneurs introduce into new niches? How does the degree of originality affect later performance. It might be hypothesised that the level of innovation is sector dependent. The study might look in detail at one particular sector or be a cross-sectional evaluation of a number of complementary sectors.

Introduction and expansion of strategic positioning

The model of strategic positioning developed above can be used to describe both the initial positioning of new entrepreneurial ventures and the selection of expansion strategies. Obtain descriptions of a number of entrepreneurial ventures with details on the stage in value addition, customer groups targeted, the particular needs of those customers and the technology adopted to serve those needs. Ideally these should cover both introduction and subsequent expansion. How focused are entrepreneurs in their entry? Do they seek unoccupied strategic positions or are they willing to compete in already occupied positions? What are the preferred modes of expansion (value addition, vertical integration, new needs with existing customers, new customers, new technologies)? Is a single mode of expansion preferred or are several tackled at once? Again, this could well be sector dependent so both detailed studies of a single sector and cross-sectional studies of several would be valuable.

Factors affecting opportunity analysis formality

This research theme investigates the degree of formality in entrepreneurs' evaluation of the market they are entering (or have entered) and their investment in detailed market research. Some ventures are based on the entrepreneur's extant and intuitive knowledge with no formal research. At the other end of the spectrum, external consultants and market research specialists may be brought in to support the entrepreneur. Some of the factors that might be postulated as important in influencing the decision about how much to invest in formal market research include the following:

- The level of initial investment in the venture. Higher levels of investment will tend to make higher levels of expenditure on market research seem more reasonable.
- The risks in the venture. The higher the risks (more specifically, the ambiguity the venture faces), the more the entrepreneur might be tempted to acquire information that brings that ambiguity under control.
- The involvement of external stakeholders. The more external stakeholders (particularly, but not exclusively, investors) are involved, the more the entrepreneur might be tempted to invest in independent evidence to bring them on board. This will tend to correlate positively with the initial investment in the venture.
- The entrepreneur's personal style. Formal research is likely to be more demanded by entrepreneurs who are familiar with the techniques and whose personal decision-making style is sympathetic with explicitly rational (information-based) decision making as opposed to an implicit, intuitive approach.
- The entrepreneur's current experience of the product technology/market sector (say, as a result of incubation in an incumbent). The lower that experience, the more the entrepreneur might be tempted to invest in additional information.

These five factors are (broadly) quantifiable (at least on a 1–5 Likert scale) and may be discovered through a survey of a pool of entrepreneurs. (Some may feel more comfortable with a tick-box banded answer than with giving an exact figure of what initial investment and expenditure on market research was.) Make an attempt to quantify the entrepreneurs' own time commitment to research as well as explicit costs. The direction of the five factors discussed should be expected to correlate positively with the entrepreneur's investment in market research (as a proportion of total initial investment in the venture). Does this hypothesis hold out empirically? Statistical analysis of variance could be used to indicate the relative importance of the five factors.

For the student interested in a good discussion and information about advanced techniques in the mapping of cognitive perceptions about strategic situations, Huff (1990) is highly recommended.

Key readings

Two articles that are quite old now, but the wisdom they relate about thinking in terms of positioning offerings against those of competitors is timeless.

Aaker, D.A. and Shansby, J.G. (1982) 'Positioning your product', *Business Horizons*, May/June, pp. 56–62.

Mattson, B.E. (1985) 'Spotting a market gap for a new product', *Long Range Planning*, Vol. 18, No. 1, pp. 87–93.

Suggestions for further reading

Abell, D.F. (1980) *Defining the Business: The Starting Point of Strategic Planning*. Englewood Cliffs, NJ: Prentice Hall.

Datta, Y. (1996) 'Market segmentation: an integrated framework', *Long Range Planning*, Vol. 29, No. 6, pp. 797–811.

Day, G.S. (1984) *Strategic Market Planning*. St Paul, MN: West Publishing.

Day, G.S., Shocker, A.D. and Srivastava, R.K. (1978) 'Customer-orientated approaches to identifying product-markets', *Journal of Marketing*, Vol. 43, pp. 8–19.

Eisenhardt, K. (1989) 'Making fast strategic decisions in high-velocity environments', *Academy of Management Journal*, Vol. 32, pp. 543–76.

Garda, R.A. (1981) 'Strategic segmentation: how to carve niches for growth in industrial markets', *Management Review*, Aug. Reproduced in Weitz, B.A. and Weley, R. (eds) (1988) *Readings in Strategic Marketing: Analysis, Planning and Implementation*. New York: Dryden Press.

Huff, A.S. (1990) *Mapping Strategic Thought*. London: Wiley.

Johnson, R.M. (1971) 'Market segmentation: a strategic management tool', *Journal of Marketing Research*, Feb., pp. 13–18.

Kast, F.E. and Rosenzweig, J.E. (1970) *Organization and Management: A Systems Approach*. New York: McGraw-Hill.

Langley, A. (1995) 'Between "paralysis by analysis" and "extinction by instinct"', *Sloan Management Review*, Spring, pp. 63–76.

Marlow, H. (1994) 'Intuition and forecasting – a holistic approach', *Long Range Planning*, Vol. 27, No. 6, pp. 58–68.

Selected case material

CASE 23.1   16 January 2006

College Friends with designs on selling arts and craft

MIRANDA GREEN

When Victoria Swan and three of her friends on design courses at Lowestoft College decided they wanted to work together, the level of their student debts was not uppermost in their minds.

'Working for ourselves is something we all wanted to do, so we decided to sell and exhibit online,' says Ms Swan. Their website, Loop-360, is being launched in March, and will undercut galleries and shops by charging artists and craftsmen only 20 per cent commission on sales of their wares. Ms Swan says they have plans to expand and eventually put on mobile exhibitions.

But with combined debts of more than £50,000 – about £14,000 each – the partners have decided to make sure their project will not be dependent on further borrowing.

'We did our homework,' says Ms Swan, explaining that as a mature student and a mother she has taken on a part-time job to fund her share of the minimal start-up costs. Having looked into and rejected the idea of applying for grants, and after taking business advice from the National Council for Graduate Entrepreneurship (NCGE) and from the local business centre, the four partners set up a limited company so they can avoid paying back their student loans while their earnings from the company are below the £15,000 repayment threshold.

'I don't think about the debt. I'm very proud that I've got a degree because I've got children – and in other countries they pay,' she says. 'If you want to work for yourself you just have to blank out the debt and it gave you something good, your education. But it's made us more determined, because we want to pay it off and make a lot of money as soon as possible.'

Paul Hannon of the NCGE says many of tomorrow's most successful graduate entrepreneurs will be those on creative courses as well as in engineering, science and technology, because they are already working on products that could be taken into the marketplace. But traditionally only business students have been exposed to the individuals who might inspire them or advise on how to start up. All that is changing, he believes.

'I think over time entrepreneurship is going to emerge from students in all sorts of subjects,' he says.

Source: Miranda Green, 'College friends with designs on selling arts and craft', *Financial Times*, 16 January 2006, p. 4. Copyright © 2006 The Financial Times Limited.

18 August 2005

Heineken increases Russian Portfolio with sixth buy in 12 months

NEIL BUCKLEY AND SARAH LAITNER

Heineken is deepening its presence in the rapidly growing Russian beer market with the purchase of Ivan Taranov Breweries in a deal understood to be worth just over $500m.

The cash acquisition by the Dutch brewer underlines the growing interest of foreign beer groups in the world's fifth-largest market by volume. The drink is increasingly popular with Russia's expanding middle classes.

The purchase of Ivan Taranov, Russia's seventh-largest brewer, will increase Heineken's market share in the country to 14 per cent, or more than 11.4m hectolitres.

Heineken said it was attracted to Ivan Taranov, which has a 3.4 per cent share of the Russian market, because it would improve its access to distribution and production units and increase its stable of brands in the country to 34.

The Dutch group will also have the option of buying Ivan Taranov's distribution business, which incorporates 23 companies across Russia.

Before this deal, Heineken had snapped up five breweries in Russia in the past 12 months – including last month's deal to buy 100 per cent of the Baikal Beer Company in Irkutsk.

United Financial Group, a Moscow-based investment bank, estimated that Heineken had spent $1.2bn in Russia since entering the market in 2002.

Foreign beer groups are rushing to expand in Russia, where the market is expected to grow more than 5 per cent to more than 89m hectolitres this year.

Heineken is the third-largest brewer in Russia after Belgium-based InBev and market leader BBH, which is jointly owned by Scottish & Newcastle and Carlsberg.

The Ivan Taranov purchase is second-largest deal in the Russian brewing industry after Inbev this year bought out Sun Interbrew. InBev followed up that deal with plans to buy Tinkoff, a St Petersburg-based brewer, for $200m.

Heineken's latest deal gives it three breweries in areas where it has been underrepresented before and popular Russian brands including PIT, Three Bears and Dr Diesel.

Heineken said the Russian brewer was 62 per cent owned by Allied Partners, run by Russian entrepreneurs Eugene Kashper and Alexander Lipshifts, and 38 per cent by US private equity group Texas Pacific.

Heineken and Ivan Taranov refused to disclose the value of the deal, though people familiar with the transaction pointed to a price above $500m.

Heineken was advised by Merrill Lynch. Lehman Brothers and Renaissance Capital advised Ivan Taranov.

Discussion points

1. What information do you think should be obtained before the venture described in Case 23.1 is initiated? Make a list of key items.

2. How would you advise an entrepreneur to locate and measure the window for a new importing opportunity?

CHAPTER 24

Opening the window: gaining commitment

Chapter overview

The fourth stage in using the strategic window is to open it. This means initiating the business and drawing the commitment of stakeholders towards it. This chapter looks at how the venture can enter and establish itself in the business network. The key issues relating to attracting financial and human support are considered along with the specific issue of gaining the commitment of distributors.

24.1 Entering the network

Key learning outcome

An appreciation of the way in which a new venture redefines the network of relationships that exist within a business community.

Having spotted the window, that is, having identified a new opportunity, and having located and measured the window, that is, having defined and quantified the opportunity, the entrepreneur must then *open* that window. This means initiating the business. Initiation demands that a variety of stakeholders be drawn into the venture. The new venture and the entrepreneur driving it must create a new set of relationships with those stakeholders. Yet, in most instances, those stakeholders will already have relationships with a variety of other (possibly competing) organisations. In effect, starting a new venture means *redefining* the relationships that stakeholders have with third parties and with one another. The new venture must enter an existing network of relationships and, in doing so, modify that network of relationships. If the venture is to enjoy long-term success it must do this in a way which *increases* the overall value of the network to those who make it up.

The relationships in this network are both competitive and collaborative. The entrepreneur must decide on the way these two dynamics are to be complemented and balanced as the network is redefined. This balancing act must be considered in relation to each and every stakeholder and stakeholder group.

Relationship with investors

Investors seek out opportunities to invest. They look for the best returns on the capital they provide, consistent with a certain level of risk. Because capital, like any resource, is both valuable and limited, investors are selective in the investments they choose to support. Investors are less interested in the cost of an investment than in its *opportunity cost*: the money that will be lost if an investment is not made *elsewhere*.

Entrepreneurs must compete for the attentions of investors. If an entrepreneur offers an investor an investment opportunity, then they are limiting the possibility for investment in other ventures by that investor. One entrepreneur's success in attracting investment capital will be another's, perhaps many others', failure. This is harsh. Yet, in the long run, this competition generates an overall increase in value for *all* entrepreneurs in two ways. First, by defining opportunity costs it provides a strong signal as to which opportunities are worth pursuing and which are not. Second, by offering investors a good return, it generates the capital that can be used to make further investments.

Relationship with suppliers

To a supplier, an entrepreneurial venture is a potential new customer. At face value this is good since a new customer offers the prospect of new business. However, the new venture may also complicate life for a supplier. The venture may be competing with an existing customer of the supplier. While the venture may be offering the potential for additional business it may also be simply threatening to replace one set of business arrangements with another. The supplier may not always see the entrepreneurial venture as new business. They can also see the costs of gaining one new (and untried) customer only to face the risks of losing an established one. Suppliers prefer entrepreneurs who intend to expand a market rather than those who intend just to replace existing producers within it.

If the business is characterised by close and strong relationships between supplier and customer then that relationship may be strained if the supplier is called upon to provide for a customer's competitor. While in many economies a legal framework exists to ensure that trading is free and fair and that strong customers do not coerce weaker suppliers, and vice versa, this is not always the case. Even if a robust legal framework exists, informal agreements and expectations can still be influential.

In short, when approaching suppliers the entrepreneur must be conscious not only of the new business they are offering them but also of the way the relationship they are proposing to build will affect the existing relationships the supplier enjoys. New business may not always be as attractive as it first appears.

Relationship with employees

Entrepreneurial ventures can be progressed only if the right human skills are in place. They demand productive labour, technical knowledge, business insight and leadership. Human inputs are traded in markets. Some categories of human skill may be in short supply. If this is the case, the entrepreneur may have to compete to get hold of them. This competition takes the form of offering potential employees attractive remuneration packages and prospects for development.

If one entrepreneur employs an individual with a skill which is valuable and in short supply then another cannot employ that individual. More critically, perhaps, it is likely that the entrepreneur will attract such a person from an existing business. Most would agree that individuals should have the right to offer their skills and insight to whomsoever they wish. Furthermore, the demand for people with rare talents, reflected by the rewards they are offered, provides an incentive for others to develop those skills.

In practice, however, individuals do not market themselves as commodities within a 'perfect' labour market. They build close relationships with the organisations for which they work. People are motivated by more than just the financial rewards of working. The 'contracts' that individuals have with their organisations go beyond the simple terms of the formal written contract of employment. They involve unwritten, often unarticulated, expectations and loyalties on both sides.

As a consequence, while an entrepreneur seeking to attract an employee from a competitor is a proper functioning of the labour market, it can also be seen in negative terms as a kind of illegitimate 'poaching'. This can be traumatic and cause ill-feeling, particularly when the business community is close knit and the employee is felt to be offering not just their general experience, skills and insights but also insider knowledge to a competitor. Some employers use formal contractual devices to restrict employees in possession of sensitive knowledge moving to competitors.

While the entrepreneur should never feel ashamed at offering individuals a good reward for the skills and talents they have invested in creating for themselves, the effective entrepreneur must be sensitive to the human dimension of the business they are operating in and its rules when recruiting people. More often than not, these rules about what is acceptable and unacceptable in recruitment practice are unwritten.

Relationship with customers

Customers are a key stakeholder group for the entrepreneur. It is their interest in what the venture offers, and their willingness to pay for it, that ultimately provides the money which the entrepreneurial venture will use to reward all its stakeholder groups. The best way to attract the interest of customers is to provide them with goods and services which *genuinely* satisfy their needs, solve their problems and meet their aspirations.

A customer will not usually have a need which is both explicit and completely unsatisfied. Rarely will the entrepreneur be offering the customer something which they need in addition to everything else they consume. It is much more likely that they will be offering something that will *replace* something else they are using. In short, even an innovative entrepreneurial business will be competing with the potential customer's existing suppliers. Suppliers and their customers do not relate solely through the medium of a market. They also interact at a human level via the business network. In some instances this relationship may be trivial. In many, however, the relationship is far-reaching, deeply established and complex. The relationship may be sustained not by economic self-interest alone but also by friendship and trust.

When a new venture approaches a customer, it is asking not only that the customer buy the offering, but also that they stop buying or replace the offering provided by a competitor. The success of the selling approach will depend on more than the way the entrepreneur's offering competes against the one they seek to oust. The wider relationship they seek to end and the new one they offer to replace it will also be important. If the entrepreneur is to be successful in marketing and selling their products and services to customers they must consider not just the product or service but also the nature of the individual and organisational relationships that exist between customer and supplier in the marketplace. The entrepreneur must be prepared to create more rewarding relationships. This point will be developed further in section 25.1.

When starting their ventures, entrepreneurs are not just offering their product or service into a melée of short-term market exchanges. They are breaking and then reforming a pattern of relationships. Those relationships are governed by rules, some formal, some informal, some based on self-interest, and others governed by altruistic motives. Some are articulated openly, whereas others are not even recognised – until they are lost. Effective entrepreneurs understand those relationships, and the rules that govern them, so that they can successfully manage their position within the network. This is not to say that the entrepreneur should not occasionally break the rules – but they should be aware that they *are* breaking the rules and know *why* they are doing it.

24.2 Gaining financial investment: key issues

> ### Key learning outcome
>
> A recognition of the main issues associated with attracting financial investment to the new venture.

An entrepreneur will be interested in obtaining a variety of different resources in order to progress their venture. However, it is money that is likely to take first place on the list of priorities. This is understandable. Money is the most liquid of resources. Once it has been obtained it can be used readily to obtain the other things the business needs.

Attracting investment capital is one of the primary functions of the entrepreneur. It is a process that raises a number of critical issues. The entrepreneur must consider these issues carefully and make some fundamental decisions in relation to them. This section looks at the issues in overview as they were dealt with in detail in Chapter 20.

What level of investment is required?

Broadly, how much money will be needed to start the venture? This will depend on the nature of the venture, the opportunity it is pursuing, the stage in its development and the plans the entrepreneur has for the future. Initial investment levels are sensitive to the strategy the business is pursuing, in terms of the initial scope the business must have and the potential this leaves for growth. Some ventures can start on a small scale and build up over time. Anita Roddick started The Body Shop with a single outlet and a loan of £4,000. The business grew as new outlets were added incrementally over time. On the other hand, when Frederick Smith started the US air freight business Federal Express, he realised that if the business was to work he needed to offer customers a full service from the start. That meant acquiring a fleet of aircraft and a relatively large administrative and support structure. He sought $90 million of start-up capital.

Where is the investment to come from?

While there is an overall 'market for capital', there are a number of sources of investment capital. For example, the entrepreneur's own funds, bank loans, government loans, venture capital, share issues, business angels (experienced manager–investors who offer their expertise to new ventures along with capital), and so on. In other words, the market for capital is a fragmented one. Different capital providers occupy different niches in the market. They are characterised by the way they look for different types of investment opportunity, accept different levels of risk, expect different types of return and assume different levels of involvement in the running of the venture. To be effective in managing the project of attracting funds the entrepreneur must understand these different markets and the ways in which they work.

What is the capital structure of the investment to be?

The *capital structure* of the venture is simply the mix of different investment sources that are used. In broad terms it refers to the ratio of 'equity' to 'debt' capital, that is, the mix of investors who expect a return that will be linked to the performance of the venture to those who expect a fixed return based on an agreed interest rate whatever the performance of the business. In addition, loan capital may be unsecured or secured against some assets of the business.

The capital structure of the venture reflects the way in which the entrepreneur is sharing risk with the investors. Clearly, a secured loan exposes the investor to a lower level of risk than an equity share. At the same time, capital which exposes the investor to risk is more expensive than capital which does not. So by adjusting the capital structure entrepreneurs can, in effect, 'sell off' the risks inherent in their venture to different degrees.

How will the investors be approached?

Entrepreneurs and investors need to get in touch with each other before they can work together. Usually, the onus is on the entrepreneur to initiate the contact. That contact must be managed. Although investors try to make rational decisions about investment opportunities they are not calculating machines. They are still human beings who are influenced by *how* things are said as well as *what* is said – and first impressions are important. The way in which the entrepreneur first approaches the potential investor can have a bearing on the outcome of that contact. In essence, three things must be considered: the *who* of the contact, the *how* of the contact and the *what* of the contact.

First, the entrepreneur must identify suitable sources of investment, that is, the *who* of contact. This involves identifying organisations that provide investment capital. However, organisations do not make decisions, *individuals* do, and the entrepreneur may find it productive to find out which individual or individuals they should approach within the organisation. They may also consider the decision-making structure within the organisation, i.e. not only who actually takes the investment decisions but who influences them in that decision and the way in which their decisions are policed and judged within the organisation.

Second, the entrepreneur must consider the *how* of the contact. Should it be formal or informal? Does the investor lay down a procedure for making contact? (Most banks and venture capital companies, for example, do.) Does the investor expect a written proposal or a verbal one in the first instance? If it is verbal, do they expect a one-to-one chat or a full-blown presentation? If it is a written one, do they lay down a format for the proposal or do they give the entrepreneur latitude in the way they communicate? Many investors will simply reject a proposal out of hand if they are not approached in the right way.

Third, they must consider *what* to tell the investor. At the first contact stage, attracting the investor's attention and encouraging their interest is likely to be as important as giving them information. This will be particularly so if the investor is receiving a large number of approaches. Is it necessary to relate a detailed picture or will a broad outline be more effective? How much room for manoeuvre is there here if the communication has to comply with a set format?

What proposition is to be made to the investors?

The entrepreneur must consider what, exactly, they are offering the investor. Some of the critical dimensions here are:

- the amount of investment required;
- how that particular investment fits with the overall investment profile for the venture;
- the nature of the investment (e.g. loan or equity, secured or unsecured);
- the level of return anticipated;
- the nature (particularly the *liquidity*) of any security being offered;
- the degree of risk to which the capital will be exposed;
- the way 'in', i.e. how the investment will be made (what amount of money at what time);
- the way 'out', i.e. how the investor will get their return (what amount of money at what time);
- the degree of *control* the investor will be given over (or be expected to contribute to) the way the venture is run.

These things constitute the 'package' that the entrepreneur is offering to the investor. It is on the basis of these factors that investors will make their judgement as to whether the investment opportunity is of the right sort for them. The entrepreneur must never forget that they are *selling* the venture to investors. The entrepreneur must put as much effort into this selling exercise as they would into selling the business's products to customers.

24.3 Gaining human commitment

Key learning outcome

An appreciation of how the commitment of key people to the venture may be gained.

On its own, investment capital can achieve nothing. It must be used by *people* to progress the venture. The money obtained by one entrepreneur is exactly the same as the money obtained by another and, indeed, exactly like that held by established businesses. If an entrepreneurial venture is successful then it must be because its people do something *different* and *better* with the money to which they have access.

While it is conventional in management theory to talk of human beings as a resource, it should always be remembered that they are a *special* type of resource. There is more to gaining human commitment than simply bringing people into the business. They must certainly be attracted to the venture in the first instance. Once in, their motivation and dedication must be maintained and constantly developed. The entrepreneur does not just *recruit* to their venture, they must also *lead* it.

The entrepreneur faces a number of decisions in relation to developing the commitment other people have towards the venture.

What human skills are required?

Businesses need a variety of different types of human input. Technical skills, communication skills, functional skills and analytical skills are all critical to the success of a venture. Different ventures need different mixes of these skills in order to progress. The entrepreneur must decide what profile of skills and experience is right for their venture as it stands now, and what profile will be needed as it grows and develops. In light of the fact that human resources are as likely to be as scarce as any other, this may mean prioritising some requirements over others.

Where will those skills be obtained from?

Where are the people with those skills? Are they working for other organisations? If so, are they working for competitors or for non-competitors? If they are working for competitors, what issues will recruiting them raise?

What will be offered to attract those who have the skills?

In the first instance, this means pay and other aspects of the remuneration package. The entrepreneur must offer a package which is competitive in light of what other employers are offering. But pay is not the entirety of what an organisation offers an employee. Human needs go beyond purely financial concerns. It is critical to ask what the venture offers people as a stage on which to build social relationships. Is it a friendly environment? Will it be fun to work for? Further, what does the venture offer in the way of potential for self-development? How can people progress within it as it expands? What roles will they play? How does the venture represent a theatre for personal growth?

An entrepreneurial venture must compete for people not just with other entrepreneurial ventures but also with established organisations. The venture offers potential employees much the same thing as it presents to financial investors, that is, risk but with the promise of higher returns. The employee is exposed to the chance of the venture failing. However, there may also be the possibility of much higher rewards in the way of personal development, experience and achievement. Of course, financial investors and employees draw upon quite different mechanisms to manage risk and their exposure to it.

The entrepreneur must be aware of why the option of working for a dynamic, fast-changing, fast-growing organisation might be attractive (and why it might be unattractive) to potential employees.

How will potential employees be contacted?

People must be recruited. There are a variety of means for doing this. In the first instance, personal contact and word of mouth can be very productive. If this is not possible then a more formal means of recruiting is called for. This may demand advertising (perhaps in a trade press). It may even be felt expedient to delegate the task of attracting people to a specialist recruitment agency.

How will potential employees be evaluated?

Having contacted and attracted the interest of potential employees, then some evaluation and selection procedure must be invoked. Taking on a new employee represents a major commitment for both the business and the employee. Any effort expended in ensuring that the person is right for the organisation, and that the organisation is right for the person, at the recruitment stage, is likely to pay dividends. Mistakes can be expensive and painful for both parties. This is a process of ensuring not just that the person has the right technical skills but also that their attitudes and approach will fit with the organisation's approach, values and culture. However, the entrepreneur should be careful: there is strength in diversity.

If the entrepreneur knows a potential employee well, and has experience of the way in which they work, then the recruitment process may be quite informal (often little more than a job offer over a drink). If they are not acquainted with the person (and the contribution they might make) then an interview of some sort is required. Some would go further and require the candidate to undertake a *psychometric* or *attitudinal* test. Of course, these tools exist to aid the entrepreneur in making recruitment decisions which they cannot make on their own.

Should a skill be in-house or should it be hired when necessary?

Resources are scarce in the entrepreneurial venture. The entrepreneur must make the resources they have work hard. One question they should always ask when faced with the need for a particular human skill is whether it is best to bring that skill in-house, i.e. to recruit someone to perform the task, or to use an external agency to provide it. For example, should the business employ a financial expert or call on the assistance of a firm of accountants? Should it take on research and development staff or delegate a project to a university?

The 'employ or hire' decision is influenced by a variety of factors. How much of a particular skill input is required? Over what timescale will it be required? Will the business have a long-term need for it? How much control does the entrepreneur need over the person contributing that skill? How much will it cost to employ someone versus hiring them?

It may often appear that the hiring option is the more expensive. However, this expense needs to be considered in the light of the costs of recruitment. There are also risks associated with bringing someone new into the business. What contribution will they *really* make? How will they fit? How will existing employees get along with them? Further, hiring someone tends to add to the business's marginal costs whereas employing them adds to fixed costs. Hiring may be more attractive from a cash flow point of view especially when the venture's output may be variable and unpredictable. In light of this, in general, employment should be considered only when there is a clear, consistent, long-term need for a particular skill or a particular expertise within the business.

The way the business will gain from the additional level of control that comes from having the skill in-house should also be considered. If the business aims to develop a competitive advantage based on knowledge and an ability to use it to deliver value to the customer then it goes without saying that this knowledge should be held by people who are dedicated to the business.

Leadership and motivation strategy

Commitment is not just given, it must be maintained. In this the entrepreneur must be conscious of their own leadership and motivational strategy and the way they use it to bring out the best in their people. Developing and applying this strategy takes practice. The entrepreneur is the venture's key human resource. The skill they provide comes from being able to manage vision and use it to lead the organisation.

24.4 Establishing a presence with distributors

> ### Key learning outcome
>
> An understanding of decision making by distributors and the issues that entrepreneurs face in gaining access to distribution channels.

Distributors are often at the neglected end of business thinking. They are sometimes regarded as a necessary evil: a part of the value addition system that (productive!) businesses must put up with. Many accounts of entrepreneurship regard distributors as hurdles that entrepreneurs must overcome if their business is to be successful.

To be sure, 'glamorous' distributors such as the major retailers get a lot of attention (albeit often critical), but far less attention is given to smaller distributors. This neglect is unfortunate. Distributors create real economic value. They do so in four ways. First, they provide a logistical efficiency. Buyers can obtain a wide variety of purchases with a single journey. Second, they provide information in that they give buyers the opportunity to compare different producers' offerings alongside each other, thus enhancing competitive efficiency. Third, they can offer support with the promotion of goods, working as partners with producers. Fourth, and this is perhaps the most important aspect of their value addition, they provide producers with *liquidity*. A manufacturer may wish to produce a quantity of a good at any one time (capitalising on economies of scale). However, if that good is stored in the manufacturer's warehouse, then capital is tied up. By agreeing to buy a quantity in advance of customer demand, then the manufacturer can turn that stock into cash to fund the next phase of production.

In principle, strategic decision making by distributors is relatively straightforward. If the distributor is concerned with maximising profit, then they should consider only three things when deciding which (producers') goods to distribute:

- the *margin* on the good – the difference between the price the good can be purchased for and the price it will be sold for;
- the *rate of sale* of the good – how many units will be sold in a period;
- the *cost of storing* (and displaying) the good for the period before it is sold.

The cost of holding items is an *opportunity cost*, given that other items might be stored and displayed. In effect, the distributor is maximising the relationship:

Profit (on stocked item) per period = (Margin on item × Number of items sold in a period) − Cost of holding items over that period

This calculation may be intuitive and based on the distributor's experience, but, increasingly, distributors (and not just large retailers) are using computer software to do this calculation (often referred to as direct product profitability or DPP). This is not to negate the effect of personal relationships in producer–distributor networks, but these are usually built and maintained on the basis of such prior (implicit or explicit) calculations. It is for this reason that most distributors (be they major retailers or small wholesalers) rarely carry more than about three competitor products in any one product category.

What does this mean for the entrepreneur seeking the support of distributors? In short, appropriate distributors will be attracted if, and only if, in light of this calculation, the entrepreneur is offering a better deal than existing suppliers are. Consider the situation from the distributor's perspective. The entrepreneur may claim to be offering an innovative product that is new, different and better than that offered by existing suppliers and that will create new benefits to buyers. But all the distributor will see is that existing sales (from existing suppliers) will be replaced by sales of the entrepreneur's new item – no gain to them, and a lot of additional cost. Why should they replace the extant competitors' products, especially if they have a good relationship with existing suppliers? How might the entrepreneur improve on the deal and encourage the distributor to switch? The calculation suggests how. Either give higher margin, so the distributor gains more from every sale; and/or promise a higher rate of sale (i.e. *faster* overall demand), or propose that storage and display costs will be lower.

Each of these three options presents the entrepreneur with a dilemma. The higher the margin offered the lower (given production costs) the revenues to the entrepreneur. In effect, the entrepreneur is *buying* (with forgone profits) a presence with distributors. A higher rate of sale is plausible only if demand for the entrepreneur's good is absolutely higher than that of competitors (i.e. an expansion of the market) and, in any case, rate of sale will be dependent on the availability of competitor products. This can reduce to a self-fulfilling 'we will sell more, provided you exclude them' scenario. Rate-of-sale may be increased by effective promotion to the end-buyer, but this has costs of its own. Storage and display costs are fundamentally about the resources the distributor must apply to maintain that storage and display, but this often reduces to the physical volume of the good (given that the distributor is displaying to capacity), so the entrepreneur must offer to support display with direct financial support (additional to that offered by competitors), something which again introduces additional costs. Of the three options – increasing margin, additional payments to support storage costs, and support with promotion – entrepreneurs usually prefer the latter and make it the mainstay of their negotiation with distributors. Margin is likely to be an irredeemable cost of sale as negotiating reduced margins is difficult; promotional support is an investment that might be scaled back in the future.

In summary, distributors create real value. However, their inherent (and quite rational) conservatism does present a barrier to entry for new entrepreneurs. Entrepreneurs will face costs in bringing distributors on board and excluding existing competitors. However, the entrepreneur who has caught the attention (and support) of a distributor has a competitive advantage in that future entrepreneurs will have to go through the same process (undertake the same investment) if they wish to replace them.

Summary of key ideas

- The fourth stage in the strategic window is *opening* it.

- Opening the window means gaining the *commitment* of stakeholders and actually starting the venture.

- Distributors may be key allies, but their decision making must be understood if they are to be used effectively.

- The key commitments are financial support from *investors*; productive support from *employees* and *network contacts*; agreements to provide inputs by *suppliers*; and agreement to purchase outputs by *customers*.

Research themes

Entrepreneurs' management of resource acquisition

What guides an entrepreneur's decision whether to bring human and operating resources into the venture on a permanent basis (hold), or, alternatively, to hire them in as and when necessary? It might be hypothesised that the following factors would be important:

- Internal demand for the resource: is it needed for only a short period or is it required regularly?
- How *important* the resource is to the venture: marginal or critical?
- How easy it is to *obtain* the resource on a short-term basis (how well developed is the external market for the resource): easy or difficult?
- To what extent *unique* access to the resource is a source of competitive advantage: not significant or significant?
- To what extent the entrepreneur must invest in *developing* the resource: to a low degree or high?
- The difference in cost between short-term hiring and long-term holding: low hire-to-hold or high hire-to-hold ratio?

In each case, the former would be predicted to encourage hiring in, the latter to encourage permanent holding and internal development of the resource. For a particular set of ventures, identify a range of human and operating resources relevant to those ventures that vary across these factors. Use questionaires or interviews with the entrepreneurs leading those ventures and inquire into their hire-or-hold decisions. Have them rationalise those decisions. Do the rationalisations meet with these hypothesised criteria?

Network modelling and entrepreneurial entry

This study adopts a case study methodology. To be effective a significant number of cases (say around 20) need to be considered, but the analysis for each is quite focused. Obtain descriptions of a number of entrepreneurial ventures. A picture may be built up by undertaking secondary research from published sources or by primary research. For each venture, summarise the organisations that form its immediate network. A network model has two parts. The first considers an entrepreneurial venture and its links to other, resource-providing, individuals and organisations such as key employees, distributors, end-users, capital providers and suppliers. The second considers the nature of those links. In particular, how significant the resource provided is to the venture, the competition between suppliers of that resource, the nature of the relationship and how tight the link is (e.g. can the venture shift to an alternative provider? How high are switching costs? What are the risks in going elsewhere? How important is trust in the relationship? How high are search, contract establishment and monitoring costs?). The theory of networks suggests that entrepreneurs find it difficult to enter tight networks but are secure once in, and find it easy to enter loose networks, but are susceptible to future entrants once in. Is this borne out in practice? Identify sectors in which linkages are tight, moderate and loose. Then consider the rate of new entry and exit by entrepreneurs into the sector. A useful source of this information is VAT registration and deregistration statistics. Looser networked sectors should have a higher rate of entry and exit compared with tighter networked sectors. Is the prediction of the model realised?

The more mathematically ambitious student may wish to formalise the analysis of entrepreneurial networks using a branch of mathematics called *graph theory*. This is finding increasing application in the management sciences. A good introduction to the theoretical ideas can be found in Chartrand (1977).

 ## Key readings

Two papers that offer an interesting contrast, one examining start-up commitment from a resource perspective, the other from a network perspective, are:

Colombo, M.G., Delmastro, M. and Grilli, L. (2004) 'Entrepreneurs' human capital and the start-up of new technology-based firms', *International Journal of Industrial Organization*, Vol. 22, No. 8/9, pp. 1183–211.

Witt, P. (2004) 'Entrepreneurs' networks and the success of start-ups', *Entrepreneurship and Regional Development*, Vol. 16, No. 5, pp. 391–412.

Suggestions for further reading

Chartrand, G. (1977) *Introducing Graph Theory*. New York: Dover.

Cook, W.M. (1992) 'The buddy system', *Entrepreneur*, Nov., p. 52.

Gartner, W.B. (1984) *Problems in Business Start-up: The Relationships among Entrepreneurial Skills and Problem Identification for Different Types of New Venture*. Babson, Wellesley Park, MA: Centre for Entrepreneurial Studies.

Hall, W.K. (1980) 'Survival strategies in a hostile environment', *Harvard Business Review*, July/Aug., pp. 75–85.

Schoch, S. (1984) 'Access to capital', *Venture*, June, p. 106.

Yamada, J. (2004) 'A multi-dimensional view of entrepreneurship: towards a research agenda on organizational emergence', *Journal of Management Development*, Vol. 23, No. 4, pp. 289–320.

Selected case material

CASE 24.1

17 September 2005

The personal touch

EDI SMOCKUM

There's a lot of pain involved in selling your house: parting with memories, leaving friends and, most of all, watching the estate agent walk off with a hefty commission for what seems to have been very little work. Estate agents are everyone's favourite grumble. Unlike accountants and lawyers, they are not even worthy of being the butt of jokes (think about it, do you know any?). So, it is little wonder that people are beginning to take the selling of their home into their own hands.

FSBOs or 'For sale by owners' have been around for some time. But, while the concept is more popular in France and Germany, in Britain the drawbacks of cutting out the intermediary have tended to be emphasised more than the advantages. Homemade signs plonked on a front garden rarely inspire confidence in a buyer, and newspaper advertising costs can mount up alarmingly if a property does not sell quickly.

But since the growth of the internet a plethora of websites has sprung up that give access to a seemingly limitless number of potential buyers and provide services to help the potential seller to market their house more professionally.

When Jade Thomas and her husband decided to sell their Buckingham home this summer, they looked at what skills they had to bring to the selling game. Thomas is a designer, so she thought that she would have a professional feel for advertising on the web and could negotiate good prices on quarter-page advertisements in her local paper. She worked from home, so was available to take telephone calls and show people around.

The couple signed up with HouseWeb.com, a company started in 1995 by a group with a mix of marketing and IT experience. The company's prices for a standard advertisement on the website start at £47; adding a virtual tour makes the package £299, and taking one of the company's professionally produced 'for sale' signs costs another £24.99. These costs are a one-off charge and you can keep your house on the website until it sells. Like many of its competitors, HouseWeb also markets its properties on other websites such as fish4 and propertyfinder, giving customers access to some 2 million potential buyers.

Mark Desvaux, HouseWeb's managing director, says that when the company started people were sceptical about ordering a book on Amazon, let alone buying a house on the internet. At first, the company only advised customers about house buying and selling, and it was not until a year later that it sold its first home. Now it has about 3,000 properties on the website.

According to Desvaux, one of the things that draws people such as Thomas to online selling is simple – they want to save money. Now that people move home much more frequently than did previous generations, and with the average sale garnering up to 2 per cent for an estate agent (which would be up to £8,000 on a £400,000 sale), anyone who moves several times stands to pay out a lot in commission to do so.

As well as the financial considerations, many people think that they can sell their house more effectively than an estate agent since they have the personal experience of living in it and the motivation to get the best price for it. 'Estate agents are all about feet and inches,' says Desvaux. 'But a person who lives in a house knows its good points. Plus, they will remember being in the same shoes as the potential buyer when they bought the house, so they can empathise with them.'

While estate agents may think about location, location, location, owners who sell their own home can talk in detail about the local schools, the doctors' surgery and nearby shops and neighbours, which gives what Desvaux believes is a more representative picture of the house.

Thomas agrees. 'Other than the initial database of local house hunters and window shoppers, we couldn't see what an estate agent could offer us on top of marketing, especially not for several thousand pounds,' she says. 'We have the greatest knowledge of and motivation to sell this property.'

So just how easy is it? Martin Charlick is managing director of The Little House Company, which has 2,000 homes on its website. He says self-sellers have always had the problem of getting 'the same broad-brush penetration as estate agents'. The internet has changed that, although he points out that it has taken time. 'It took a while for people to get their head around the fact that they could sell a house themselves,' he says. The process has been helped, he adds, by growing confidence in doing business on the net.

Another factor, according to HouseWeb's Mark Desvaux, is that people are beginning to take much more control of their finances through self-trading and self-directed pensions, and have begun to see house selling as an extension of this. Both men say that so much of the process will be in the hands of sellers when Home Information Packs become mandatory in 2007, that it will make selling your own home feel even easier.

On the other hand, Charlick points out that self-selling isn't right for everyone – many people don't have the time to do the same preparatory work that an estate agent would do. 'You still need a good description and a good set of photographs,' he says, 'and it helps if you are a good communicator.' All too often, some of his customers fail to understand that the 'buck stops with them'. If a house doesn't sell, the underlying reasons tend to be just the same as with properties listed with estate agents – 'the price is too high or people are just too attached to their property. We try to tell them that they have to be objective. They may love their house, but they have to see it through someone else's eyes and recognise its shortcomings.'

One vital issue is pitching the price of the house at the right level: get that wrong and sellers could lose more money than they save. The Thomases got quotes from three estate agents before choosing the 'middle' price on their house. HouseWeb suggests that people research what price houses on their street are being sold at and use the new database provided by the Land Registry.

But what about the nitty-gritty bits of real estate – the negotiation and liaising – isn't that better done by an agent? Not always, according to Desvaux. 'I think there is a fundamental flaw in the UK process of house buying and selling – and a fair amount of smoke and mirrors. An estate agent holds all the information – and, working from commission, they can use that information for their own gain.'

Once a price has been negotiated, the process is the same as it is with an estate agent – a solicitor or conveyancer has to be appointed to do the legal work. Charlick says that he finds it extraordinary that some people are willing to do this phase of the transaction to save money – at some risk if they get it wrong – but are afraid of trying to sell their home themselves.

Police officer Richard Tribe did sell his mother's house himself, and found the conveyancing to be no easier than it is when you go through an estate agent. 'It still took it out of me,' he admits. But, otherwise, he found the rest of the process very easy and wouldn't use an estate agent again. 'I think they are soon going to be a thing of the past. They've made too much money for too long.'

Sellers also have the option of choosing both routes – engaging an estate agent and trying to sell their house themselves through a website. The Office of Fair Trading clearly states in its guide to house buying and selling that if you find a buyer yourself, you don't have to pay commission because you are not an agent. Only if the estate agent has put in a clause retaining 'sole selling rights' rather than 'sole agent rights' are they entitled to commission on any sale. About two-thirds of The Little House Company's customers, for example, are listed with an estate agent as well.

Will selling on the web come to dominate house sales in the future? Most people already start their house search on the web and there are many new entrants to the online selling business – often offering very cheap rates to list a house. Entrepreneurs are also beginning to see gaps in the self-sell market and are providing complementary services. Charlick was contacted by a company recently offering to do the 'chain chasing' for people selling their own homes. The irony was not lost on him: 'I do hope we don't come full circle, so that we end up in a situation where an estate agent will say, "Come back to us because we'll do it all for you."'

Source: Edi Smockum, 'The personal touch', *Financial Times*, 17 September 2005, p. 22. Copyright © 2005 Edi Smockum.

CASE 24.2

17 September 2005

FT

Candy-coloured 'blobjects' for all

DALIA FAHMY

Karim Rashid's living room in an old New York town house looks like a toyshop in outer space. The glossy white epoxy floor is strewn with candy-coloured 'blobjects', to use a term he coined, and it takes me a few seconds to recognise furniture: a lime green television console shaped like a bean, and seating for five on a phallic orange sack called the Superblob.

Almost everything in sight was conceived by the Egyptian-born, Canadian-bred industrial designer, down to the prize-winning hour-glass bottle of Method dish soap that stands on its head by the kitchen sink. (He even helped concoct the liquid inside. 'It's all natural; you can drink the whole bottle,' he explains. 'Not that you'd want to.')

Stunningly prolific, Rashid has fashioned thousands of objects that people use every day. Millions have bought the plastic Oh Chair and Garbo garbage bin he created for Canadian houseware company Umbra.

He has designed Issey Miyake perfume bottles, Sony CD players and Target dog bowls. The list of his work seems endless and spans everything from hotels to kettles to sunglasses. Yet few outside the design world would recognise his name.

That may change this month as the 45-year-old makes his television debut as a judge on the new reality show *Made in the USA* from US cable channel USA Network. Rashid will be one of three experts who rate the work of aspiring inventors; his job will be to comment on design and packaging.

'The show allows me to continue with my agenda, which is to get everybody in this country to recognise design,' he says, gesticulating with tan arms covered in tattoos of a hieroglyphic alphabet he invented. Rashid is fascinated by symbols and often embeds them in his work. He tells me he sees them as proof of a language shared by the first humans, who, he says, descended to Earth on a spaceship. (Suddenly, the decor makes more sense.)

But the origin of life is not a subject on which he wants to dwell. The rise of good design is.

'It's almost like design is the new art form,' he says. 'Architecture was at the pinnacle of the major arts for a while, and now I think design is at the top.'

We are sitting on a womb-like green couch Rashid calls Orgy ('because it brings people together') and the designer's white nail-polish and clunky rings glint in the sun as we talk. Tall and thin, he wears a white shirt with sleeves rolled up, pink Converse sport shoes and matching pink trousers.

Rashid is known for work that mixes colours and shapes for a distinctively futuristic look. Critics write it off as a 1960s version of the future, but it's much sleeker than that. Anthropomorphic, sexually suggestive forms are softened by smooth glossy surfaces. Bright colours are offset by lots of white.

Above all, he likes to use technology and synthetic materials, often plastic, to make design affordable.

'Craft is dead,' he says, arguing that the ever-improving quality of mass-produced goods has made traditional handmade luxuries obsolete. In the past, he says, one had to spend thousands of dollars on a Rolex to get a watch that looked good and kept time accurately. Now, anybody can get precision and aesthetics for much less. Incidentally, Rashid has just finished designing plastic watches for the Italian firm Alessi, which will go on sale for $80 in the US this autumn.

'I've always been a big advocate of democratic design,' he says. 'I would like to surround people with the best quality and most inexpensive goods.'

The Oh Chair and Garbo bins succinctly embody this philosophy. Made of plastic, they are light, stackable, and inexpensive, widely available for just $40 and $5 respectively. Even cheap, well-designed objects provide physical and psychological comfort, Rashid says, and he wants to help people live healthier and happier lives.

This drive to design for the masses and Rashid's unapologetic salesmanship have made him an immensely successful entrepreneur, but they have also roused considerable hostility. 'He's somewhat controversial in the design world and is becoming more controversial,' says Christopher Mount, director of exhibitions and public programmes at the Parsons School of Design. 'He's spent so much time promoting himself.'

Mount says Rashid is often criticised for producing work of 'varying quality': objects that don't follow traditional rules of good design, contain too much superfluous detail or are made too cheaply.

Rashid says he consciously breaks rules and no longer believes in any particular school of thought. 'The design profession is so steeped in a nepotistic insular world,' he says. Design doesn't neatly fall into categories of 'good' and 'bad' the way it used to. 'I have always believed that design is for everyone, and I do not agree with those who see it as elitist.'

Prize juries seem to like his work well enough, and he rakes in several awards each year. Michelle Berryman, executive vice-president of the Industrial Designers Association of America, which has honoured him six times, says Rashid is popular because his work is unconventional. 'He's really into challenging traditional ideas of what things should look like.'

Even critics admit that Rashid has significantly helped to raise the public's awareness of industrial design, and Mount suggests that this might be his biggest contribution to the field.

In 1993, when Rashid moved to New York after training under Ettore Sottsass in Italy, few consumers knew or cared who had designed their toaster or shower curtain. Now, people such as Michael Graves and Martha Stewart have become celebrities who sign their names on exactly these items at discount stores such as Target and K-Mart. 'Especially in America, I would like to take credit for pushing the larger audience to embrace design,' Rashid says.

There is no question that he is a tireless advocate and promoter through lectures, publicity events and now in the forthcoming television show. He has also published four books, including *I Want To Change the World*, in 2001.

Last year, Rashid decided to open his first retail outlet in New York's Chelsea. He concedes that Americans lag slightly behind Europeans in embracing innovative design (Galeries Lafayette in Paris, for example, carries a good portion of his collection while comparable department stores in New York carry none). But he blames a lack of affordable choices rather than US conservatism.

'Americans have created the phenomenon of Target, Apple or Nike. These are huge design-driven companies and they've influenced the rest of the world,' he says. 'The difference is that Americans like design

CASE 24.2 CONT.

when it's at the right price. As soon as it's more democratic, it's more acceptable.'

Rashid says that living in Canada and now the US has instilled in him an appreciation of casualness and comfort, but also a sense of freedom. 'Knowing that life is short, you should be able to embrace it the way you want,' he says. 'Design can influence that, because it makes you rethink the way you live.'

Source: Dalia Fahmy, 'Candy-coloured "blobjects" for all', *Financial Times*, 17 September 2005, p. 13. Copyright © 2005 Dalia Fahmy.

Discussion points

1. What do you see are the specific challenges in getting stakeholders to commit to an internet venture as opposed to a 'conventional' venture?

2. What issues might Karim Rashid face in gaining the commitment of stakeholders to his venture?

CHAPTER 25

Closing the window: sustaining competitiveness

Chapter overview

The final stage in using the strategic window metaphor is to close it. This means giving the venture some unique and valuable character so that competitors cannot follow through the window and exploit the opportunity it has identified as well. The concept of competitive advantage is introduced; what it is, how it can be established and how it can be maintained are considered.

25.1 Long-term success and sustainable competitive advantage

Key learning outcome

An appreciation of how business success is dependent on creating, developing and sustaining competitive advantage in the marketplace.

Having opened the strategic window by gaining financial and human commitment to the venture, the entrepreneur must ensure that the long-term potential for success is not eroded by competitors moving in. Entrepreneurs must close the strategic window to limit the possibility that competitors will follow them and exploit the opportunity as well.

The notion of *sustainable competitive advantage* provides a powerful conceptual approach to recognising the ways in which the strategic window can be closed to help guarantee long-term success in the marketplace. It provides an insight into the decisions that must be made in order to keep the business in a position where it can compete effectively. Competitive advantage is a central pillar of strategic thinking, which has been developed by Michael Porter (1985) in particular.

It is important to distinguish between a *competitive advantage*, which must be understood in terms of what the business offers to the marketplace, and the *source* of that competitive advantage, which relates to how the business is set up to deliver that offering to the marketplace. Business life is, by definition, competitive. A particular competitive advantage may be imitated, in which case it loses its value. If a business is to enjoy a competitive advantage over the long term it must be one which competitors find difficult, and in business that means *expensive*, to copy. Consequently, a full delivery of competitive advantage demands decisions at three levels (Figure 25.1):

Figure 25.1 The structure of competitive advantage

- what will be offered to the marketplace that is unique and valuable – the *competitive advantage*;
- how that offering will be maintained by the business – the *source* of the competitive advantage;
- how that competitive advantage will be protected from imitation by competitors – the way it will be *sustained*.

Competitive advantage

Competitive advantage is located in what is offered to the marketplace. A competitive advantage is present if the business consistently offers the customer something which is *different* from what competitors are offering, and that difference represents something *valuable* for the customer. In short, a competitive advantage is the reason why customers spend their money with one business rather than another.

The entrepreneur must decide what type of competitive advantage they aim to pursue. Some of the more important are:

- offering the customer a *lower price*, that is, better value for money;
- differentiating the offering through its *features* or *performance*, that is, an offering which satisfies needs or solves problems for its customers better than a competitor's product does;
- differentiating the offering through *service*, that is, addressing needs or solving problems in a more effective way, or supporting the use of the product more effectively;
- differentiating the offering through *branding*, that is, through investment in communicating quality and the business's commitment to the offering;
- differentiating the offering through *brand imagery*, that is, by building in associations which address social and self-developmental needs as well as functional needs;
- differentiating through *access* and *distribution*, that is, by giving the customer easier, more convenient, less disruptive or less time consuming access to the offering.

The sources of competitive advantage

Being able to *consistently* offer something different and meaningful in the ways described above will occur only if the business is itself different from its competitors in some way.

A competitive advantage in the marketplace must be delivered from within the business and be supported by it.

John Kay (1993) has developed a perspective on competitive advantage which sees it as having its source in one of four distinct capabilities:

- the *architecture* of the business – i.e. its internal structure;
- the *reputation* of the business – i.e. the way key stakeholders view it;
- the way the business *innovates* – i.e. its ability to come up with new and valuable ideas;
- the business's *strategic assets* – i.e. valuable assets to which it has access but its competitors do not.

These four distinctive capabilities are quite general and apply to all businesses. They can be related to four specific sources of competitive advantage for the entrepreneurial venture making its presence felt in the marketplace. These are *costs*, *knowledge*, *relationships* and *structure*.

Cost sources

The business may enjoy an advantage owing to lower costs. In economic terms this means that the business will be able to *add value* more efficiently. Cost advantages may be gained from four main areas:

- *Lower input costs* – the business may have access to input factors which are cheaper than those available to competitors. This can include raw materials, energy or labour. Lower input costs can be gained by a number of means. Particularly important are access to unique sources of inputs (say, through special contractual arrangements or from geographical location) and achieving buying power over suppliers.
- *Economies of scale* – a business must dilute its fixed costs (which are independent of output) over revenues (which are dependent on output). Hence, *unit* costs tend to fall as output increases. Fixed costs are those which must be borne regardless of the output achieved. These typically include 'head office' costs and often much of the marketing, sales and development activity. A larger output means that these costs are being used more productively. It may then give a business an overall cost advantage over competitors.
- *Experience curve economies* – these are a consequence of the business's learning how to generate its outputs. As a business gains experience in adding value, the cost of adding that value is reduced. In short, practice pays. A large number of studies over a variety of different industries has found that a strict mathematical relationship holds between unit cost and output experience. This relationship is exponential, that is, costs fall by a fixed amount every time output is doubled. This means that, for a linear output, the cost reductions achieved in a particular time period are seen to fall off as time goes on. This exponential relationship is shown in Figure 25.2.

Like economies of scale, experience curve economies are related to output. However, the two should not be confused. Whereas economies of scale depend on output in a particular *period*, experience curve economies are a result of *cumulative* output. In general, the firm with the highest cumulative output in a market will be in a position to have developed the lowest unit cost. Most studies of experience curve economies have concentrated on production costs. However, the principle is a general one and applies to any cost of adding value. So experience curve economies may be sought in other parts of the firm's value addition process such as sales, marketing, procurement, etc.

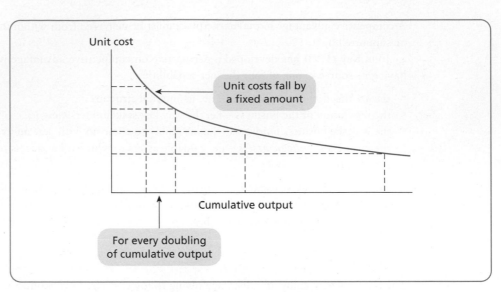

Figure 25.2 The experience curve: costs fall exponentially as experience is gained

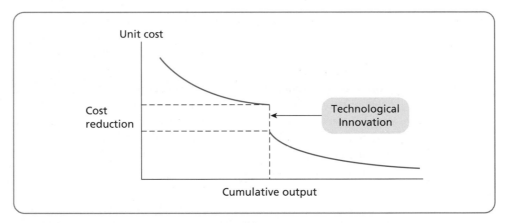

Figure 25.3 The experience curve and technological innovation

- *Technological innovation* – a firm's costs are, technically, the cost of adding a particular amount of value to an input in order to create a saleable output. Costs are related to the technology used by the business to add value. A technological innovation can provide a cost advantage by enabling value to be added more efficiently. In practice, a technological innovation can be used to 'reset' the experience curve at a lower level (Figure 25.3). Such innovation often relates to production technology but in principle it can apply to any value-adding activity within the organisation.

Knowledge sources

Knowledge can be valuable. A firm may enjoy a competitive advantage if it knows things that its competitors do not. This knowledge might be in any one of a number of areas:

- *Product knowledge* – a special understanding of the products (or services) that make up the market. Critically, this knowledge must be used to create offerings which are more attractive to buyers. Product knowledge must be used in conjunction with knowledge of the *market*.
- *Market knowledge* – special insights into the way the market functions. This includes areas such as the needs of the consumer, the way in which customers buy and what can be used to influence them. This knowledge can be used to create effective marketing and selling strategies.
- *Technical knowledge* – a special understanding and competence in making and delivering the offering to the marketplace. This knowledge is not valuable on its own. Rather, it must be used to offer the customer something different: a better product, a lower-cost product or a better service.

Knowledge does not come for free. It is the result of investment. Product and technical knowledge arise from research and development activities. Market knowledge comes from market research and market analysis. It should be remembered that knowledge is not in itself valuable. It only forms the basis of a competitive advantage if it is used to deliver new value to the customer.

Relationship sources

Relationships are not just a 'nice to have' add-on to business activity, they are fundamental to it. A relationship establishes trust and trust adds value by reducing the need for contracts and monitoring. A business may be able to build a competitive advantage on the basis of the special relationships it enjoys with its stakeholders. Building relationships is essential if the business is to locate itself in a secure, and supportive, network.

The idea of entrepreneurial networks has been considered earlier in section 13.4. The notion of building competitive advantage on the basis of relationships resonates with the idea of locking the venture into a set of secure and rewarding network links that competitors find it hard, or at least expensive, to break. Networks built on trust and confidence are valuable because they minimise transaction costs. Kay (1996) considers the role of trust in developing and maintaining economic relationships.

- *Relationship with customers.* A firm's relationship with its customers is a critical dimension of its success. The relationship can be built in a number of ways. Much depends on the nature of the products being sold to the customer and the number of customers the firm has to deal with. A business selling a small number of highly valuable products to a few customers is in a different situation from one selling a large number of relatively low-value items to a great number of customers.

  Relationships can be personal, that is, created through individual contact. Account management and sales activities are important in this respect. The sales–buyer interaction is both a one-to-one contact and a conduit through which value can flow from the business to its customers. If a large number of customers are involved, and personal contact is not possible, then contact may be sustained via the media through advertising and public relations.

  Critical to the relationship with customers is *reputation*. A reputation for delivering products which do what they say they will, and for delivering them with a high degree of service, and for undertaking business in a fair and equitable way, is invaluable. Reputation can be hard to build up. It is, however, quite easy to lose.

*   *Relationship with suppliers.* Suppliers are best regarded as partners in the development of an end-market. They are integral to the network the business needs to build up around itself. A business can put itself in a stronger position to deliver value to its customers if its suppliers themselves show flexibility and responsiveness. Further, suppliers can be encouraged to innovate on behalf of the business. All of this means that the relationship with suppliers has to go beyond just the concern with negotiating over prices. Although suppliers need to share value with their customers, the game need not be a zero-sum one. A customer working with its suppliers can address the end-market better and create more overall value to be shared than one working against its suppliers.

*   *Relationship with investors.* Of all stakeholders it is, perhaps, investors who have the most transparent relationship with the entrepreneurial venture. In economic terms their concern is the most one-dimensional: they are concerned to maximise their returns. Investors are, however, still human beings. They engage in communication and relationship building with the entrepreneur. They respond not only to actual returns but also if they feel their interests are being properly addressed by the entrepreneur.

    The support of investors can be critical to success. Any venture will have its ups and downs, especially in its early stages. When things are not going too well, the support of investors is invaluable. If they insist on liquidating their investment then, at best, problems will be exacerbated; at worst, the business may not survive. The support of investors can be maintained by developing a strategy to communicate actively with them. This will involve managing the investors' expectations, building their confidence in the venture and avoiding 'surprises' which lead investors to make hasty judgements.

*   *Relationship with employees.* Building a motivating and productive relationship with employees is one of the entrepreneur's most important activities. It is the employees who deliver the actions which convert the entrepreneur's vision into reality. The entrepreneurial venture may not enjoy many of the cost, technical and relationship advantages that established players can call upon. All it has is its people, and their interest, motivation and drive on behalf of the business. The entrepreneur must draw this out by understanding their employees' motivations and adopting the right leadership strategies.

Structural sources

The final area in which the entrepreneurial business can aspire to develop a basis for competitive advantage is in its structure. Structural advantages arise as a consequence not so much of *what* the business does as of the *way* it goes about doing things. This is a function not only of its formal structure, the predefined way in which individuals will relate to each other, but also of its informal structure, the unofficial web of relationships and communication links which actually define it, and its *culture*, which governs how those relationships will function and evolve. Since new entrants are unlikely to enjoy cost advantages in the early stages of the business, and because relationship advantages take time to build up and knowledge advantages require investment, the entrepreneurial business is likely to be highly dependent on structural advantages.

A business can gain a competitive advantage from its structure if that structure allows it to perform better in the marketplace. Such a structural advantage may arise from having the

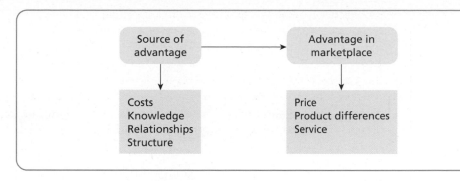

Figure 25.4 Competitive advantage and its sources

business co-ordinated by a strong leader who keeps the business on track and focuses it on the opportunities at hand. Such leadership ensures that resources are used effectively. The business may also be better at gaining information from the marketplace and using it to make decisions. This might allow it to be more responsive to the needs of customers and so be quicker to offer them new products and services.

Another structural advantage can arise if the individuals who make up the business emphasise *tasks* (what needs doing) rather than *roles* (what they feel their job descriptions say they should do). Such an attitude enables the business to be flexible, to focus on its customers and keep fixed costs to a minimum.

Competitive advantages in the marketplace can be built on a number of platforms within the organisation (Figure 25.4). Costs, knowledge, relationships and structures may all be used to offer the customer value in a way that competitors cannot. This makes them sources from which a competitive advantage may be developed in the marketplace. They have the potential to bring success to the venture. However, if this success is to be long term, the competitive advantages must be maintained in the face of competitive activity. They must be *sustained*.

25.2 How competitive advantage is established

Key learning outcome

An appreciation of the ways in which competitive advantages may be established but can be lost to competitors.

The business world does not stand still. Competitors are aware of each other to varying degrees. They become *acutely* aware if they lose business, or at least are prevented from gaining it, by the activities of a competitor. They may go on to develop an understanding of *why* that business is performing better than they are. A successful business cannot hide its competitive advantage for long. Competitors will then be tempted to imitate and recreate that competitive advantage for themselves. This may be easier said than done. If competitors find a competitive advantage hard to imitate, then the entrepreneurial firm may go on enjoying the rewards that that advantage offers. If the advantage is hard to imitate it is said to be *sustainable*.

A reverse perspective is illuminating in this instance. To understand how competitive advantage may be sustained demands an appreciation of how it can be *lost*. Quite simply, a

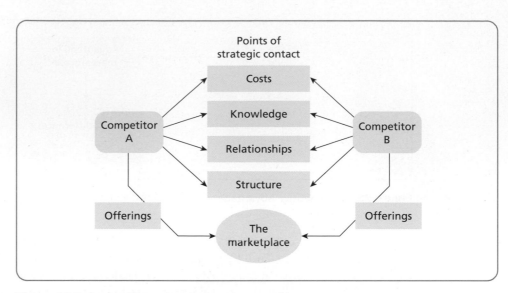

Figure 25.5 Competitive advantage and competition

competitive advantage is lost if a competitor *gains* it. In order to offer something that gains an advantage in the marketplace, a business must create for itself the *source* of that advantage. The framework developed in the previous section applies, so competitive advantage is lost to competitors if they achieve lower *costs*, or gain *knowledge* that was exclusive to and valuable to the venture, or build a stronger network of *relationships* than the venture enjoys, or develop *structural* advantages (advantages in the way the business organises itself).

An entrepreneurial venture must constantly strive to prevent competitors gaining a relative advantage in these areas. While the venture actually meets its competitors in the marketplace the basis of competitive advantages provides the points of *strategic contact* between the venture and its competitors. It is these things which give the venture the *power* to compete (Figure 25.5).

The entrepreneur must be on their guard as to the ways in which competitors might gain the upper hand in terms of competitive advantage. They must consider the ways in which competitors might gain the advantage, and be aware of these when they are developing their strategy. A sound strategy must be built on a competitive advantage which can be sustained. Knowing this is part of understanding the nature of the market, the players who make it up and competition within it. The decisions which relate to developing a competitive advantage must be made in relation to the considerations on how *costs*, *knowledge*, *relationships* and *structure* deliver advantages in the marketplace.

Considerations in relation to cost advantages

Here the chief considerations relate to how cost advantages may be used in the marketplace to achieve volume gains (in other words, how price sensitive the customer is); how competitors can use factor prices to their advantage; and how volume gains are rewarded with further cost reductions (i.e. to what extent volume and cost are linked in a virtuous circle via economies of scale and experience effects). Also important is how established the cost structure of the industry is. In particular, is a technological innovation that changes the cost rules likely to occur, and if so, how quickly will it spread through the sector?

Some important specific questions are:

- How important is price to the customer?
- How important is price to intermediaries and distributors?
- Can volume be gained if price is reduced (i.e. is demand elastic)?

These questions may be answered by the use of appropriate market research techniques. Some further discoveries to be made through market research are:

- Have all the players in the market access to the same inputs?
- Do some players enjoy exclusive access to low-cost inputs?
- Are economies of scale important?
- If so, does one player have a significant *period* volume advantage?
- Are experience economies important?
- If so, has one player a *cumulative* volume advantage?
- Do any players have a *technological advantage* that influences costs?
- Is a technological innovation that will alter costs likely in the future?
- If so, how quickly would such a technological innovation spread through the industry?
- How expensive would it be to adopt any such cost-reducing technological innovations?

These questions may be answered by an analysis of the industry's structure and from knowledge of its technological base. The answers will illuminate the possibility of sustaining a cost-based advantage. In short, it will be sustainable if price is important to the customer and one player can gain a cost advantage from experience or technological sources.

Considerations in relation to knowledge advantages

Here the considerations relate to how exclusive knowledge may be gained, used and protected by the players in a sector.

Some important specific questions are:

- Is the knowledge the industry uses established or is it in a state of rapid development? (This involves consideration of whether the industry is a high-tech one which spends heavily on product research and development or marketing research.)
- Do the businesses in the industry use a common pool of knowledge or do they rely on their own localised knowledge?
- Is knowledge developed in-house or are external organisations (for example, business service firms such as market research agencies and consultancies and not-for-profit organisations such as universities) important?
- How important to the industry are knowledge protection devices such as patents, copyrights and registered designs?

Again, these questions can be answered through an appropriate analysis of the industry, its environment and its technology. Clearly, knowledge which is important to delivering customer value, is localised and is protectable offers a more sustainable basis for competitive advantage than knowledge which is accessible to all.

Considerations in relation to relationship advantages

Relationships are the glue that holds the business network together. If relationships are long term and secure, then the network can be thought of as tight. If relationships are transitory and easily broken, then the network is loose. A new entrant will find a tight network hard to break into. It may be expensive to break old relationships and establish new ones. On the other hand, once a location in that network has been established the business will find it easy to defend its position. Conversely, a loose network, while being easy to enter, will offer little security from competitors.

Some important specific questions are:

- What means are used to establish and maintain relationships with customers? (Personal contact (e.g. sales activity) or contact via the media (e.g. advertising)?)
- Are relationships with customers long term or short term? (Consider whether purchases are one-off or repeat. Is after-sales support important?)
- What *risks* does the buyer face in buying and using the product? (What sort of investment does it entail? What can go wrong when using it?)
- How can a sense of *trust* between the buyer and seller aid the management of those risks?
- How important is the seller's *reputation* to the buyer?
- On what basis can reputation be built? (Consider issues such as product quality, service, ethical standards, behaviour.)

A particularly effective entrepreneurial strategy is to identify a sector in which the network is loose and to create value through 'tightening it up' by offering a higher level of commitment and service. This also locks out competitors and makes the advantage gained sustainable.

Considerations in relation to structural advantages

As noted in section 25.1, structural advantages arise as a consequence not so much of *what* the business does as of the *way* it goes about doing things. A business can gain an advantage over its competitors by having a structure in which roles are more flexible (which can lead to lower costs), by being more focused on the market and so more responsive to signals from customers and competitors, and then by using those signals to make faster and better decisions about how to serve the customer.

Some important specific questions are:

- What kind of organisational *structures* do businesses in the sector adopt? (Consider, in particular, how important are functional departments, team working, ad hoc structures.)
- How important are *formal* structures? (Consider how the way things *really* happen compares with the way businesses say they *should* happen.)
- What kinds of *decision-making processes* are used? (Over what timescale are plans made? Who is involved in decision making? How are particular decisions justified within organisations?)
- How do firms in the sector identify, process and respond to market signals? (Consider whether the market research is formalised. How is pricing policy determined? How is new product development organised?)
- What *cultures* are adopted by businesses in the sector? (Consider customer focus versus internal concerns; entrepreneurial versus bureaucratic attitudes; the importance of tasks versus roles.)

- What leadership styles are adopted? (Consider whether they are authoritarian or consensus based. Is power exercised through the control of resources or the communication of vision? Is there a focus on tasks or a focus on people?)

Rigid structures provide the entrepreneur with a means of focusing and directing their organisation but they are ambivalent as a source of competitive advantage. It may be better to allow people to use their skills and insights by pushing decision making down the organisation – particularly when it is in a turbulent environment.

Understanding the answers to all of these questions gives the entrepreneur an insight into how they can establish a competitive advantage in the marketplace in a way which has a secure and distinctive base within their business. Further, it indicates the potential which a particular competitive advantage has to be *sustainable* in the face of competitive pressure.

25.3 Maintaining competitive advantage

> ### Key learning outcome
>
> An understanding of the ways in which competitive advantage may be sustained.

Identifying a competitive advantage, that is, something the customer finds both different and attractive, and securing that on the basis of some aspect of the business, be it *costs*, *knowledge*, *relationships* or *structure*, in a way which both provides a source for that advantage and differentiates the business from competitors is the *starting point* for long-term success. In order to *ensure* that it happens, the business must make sure that the competitive advantage cannot be imitated, and so the profits it promises cannot be eroded, by competitors. The entrepreneur must decide not only what the competitive advantage of the venture they establish will be but also how that advantage will be *sustained*.

Sustaining cost advantages

The key decision here is how will the business keep its costs lower than those of competitors? There can only be *one* cost leader in a market. If it is to be based on scale and experience curve economies, cost leadership demands *output volume* leadership. This means gaining and maintaining the highest (or at least highest volume) market share. This can prove to be expensive if the market is price sensitive. Competitors will be willing to compete by cutting their prices. The cost leader will have to use their cost advantage to establish a price below that of competitors' costs. This may mean a low, or even zero, profit margin. A cost leadership strategy may mean a long haul with poor profit levels until competitors have been 'seen off'.

The temptation to increase prices to gain short-term profits must be resisted since this will create a 'price umbrella' under which less efficient competitors can shelter. If the entrepreneur is a late entrant to the market and coming in from behind, then they may need to invest heavily in the short term to gain a rapid cumulative volume advantage over competitors. Again, this can prove to be expensive in the short run, with substantial returns offered only in the long term. This, of course, introduces a number of risks.

Further, even though experience cost reductions are a function of output volume, they do not occur by right. They have to be *managed*. For the cost leader, cost control has to take centre stage, i.e. driving costs down must take priority over all other considerations. This demands that powerful cost control systems be in place. This in turn will influence the leadership and motivation strategies adopted by the entrepreneur and the culture of the organisation they create. Such 'single-minded' organisations are not to everyone's taste: a factor which needs to be considered when recruiting and building the management team.

If the cost leadership is to be established on the basis of a technological innovation then the entrepreneur needs to be sure why they, and they alone, will have access to that technology. It is best to assume that competitors will eventually gain access to the innovation even if it is secured through patents and other intellectual property devices (see below). In respect to this it is best to use the innovation as the *starting point* to gain an initial cost advantage, which can be built on and sustained using scale and experience effects.

Even if all this is achieved, the entrepreneur must be sensitive to the attentions of anti-trust regulators. A strategy which achieves a large market share on the basis of squeezing competitors out on price may be a just reward for doggedly pursuing efficiency. To outsiders, however, it may seem like an unfair monopoly.

In conclusion, there can only be one cost leader in a market. A cost leadership strategy is one which is challenging and, in the short term at least, expensive, to sustain.

Sustaining knowledge advantages

Knowledge advantages are based on an understanding of both the product and the market. These two things operate in tandem with one other. An understanding of what is offered must be tempered with an understanding of why the customer wants it. Generally in business, knowledge soon becomes public. Even if knowledge is 'secure' within the business, the process of launching products and promoting them to the customer sends clear signals to competitors.

Knowledge may be protected by means of patents and other intellectual property devices such as copyrights and registered designs. In principle, these prevent competitors from using the knowledge. They grant the holder a monopoly over the innovation arising from the knowledge. In some industries, intellectual property is very important, for example in the biotechnology industry. In others, such as engineering, it is less so. However, the use of intellectual property devices as a means of securing a competitive advantage should be approached cautiously. Patents and other devices are not granted for every new idea; rather, they must reflect a *significant* technological innovation. Even if the new idea is significant, the registration process is time consuming, demands the aid of experts and can be expensive. Registration may also involve the public posting of the invention prior to any patent being granted. In effect this means presenting the patent to challenge by holders of other patents. This can tip off competitors. Often, not just one but a number of variations of the idea will have to be patented in order to ensure that competitors do not get round the patent by presenting minor variations to the market.

Furthermore, the patent registration will have to be obtained in a variety of regions if global cover is desired. If comprehensive cover is not obtained then competitors may get round the patent by producing the product in an area where the patent does not hold. Even if global cover is obtained, some countries are lax (because of weak legal structures or even, in some cases, as a matter of policy) in enforcing intellectual property law. If the law-enforcement mechanisms will act to protect the patent, it is still down to the patent holder to police their property and challenge infringements. Even if all this is done, there are strict time limits on the protection offered.

These drawbacks do not mean that patents are not valuable, just that they should not be relied upon to provide a source of competitive advantage on their own terms. Rather, they should be used *tactically* to provide an initial advantage which can then be used to develop other advantages based on cost and relationships.

Sustaining relationship advantages

Relationships are valuable because they establish *trust* and trust brings down costs for a variety of reasons. First, it reduces the need for a buyer to be constantly scanning the market for offerings. They simply go to a supplier they know. Second, it eliminates the need to establish detailed contracts between buyer and seller. Third, it eliminates the need for a constant *policing* of those contracts. In this context, we may consider *all* stakeholders, not just customers, to be engaged in contract building with the venture, although a trusting relationship with the customer is particularly important and has immediate payoffs.

If trust is built up, it can then form the basis for sustaining competitive advantage. Given that cost and knowledge advantages are most easily accrued by the large (and that usually means the established) business, trust can be a potent ingredient in entrepreneurial success, particularly in the early stages of the venture.

Trust can only be built by establishing and developing relationships which exist on a number of levels. At one level is the experience the parties have of each other through personal contact, say as a result of direct selling activities. The salesperson is not just informing the buyer of a firm's outputs; they are also acting as an ambassador for the business as a whole. At the next level is communication through the media using advertising and public relations activity. Product branding and company image are important mediators. At another level is the general *reputation* that a business builds in the mind of the buyer through their wider experience of it. Reputation is established not through absolute outcomes but through outcomes in relation to *expectations*. Quite simply, if expectations are exceeded then a stakeholder will be very satisfied by the outcome; if they are not met then the stakeholder will be disappointed and feel let down.

Thus a strategy for building and maintaining trust must have three interlocking aspects:

- *The management of expectations*. The entrepreneur must take charge of what the other party (be they a customer, an investor, a supplier or an employee) expects to come out of the relationship. While entrepreneurs are right to strive to deliver on behalf of the stakeholders in their venture, they must avoid 'overpromising' as this can easily lead to disappointment, dissatisfaction and a feeling that trust has been broken if what has been promised is not delivered.
- *The management of outcomes*. Entrepreneurs must take responsibility for what their venture delivers to its stakeholders. They must ensure that these outcomes at least meet the stakeholder's expectations, even if they do not exceed them. If for any reason they underdeliver (and no one, not even the most effective entrepreneur, can control all contingencies), then the entrepreneur is faced with the challenge of addressing the stakeholder's disappointment and managing the process of rebuilding trust. The details of how this must be done will vary depending on the stakeholder, the circumstances and the extent of failure that has occurred. The golden rule, however, is that disappointment should never be ignored.

- *The management of communication.* Expectations and the delivery of outcomes occur on a stage built by communication. Communications between the entrepreneur (and the venture's staff) and stakeholders can take a variety of forms. They can be formal or informal, personal or impersonal, directed to a specific stakeholder or widely broadcast. They may take place via a variety of media. The entrepreneur must be aware of the communication channels that connect and draw the venture's stakeholders together, learning how to use them and how to reinvigorate them constantly. They must also take control of how those channels are used. In particular, the entrepreneur must take clear responsibility for the promises that are being made on behalf of the venture: not just the promises they make themselves, but also those being made by other people on behalf of the venture.

Sustaining structural advantages

Structural advantages arise when a business, by virtue of the way it organises itself, becomes more attuned to signals from the marketplace, more acute in its decision making and more flexible in responding to the needs of customers. Such responsiveness is a product of the organisation's structure, that is, the network of responsibilities and communication links which give the business its form.

As with relationship advantages, the entrepreneurial business is in a strong position to enjoy structural advantages over larger businesses. Established, older businesses may be hampered by internal structures. These structures may serve an important function, but once started they tend to develop a momentum of their own. This can mean that they continue to exist after their usefulness has declined. In the entrepreneurial business, on the other hand, internal structures will be in a state of flux and will be forming in response to market demands.

Decision making within the established firm may also be less acute. Key decision makers may be insulated from the realities of the market, the signals it is sending and the opportunities it is presenting. Decision making may also be distorted by internal 'political' concerns which put internal factional interests ahead of those of the customer and the business as a whole. The entrepreneur, however, should be using the venture's organisation to facilitate and focus decision making, rather than to hinder it. In addition, they are in a position to use strong leadership to draw disparate groups together and co-ordinate their actions.

This demands that entrepreneurs keep themselves in touch with their market and that they do not allow themselves to be 'swamped' by their organisations. Communication systems should be designed with the primary objective of feeding information about the market to decision makers. While information on the internal state of the business is important, this should be used to support market-orientated decision making, not to compromise it.

Competitive advantage is *dynamic* not static. Once a venture gains a competitive advantage in the marketplace it must use the success this brings to constantly reinvent the advantage. Success offers rewards in excess of market norms. These rewards must be reinvested in the business. This investment should be aimed not merely at reinforcing the existing competitive advantage but at modifying it and, if need be, creating the basis for entirely new ones.

If the venture aims to become a *cost leader* then it must invest in volume leadership and cost control. If it aims to use *exclusive knowledge* then it must invest in developing its understanding of the products and services offered to the market, the way in which they meet the

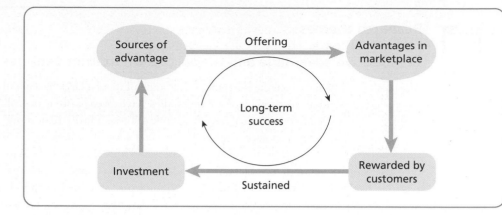

Figure 25.6 Sustaining competitive advantage

needs of customers and the way in which customers decide to buy. If *relationships* are to be used then investment must take place in developing existing relationships and creating new ones. This means managing expectations, outcomes and communication, and all of these in turn mean investment in the people who communicate to customers on behalf of the business. Maintaining a *structural advantage* demands investment in human and communication systems. The business cannot afford to become stale, that is, to let its structures gain a life and a *raison d'être* independent of their function in serving the market. It also demands investment in *change*. Change is more than just a structural phenomenon, it also represents development in individual attitudes and organisational culture. The rewards gained from a competitive advantage must be reinvested to maintain, develop and renew the basis of that advantage within the business (Figure 25.6).

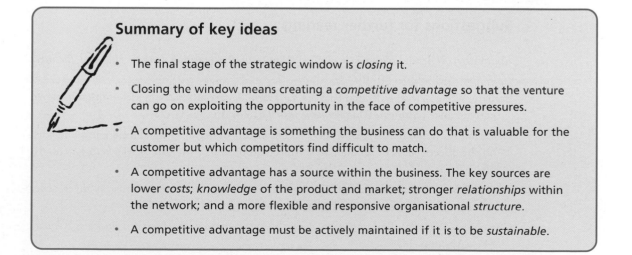

Summary of key ideas

- The final stage of the strategic window is *closing* it.

- Closing the window means creating a *competitive advantage* so that the venture can go on exploiting the opportunity in the face of competitive pressures.

- A competitive advantage is something the business can do that is valuable for the customer but which competitors find difficult to match.

- A competitive advantage has a source within the business. The key sources are lower *costs*; *knowledge* of the product and market; stronger *relationships* within the network; and a more flexible and responsive organisational *structure*.

- A competitive advantage must be actively maintained if it is to be *sustainable*.

Research themes

Competitive advantage and the success of Internet ventures

The past few years have seen the start-up, success and failure of a large number of internet-based entrepreneurial ventures. Good case studies have been written describing these ventures in detail. Undertake an analysis of a sample of these (ideally 10 or more), describing ventures that have been successful and some that have not, looking for sources of competitive advantage, the firm's core competences and how these were used to underpin the success of the venture. As a comparator, also evaluate incumbent non-internet-based ventures in the same sectors. Use John Kay's framework described in this chapter and Prahalad and Hamel's competence-based approach described in section 6.1 to guide this evaluation. How does the presence of sources of competitve advantage and core competences correlate with the long-term performance of the venture? What are the implications for planning and developing strategy for new internet-based ventures?

Key readings

The notion of competitive advantage was originally developed with an eye to large firms. However, it is just as relevant to the small and entrepreneurial. Two excellent papers that consider competitive advantage from the specific perspective of the small business are:

Bamberger, I. (1989) 'Developing competitive advantage in small and medium-sized firms', *Long Range Planning*, Vol. 22, No. 5, pp. 80–8.

Snell, R. and Lau, A. (1994) 'Exploring local competencies salient for expanding small businesses', *Journal of Management Development*, Vol. 13, No. 4, pp. 4–15.

Suggestions for further reading

Abernathy, W.J. and Wayne, K. (1974) 'Limits of the learning curve', *Harvard Business Review*, Sept./Oct., pp. 109–19.

Barnett, W.P., Grieve, H.R. and Park, D.Y. (1994) 'An evolutionary model of organisational performance', *Strategic Management Journal*, Vol. 15, pp. 11–28.

Brock Smith, J. and Barclay, D.W. (1997) 'The effects of organisational differences and trust on the effectiveness of selling partnership relationships', *Journal of Marketing*, Vol. 61, pp. 3–21.

Doney, P.M. and Cannon, J.P. (1997) 'An examination of the nature of trust in buyer–seller relationships', *Journal of Marketing*, Vol. 61, pp. 35–51.

Ghemawat, P. (1985) 'Building strategy on the experience curve', *Harvard Business Review*, Mar./Apr., pp. 143–9.

Kay, J. (1993) *Foundations of Corporate Success*. Oxford: Oxford University Press.

Kay, N.M. (1996) 'The economics of trust', *International Journal of the Economics of Business*, Vol. 3, No. 2, pp. 249–60.

Lieberman, M.B. and Montgomery, D.B. (1988) 'First mover advantages', *Strategic Management Journal*, Vol. 9, pp. 41–58.

Pitt, L.F. and Jeantrout, B. (1994) 'Management of customer expectations in service firms: a study and checklist', *The Service Industries Journal*, Vol. 14, No. 2, pp. 170–89.

Porter, M. (1980) *Competitive Strategy: Techniques for Analysing Industries and Competitors*. New York: Free Press.

Porter, M. (1985) *Competitive Advantage: Creating and Sustaining Superior Performance*. New York: Free Press.

Prahalad, C.K. and Hamel, G. (1990) 'The core competencies of the corporation', *Harvard Business Review*, May/June, pp. 79–91.

Russell, M. (1984) 'Scales true economies', *Management Today*, May, pp. 82–4.

Stevens, H.H. (1976) 'Defining corporate strengths and weaknesses', *Sloan Management Review*, Spring, pp. 51–68.

Teas, R.K. (1993) 'Expectations, performance evaluation and consumer's perceptions of quality', *Journal of Marketing*, Vol. 57, pp. 18–34.

Tellis, G.J. and Golder, P.N. (1996) 'First to market, first to fail? Real causes of enduring market leadership', *Sloan Management Review*, Winter, pp. 65–75.

Voss, C. (1992) 'Successful innovation and implementation of new processes', *Business Strategy Review*, Spring, pp. 29–44.

Zahra, S.A., Nash, S. and Bickford, D.J. (1995) 'Transforming technological pioneering into competitive advantage', *Academy of Management Executive*, Vol. 9, No. 1, pp. 17–31.

Zeithaml, V., Berry, V. and Parasuraman, A. (1993) 'The nature and determinants of a customer's expectations of a service', *Journal of the Academy of Marketing Science*, Vol. 21, No. 1, pp. 1–12.

Selected case material

23 March 2005

How the Mittelstand found its champion

BERTRAND BENOIT

Not twelve weeks in office, and Jürgen Thumann can already tick off the top item on his to-do list.

One month after taking the helm at the BDI, Germany's mighty industry federation and the country's most powerful lobbying organisation, the 63-year-old manager set corporate tax cuts as his priority.

Then, last week, having brushed aside objections from his finance minister and secured the backing of opposition leaders at a rare cross-party meeting, Gerhard Schröder, the chancellor, pledged to slash the tax burden weighing on German businesses.

As he sits down for dinner in a corner office of the BDI's headquarters, a lofty glass cathedral in Berlin's run-down Museum Quarter, Mr Thumann radiates satisfaction.

After floating his proposal for a cut in taxes on retained earnings on a talk show last month, Mr Thumann swiftly assembled a broad coalition of supporters, ranging from Wolfgang Clement, the business-friendly economics minister, to Michael Sommer, head of the DGB trade union federation – a remarkable achievement in the slow-moving world of German politics.

Yet this is not just a personal victory, but a vindication for the cultural revolution Mr Thumann has set in motion at the start of his two-year term as German business's chief lobbyist and head of Europe's most influential gathering of industrialists.

While his predecessors, Hans-Olaf Henkel, an IBM manager, and Michael Rogowski, former chief executive of Voith, an industrial conglomerate, had turned the BDI into the mouthpiece of big business, Mr Thumann has vowed to speak for the Mittelstand, the small and medium-sized business backbone of the German economy.

'There are 3.5m companies in Germany, and 1.5m of these are solitary fighters, one-person operations that account for a total of 10m jobs,' he says.

Born in the Westphalian village of Schwelm during the second world war, Mr Thumann took over his father's steelmaking business at the age of 19. The Heitkamp & Thumann (H&T) group he went on to create with a cousin in 1978 is now home to 25 companies.

Although small, with a turnover of €350m ($461m), the group's businesses are nearly all market leaders in their fields. H&T accounts for half of all battery cases manufactured in the world and dominates the market for aerosol cans. Its five-strong management board includes a US and a British manager, and half of its 2,000 workers are outside Germany. Lean, secretive, conservative and successful, the group is stereotypical of the 'hidden champions' Mr Thumann has pledged to defend.

His support of the Mittelstand, however, is not just born of personal experience. While they account for 90 per cent of all German businesses and provide the bulk of the country's jobs, he says, small and medium-sized companies – the bulk of them family-owned and bank-financed – have suffered most from political neglect and Germany's gradual loss of competitiveness over the past decades.

The blue chip companies of the Dax-30, the Frankfurt stock exchange's top index, have long gone global, shifting production assets and profits around the world in search of a cheaper workforce, the lowest tax rates and access to international markets for capital. Yet their junior peers have struggled to keep up with mounting labour costs, crushing levies, tighter bank lending and crippling regulation.

'Most of these businesses are so anchored in their *terroir* that they could not relocate production abroad if they wanted to . . . Of the 70,000 companies that are inherited each year, many don't even have enough capital to cover the death duties,' says Mr Thumann.

His core belief that large and small companies now face both diverging interests and challenges has not only informed Mr Thumann's anti-tax stance. It is also behind his crusade against German red tape.

'Why should it take an entrepreneur in the Ruhr region 24 months to obtain the necessary authorisations to set up a chemical laundry service while it takes eight months across the border in Metz?' asks the Francophile manager, who spends much of his holiday time south of the Rhone.

'That is because you have a one-stop shop in France. Once an investment decision is made, one civil servant will file all the necessary administrative applications.'

Controversially, Mr Thumann's championing of the Mittelstand and his back-to-basics style have not only refreshed the BDI's agenda but heralded a harsher tone against what both he and a large segment of the public perceive as market-inspired excesses.

He stigmatises the 'short-termism' of quarterly reporting and rails against both inflationary executive pay and a draft bill introduced by the government two weeks ago that would force listed companies to publish their directors' compensation – a 'bureaucratic move', he says, that goes against the Protestant discretion inherent in Rhineland capitalism.

'As far as I am concerned I invest partly out of a sense of duty to my workers. But I also have the luxury of not being bound by the short-term focus that constrains listed companies,' he says. 'Luckily, we still have . . . Mittelstand businesses that can afford to pursue longer-term goals.'

Early last month Josef Ackermann, the head of Deutsche Bank, unleashed the ire of the tabloid press by announcing 6,400 job cuts despite a steep rise in profits. Mr Thumann responded by telling an exclusive gathering at the Berlin Capital Club he did not 'think companies should subordinate everything to the goal of profit maximisation'.

This was no criticism of Mr Ackermann, he now says, diplomatically. 'Deutsche Bank has no choice but to aim for 25 per cent return on equity. The most successful banks, like Citigroup, HSBC, Royal Bank of Scotland, Crédit Suisse or UBS, all have rates of return of 30 per cent or more. This is the kind of competitive pressure Deutsche Bank is under.'

Yet, he says 'business should strive to create role models' and that companies should rise to their social duties, for instance, by creating foundations to finance student grants when, as is expected, German universities begin charging fees. Better education, he says, is the second item on his list, just below corporate tax reform.

If Mr Thumann's cultural revolution has already resulted in a rebalancing of power within the BDI, a question mark remains over its broader political implication. Under Mr Rogowski, it drifted away from its traditional alliance with the Christian Democratic Union and became a robust supporter of Mr Schröder's market-oriented reforms.

Although he has so far cultivated a prudent even-handedness in his political pronouncements, Mr Thumann describes himself as a conservative. In private, he

CASE 25.1 CONT.

shows scant regard for the economic achievements of the Social Democratic Party, whose rule saw unemployment rise to its highest level in 70 years. He sees Mr Schröder's Green coalition partner as a left-wing faction driven mainly by ideological considerations in its policy decisions.

He is a passionate critic of the government's fight against discrimination at work; he has denounced the chancellor's efforts to water down the European Union's stability pact and dismantle the European Commission's plans for services liberalisation; and he wants to scrap the Green-inspired ban on nuclear power as a way to counter rising energy prices.

A tuxedo-clad Mr Schröder may already have sensed the wind turning when he addressed Mr Thumann's introductory gala at Berlin's Concert House in January. 'I wish him', he told the 900 guests, flashing his trademark grin, 'the wisdom to accept that some things are not easily changed.'

The battle fronts for the Mittelstand

Germany's small and medium-sized companies – commonly known as the Mittelstand – have been under pressure on several fronts:

1. An underdeveloped stock exchange, the reluctance of retail investors to hold equity and of entrepreneurs to sell it and a plentiful supply of cheap credit explain why Mittelstand companies were reliant on bank loans for financing throughout the post-war period. When banks tightened lending in the 1990s, a credit crunch ensued. Businesses have been exploring other funding sources, from leasing to private equity and mezzanine financing.

2. With a total corporate tax rate of 38.6 per cent, German companies are the most heavily taxed in Europe. For one-person companies, which are subject to income tax, the rate can rise to 44.3 per cent of profits – hence the BDI's support for a model that would allow smaller companies to choose between paying income or corporate tax.

3. Despite wage moderation and the government's efforts to keep non-wage labour costs in check, German workers remain the most expensive in the world after Norway. With limited possibilities of shifting activities to cheaper labour markets, the Mittelstand faces excessive costs.

4. Rather than resort to mass lay-offs, smaller companies have tended to reduce high costs by slashing investment in research and development. Once highly innovative, the Mittelstand has continuously lost ground to bigger companies in terms of R&D investment since 1998, according to a recent study by the ZEW economic institute.

5. The number of insolvencies in Germany has risen steadily over the past two decades to reach 40,000 last year. The BDI names undercapitalisation, stagnating demand, excessive taxation and labour costs as the main reasons.

CASE 25.2

18 August 2005

Rank to buy control of CCH Wood Products

TIM JOHNSTON

New Zealand entrepreneur Graeme Hart yesterday secured agreement to buy a NZ$1.65bn (US$1.15bn) controlling stake in wood products company Carter Holt Harvey (CHH) from International Paper, and said he would launch a bid for the outstanding shares.

Mr Hart's investment company, Rank Group, has trumped other consortia, including CVC Asia and Newbridge Capital, and Carlyle and JPMorgan, securing the most sought-after asset in International Paper's $10bn sale of non-core businesses.

International Paper yesterday said it had signed a lock-in agreement to sell its stock into a NZ$2.50 a share full takeover offer expected to be launched by Rank Group in four to six weeks.

Mr Hart's offer represents premium of about 30 per cent on the value of International Paper's 50.5 per cent holding in CHH as at June, when it was put up for sale. International Paper is selling to help pay down debt and concentrate on coated papers and packaging.

CHH is Australasia's largest paper and wood products company, and there was speculation yesterday that Mr Hart might try to sell off some of the assets.

Mr Hart built his reputation, and a considerable fortune, buying undervalued assets and turning them round. This month he sold New Zealand Dairy Foods, which he bought in 2002 for NZ$310m, for a mixture of cash and assets valued at NZ$754m.

Analysts estimate CHH's underlying asset value at NZ$2.50 to NZ$2.90 a share, and said they thought it unlikely that Mr Hart would maintain the company in its current form, which is fully vertically integrated.

Paper products groups such as Australia's Amcor or Visy Group have expressed qualified interest in the CHH's packaging assets.

Mr Hart is believed to be most interested in CHH's 220,000 acres of plantation forest, and some observers have said the company's land bank could be revalued.

It has underperformed the stock market, largely because of the difficult trading conditions in the pulp and paper market. Rising demand in China has not led to any marked improvement in prices because of supplies of wood from Russia.

The company is also sitting on cash. This year it raised NZ$441m by selling some of its forests.

Standard & Poor's placed its BBB/A-2 ratings on CHH on CreditWatch in the wake of the news. S&P said its move reflected 'the uncertainties surrounding the proposed transaction, including the impact of the potential new owner on the group's capital structure and financial policies, and the future strategic direction of the company'.

Source: Tim Johnston, 'Rank to buy control of CCH Wood Products', *Financial Times*, 18 August 2005, p. 27. Copyright © 2005 The Financial Times Limited.

Discussion points

1. In what ways might 'excessive' government regulation ('red tape') disadvantage the smaller, entrepreneurial business versus the larger, established incumbent?

2. How might an entrepreneur close the window with a commodity business?

CHAPTER 26

The dimensions of business growth

Chapter overview

The potential for growth is a defining feature of the entrepreneurial venture. This chapter is concerned with evaluating growth as a specific opportunity for the venture and approaches to evaluating the process of business growth. A multifaceted approach is developed and the growth of the entrepreneurial venture is considered from financial, strategic, structural and organisational perspectives. The management of these four facets is considered. How the growth of the venture creates opportunities for, and impacts on, the lives of its stakeholders is considered. The chapter concludes with an exploration of the different ways in which growth may be conceptualised metaphorically.

26.1 Growth as an objective for the venture

Key learning outcome

An appreciation of the issues associated with setting growth as an objective for the venture.

The entrepreneurial venture is characterised by its growth potential, but why might an entrepreneur wish to take advantage of that potential and grow their venture? There are a number of answers to this question. It might be the result of a desire to increase personal wealth, but this is not usually the main motivation of an entrepreneur. More usually it relates to a sense of achievement. In a sense, the size of the venture is a way of 'keeping the score'. Entrepreneurs are also driven by a desire to make a difference to the world. And in general, the larger the venture they create, the bigger the difference they have made. Driving growth can also relate to the desire for personal control. The bigger the venture, the greater the domain over which the entrepreneur can express their power.

For these reasons, growth is often an important objective for the venture. However, setting growth targets creates challenges in relation to the venture's strategy and resources and the risk to which it is exposed.

Growth and strategy

Growth has to be achieved. It must be delivered by obtaining a greater volume of business. Ultimately, it must be driven by increased sales. The venture must have a strategy in place to develop its sales base. As we shall discuss in this chapter, such a strategy may be based on exploiting market growth, increasing market share, developing new products or entering new markets.

An expansion strategy must be consistent with the capabilities of the venture, it must draw upon and develop the venture's competitive advantages and be viable given the competitive situation it will have to face. Growth targets must be demanding but they must also be reasonable given the strategic constraints the venture faces.

Growth and resources

Growth is dependent on the venture's ability to attract new resources. The ultimate source of resources is customer money. Investment and loan capital can only be a means to the end of attracting customers.

Capital is not useful in itself. It must be converted into productive assets in terms of people and operating resources. Growth targets must take account of the resources the venture will be able to acquire. Consideration must be made not just of the ability to attract capital from customers, lenders and investors but also of the ability of the venture to *use* that capital to bring in the people and specialist assets the venture depends on. If these are in short supply, then any limitations imposed on growth must be taken into account.

Growth and risk

There is a complex relationship between growth and risk. In general, the larger a firm, the less risk it is exposed to. There are two reasons for this. First, size reflects *success*. A large firm is successful which implies that it is good at what it does. Clearly, being effective in the marketplace is the best way to reduce risk. Second, the larger the firm, the more resources it will have. In particular, larger firms tend to have more 'slack' resources. These are resources that are not dedicated to specific projects and can be moved around quickly. The large business can use these resources to buffer itself from short-term environmental shocks better than can the small firm.

However, growth carries some risk in itself. Growth implies developing new business which means venturing into the unknown. The degree of risk depends on the way in which the expansion draws upon the venture's capabilities, its knowledge of products and markets and the environment in which it competes. Using resources to fuel growth is an *investment* regardless of whether new investment capital is obtained or profits are reinvested rather than distributed back to shareholders. As an investment, growth must be judged like any other in light of the risks it presents, the returns it offers and the opportunity costs it imposes.

The growth objective for the venture must be set following consideration of these factors. It must define the growth of the venture in terms of increased sales, increased income (including new investment capital) and how these revenues will be converted to assets. Growth targets must be consistent with a strategy to achieve that growth, they must be feasible and they must be acceptable to the venture's stakeholders in terms of the risks this creates.

Not all entrepreneurs set out with high growth objectives in mind. When Anita Roddick established The Body Shop in Brighton she intended to start only a small business capable of providing an income for her and her family. However, once the potential of her innovation became evident, growth (particularly through franchising) became a strategic priority for the business.

26.2 The process of growth

Business growth is critical to entrepreneurial success. The potential for growth is one of the factors which distinguishes the entrepreneurial venture from the small business. Organisational growth, however, means more than just an increase in size. Growth is a dynamic process. It involves development and change within the organisation, and changes in the way in which the organisation interacts with its environment. Although an organisation grows as a coherent whole, organisational growth itself is best understood in a multifaceted way. It has as many aspects as there are aspects of organisation itself. The case for a multi-perspective approach to understanding organisational growth and change was made very effectively by Henry Mintzberg in his book *The Structuring of Organizations* (1979).

Given the multifaceted nature of organisation, the entrepreneur must constantly view the growth and development of their venture from a number of different perspectives. Four perspectives in particular are important: the *financial*, the *strategic*, the *structural* and the *organisational*.

- *Financial growth* relates to the development of the business as a commercial entity. It is concerned with increases in *turnover*, the *costs* and *investment* needed to achieve that turnover, and the resulting *profits*. It is also concerned with increases in what the business owns: its *assets*. Related to this is the increase in the *value* of the business, that is, what a potential buyer might be willing to pay for it. Because financial growth measures the additional value that the organisation is creating which is available to be distributed to its stakeholders, the value of the business is an important measure of the *success* of the venture.
- *Strategic growth* relates to the changes that take place in the way in which the organisation interacts with its environment as a coherent, *strategic*, whole. Primarily, this is concerned with the way the business develops its capabilities to exploit a presence in the marketplace. It is the profile of opportunities which the venture exploits and the assets, both tangible and intangible, it acquires to create *sustainable competitive advantages*.
- *Structural growth* relates to the changes in the way the business organises its internal systems, in particular, managerial *roles* and *responsibilities*, reporting *relationships*, *communication* links and resource *control systems*.
- *Organisational growth* relates to the changes in the organisation's *processes*, *culture* and *attitudes* as it grows and develops. It is also concerned with the changes that must take place in the entrepreneur's role and leadership style as the business moves from being a 'small' to a 'large' firm.

The four aspects of growth described are not independent of each other. They are just different facets of the same underlying process. At the heart of that process is the awarding of valuable resources to the venture by external markets because it has demonstrated that it can make better use of them, that is, create more value from them, than can the alternatives on offer. That better use of resources is a consequence of the entrepreneur's decision making.

The *strategic* perspective must take centre stage. It is this which relates the needs of customers to the ability of the business to serve them. *Financial* growth is a measure of the business's performance in serving the needs of its markets, thus it is a measure of the resources

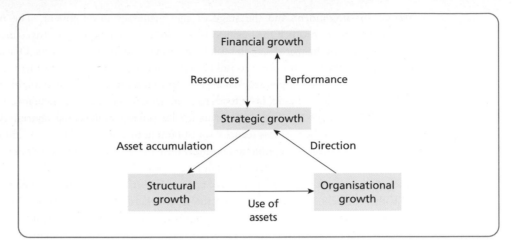

Figure 26.1 The dynamics of growth for the entrepreneurial venture

that the market has allocated to the firm. The firm must convert those resources into assets. These assets are configured by the structure of the organisation. Additional resources means increasing the *assets* that the business holds which in turn demands changes to the *structure* in which they are held.

This structure provides only a framework, however (Figure 26.1). The decisions that the individuals who make up the organisation make and the actions that they take in relation to the assets it owns are governed by wider dimensions of the organisation such as its culture and attitudes. Strategic growth has a *direction* and that direction results from the vision and leadership the entrepreneur offers.

It must also be added that although growth is a *defining* feature of the entrepreneurial venture, this does not mean that an entrepreneurial business has a *right* to grow. It merely means that, if managed in the right way, it has the *potential* to grow. Growth must be made an objective for the venture. It is an opportunity that must be managed effectively if it is to be capitalised upon. For the entrepreneur, growth is a reward for identifying the right opportunities, understanding how they might be exploited and competing effectively to take advantage of them.

26.3 Financial evaluation of growth

Key learning outcome

An understanding of the way in which financial growth is recorded, reported and analysed.

The financial performance of a firm is important to all its stakeholders. A sound financial position brings security for employees, offers customers the prospect of good service and investment in future offerings, and promises suppliers a demand for their outputs. Investors, of course, have an interest in seeing a good return on their capital. They will take particular note of the financial performance of the businesses they have chosen to back.

Investors and businesses communicate in a number of ways. The degree of personal contact will depend on the type of investors, the

517

amount of investment and the stage of the business's development. The nature of the economic system in which the business is operating is also important. Investment systems in different parts of the world vary in both their formal and informal aspects. One key difference is in the way the investor seeks to influence the management of the business. If the business seeks investment in an open stock market then two main means are available to effect this. If the stock market is 'liquid' (as it tends to be in the UK and the USA) then investors can signal their assessment of the firm's performance by buying and selling shares. An increasing share price offers the business security for obtaining further investment. A falling share price can make a business susceptible to takeover. Other economies (typically those in continental Europe) tend towards a greater degree of intervention by investors. Institutional shareholders (such as pension funds and banks) may appoint directors to act on their behalf.

If the business has not yet reached the stage where it is ready to offer investment stock to the stock market and is reliant on private and institutional investment such as banks and venture capital instead, then a high degree of both investor scrutiny and involvement is likely.

Whatever the nature and means of the interaction between business and investor, financial reporting provides a common language by which they can communicate with each other. At the centre of this communication are two documents: the *balance sheet* and the *profit and loss account* (Figure 26.2). The balance sheet is a summary of *what the business owns*, that is, its *assets* and *liabilities*. It represents the state of the business at *a point in time*, specifically the date of the report. The profit and loss account is a report on *what the business has done* over the previous period, that is, its trading activity in terms of *sales* (or *turnover*), the *expenditure* involved in achieving those sales and the resulting *profits*. The reporting period is normally one year but can be shorter if investors see the need for more detailed tracking.

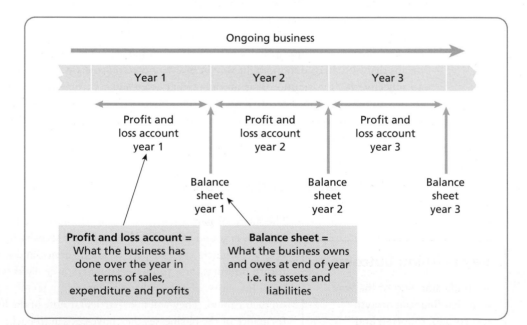

Figure 26.2 The structure of financial reporting: the balance sheet and profit and loss account

Table 26.1 The balance sheet

Assets	Liabilities
Tangible assets The value of all buildings and machinery etc. owned by the firm + *Intangible assets* The valuation of the things 'owned' by the firm, which have no physical form but can, potentially, be bought and sold, e.g. brand names and goodwill	*Short-term creditors* All creditors (people and organisations to whom the firm owes money) due for payment within one year + *Long-term creditors* All creditors due for payment after one year. Important elements include: • loan repayment due after one year • dividends planned for investors (including the entrepreneur's remuneration) • long-term repayments agreed with suppliers • taxes owed to the government
+ *Current assets* Cash in hand, stock (including finished goods, work in progress and raw materials), creditor and trade debts owed to the firm	+ *Called-up share capital* The permanent capital of the firm in the form of the face value of issued shares
+ *Investments* Investments held by the firm in other businesses, government stock and other financial instruments	+ *Capital reserves* The profits held by the firm. Strictly, these are the property of the investors in the firm. Some may be distributed to investors in the form of dividends; others may be retained for future investment
= **Total assets**	= **Total liabilities**

The balance sheet

The balance sheet is so called because it is usual to show the assets and liabilities of the firm as being equal (i.e. balancing). The details presented on the balance sheet vary across different countries; however, some of the key lines are as indicated in Table 26.1.

The profit and loss account

The profit and loss account provides a summary of the revenues obtained as a result of trading activity over the period in question. The key lines are shown in Table 26.2.

Table 26.2 The profit and loss account

Income

Turnover from normal trading activities
The income generated as a result of the firm's normal business activities

Extraordinary income
Additional income which is a result of activities that are not part of the firm's usual profile of business

Income from investments
Income received as a result of investments owned by the firm in other businesses or other investment instruments

Outgoing

Cost of sales
The expenditure that was necessary to deliver the sales that were achieved. Important cost elements are:

- raw materials and factors
- salaries
- purchase (or rental) of machinery and equipment
- depreciation charges on machinery and equipment
- sales and marketing expenditure

Interest on debt
Payments to cover interest charges on outstanding debts

Extraordinary expenditure
Expenditure that has been made but which is not typical of the expenditure the business normally faces. It is a result of special circumstances or a one-off activity. Critically, it is expenditure the business does not expect to face again

Taxation
Money owed to the government as a result of taxation

Dividends
Money to be paid to investors as a return on their investment. (This may include some of the entrepreneur's remuneration in so far as the entrepreneur is an investor.)

Ratio analysis

The performance of the entrepreneurial venture must be measured not only in terms of absolutes – the new value it generates – but also in relative terms, i.e. the new value created given the resources the entrepreneur has to hand. An investor in the venture is interested not so much in 'profits' as in the *returns* the venture will offer for a *given level of investment*.

Ratio analysis can be used to provide a valuable insight into the performance, condition and stability of the venture. As its name suggests, it is based on an evaluation of the ratios between different lines on the balance sheet and profit and loss account.

Three types of ratio are important. *Performance ratios* indicate the way the business is performing, that is, the value it is creating from the resources to hand. *Financial status* ratios provide an indication of the financial security of the venture and how exposed a backer's investment is. If the venture has a stock market listing, then *stock market ratios* can be used to compare the performance of an investment in the venture with alternative investment opportunities.

26.4 Financial growth

> ### Key learning outcome
>
> An appreciation of how financial analysis provides a context for understanding the financial growth and development of the venture.

The report of the financial situation, that is, the balance sheet and the profit and loss account and the ratios that can be derived from these items, provides those interested in the venture (the entrepreneur, other managers, investors and taxing authorities) with a wealth of information on which decisions may be based. However, decisions must be made within a broader context which needs to consider both the firm's performance *relative to its particular business sector* and the overall *trends* in the firm's performance.

There are no absolute measures of performance. The profit margin or return on investment (or any other performance measure) to be expected from a venture will depend on the sector in which the business operates. What matters is not so much the performance of the venture as its performance *relative* to key competitors and to market norms. Similarly, the expected financial status ratios will vary across different industry sectors. The factor which determines how investment capital is distributed between sectors offering different levels of return is, of course, *risk*. The way in which risk is anticipated by investors can be gleaned from a close examination of the stock market ratios of players within a particular sector. An entrepreneurial venture is not static. It is undergoing constant growth and development. Investors and other decision makers will colour their decisions not just by reference to the indicators for the business at a single point in time but also by evaluating the *trends* in its performance. This will be particularly important for investors who are not expecting immediate returns from the venture but who are willing to accept some risk for the promise of higher returns in the future. Investors' decision making (particularly the key decision of whether to hold or exit from their investment) will be influenced by four main factors: the venture's underlying performance, its growth in value, the trend in its risk, and its dividend yield.

The underlying performance (return on investment) of the venture

Investors will be interested in the performance of the venture not just in absolute terms but relative to their *expectations* of that performance, which will usually be expressed in terms of the return on investment (ROI) that they would like to achieve. Their expectations will be a result of their knowledge of the business and the sector it operates in, and of the promises offered by the entrepreneur driving the venture.

The growth in the value of the venture

The *growth* of the venture can be qualified by a number of financial criteria. Growth in *income* (and by implication, *outgoings*), *assets* and *capital* are equally important. Some of the key indicators to follow include changes in turnover, changes in cash profits, changes in tangible assets, changes in total assets and changes in shareholders' capital. Growth in these measures can be followed both in absolute terms and as a proportion of absolute values. Proportional changes can be indicated as an index or as a percentage. A *growth index* is calculated as:

$$\text{Growth index} = \frac{\text{Value of measure in year}}{\text{Value of measure in previous year}}$$

Growth as a *percentage* is given by:

$$\text{Growth \%} = \frac{(\text{Value of measure in year} - \text{Value in previous year})}{\text{Value of measure in previous year}} \times 100\%$$

When making a comparison it is often useful to *discount* for general inflation in an economy. This enables the *real* growth of the venture to be measured. To discount for inflation the *nominal* growth calculated for the venture must be divided by the inflation index for the period under consideration:

$$\text{Real growth} = \frac{\text{Nominal growth}}{\text{Inflation index}}$$

Usually, the general retail price index is used, but other more specialist inflation measures may be adopted. If inflation is quoted as a percentage it can be converted by the following formula:

$$\text{Inflation index} = \frac{[(\text{Inflation as \%}) + 100]}{100}$$

Growth by the venture is usually received positively. Expansion of the venture drives an increase in the underlying value of a shareholder's investment. Growth also indicates that the venture has a successful formula and so, *in general*, it signals a reduction in risk. Growth does not, however, come for free. It must be *paid for* and a high level of growth may make cash flow tighter and so lead to less favourable financial status ratios. This may make the venture slightly more risky in the short term, particularly if there is a crisis and short-term liabilities have to be met.

The trend in the risk of the venture

While growth tends to reduce risk overall, the specific level of risk faced by the business is, to a degree, under the control of the entrepreneur and other managers. An important factor is the debt ratio (or, alternatively, gearing) of the venture. Debt, on the whole, is cheaper than equity finance. However, debt must be repaid whatever the performance of the business. Debt repayment must take priority over the repayment of equity or dividends. Therefore a high debt ratio does expose the business (and that means its investors) to more risk.

No generalisation can be made about the optimum level of debt to equity. This is a complex issue and not only are interest rates and industry risk relevant, but taxation effects also have an influence. Comparison with industry norms can provide a rough and ready guide.

Financial status and (if the firm has floated shares) stock market ratios provide an insight into the overall risk status of the venture. In general, as the business grows, matures and

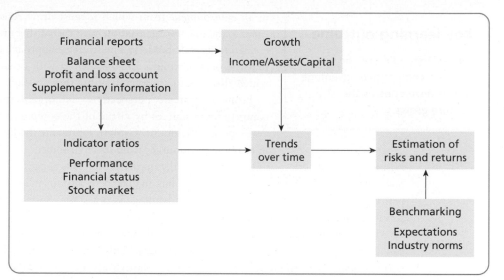

Figure 26.3 A model of financial appraisal for the entrepreneurial venture

stabilises, investors will expect risk to be reduced. Having faced risk initially they become ready to enjoy the return they are owed.

The dividends yielded by the venture

At the end of the day, investors will wish to see a capital gain through their investment. This may be realised by their receiving dividend payments on the shares they hold or by selling those shares. These two approaches to liquidating investment differ in timing rather than substance. The buyer of the share does so in the expectation of a future flow of dividends. An independent market values the investment on the basis of the cash flow it can generate.

Managers in the venture will make a decision about how much of the profits generated is to be passed on to the shareholders and how much is to be retained within the business for future investment. Shareholders will either agree to this split or will not. They will show their approval (or otherwise) either by direct interference in the firm or, if their investment is liquid, by buying or selling their shares thus raising or depressing the share price. In general, while investors may be willing to see managers recycle profits back into a young, fast-growing venture, they will at some point expect to see a real cash reward for their investment. As the firm matures, it is likely that investors will expect a greater proportion of profits to be given back to them.

A general scheme for analysing the financial growth of an entrepreneurial venture is indicated in Figure 26.3.

26.5 Strategic growth

The strategic approach to organisational management regards the organisation as a single *coherent* entity which must be managed in its entirety. It locates the organisation conceptually in an *environment* from which it must draw resources and *add value* to them. The organisation must then distribute the new value created to its stakeholders. The strategic approach also recognises that the organisation is in *competition* with other organisations which also seek to attract and utilise those resources.

From a strategic perspective, the organisation is able to compete for resources by virtue of the *competitive advantages* it develops and maintains. Growth represents the business's success in drawing in resources from its environment. It is a sign that the business has been effective in competing in the marketplace. This suggests that the business has built up a competitive advantage and has managed to sustain it in the face of competitive pressure. However, a competitive advantage is not static. Sustaining an advantage simultaneously develops and enhances it.

All advantages are sensitive to business growth. In general, expansion of the business can be used to enhance a competitive advantage. This will only occur, however, if the entrepreneur is sensitive to the nature of the competitive advantages that their venture enjoys and strives to actively manage that advantage as the business grows and develops.

Growth and cost advantages

The main source of cost advantages are experience effects. Practice in delivering the outputs leads to a reduction in cost (strictly, the cost of adding a particular amount of value). Costs tend to fall in an exponential way as output increases linearly. Hence, experience cost advantages are (usually) held by the business which has achieved the greatest cumulative output. This can lead to a 'virtuous circle' (Figure 26.4). Cost leadership means that the customer can be offered a lower price. This increases demand for the firm's outputs relative to those of

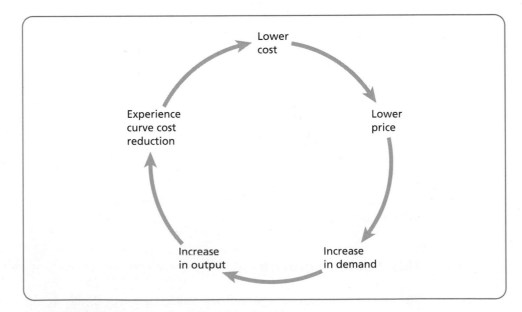

Figure 26.4 The virtuous circle of cost leadership

competitors. This leads to the firm developing a volume output lead over competitors. In turn, this volume advantage leads to enhanced cost leadership and the ability to offer customers an even lower price, and so on.

Clearly, the entrepreneur can build in cost advantages as the business grows. Such a strategy offers the potential for a consistent and sustainable advantage in the marketplace. It is, however, a strategy which requires certain conditions to be met and it is not without risk. If the strategy is to work, the entrepreneur must be sure of a number of features of the market they are developing.

Cost advantages have not already been established in the market

If cost advantages have already been established in the market, then the business will risk being a follower rather than a leader. If the venture's costs are not *genuinely* lower than those of the leading competitor then undercutting the leader to subsidise costs and offer the customer a lower price will demand a high level of investment. In some instances such undercutting will be construed as anti-competitive by regulatory bodies. It is, in any case, always expensive.

In order to become a cost leader it is better if the entrepreneur is first into a market. In effect, what this means is that the innovation on which the venture is based is sufficiently different to constitute a 'new' market.

Potential volume outputs make entry into the market worthwhile

Experience curve cost reductions become meaningful only when the output volumes are quite high. Consequently, a cost leadership strategy is not a realistic option for a small, or even a medium-sized, business serving a local market. In reality, cost leadership becomes a serious option only for the business which is an industry maker and which aims to deliver its outputs to a wide (which increasingly today means *global*) market. This is not to say that price is not an important factor for smaller businesses or that they should not manage costs; rather, that cost as the *mainstay* of competitive advantage is really the prerogative of the large player.

A corollary of this fact is that the entire market must be ready to accept a fairly homogeneous product. If too much specialisation is required at a local level then the extent to which production is repetitive will be lost and hence the possibility of cost-reducing experience will also be lost.

Sales of the product they are offering are sensitive to price

Experience cost advantages are gained via volume output. The virtuous circle will be followed only if customers respond to lower prices by buying more of the price leader's offerings. This demands that the products offered are *price sensitive*, which means that the firm's products must be *substitutable* with those of competitors. Substitutability implies that the products of different suppliers are pretty much equivalent (from the buyer's perspective) and can replace one another in use. To be substitutable, products not only must be similar in a technical sense but also must not have any switching costs associated with them, that is, there should be no additional expense for the customer when moving from one supplier to another.

If switching costs are present *and* the entrepreneur is the first to get customers on board then they may use these costs as the basis of a competitive advantage. Again, this emphasises the importance of innovation in entrepreneurial success.

The experience curve will be steep enough (but not too steep)

An experience curve has a *gradient*. This is the rate at which increasing output reduces costs, that is, the speed at which learning takes place. The experience curve needs to be steep enough for the volume advantages that the pioneering entrepreneur can gain to lead to cost advantages which have a meaningful impact on prices in the marketplace. If, however, the curve is too steep then followers will find it easy to catch up, and any advantage gained initially will be quickly eroded.

Distribution can be maintained

A price advantage offered to the customer is useful only if the customer can get hold of the product. This implies that distribution can be readily achieved. If independent agencies (e.g. wholesalers or retailers) are involved in the distribution process then there is always the danger that a follower will, in some way or other, interfere with the cost leader's ability to distribute. In effect, the entrepreneur is looking towards distributors as the basis for developing a non-cost competitive advantage. If a distributor 'lock-out' occurs, then the leader will lose volume and any cost advantage can be rapidly lost. Often, such actions are restricted by anti-trust legislation. However, such legislation is difficult to enforce. If the business is multinational, then distributors may be tempted to favour local suppliers. Governments that have seen a 'strategic' advantage in supporting local producers have been known to resist pressure to open their markets by accusing global cost leaders of 'dumping' (i.e. of selling below cost to establish their presence in a market). Even if such accusations are eventually disproved, volume sales may have been lost already. With a cost leadership strategy, time equals volume, which means costs, which equals money.

Technological innovation will not reset the experience curve

Experience is gained by repetitive utilisation of a particular operational technology to manufacture or deliver a service. If the technological basis of an industry changes then descent down a new experience curve begins. In cost terms, all bets are off! Innovation, both in the type of product offered to the customer and the means for its delivery, offers both an opportunity and a threat. It may be the means by which the entrepreneur first enters the market and gains an advantage over existing players; but, once they are established, and competitive advantage has been built on a particular technology, they are vulnerable to a new generation of innovators. This means that the entrepreneurial business, even if it is following a cost leadership strategy, must still look towards maintaining innovation.

The entrepreneur (and financial backers) have patience

Cost leadership is not a short-term strategy. The payoffs are far from immediate. While competing on a price leadership basis, profit margins must be kept slim, i.e. just sufficient to cover overhead costs. This is the only way in which the business can be sure that it is reflecting its cost advantage with the most competitive market price. However, it will be tempting to raise prices and to increase short-term profit margins. The entrepreneur may be looking for additional returns to invest in the growth of the business. Investors may be eager to see a positive

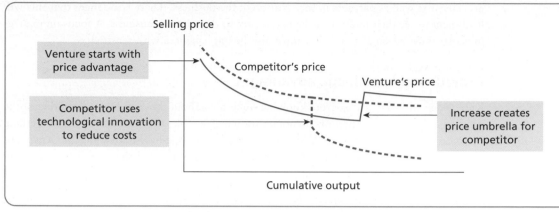

Figure 26.5 Risks in a cost leadership strategy

return on their investment. The business may see a price increase as a viable option. It will be in a market-leading position (certainly in volume terms). It may have established a strong relationship with customers. Competitors may have found it hard to gain a foothold in the market. However, the temptation to increase prices must still be resisted.

All these advantages are a *consequence* of keeping prices low. They are the basis on which the business can gain a future reward for maintaining tight profit margins. If the business increases its prices too early then it can create a 'cost umbrella' under which less efficient competitors may shelter. It may be just the gap a competitor needs in order to gain a toehold in the market. If a cost leadership strategy is to be effective then the business pursuing it must keep its nerve and keep prices as low as possible for as long as possible. Optimally, prices should be kept to a minimum until market growth has stopped. After this the market will start to lose its attractiveness to new entrants as gaining market share will tend to require the conversion of existing customers rather than drawing new ones into the market. At this point the cost-leading business can start to raise prices above costs, to increase profit margins and to harvest its investment.

Figure 26.5 shows how both technological innovation and the creation of cost umbrellas present risks for a cost leadership strategy.

Costs are actively managed

Even though costs often follow a mathematical relationship to output volume this does not mean that increasing output *automatically* drives down costs. Increasing output gives the firm's managers the *opportunity* to drive down costs but that is an opportunity they must grasp actively. The management of cost must become the focus of managerial activity. In fact, it must become the key criterion around which decisions are made.

Cost leadership is a strategy which has an impact on, and must be supported by, all the firm's stakeholders. As noted above, customers must be responsive to price and investors must be willing to play a long game. In addition, suppliers must recognise that they need to be competitive in the price at which they offer inputs to the business. Further, employees will become aware (and if not managed properly, *acutely* aware) of the fact that they themselves are 'costs' as well as partners in the creation of the business. There is a danger that this will lead them to see their interests as being counter to those of the business. A focus on managing costs must be single-minded. It must also be implemented with sensitivity.

Growth and knowledge advantages

Knowledge advantages arise from knowing something about the customer, the market or the product offered that competitors do not know, which enables the business to offer something of value to the customer. The development of a knowledge-based advantage is dependent on two factors: the *significance* of the knowledge advantage and the rate at which it will be *eroded*.

- *How significant is the knowledge advantage?* How *valuable* is what is known? Is the knowledge sufficient in scope and does it have significance to enough customers in order to sustain the growth of the business? If so, what level of growth can it sustain?
- *How will the knowledge advantage be eroded?* How long will it take competitors to *gain* the knowledge and use it themselves? Can they discover it for themselves or through others? Will the venture's activities *signal* it to them?

Clearly, these two factors work against each other. The more valuable the knowledge, the more that competitors will be encouraged to get hold of it for themselves. Knowledge is difficult to protect. A particular piece of knowledge rarely offers more than a transient advantage. If the business aims not just to survive, but also to *grow*, on the back of knowledge advantages, then it must be active in a process of constant rediscovery about what it is offering the market and why the market buys it.

To do this the business needs to position itself in a market where discovery and innovation are well received and rewarded. This is certainly the case in high-tech markets where technological innovation is the norm. However, the market does not have to be high-tech. More generally, knowledge-based advantages can be gained in any market where customer expectations are in flux and they are likely to respond well to new offerings.

In order to respond to this the entrepreneurial business must ensure that two activities are given priority. First, it requires that resources are put into understanding the market and its customers. In a functional sense this means *market research*. More broadly, it means that the whole organisation must be attuned to new ideas and new initiatives. It particularly demands that the organisation be responsive to the signals sent out by customers about their needs and desires. Second, it requires that the organisation be active in creating, developing and offering new products and services to the customer. Product development activity must be supported by the processes and systems within the organisation. Indeed, it must be *prioritised* by them. These systems must be given centre stage as the growth and development of the organisation is managed.

Growth and relationship advantages

Relationships exist between *people*, not just organisations. During its early stages, the business may be 'fronted' directly by the entrepreneur. They will be directly responsible for building productive relationships with the venture's stakeholders. Indeed, tying together and securing the threads of the network into which they have entered may be the entrepreneur's key role. Customers, suppliers, employees and investors will be drawn to the venture as a result of the positive relationship they develop with the entrepreneur. The question becomes, how can the entrepreneur maintain relationship advantages as the business grows and develops? Further, how can the entrepreneur use such advantages to *drive* growth in the business?

This challenge is acute. In the first instance, the entrepreneur will be located at the centre of the web of relationships and will be in control of them all. As the organisation grows and develops then the web of relationships becomes much more complex. The entrepreneur can no longer represent the organisation to all the parties who have an interest in it. New individuals must develop the organisation's relationships on a specialist basis. For example, salespeople will make representations to customers. Procurement and purchasing specialists must work with suppliers. At some stage it may even be necessary to have finance specialists to manage the venture's relationship with its investors.

To understand how relationship advantages may be maintained and developed as the business grows, it is necessary to have a deep understanding of the ways in which the relationships the business has with its stakeholders are *different* from those of competitor organisations; why that difference is important in offering *value* to those stakeholders; and why competitors find it hard to *imitate* those relationships. In particular, the entrepreneur must ask the following questions.

Why are the relationships valuable?

What aspect of the relationship creates value for the stakeholder? Does the relationship provide trust which reduces the need for monitoring costs? Does the relationship offer benefits which satisfy social needs? Does the relationship promise the potential to satisfy self-developmental needs? Are these benefits carried as part of the product (say, through *branding*) or are they supplementary to it (say, through working in *association* with the business)?

What are the expectations of the relationships?

What matters in a relationship is not actual outcomes but outcomes in relation to *expectations*. If expectations are met (or even better, exceeded) then satisfaction will occur. If they are not met then disappointment will result. Human relationships are complex. The expectations they generate are multifaceted. They may be manifest at economic, social and self-developmental levels. Often, these interact with each other and the effective entrepreneur must manage relationships at each level.

What practices sustain the relationships?

Relationships are acted out. The parties to the relationship play *roles*. To a greater or lesser extent, relationships are *scripted*. Selling, for example, involves a series of reasonably well-defined steps: first approach, introduction, product presentation, close, etc. Internally, employee motivation may be sustained through appraisal and reward procedures. Not all the practices that sustain relationships are explicit. Some may not even be noticed until the practice is broken. Practices, even quite trivial ones, may almost become ritualised. In this, they are one of the building blocks out of which expectations are created. Changing a routine may have an impact on a relationship at a deep level.

By way of an example, consider an entrepreneur whose business is doing quite well. The venture's backers are very happy. Their expectations have been more than met. The entrepreneur provides the backers with a financial report every three months. After a while, this becomes routine. The backers, acknowledging that the business presents them with no concerns, stop examining the report in any detail. After a while the entrepreneur recognises this and decides that the report is 'a waste of time', so the entrepreneur, without informing the backers, stops sending it.

What are the backers to think? Should they be concerned? They contact the entrepreneur who informs them that they should not worry, that the business is still doing well and that the report was stopped because it was not giving them any new information and so the communication 'was not important'. How are the backers likely to interpret the attitude of the entrepreneur towards them?

What relationship skills are required to maintain them?

Relationships must be managed and this management, like any other form of management, calls upon knowledge and skills. As discussed fully in section 5.3, the key skill areas for managing the relationships in and around the entrepreneurial venture include *communication* skills, *leadership* skills, *negotiating* skills and *motivational* skills.

What behaviour standards are demanded?

Behaviour standards (which are as much about what should *not* be done as what should be) are a critical dimension of relationships. A society will, in general, define the behavioural standards expected for business practice. This is only a minimum guide. The entrepreneur may always look for competitive advantage in accepting discretionary responsibilities that go *beyond* those normally expected for a business in the sector (see section 9.4).

Growth and structural advantages

Structural advantages arise when the business organises itself in a way which gives it more flexibility and responsiveness in the face of competitive pressures. This is often a key area of advantage for the entrepreneurial business. Lacking the cost and possibly the relationship advantages enjoyed by established businesses, the entrepreneurial venture must prosper by being more acute to the market's needs and innovating to satisfy them.

The challenge to the entrepreneurial business is to retain this responsiveness and drive for innovation as the business grows and matures. The key to this is understanding the nature of the structural advantages the business has gained and designing the development of the business's structure and organisation so that these are sustained and encouraged to flourish. This important idea will be developed in sections 26.6 and 26.7.

26.6 Structural growth

Every organisation has a unique *structure*. An understanding of this structure is best approached from a broad perspective. It has both static and dynamic aspects. At one level it

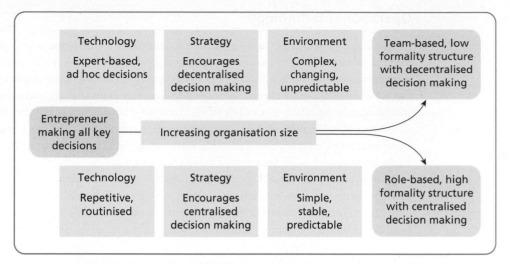

Figure 26.6 Factors influencing organisational structure

is the framework of reporting relationships (who is responsible to whom) that describes the organisation. This is how the organisation is often depicted in hierarchical 'organigrams'. This formal structure is, however, just a skeleton. The organisation gains its flesh from the way in which those reporting relationships are played out in terms of the *communications* that take place, the *roles* that must be performed and the *power structures* that define, support and confine those roles. Some of these are formal and explicit, others are informal and implicit, but the entrepreneur must learn to manage all of them.

The structure of the organisation, and the way that structure develops as the organisation grows, is both a response to the circumstances in which the organisation finds itself and a reaction to the opportunities with which it is presented. One well-explored approach to understanding how the particular situation of an organisation defines its structure is provided by *contingency theory*. In essence, contingency theory regards the structure of an organisation as dependent on five 'contingencies', or types of factor. These are the organisation's *size*, the operational *technology* it uses to create value, the *strategy* it adopts, the *environment* it is in, and the way *power* is utilised within it (Figure 26.6).

Organisation size

In general, the larger the organisation, the more complex its structure will be. A larger organisation provides more scope for tasks to be differentiated. As more information needs to be passed up to decision makers and more instructions passed back down again, there will be room for more layers of management. Once a certain size is reached, the complexity of the organisation may become so great that it is better to break it up into a series of sub-organisations (functions or departments), each reporting to a common centre.

Operational technology

In broad terms, an organisation's operational technology is simply the way it goes about performing its tasks. Some organisations are involved in repeating a series of relatively straightforward tasks. For example, McDonald's restaurants are involved in producing and retailing fast food through a large number of outlets. Others face tasks that are more complex but are still ultimately repetitive. For example, easyJet must transport air passengers from one place to another. On the other hand, some businesses, particularly high-tech ones, undertake a small number of complex tasks, possibly with very few repetitive elements. An example here might be Microsoft's development of software packages.

Contingency theory predicts that organisations which undertake a large number of repetitive tasks will have a more formal structure, with well-defined roles and responsibilities, than an organisation undertaking less repetitive and predictable tasks, which will tend to have a less formal structure. Individuals will tend to define their roles in relation to the demands of a particular project, rather than the expectation of a routine. In this case the organisation may develop expert roles and ad hoc team structures.

Organisation strategy

The strategy adopted by a business is the way it goes about competing for its customers' attention. It is, in essence, what it offers, to whom and the reasons it gives customers to buy. Some organisations, having established their business, take up a defensive posture. They understand their products and the reasons why customers buy. They compete by being better at serving 'their' niche than anyone else and they react to competitors only when they move in on 'their' territory.

Other businesses – and entrepreneurs must be in this class – are more aggressive. They aim to grow their business by attacking entrenched competitors. They compete by offering the customer an innovation which serves a need, or solves a problem, better than existing offerings. Some organisations may combine both these generic strategies: defending established business and using the resources gained to attack in other areas.

More specifically, the organisation's strategy is the way it goes about developing and sustaining competitive advantage, in particular *cost advantages*, *knowledge advantages*, *relationship advantages* and *structural advantages*.

There is no simple relationship between strategy and structure. The defining tension is the way in which decision making within the organisation drives the strategy. In short, if decision making can be centralised then a more regular, and formal, structure should be expected. If, on the other hand, decision making must be 'pushed down' to lower levels of the organisation then a less formal, more flexible, structure might be expected. Organisations pursuing cost leadership (for example, the Japanese engineering conglomerate Minebea) tend to centralise control in order to ensure that costs are managed. Retail organisations which depend on a strong brand presence (for example, The Body Shop) may also enact strong central control in order to ensure that the brand, and the products and services it endorses, are carefully managed.

Businesses based on knowledge advantages, especially where there is a lot of expertise involved, may avoid strong central control systems. Decision making may be localised. Actions may, however, be guided by a strong organisational culture. Team structures may be important, as may informal mentoring of less experienced employees by more experienced. Many professional organisations with an entrepreneurial background (for example, Saatchi and Saatchi) have adopted this approach.

The organisation's environment

Organisations find themselves in an environment made up of macroeconomic features, stakeholders and competitors. This environment both offers resources and challenges their availability. Opportunities offer new possibilities whereas threats present the danger that what is enjoyed now may be lost in the future. The environment is defined by a number of factors, in particular how *complex* it is (i.e. how much information must be processed in order to understand it), how *fast* it is developing or changing, and how *predictable* those changes are. As with strategy, the influence of the environment on structure impacts through the way in which decision making is shaped. A known, slow-changing, predictable environment encourages centralised decision making. A new or fast-changing and unpredictable environment encourages decision making to be passed down to those at the cutting edge of the organisation who are 'in contact' with the environment.

Power, control and organisational politics

The structure of an organisation represents a response to the contingencies of size, technology, strategy and environment. But the extent to which it represents a controlled, deliberate and rational response depends on the extent to which, and the way in which, the entrepreneur can exert control over the organisation as it grows. A powerful central entrepreneur can be a great asset to a business. They can provide vision and leadership and keep the organisation focused on the opportunities with which it is presented. In the absence of this, the organisation may lack direction and so lose its momentum. Individuals, and informal coalitions of individuals, can begin to see their interests as being different from those of the organisation as a whole and the organisation can become *politicised*.

On the other hand, if the power the entrepreneur enjoys is misdirected, then the organisation may be led down the wrong path. Entrepreneurial power brings responsibility. It is important that the entrepreneur uses their position and power to create an organisational environment in which individuals are free to express, and act upon, their own analysis and decision-making skills. This is particularly important for the fast-growing, innovative business pursuing an aggressive strategy in a changing, unpredictable environment where localised decision making can offer an advantage. Even if the organisation can benefit from a degree of centralisation of decision making, the entrepreneur will face practical limitations in the range and number of decisions they can make personally. Once the organisation reaches a certain size (and it need not be that large) the entrepreneur is well advised to call upon the skills of a supporting management team. A summary of the influence of contingency factors on structure is provided in Table 26.3.

26.7 Organisational growth

The entrepreneur is faced with the task of designing and creating an organisation. A study by Chaganti *et al.* (2002) suggests that the entrepreneur's leadership style and strategy are

Table 26.3 The influence of contingency factors on organisational structure

Contingency	Influence on organisational development
Size	Organisational complexity tends to increase with size; development of internal structure occurs. Roles and responsibilities become more specialised
Technology	Structure driven by nature of organisation's tasks: are they repetitive, ad hoc or based on expert judgement?
	Repetitive tasks tend to favour routinised activities and repeated unit structure with centralised decision making
	Ad hoc and expert tasks encourage delocalised decision making, perhaps within a strong 'organisational cultural' framework
Environment	Well-understood, stable and predictable environment favours centralised decision making and formal, routinised structures
	Poorly understood, unstable and unpredictable environment favours decentralised decision making and empowerment at low levels in the organisational hierarchy
Strategy	Influence depends on how strategy is sustained through decision making
	Does strategy adopted demand strong central control or does it favour decentralised decision making?
Power	Can entrepreneur impose strong central control? By what means?

Key learning outcome

An appreciation of how the resource requirements of the organisation can be used as a guide to its design.

important factors in shaping the dynamics of small business growth. Contingency theory provides a valuable insight into the variables that mould the organisation but it does not provide a detailed guide to shaping a particular organisation. A better approach is to consider the resource requirements of the organisation and to design its structure around them.

The 'traditional' path of development for an entrepreneurial venture is sometimes related as follows. At its inception, the business consists of just the entrepreneur and perhaps one or two others. The entrepreneur makes the decisions and undertakes the task of performing the business's activities, perhaps with a little delegation. In its early growth stages, as the business takes on more staff, the entrepreneur is freer to undertake the decision making and delegate more of the actual business-generating activity. As growth continues, the entrepreneur may develop a management team to support their own decision making. In time, the members of this management team may act as the nucleus for more formal departments or business functions. As this process continues, the entrepreneur's role becomes that of the chief executive and the organisation settles down to maturity.

While this presents a plausible story for the growth of a business it is, at best, retrospective. Models that define the development of an organisation in terms of definite stages should be met with some caution. An important example is Greiner's (1972) model that describes organisational growth in terms of five growth phases in which the business can expand with its resource base and structure intact, and five intermittent crisis phases during which the business must acquire new resources and radically modify its structure if it is to survive and move into the next growth phase. Failure to do so leads to decline.

While such models may provide an account of what *has* happened they have little power to predict what *will* happen. Even if particular stages of development do exist, an individual business will move through different stages at different rates and may miss out some stages altogether. Such models are of limited use as a guide to decision making. It is hard to say at a particular time exactly what stage a business has reached or when it can be expected to move on to the next stage.

For the decision maker attempting to design an organisation, it is more profitable to ask what governs the structures a particular business should adopt given the (unique) situation with which it is faced. One option is to consider the *resource requirements* of the organisation.

The resource requirement approach

The nature of the resources available to the entrepreneur have been considered in Chapter 12. In essence, the entrepreneurial venture needs only three things: *information* from which an innovation can be developed, *capital* (money) for investment and *people* to make the venture happen. The initial resource requirements of an organisation are shown in Figure 26.7. In practice, the venture will obtain these things through a variety of routes.

Information

In the first instance, information will be obtained via the entrepreneur's experience within a particular business sector. As the business grows, market intelligence gathering will become

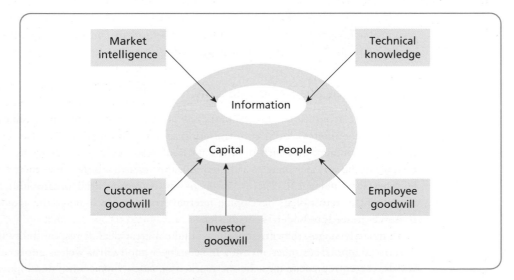

Figure 26.7 The resource dependency model of organisation

increasingly important. As it develops further, this may be supplemented by formal market research to provide market information and a research and development programme to provide information on products and technology.

Capital

The entrepreneur may use their own money to initiate the business. This may be supplemented by formal and/or informal investment capital. If the business is to be sustained, however, it must attract money from customers. This will, of course, be a result of the business selling its products to them. If this is to occur then the customer's interest and *goodwill* towards the business, and what it offers, are needed. If the business is to grow at a sustainable rate then additional capital may be needed from investors. Again, their interest and goodwill towards the venture are needed.

People

In the early stages of the business the entrepreneur may invite close associates to join the venture. However, as the business grows, more formal, procedures for identifying and recruiting personnel and gaining their goodwill will be needed.

The structure adopted by a particular organisation can be thought of as a response to its requirements in relation to these three key resources. Particular functions appear within the organisation in order to manage the acquisition of these resources. The 'conventional' response for the large, mature organisation is to set up *departments* with specific responsibility for the acquisition of particular resources. Thus customer goodwill is captured by marketing and sales; investor goodwill by the finance department; market knowledge by the marketing research function (perhaps integrated into the marketing department); technical knowledge by the research and development function; and so on.

The complete organisation will include two additional functions. The operational system which actually produces the outputs of the business (i.e. production or service provision) is responsible for adding value to the inputs, and a strategic control function co-ordinates the operation of the organisation as a whole.

The resource acquisition approach

The resource acquisition approach to growth is only *one* of a range of possible responses. It represents the limitation of the organisation as it reaches maturity. It also reflects a traditional environment in which different types of resource are independent and quite predictable in the way they may be acquired. It is this feature which allows them to be acquired by 'specialist' managers. The evolution of the entrepreneurial organisation can thus be thought of in terms of its developing internal structures to manage the acquisition of the resources it needs to undertake its business.

In its early stages, the entrepreneur will take a great deal of responsibility for attracting the critical inputs: customer, investor and employee goodwill as well as information. In other words, the entrepreneur must be the marketing, sales, finance and development specialist rolled into one. The entrepreneur must also maintain strategic control over the business and

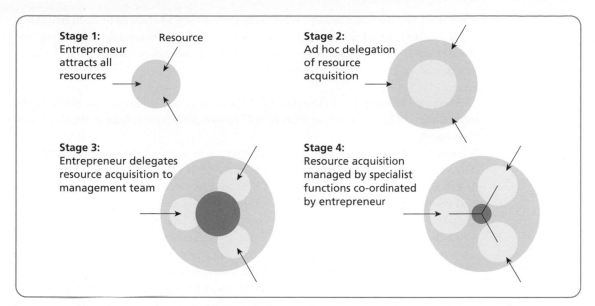

Figure 26.8 The development of resource acquisition in the growing venture

may be responsible for undertaking operations as well. At this early stage, the entrepreneur's role is a challenging one.

As the business grows, tasks can be differentiated, and the role of the entrepreneur can become more distinct. Usually, they will relinquish participation in operational activities and concentrate on managing the business as a whole. As the business grows further, roles can become even more specialised. Individuals can focus their attention on obtaining critical resources. As a result, specific resource acquisition functions can start to emerge. The evolution of input-acquiring functions in the development of the entrepreneurial business is shown in Figure 26.8.

This approach can be used as a guide for decision making about the structure the organisation should adopt. The key issues in relation to deciding on structure are:

- *How large is the organisation?* How many people work for the organisation? How much latitude is there for individuals to take on specialist roles? To what extent is it possible to use outside specialists? (Consider here the points raised in section 23.6 in particular.)

   As a rule, tasks, roles and responsibilities should be specialised, if possible.

- *What are the critical inputs?* All inputs are important. However, the acquisition of some will take priority at any one point and this will alter at different stages of development. The question is, what matters *most* at this point in time: information on markets and product technology, or investment capital, or sales to customers, or people? Is the lack of any *particular* one of these responsible for limiting the venture's potential? To what extent is it possible to dedicate available resources to the acquisition of a particular input? How might this situation change in the near future?

   As a rule, attention should be focused on critical inputs – but it is important not to neglect other inputs.

- *What is the venture's skill profile?* What skills are available in order to be dedicated? How is the venture served for people with selling, marketing, financial, negotiating and research skills, etc.? How might these be acquired (e.g. through training, new recruitment or external support)? What does this say about the venture's skill requirements for the future?

  As a rule, the venture's skill profile should be built up (but an awareness of fixed costs is important). The entrepreneur must be willing to call on outside help in the short term if necessary.

- *What is the nature of the inputs needed?* The nature of inputs that the venture needs will differ depending on the environment in which it finds itself. Are the inputs well defined? (If the business is very innovative or if it is in a business environment which is not well developed then they might not be.) Are they easily obtainable? How intense is the competition for them? On what basis does competition take place?

  The key issue here is how *specialist* the task of managing the acquisition of a particular input needs to be in order to be successful. As a rule, the possibility of gaining competitive advantage by building in-house specialisation should be considered.

- *How do different inputs interact?* The acquisition of any one input cannot be considered in isolation, since how one input is acquired affects how the others will be. Technical knowledge means little without consideration of what the market wants. The acquisition of investors' capital will be facilitated if the venture has a good knowledge of market conditions. Similarly, the goodwill of employees will provide a strong platform on which to build a culture which attracts the goodwill of customers.

  This means that one input-attracting function must communicate with the others. Those responsible for market research must talk to those responsible for development. The finance department must talk to those responsible for marketing. Inter-function communication is facilitated (or hindered) by organisational structure. If the acquisition of inputs can be considered largely in isolation of each other, then a structure which features dedicated specialist functions co-ordinated centrally (perhaps supplemented by informal inter-functional communication) may be suitable. On the other hand, if detailed co-ordination of input acquisition is necessary, then a matrix or a team structure may be more effective and offer a better route to developing a structural competitive advantage.

26.8 Controlling and planning for growth

Key learning outcome

A recognition of the ways in which growth can be controlled by the entrepreneur.

The fact that growth presents strategic, resource and investment decision-making issues to the entrepreneur means that it is a process which must be both planned for and controlled. Indeed, the objective of growth, once it has been established, should lie at the heart of and drive forward the venture's planning and control process. The idea of controlling growth is critical to entrepreneurial success. It draws together a number of themes which have been developed in this book.

The *desirability* of growth must be reflected in the entrepreneur's vision (see Chapter 16). This vision must act as a force which co-ordinates and focuses the whole organisation on the tasks it faces. To do this, the vision must not only illuminate the *what* of growth but also the *why*, that is, not only what is in it for the organisation but also why the stakeholder will gain from it.

The *potential* for growth must be recognised in the venture's mission (see Chapter 17). This mission should be reasonable given the venture's capabilities and competitive situation but it should also stretch the organisation to make maximum use of its capabilities and exploit its competitive potential.

The *direction* of growth must be indicated by the venture's strategy (see Chapter 18). This should indicate the products that the business will offer, the markets it will operate in and the competitive advantages it will develop and exploit in order to serve the customer better than do competitors in those markets.

The *management* of growth demands the management of resource flows within the organisation. It means designing the organisation so that appropriate resource-acquiring functions are in place to co-ordinate resource-acquiring activities effectively. This relates to the ideas developed earlier in this chapter.

In summary, the *achievement* of growth is a result of the decision-making processes that go on within the venture. The entrepreneur must control these through their power and leadership strategies. The entrepreneur's need (and desire) to impose their will on the organisation must always be tempered by the value to be gained from letting individuals use their own insights and initiative.

26.9 The venture as a theatre for human growth

Key learning outcome

A recognition of the importance of the human dimension in organisational growth.

Business organisations are not just systems for generating wealth; they are the stages on which human beings live their lives. Individuals use their organisational role to create images of themselves. For many people, what you *do* is who you *are*. In building an organisation, an entrepreneur is not just generating employment opportunities but also creating a theatre in which people will play out the parts that are critical to their personal development. Organisations are the places where people meet and interact. The entrepreneur is offering not only economic rewards but social and personal development ones as well.

Effective entrepreneurs will recognise this. They will understand that an individual working in the organisation is bringing with them a number of different expectations operating at different levels. Entrepreneurs should be aware of the meaning that the organisation offers to the people who are part of it and, critically, of how that meaning changes as the organisation grows.

The small, informal organisation will offer a different environment from that offered by the larger one where roles and relationships are more formal. Of course, there is a trade-off. The larger organisation offers more security and the possibility for employees to use and develop specialist skills, whereas the smaller one may offer a more flexible and intimate environment. The entrepreneur must recognise the balance of benefits from the perspective of the individual employee.

An entrepreneur, like any good manager, recognises that the development of the organisation is also the development of the people within it. Its growth offers them the potential for their growth. Developing and communicating vision means writing the story of how the organisation will develop, the roles that particular individuals will play in that development, and what those roles will mean for them.

In practice this means that the entrepreneur must discuss with employees the changes that are taking place within the organisation, and use those discussions to develop an understanding of what those changes mean for them. Presenting the future possibilities offered by, and removing the fear of, change is the platform on which motivation is built. Such discussions may be quite formal (for example, regular appraisals and objective setting) or informal chats.

An understanding of what the prospects and achievement of growth offer and of the fears and apprehensions they create for the individual within the organisation is crucial since these factors form the platform upon which the entrepreneur builds their leadership strategy.

26.10 Conceptualising growth and organisational change

Key learning outcome

An understanding of the metaphors used to describe organisational growth.

The idea that organisations and organising are best understood through the use of metaphor was introduced in section 13.1. The point was made that the way in which management is approached is dependent, to some extent, on the metaphor being used to provide an image of organisation by the entrepreneurial decision maker. As well as influencing the way in which organisation is perceived in a static sense, metaphors also influence the way in which organisational *growth* and *change* are seen to take place. Again, such metaphors provide a basis for recognising the challenges the organisation faces and the approaches the entrepreneur might take to meet them.

Van de Ven and Scott Poole (1995) have summarised the most important metaphors of organisational change. These are based on the notions of *life cycle*, *evolution*, the *dialectic* and *teleology*. In addition, the metaphors of the trialectic and chaos complement the picture.

Life cycle

The notion of life cycle suggests that the organisation undergoes a pattern of growth and development much like a living organism does. Life for an organism consists of a series of different stages: it is born, grows, matures and eventually declines and dies (Figure 26.9). This pattern is pre-programmed and the changes that take place are both unavoidable and irrevocable. Drawing on the experience of living things, this metaphor accounts for the view that youthful entrepreneurial organisations are dynamic whereas older organisations are more sedate and sluggish and that this is a fate that will eventually befall the entrepreneurial venture as it matures. The metaphor does not give a definite lifespan, however; it does not say *when* this must happen.

This metaphor is limited in that it (falsely) suggests that organisational decline is inevitable. It does, however, serve to warn the entrepreneur against complacency as the venture becomes successful.

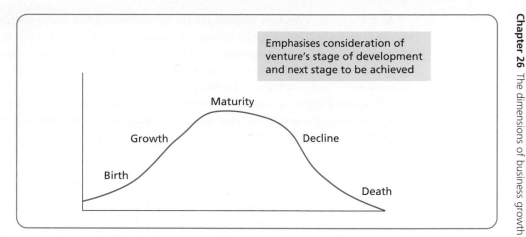

Figure 26.9 Life cycle growth metaphor

Evolution

Evolution is a theoretical scheme which explains changes over time of the morphology of biological populations. It is founded on the concepts of *competition, fitness, selection* and *survival*. This scheme has been co-opted from biological science to describe changes in populations of business firms (Figure 26.10).

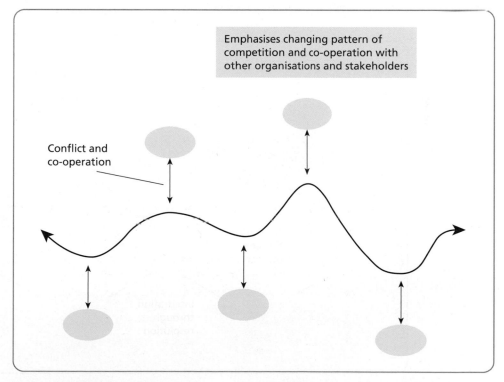

Figure 26.10 Evolutionary growth

As a metaphor, evolution reminds the entrepreneur that they are operating in a competitive environment, that they must compete for scarce resources and that the venture must be efficient ('fit') in the tasks it undertakes. While evolution may conjure up an image of untrammelled competition – of a nature 'red in tooth and claw' in the words of Tennyson's *In memoriam* – a more sophisticated reading reminds us that co-operation within and between species is also a feature of the natural world. This is similar to the entrepreneurial venture which not only competes, but also grows within a stakeholder network which may be supportive as well as competitive.

The dialectic

The dialectic is a concept which can be traced back to classical Greek philosophy. It has been extensively developed by thinkers such as Marx and Freud and is based on a notion of progression through conflict and resolution. A system is initially unified but, over time, distinct parts begin to distinguish themselves. These parts recognise that their interests conflict and so they begin to oppose each other. Neither part can actually win the conflict and what eventually emerges is a newly unified system in which both parts have been changed and reintegrated (Figure 26.11).

As a metaphor of organisational development, the dialectic illuminates conflict and conflict resolution at a number of levels, for example between the entrepreneurial venture and competitor firms; between different stakeholder groups within the venture such as between investors and employees; and within stakeholder groups. This latter level would include, for example, political manoeuvring by managerial factions within the business.

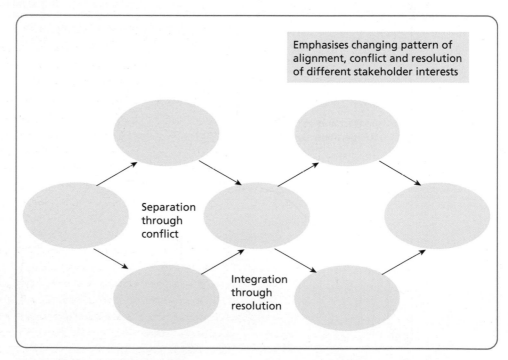

Figure 26.11 Dialectical growth

The importance of this metaphor for the entrepreneur is not so much its emphasis on the inevitability of conflict as in the idea that value can be created by resolving that conflict. The entrepreneur brings stakeholders (whose interests may differ) together in a way in which all benefit.

The trialectic

Ford and Ford (1994) have drawn upon a development of the dialectic to present a new metaphor for describing organisational growth. This is the *trialectic*. The dialectic suggests that a system separates into two conflicting parts. As its name implies, the trialectic suggests that systems have a dynamic consisting of three parts. However, the way that these three parts attract rather than conflict with each other is emphasised.

A trialectic takes as its starting point the notion that all things are in a state of flux. This flux is the fundamental 'stuff' of the universe, not the objects we see. When we recognise objects or systems, we do so only as a result of our seeking out transient 'resting points' or 'material manifestations'. The three aspects that are important to the growth of an organisation are its current state or 'manifestation' and two alternative possible futures or potential manifestations. These possible future states act to attract the venture and pull it forward. In pursuing these, the organisation creates new pairs of possible future states (Figure 26.12). This process is ongoing, continuous and dynamic. Again, we notice these states only because we continually seek out the transient manifestations.

The metaphor of trialectical change calls upon some deep philosophical ideas. As a metaphor for growth in the entrepreneurial venture it does, however, emphasise the fact that change is not just an aspect of the organisation; it is fundamental to it. It also emphasises the possibility of choosing a number of different future states and the freedom the entrepreneur has to create their own entirely new world.

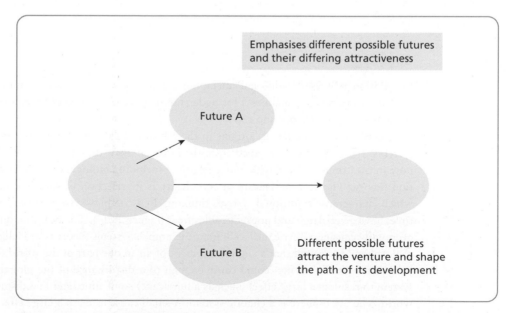

Figure 26.12 Trialectical growth

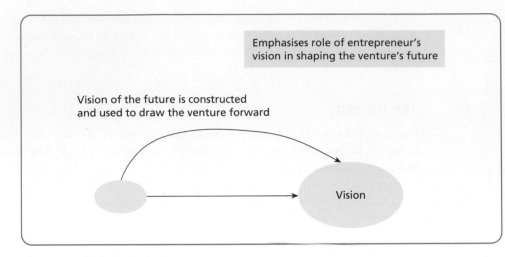

Figure 26.13 Teleological growth

Teleology

Teleology suggests a process of change in which a system is progressing toward some future state or *teleos*. This future state both attracts the system or pulls it forward, and defines the shape the system takes as it progresses (Figure 26.13). More than any other metaphor, teleology introduces the notion of *purpose* to organisational change and growth. The entrepreneur can use their vision as the future state which pulls the organisation forward. It can be used to define goals and objectives and it is a critical element in leadership. Visionary leadership is a teleological process.

Chaos

In addition to these 'traditional' metaphors, a new perspective is becoming increasingly important in providing a context for understanding organisational change. This is based on the notions of *complexity* and *chaos*.

Complexity science has its origins in the physics of turbulent and far-from-equilibrium systems. Its insights have escaped from the boundaries of these narrow concerns and they now inform thinking on a wide range of topics including biology, economics and organisation theory. The defining feature of complexity is its rejection of simple lines of causality which characterise traditional systems thinking. In a complex system a small cause may, in time, have a very large and unpredictable effect (Figure 26.14). The beat of a butterfly's wing eventually causing a hurricane is a dramatic example. Systems theorists modelling the earth's atmosphere discovered that a slight movement of air in one part of the world (say, from the beat of a butterfly's wing) could cause enough of a disturbance of the global atmospheric system to result in a large effect (such as a hurricane) some time later in a distant part of the world. The atmosphere is a chaotic system. A small cause leads to a large effect that cannot be predicted *ex ante*. Complex systems are not simply disorganised, however. They may

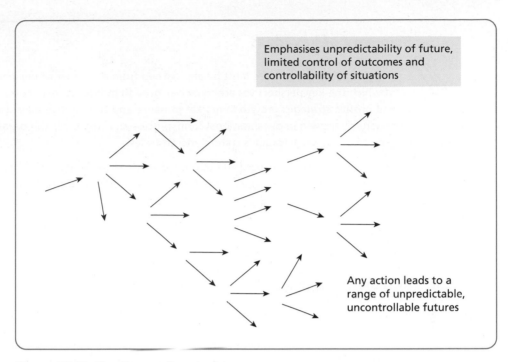

Emphasises unpredictability of future, limited control of outcomes and controllability of situations

Any action leads to a range of unpredictable, uncontrollable futures

Figure 26.14 Chaotic growth metaphor

show higher levels of form and order as a result of 'emergent' features which do not have a straightforward one-to-one relationship with lower levels of order. This is a perspective which has been developed extensively by Stacey (2000).

The main question which complexity theory poses to management thinking is, if organisations are chaotic systems, can they be 'managed' at all? The answer usually leads not to a rejection of management but to demands to view it in a more sophisticated light. What is rejected is the idea that management can be reduced to a simple process of moving the venture to a predetermined end-point by a series of controlled steps.

The entrepreneurial venture is inherently unpredictable. By its very nature, it creates a future which is uncertain. Systems emerge to manage this uncertainty, for example the network of stakeholder relationships which define the venture, but they cannot eliminate it completely. The chaos metaphor reminds the entrepreneur that control and direction cannot be 'programmed' into the organisation. Events cannot be foreseen and each contingency must be responded to on its own terms. Entrepreneurial management is a *dynamic* process and it demands a 'hands on' approach. The future of the venture is not predetermined by its present; rather, it is actively shaped by the entrepreneur as new, unseen and often unseeable possibilities emerge.

As with metaphors of static organisation, entrepreneurs must learn to enrich their decision making by recognising the metaphors they are using and by drawing on as wide a variety of metaphors of organisational change as possible.

Summary of key ideas

- The growth of the venture must be approached from a number of perspectives of which the key perspectives are: *financial*: growth in income, expenditure and profits; *strategic*: growth in market presence and competitive advantages; *structural*: growth in organisational form, process and structure; and *organisational*: growth in the organisation's culture and attitudes.

- Effective entrepreneurs recognise that the growth of the venture provides all of its stakeholders with an opportunity for personal growth and development.

Research themes

Entrepreneurs' growth objectives

It is often assumed that all entrepreneurs wish to grow their businesses. However, as pointed out in the discussion of differential advantage theory (section 6.1), growth may be one objective among many and may be a means of achieving other objectives rather than an objective in itself. Select a sample of entrepreneurs and survey them to ascertain their attitudes towards the growth of their ventures. Issues to be explored include whether the entrepreneur sees growth as a priority or not, to what extent growth should take precedence over other objectives (such as short-term profitability and consolidation of existing position), what level of risk is acceptable to achieve growth, what managerial challenges does growth entail and what long-term rewards does the entrepreneur expect for delivering growth. Further, inquire into how growth might conflict with wider stakeholder concerns (including those of the entrepreneur themself) and perhaps its impact on broader social responsibilities. Do all entrepreneurs hold the same attitudes towards growth? Is growth an objective in itself or is it a means to an end? Summarise by considering the implications for supporting entrepreneurs in achieving growth.

Patterns of growth in entrepreneurial businesses

A large body of financial data is now available on the internet. Many businesses publish their accounts on the web, and specialist databases such as FAME provide stock market information. This availability is creating the opportunity for studies into the patterns of growth achieved by fast-growing entrepreneurial businesses. Such a study could examine the shape of growth profiles using metrics such as turnover, profits and asset base. The methodology would be to examine growth in these measures against time. What patterns are evident? Is growth generally smooth and incremental, or does it tend to be erratic? What rates of growth are seen? Do fast-growing businesses tend to have downturns as well as upturns? How does change in turnover relate to change in profits and assets? Quite a number of different patterns are likely to be seen. Can these be grouped and classified in any meaningful way? There are mathematical techniques for comparing such patterns in a rigorous way, but quite a lot can be achieved with simple visual inspection. Conclude by suggesting a generic scheme for patterns of growth. The more businesses introduced into the study, the more general and valuable will be the findings. A sample of at least 100 drawn either from one particular sector or on a cross-sectional basis should be used.

Financial growth and strategic and organisational turbulence

Models of growth such as Greiner's (discussed above) suggest that fast-growing organisations experience growth as periods of incremental increase based on relatively stable organisational forms and strategic approach interspersed with periods of crisis during which significant changes in organisational form and strategic approach must be made if the organisation is to continue growing. One way of validating such a view would be to correlate a detailed history of a business with financial measures of size. Use the historical information (which might be obtained from good, detailed case studies or primary research) to define growth and crisis phases. You should be explicit and rigorous in your criteria for identifying these. Do this before examining the financial information on the business. Is there a correlation between the historical phases and size as measured financially? Does this confirm Greiner's concept? A sample of at least five businesses (either from one sector or cross-sectional) should be considered. The more organisations studied, the more robust will be the findings.

Entrepreneurs' metaphors for growth

As outlined in section 26.10, growth is often understood through the mirror of metaphor. The metaphors described can be translated into propositions about growth. For example, the teleological metaphor can be related as, 'I know where I want to be in growing this business'; the dialectic as, 'growth always results in conflict'; the biological as, 'all businesses eventually die'; and so on. Work on a series of propositions relating the metaphors in this way, creating several for each metaphor. Present these to entrepreneurs (nascent or experienced) and have them indicate their agreement or disagreement with them (use a Likert scale). In order to discriminate between different metaphorical representations, pairs of propositions drawn from different metaphors can be presented, with the subject indicating which of the pair they most agree with. Additionally, have the entrepreneur detail their growth objectives and ambitions as well as approach and perceived issues in achieving growth for their venture (this study might well follow on from the one above). Do individual entrepreneurs tend towards a single metaphor, or do they draw from several? How does the dominant metaphor relate to approaches to and understanding of growth management? Conclude by making recommendations about how supporters of entrepreneurs may use an understanding of the individual entrepreneur's declared underpinning metaphor for growth to enhance communication with entrepreneurs about growth and its management.

Key readings

Growth is a complex and elusive concept. A good paper to explore the idea of growth while engaging with the challenge of developing models for its analysis is:

Gibb, A. and Davies, L. (1991) 'In pursuit of frameworks for the development of growth models of the small business', *International Small Business Journal*, Vol. 9, No. 1, pp. 15–31.

Metaphors present one way of developing an understanding. A substantive analysis of one growth metaphor is provided by:

O'Rand, A.M. and Krecker, M.L. (1990) 'Concepts of the life-cycle: their history, meanings and uses in the social sciences', *Annual Review of Sociology*, Vol. 16, pp. 241–62.

Suggestions for further reading

Birley, S. and Westhead, P. (1990) 'Growth and performance contrasts between "types" of small firm', *Strategic Management Journal*, Vol. 11, pp. 535–57.

Bitner, L.N. and Powell, J.D. (1987) 'Expansion planning for small retail firms', *Journal of Small Business Management*, Apr., pp. 47–54.

Brocklesby, J. and Cummings, S. (1996) 'Designing a viable organisational structure', *Long Range Planning*, Vol. 29, No. 1, pp. 49–57.

Chaganti, R., Cook, R.G. and Smeltz, W.J. (2002) 'Effects of styles, strategies and systems on the growth of small businesses', *Journal of Developmental Entrepreneurship*, Vol. 7, No. 2, pp. 175–92.

Ford, J.D. and Ford, L.W. (1994) 'Logics of identity, contradiction and attraction in change', *Academy of Management Review*, Vol. 19, No. 4, pp. 756–85.

Gaddis, P.O. (1997) 'Strategy under attack', *Long Range Planning*, Vol. 30, No. 1, pp. 38–45.

Glancey, K. (1998) 'Determinants of growth and profitability in small entrepreneurial firms', *International Journal of Entrepreneurial Behaviour and Research*, Vol. 4, No. 2, pp. 18–27.

Greiner, L.E. (1972) 'Evolution and revolution as organisations grow', *Harvard Business Review*, July/Aug., pp. 37–46.

Hunsdiek, D. (1985) 'Financing of start-up and growth of new technology based firms in West Germany', *International Small Business Journal*, Vol. 4, No. 2, pp. 10–24.

McKergow, M. (1996) 'Complexity science and management: what's in it for business?', *Long Range Planning*, Vol. 29, No. 5, pp. 721–7.

Mintzberg, H. (1979) *The Structuring of Organizations: A Synthesis of the Research*. Englewood Cliffs, NJ: Prentice Hall.

Oakley, R. (1991) 'High-technology small firms: their potential for rapid industrial growth', *International Small Business Journal*, Vol. 9, No. 4, pp. 30–42.

Petrakis, P.E. (2005) 'Growth, entrepreneurship, structural change, time and risk', *Journal of the American Academy of Business*, Vol. 7, No. 1, pp. 243–50.

Scott, M. and Bruce, R. (1987) 'Five stages of growth in small business', *Long Range Planning*, Vol. 20, No. 3, pp. 45–52.

Smallbone, D., Leigh, R. and North, D. (1995) 'The characteristics and strategies of high-growth SMEs', *International Journal of Entrepreneurial Behaviour and Research*, Vol. 1, No. 3, pp. 44–62.

Stacey, R. (1996) 'Emerging strategies for a chaotic environment', *Long Range Planning*, Vol. 29, No. 2, pp. 182–9.

Stacey, R. (2000) *Strategic Management and Organisational Dynamics* (3rd edn). London: Pitman Publishing.

Tuck, P. and Hamilton, R.T. (1993) 'Intra-industry size differences in founder controlled firms', *International Small Business Journal*, Vol. 12, No. 1, pp. 12–22.

van de Ven, A.H. and Scott Poole, M. (1995) 'Explaining development and change in organizations', *Academy of Management Review*, Vol. 20, No. 3, pp. 510–40.

Selected case material

CASE 26.1   17 October 2005

Ban the bureaucracy and bring in the bulldozers

MARTIN ARNOLD AND ANDREW JACK

A small grey marble table sits in the corner of Jean-François Dehecq's spartan chief executive suite in Paris, with room for no more than a handful of people to gather round.

Sanofi-Aventis, the company he runs, may have become one of the world's largest pharmaceutical companies, but he believes this table remains big enough for all those needed to take the key decisions.

Apart from Mr Dehecq, that means just three other long-standing colleagues in whom he has total confidence: Gérard Le Fur, head of research; Jean-Claude Leroy, head of finance; and Hanspeter Spek, head of pharmaceutical operations.

'We don't need to talk to understand each other,' he says, speaking in a French rich in colloquialisms. 'We sit around this little table and make decisions and apply them the next morning. There are no committees, no mucking around.'

This is one of a number of his defiantly distinctive approaches to management. While executives in many 'big pharma' groups complain that they are spending too much time bogged down in large committees and ensnared by cumbersome bureaucracy, Mr Dehecq believes he can best keep his company alive by retaining a direct approach that cuts away bureaucracy.

He cites the plan of a group of his managers to build a new $100m (£57m) vaccines plant in the US. 'We challenged it, and then we said "Right, let's go". The reaction of these guys was, "So which committee do we go to now?" I said tomorrow morning you get the bulldozers on the site and start building. We just took the decision.'

▶

Such speed was just as useful to plan a response when Barr Pharmaceuticals of the US and Teva Pharmaceutical Industries of Israel launched a generic rival to Sanofi-Aventis's Allegra anti-allergy drug last month – even as legal proceedings to challenge its patent were continuing. That led to the introduction of its own lower-priced generic equivalent to win back the market.

'We were not expecting it at all,' he recalls of the move. 'It took us four days to sign an agreement with a generic company and ten days to produce the first product. I did it all by telephone and Spek went over to the US to fix it over the weekend. We agreed and went for it, no need for discussions or committee meetings.'

More than at any time before, that same small group of executives came into play when engineering Sanofi's largest takeover, with the purchase of the rival French group Aventis last year in a highly unusual, hostile takeover battle.

Mr Dehecq says the saga began as a survival strategy for Sanofi, indicating that Pfizer, the world's largest drugs group, was among a number of pharmaceutical companies eyeing his business for acquisition because of its profitability.

Despite the fact that Aventis was larger, Mr Dehecq makes clear that he was happy to launch an aggressive takeover, dispensing with the usual diplomatic niceties associated with the nominal 'mergers' of equals. 'If you do not go hostile, you get bogged down as with the big mergers in recent years.'

The result was a purge of Aventis's top management, as he has imposed Sanofi's vision and style. Asked to cite who remains in senior positions from the other side, he mentions only the heads of regional operations in Brazil, Spain and Italy.

'The people at Aventis are happy, except for the ones we kicked out,' he says. 'But it's only ever the top level that gets cut. It's not for incompetence; simply, there were two groups with completely opposing views. It's not a judgement on their management, it is just they could not find their place, they had a different approach and were not prepared to support mine.

'You are going to say that my strongmen are Le Fur, Spek and Leroy. I reply "yes". Otherwise we would be stuck in the mud like all the big mergers with only 2 or 3 per cent [revenue] growth this year, while we are generating 11 per cent.'

Many pharmaceutical companies might concede that serendipity plays an important role in the development of successful new drugs. Mr Dehecq's path also exemplifies serendipity. He says it was far from preordained that he would be in charge of a drugs company when he first joined Elf Aquitaine, the oil group, in 1973.

Previously an engineer and rocket scientist, he has since built the company through a series of ambitious acquisitions. He says: 'I nearly went into wall and floor refurbishment. If I had, I think I would have done the same thing. If you decide to be an entrepreneur, you must not be afraid, you take risks, mobilise your people, get them behind you. You can't build an empire if people do not run faster with you than with others.'

Once he decided to focus on pharmaceuticals, he says, he got to work educating himself by 'hitting the books' and talking extensively to Mr Le Fur, whose instinct for new drugs he trusts absolutely, and whom he describes as a mixture of 'brother and son'. 'I bring him some common sense, and the requirement to take measured risks.'

If Sanofi's cardiovascular blockbuster Plavix has been one of the company's great successes to date, Mr Dehecq talks with particular excitement about innovative treatments as central to the company's future. That includes its anti-obesity medicine Acomplia, which is gearing up for regulatory approval.

A series of takeovers has helped him create an international company, but he stresses that Sanofi-Aventis remains firmly rooted in Europe. By contrast, his fellow Frenchman, Jean-Pierre Garnier, the head of UK-based GlaxoSmithKline, is based in Pennsylvania, and Novartis of Switzerland has shifted its research and development centre to Boston.

While conceding that margins remain higher in the US, he suggests that after discounts, prices are not so different in Europe. He warns that sales are slowing in the US, the growing pressure from generic drugs is destabilising the market in that country and pricing pressures are in any case creating convergence towards European levels.

Pure business aside, Mr Dehecq defends the role of his group as part of Europe's future, even while the politicians are lagging behind. 'Europe will realise that it is extremely important to keep [industrial research], providing higher salaries and value added. I have built a company for Europe. One day Europe will exist.'

Today, he suggests that as Europe's largest pharmaceuticals group, and one of the bigger companies in the US, Sanofi-Aventis only has 'a hole' in Japan. 'It would be stupid to say we are not big enough. You have to guard against creating unmanageable monsters,' he says.

'I remain convinced the productivity of research is the key. If [it] is continuing to have a rhythm of success, perhaps we can build a bigger boat. But the problem is, can we find an asset to feed the boat?'

As for the future, he hints that any of his three close colleagues could take on his mantle when he comes up for retirement in three years, and with the board's approval he has chosen a preferred 'dauphin' – whose identity he will not reveal – who shares his vision. 'The essential thing is that we don't end up working by committees. If we do that, we are dead.'

Source: Martin Arnold and Andrew Jack, 'Ban the bureaucracy and bring in the bulldozers', *Financial Times*, 17 October 2005, p. 13. Copyright © 2005 The Financial Times Limited.

CASE 26.2

1 February 2006 **FT**

South Beauty's chic chow plans to win the West

GEOFF DYER

A couple of decades ago, just about the only thing that China successfully exported to the rest of the world was the Chinese restaurant.

As Chinatowns sprang up in large cities in Europe and the US, chow mein and sweet and sour pork became household names, even if the dishes might not have been recognisable in their homeland.

Nowadays the world is bursting at the seams with China-made DVD players, cosmetics and T-shirts as the country has turned itself into an exporting powerhouse. But one Beijing entrepreneur believes the mainland

CASE 26.2 CONT.

touch is required to upgrade the western experience of the Chinese restaurant.

Zhang Lan owns a chain of restaurants called South Beauty that already has 20 branches in mainland China, mostly in Beijing and Shanghai. As well as an aggressive expansion plan in her home market, she has decided it is time to take the South Beauty brand overseas to Europe and the US.

With the sort of bravado that many Chinese entrepreneurs demonstrate, she has ambitions for her company that are a far cry from dingy Chinatown dives with bad-tempered waiters and lukewarm noodles. 'We want to become the Louis Vuitton of the restaurant business,' says Ms Zhang.

The dramatic growth of the Chinese economy has led to an explosion in the mainland restaurant business. With disposable incomes rising at double-digit rates every year for more than a decade, Chinese are eating out much more, especially the younger people in cities, the group with the fastest-rising salaries.

South Beauty has been one of the beneficiaries. With its combination of spicy Sichuan food and distinctive, open-plan decor, the chain has become a favourite of well-to-do diners and has used direct marketing to attract clientele from nearby offices. It has also built up a strong following among the expatriate community – an important indicator given its overseas ambitions.

Ms Zhang says the company will open a restaurant in the Chelsea area of Manhattan later this year and she will shortly travel to Paris to choose a location there. Branches will be opened in Hong Kong and Singapore, while Milan and London are also candidates for the South Beauty treatment. 'I want to take the Chinese restaurant out of Chinatown,' she says.

Of the interesting new companies in China, many were founded by Chinese who have brought relevant experience back from overseas. Ms Zhang is also a 'returnee'. After graduating with a business degree in Beijing, she moved to Canada where she worked as a maid for a Taiwanese family and as a waitress. It was there, she says, that she had the idea to try to combine traditional Chinese cooking with western design.

With $20,000 in her pocket, she moved back to Beijing in 1991 and opened her first restaurant, A'lan. Most restaurants at the time were either vast halls with bright neon lights or grubby back rooms in private houses. To give her new venture a distinctive look, she travelled to Sichuan in the south-west of the country and collected 13 feet long bamboo shoots, which she then painted white.

The bamboo has remained part of the design scheme at South Beauty, which she founded five years ago. As the restaurants have become successful, the locations have become more glamorous. The newest branch in Shanghai has a cigar bar with a jazz band and is in a 1930s mansion; the glass building in the garden that houses the restaurant was designed by Super Potato, a funky Japanese design company. A new branch in Beijing – to be the largest yet – is being designed by Philippe Starck, one of the biggest names in the design field.

'We want to make this branch into one of the top ten restaurants in the world,' says Ms Zhang.

Ms Zhang has set a giddy target of 100 branches by the time the 2008 Olympics open in Beijing. The company's annual revenues are now about Rmb500m ($62,000).

Like many Chinese of her generation, her quiet determination belies some tough experiences earlier on. During the Cultural Revolution, her civil servant mother was branded an intellectual, and the family was sent to the countryside for 're-education' in central Hubei province. This experience gave Ms Zhang – an accomplished cook herself – a taste for the spicy cuisine of the region.

The menu at South Beauty is mostly from Sichuan province, which over the last decade has become one of the most popular cuisines in the country. The restaurant's signature dish is stone-grilled beef, where slices of meat are cooked on the table in a bowl of hot oil and stones, with a sauce of chillies, garlic, coriander and peanuts.

Taking a restaurant chain to New York, Paris or London – no matter how popular the original concept – is no easy task, however. Failure rates are high, the customers fickle.

In most international cities, the Chinese restaurant has long broken out of the Chinatown ghettos to offer a more upmarket version of traditional cooking. Chinese restaurants have been in the US since the California gold rush in 1849 and Sichuan food is already commonplace there. London, meanwhile, has two Chinese restaurants with a Michelin star.

Mainland Chinese companies have struggled in recent years to establish brands with a reputation for high quality. South Beauty's competition will include a number of restaurant groups from Hong Kong, where service levels are much higher than on the mainland.

Ms Zhang says that the group's innovative designs will attract customers to the overseas branches. Grabbing my notebook, she starts to draw diagrams of open-plan restaurant layouts with the kitchen usually in the centre. 'With this type of concept, we can take leading Chinese chefs abroad and show customers traditional Chinese cooking skills,' she says. 'It will give them a surprise.'

Collaboration with luxury goods companies – the precise nature of which she refuses to disclose – could be one strategy to boost the South Beauty brand. Another option might be to sign a partnership with a leading hotel chain to put several branches in five-star locations, she says.

Even if the group manages to carve itself a niche in the restaurant market in its target cities, such aggressive expansion plans inevitably raise questions about the management capabilities of a family business. Ms Zhang says she does not want to use franchises yet because she wants to retain control.

The overseas expansion is being led by her 25-year-old son, Wang Shaofei. But a small group of people can manage only so many branches. Some regular customers have complained that quality is slipping in the newer restaurants.

Financing such plans is a further obstacle. A flotation has been mooted before, but Ms Zhang says the idea is on the back burner at the moment. She says retained profits have been sufficient so far, and the group has been talking to a number of potential investors.

Private equity groups are currently scouring China for deals. A capital-hungry company in need of foreign management and marketing skills could be just the recipe they are looking for.

Source: Geoff Dyer, 'South Beauty's chic chow plans to win the West', *Financial Times*, 1 February 2006, p. 9. Copyright © 2006 The Financial Times Limited.

 ## Discussion points

1. Under what circumstances would you regard acquisition as not being appropriate as an entrepreneurial growth strategy?

2. Under what circumstances would you regard international expansion as not being appropriate as an entrepreneurial growth strategy?

CHAPTER 27

Consolidating the venture

Chapter overview

The entrepreneurial venture is characterised by growth, but at some
stage growth slows and the venture becomes a mature organisation. This chapter
is concerned with describing the process of consolidation, how the rules of success
change and how some of the entrepreneurial vigour of the venture might be
retained through intrapreneurship.

27.1 What consolidation means

Key learning outcome

A recognition that maturity is
accompanied by significant
changes in the way the venture
functions at a financial,
strategic, structural and
organisational level.

No business can grow for ever. There must come a point at which
its expansion slows. In the same way the entrepreneurial venture
must *mature*. However, maturity is associated with more than
a simple cessation of growth. As discussed in Chapter 26, the
growth of a business is a complex and multifaceted phenomenon.
It has financial, strategic, structural and organisational dimensions. As the venture matures, the slowing of growth is associated
with a number of changes in each of these aspects of the organisation. Together these changes are referred to as *consolidation*.

At the *financial* level, consolidation means that turnover (and
profits) begin to plateau. Turnover should still increase, at a rate
not less than the overall expansion of the economy in which the business operates (which
would imply a contraction in real terms), and it is not unreasonable to set growth objectives
above this. But dramatic increases in turnover are not to be expected (unless, perhaps they
are achieved through acquisitions). Growth in the assets supporting turnover will also slow to
a similar level. New assets will tend to be a replacement for the depreciation of existing assets.

Consolidation means that *investment* in the growth of the business can be reduced. So it
is at this point that financial backers will be looking for their returns. Shareholders will
expect to receive a greater share of the profits and to see their dividends increase. Venture
capitalists will look to exit and liquidate their investment.

Strategically, consolidation means that the venture has successfully defined its position in
the market. The place it occupies in the industry value addition chain, the customer groups

it serves and the technology it uses to serve them will be *largely* established – only largely because there is always room for development of the strategic position through organic developments and acquisition. The business's attention will shift from aggressive strategies aimed at encroaching into competitors' territory to more defensive postures aimed at preventing competitors (including new entrepreneurial ones) from taking business away.

In *structural* terms, consolidation means that the internal configuration of the business develops some permanence. During the growth phase, organisational structures and the roles and responsibilities they define will tend to shift, merge and fragment as the business's complexity increases. Consolidation allows the venture to give key roles and responsibilities a longer-term definition. These roles and responsibilities will tend to be defined around the resource needs of the organisation with structures emerging to manage the acquisition of key inputs.

Alongside structural consolidation there will also be *organisational* consolidation. Growth means that the organisation's systems, procedures and operating practices must be in a state of constant flux. Maturity allows these systems to settle down into more permanent patterns of activity. Out of the complex interaction between the entrepreneur, the venture's stakeholders and the wider social world, the organisation's culture will take a final shape.

The prospects and rewards the business offers its employees will also change as it consolidates. Risks will be lowered and job security may be higher. The positions within the organisation will be better defined and career pathways will become more predictable. Change will be at a slower pace. On the other hand, some may miss the challenge that comes from managing rapid growth, including the day-to-day changes this brings and the excitement of not knowing, exactly, what the future might bring.

27.2 Building success into consolidation

Key learning outcome

An appreciation of how the rules of success change as the venture matures.

The rules of success change as the entrepreneurial venture consolidates. The business becomes less concerned with making rapid strides forward and more concerned with progressing in a measured and sure-footed way. Success is measured not so much by what might be achieved tomorrow as by what is being achieved today. This is not to say that the mature business can afford to forget about the future. Far from it. All businesses must plan for an uncertain tomorrow and invest accordingly. It is to suggest, however, that the balance of interest shifts from the possibility of long-term returns towards the reality of short-term rewards.

In section 9.1, the success of the venture was defined in terms of the *stakeholders* with an interest in it, their *needs* and their *expectations* of what it will offer them. This framework provides an insight into how the terms of success change as the venture consolidates.

For investors, the main shift in their expectations is in relation to the risks and returns offered by the venture. After initiation, and while it is growing strongly, the entrepreneurial venture is offering the prospect of high returns for the investor at some point in the future. Returns cannot be offered immediately because any profits generated will need to be ploughed back into the business. In any case, profits are often low during growth. This is certainly the case if a cost leadership strategy is being pursued (described in section 20.3). The

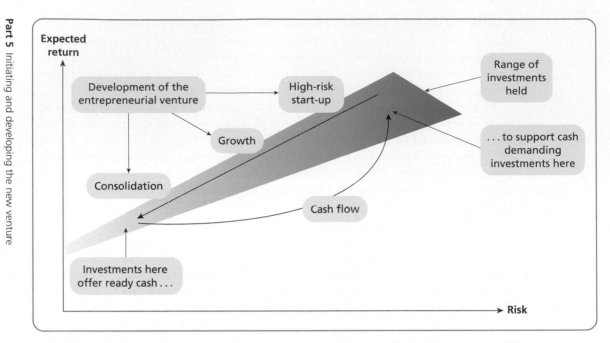

Figure 27.1 The changing position of the entrepreneurial venture in the investor's portfolio

future is uncertain: profits promised in the future carry a higher risk than those on offer today. The plan for the venture must be based on assumptions. Risk enters the equation because there must be some doubt about the validity of those assumptions.

Investors accept risk if the future returns, properly discounted, are attractive enough. There will come a point, however, when they will want to see those returns. Many investors hold a *portfolio* of investments. This portfolio mixes investments which are currently net generators of money (and are therefore low risk) with those demanding money on the basis of future return (high risk). The entrepreneurial venture starts as a high-risk absorber of capital. If it is to remain in the investor's portfolio long-term it must eventually move to become a lower-risk generator of capital (Figure 27.1).

From the perspective of the investor, the success of the venture stops being measured in terms of the way it is growing its sales and assets and establishing its position in its marketplace to the short-term return it is generating on the (investor's) capital it is using. The key measures of performance become the *profit margin* and *return on capital employed*.

Stakeholders other than investors also share in the risks taken on by the entrepreneurial venture. Employees who make a contribution to the venture in its early stages are called upon to make a special effort. The demands will be high. Roles and responsibilities may be poorly defined. Job security will be relatively low. The immediate financial rewards may be less than can be obtained elsewhere. In return for this commitment, employees will, in general, expect an increase in remuneration, a well-defined role and an improvement in job security as the venture consolidates.

While the financial and security rewards of the entrepreneurial venture may be more limited than those offered by the established business, working with a fast-growing and dynamic organisation brings its own rewards at the social and personal development level. For some employees, consolidation may imply a loss in the way the organisation can satisfy these needs, and they may feel it is time to move on to new entrepreneurial pastures.

Suppliers and customers may also have offered a commitment to the venture in its early stages. The turnover of the business will have been quite low. Many suppliers may nonetheless have made a commitment to supplying it with a high level of customer service even though it may have cost more in real terms than they received. Customers may have taken on the business as a supplier even though switching costs had to be faced and continuity of supply was not assured. Such suppliers and customers will see the venture as successful if it returns this early commitment by operating within the business network as a fair, effective and rewarding customer/supplier itself.

27.3 Encouraging intrapreneurship

> ### Key learning outcome
>
> An appreciation of the potential and limits to intrapreneurship in the consolidating organisation.

In recognising the power of the entrepreneurial organisation, it is important not to be too dismissive of what the established 'non-entrepreneurial' organisation has to offer its stakeholders. After all, an established business is only established because it has enjoyed success. The entrepreneurial organisation and the established organisation both have advantages. The entrepreneurial shows an acceptance of (even a need for) change and an ability to exploit new opportunity. The established demonstrates an ability to consolidate around success, manage risk and control resource flows.

A combination of the two, that is, an organisation which recognised the basis of its success and was able to manage it to reduce risk and yet at the same time was flexible to the shifting needs of its stakeholders, remained attuned to new market opportunities and responsive to the need for change, would suggest itself as an ideal type of business. The *intrapreneur* provides a means of achieving the established–entrepreneurial synthesis. The intrapreneur is a role defined by Gifford Pinchot (1985) in his book *Intrapreneuring*. In essence, the intrapreneur is an entrepreneur who works within the confines of an established organisation. The intrapreneur's role would parallel that of the entrepreneur. In particular they would be responsible for developing and communicating organisational vision; identifying new opportunities for the organisation; generating innovative strategic options; creating and offering an organisation-wide perspective; facilitating and encouraging change within the organisation; challenging existing ways of doing things and breaking down bureaucratic inertia. This role has also been described as that of a 'change master' (Kanter, 1985).

Intrapreneurial activity can be directed at four levels within and outside the organisation. These differ in the impact they will have on the organisation and its surroundings, their effect on the venture's stakeholders, the resources they will require and the level of risk they entail.

- *The management of specific projects.* All businesses engage in new projects of some type. Projects such as new product development, the exploitation of a new market opportunity (perhaps international through exporting or strategic alliance), the integration of a new technology into the firm's operations or the acquiring of new funding are especially important to the maturing entrepreneurial venture that wants to keep its competitive edge. Such projects may be best managed in an entrepreneurial way that cuts across conventional organisational boundaries. They may be made the responsibility of a particular cross-disciplinary team that operates with intrapreneurial flair. Ahuja and Lampert (2001) develop a model of how intrapreneurism helps large firms achieve breakthrough inventions.

- *The setting up of new business units.* As the venture becomes larger, new and distinct business functions and units come into their own. A particular part of the business may operate best if it has a distinct character and a degree of independence. The setting up of new business units is a demanding project. Not only must the structural and external strategic issues be considered, but there are also the resourcing issues (including human) and the relationship with the parent business to be taken into account. Again, an intrapreneurial team, the members of which may have a future role in the new unit, may best manage this sort of project.

- *Reinvigorating the whole organisation.* The success of entrepreneurial ventures is largely based on their flexibility and responsiveness to new and unmet customer demands. Such flexibility can be lost as the business grows and its attention is drawn to internal concerns. Injecting the inventive spirit back into the business may be a radical process. Making the organisation entrepreneurial again is clearly an intrapreneurial project. An intrapreneur must lead such a project with entrepreneurial vision for the organisation's future, with an entrepreneurial approach to using power, leadership and motivation, and an ability to overcome organisational resistance to change.

- *Reinventing the business's industry.* Entrepreneurs make a difference. The world is not the same after they have built their venture. The most successful entrepreneurs do not just enter a market: they reinvent the industry in which they operate by introducing new technology, delivering new products or operating in a new, more effective way. There is no reason why the maturing entrepreneurial venture should not hold on to this ambition. A business can win by playing to the rules well; but it can also win by changing the rules to suit itself. Clearly though, such a project is wide in its scope and challenging to implement. It demands an eye on the future, strategic vision, comfort with risk and an ability to lead people forward. It is at this level that intrapreneurship meets up with and becomes entrepreneurship.

Intrapreneurism offers an exciting option for the consolidating entrepreneurial venture. It promises a way to build on success while retaining the original dynamism of the venture. It suggests a way to reduce risk while still pursuing fleeting opportunities. However, any organisational form which promises such high rewards must also present some challenges. There are limitations to intrapreneurship, a point developed by Ross (1987).

Entrepreneur's comfort

Allowing a role for the intrapreneur to develop demands that the entrepreneur actually create space for the intrapreneur to operate. That means letting go of some control. The entrepreneur, having brought the organisation to where it is by exerting control, may not feel comfortable with this. In effect, allowing the intrapreneur to operate means that the entrepreneur must share a part of their own role at a core rather than at a peripheral level. After all, as Young (1999) points out, intrapreneurial management is about breaking rules. And this means the rules that the entrepreneur has created.

Decision-making control

Entrepreneurs exist to challenge orthodoxies. They seek a better way of doing things. They must be dissatisfied with the status quo. This same dissatisfaction must also motivate the intrapreneur. Unlike the entrepreneur, however, the intrapreneur must operate within an organisational decision-making framework. If they did not, then they would not actually be working for the organisation at all. The question here is to what extent the intrapreneur can be allowed to challenge existing decision-making procedures and to what extent they must be bound by them. A balance must be created between allowing the intrapreneur freedom to make their own moves and the need to keep the business on a constant strategic path.

Internal politics

The intrapreneur must question the existing order and drive change within the organisation. For many individuals and groups within the organisation, such change will present a challenge. As a result, the intrapreneur is likely to meet resistance, both active and passive, to the ideas they bring along. An ability to predict and understand that resistance, and developing the leadership skills necessary to overcome it, presents a considerable challenge to the manager. Intrapreneurs are a rare breed. Tom Peters (1989) has suggested that intrapreneurs must be able to 'thrive on chaos'.

Rewards for the intrapreneur

This point really results from the latter. The intrapreneur, if they are to be effective, must bring along the same type, and level, of skills that entrepreneurs themselves offer. The question is, can the organisation *really* offer the intrapreneur the rewards (economic, social and developmental) they might come to expect in return for using them? In short, if someone is an effective intrapreneur how long will it be before the temptation of full-blown entrepreneurship is felt and they move off to start a venture of their own?

Clearly intrapreneurship presents itself as a spectrum which, as a style of management, acts to connect 'conventional' management with entrepreneurial management. It offers a way to bring the advantages of both types of management together. In this it is a compromise. The entrepreneur can facilitate intrapreneurship within the business only by recognising the nature of this compromise and making decisions in relation to it. The central question relates to how much latitude the venture's strategy gives individuals to make their own decisions. The question is not just strategic; an entrepreneur must decide to what extent they will be willing to accept dissent from the intrapreneur. Will it be received as a challenge? How does active dissent fit with the leadership strategy that the entrepreneur has nurtured?

Entrepreneurs must also ask how the reward structure they have set up encourages and discourages individual decision making. What does the individual get in return for venturing on behalf of the business? What sanctions come into force if things go wrong? The entrepreneur must remember that such rewards and sanctions are not always formal and explicit. Further, the entrepreneur must recognise the level of resistance that agents driving change meet from the organisation and accept responsibility in helping the intrapreneur to overcome this. No less than any other member of the organisation, the intrapreneur needs support, encouragement and leadership.

Summary of key ideas

- As the venture matures, its rate of growth slows. This process is known as *consolidation*.

- Consolidation involves changes to the *financial*, *strategic*, *structural* and *organisational* dynamics of the venture.

- Consolidation offers the venture a chance to create a defendable competitive position in the marketplace. This offers the promise of rewarding the commitment that stakeholders have shown towards the venture.

- *Intrapreneurism* is a form of management which, potentially, offers the venture a way of combining the flexibility and responsiveness of the entrepreneurial with the market power and reduced risk of the established organisation.

Research themes

Entrepreneurs' anticipation and experience of venture consolidation

Consolidation offers both opportunities and challenges to the entrepreneur. It would be interesting to compare and contrast the anticipation of these prior to consolidation and the remembered experience of them afterwards. Select two samples of entrepreneurs, one group whose venture is in an early growth stage, the other whose ventures have reached maturity and have consolidated. This distinction may be judged by considering the history of the ventures. With the former group, conduct interviews to ascertain their expectations of consolidation, the positive and negative experiences they expect and the managerial issues these will entail. Consider strategic, financial and human issues. Conduct similar interviews with the post-consolidation group, ascertaining the entrepreneurs' experience in terms of its positive and negatives, again in strategic, financial and human terms. What generic issues are identified by each of the two groups? A positive–negative versus type-of-issue grid may aid coding of responses. How do these compare between the two groups? Do entrepreneurs have realistic expectations about the consolidation experience? Do entrepreneurs in the growth phase even think about consolidation? In what respects are they being optimistic or pessimistic? Does any mismatch go on to encourage serial entrepreneurship? Summarise by making recommendations about how entrepreneurs may be supported in managing the consolidation process.

Key readings

An interesting study comparing the role and approach of the chief executive versus that of the entrepreneur is:

Mauruca, R.F. (2000) 'Entrepreneurs versus chief executives at Socaba.com', *Harvard Business Review*, July/Aug., pp. 30–8.

A good review of the reasons why entrepreneurs retire prematurely is:

Ronstadt, R. (1986) 'Exit, stage left: why entrepreneurs end their entrepreneurial careers before retirement', *Journal of Business Venturing*, Vol. 1, No. 3, pp. 323–38.

Suggestions for further reading

Adams, M. (2004) 'Exit pay-offs for the entrepreneur', *Mergers and Acquisitions*, Vol. 39, No. 3, pp. 24–8.

Ahuja, G. and Lampert, C.M. (2001) 'Entrepreneurship in the large corporation: a longitudinal study of how established firms create breakthrough intentions', *Strategic Management Journal*, Vol. 22, pp. 521–43.

Capon, A. (1997) 'Exit strategies for entrepreneurs', *Global Investor*, No. 107, pp. 16–19.

Chiyyipeddi, K., Grasso, E., Kotha, S., Swamidass, P., Lawrence, J.J. and Hottenstein, M.P. (1992) 'Entrepreneur's exit decisions: the role of threshold expectations', *Academy of management Proceedings*, pp. 75–9.

Kanter, R.M. (1985) *The Change Masters*. London: Unwin Hyman.

Osborne, R.L. (1991) 'The dark side of the entrepreneur', *Long Range Planning*, Vol. 24, No. 3, pp. 26–31.

Osborne, R.L. (1992) 'Building an innovative organisation', *Long Range Planning*, Vol. 25, No. 6, pp. 56–62.

Peters, T. (1989) *Thriving on Chaos*. London: Macmillan.

Pinchot, III, G. (1985) *Intrapreneuring*. New York: Harper & Row.

Ross, J. (1987) 'Corporations and entrepreneurs: paradox and opportunity', *Business Horizons*, July/Aug., pp. 76–80.

Vrakking, W.J. (1990) 'The innovative organization', *Long Range Planning*, Vol. 23, No. 2, pp. 94–102.

Selected case material

CASE 27.1

25 January 2006 FT

When Disney wishes upon a Pixar

FRANK PARTNOY

The Disney brand was built on fairy tales: princesses who suffer unimaginable hardships, princes who save them and cartoon characters who inhabit strange, wonderful worlds. When Walt Disney came to Hollywood in 1923, his pilot film was called *Alice's Wonderland*.

The Walt Disney Company's latest fantasy is the plan to reawaken its film business by paying $7bn (£3.9bn) for Pixar, a 775-employee company that has made six computer-animated films since its founding 20 years ago. Robert Iger, Disney's new chief executive, says animation is the key to his company's future, and Pixar is the top digital animation studio: it has 18 Academy Awards and its films have grossed more than $3bn.

Most reports have portrayed the Disney–Pixar negotiations as a personality play, between Mr Iger and Steven Jobs, Pixar's head. Both have much to gain from a deal. Mr Iger could secure top animation talent, something his predecessor, Michael Eisner, could not do; and Mr Jobs would be Disney's largest shareholder, at 7 per cent, with a platform for cross-selling products from Apple, the other company he leads.

But like a classic Disney feature, this deal, if it comes off, would be about much more than the main characters. It is an allegory of what is right and wrong with large companies, particularly in media and technology.

Disney has become a pathologically dysfunctional organisation. Like IBM of the 1970s or AT&T in the 1980s, Disney grew fat and bureaucratic in the 1990s, long after cementing its lucrative entertainment franchise.

Some of Disney's problems are endemic to large corporations. When a company has 133,000 employees, it cannot be governed by human beings. Instead, it must rely on a culture to preserve its earlier entrepreneurialism, while focusing workers on the continuing mission.

Unfortunately, Disney's culture, like that of IBM and AT&T, encouraged inefficiency and stifled creativity. Over the past five years, Disney's shares have lost a third of their value and the company has became a corporate governance pariah. Many thought the low point was the fiasco surrounding Michael Ovitz, who left Disney with $140m after just 14 months. But more troubling was the release of the abysmal *Treasure Planet*, a film that cost about as much as Mr Ovitz and avoided universal ignominy only because so few people saw it.

To survive and prosper, large organisations must be divided into manageable pods, whose workers have independence and incentive. In contrast to Disney, Pixar was just such a free-standing, free-spirited group with a relaxed, open-plan office and no signs of managerial hierarchy. John Lasseter, Pixar's creative leader, wore Hawaiian shirts and rode a scooter inside. When Pixar won Oscars, employees displayed the statues proudly but dressed them in Barbie doll clothing. Whereas Disney executives micromanaged films, including those with Pixar, Mr Lasseter let his crew run free and encouraged ideas.

In many ways, Pixar was an old-fashioned, entrepreneurial company, built on the foundational incentives that Frank Knight, the early 20th century economist, had described as the linchpin of successful corporate activity. Mr Knight argued that companies would be best managed when a single human being held a large stake. This view makes especially good sense for today's technology companies, where production is driven by small groups of entrepreneurs with the incentives and skills to innovate. Mr Jobs owns more than half of Pixar's shares and has been the driving force to maximise share value. He is a proven risk-taker, a quintessential Knightian entrepreneur. Unlike Disney's top executives, who were handsomely rewarded with salary, bonus and stock options, Mr Jobs has earned a total salary at Pixar over three years of just $157, not even enough to buy a new iPod, and he did not receive stock options.

Even if the deal is concluded, no one, including Mr Jobs, will have a large enough stake in the game at Disney to play entrepreneur. Besides, Mr Jobs is more likely to focus on running Apple. In general, companies without an entrepreneur suffer when they grow. Examples abound today. Large techno-logy groups do defensive patenting, building thickets of intellectual property, not because they have good ideas but because they want protection from smaller rivals who might. Big drug companies do not invent new drugs; they buy companies that do. And so on.

The key question for a possible Disney–Pixar deal is, which company's culture would survive: large or small? Would Pixar become 'Disneyfied'? Or would Disney apply Pixar's model and unshackle its other business units? In its formative years, Disney was a creative hotbed, led by a handful of brilliant minds. Over time, the leaders lost sight of their mission and product. Mr Iger's challenge is to remake Disney with a small-company culture that rewards experimentation and encourages innovation. As a Pixar employee noted: 'What you need to create is the most trusting environment possible where people can screw up.' And, one might add, live happily ever after.

Source: Frank Partnoy, 'When Disney wishes upon a Pixar', *Financial Times*, 25 January 2006, p. 21. Copyright © 2006 Frank Partnoy.

> ## CASE 27.2

29 January 2005 **FT**

The calm reinventor: man in the news A.G. Lafley

NEIL BUCKLEY

Two days after taking over as Procter & Gamble's (P&G) chief executive in 2000, A.G. Lafley walked unannounced into a Chicago dinner party of P&G's 'alumni' – former executives of the consumer goods giant. With his spiky, silver-grey hair and quiet charisma, Mr Lafley's arrival caused quite a stir.

There was good reason for those present to be surprised. P&G was famous for recruiting high-flyers from the top universities and promoting only from within. But it was equally well known for treating as outcasts any who chose to leave the Cincinnati-based company, despite a roll-call of alumni that included many stars of US business, including Jeffrey Immelt of General Electric, Jim McNerney of 3M, Meg Whitman of eBay and Steve Ballmer of Microsoft. Mr Lafley was the first P&G chief executive ever to embrace the alumni organisation and attend one of its meetings.

The gesture was symbolic of the changes he would bring to the company that this week's planned $57bn (£30bn) purchase of Gillette will transform into the world's biggest household goods and personal care business by far.

Mr Lafley has not only pruned costs, rebuilt the corporate structure in a way that has become a model for many other consumer goods groups, and rekindled P&G's spirit of innovation. He has also reinvented the culture, turning a hidebound, introspective company, whose besuited executives were nicknamed 'Proctoids', into one that is open and outward-looking.

Yet Alan George Lafley, known universally as AG, took P&G's top job almost by accident – and found a company in crisis. Durk Jager,

his predecessor, had been ousted after barely 18 months in the job, having attempted to drive through a restructuring plan that had brought chaos to the company and resulted in three profit warnings in three months.

Mr Lafley, then a 23-year veteran of P&G who had headed both its Asian and North American operations, represented, above all, a change of style.

The aggressive Mr Jager tended to intimidate employees. His style was similar to that of Ed Artzt, his predecessor-but-one, nicknamed the 'Prince of Darkness' within P&G. Mr Lafley is, by contrast, affable and consensual in his approach. He speaks quietly, with a slightly nasal New England twang, and with a calm self-assurance.

The shake-up of P&G launched by Mr Jager in 1999 was the product of a 1997 'think-in' involving half a dozen senior executives, including Mr Lafley and John Pepper, the previous chief executive. It aimed to jolt P&G out of its torpor of the 1990s, when innovative products were thin on the ground and the company looked in danger of running out of steam.

National P&G fiefdoms were to be swept away by a 'matrix' of global business units managing product areas such as health and beauty, and fabric and homecare. These would work with a network of regional market development organisations charged with marketing and distribution at local level.

The structure would ultimately prove to be the right one, but Mr Jager attempted to introduce it too fast and set goals that were too demanding, causing dislocation and a loss of focus on its key products. Mr Lafley reduced

Mr Jager's over-ambitious targets of 7 to 9 per cent growth in annual sales to a more realistic 4 to 6 per cent, and its 13 to 15 per cent earnings per share growth target to 10 per cent.

Within two years, P&G was outperforming both its new targets and many of its competitors.

Yet perhaps more important than the structural revamp were the cultural changes Mr Lafley brought in. Out went suits in favour of the open-necked shirts that Mr Lafley usually sports. Out, too, went the 11th-floor, wood-panelled executive offices in the Cincinnati headquarters, replaced by open-plan meeting and training areas.

He restored the company's focus on responding to consumers' needs, rather than just coming up with ideas and trying to find ways to market them. 'The consumer is boss' is the mantra he repeats endlessly.

Most important, Mr Lafley insisted P&G should no longer refuse to look at ideas from outside but be prepared to buy in ideas and technology – as well as sell or license out technology it developed but could not use itself. It now has a unit devoted to doing those things and a team of scientists whose job is to scour the internet and scientific publications for breakthroughs P&G may be able to use. Nabil Sakkab, head of research and development at P&G's fabric and homecare division, says the company's attitude towards its intellectual property has changed from 'the Kremlin to the Acropolis'.

The result has been a string of successful product introductions, such as the Crest Spinbrush, a battery-powered toothbrush brought to P&G by an entrepreneur, Whitestrips tooth-whitening strips, Swiffer electrostatic cleaning products and an extension of the Mr Clean household cleaning brand into a car-washing system, Mr Clean Autodry.

But Mr Lafley's understated style masks a keen strategic mind and ambition. He led P&G through what were, until this week, its two biggest acquisitions – of the Clairol and Wella hair care businesses. Those deals shifted the company's focus decisively towards higher-margin health and beauty businesses.

But the Gillette purchase dwarfs them, and will represent a far bigger integration challenge. Mr Lafley's quietly authoritative approach will be one key to making the takeover work. Another will be the successful application to the enlarged group of the consumer focus that he has restored to P&G. 'We want to be consumer-driven,' he says. 'We want to be market-driven. We don't want to be pushing something out of an ivory tower somewhere.'

Source: Neil Buckley, 'The calm reinventor: man in the news A.G. Lafley', *Financial Times*, 29 January 2005, p. 11. Copyright © 2005 The Financial Times Limited.

Discussion point

1. Discuss the challenges that arise in instilling an entrepreneurial culture and ethos in (a) Pixar and (b) Gillette.

(CHAPTER 28)

Making your contribution: researching entrepreneurship

Chapter overview

Entrepreneurship is an active field of research. Like all other disciplines, entrepreneurship has six aspects: phenomena of concern, knowledge, theory, methodology, philosophical concerns and an institutional system. The study of entrepreneurship is a new field and it is very much an 'adolescent' discipline. This chapter considers the field in terms of its core scope, concerns and approach. It concludes with an overview of research paradigms and methodology in entrepreneurship.

28.1 Entrepreneurship: an adolescent discipline

Key learning outcome

An understanding of what constitutes an academic discipline, a recognition of the study of entrepreneurship as a distinct discipline and an appreciation of its connections to other disciplines in the social sciences.

Entrepreneurship is now widely regarded as an independent subject within the social sciences. It is a relatively new subject. It fully blossomed within the field of management about 25 years ago (albeit with important antecedents before that) and has only started to become truly distinct from other management studies in the past 15 years or so. As an independent field of study it is much younger than subjects sociology and anthropology and very much younger than 'traditional' subjects in the natural sciences or the humanities. Low (2001) has called entrepreneurship 'an adolescent discipline'. What do we mean when we talk about a discipline (subject, or field of inquiry)? Essentially, six interconnected, but distinct, things are implied.

First of all, a subject has a particular *range of phenomena* that are its concern. This range of phenomena is the list of objects, causes and effects in the world that the subject sets out to investigate. Biology is concerned with living organisms, history with man's past, mathematics with the patterns in nature, and so on. Clearly, entrepreneurship is concerned with the economic effects of, and the management practice of, *entrepreneurs*. However, not all subjects have clear boundaries defining where their phenomena of interest

566

begin and end. For example, there is debate as to how distinct the areas of concern of sociology and social anthropology are. The list of things that entrepreneurship is concerned with will depend on the way in which entrepreneurs and entrepreneurship is defined. There is no neat 'bag' that contains what entrepreneurship, and only entrepreneurship, should be concerned with. There is considerable latitude as to where entrepreneurship ends and other management disciplines, economics and the broader social sciences begin.

The second aspect of a subject is a collection of statements or propositions about the world. This collection of propositions is what constitutes the *knowledge* that the discipline has accumulated about the range of phenomena it sets out to explore, such as might be found in a textbook. Most philosophers of science doubt that such propositions are straightforward, neutral, statements about the world. How do we know that the knowledge is true knowledge? Philosophers disagree about what the notion of truth actually means. A major issue for some philosophers of science is that discoveries are *theory laden*. This view, known as *constructivism*, implies that the propositions only make sense in light of some theory, or set of theories, about the world and so their truth depends on the assumption that the theory is true in the first place.

The set of *theories* used to account for the phenomena constitutes the third aspect of a subject. A theory is a framework that both accounts for and predicts how causes are linked to effects. Not all social scientists would agree that physical scientists' concern with causes and effect is appropriate to the study of human behaviour. While what happens in the outside world are cause–effect *events*, humans engage in premeditated *actions*. An effect has no choice over whether it will occur or not given a particular cause, but a human being can (apparently) choose whether to act. So a deterministic causality is replaced with a motivation–action concern: what 'leads' people to do what they do, rather than the causes that 'determine' their actions.

In some disciplines a set of incompatible and perhaps competing theories are present. Following the work of the philosopher Thomas Kuhn, such theories are referred to as *paradigms*. These paradigms not only guide the making of particular propositions (and the rejection of others), but also the way in which different propositions are related to each other. Some subjects, the natural sciences come to mind, are dominated by a single, widely accepted paradigm. There is general acceptance as to the theoretical frame within which inquiry should be made. Other subjects, though, are multi-paradigm. There is no dominant theoretical frame. Many social sciences are like this. Psychology is an example (as was seen in section 3.1 where the entrepreneurial personality was discussed). There is a tendency for younger subjects in general, and the social sciences in particular, to be richer in paradigms. There has been less time for the subject to 'settle down' to a single accepted paradigm. Some thinkers may appreciate paradigm diversity for its own sake and so seek to retain it; others may regard it as a failure of the subject to develop proper understanding of the world and as a distraction. As an adolescent discipline, entrepreneurship is paradigm rich.

Theories are constructed on the back of some sort of inquiry into the world. But inquiry must follow certain rules if it is to be accepted as a legitimate form of truth-generating inquiry. This fourth aspect of a subject is called its *methodology*. A methodology is a set of rules about how investigations are to take place. Within a subject, claims to new knowledge discoveries will be accepted only if that knowledge has been obtained through the application of a proper methodology. Different paradigms often have their own methodology. So within multi-paradigm disciplines there will often be debate about methodology as well as about theory. In the following sections, the concerns of entrepreneurship (its domain), research paradigms, methodologies and a selection of specific research themes will be considered.

In addition, a subject may be associated with some *philosophical perspective* and even a *social agenda*. Knowledge, and the theories it is embedded in, suggests (to the human imagination at least) that the world is a certain way. The physical and biological sciences, for example, suggest that the world is in essence *material* (made up of physical substances and physical substances only) and that all effects have a specific cause, that is, it is *deterministic*. History, on the other hand, traces historical situations to actions that individuals might or might not have taken. History suggests that the world is quite *contingent*. Entrepreneurship bridges these concerns. In seeking the general causes that lead to business success (an effect), it is, on the one hand, presuming determinism. On the other hand, each entrepreneurial venture has its own, unique characteristics and history and so is contingent.

The discipline of entrepreneurship, then, deals with a complex phenomenon. The two perspectives – determinism and contingency – might not conflict if we were to confine deterministic and contingent propositions about entrepreneurship to particular aspects of the phenomena: to recognise contingency in individual ventures, but to seek generalisations by comparing many ventures.

The pictures of the world (philosophical perspectives) that a subject engenders can also have moral and political implications. Classical economics, in attempting to be a dispassionate and scientifically neutral account of the way in which humans interact, suggests that unconstrained markets in which individuals make free and personal-wealth-maximising decisions is optimal, or Pareto efficient. As noted in section 6.2, while this may strictly be *only* a formal statement about the mathematical properties of such a system, it is very easy to make the move to suggesting that such a system is *morally* or *politically* optimal as well. Many social scientists are concerned that a reductive account of human behaviour in terms of our genetic complement suggests that actively manipulating the genetic character of future generations (eugenics) is morally acceptable and that this alone is sufficient reason for resisting such reductionist accounts.

While entrepreneurship borrows heavily (and quite properly) from economic thinking, economics is not the only disciple that informs debate within the subject. Many (I think most) researchers in entrepreneurship study it in a belief that entrepreneurship is not only morally acceptable, but also morally *desirable*. They study the subject not only with the intent of discovering things about the world that entrepreneurs have created (important enough), but also with an intent to contribute to the future development of it. Entrepreneurship is an applied as well as an academic discipline. However, there are a number of researchers who have made important contributions who are critical (sometimes radically) of entrepreneurship and its effects.

The final aspect of a subject is its *institutional system*. The discovery of new knowledge is a human activity. It is structured. One of the distinctive features about our current age is the way in which research activity is organised. Not that long ago, only a few hundred years or so, it was possible for one person to know pretty much all of what the sciences, history and the humanities had to say. The encyclopaedists were scholars who attempted to summarise all of what was known into a single or few volumes. Inquiry into the world was undertaken pretty much as a hobby. Things changed with the Enlightenment in the eighteenth century. Rapid discoveries based on new and rational modes of inquiry led to an exponential growth in human understanding – far more than any one person could hope to master. This led directly to the fragmentation of inquiry into different disciplines. Inquiry became professionalised. In the modern age, scholars not only restrict themselves to a single discipline but increasingly a sub-discipline or even a sub-sub-discipline. Along with this fragmentation, new disciplines arose to study newly discovered phenomena in new ways. As well as fragmentation, there was integration. Some new disciplines studied specific phenomena using ideas from a range of other, more established disciplines. The social sciences are notable here. And within the social sciences, entrepreneurship is a case in point. The study of entrepreneurship calls upon economics, psychology, management science, sociology, anthropology, technology studies, systems theory and political science, among others, to provide both theoretical insights and methodological guidance. Individuals will often take up the study of entrepreneurship from a base in one of these subject areas.

The institutional aspect of a subject includes the set of individual teachers and researchers who contribute to the subject, their organisational context such as university departments or consulting firms, and their communication system, including dedicated journals and 'the conference circuit'. These institutions are now global. Applied subjects (and this is particularly the case with entrepreneurship) also have institutional links outside the university system to government and commerce. A (loosely knit) group of philosophers, sometimes known as the new sociologists of knowledge, place emphasis on this institutional aspect of a subject and (in their most radical manifestation) claim that knowledge within the discipline is entirely the result of the institutional system and that there is no such thing as truth independent of socially mediated agreements. As might be imagined, such views are highly controversial and are not widely accepted, but they have been influential. By way of a summary, these six aspects of entrepreneurship as a discipline are detailed in Table 28.1.

Adolescence is at once the most wonderful and most troubling time of our lives. Every new discovery is fresh and exciting. The future is full of potential. We are confident in ourselves and in our ability to make a real difference. No challenge seems too great. But we may be inexperienced, naive even. We make mistakes. We may be awkward and lack confidence compared with our elders. All of these things apply to entrepreneurship as an adolescent discipline. And they all, both positive and negative, add to its excitement.

28.2 Entrepreneurship: the research field

> ### Key learning outcome
>
> Recognition of the main themes in entrepreneurship research and how they are categorised.

What is the range of phenomena with which entrepreneurship should concern itself? There is no hard and fast answer to this question. If we look at the entrepreneurship literature, however, we do see a central 'core' of concerns with a number of other, more peripheral, issues occurring with varying degrees of frequency. This central core has been defined (Bygrave and Hofer, 1991) as 'all functions, activities and actions associated with the perception of opportunities and creation of organisations to pursue them'. As will be evident from this definition, even this central core is very large. Although it suggests a broad range of research agendas, it does not commend any specifically. Within this core there are a number of distinct sub-fields that are more focused on specific research programmes.

Table 28.1 The six aspects of entrepreneurship as an academic discipline

Aspect of the discipline	Generally concerned with	Specifics of entrepreneurship research
Range of phenomena	Objects, causes and events (or motivations and actions) the discipline attempts to explain	Creation of new wealth and new organisations by entrepreneurs
Knowledge	The corpus of propositions about the world the discipline (or at least general agreement within it) regards as true (or otherwise)	Propositions ('truths' and 'falsehoods') about entrepreneurship in academic textbooks, journal articles, etc. held by entrepreneurs and those who interact with them
Theoretical systems	Frameworks of explanation that connect causes to events (or motivations to actions)	Drawn from economic, strategic, psychological, sociological and anthropological theory
Methodology	The (generally accepted) 'rules' that govern proper (truth guaranteeing) investigations leading to new knowledge within the discipline	Positivistic versus Anti-positivistic
Philosophical perspective	The general 'world view' that underpins the discipline and governs any ethical and moral assertions it makes	Entrepreneurship brings benefits and should be encouraged versus Entrepreneurship reduces human (overall) welfare and should be controlled, discouraged or inhibited
Institutional system	The human organisation within a social and economic system that co-ordinates the discovery of new knowledge within the discipline	Knowledge creation, co-ordination and transfer through teaching and research in universities and consulting firms and through network links to practising entrepreneurs and their supporters

The Low and MacMillan classification scheme

In 1988, Low and MacMillan suggested in an influential paper that there are three essential sub-fields within entrepreneurship. These are as follows.

Process

Process refers to the series of actions taken by, and elicited by, the entrepreneur in the identification and pursuit of new opportunities. Process includes both the explicit and public aspects of opportunity identification by entrepreneurs and, at a cognitive level, the innate psychological and decision-making facets of the entrepreneur.

Context

Context refers to the situation within which entrepreneurs work. Context includes the organisational, regional, national and international setting for the entrepreneur's activities with reference to the economic, social and cultural conditions, the availability of resources, the competitive environment and the opportunities and challenges they present.

Outcomes

Outcomes refer to the performance of the entrepreneur in financial, organisational and human terms. A single point-in-time 'snapshot' of outcomes may be significant, but outcomes have real meaning only in a comparative sense. Two sorts of study compare outcomes. *Longitudinal studies* follow a single or small group of businesses over time to observe how their performance develops. Being a defining characteristic of the entrepreneurial firm, growth of the business is a significant variable here. *Cross-sectional studies*, on the other hand, compare a large group of businesses in a single or small group of sectors over a relatively short period. The competitiveness of entrepreneurial businesses relative to their established counterparts is important here. Performance may mean more than just financial performance. 'Softer' organisational benefits such as employee satisfaction and wider ethical or social performance may also be of interest.

The Ucbasaran *et al.* classification scheme

Ucbasaran *et al.* (2001) have suggested that the core of entrepreneurship research might be better described as having five sub-fields. These they describe as follows.

Theoretical antecedents

Theoretical antecedents are those aspects of entrepreneurship research that concentrate on important theoretical departures. As entrepreneurship is influenced by a number of social sciences, these theoretical insights are usually developed from a base in one of the social sciences. Economics, finance and psychology are important. Sociology and anthropology are also influential. Theoretical studies may be quite conceptual in nature. They may be concerned with proposing new theoretical perspectives or gathering empirical evidence to support or disprove existing theoretical ideas.

Types of entrepreneur

A number of studies are concerned with defining and classifying different types of entrepreneur (see Chapter 2). This is important because different types of entrepreneur may need different theoretical antecedents. For example, are all entrepreneurs motivated in the same way? How do the entrepreneurial processes they initiate and are guided by, differ? Do they create similar or dissimilar organisations? Do they produce the same type of outcomes? In a more practical sense, do they all respond to the same type of support and encouragement from, say, government? Do they need different systems to provide financial support? Again, insights can be developed from economic, finance, psychological and sociological perspectives. An important level of distinction is among nascent (prospective entrepreneurs, not yet having started a business), novice (entrepreneurs who have started a business recently), serial (entrepreneurs who have created a series of businesses, one after the other), and portfolio (entrepreneurs who are managing a collection of businesses) entrepreneurs.

The entrepreneurial process

This is parallel to Low and MacMillan's process sub-field. Process studies are usually centred on the process of opportunity recognition, evaluation and exploitation both from an external to the entrepreneur (social, economic, cultural) and internal to the entrepreneur (cognitive, psychological) perspective.

Types of entrepreneurial organisation

What makes an organisation entrepreneurial? What differences do individual entrepreneurs make to the organisations they manage and come into contact with? Organisations can be defined and categorised in a number of ways. Of particular interest in entrepreneurship studies is categorisation by type of innovation (e.g. high-tech, low-tech), rate of organisational growth (e.g. fast growing, slow growing), stage in life cycle (e.g. start-up, early growth, maturity, exit) and origins of the business (e.g. new start-up, franchising, management buyout, inheritance).

Entrepreneurial outcomes

This is in a similar vein to Low and MacMillan's outcomes. Studies are concerned with growth and performance trends over time and in comparison to competitors.

Ucbasaran *et al.* (2001) suggest a complementary approach. They go on to categorise entrepreneurial research in a hierarchical manner: research dealing with the *individual entrepreneur*, the *entrepreneur's firm*, the *sector* and *industry* the firm is in. Paralleling this is the geographical regional, national and international context of the firm. A development of this scheme is illustrated in Figure 28.1.

The Meyer *et al.* classification scheme

In 1999, Meyer and colleagues worked as part of a taskforce entitled Doctoral Level Education in Entrepreneurship. This taskforce concluded that entrepreneurship is essentially about *creation*. As such, they recommended that the domain of entrepreneurial research should be centred on four issues:

- the creation of new ventures and organisations;
- the creation of new combinations of goods and services, methods of production, markets and supply chains;

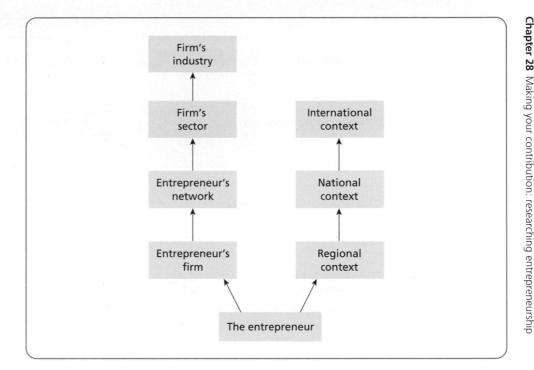

Figure 28.1 The Ucbasaran *et al.* (2001) model of entrepreneurial research

- creative recognition of new and existing opportunities; and
- cognitive processes, behaviours and modes of action (especially those that might be regarded as creative) to exploit new and existing opportunities.

As a development of this, Meyer *et al.* (2002) suggested that it was fruitful to consider the intersection of entrepreneurship studies with strategic management. Entrepreneurship is about *creation*, whereas strategic management is about *performance*. Entrepreneurship relates to how opportunities to create new goods and services come into being and are exploited. Strategic management relates to how decisions and actions bring about competitiveness and above-average returns. These issues crossed with the concern for new, smaller businesses and large corporations give a fourfold classification. With some modifications, this scheme is presented in Figure 28.2.

Entrepreneurial creation

Entrepreneurial creation is concerned with all aspects of the entrepreneur and entrepreneurship that address the issue of how entrepreneurs devise and implement innovative products, ideas and ways of doing things. It includes studies into the cognitive make-up of individual entrepreneurs, the discovery and exploitation of new opportunities, and the creation of new organisational forms.

	Small and medium firms	Large corporations
Entrepreneurship	Entrepreneurial creation	Intrapreneurial creation
Strategic management	SME performance	Corporate performance

Figure 28.2 Meyer *et al.*'s (2002) classification of the domain of entrepreneurship

SME performance

SME performance is that aspect that examines how small and medium-sized businesses (especially those that have the potential to be entrepreneurial ventures) perform in both financial and wider terms over time and in comparison with other business organisations. In this respect it has parallels to entrepreneurial outcomes of Low and MacMillan's (1988) and Ucbasaran *et al.*'s (2001) classification schemes.

Intrapreneurial creation

Intrapreneurs are managers who work in an entrepreneurial way as employed managers within larger, established organisations. For obvious reasons, the combination of the entrepreneur's creativity and drive with the financial and market power of the large organisation is something of a holy grail in management. This aspect of the discipline looks at the possibility of such a combination, the opportunities it presents and the impediments to achieving it.

Corporate performance

This aspect is concerned with examining the performance of large, established organisations that are not normally regarded as entrepreneurial (in the conventional sense of the word). Again, such studies might be purely financial, or take on wider concerns and be cross-sectional or longitudinal in nature. For those with a more exclusive interest in entrepreneurship such studies provide important reference points and comparisons for evaluation of, and explanation of, entrepreneurial performance.

Combining these four primary categories suggests particular research programmes. Entrepreneurial creation–SME performance suggests studies into how SMEs compete against, and win against, larger competitors through first-mover advantages. The entrepreneurial creation–intrapreneurial creation intersection suggests studies looking at how the decision making and practice of entrepreneurs can be imitated to advantage by large corporations trying to overcome the obstacles of bureaucracy, and, through the intrapreneurial creation–corporate performance intersection, looks at the impact this has. Is, for example, entrepreneurial management always better than conventional management, even for the large firm? Finally, the SME performance–corporate performance intersection suggests studies into how business performance is, in general, measured – whether purely financial measures suffice, or whether a broader balance card taking account of other stakeholder issues may also be needed (a point discussed further in section 9.5). Also suggested is the specific issue of whether performance measures designed for large corporations are appropriate for SMEs (where the entrepreneur's personal goals are significant), and vice versa.

It should be recognised that all these categorisations represent *elements* of individual studies, not their entirety. Many studies adopt two or more categories. For example, a study might look at how different types of entrepreneur manage the entrepreneurial process, or at how context influences outcomes. Theoretical antecedents might be developed to explain outcomes, and so on. When designing a new research programme, it is fruitful to consider the questions that are raised by the intersection between different categorisations of the sub-domains of the discipline, as well as the interrelationship of the discipline with other areas of the social sciences. In an immediate sense, entrepreneurship draws from other areas of management studies. For example, Brophy and Shulman (1992) and Hills and LaForge (1992) reflect on what finance and marketing, respectively, have to offer the field.

28.3 Research paradigms in entrepreneurship

Key learning outcome

An understanding of the notion of a research paradigm, the different paradigms adopted in entrepreneurship research and the issue of their commensurability.

The concept of a *paradigm* – a collection of theories with a dominant meta-theory connecting them that guides inquiry within a discipline – introduced above – was proposed by Thomas Kuhn as a way of explaining the way in which physics had developed. While the concept of a paradigm had little impact in the natural sciences, social scientists took to it with enthusiasm. Kuhn originally intended the concept to explain how one theory gave way to another over time, but social scientists saw it as a way of accounting for the wide variety of approaches within the social sciences at any one time.

A seminal study of paradigm variety in organisational science was undertaken by Burrell and Morgan (1979). They suggested that the different paradigms could be related in terms of two dimensions. The first is the *objective–subjective* dimension. *Objective* inquiry was concerned with external, verifiable facts about the world that are assumed to be independent of human experience, whereas *subjective* inquiry was concerned with the interpretation of individual human experience. These may be 'verifiable' only in terms of internalised experience and not be repeatable in a traditional scientific way.

Burrell and Morgan suggest that there are four aspects to this objective–subjective distinction:

- *Ontology* refers to the nature of the phenomena under inquiry. Are they *realist* – external to the individual that impinge on experience from outside – or *nominalist* – an internal, personal reality constructed by individual consciousness?
- *Epistemology* refers to the nature of knowledge about those phenomena. Positivism regards proper knowledge as being true timelessly and independently of any one individual

and verifiable by independent observation. Anti-positivism is a collection of beliefs that knowledge is, fundamentally, true only in a personal sense, to one individual at one time and that such truth cannot (always, ever?) be established through traditional 'scientific' methods. Rather it is revealed by introspection and interaction with experiencing subjects.

- *Belief about human nature* concerns whether human beings are seen as 'just' another object in the universe with behaviour that is causally determined in the same way as all other events in the universe are, or, alternatively, if humans are to be regarded as a special phenomenon in which free will negates deterministic causality: humans *choose* to act, they are not *made* to act by external natural forces (although their actions may be guided by social forces). This distinction is often brought into debates about the relationship between man and society.

- *Methodology* is the means of inquiring into the world: whether it is believed that the social world can be inquired into in the same way the physical world is, through repeated experiments in which causal variables are manipulated to test hypotheses – a *nomothetic* methodology – or if it requires a distinct – *ideographic* – methodology in which individual human experience is placed centre stage and the issue is one of revealing that experience rather than testing pre-claimed hypotheses.

The second dimension distinguishes among the different philosophical concerns or social agendas for the paradigms. Some – referred to as *sociologies of regulation* – are largely uncritical of existing society or claim only a need for marginal changes. Their application is in explaining society as it is and how it can be managed better. Other paradigms – referred to as *sociologies of radical change* – are critical of existing society and see the need for it to be modified or reconstructed in a dramatic way if human life is to be improved.

These two dimensions are independent and can be combined into four basic types of paradigm:

- *Functionalism* – the objective-regulation paradigm. This is perhaps the dominating paradigm in entrepreneurship studies and certainly accounts for the majority of studies. It regards entrepreneurship as something that is amenable to scientific (positivistic) investigation and believes that the findings may be used to improve entrepreneurial management. It is represented by all studies that use mainstream economic thinking, cognitive psychology and the more scientific aspects of the other social sciences.

- *Radical structuralism* – the objective-radical paradigm. This paradigm is motivated by a belief in the necessity of radical change in society but believes that the best way to achieve this is through a better scientific understanding of society. The works of Karl Marx (who was critical of the effects of entrepreneurship, but not actually of entrepreneurs themselves) and other socialist economists are influential in this paradigm. At the other end of the political spectrum, it is reflected in the views of some libertarians influenced by the Austrian School view of entrepreneurs who argue that all economic knowledge is fundamentally held by individuals at a local level and that a 'higher-level' knowledge of economic systems does not have substantive meaning.

- *Interpretism* – the subjective-regulation paradigm. This paradigm does not demand a radical change in how society works, but does suggest that there are other (perhaps better) ways to understand society in general, including entrepreneurship, than through adherence to scientific method. Concern is often expressed with 'science's' inability to get to grips with personal human experience. Studies within this paradigm often resort to *ethnomethodological*, *phenomenological* and *symbolic interactionist* methodologies.

- *Radical humanism* – the subjective-radical paradigm. A rejection of scientific method also characterises this paradigm. Given the radical dimension, though, often associated with this paradigm is a rejection of 'science' not just because of its methodological limitations but also because it is a 'power structure' used to 'create knowledge' that can be used for purposes of 'domination and exploitation'. Some approaches within radical feminist and anti-capitalist criticism of business practice are located within this paradigm.

The existence of, and value of, these alternative paradigms is an issue of extensive (and often ill-tempered) debate within the organisational sciences. This debate centres on whether the paradigms are all necessary and whether they may, or may not, be integrated into broader paradigms that can share their methodology, differing concerns and insights. This is an issue referred to as *paradigm commensurability*. Three positions have emerged. The first is that only one paradigm constitutes a proper form of inquiry and that the others are a distraction, leading at best to irrelevant and meaningless findings. This position is often taken by the objective-regulation school, who insist that normal levels of scientific rigour should be applied to the study of entrepreneurship (a position clearly exemplified by Donaldson (1985) and Pfeffer (1993), who both regard paradigm proliferation as something that hinders the development or organisational science), and at times by proponents of both the subjective paradigms, who believe that scientific method is inappropriate to discovery in the *human* sciences. The radicals might add that conventional science is a power structure used to maintain (inequitable and exploitative) social relationships.

The second position proposes that the claim of incommensurability implies that, while all paradigms may be of value, they are so fundamentally different that they cannot be integrated into a single, overarching paradigm. Some of this position (notably Jackson and Carter (1991) and Cannella and Paetzold (1994)) argue that paradigm incommensurability is an insurance against the domination of a positivist 'elite' in organisational science intending to gain an 'imperialistic' hold over all forms of inquiry into it.

The final position takes the view that the paradigms are commensurable and that integrating them can lead to new knowledge. Examples here are Hassard (1988, 1991), Willmott (1993), Weaver and Giola (1994), and Mir and Watson (2000, 2001); see also Kwan and Tsang (2001). A good flavour of the overall debate is provided by Hickson (1988). Gorton (2000) argues that the structure–agency divide between functional and behavioural factors in entrepreneurship research is unhelpful and should be overcome in future projects.

Research methodology is a broad and often technical subject. Given that it is usually dealt with in specialist courses within business education programmes and is the subject of a number of excellent texts in its own right, I shall confine the discussion here to generalities. The Burrell–Morgan distinction between objective and subjective paradigms is partly based on researchers' confidence in different methodological approaches. Objective inquiry is *nomothetic* and is based on prior and external theoretical frames. It can be both qualitative and quantitative (often in combination). Qualitative studies are usually based on categorical descriptions whereas quantitative studies are based on numerical data. The data may be derived from case studies of the development of a single or small group of ventures, longitudinal studies of the development of a single venture over time, or cross-sectional studies of a large number of businesses at any one time. Subjective studies use different – *ideographic* –

methodologies. *Ethnomethodological* approaches prioritise the 'methodology' that individual subjects adopt to make sense of, and make their way in, the world. Inquiry should be focused on revealing these personal methods, not on substantiating preconceived and externally imposed theories. *Phenomenological* approaches share this emphasis, but add that the way in which individuals negotiate their realities through social interaction and within broader social systems is more important than isolated individual experience.

28.4 Research methodology in entrepreneurship

Key learning outcome

An appreciation of the range of research methodologies – strategies of inquiry – that are adopted to create understanding about the entrepreneur and the entrepreneurial process.

A research methodology might be described as a strategy of inquiry. It is an approach that has been demonstrated to be, or can otherwise be justified (perhaps on philosophical grounds) as a way of obtaining reliable knowledge. Broadly speaking there are two classes of methodology: quantitative and qualitative, although there are some overlaps. These terms should not be confused with the same terms used in market research, although there are tenuous links.

Quantitative methods, often favoured within the positivistic perspective, rely on representative sampling of subjects, often with statistical support. The aim is that results may be generalised. Qualitative methods, on the other hand, rarely rely on statistical sampling. Generalisation of findings is of less importance. The claim may be only to 'local' knowledge upon which no demand for generalisation is made, or a claim is made for 'natural' generalisation that does not look towards positivism for justification. There is a vigorous, and at times ill-tempered, debate about the relative merits of these two classes of methodology and how they might be related. There is no need to engage in that debate here: both play an important part in the study of entrepreneurship. Because most the methods discussed below might be used in either a positivistic or non-positivistic way (although experimentation is entirely – canonically – positivistic, and hermeneutics entirely non-positivistic; (ethnomethodology is largely non-positivistic, but its techniques are often borrowed by sociolinguists who are usually positivists), I have avoided unnecessary controversy by not categorising them as either quantitative or qualitative.

Deductive–inductive theorising

Theorising is the oldest way of creating knowledge known to man. It pre-dates all other methods by at least 2,000 years. All research involves a reflective theorising stage, at least to develop hypotheses that will be tested by other methods. It can, however, feature on its own as a way of consolidating existing knowledge or developing insights into relationships.

Survey methods

A survey is a methodology that seeks answers (either open, or selected from a restricted menu) to a specific series of questions. The survey may be distributed in written form, by telephone or by interview (which does allow some latitude for free exploration of answers) or, increasingly, by e-mail to a selected (perhaps statistically representative) sample of respondents. The methodology is quantitative and can be statistically robust for generalisation. The depth of inquiry is, however, limited and results may be distorted by the fact that not all targeted respond.

Delphi analysis

Delphi analysis is a specialist form of survey in which expert opinion is elicited. It is particularly useful for developing a picture of opinions on controversial or ill-defined issues. A pool of experts is selected. An initial survey is sent out, with perhaps quite open questions to garner initial opinions on the issue. On return, this is analysed and a summary produced. This summary is then re-sent to the expert pool with a series of questions (perhaps more specific this time) that have been generated by the analysis. This process may be repeated several times until no further information appears to be forthcoming (or the respondents get bored). A final summary is produced which identifies consensus (and dissention) on the question in hand.

Econometrics

Econometrics is a highly formal technique that takes secondary quantitative data and then uses mathematical analysis to develop an insight into correlations (and perhaps causal directions) between variables. It might be used, for example, to study the relationship between the number of self-employed in an economy and economic growth, or the effect of interest rates on small business failure. Quite technical, it is not for the mathematically uninitiated.

Experimentation

Experimentation is a methodology in which the causal relationship between variables is identified by fixing one set of variables, controlling others and observing the effects. Commonplace in the natural sciences, it has not, until recently, had any real place in the social sciences (except for psychology). Its use in entrepreneurship studies is growing, not least because of the use of the experimental method in behavioural economics and growing interest in entrepreneurial cognition. The methodology is usually based on presenting the subject with highly structured tasks and observing their responses, either conscious (e.g. the actual decision made) or non-concious (e.g. the time taken to make a decision).

The main criticisms of experimentation are that: (a) the tasks presented are rather simple and 'semantically impoverished' compared with real world (so called 'ecological') decisions; (b) real-world decisions have significant consequences and laboratory decisions do not, and (c) it takes a too 'scientistic' view of human behaviour.

Content analysis

Content analysis is a methodology for analysing communications (be they written, verbal or even visual). A collection of pieces of communication (transcripts if they are verbal) of interest (say, business plans or entrepreneurs' presentations to venture capitalist) are taken. They are then analysed to identify key words, phrases or concepts. A statistical evaluation is then undertaken to identify the prevalence and relationship between these words, phrases or concepts.

To be effective, content analysis must be undertaken with proper statistical rigour. One criticism is that, beyond the identification of single words or predefined phrases, a degree of interpretive latitude opens up on the part of the analyst (looking for the word 'opportunity' is one thing, but looking for 'phrases that emphasise the positives' is another). This may be overcome by having strict, and justified, criteria for identification in place before the analysis is made, having more than one analyst, and ensuring that all analyses agree to a sufficient degree before the results are interpreted.

Discourse analysis

Discourse analysis has some links to content analysis but its concerns are somewhat broader. It is based on a detailed and structured observation of communication in an active social setting. It borrows from sociolinguistics and, as well as looking for key words and phrases, it may also take account of paralanguage (intonation, facial expressions and body language) and evidence of power relations in communication.

Discourse analysis has been used to analyse entrepreneurs' leadership strategies and their dealings with key supporters, especially investors. The technique demands skill, and practice is essential if it is to be used effectively.

Cognitive mapping

Cognitive mapping is a collection of related techniques that aim to create a picture of an individual's cognitive representation of the world. As its title suggests, it is borrowed from cognitive psychology. There are a number of variants, from simply getting a subject to brainstorm or to draw a mind map, to more sophisticated techniques such as repertory grid analysis. The methodology is growing in importance and has been used to create pictures of entrepreneurs' cognitive representations of their competitive world and to make representations of their 'visions'. One criticism is that it is assumed that the picture created is in some way a true mapping of a cognitive structure.

Case study construction and analysis

Originally borrowed from the medical sciences, case studies have long been used for teaching in management. They do, however, have a major role to play in research. A case study is usually a highly structured narrative (story) of a series of events. It is constrained in two dimensions: the level of agency (is it about an individual, a small group, an organisation, a group of organisations?), and temporal extent (What period does it cover? A single decision? A particular period in the life of an organisation? The entire life of the organization?) Case studies may be *descriptive* (they 'capture' the important issues and events), *illustrative* (provide an account of how a particular theory applies in a particular instance), *exploratory* (revealing the particular issues that are of concern in the case instance), *explanatory* (attempting to draw the threads of cause–effect relationships), *experimental* (looking at what happens when a particular variable is changed), *comparative* (what are the similarities and differences between case instance A and case instance B?) and *confirmatory–refutational* (does this case support the predictions of theory X?)

A major criticism of the case methodology is that there is no justification for generalising the findings of a single case beyond the bounds of that case. Hence any knowledge gained from the case study method is, at best, anecdotal. A number of responses have been made to this criticism. One is that generalisation is not important – it may be something the natural sciences aspire to, but its role in the human sciences is limited. Another response is that case study findings can be generalised, but in a 'natural generalisation' way, not the statistical way that quantitative methods (experimentation, survey) are. Some argue that the non-generalisability of the case method is overstated, or that case methodology is not meant to be isolated from other methodologies than can validate its generalization.

Ethnomethodology and hermeneutics

Ethnomethodology is borrowed from anthropology and some aspects of social psychology. The term covers a number of approaches. In its essence, it refers to a highly detailed, and sympathetic, observation of actors in their social setting. It does not insist on observer detachment as quantitative methods do (many ethnomethodologists would claim such is not possible anyway). The ethnomethodologist will rarely enter into a study with structured questions or hypotheses framed in advance, but will be content to let these emerge as observation/interaction unfolds. Rather than seek a single perspective, the ethnomethodologist will attempt to find as many perspectives as possible, a different one for every actor if need be.

The hermeneutic approach moves even further towards anti-positivism. It is perhaps true to say that it represents a philosophical stance rather than a particular method. It insists that there are no such things as facts, only values, and that any actor's values are as valid as those of any other. The observer is an intimate part of what is observed. The aim of the research (such as there is one) is to identify 'local' knowledge. This local knowledge is holistic, it cannot be broken down into a series of propositions.

The key criticism of ethnomethodology (and particularly of hermeneutics) is that it does not produce any knowledge of anything of any real value. Certainly not knowledge that is in any way generalisable. 'So what!', cry its advocates. 'Positivistic imperialism!' While there have been some studies into entrepreneurship using ethnomethodological and hermeneutic methodologies, those studies tend to find their way to their own journals.

The philosophical debate about the nature and reliability of knowledge generated by these methods is engaging, and often entertaining. At the end of the day, however, the student of entrepreneurship wants to create new understanding. Consider your research question and use what works to answer it!

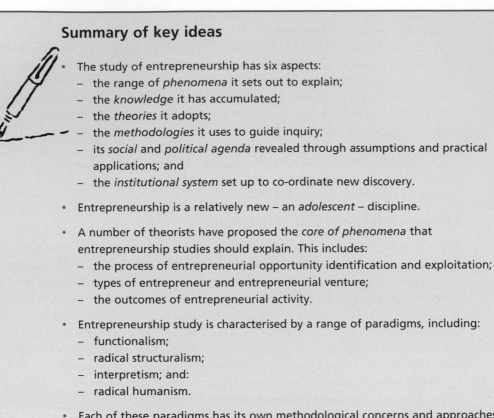

Summary of key ideas

- The study of entrepreneurship has six aspects:
  - the range of *phenomena* it sets out to explain;
  - the *knowledge* it has accumulated;
  - the *theories* it adopts;
  - the *methodologies* it uses to guide inquiry;
  - its *social* and *political agenda* revealed through assumptions and practical applications; and
  - the *institutional system* set up to co-ordinate new discovery.

- Entrepreneurship is a relatively new – an *adolescent* – discipline.

- A number of theorists have proposed the *core of phenomena* that entrepreneurship studies should explain. This includes:
  - the process of entrepreneurial opportunity identification and exploitation;
  - types of entrepreneur and entrepreneurial venture;
  - the outcomes of entrepreneurial activity.

- Entrepreneurship study is characterised by a range of paradigms, including:
  - functionalism;
  - radical structuralism;
  - interpretism; and:
  - radical humanism.

- Each of these paradigms has its own methodological concerns and approaches. All have something to offer towards enhancing understanding of entrepreneurship.

Research themes

Trends in entrepreneurship research

Given its fragmented, multi-disciplinary and multi-paradigmatic nature, entrepreneurship is a diverse field of study. The claim has been made that the functionalist paradigm dominates. I am confident that this is true, but to what extent is not clear. A useful research project would take a collection of journals that deal with entrepreneurship, either specifically or as part of a broader concern with management studies, or beyond into the social sciences generally, and evaluate the trends in entrepreneurship research. From the selected set of journals, review the articles over a time period (the publication of Burrell and Morgan's book in 1979 would be a good starting point, though this means a lot of articles so don't be too ambitious in the range of journals considered). Assess what proportion of articles address entrepreneurship directly (if just journals dedicated to entrepreneurship are chosen, this would clearly be all), and the paradigmatic approach they take (using the Burrell and Morgan scheme above to make a judgment). What proportion adopts which paradigm? How many articles express explicitly their paradigmatic assumptions, or, alternatively, leave these implicit? How many attempt to integrate different paradigms? How often are views about paradigm commensurability expressed? If so, which views? What are the overall trends? Conclude by making projections (and recommendations) for the future of entrepreneurship research.

Entrepreneurs' views on research priorities

Entrepreneurship is very much an applied science. The idea that research into entrepreneurship can lead to improved performance for entrepreneurial ventures dominates. But this is a presupposition. How do practicing entrepreneurs feel about (formal, academic) research into what they do? Do they feel that it has value? If it does, how do researchers help? What should researchers be looking at? What kind of research findings might be valuable? These are important questions. A survey of a sample, either general or of a specific group of entrepreneurs (either from a specific sector or of a particular type – refer back to chapter 2) could provide answers. A Delphi analysis approach would be effective. Conclude by making recommendations for future directions in entrepreneurship research given practising entrepreneurs' priorities.

Key readings

Two seminal papers that have done most to define the future research agenda for the entrepreneurship field are:

Bygrave, W.D. and Hofer, C.W. (1991) 'Theorizing about entrepreneurship', *Entrepreneurship Theory and Practice*, Summer, pp. 13–22.

Hofer, C.W. and Bygrave, W.D. (1992) 'Researching entrepreneurship', *Entrepreneurship Theory and Practice*, Spring, pp. 91–100.

Suggestions for further reading

Aldrich, H.E. and Martinez, M.A. (2001) 'Many are called, but few are chosen: an evolutionary perspective for the study of entrepreneurship', *Entrepreneurship Theory and Practice*, Summer, pp. 41–56.

Amit, R., Glosten, L. and Muller, E. (1993) 'Challenges to theory development in entrepreneurship', *Journal of Management Studies*, Vol. 30, pp. 815–34.

Brophy, D.J. and Shulman, J.M. (1992) 'A finance perspective on entrepreneurship research', *Entrepreneurship Theory and Practice*, Spring, pp. 61–71.

Burrell, G. and Morgan, G. (1979) *Sociological Analysis and Organisational Paradigms*. Aldershot: Arena.

Bygrave, W.D. and Hofer, C.W. (1991) 'Theorizing about entrepreneurship', *Entrepreneurship Theory and Practice*, Summer, pp. 13–22.

Cannella, A.A. and Paetzold, R.L. (1994) 'Pfeffer's barriers to the advance of organizational science: a rejoinder', *Academy of Management Review*, Vol. 19, No. 2, pp. 331–41.

Chandler, G.N. and Lyon, D.W. (2001) 'Issues of research design and construct measurement in entrepreneurship research: the past decade', *Entrepreneurship Theory and Practice*, Summer, pp. 101–13.

Davidson, P. and Wilkund, J. (2001) 'Levels of analysis in entrepreneurship: current research practice and suggestions for the future', *Entrepreneurship Theory and Practice*, Summer, pp. 81–99.

Dess, G.D. (1999) 'Linking corporate entrepreneurship to strategy, structure and process: suggested research directions', *Entrepreneurship Theory and Practice*, Spring, pp. 85–103.

Dodd, S.D. (2002) 'Metaphors and meaning: a grounded cultural model of US entrepreneurship', *Journal of Business Venturing*, Vol. 17, No. 5, pp. 519–37.

Donaldson, L. (1985) *In Defence of Organization Theory: A Reply to the Critics*. Cambridge: Cambridge University Press.

Fadahunsi, A. (2000) 'Researching informal entrepreneurship in sub-Saharan Africa: a note on field methodology', *Journal of Developmental Entrepreneurship*, Vol. 5, No. 3, pp. 249–60.

Fay, B. (1996) *Contemporary Philosophy of Social Science*. Oxford: Blackwell.

Gorton, M. (2000) 'Overcoming the structure–agency divide in small business research', *International Journal of Entrepreneurial Behaviour and Research*, Vol. 6, No. 5, pp. 276–92.

Guzmán Cuevas, J. (1994) 'Towards a taxonomy of entrepreneurial theories', *International Small Business Journal*, Vol. 12, No. 4, pp. 77–88.

Harrison, D.E. and Krauss, S.I. (2002) 'Interviewer cheating: implications for research on entrepreneurship in Africa', *Journal of Developmental Entrepreneurship*, Vol. 7, No. 3, pp. 319–30.

Hassard, J. (1988) 'Overcoming hermeticism in organizational theory: an alternative to paradigm incommensurability', *Human Relations*, Vol. 41, No. 3, pp. 247–59.

Hassard, J. (1991) 'Multiple paradigms and organizational analysis: a case study', *Organization Studies*, Vol. 12, No. 2, pp. 275–99.

Hickson, D. (1988) 'Offence and defence: a symposium with Hinings, Clegg, Child, Aldrich, Karpick and Donaldon', *Organization Studies*, Vol. 9, No. 1, pp. 1–31.

Hill, J. and McGowan, P. (1999) 'Small business and enterprise: questions about research methodology', *International Journal of Entrepreneurial Behaviour and Research*, Vol. 5, No. 1, pp. 5–18.

Hills, G.E. and LaForge, R.W. (1992) 'Research at the marketing interface to advance entrepreneurship theory', *Entrepreneurship Theory and Practice*, Spring, pp. 33–58.

Hollis, M. (1994) *The Philosophy of Social Science*. Cambridge: Cambridge University Press.

Jackson, N. and Carter, P. (1991) 'In defence of paradigm incommensurability', *Organization Studies*, Vol. 12, No. 1, pp. 109–27.

Jobber, D. and Lucas, G.J. (2000) 'The modified Tichy TPC framework for pattern matching and hypothesis development in historical case study research', *Strategic Management Journal*, Vol. 21, pp. 865–74.

Kiggundu, M.N. (2002) 'Entrepreneurs and entrepreneurship in Africa: what is known and what needs to be done?' *Journal of Developmental Economics*, Vol. 7, No. 3, pp. 239–58.

Kwan, K.M. and Tsang, W.K. (2001) 'Realism and constructivism in strategy research: a critical realist response to Mir and Watson', *Strategic Management Journal*, Vol. 22, pp. 1163–8.

Low, M.B. (2001) 'The adolescence of entrepreneurship research: specification and purpose', *Entrepreneurship Theory and Practice*, Summer, pp. 17–25.

Low, M.B. and MacMillan, I.C. (1988) 'Entrepreneurship: past research and future challenges', *Journal of Management*, Vol. 14, No. 2, pp. 139–61.

Lyon, D.W., Lumpkin, G.T. and Dess, G.G. (2000) 'Enhancing entrepreneurial orientation research: operationalizing and measuring a key strategic decision-making process', *Journal of Management*, Vol. 26, No. 5, pp. 1055–85.

May, T. (1993) *Social Research: Issues, Methods and Process*. Buckingham: Open University Press.

Meyer, G.D., Venkataraman, S. and Gartner, W. (1999) *Task Force on Doctoral Education in Entrepreneurship*. Entrepreneurship Division of the Academy of Management, Seattle, USA.

Meyer, G.D., Neck, H.M. and Meeks, M.D. (2002) 'The entrepreneurship–strategic management interface', in Hitt, M.A., Ireland, R.D., Camp, S.M. and Sexton, D.L. (eds) *Strategic Entrepreneurship: Creating a New Mindset*. Oxford: Blackwell.

Mir, R. and Watson, A. (2000) 'Strategic management and the philosophy of science: the case for a constructivist methodology', *Strategic Management Journal*, Vol. 21, No. 9, pp. 941–53.

Mir, R. and Watson, A. (2001) 'Critical realism and constructivism in strategy research: toward a synthesis', *Strategic Management Journal*, Vol. 22, pp. 1169–73.

Mitchell, J.R., Friga, P.N. and Mitchell, R.K. (2005) 'Untangeling the intuition mess: intuition as a construct in entrepreneurship research', *Entrepreneurship: Theory and Practice*, Vol. 29, No. 6, pp. 653–79.

Morris, M.H. (2000) 'New directions and streams of research', *Journal of Developmental Entrepreneurship*, Vol. 5, No. 1, pp. v–vi.

Pfeffer, J. (1993) 'Barriers to the advancement of organisational science: paradigm development as a dependent variable', *Academy of Management Review*, Vol. 18, No. 4, pp. 599–620.

Schwartz, R.G. and Teach, R.D. (2000) 'Entrepreneurship research: an empirical perspective', *Entrepreneurship Theory and Practice*, Spring, pp. 77–81.

Ucbasaran, D., Westhead, P. and Wright, M. (2001) 'The focus of entrepreneurial research: contextual and process issues', *Entrepreneurship Theory and Practice*, Summer, pp. 57–80.

Weaver, G.R. and Giola, D.A. (1994) 'Paradigms lost: incommensurability vs structurationist inquiry', *Organization Studies*, Vol. 15, No. 4, pp. 565–90.

Willmott, H. (1993) 'Breaking the paradigm mentality', *Organization Studies*, Vol. 14, No. 5, pp. 681–719.

 Index